AMERICA

THE
UNITED STATES

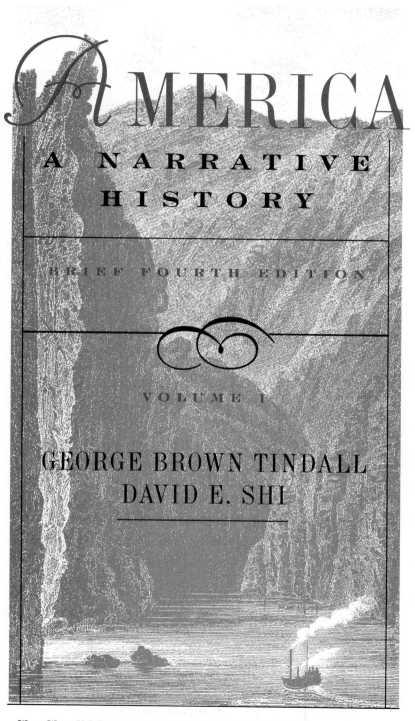

AMERICA

A NARRATIVE
HISTORY

BRIEF FOURTH EDITION

VOLUME I

GEORGE BROWN TINDALL
DAVID E. SHI

W · W · NORTON & COMPANY · NEW YORK · LONDON

The text of this book is composed in Fairfield Light
with the display set in Torino
Composition by Compset Inc.
Manufacturing by R. R. Donnelley
Book design by Antonina Krass
Cover aquatint by William James Bennett,
South Street from Maiden Lane, c. 1834.
Courtesy of The New York Public Library, Prints Collection,
Miriam and Ira D. Wallach Division of Art,
Astor, Lenox and Tilden Foundation.

The Library of Congress has cataloged the one-volume edition as follows:

Tindall, George Brown.
    America : a narrative history / George Brown Tindall, David E.
Shi.—Brief 4th ed.
        p.   cm
    Includes bibliographical references and index.
    ISBN 0-393-97063-9 (pbk.)
    1. United States—History.   I. Shi, David E.   II. Title.
E178.1.T55   1997
973—dc20   96–25530

ISBN 0-393-97065-5

W. W. Norton & Company, Inc., 500 Fifth Avenue, New York, N.Y. 10110
http://www.wwnorton.com

W. W. Norton & Company Ltd., 10 Coptic Street, London WC1A 1PU

2 3 4 5 6 7 8 9 0

FOR BRUCE AND BLAIR

FOR
JASON AND JESSICA

CONTENTS

PART TWO / **BUILDING A NATION**

$\mathscr{P}$ART FOUR / **A HOUSE DIVIDED**

MAPS

PREFACE

Just as history is never complete, neither is a historical textbook. We have learned much from the responses of readers and instructors to the first three editions of Brief *America*. Perhaps the most important and reassuring lesson is that our original intention has proved valid: to provide a compelling narrative history of the American experience, a narrative animated by human characters, informed by analysis and social texture, and guided by the unfolding of events. Readers have also endorsed the book's unique format. *America* is designed to be read and to carry a moderate price.

   In a significant attempt to help students grasp the major themes and developments throughout the text, without compromising its intellectual integrity, Brief *America* now contains a new pedagogical program. Students will receive additional guidance when reading the text from new part openers, which lay out the major ideas emphasized in upcoming chapters. Chapter organizers appear on the first page of each chapter and present key idea statements that serve as a guide through the narrative. "Making Connections" boxes appear on the final page of each chapter (except the last) to link significant events in the current chapter to issues in surrounding chapters. The new pedagogical program with the larger format and the new two-color design result in an attractive, easy-to-read text that instructors and students should find inviting.

   The revisions that set off the Brief Fourth Edition of *America: A Narrative History* highlight frontiers: the experiences of men and women on America's frontiers and the significance of frontiers in shaping the nation's history. Frontiers can be understood in many ways. In announcing that the American frontier had closed in 1893, the historian Frederick Jackson Turner described the frontier as the source of American democratic values and institutions. For Turner the frontier was the place where Americans reinvented themselves, made better lives, tamed the wilderness, and set it on the path to civilized development. The frontier experience forged the distinctive American character and the independence, acquisitiveness, and boldness often attributed to it. Turner's frontier incorporated images already being conjured in American popular culture: savage Indians, virtuous settlers, gritty desperadoes, and gallant mothers and wives.

Turner's "frontier thesis" dominated the teaching of American history for almost half a century. Yet his uncritical celebration of the dramatic process of westward expansion overlooked many tragedies and failures along the way. It also was highly selective. His cast of characters was made up almost exclusively of white males. He left out many other important actors: Indians, women, Hispanics, Asians, and African Americans, among others.

Despite the flaws in Turner's version of the frontier, the concept itself remains viable. Many historians still find the frontier a useful frame for understanding important aspects of the American experience (not to mention other societies as well). In tracing the significance of the frontier experience in the development of American society and culture, we adopt an expansive definition and an inclusive treatment of its participants.

America has had many frontiers. They were places of fast-paced change. The unsettled conditions in many areas helped alter social relations, including those between women and men. Frontiers also served as crossroads where ethnic and racial groups formed new configurations, often with violent overtones. And the frontier exists in the minds of Americans as a powerful metaphor for change, for the chance to start anew.

There is much that is new in the Brief Fourth Edition of *America*. The frontier theme surfaces in fresh treatments of the Spanish Southwest in the colonial period and the ways Native Americans and Spanish settlers reacted and adapted to each other (Chapters 1 and 4). In Chapter 1 there are new discussions of Indian cultures and societies in the colonial Atlantic region. The French empire in America and its interactions with the Native Americans receive fresh attention in Chapter 3. There are new sections detailing Anglo-Indian relations (Chapters 1, 3, and 4), and expanded treatments of the old Southwest (Chapters 13 and 14), the mining frontier (Chapters 15 and 18), the Civil War in the

West (Chapter 16), and the development of the West in the late nineteenth century (Chapter 18). This edition of *America* also provides more extensive coverage of the West in the twentieth century, with new discussions of the West during the Great Depression of the 1930s and World War II, and the particular experiences of Hispanics.

This Brief Fourth Edition, like its predecessor, integrates more social history into the narrative of American experience, detailing the folkways and contributions of those groups often underrepresented in historical treatments—women, blacks, and ethnic Americans. New sections have been added dealing with the Salem witch trials, Andrew Jackson, Clara Barton, Woodrow Wilson, Eleanor Roosevelt, the D-Day invasion, the social impact of the GI Bill, the "black power" movement, cultural conservatism, and the Clinton administration. This edition also features new material about religious life in general and revivalism in particular.

In preparing this Brief Fourth Edition of *America* we have benefitted from the insights and suggestions of many people. The following scholars provided close readings of the manuscript at various stages: Holly Mayer (Duquesne University), Jean B. Lee (University of Wisconsin, Madison), Elizabeth Leonard (Colby College), Bruce Field (Northern Illinois University), Virginia DeJohn Anderson (University of Colorado), Fred Anderson (University of Colorado), Charles Eagles (University of Mississippi), and David Parker (Kennseaw College). Once again we thank our friends at W. W. Norton, especially Margaret Farley, Mary Kelly, Kate Nash, and Steve Forman, for their care and attention along the way.

—George B. Tindall
—David E. Shi

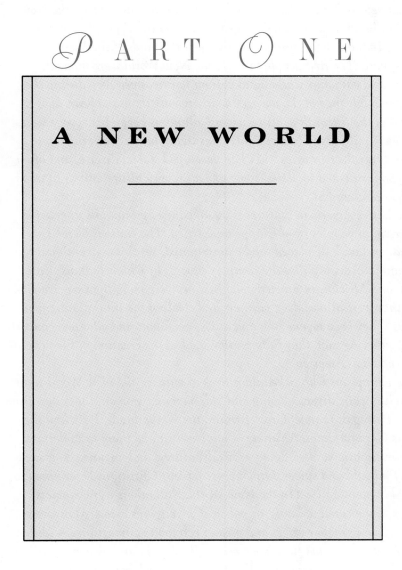

A NEW WORLD

Long before Christopher Columbus accidentally discovered the New World in his effort to find a passage to Asia, the tribal peoples he mislabeled "Indians" had occupied and shaped the lands of the Western Hemisphere. The first people to settle the New World were nomadic hunters and gatherers who migrated from northeastern Asia during the last glacial advance of the ice age, nearly twenty thousand years ago. By the end of the fifteenth century, when Columbus began his voyage west, there were millions of Native Americans living in the Western Hemisphere. Over the centuries, they had developed stable, diverse, and often highly sophisticated societies, some rooted in agriculture, others in trade or imperial conquest.

The native American cultures were, of course, profoundly affected by the arrival of peoples from Europe and Africa. The Indians were exploited, enslaved, displaced, and exterminated. Yet this conventional tale of conquest oversimplifies the complex process by which Indians, Europeans, and Africans interacted. The Indians were more than passive victims; they were also trading partners and rivals of the transatlantic newcomers. They became enemies and allies, neighbors and advisors, converts and spouses. As such they fully participated in the creation of the new society known as America.

The Europeans who risked their lives to settle in the New World were themselves quite diverse. Young and old, men and women, they came from Spain, Portugal, France, Great Britain, the Netherlands, Italy, and the various German states. A variety of motives inspired them to undertake the transatlantic voyage. Some were adventurers and fortune seekers, eager to find gold and spices. Others were fervent Christians determined to create kingdoms of God in the New World. Still others were convicts, debtors, indentured servants, or political or religious exiles. Many were simply seeking higher wages and greater economic opportunity. A settler in Pennsylvania noted that "poor people (both men and women) of all kinds, can here get three times the wages for their labour than they can in England or Wales."

Yet such enticements were not sufficient to attract enough workers to keep up with the rapidly expanding colonial economies. So the Europeans began to force Indians to work for them. But there were never enough of them to meet the unceasing demand. Moreover, they often escaped or were so obstreperous that several colonies banned their use. The Massachusetts legislature did so because Indians were of such "a malicious, surly and revengeful spirit; rude and insolent in their behavior, and very ungovernable."

Beginning early in the seventeenth century, more and more colonists turned to the slave trade for their labor needs. In 1619 white traders began transporting captured Africans to the English colonies. This development would transform American society in ways that no one at the time envisioned. Few Europeans during the colonial era saw the contradiction between the New World's promise of individual freedom and the expanding institution of race slavery. Nor did they reckon with the problems associated with introducing into the new society a race of peoples they considered alien and unassimilable.

The intermingling of peoples, cultures, and ecosystems from the three continents of Africa, Europe, and North America gave colonial American society its distinctive vitality and variety. In turn, the diversity of the environment and climate led to the creation of quite different economies and patterns of living in the various regions of North America. As the original settlements grew into prosperous and populous colonies, the transplanted Europeans had to fashion social institutions and political systems to manage growth and control tensions.

At the same time, imperial rivalries among the Spanish, French, English, and Dutch produced numerous intrigues and costly wars. The monarchs of Europe had a difficult time trying to manage and exploit this fluid and often volatile colonial society. Many of the colonists, they discovered, brought with them to the New World a feisty independence that led them to resent government interference in their affairs. A British official in North Carolina reported that the residents of the Piedmont region were "without any Law or Order. Impudence is so very high [among them], as to be past bearing." As long as the reins of imperial control were loosely applied, the two parties maintained an uneasy partnership. But as the British authorities tightened their control during the mid-eighteenth century, they met resistance, which escalated into revolt, and culminated in revolution.

1   DISCOVERY AND SETTLEMENT

CHAPTER ORGANIZER

This chapter focuses on:

- the reasons for the founding of the different colonies

- the ways in which Europeans and Native Americans adapted to each other's presence

- the factors making for England's success in North America

    he Western Hemisphere was originally an uninhabited frontier. But like all frontiers, it served as a powerful magnet for dreamers and adventurers. Its first human inhabitants were immigrants whose origins are lost in the mists of time, where legends abound. Over the centuries these so-called Native Americans have passed down various creation myths. Some of these stories claim that the first people descended from the sky; others have insisted that they drifted across from Asia, Africa, or Europe. The most plausible explanation is that nomadic people entered the New World from Siberia to Alaska, either by island-hopping across the Bering Strait or by traversing a fifty-mile land bridge (Beringia) exposed by receding waters during the Ice Ages. They probably arrived some 16,000–18,000 years ago; for thousands of years small bands of these Asian immigrants split off from one another and filtered southward from the desolate, frigid, and windswept Yukon, following migrating mammoths and giant bison toward warmer regions, eventually reaching the tip of South America and the Atlantic coast of North America.

PRE-COLUMBIAN INDIAN CIVILIZATIONS

Once the ice sheets melted and the sea rose again, these migrants were cut off from the rest of humanity, except for the short-lived Viking settlements on Greenland (A.D. 985) and Newfoundland (A.D. 1001). Archeological digs add yearly to the fragments of knowledge about the varied and complex societies of pre-Columbian America. The most illuminating artifacts have been found in the high altitudes of Mexico and Peru, where the Olmecs, Mayas, Aztecs, Incas, and others built great empires and a monumental architecture, supported by large-scale agriculture and a far-flung commerce.

THE MAYAS, AZTECS, AND INCAS   By about 2000–1500 B.C., the nomadic Indian tradition began to give way in what is today Central America to more permanent farming settlements. The more settled life in turn fostered more complex cultures through the cultivation of religion, crafts, art, science, civic administration—and organized warfare.

A stratified social structure also developed. From about A.D. 300–900, this Middle American region reached its cultural peak, with great religious centers, gigantic pyramids, temple complexes, and ceremonial courts, all supported by the surrounding villages. The Mayas, living in present-day Yucatán, Guatemala, Belize, and western Honduras and El Salvador, were a warlike people who ruled a far-flung and loosely controlled empire. They built dozens of pyramids, devised a complex writing system based on hieroglyphs, and developed enough mathematics and astronomy to devise a calendar more accurate than that used by Columbus.

Then, about A.D. 900, for reasons unknown, Mayan culture abruptly collapsed and the religious centers were abandoned. The disappearance of Mayan culture has baffled scholars. Numerous civil wars helped weaken the social fabric, but other factors also played a role. There is evidence that the Mayas overexploited the rain forest upon whose fragile ecosystem they depended for survival. Overpopulation placed added strain on Mayan society. Skeletal remains reveal evidence of widespread malnutrition. Whatever the reasons, the Mayas succumbed to the Toltecs, a warlike people who conquered most of the region in the tenth century. But around A.D. 1200, they too mysteriously withdrew.

The equally warlike Aztecs, who arrived from the northwest, founded the city of Tenochtitlán (now Mexico City) in 1325 and gradually extended their control over central Mexico. When the Spaniards invaded in 1519, the Aztec Empire under Montezuma II ruled over 5 million people. A hereditary elite of warrior-priests held them in fairly loose subjugation. Their economy depended on agriculture, and their religious practices included human sacrifices to the sun god. (More than 5,000 people were supposedly sacrificed to celebrate the coronation of Montezuma II in 1502.) Farther south, Incas by the fifteenth century controlled an empire that stretched a thousand miles along the Andes mountains from Ecuador to Chile, connected by an elaborate system of roads and organized under an autocratic government that dominated community life.

INDIAN CULTURES OF NORTH AMERICA   Of the hundreds of Indian tribes inhabiting the present-day United States, the ancestors of only a few such as the Pueblos, Creeks, and Iroquois ever approached the level of social organization or cultural sophistication achieved by the Mayas or Aztecs. North American tribes tended to be smaller, more scattered, and less settled. Most of them migrated with the seasons in search of food—fish, deer, rabbits, maize (corn), nuts, berries—and temperate locales. They built few permanent structures and tended to own land communally, although individuals were allowed to own the food they produced or gathered.

In the Ohio and Mississippi River valleys many tribes did develop a thriving village culture. While still primarily dependent on hunting and gathering for subsistence, they also cultivated squash, beans, and maize. But even the most developed Indian societies of the sixteenth century were ill-equipped to resist the dynamic European cultures invading their world. There were fatal gaps in Indian knowledge and technology. The Indians of Mexico, for example, had copper and bronze but no iron, except a few specimens of meteorites. They had domesticated dogs, turkeys, and llamas, but horses were unknown until the Spaniards arrived. When fighting erupted, arrows and tomahawks were seldom a match for guns.

A wooden carving of a mother carrying a child, found in a Hopewell burial mound in southern Ohio.

Despite such disadvantages, however, the Indians resisted European invaders for centuries. They displayed an amazing capacity for adapting to changing circumstances, incorporating European technology and weaponry, forging new alliances, changing their own community structures, and often converting whites to their way of life. Many Spanish, English, and French settlers voluntarily joined Indian society or chose to stay after being captured. As a French colonist in America noted, "thousands of Europeans are Indians," yet "we have no examples of even one of those Aborigines having from choice become Europeans."

THE COLLISION OF CULTURES

The discovery of the New World coincided with the opening of the modern period in European history which saw Europe spread its power and culture around the world. The expansion of Europe derived from, and in turn affected, the peculiar patterns and institutions that distinguished modern times from the medieval: the revival of learning and the rise of the inquiring spirit; the explosive growth of trade, towns, and modern corporations; the decline of feudalism and the rise of national states; the religious zeal generated by the Protestant Reformation and the Catholic Counter-Reformation; and on the darker side, some old sins—greed, conquest, racism, and slavery.

By the fifteenth century these forces had combined to focus European eyes on new lands to conquer or settle and on new peoples to convert, civilize, or exploit. They were especially attracted by the lure of Asia, a near-mythical land of spices, silks, jewels, and millions of "heathens" to be Christianized. Marco Polo had returned from the Orient bedazzled by a region where "sands sparkled and glittered with gems and precious ores." Equally valued were the spices—pepper, nutmeg, clove—so essential to the preserving of food, especially in southern Europe, where the warm and humid climate accelerated spoilage.

THE VOYAGES OF COLUMBUS   The Orient's mythic wealth caught the expansive vision of Christopher Columbus. Born in 1451, the son of an Italian weaver, Columbus took to the sea at an early age. As a young man he went on voyages to England and Iceland, and during the 1480s he hatched a scheme to reach Asia by sailing west. After Portugal, England, and France showed little interest in his plan, Columbus turned to Spain for backing, and after years of disappointment, he finally won the support of Ferdinand and Isabella, the Spanish monarchs. The legend that the queen had to hock the crown jewels is as outrageous as the fable that Columbus had to prove the earth was round.

Columbus, a tall, robust, red-haired, and long-faced man with a ruddy complexion, oval eyes, and huge nose, chartered one ship, the *Santa María,* and the Spanish city of Palos supplied two smaller caravels, the *Pinta* and *Niña.* From Palos this little squadron, with eighty-seven men, set sail on August 2, 1492. It headed by dead reckoning westward for what Columbus thought was Asia. The first leg of the journey went well, thanks to a strong trade wind. Then the breeze lagged, the days passed, and the crew began to grumble about their captain's far-fetched plan. To rally flagging morale Columbus reminded the crew of the dazzling riches awaiting them. Yet skepticism remained rife, and he finally promised that the expedition would turn back if land were not sighted in three days.

Early on October 12, 1492, a lookout called out, *"Tierra! Tierra!* [Land! Land!]" It was an island in the Bahamas that Columbus named San Salvador (Blessed Savior). According to Columbus's own reckoning he was near the Indies, so he called the islanders "Indios," Indians. He

NORTH AMERICA

ATLANTIC OCEAN

ENGLAND

FRANCE

PORTUGAL SPAIN

AZORES

CANARY ISLANDS

1492

GULF OF MEXICO

BAHAMAS

SAN SALVADOR

CUBA

HISPANIOLA

1493

JAMAICA

1502

CARIBBEAN SEA

LESSER ANTILLES

TRINIDAD

1498

CAPE VERDE ISLANDS

AFRICA

CENTRAL AMERICA

PACIFIC OCEAN

SOUTH AMERICA

COLUMBUS'S VOYAGES

0   1000 Miles
0   1000 Kilometers

described them as naked people, "very well made, of very handsome bodies and very good faces." The Indians paddled out in dugout logs, which they called *canoa,* and offered gifts of parrots and javelins to the strangers. Their warm generosity and docile temperament led Columbus to write in his journal that "they invite you to share anything that they possess, and show as much love as if their hearts went with it." Yet he added that "with fifty men they could all be subjugated and compelled to do anything one wishes."

At the moment, however, Columbus was not interested in enslaving "noble savages"; he was seeking the Indies and their fabled riches. He therefore continued to search through the Bahamian Cays down to Cuba, a place name that suggested Cipangua (Japan), and then eastward to the island he named Española (or Hispaniola), where he first found significant amounts of gold jewelry. Columbus learned of, but did not encounter until his second voyage, the fierce Caribs of the Lesser Antilles. The Caribbean Sea was named after them, and, because of their alleged bad habits, the word "Cannibal" derived from a Spanish version of their name (Caníbal).

On the night before Christmas 1492, the *Santa María* ran aground off Hispaniola, and Columbus, still believing he had reached Asia, decided to return home. He left about forty men behind and seized a dozen natives to present as gifts to Spain's royal couple. After Columbus reached Palos, the news of his discovery spread rapidly throughout

Europe, and Ferdinand and Isabella instructed him to prepare for a second voyage. Columbus returned across the Atlantic in 1493 with seventeen ships and some 1,200 men, as well as royal instructions to "treat the Indians very well and affectionately without causing them any annoyance whatever."

Once back in the New World, Admiral Columbus discovered the camp in chaos. The unsupervised soldiers had run amok, raping native women, robbing Indian villages, and, as Columbus's son later added, "committing a thousand excesses for which they were mortally hated by the Indians." The Indians finally struck back and killed ten Spaniards. A furious Columbus immediately launched a wholesale attack on the Indian villages. The Spaniards, armed with crossbows, guns, and ferocious dogs, decimated the native defenders and loaded 500 of them onto ships bound for the slave market in Spain.

After two more voyages to the New World, Columbus finally returned to Spain in 1504, and two years later he died. To the end Columbus refused to believe that he had discovered anything other than outlying parts of Asia. Ironically, the New World was named not for its discoverer but, in what one writer has called a comedy of errors, for another Italian, Amerigo Vespucci.

Vespucci was a Florentine merchant and navigator who knew Columbus and helped outfit his ships for the transatlantic crossing. Later, Vespucci himself made several voyages to the New World. In 1507 a young geographer named Martin Waldseemuller published a book in which he mistakenly credited Vespucci with having reached South America in 1497, one year before Columbus. For that reason, Waldseemuller suggested that the new continent be named "America" in his honor.

Actually, Vespucci's first voyage began in 1499, and there is no firm evidence that he, any more than Columbus, ever believed he had discovered anything other than a part of East Asia. Waldseemuller's idea stuck, however, and the name for the New World took hold before Vespucci's right to the honor could be questioned.

THE GREAT BIOLOGICAL EXCHANGE   The first European contacts with this New World produced a remarkable diffusion of cultures, an exchange of such magnitude and rapidity as humanity had never known before. It was in fact more than a diffusion of cultures: it was a diffu-

A tortoise, drawn by John White, one of the earliest English settlers in America.

sion of distinctive biological systems. If anything, the plants and animals of the two worlds were more different than the people and their
ways of life. Europeans, for instance, had never seen such creatures as
the iguana, flying squirrel, catfish, rattlesnake, or anything quite like
several other species native to America: bison, cougars, armadillos,
opossums, sloths, anacondas, electric eels, vampire bats, toucans, con-
dors, or hummingbirds. Among the Indians' few domesticated animals
they could recognize the dog and the duck, but turkeys, guinea pigs, llamas, and alpacas were all new. Nor did the Indians know of horses, cattle, pigs, sheep, goats, and (maybe) chickens, which soon arrived from
Europe in abundance.

The transfer of plant life worked an even greater change, a revolution
in the diets of both hemispheres. Before 1492 three main staples of the
modern diet were unknown in the Old World: maize (corn), potatoes
(sweet and white), and many kinds of beans (snap, kidney, lima, and
others). When Columbus first sampled corn in Cuba, he declared it
"most tasty boiled, roasted, or ground into flour." He returned to Spain
with a handful of corn kernels, and within a few years corn had become
a staple crop throughout Europe. The white potato, although commonly
called "Irish," actually migrated from South America to Europe and only
reached North America with the Scotch-Irish immigrants of the 1700s.
Other New World food plants were peanuts, squash, peppers, toma-

toes, pumpkins, pineapples, papayas, avocados, cacao (the source of chocolate), and chicle (for chewing gum). Europeans in turn soon introduced rice, wheat, barley, oats, wine grapes, melons, coffee, olives, bananas, "Kentucky" bluegrass, daisies, and dandelions.

The beauty of the ecological exchange between old and new worlds was that the food plants were more complementary than competitive. They grew in different soils and climates, or in different seasons. Indian corn, it turned out, could flourish almost anywhere—high or low, hot or cold, wet or dry. It spread quickly throughout the world. Before the end of the 1500s American maize and sweet potatoes were staple crops in China. The green revolution exported from the Americas thus helped nourish a worldwide population explosion probably greater than any since the invention of agriculture. Plants initially domesticated by American Indians now make up about a third of the world's food crops.

Europeans also adopted many Indian devices, such as canoes, snowshoes, moccasins, hammocks, kayaks, ponchos, dogsleds, toboggans, and parkas. The rubber ball and the game of lacrosse had Indian origins. New words entered European languages: wigwam, teepee, papoose, succotash, tobacco, moose, skunk, opossum, woodchuck, chipmunk, tomahawk, hickory, pecan, raccoon, and hundreds of others. And the natives left the map dotted with place names of Indian origin long after they were gone, from Miami to Yakima, from Penobscot to Yuma. There were still other New World contributions: tobacco and a number of other drugs, including coca (for cocaine and novocaine), curare (a muscle relaxant), and cinchona bark (for quinine).

Unfortunately, the Europeans in exchange presented the Indians with illnesses they could not handle. Even minor diseases such as measles turned killer in the bodies of Indians who had never encountered them and had built no immunity. Major infections such as smallpox and typhus killed all the more speedily. The first contacts with some of Columbus's sailors devastated whole Indian communities. In the quarter century after Columbus colonized Hispaniola, the island's Indian population plummeted from 500,000 to 500. The epidemics spread rapidly into the interior, and some tribes lost 90–95 percent of their population within the first century of European colonization. In central Mexico alone, some 8 million people, perhaps a third of the entire population, died of disease within a decade after the Spaniards arrived. In what is now Texas, one Spanish explorer noted, "half the natives died from a disease of the bowels and blamed us."

A devastating smallpox epidemic depicted in an Aztec manuscript.

THE SPANISH EMPIRE   Excited by Columbus's discoveries, professional explorers, mostly Italians, hired themselves out to look for a western passage to Asia. One after another of these men probed the shorelines of America during the early sixteenth century in the vain search for a passage to China, and in the process greatly increased European knowledge of the New World. The first to sight the North American continent was John Cabot, a Venetian sponsored by the English king, Henry VII. Cabot sailed across the North Atlantic in 1497. His landfall at what the king called "the newe founde lande" gave England the basis for a later claim to all of North America. During the early sixteenth century, however, the British became so preoccupied with internal divisions and conflicts with France that they failed to follow up Cabot's discoveries for several decades.

The New World thus was a Spanish preserve, except for Brazil, which was a Portuguese colony. The Caribbean Sea served as the funnel through which Spanish power entered the New World. After establishing colonies on Hispaniola and at Santo Domingo, which became the capital of the West Indies, the Spanish proceeded eastward to Puerto Rico (1508) and westward to Cuba (1511–1514). Their motives were explicit. Said one soldier: "We came here to serve God and the king, and also to get rich."

A CLASH OF CULTURES   The encounter between Spaniards and Indians in North America involved more than a clash between different peoples. It also brought together quite different forms of technological development. Where Indians used dugout canoes for transport, Europeans sailed on heavily armed, oceangoing vessels. The Spanish ships not only carried human cargo; they also brought with them steel swords, firearms, explosives, and armor. These advanced military tools struck fear into many Indians and help explain why the Europeans were able to defeat far superior numbers of Indians.

The Europeans also enjoyed other cultural advantages. The only domesticated four-legged animal in North America, for example, was the dog. The Spaniards, on the other hand, brought with them horses, pigs, and cattle, all of which offered sources of food and leather. Horses provided greater speed in battle and also introduced a decided psychological advantage. "The most essential thing in new lands is horses," reported one of Coronado's soldiers. "They instill the greatest fear in the enemy and make the Indians respect the leaders of the army."

The great adventure of mainland conquest began in 1519, when Hernando Cortés and 600 men landed on the site of Vera Cruz, Mexico, which he founded. Cortés then set about a daring conquest of the Aztec Empire. The 200-mile march from Vera Cruz through difficult mountain passes to the magnificent Aztec capital of Tenochtitlán (Mexico City), and the subjugation of the Aztecs, were two of the most remarkable—and tragic—feats in human history.

Cortés made the most of his few assets. An acute judge of character and a gifted diplomat as well as military leader, he landed in a region where the natives were still resisting the spread of Aztec power and were ready to embrace new allies, especially those who possessed strange animals (horses) and powerful weapons. By a combination of threats and deception, Cortés entered Tenochtitlán peacefully and made the emperor, Montezuma, his puppet. This state of affairs lasted until the spring of 1520, when the Aztecs rebelled and stoned Montezuma to death. The Spaniards lost about a third of their men as they fought their way out of the city. Their Indian allies remained loyal, however, and Cortés gradually regrouped his forces; in 1521 he took the city again. Thereafter Cortés and his officers simply replaced the former Aztec overlords as rulers over the Indian empire.

In doing so they set the style for other conquistadors to follow, and within twenty years the Spanish had established an empire far larger than Rome's had ever been. Between 1522 and 1528 various lieutenants of Cortés conquered the remnants of Indian culture in Yucatán and Guatemala. In 1531 Francisco Pizarro led a band of soldiers down the Pacific coast from Panama toward Peru, where they attacked and subdued the Inca Empire. From Peru, conquistadors extended Spanish authority through Chile, and to the north, in present-day Colombia.

SPANISH AMERICA The conquistadors transferred to America a system known as the *encomienda,* whereby favored officers took over entire Indian villages or groups of villages. They were called upon to protect and care for the villages and support missionary priests. In turn they could require tribute from the native villagers in the form of goods and labor. Spanish America therefore developed from the start a society of extremes: affluent European conquistadors and subject native peoples who were held in poverty.

Those who remained, that is. By the mid-1500s Indians were nearly extinct in the West Indies, killed more by European diseases than by Spanish exploitation. To take their place the colonizers as early as 1503 began to import slaves from Africa, a tragic practice that eventually would transport over 9 million people across the Atlantic in bondage. In all of Spain's New World empire, the Indian population dropped from about 50 million at the outset to 4 million in the seventeenth century, and slowly rose again to 7.5 million. Whites, who totaled no more than 100,000 in the mid-sixteenth century, numbered over 3 million by the end of the colonial period.

The Indians, however, did not always lack advocates. Many Catholic missionaries offered a sharp contrast to the conquistadors. They ventured into remote areas, often without weapons or protection, to spread the gospel—and sometimes suffered martyrdom for their efforts. Where conquistadors sought to wrest gold, land, and labor from the Indians, the Spanish missionaries—as well as their French Jesuit and English Protestant counterparts of later years—wanted their souls, and they had a tremendous impact upon native American culture. At their worst the missionaries were bigots determined to rid "heathen" people of their native religions and many of their cultural practices. At their best, however, the missionaries were impassioned defenders of the Indians.

For most of the colonial period, much of what is now the United States belonged to Spain, and Spanish culture has left a lasting imprint upon American ways of life. Spain's colonial presence lasted more than three centuries, much longer than either England's or France's, and its possessions were much more far-reaching. The viceroyalty of New Spain was centered in Mexico, but its frontiers extended from the Florida Keys to Alaska and included areas not currently thought of as formerly Spanish, such as the Deep South (Memphis was founded as San Fernando, Vicksburg as Nogales) and the lower Midwest. Hispanic place names—San Francisco, Santa Barbara, Los Angeles, San Diego, Tucson, Santa Fe, San Antonio, Pensacola, and St. Augustine—survive to this day, as do Hispanic influences in art, architecture, literature, music, law, and cuisine.

The Spanish encounter with native Indian populations and their diverse cultures produced a two-way exchange by which the two societies blended, coexisted, and interacted. To be sure, each side was more concerned with preserving its own integrity and dealing with its own needs than with understanding the other. But even when locked in mortal conflict and riven with mutual suspicion, the two cultures necessarily affected each other. The imperative of survival forced both natives and conquerors to devise creative adaptations. For example, the Pueblo Indians of the Southwest practiced two religious traditions simultaneously, adopting Spanish Catholicism while at the same time retaining the essence of their own inherited faith.

Although Spain's influence was strongest from Mexico southward, the "Spanish borderlands" of the southern United States from Florida to California preserve many reminders of Spanish presence. The earliest known exploration of Florida was made in 1513 by Juan Ponce de León, then governor of Puerto Rico. He sought the mythic fountain of youth but instead found alligators, swamps, and abundant wildlife. Meanwhile Spanish explorers skirted the Gulf coast from Florida to Vera Cruz, scouted the Atlantic coast from Cuba to Newfoundland, established a town at St. Augustine, Florida, and a mission at Santa Fe, New Mexico, and planted a short-lived colony on the Carolina coast. Spanish settlements along the Gulf coast and in California did not appear until the eighteenth century.

The Spanish established provinces in North America not so much as commercial enterprises but as defensive buffers protecting their more lucrative trading empire in Mexico and South America. They were concerned about French traders infiltrating from Louisiana, English settlers crossing into Florida, and Russian seal hunters wandering down the California coast. Yet the Spanish settlements in what is today the United States never flourished. The Spaniards failed to realize that a prosperous and enduring colonial empire depended on self-sustaining economic development. Preoccupied with exploitative and extractive economic objectives, they never understood the central significance of developing a viable market economy. The primary reason why England and France surpassed Spain in the development of an American presence was that Spain failed to embrace what the other imperial powers decided early on: that developing a thriving Indian trade in goods was more important than the conversion of "heathens" and the vain search for gold and silver. Free enterprise, rather than a state-controlled mercantilism, became the fulcrum of successful colonial development.

THE SPANISH SOUTHWEST   The Spanish eventually established other permanent settlements in what is now New Mexico, Texas, and California. Eager to pacify rather than fight the far more numerous Indians of the region, the Spanish used religion as an effective instrument of colonial control. Missionaries representing the various monastic orders, particularly the Franciscans and Jesuits, ventured into the frontier to establish isolated Catholic missions where they taught Christianity to the Indians. A successful mission gradually became a secular settlement: its lands were divided among the converted Indians, the mission chapel became a parish church, and the inhabitants were given full Spanish citizenship—including the privilege of paying taxes. The soldiers who were sent to protect the missions were housed in *presidios,* or forts, while their families and the merchants accompanying the soldiers lived in adjacent villages.

The Franciscans were a Catholic order of ascetic belief founded in 1209. To be eligible for the order, applicants—all male—had to surrender all their personal property and live only on charitable contributions. The friars donned simple robes, wore sandals rather than shoes, and walked rather than rode. To demonstrate the intensity of their piety, some wore hairshirts, walked barefoot, or flagellated themselves. All took vows of celibacy. In 1526 the Spanish monarchy ordered that at least two Franciscan friars accompany each colonial expedition to ensure that the "conquest be a Christian apostolic one and not a butchery," as Mexico's first bishop explained. The Franciscans not only wanted to save the souls of "heathen" Indians; they also sought to transform their cultures. They smashed, burned, or confiscated the objects deemed sacred by the Indians and suppressed spiritual rituals and ceremonial dances. The Franciscans regarded the Indians as childlike innocents who could form the basis for ideal Christian communities in which property was owned in common and worked together, not unlike the original Puritan utopia envisioned by John Winthrop and the settlers of Massachusetts Bay.

The land that would later be called New Mexico was the first center of mission activity in the American Southwest. In 1598 Juan de Oñate, the wealthy son of a prominent family in Mexico, received a patent for the territory north of Mexico above the Rio Grande. With an expeditionary military force, he took possession of New Mexico, established a capital at San Gabriel, and sent out search parties looking for evidence of gold and silver deposits. He promised the Pueblo Indian leaders that Spanish dominion would bring them peace, justice, prosperity, and protection. Conversion to Catholicism offered even greater benefits: "an eternal life of great bliss" instead of "cruel and everlasting torment." One of Oñate's aides recorded that the Indians thereupon "spontaneously" agreed to become Spanish vassals and Christians.

Some Indians welcomed the missionaries as "powerful witches" capable of easing their burdens. Others tried to use the Spanish as allies against rival Indian tribes. Still others saw no alternative but to submit. The Indians living in Spanish New Mexico were required to pay tribute to their *encomenderos*—privileged landowners given control over a specified number of natives. The annual tribute was usually a bushel of maize and a blanket or deer hide. But Indians were often required to perform personal tasks for the *encomenderos,* including sexual favors. Disobedient Indians were flogged by both soldiers and priests.

Before the end of the province's first year, the Indians discovered that the Spanish were not keeping their promises of just treatment. They revolted, killing several soldiers and incurring Oñate's wrath. During three days of relentless fighting, the Spanish killed 500 Pueblo men and 300 women and children. Surviving women were enslaved. Indian males over the age of twenty-five had one foot severed in a public ritual intended to strike fear in the hearts of the Indians. Children were taken from their parents and placed under the care of a Franciscan mission where, Oñate remarked, "they may attain the knowledge of God and the salvation of their souls."

During the first three-quarters of the seventeenth century, Spanish New Mexico expanded very slowly. The hoped-for deposits of gold and silver failed to materialize, and a limited food supply also helped dull interest among potential colonists. In 1608 the Spanish government decided to turn New Mexico into a royal province. The following year it dispatched a royal governor, and in 1610, at the same time the English settlers were struggling to survive at Jamestown, the Spanish moved the capital of New Mexico to Santa Fe, the first seat of government in the present-day United States. By 1630 there were fifty Catholic churches and friaries in New Mexico and some 3,000 Spaniards. The leader of the Franciscan missionaries claimed that 86,000 Pueblo Indians had been converted to Christianity.

In fact, however, resentment among the Indians increased with time. In 1680 a charismatic Indian leader named Popé organized a massive rebellion that involved some 17,000 Indians living in separate villages spread across hundreds of miles. Within a few weeks, the Spaniards had been driven from New Mexico. Almost 400 of the 2,500 Europeans were killed in the uprising. The outraged Indians burned churches, tortured and executed priests, and destroyed all relics of Christianity. "The heathen," wrote one Spanish officer, "have concealed a mortal hatred for our holy faith and enmity for the Spanish nation." It took fourteen years and four military assaults for the Spaniards to reestablish their control over New Mexico. Thereafter, except for sporadic raids by Apaches and Navajos, the Spanish exercised stable control over New Mexico.

THE PROTESTANT REFORMATION   While Spain built her empire, a new movement flourished elsewhere in Europe, the Protestant Reformation. It would embitter national rivalries, and, by encouraging serious challenges to Catholic Spain's power, profoundly affect the course of early American history. When Columbus sailed in 1492, all of western Europe acknowledged the Catholic church and its pope in Rome. The unity of Christendom, however, began to crack in 1517, when

Martin Luther, a German monk and theologian, launched his protest against abuses in the church and especially against the sale of indulgences for the remission of sins. Sinful people, Luther argued, could win salvation neither by good works nor through the mediation of the church, but only by faith in the redemptive power of Christ and through a direct relationship to God—the "priesthood of all believers." The only true guide to the will of God, he insisted, was the Bible, not corrupt Catholic priests.

In Geneva the reform movement looked to John Calvin, a French theologian who brought his adopted city under the sway of his stern beliefs. All people, he taught, were damned by Adam and Eve's original sin, but the sacrifice of Christ made possible redemption by faith. The gift of grace, however, was offered only to those who had been elected by God and thus predestined to salvation from the beginning of time. Calvinism was a hard doctrine requiring a rigid moral code, for the outward sign of having been "elected" for salvation was correct behavior. If this did not necessarily prove that one was saved, an immoral life clearly proved the opposite. This Calvinist doctrine provided the basis for the beliefs of the German Reformed and Dutch Reformed churches, the Presbyterians in Scotland, some of the Puritans in England, and the Huguenots in France.

THE REFORMATION IN ENGLAND   In England the Reformation, like so many other events, followed a unique course. There the rejection of papal authority occurred for purely political reasons. King Henry VIII (1509–1547), the second of the Tudor dynasty, requested an annulment of his marriage, which had not produced a male heir. When the pope refused, Henry severed the connection with Rome, named a new archbishop of Canterbury, who granted the annulment, and married the lively Anne Boleyn. In one of history's great ironies, she presented him not with the male heir he sought, but with a daughter, who as Elizabeth I would reign from 1558 to 1603 over one of England's greatest eras.

Elizabeth could not be a Catholic, for in the Catholic view she was illegitimate. During her reign, therefore, the Church of England became Protestant, but in its own way. The organizational structure, the bishops and archbishops, remained much the same, but the doctrine and practice changed: the Latin liturgy became, with some changes, the English

Book of Common Prayer, the cult of saints was dropped, and the clergy were permitted to marry. For the sake of unity the "Elizabethan Settlement" allowed some latitude in theology and other matters, but this did not satisfy all. Some tried to enforce the letter of the law, stressing traditional practice.

Many others, however, especially those under Calvinist influence from the Continent, wished to "purify" the Church of England of its Catholic remnants so that it more nearly fit their views of biblical authority. These so-called Puritans wanted to scrap the Anglican prayer book in favor of the Bible, simplify the rituals of worship, and strictly observe the sanctity of the Sabbath. Some Puritans would later despair of the effort to reform the Anglican church and would leave England to build their own churches and communities in America. Those who broke altogether with the Church of England were called Separatists. The religious controversies associated with the English Reformation so dominated the political life of the nation that interest in colonizing the New World drifted to the periphery of concern.

CHALLENGES TO SPANISH EMPIRE   The Spanish monopoly of the New World colonies remained intact throughout the sixteenth century, but not without challenge from national rivals lusting for New World booty. The French were the first to pose a serious threat. In 1524 the French king sent an Italian named Giovanni da Verrazano in search of a passage to Asia. Sighting land (probably at Cape Fear, North Carolina), Verrazano ranged along the coast as far north as Maine, but it was not until a decade later that the French made their first colonization effort. On three voyages Jacques Cartier explored the Gulf of St. Lawrence and ventured up the St. Lawrence River as far as present-day Montréal. Near Québec he established a short-lived colony in 1542.

Thereafter, however, French interest in Canada waned, as the French were preoccupied with the religious civil wars wracking their country. Not until the early seventeenth century, when the bold explorer Samuel de Champlain established new settlements in Acadia (Nova Scotia) and at Québec, did French colonization in America begin in earnest. Enterprising French traders negotiated with Indians, mostly Micmacs and other Algonquian tribes, for their fur pelts, and French Jesuit missionaries cultivated their souls. Those seeking profits frequently clashed with those promoting piety, as many Jesuits deplored the crass exploitation of the Indians. Unlike many English missionaries, the Jesuits were not determined to strip their converts of all vestiges of Indian culture. Instead they displayed considerable respect for Native American values.

Acquiring furs and ministering to heathens took the French southward as well. In 1673 Père Jacques Marquette, a Jesuit priest, took the first expedition down the Mississippi River. Nine years later Robert Cavalier, sieur de la Salle, did the same, but he ventured all the way to the Gulf of Mexico. There, near the river's delta, the French in the early eighteenth century would establish a settlement called New Orleans. The French thereby came to control not only Canada but also the major inland waterway in North America. But it was a deceptive control, because the French monarchy never emphasized permanent settlement. Instead it viewed the region almost solely as a source for trade, and French America remained only sparsely populated.

From the mid-1500s forward, greater threats to Spanish power in the New World arose from the growing strength of the Dutch and English. The prosperous provinces of the Netherlands, which had passed by inheritance to the Spanish king, and which had become largely Protestant, rebelled against Spanish rule in 1567. A protracted, bloody struggle for independence was interrupted by a twelve-year truce, but Spain did not accept the independence of the Dutch republic until 1648.

Almost from the beginning of the revolt, Dutch privateers plundered Spanish ships. The Dutch raiders soon had their counterpart in England's Elizabethan "Sea Dogges": John Hawkins, Francis Drake, and others. While Elizabeth steered a tortuous course to avoid open war with Catholic Spain, she encouraged both Dutch and English sea captains to attack the Spanish. In 1577 Drake set out on his famous adventure around South America to raid Spanish towns along the Pacific coast. Three years later he returned in triumph. Elizabeth, who had secretly backed the voyage, shared a profit of 4,600 percent, and knighted Francis.

THE ARMADA'S DEFEAT   Sporadic British piracy against the Spanish continued for almost twenty years before circumstances provoked open war. In 1568 Queen Elizabeth's Catholic cousin Mary, "Queen of Scots," ousted by Scottish Presbyterians in favor of her infant son, fled to England. Mary claimed the English throne by descent from Henry VII, and she soon became the focus for Spanish-Catholic intrigues to overthrow Elizabeth. Finally, after an abortive plot to kill the queen and elevate Mary to the throne, Elizabeth yielded to the demands of her ministers and had Mary beheaded in 1587.

In revenge, Spain's Philip II decided to crush Protestant England and began to gather his ill-fated Armada. The ambitious enterprise quickly became a case of incompetence and mismanagement accompanied by bad luck. The heavy Spanish galleons could not cope with the smaller, faster English vessels commanded by Drake and others. The English harried the Spanish ships through the English Channel on their way to the Netherlands, where the Armada was to pick up invasion troops. But, caught up in a powerful "Protestant Wind," the storm-tossed Spanish fleet was swept into the North Sea, and what was left of it finally found its way home around the British Isles, leaving wreckage scattered on the shores of Scotland and Ireland.

Defeat of the Armada convinced the English that the Spanish navy was no longer invincible and cleared the way for English colonization of the Americas. England at the end of the sixteenth century entered the springtime of her power, filled with a youthful zest for the new worlds and wonders that were opening up before her.

ENGLISH EXPLORATIONS   English colonization in North America began in 1584 when Sir Walter Raleigh, eager "to seek new worlds for gold, for praise, for glory," sent an expedition to explore prospects for founding a colony in America. Sailing by way of the West Indies, they came to the Outer Banks of North Carolina and discovered Roanoke Island, where the soil seemed fruitful and the natives friendly. Three years later 117 settlers arrived, including women and children, under the leadership of Governor John White. After a month in Roanoke, White returned to England to get supplies, leaving behind his daughter, Eleanor, and her baby, Virginia Dare, the first English child born in the New World. White, however, was long delayed because of the war with Spain. When he finally returned in 1590, he found the village of "Ralegh" abandoned and pillaged.

No trace of the "lost colonists" was ever found. Hostile Indians or Spaniards may have destroyed the infant colony. The main body of colonists may have gone north to the southern shores of the Chesapeake Bay, where they lived for some years until killed by Indians. But not one of them was ever seen again, and there were no English settlers in North America when Queen Elizabeth died in 1603.

SETTLING THE CHESAPEAKE

With the death of Elizabeth, the Tudor line ended and the throne fell to her cousin James I, the son of the ill-fated Mary, Queen of Scots, and the first of the Stuarts. Their dynasty spanned most of the seventeenth century, a turbulent time of religious and political tensions, civil war, and foreign intrigues. During these eventful years in English history, all but one of the thirteen North American colonies and several more in the Caribbean had their start. They were quite diverse in geography, motives, and composition, a diversity that has since been a trademark and strength of American society.

In 1606, having made peace with Spain and thereby freeing up resources and men for colonization, James I chartered the Virginia Company with two divisions, the First Colony of London and the Second Colony of Plymouth. The stockholders expected a potential return from gold and products such as wine, citrus fruits, olive oil, pitch, tar, potash, and other forest products needed for naval stores. Many also still hoped to discover a passage to India. Few if any investors foresaw what the first English colony would become: a fertile place to grow tobacco.

VIRGINIA The London Company planted the first permanent colony in Virginia, named after Elizabeth I, the "Virgin Queen." On May 6, 1607, three ships loaded with about 100 men reached Chesapeake Bay after four storm-tossed weeks at sea. They chose a river with a northwest bend—in hope of a passage to Asia—and settled about 40 miles from the sea to hide from marauding Spaniards. One of the settlers noted that they found "fair meadows and goodly, tall trees, with such fresh waters running through the woods as I was almost ravished with the first sight thereof."

The river they called the James, and the colony Jamestown. After building a fort, thatched huts, a storehouse, and a church, the sea-weary colonists then began planting, but most were either townsmen unfamiliar with farming or "gentlemen" adventurers who scorned manual labor. They had come to find gold, not to establish a farm settlement. Ignorant of woodlore, they did not know how to exploit the area's abundant game and fish. Supplies from England were undependable, and only firm leadership and their trade with the Indians, who taught the colonists to grow maize, enabled them to survive.

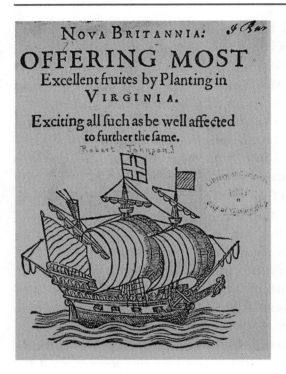

A 1609 handbill of the Virginia Company attempts to lure settlers to Jamestown.

The Indians of the region were loosely organized. Powhatan, chief of the Pamunkey tribe, had gained shaky control over some thirty tribes (14,000 people) in the coastal area. Largely an agricultural people, they raised several varieties of corn. They lived along rivers in fortified towns and resided in framed houses sheathed with bark. Despite occasional clashes with the colonists, the Indians of Virginia initially adopted a stance of nervous assistance and watchful waiting. Powhatan apparently hoped to develop a lucrative trade and military alliance with the newcomers; he realized too late that the newcomers intended to expropriate his lands and subjugate his people. As one Indian said in 1608, "We hear you are come from under the World to take our World from us."

The colonists, as it happened, had more than a match for Powhatan in Captain John Smith, a swashbuckling soldier of fortune with rare powers of leadership and self-promotion. Smith had earlier fought as a mercenary with the Austrians in Hungary against the Turks. There, the story goes, he had beheaded three Turks in hand-to-hand challenges staged in front of a Turkish fortress, and the grateful Austrians awarded him the title of captain, a horse, a scimitar, and a coat of arms. Smith was then wounded, captured, and enslaved in Turkey, but he freed himself by killing his overseer. After fleeing across Russia and sailing in a pirate ship off the coast of Africa, the twenty-four-year-old Smith was "befriended by a gentlewoman" who facilitated his return to England in 1604.

The Virginia Company, understandably impressed by Smith's exploits, appointed him a member of the resident council to manage the new colony in America. It was a wise decision. With the colonists on the verge of starvation, Smith imposed strict discipline and forced all to labor, declaring that "he that will not work shall not eat." Smith also bargained with the Indians and explored and mapped the Chesapeake region. Through his efforts, Jamestown survived, but Smith's dictatorial acts did not endear him to many of the colonists. One called him "ambitious, unworthy, and vainglorious."

John Smith's efforts to control the struggling colony abruptly ended when he suffered a gunpowder burn and sailed back to England in 1609. The colony lapsed into anarchy and suffered the "starving time" of the winter of 1609–1610, during which most of the colonists, weakened by hunger, fell prey to disease. A relief party found only about sixty settlers still alive in 1610. All poultry and livestock (including horses) had been eaten, and one man reportedly had dined on his wife.

For the next seven years the colony limped along until it gradually found a reason for being: tobacco. In 1612 John Rolfe had begun to experiment with the harsh Virginia tobacco, and by 1616 a smoother variety of the weed had become an export staple. Meanwhile Rolfe had made another contribution to stability by marrying Pocahontas, the daughter of Powhatan. Distinguished Virginians still boast of their descent from the Indian "princess," who died of smallpox in London in 1620.

In 1618 officials in London initiated a series of reforms intended to shore up their struggling American colony. They first inaugurated a new "headright" policy. Anyone who bought a share in the company, or who could transport himself to Virginia, could have fifty acres, and fifty more for any servants he might send or bring. The following year, 1619, the company relaxed its tight legal code and promised that the settlers should have the "rights of Englishmen," including a representative assembly. On July 30, 1619, the first General Assembly of Virginia met in the Jamestown church and deliberated for five days, "sweating and stewing, and battling flies and mosquitoes." It was an eventful year in

Engraving of Pocahontas, from John Smith's Generall Historie.

two other respects. During 1619 a ship arrived with ninety "young maidens," to be sold to likely husbands of their own choice for the cost of transportation (about 125 pounds of tobacco). And a Dutch man-of-war dropped off "20 Negars," the first blacks known to have reached English America.

Yet despite its successes, Jamestown again fell upon evil days. The profitable tobacco trade intensified the settlers' lust for land. The colonists especially coveted Indian fields because they had already been cleared and were ready to be planted. In 1622 the Indians, led by Opechancanough, Powhatan's brother and successor, tried to repel the land-grabbing English. They killed some 350 colonists, including John Rolfe, only to provoke a vengeful counterattack. John Smith denounced the Indian assault as a "massacre" and dismissed the "savages" as "cruel beasts" whose "brutishness" exceeded that of wild animals. Whatever moral doubts had earlier plagued English settlers were now swept away. Said one settler: "We shall enjoy their cultivated places. . . . Now their cleared grounds in all their villages (which are situated in the fruitfulest places of the land) shall be inhabited by us."

The English thereafter sought to wipe out the Indian presence along their frontier. In 1623 Captain William Tucker led a band of soldiers into a Powhatan village, ostensibly to negotiate a settlement. After signing a treaty, Tucker invited the Indians to drink a toast to celebrate their truce. Unwittingly, the Indians drank the proffered wine, only to realize too late that it had been poisoned. Two hundred Indians died from the doctored brew. The soldiers then killed another fifty and "brought home part of their heads." This process of "continual incursions" into Indian territory continued throughout the decade.

Yet the English foothold in Virginia remained tenuous. Some 14,000 people had migrated to the colony since 1607, but the population in 1624 stood at a precarious 1,132. The king appointed a commission to investigate the struggling colony, and on its recommendation a court dissolved the company. In 1624 Virginia became a royal colony.

After 1622 relations with the Indians continued in a state of what the governor's council called "perpetual enmity" until the Indians staged another concerted attack in 1644. The English suffered as many casualties as they had twenty-two years before, but they put down the uprising with such ferocity that nothing quite like it happened again.

MARYLAND   In 1634, ten years after Virginia became a royal colony, a neighboring settlement named Maryland appeared on the northern shores of Chesapeake Bay. It was the first so-called proprietary colony, granted not to a joint-stock company but to an individual, Lord Baltimore. Sir George Calvert, the first Lord Baltimore, had announced in

0 ———— 100 Miles
0 ———— 100 Kilometers

Susquehanna R.

Delaware R.

MARYLAND

DELAWARE BAY

Potomac R.

VIRGINIA

St. Mary's (1634)

CHESAPEAKE BAY

James R.

Henrico (1610)

York R.

ATLANTIC OCEAN

Jamestown (1607)

EARLY VIRGINIA AND MARYLAND

▮ Original grant to Lord Baltimore

---- Present-day boundary of Maryland

ROANOKE ISLAND (1580s)

1625 his conversion to Catholicism and sought the colony as a refuge for English Catholics, who were subjected to discriminations at home. The charter for such a colony was finally issued in 1632, after his death.

His son, Cecilius Calvert, the second Lord Baltimore, actually founded the colony in 1634 at St. Mary's on a small stream near the mouth of the Potomac. Calvert brought along Catholic gentlemen as landholders, but a majority of the servants were Protestants. The charter gave Calvert power to make laws with the consent of the freemen (all property holders). The first legislative assembly met in 1635 and later divided into two houses, with governor and council sitting separately. The charter also empowered the proprietor to grant manorial estates, and Maryland had some sixty before 1676. But the Lords Baltimore soon found that to draw large numbers of settlers they had to offer small farms. The colony was meant to rely on mixed farming, but its fortunes, like those of Virginia, soon came to depend on tobacco.

SETTLING NEW ENGLAND

PLYMOUTH Meanwhile, far to the north of the Chesapeake, quite different colonies were taking shape. The Pilgrims who established Plymouth Colony were bent not on finding gold or making a fortune but on building a Christian commonwealth. They belonged to the most extreme and uncompromising sect of Puritans, the Separatists, who had severed all ties with the Church of England. Persecuted by James I and Anglican officials, they fled to Holland in 1607. The Calvinistic Dutch granted them asylum and toleration, but restricted them mainly to unskilled laboring jobs. After ten years in Leyden, the Pilgrims had wearied of such discrimination. Watching their children adopt Dutch customs and become sailors, soldiers, or worse, so that "their posterity would be in danger to degenerate and be corrupted," they longed for English ways and the English flag. If they could not have them at home, perhaps they might transplant them to the New World. King James would not promise outright toleration if they set up a colony, but he did agree to leave them alone.

The Leyden group secured a land patent from the Virginia Company, and in 1620, 101 men, women, and children, led by William Bradford, crammed into the *Mayflower* for the transatlantic voyage. Only half of

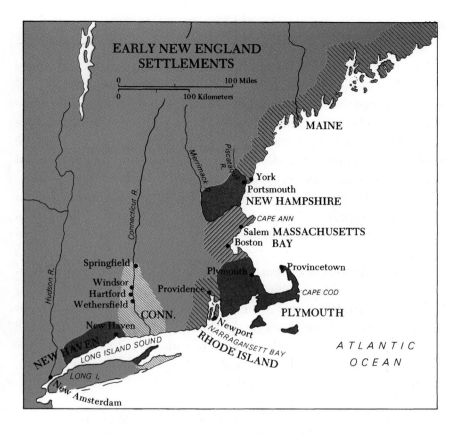

EARLY NEW ENGLAND SETTLEMENTS

0 — 100 Miles
0 — 100 Kilometers

MAINE

Merrimack R.
Piscataqua R.
Connecticut R.
Hudson R.

York
Portsmouth
NEW HAMPSHIRE

CAPE ANN
Salem MASSACHUSETTS
Boston BAY

Springfield
Windsor
Hartford
Wethersfield
CONN.
New Haven
NEW HAVEN

Providence
Plymouth

Provincetown

CAPE COD

PLYMOUTH

Newport
NARRAGANSETT BAY
RHODE ISLAND

LONG ISLAND SOUND
LONG I.
New Amsterdam

ATLANTIC
OCEAN

the voyagers were Pilgrim "Saints"—people recognized as having been elected by God for salvation; the rest were non-Pilgrim "Strangers"—ordinary settlers, hired hands, and indentured servants. The leaders undertook the voyage, as Bradford asserted, "for the glorie of God, and advancements of the Christian faith and honour of our king & countrie."

A stormy voyage led them to Cape Cod, far north of Virginia. Heading south, they encountered rough waters and turned back to seek safety at Provincetown. "Being thus arrived at safe harbor, and brought safe to land," Bradford wrote in his history, *Of Plymouth Plantation*, "they fell upon their knees and blessed the God of Heaven who had brought them over the vast and furious ocean." Exploring parties then scouted Cape Cod Bay and hit upon a place called Plymouth for their settlement. Since they were outside the jurisdiction of any organized government, forty-one of the Pilgrims entered into a formal agreement to abide by laws made by leaders of their own choosing—the Mayflower Compact of November 21, 1620. Later used as a model by other New England settlers, the compact helped establish the distinctive American tradition of consensual government.

The Pilgrims built and occupied their dwellings amid the winter snows, but many failed to see the arrival of spring. It "pleased God," Bradford noted, "to visit us with death daily, and with so general a disease that the living were scarce able to bury the dead." Nearly half the colonists died of exposure and disease, but friendly relations with the neighboring Wampanoag Indians proved their salvation. In the spring of 1621, the colonists met Squanto, who showed them how to grow maize. By autumn the Pilgrims had a bumper crop of corn, a flourishing fur trade, and a supply of lumber for shipment. To celebrate they held a harvest feast with the Wampanoag, which later would be dubbed Thanksgiving.

Throughout its separate existence, until it was absorbed into Massachusetts in 1691, Plymouth Colony's government grew out of the Mayflower Compact, which was not a formal constitution but an agreement among members of a religious group who believed that God had made a covenant (or agreement) with people to provide a way to salvation. Thus the civil government evolved naturally out of the church government, and the members of each were initially identical.

JOHN WINTHROP AND THE BEGINNINGS OF MASSACHUSETTS BAY   Plymouth colony's population never rose above 7,000, and after ten years it was overshadowed by its larger neighbor, Massachusetts Bay colony. It, too, was intended to be a holy commonwealth made up of religious folk bound together in the harmonious worship of God and pursuit of their "callings." And, like the Pilgrims, the Puritans who colonized Massachusetts Bay were primarily Congregationalists who wanted self-governing churches whose members would be limited to "visible saints," those who could demonstrate their receipt of the gift of God's grace. Unlike the Plymouth Separatists, however, the Puritans who settled Massachusetts hoped that the Church of England could be reformed. Thus they were called Non-Separating Congregationalists.

In 1629 a group of Puritans and merchants convinced King Charles I to grant their newly formed Massachusetts Bay Company an area north of Plymouth colony for settlement. Leaders of the company at first looked upon it mainly as a business venture, but a majority faction led by John Winthrop, a respected lawyer, resolved to use the colony as a refuge for persecuted Puritans and as an instrument for building a "wilderness Zion" in America.

Governor John Winthrop, in whose vision the Massachusetts Bay colony would be as "a city upon a hill."

Winthrop was a courageous and committed leader who reflected the strengths and weaknesses of the Puritan movement. He remembered that as a youth he had been "very wild and dissolute, and as years came on my lusts grew stronger." But in 1606 he experienced an intense religious conversion and soon joined the Puritan movement, determined to rid the Church of England of its Catholic trappings and to lead a life of intense piety.

By 1629 Winthrop was forty years of age, had a large family, and found himself managing a floundering English estate that could not support his seven sons. Even more unsettling was the government's heightened persecution of Puritans and other dissenters. Hence he eagerly supported the idea of establishing a spiritual plantation in the New World, and he agreed to head up the enterprise. Winthrop shrewdly took advantage of a fateful omission in the charter for the Massachusetts Bay Company: the usual proviso that the company maintain its home office in England. Winthrop's group thus decided to take the charter with them, thereby transferring the entire government of the colony to Massachusetts Bay, where they hoped to ensure Puritan control.

In 1630 the *Arbella,* with Governor John Winthrop and the charter aboard, embarked with six other ships for Massachusetts. In a sermon, "A Model of Christian Charity," delivered on board, Winthrop told his fellow Puritans "we must consider that we shall be a city upon a hill"— an exemplary beacon showing all people what a truly godly community could be. By the end of 1630 seventeen ships bearing 1,000 more colonists arrived. As settlers—Puritan and non-Puritan—poured into the region, Boston became the chief city and capital. The *Arbella* migrants were the vanguard of a massive movement, the Great Migration that carried some 40,000–50,000 English settlers to the New World over the next decade, fleeing persecution and economic depression at home.

The transfer of the Massachusetts charter, whereby an English trading company evolved into a provincial government, was a unique venture in colonization. Under this royal charter, power rested with the General Court, which elected the governor and assistants. The General Court consisted of shareholders, called freemen (those who had the "freedom of the company"), but of those who came, few besides Winthrop and his assistants had such status. This suited Winthrop and his friends, but soon other settlers demanded a share of political power. Rather than risk trouble, the inner group invited applications and finally admitted 118 additional freemen in 1631. They also stipulated that only official church members, a limited category, could become freemen.

At first the freemen had no power except to choose assistants, who in turn elected the governor and deputy governor. The procedure violated provisions of the charter, but Winthrop kept the document hidden, and few knew of its exact provisions. Controversy simmered until 1634, when each town sent two delegates to Boston to confer on matters coming before the General Court. There they demanded to see the charter, which Winthrop reluctantly produced, and they read that the power to pass laws and levy taxes rested in the General Court. Winthrop argued that the body of freemen had grown too large, but when it met, the General Court responded by turning itself into a representative body with two or three deputies to represent each town. They also chose a new governor, and Winthrop did not resume the office un- til three years later. A final stage in the evolution of the government, a two-house legislature, came in 1644, with the deputies and assistants sitting apart and all decisions requiring a majority in each house.

Thus over a period of fourteen years, the Massachusetts Bay Com- pany, a trading corporation, evolved into the governing body of a com- monwealth. Membership in a Puritan church replaced the purchase of stock as a means of becoming a freeman, which was to say a voter. The General Court, like Parliament, became a representative body of two houses, the House of Assistants corresponding roughly to the House of Lords, the House of Deputies to the House of Commons. The charter remained unchanged, but practice under the charter differed consider- ably from the original expectation.

ROGER WILLIAMS AND ANNE HUTCHINSON More by accident than design Massachusetts became the staging area for the rest of New England as new colonies grew out of religious quarrels within the fold. Puritanism created a volatile mixture: on the one hand the search for God's will could lead to a rigid orthodoxy; on the other hand it could lead troubled consciences to diverse, radical, or even bizarre convic- tions.

Young Roger Williams, who arrived in 1631, was among the first to cause problems, precisely because he was the purest of Puritans, a Sep- aratist troubled by the failure of the Massachusetts Nonconformists to repudiate the Church of England entirely. He held a brief pastorate in Salem, then tried Separatist Plymouth. Governor Bradford found Williams to be gentle and kind in his personal relations and a charis- matic speaker, but he "began to fall into strange opinions." A quarrel with the authorities over their treatment of Indians led Williams to re- turn to Salem. There he continued to challenge the social and religious status quo. Williams's belief that a true church must have no relations with the English government, the Anglican establishment, or with the unregenerate led him eventually to the conclusion that no true church was possible, unless perhaps consisting of his wife and himself—and he may have had doubts about her.

But eccentric as some of Williams's beliefs may have been to the au- thorities, they led him to establish principles that later generations would honor for other reasons. The purity of the church that he espoused required complete separation of church and state and freedom from coercion in matters of faith. Such views were too advanced even for the radical church of Salem, which finally removed him, whereupon Williams charged that the churches were "ulcered and gangrened." In 1635 a provoked General Court banished him to England. Aided by Narragansett Indian friends, Williams and a few followers headed into the wilderness in the dead of winter and eventually were taken in by the Narragansetts. In the spring of 1636 Williams bought some land from the Indians and established the town of Providence at the head of Narragansett Bay, the first permanent settlement in Rhode Island, and the first in America to legislate freedom of religion.

Anne Hutchinson quarreled with the Puritan leaders for different reasons. She was married to a prominent merchant and had given birth to thirteen children. Strong-willed and articulate, she also worked as a healer and midwife and hosted meetings in her Boston home to discuss sermons. Soon, however, those discussions turned into forums for Hutchinson to provide her own commentaries on religious matters. She claimed to have had direct revelations from the Holy Spirit that convinced her that only two or three Puritan ministers actually preached the appropriate "covenant of grace." The others, she charged, were deluded and incompetent and were promoting a "covenant of works" that led people to believe that good conduct would ensure their salvation.

Hutchinson's beliefs were provocative for several reasons. Puritan theology affirmed the Calvinist doctrine that people could be saved only by God's grace rather than through their own willful actions. But Puritanism in practice also insisted that ministers were necessary to interpret God's will for the people so as to "prepare" them for the possibility of salvation. In challenging the very legitimacy of the ministerial community as well as the hard-earned assurances of salvation enjoyed by current church members, Hutchinson was undermining the stability of an already fragile social system and theological order. Moreover, her critics likened her claim of direct revelations from the Holy Spirit to the Antinomian heresy, technically a belief that one is freed from obeying the moral law by one's own faith and by God's grace. What made the situation worse in such a male-dominated society, of course, was that a *woman* had the audacity to make such charges and assertions. Anne Hutchinson had both offended authority and sanctioned a disruptive individualism.

Hutchinson, again pregnant, was hauled before the General Court in 1637, and for two days she verbally sparred on equal terms with the presiding magistrates and testifying ministers. Her skillful deflections of the charges and her ability to cite chapter and verse defenses of her actions led an exasperated Governor Winthrop to explode: "We do not mean to discourse with those of your sex." He found Hutchinson to be "a woman of haughty and fierce carriage, of a nimble wit and active spirit, and a very voluble tongue."

As the intense trial continued, an overwrought Hutchinson was eventually lured into convicting herself by claiming direct divine inspiration. Banished in 1638 as "a woman not fit for our society," she walked through the wilderness to Providence and then settled with her family and a few followers on an island near what is now Portsmouth. The arduous journey had taken a toll, however. Hutchinson grew sick and her baby was stillborn, leading her critics back in Massachusetts to assert that the "monstrous birth" was God's way of punishing her for her sins. Hutchinson's spirits never recovered. After her husband's death in 1642 she moved to Long Island, then under Dutch jurisdiction, and the following year she and five of her children were massacred during an Indian attack. Her fate, wrote an unusually vindictive Winthrop, was "a special manifestation of divine justice."

Thus the colony of Rhode Island, the smallest in America, grew up in Narragansett Bay as a refuge for dissenters who agreed that the state had no right to coerce religious belief. In 1640 they formed a confederation and in 1644 secured their first charter. Williams lived until 1683, an active and beloved citizen of the commonwealth he founded in a society which, during his lifetime at least, lived up to his principles of religious freedom and a government based on the consent of the people.

CONNECTICUT, NEW HAMPSHIRE, AND MAINE   Connecticut had a more orthodox beginning. It was founded by groups of Massachusetts Puritans seeking better lands and access to the fur trade farther west. In 1636 three entire church congregations trekked westward by the "Great Road," driving their hogs and cattle before them, and moved to the Connecticut River towns of Wethersfield, Windsor, and Hartford, which earlier arrivals had laid out the previous year.

Led by Thomas Hooker, they organized the self-governing colony of Connecticut in 1637 as a response to the danger of attack from the Pequot Indians, who lived east of the river. In 1639 the Connecticut General Court adopted the "Fundamental Orders of Connecticut," a series of laws providing for a government like that of Massachusetts. Voting in the Connecticut colony, however, was not limited to church members. New Haven had by then appeared within the later limits of Connecticut. A group of English Puritans, led by their minister, John Davenport, had migrated first to Massachusetts and then, seeking a place to establish themselves in commerce, to New Haven on Long Island Sound in 1638. The New Haven colony became the most rigorously Puritan of all. Like all the other offshoots of Massachusetts, it too lacked a charter and maintained a self-governing independence until 1662, when it was absorbed into Connecticut under the terms of that colony's first charter.

To the north of Massachusetts, most of what is now New Hampshire and Maine was granted in 1622 by the Council for New England to Sir Ferdinando Gorges and Captain John Mason and their associates. In 1629 Mason and Gorges divided their territory at the Piscataqua River, Mason taking the southern part, which he named New Hampshire. In the 1630s Puritan immigrants began filtering in, and in 1638 the Reverend John Wheelwright, one of Anne Hutchinson's group, founded Exeter. Maine consisted of a few scattered and small settlements, mostly fishing stations, the chief of them being York.

RENEWED SETTLEMENT

Before 1640 English settlers in New England and around Chesapeake Bay had established two great beachheads on the Atlantic coast, separated by the Dutch colony of New Netherland. After 1640, however, the struggle between king and Parliament distracted attention from colonization, and migration dwindled to a trickle for more than twenty years. During the time of civil war and Oliver Cromwell's Puritan dictatorship, the struggling colonies were left pretty much alone, especially in New England, where English Puritans saw little need to intervene. Virginia and Maryland remained almost as independent from British authority as New England.

The Restoration of King Charles II in England in 1660 involved scarcely any changes in colonial governments, since little had occurred there under Cromwell. Emigration rapidly expanded the populations of

Virginia and Maryland. Fears of reprisals against Puritan New England by the reestablishment of the Anglican Church as the official church proved unfounded, at least for the time being. Massachusetts gained reconfirmation of its charter in 1662, and Connecticut and Rhode Island received the first royal charters in 1662 and 1663. All three retained their status as self-governing corporations. New Haven disappeared as a separate entity and was absorbed into Connecticut.

SETTLING THE CAROLINAS   The Restoration of Charles II, the Merry Monarch, opened a new season of enthusiasm for colonial expansion, directed mainly by royal favorites. Within twelve years the English had conquered New Netherland, had settled Carolina, and had very nearly filled out the shape of the colonies. In the middle region formerly claimed by the Dutch, four new colonies sprang into being: New York, New Jersey, Pennsylvania, and Delaware. Without exception the new colonies were proprietary, awarded by the king to "proprietors," men who had remained loyal during the civil war.

Carolina from the start comprised two widely separated areas of settlement. The northernmost part, long called Albemarle, remained a remote scattering of settlers along the shores of Albemarle Sound, isolated from Virginia by the Dismal Swamp and lacking easy access for oceangoing vessels. Albemarle had no governor until 1664, no assembly until 1665, and not even a town until a group of French Huguenots (Protestants) founded the village of Bath in 1704.

The eight Lords Proprietors to whom the king gave Carolina neglected Albemarle from the outset and focused on more promising sites to the south. Eager to find settlers who had already been seasoned in the colonies, they looked first to Barbados. The rise of large-scale sugar production in Barbados had persuaded small planters to try their luck elsewhere. Sir Anthony Ashley-Cooper finally spurred the enterprise by convincing his fellow proprietors to take on more of the financial burden of settlement. In 1669 three ships left London with about 100 settlers recruited in England; they sailed first to Barbados to pick up more settlers and then north to Bermuda. The expedition finally landed in America at a place several miles up the Ashley River. There Charles Town remained from 1670 to 1680, when it was moved across and downstream to Oyster Point, overlooking a fine harbor where, as proud

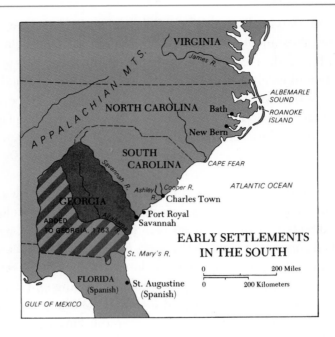

Charlestonians later claimed, the Ashley and Cooper Rivers "join to form the Atlantic Ocean."

The government rested on one of the most curious documents of colonial history, the "Fundamental Constitutions of Carolina," drawn up by Lord Ashley-Cooper with the help of his secretary, the philosopher John Locke. Its cumbersome form of government and its provisions for an almost feudal social system and an elaborate nobility had little effect in the colony except to encourage a practice of large land grants, but from the beginning smaller "headrights" were given to immigrants who paid their own way. The provision that had greatest effect was a grant of religious toleration, designed to encourage immigration, which gave South Carolina a distinctive degree of indulgence (extending even to Jews and heathens) and ethnic pluralism.

Ambitious English planters from Barbados dominated the colony and soon organized a major trade in Indian slaves, whom the Westo Indians obligingly drove to the coast for shipment to the Caribbean. The first major export other than furs and slaves was cattle, and a true staple crop was not developed until the introduction of rice in the 1690s.

South Carolina became a separate royal colony in 1719. North Carolina remained under the proprietors' rule for ten more years, when they surrendered their governing rights to the crown.

THE SOUTHERN INDIAN TRADE   The major Indian tribes in the Carolinas—the Catawba, Cherokee, Chickasaw, Choctaw, Creek, and Tuscarora—combined farming with hunting and fishing to produce a thriving culture. Like the other North American tribes, however, they were unprepared for the diseases that the Europeans brought with them from the Old World. They were also ill equipped to deal with the commercial challenges posed by white settlement. The English settlers in the Carolinas exchanged their manufactured goods—hoes, kettles, knives, beads, and cloth—for deerskins.

In the late seventeenth century English merchants—mostly illiterate adventurers—began traveling southward from Virginia down the Occaneechi trading path into the Piedmont region of Carolina, where they developed a flourishing exchange with the Catawbas. By 1690 traders from Charleston, South Carolina, made their way up the Savannah River to arrange deals with the Cherokees, Creeks, and Chickasaws. Between 1699 and 1715 Carolina exported an average of 54,000 deerskins per year. The voracious demand for the soft skins almost exterminated the deer population.

The flourishing trade with the English exposed the Indians to contagious diseases and also entwined them in a dependent relationship that would prove disastrous to their traditional way of life. Eager to receive more finished goods, weapons, and ammunition, the Indians became pliable trading partners, easily manipulated by wily English entrepreneurs and government officials. The English traders began providing the Indians with firearms and rum as incentives to convince them to capture rival tribesmen to be sold as slaves.

The continuing Indian trade led to repeated troubles. In 1715, Creeks, Choctaws, and members of smaller tribes organized a more massive revolt against English control. This so-called Yamasee War began when Indians killed several English traders, including the Indian agent for South Carolina. When a war party arrived at John Hearn's outpost, he gave them food "according to our Usual friendly manner"—and then they killed him. A similar incident resulted in twenty-two whites being killed. Word of the uprising provoked similar attacks on traders throughout South Carolina. The English attributed the attacks to French and Spanish intrigues, but it now seems likely that the Indians acted on their own. The English colonists won out by playing the Indians against one another, convincing the Cherokees to join their side.

When the Creek leaders visited the Cherokees in an effort to gain their support, the Cherokees killed them, an incident that engendered hatred between the two tribes for years thereafter. The Yamasee War ended in 1717, when the Creeks signed a peace treaty. But infighting among the Indians continued. For the next ten years or so, the Creeks and Cherokees engaged in a costly blood feud, much to the delight of the English. One Carolinian explained that their challenge was to figure "how to hold both as our friends, for some time, and assist them in cutting one another's throats without offending either. This is the game we intend to play if possible." The French played the same brutal game, doing their best to excite hatred between the Choctaws and the Chickasaws.

NEW NETHERLAND BECOMES NEW YORK   Charles II resolved early to pluck out that old thorn in the side of the English colonies—New Netherland. The Dutch colony was older than New England and had been planted when the two Protestant powers enjoyed friendly relations in opposition to Catholic Spain. The Dutch East India Company (organized in 1620) had hired an English captain, Henry Hudson, to seek the elusive passage to China. In 1609 Hudson had discovered Delaware Bay and had explored the river named for him to a point probably beyond Albany, where he and a group of Mohawks made merry with brandy. From that contact stemmed a lasting trade between the Dutch and Iroquois nations. In 1614 the Dutch established fur-trading posts on Manhattan Island and upriver at Fort Orange (later Albany). Ten years later a newly organized West India Company began permanent settlements. In 1626 Governor Peter Minuit purchased Manhattan from the Indians, and the new village of New Amsterdam became the capital of New Netherland.

Like the French, the Dutch were interested mainly in the fur trade and less in agricultural settlements. In 1629, however, the Dutch West India Company provided that any stockholder might obtain a large estate (a patroonship) if he peopled it with fifty adults within four years. The patroon supplied cattle, tools, and buildings. His tenants, in turn, paid him rent, used his gristmill, gave him first option on surplus crops, and submitted to a court he established. It amounted to transplanting the feudal manor into the New World and met with as little luck as similar efforts in Maryland and South Carolina. Volunteers for serfdom

New Amsterdam in 1667.

were hard to find when there was land to be had elsewhere, and most settlers took advantage of the company's provision that one could have as farms all the lands one could improve.

The colony's government was under the almost absolute control of a governor sent out by the company, subject to little check from his council or from the directors back in Holland. The governors were mostly stubborn autocrats, either corrupt or inept, especially at Indian relations. They depended on a small professional garrison for defense, and the inhabitants (including a number of English on Long Island) betrayed almost total indifference in 1664 when Governor Peter Stuyvesant called them to arms against a threatening British fleet. Almost defenseless, old soldier Stuyvesant blustered and stomped about on his wooden leg, but he finally surrendered without firing a shot.

The plan of conquest had been hatched by Charles II's brother, James, the duke of York, later King James II. As lord high admiral and an investor in the African trade, the duke of York had already engaged in harassing Dutch shipping and Dutch forts in Africa. When he and his advisers counseled that New Netherland could easily be conquered, Charles II simply granted the region to his brother. The English transformed New Amsterdam into New York and Fort Orange into Albany, and they held the country thereafter, except for a brief Dutch reoccupation in 1673–1674. The Dutch, however, left a permanent imprint on the land and the language: the Dutch vernacular faded away, but places like Wall Street (the original wall provided protection against Indians) and Broadway (Breede Wegh) remained, along with family names like Rensselaer, Roosevelt, and Van Buren. The Dutch presence lingered in the Dutch Reformed church; in words like boss, cookie, crib, snoop, stoop, and spook; and in the legendary Santa Claus and Rip Van Winkle.

THE IROQUOIS LEAGUE   One of the most significant effects of European settlement in North America during the seventeenth century was the intensification of warfare between Indian peoples. The same combination of forces that weakened the Indian population of New England and the Carolinas befell the tribes around New York City and the lower Hudson valley. Dissension among the Indians and susceptibility to infectious disease left them vulnerable to exploitation by whites and by other Indians.

In the interior of New York, however, a different situation arose. There the Iroquois (an Algonquian term signifying "snake" or "terrifying man") nation would eventually forge an alliance so strong that the outnumbered Dutch and, later, English traders were forced to work with the Indians in exploiting the lucrative fur trade. Initially, the Mahicans (an offshoot of the Pequots) supplied the Dutch with pelts. By 1625, however, the game animals in the Mahican territory had been killed off, so the Dutch turned to the Iroquois, a federation of five tribes who spoke related languages—the Mohawk, Oneida, Onondaga, Cayuga, and Seneca (a sixth tribe, the Tuscaroras, joined them in 1712). Legend has it that a Mohawk sachem (chief) named Hiawatha unified the "Five Nations" in the early fifteenth century.

By the early 1600s, some fifty chiefs governed the 12,000 members of the Iroquois League. The sachems made decisions for all the villages and served to minimize tribal rivalries and dissension within the confederacy. The well-organized, firmly knit Iroquois tribes lived in rectangular "long houses" sheathed in bark. These multifamily dwellings could house fifty or sixty members of an extended family. Iroquois men hunted deer, bear, and beaver; women grew corn, beans, and squash. They used belts of colored beads, known as wampum, to symbolize words intended to certify treaties or record transactions with other Indians and whites. The rejection or return of a wampum belt meant that its message or proposal was unacceptable. Although a patriarchal society, the Iroquois granted considerable powers to women; they controlled the nominations for the tribal councils and could remove ineffective or corrupt leaders.

When the Iroquois began to deplete the local game during the 1640s, they used firearms supplied by their Dutch trading partners to seize the Canadian hunting grounds of the neighboring Hurons and Eries. During the so-called Beaver Wars, the Iroquois defeated the western tribes and thereafter hunted the region to extinction. Other Indian nations such as the Fox, Sac, and Kickapoo fled in terror at the approach of the Iroquois.

Iroquois men were proud, ruthless warriors. Participation in a war party served as the crucial rite of passage for young men. They fought opponents to gain status and revenge and to ease the grief caused by the death of friends and relatives. Their skill and courage in battle determined their social status. A warrior's success was not only measured by his fighting prowess but also by his ability to capture prisoners and bring them back alive for adoption or ritual execution. This helps explain the Indian preference for surprise attacks and ambushes rather than conventional frontal assaults. If captured themselves, the Iroquois expected to be tortured; they, in turn, tortured their foes.

While providing profitable new hunting grounds, wars against other Indian tribes caused great losses. This led the Iroquois to replace lost relatives by allowing elder women to "adopt" able-bodied captives after they had been tortured so as to break their allegiance to their native group or culture. In 1657 a French missionary noted that "more Foreigners than natives of the country" resided in Iroquoia. By the 1660s more than two-thirds of the residents of some Iroquois villages were adoptees.

During the second half of the seventeenth century, the relentless search for furs and captives led Iroquois war parties to range far and wide across what is today eastern North America. They gained control over a huge area from the St. Lawrence River to Tennessee and from Maine to Michigan. These wars helped reorient the political relationships in the whole eastern half of the continent, especially in the area from the Ohio Valley northward across the Great Lakes basin. Besieged by the Iroquois Confederacy, the western tribes forged defensive alliances with the French.

In the 1690s the French and their Indian allies gained the advantage over the Iroquois. They destroyed their crops and villages, infected them with smallpox, and reduced the male population by more than a third. Facing extermination, the Iroquois made peace with the French in 1701. They claimed to be tired of serving the English as a "Pack of Hounds" to harass the French. During the first half of the eighteenth century, they maintained a shrewd neutrality between the two rival European powers that enabled them to play the British off against the French, all the while creating a thriving fur trade for themselves. Iroquois warriors intermarried and intermingled with women of the western tribes and occasionally went to war against reluctant trading partners such as the Catawbas to the south.

NEW JERSEY   Shortly after the conquest of New York, still in 1664, the duke of York granted his lands between the Hudson and the Delaware Rivers to Sir George Carteret and Lord John Berkeley and named the territory for Carteret's native island of Jersey. In East New Jersey, peopled at first by perhaps 200 Dutch who had crossed the Hudson, new settlements gradually arose: disaffected Puritans from New Haven founded Newark, and a group of Scots founded Perth Amboy. In the west, which faced the Delaware, a scattering of Swedes, Finns, and Dutch remained, soon to be overwhelmed by swarms of English Quakers. In 1702 East and West Jersey were united as a royal colony.

PENNSYLVANIA AND DELAWARE   The Quaker sect, as the Society of Friends was called in ridicule, was the most influential of many radical groups that sprang from the turbulence of the English Civil War. Founded by George Fox about 1647, the Quakers carried further than any other group the doctrine of individual spiritual inspiration and interpretation—the "inner light," they called it. Discarding all formal sacraments and formal ministry, they refused deference to persons of rank, used the familiar "thee" and "thou" in addressing everyone, declined to take oaths because that was contrary to Scripture, and embraced simple living and pacifism. Quakers experienced intense persecution—often in their zeal they seemed to invite it—but never inflicted it on others. Their toleration extended to complete religious freedom for all and the equality of the sexes, including the full participation of women in religious affairs.

In 1673 George Fox returned from an American visit with the vision of a Quaker commonwealth in the New World and enticed others with his idea. The entrance of Quakers into the New Jersey proprietorships encouraged others to migrate, especially to the Delaware River side. And soon, across the river, arose Fox's "Holy Experiment," the Quaker Commonwealth, the colony of Pennsylvania. William Penn, the colony's founder, was born in 1644 and raised as a proper gentleman, but in 1667 he converted to Quakerism. "God took me by the hand," he later recalled, "and led me out of the pleasures, vanities and hopes of the world."

Upon his father's death, Penn inherited the friendship of the Stuarts and a substantial estate, including claim to a sizable loan his father had made to the crown. Whether in settlement of the claim or out of simple friendship, he received from Charles II in 1681 proprietary rights to a huge tract of land in America and named it, at the king's insistence, for his father: Pennsylvania (literally Penn Woods). Penn vigorously recruited settlers to his new colony, and religious dissenters from England and the Continent—Quakers, Mennonites, Amish, Moravians, Baptists—flocked to the region. Indian relations were good from the beginning because of the Quakers' friendliness and Penn's careful policy of purchasing land titles from the Indians.

Pennsylvania's government resembled that of other proprietary colonies, except that the councilors as well as the assembly were elected by the freemen (taxpayers and property owners) and the governor had no veto—although Penn as proprietor did. "Any government is free . . . where the laws rule and the people are a party to the laws," Penn wrote in the 1682 Frame of Government. He hoped to show that a government could run in accordance with Quaker principles, that it could maintain peace and order without oaths or wars, that religion could flourish without an established church and with absolute freedom of conscience.

In 1682 the duke of York also granted Penn the area of Delaware, another part of the Dutch territory. At first Delaware became part of Pennsylvania, but after 1701 the settlers were granted the right to choose their own assembly. From then until the American Revolution, Delaware had a separate assembly but had the same governor as Pennsylvania.

GEORGIA   Georgia was the last of the British continental colonies to be established, half a century after Pennsylvania. In 1732 George II gave the land between the Savannah and Altamaha Rivers to the twenty-one trustees of Georgia. In two respects Georgia was unique among the colonies: it was set up both as a philanthropic experiment and a military buffer against Spanish Florida. General James E. Oglethorpe, who accompanied the first colonists as resident trustee, represented both concerns: as a soldier who organized the colony's defenses, and as a philanthropist who championed prison reform and sought a colonial refuge for the poor and persecuted.

In 1733 Oglethorpe and a band of 120 colonists founded Savannah near the mouth of the Savannah River. Soon thereafter they were joined by Protestant refugees from central Europe, who made the colony for a time more German than English. The addition of Scottish Highlanders, Portuguese Jews, Welsh, and others gave the early colony a cosmopolitan character much like that of South Carolina.

As a buffer against Spanish Florida the colony succeeded, but as a philanthropic experiment it failed. Efforts to develop silk and wine production floundered. Landholdings were limited to 500 acres, rum was prohibited, and the importation of slaves forbidden, partly to leave room for servants brought on charity, partly to ensure security. But the utopian rules soon collapsed. The regulations against rum and slavery were widely disregarded and finally abandoned. By 1759 all restrictions on landholding were removed.

In 1753 the trustees' charter expired and the province reverted to the crown. As a royal colony Georgia acquired for the first time an effective government. The province developed slowly over the next decade, but grew rapidly in population and wealth after 1763. Instead of wine and silk, Georgians exported rice, indigo, lumber, naval stores, beef, and pork, and carried on a lively trade with the West Indies. The colony finally had become a roaring success.

THRIVING COLONIES

After a late start and with little design, the English outstripped both the French and the Spanish in the New World. The lack of plan marked the genius of English colonization, for it gave free rein to a variety of human impulses. The centralized control imposed by the monarchs of Spain and France got their colonies off the mark more quickly but eventually brought their downfall because it hobbled innovation and responsiveness to new circumstances. The British preferred private investment with a minimum of royal control. Not a single colony was begun at the direct initiative of the crown. In the English colonies poor immigrants had a much greater chance of getting at least a small parcel of land, and a degree of self-government made the English colonies more responsive to new challenges—if sometimes stalled by controversy.

Moreover, the compact model of English settlement contrasted sharply with the pattern of Spain's far-flung conquests or France's far-reaching trade routes to the interior by way of the St. Lawrence and Mississippi Rivers. Geography reinforced England's bent for concentrated occupation and settlement of its colonies. The rivers and bays indenting the coasts served as veins of communication along which colonies first sprang up, but no great river offered a highway to the far interior. About a hundred miles back in Georgia and the Carolinas, and nearer the coast to the north, the "fall line" of the rivers presented rocky rapids that marked the head of navigation and the end of the coastal plain. About a hundred miles beyond that, and farther back in Pennsylvania, stretched the rolling expanse of the Piedmont, literally the foothills. The final backdrop of English America was the Appalachian Mountain range running from New England to Georgia. For 150 years the western outreach of settlement stopped at the slopes of the mountains. To the east lay the wide expanse of ocean, which served as a highway for the transit of European culture to America, but also as a barrier beyond which Old World values and folkways took to new paths in a new environment.

MAKING CONNECTIONS

- What we now know about the early settlements sets the stage for regional differences in social patterns discussed in the next chapter.

- This chapter concludes with the observation that "The lack of plan marked the genius of English colonization. . . ." This will change in Chapter 3 as England begins to take control of the American colonies.

- Later relations between colonists and Native Americans, described in Chapter 3, had their roots in the history of these early settlements.

FURTHER READING

A comprehensive anthropological account of American Indian life is Harold E. Driver's *Indians of North America* (2nd ed., 1969). On the theme of cultural conflict, see James Axtell's *The Invasion Within* (1986)* and *Beyond 1492: Encounters in Colonial North America* (1992).* Karen O. Kupperman's *Settling with the Indians: The Meeting of English and Indian Cultures in America, 1580–1640* (1980)* stresses the racist nature of the conflict. Alfred W. Crosby, Jr.'s *The Columbian Exchange* (1972)* discusses the biological aspects of the cultural collision.

The most comprehensive overviews of European exploration are two volumes by Samuel E. Morison, *The European Discovery of America: The Northern Voyages, A.D. 500–1600* (1971), and *The Southern Voyages, A.D. 1492–1616* (1974). Scholarship on Columbus is best handled by Foster Provost's *Columbus: An Annotated Guide to the Scholarship on His Life and Writings* (1990), and Vincent Sinovcic's *Columbus—Debunking of a Legend* (1990).

*These books are available in paperback editions.

David J. Weber offers a comprehensive survey of Spanish colonization in *The Spanish Frontier in North America* (1993). For background
on the motives for English exploration and settlement, see Alfred L.
Rouse's *The Expansion of Elizabethan England* (1955) and Carl Bridenbaugh's *Vexed and Troubled Englishmen, 1590–1642* (1968). Bernard
Bailyn's *Voyagers to the West: A Passage in the Peopling of America on the
Eve of the Revolution* (1986),* provides a comprehensive view of European migration. A valuable summary of recent scholarship is *Colonial
British America* (1984),* edited by Jack P. Greene and J. R. Pole. For
the effect of English settlement on Native Americans see D. W. Mein-
ing's *Atlantic America* (1986).* English constitutional traditions and
their effect on the colonists are examined in Edmund S. Morgan's *Inventing the People: The Rise of Popular Sovereignty in England and
America* (1988).*

Carl Bridenbaugh's *Jamestown, 1544–1699* (1980) traces the English
experience on the Chesapeake. See also *The Chesapeake in the 17th
Century: Essays on Anglo-American Society and Politics* (1980),* edited
by Thad Tate and David Ammerman.

See Daniel K. Richter's *The Ordeal of the Longhouse: The Peoples of
the Iroquois League in the Era of European Colonization* (1992) for a history of the northeastern Iroquois Nation.

Scholarship abounds on Puritanism. The problem of translating idea
into governance is treated elegantly in Edmund S. Morgan's *The Puritan Dilemma: The Story of John Winthrop* (1958).* Andrew Delbanco's
The Puritan Ordeal (1989)* is a powerful study of the tensions inherent
in the Puritan outlook.

Useful works on the problem of dissent in a theocracy include Edmund S. Morgan's *Roger Williams, the Church, and the State* (1967)*
and Emery Battis's *Saints and Sectaries: Anne Hutchinson and the Antinomian Controversy in Massachusetts Bay Colony* (1962).

Randall Balmer's *A Perfect Babel of Confusion: Dutch Religion and
English Culture in the Middle Colonies* (1989) describes how the English conquest of New Netherland intensified the cultural complexity of
the middle colonies. The influence of Quakers can be studied through
Gary B. Nash's *Quakers and Politics: Pennsylvania, 1681–1726* (1968).

Settlement of the areas along the south Atlantic is traced in Clarence
L. Ver Steeg's *Origins of a Southern Mosaic* (1975). The early chapters

*These books are available in paperback editions.

of Robert M. Weir's *Colonial South Carolina* (1983) cover the activities of the Lords Proprietors. For an imaginative study of race and the settlement of South Carolina, see Peter Wood's *Black Majority: Negroes in Colonial South Carolina from 1670 through the Stono Rebellion* (1975).* To study Oglethorpe's aspirations, consult Paul S. Taylor's *Georgia Plan: 1732–1752* (1971). A brilliant book on relations between the Catawba Indians and their black and white neighbors is James H. Merrell's *The Indians' New World: Catawbas and Their Neighbors from European Contact Through the Era of Removal* (1989).*

*These books are available in paperback editions.

2 ∂ COLONIAL WAYS OF LIFE

CHAPTER ORGANIZER

This chapter focuses on:

- the social and economic differences among the southern, middle, and New England colonies

- how various groups of people of different genders, races, and classes fit into colonial society

- the impact of the Enlightenment and the Great Awakening on the American colonies

THE SHAPE OF EARLY AMERICA

It is well to remember the prominent leaders and colorful figures of the colonial period—John Smith, Pocahontas, William Bradford, John Winthrop, Roger Williams, Anne Hutchinson, and others. But the process of carving a new civilization out of an abundant yet menacing and violent frontier was largely the story of thousands of diverse folk engaged in the everyday tasks of building homes, planting crops, raising families, enforcing laws, and worshipping their God.

Those who colonized America during the seventeenth and eighteenth centuries were part of a massive pattern of social migration occurring throughout Europe and Africa. Everywhere, people were on the move.

They were migrating from farms to villages, from villages to cities, and from homelands to colonies. They moved for different reasons. Most were responding to powerful social and economic forces: rapid population growth, the rise of commercial agriculture, and the early stages of the industrial revolution. Others sought political security or religious freedom. Of course, Africans were moved to new lands against their will.

Migrants to America came from diverse locales—the streets of London and other cities in southern and central England, the farms of Yorkshire and the Scottish Highlands, the villages of Germany, Switzerland, and Protestant Ireland, and the savannas and jungles of west Africa. Most who came to America were young (over half were under twenty-five) and most were male. Almost half were indentured servants or slaves, and, during the eighteenth century, England transported some 50,000 convicted felons to the North American colonies. About a third of the settlers journeyed with their families; most arrived alone. A very few were wealthy; more were impoverished. Most immigrants were of the "middling sort," neither very rich nor very poor. Whatever their status or ambition, however, this extraordinary mosaic of ordinary yet adventurous people was primarily responsible for creating America's enduring institutions and values.

BRITISH FOLKWAYS   The vast majority of early settlers came from Great Britain. Four mass migrations from distinct regions of Britain occurred over the seventeenth and eighteenth centuries. The first involved some 20,000 Puritans who settled Massachusetts between 1629 and 1641, most of whom hailed from the East Anglian counties east of London. A generation later, a smaller group of wealthy royalist cavaliers and their indentured servants migrated from southern England to Virginia. These English aristocrats, mostly Anglicans, were already accustomed to severe social inequalities and so had few qualms about the introduction of African slavery.

The third migratory wave brought some 23,000 Quakers from the north midlands of England to the Delaware Valley colonies of West Jersey, Pennsylvania, and Delaware. They imported with them a social system distinctive for its sense of spiritual equality, suspicion of social hierarchy and powerful elites, and commitment to plain living and high thinking. The fourth and largest surge of colonization occurred between

1717 and 1775 and included hundreds of thousands of Celtic Britons and Scotch-Irish from northern Ireland, the Scottish lowlands, and the northern counties of England; these were mostly coarse, feisty, clannish folk who settled in the rugged backcountry along the Appalachian Mountains.

It was long assumed that the strenuous demands of the American frontier environment served as a great "melting pot" that stripped such immigrants of their native identities and melded them into homogeneous Americans. In the late eighteenth century, J. Hector St. John de Crèvecoeur, an articulate Frenchman who took up farming in Orange County, New York, sounded this theme when he wrote that the American was a European who, "leaving behind him all his ancient prejudices and manners, receives new ones from the new mode of life he has embraced. . . . Here individuals of all nations are melted into a new race of men, whose labors and posterity will one day cause great changes in the world."

But it was not that simple. For all of the transforming effects of the New World, the persistence of disparate British ways of life was remarkable. Although most British settlers spoke a common language and shared the Protestant faith, they were in fact diverse people who carried with them—and retained—sharply different cultural attitudes and customs from their home regions. They spoke distinct dialects, cooked different foods, named and raised their children differently, adopted divergent educational philosophies and attitudes toward time, built their houses in contrasting architectural styles, engaged in disparate games and forms of recreation, and organized their societies differently.

Echoes of these regionally based folkways still resonate through American culture. Houses in New England still favor two styles brought from East Anglia: the "saltbox"—featuring two stories in front and one in back—and the one-and-a-half-story Cape Cod. People in the South prefer fried foods in part because their ancestors from southern and western England did so. And people in the hollows of Appalachia who manufacture "moonshine" are simply continuing a pattern of home distilling begun in the borderlands of northern Britain.

Other examples of cultural continuity abound. The distinctive high-pitched nasal whine associated with the New England dialect, for instance, is a product not of the American environment but of the "Norfolk whine" still evident in England's East Anglia region. Likewise, the slow drawl associated with Virginia cavaliers replicates a dialect common in southern and western England, and the speech pattern common in Appalachia that pronounces *where* as *whar* and *there* as *thar* is a product of the Scottish and Irish borderlands. Terms common to the Appalachian backcountry such as "hoosier," "redneck," and "cracker" were also imported from England rather than homegrown.

But the British cultural legacy extends well beyond linguistics. In gender relations, religious practices, criminal propensities, and dozens of other ways, many Americans in the 1990s still reflect age-old British customs. Of course, such cultural continuity is not unique to British-Americans. Enduring folkways are also evident among the descendants of settlers from Africa, Europe, Latin America, the Middle East, and Asia. Americans thus constitute a mosaic rather than a homogeneous mass, and they share a diverse social and cultural heritage.

SEABOARD ECOLOGY A cherished American legend asserts that those settling British America arrived to find a pristine environment, an unspoiled wilderness little touched by human activity. But that was not the case. For thousands of years, the pre-Columbian inhabitants of the eastern seaboard had modified their environment. Indian hunting practices over the centuries had produced what one scholar has called the "greatest known loss of wild species" in American history. In addition, the Indians had burned woods and undergrowth to provide cropland, to ease travel through hardwood forests, and to nourish the grasses, berries, and other forage for the animals they hunted. This "slash and burn" agriculture had halted the normal forest succession and, especially in the Southeast, created large stands of longleaf pines, still the most common source of timber in the region.

Equally important in shaping the ecosystem of America was the European attitude toward the environment. Where the native Americans tended to be migratory, considering land and animals as communal resources to be shared and consumed only as necessary, many European colonizers viewed natural resources as privately owned commodities. Settlers thus looked with disdain upon the subsistence level of Indian agriculture and quickly set about evicting Indians, clearing, fencing, improving, and selling land, growing surpluses, and trapping game for commercial use.

In many places—Plymouth, for instance, or St. Mary's, Maryland— settlers occupied the sites of former Indian towns, and corn, beans, and squash quickly became colonial staples, along with new crops brought from Europe. In time a more dense population of humans and their domestic animals created a landscape of fields, meadows, fences, barns, and houses.

Such innovations radically altered the ecology of the New World environment. Cleared and grazed land is warmer and drier, more subject to flooding and erosion. Foraging cattle, sheep, horses, and pigs gradually changed the distribution of trees, shrubs, and grasses. Indians, far from being passive observers, contributed to the process of environmental change by trading furs for metal or glass trinkets. This decimated the populations of large mammals that had earlier been central to Indian culture. By 1750 such unintended consequences had changed markedly the physical environment from what it had been in 1600. New England, for example, by then had become a commercial success but essentially an agricultural wasteland.

POPULATION GROWTH England's first footholds in America were bought at a fearful price. The ocean crossing aboard crowded, disease-ridden ships was anything but pleasant, and the early settlements were even more threatening. But once the brutal seasoning time was past and the colony was on its feet, Virginia and its successors grew at a prodigious rate. After the last major Indian uprising in 1644, Virginia's population quadrupled from about 8,000 to 32,000 over the next thirty years, then more than doubled, to 75,000, by 1704.

Throughout the mainland colonies, the yearly growth rate during the eighteenth century ran about 3 percent. In 1625 the English colonists numbered little more than 2,000 in Virginia and Plymouth together; by 1700 the population in the colonies was perhaps 250,000, and during the eighteenth century it doubled at least every twenty-five years. By 1750 the number of colonists had passed 1 million; by 1775 it stood at about 2.5 million. In 1700 the English at home outnumbered the colonists by about 20 to 1; by 1775, on the eve of the American Revolution, the ratio was about 3 to 1.

America's plentiful land beckoned immigrants and induced them to replenish the earth with large families. Where labor was scarce, chil-

Mr. John Freake, and Mrs. Elizabeth Freake and Baby Mary. Elizabeth married John at age nineteen; Mary, born when Elizabeth was thirty-two, was the Freakes' eighth and last child.

dren could lend a hand, and once grown, they could find new land for themselves if need be. Colonists tended, as a result, to marry and start new families at an earlier age than their European counterparts.

BIRTH AND DEATH RATES The initial scarcity of women in the colonies had significant social effects. While in England the average age of women at marriage was twenty-five to twenty-six, in America it dropped to twenty or twenty-one. Men also married younger in the colonies than in the Old World. The birth rate rose accordingly, since those who married earlier had time for about two additional pregnancies during the childbearing years. Later a gradual reversion to a more even sex ratio brought the average age at marriage back toward the European norm. Even so, given the better economic prospects in the colonies, a greater proportion of American women married, and the birth rate remained much higher than in Europe. In eighteenth-century Virginia, Col. William Byrd of Westover asserted, matrimony thrived "so excellently" that an "Old Maid or an Old Bachelor are as scarce among us and reckoned as ominous as a Blazing Star." Early marriage remained common. The most "antique Virgin" Byrd knew was his twenty-year-old daughter.

Equally important in explaining rapid population growth in the New World was its much lower death rate. After the difficult first years of settlement, infants generally had a better chance to reach maturity, and adults had a better chance to reach old age than their counterparts in England and Europe. This greater longevity resulted less from a more temperate climate than from the character of the settlements themselves. Since the land was more bountiful, famine seldom occurred after a settlement's first year. While the winters were more severe than in England, firewood was plentiful. Being younger on the whole—the average age in the colonies in 1790 was sixteen!—Americans were less susceptible to disease than were Europeans. More widely scattered, they were also less exposed to disease. This began to change, of course, as cities grew and trade and travel increased. By the mid-eighteenth century the colonies were beginning to experience levels of contagion much like those in Europe.

SOCIAL STATUS   The earliest settlers brought with them fixed ideas of social hierarchy and rank. People deferred to their "betters" almost without question. John Winthrop asserted it to be God's will that "in all times some must be rich, some poore, some high and eminent in power and dignitie, others meane and in subjection." But from Jamestown onward persons of "meane" birth like John Smith revealed rare qualities when confronted with the wilderness. The breadth of opportunity to be plucked from danger impelled more and more settlers to shake off the sense of limitations that haunted the more crowded lands of Europe.

WOMEN IN THE COLONIES   Colonists brought to America deeply rooted convictions concerning the inferiority of women. God and nature, it was widely assumed, had stained women with original sin and made these "weaker vessels" smaller in stature, feebler in mind, and prone to both excited emotions and psychological dependency. Women were expected to be meek and model housewives. Their role in life was clear: to obey and serve their husbands, nurture their children, and maintain their households. As John Winthrop insisted, "A true wife accounts her subjection [as] her honor and freedom" and would find true contentment only "in subjection to her husband's authority."

Such commonly held attitudes meant that most women were conditioned to accept their subordinate status in a male-dominated society.

A Virginia woman explained that "one of my first resolutions I made after marriage was never to hold disputes with my husband." Both social
custom and legal codes ensured that women remained deferential and
powerless. They could not vote, preach, hold office, attend public
schools or colleges, bring suits, make contracts, or own property except
under extraordinary conditions.

"WOMEN'S WORK"   In the eighteenth century, "women's work" typically involved activities in the house, garden, and yard. Farm women
usually rose at four in the morning and prepared breakfast by five-thirty.
They then fed and watered the livestock, awakened the children,
churned butter, tended the garden, prepared lunch, played with the
children, worked the garden again, cooked dinner, milked the cows,
readied the children for bed, and cleaned the kitchen before retiring
about nine. Women also combed, spun, spooled, wove, and bleached
wool for clothing, knitted linen and cotton, hemmed sheets, pieced
quilts, made candles and soap, chopped wood, hauled water, mopped
floors, and washed clothes. Martha Ballard, a farm woman in Maine,
reported in her diary that when a sheep returned from the pasture with
a gash in its neck, she "drest it with Tarr," and when a lamb was born
with its "entrails hanging out," she sewed it up.

Despite the conventional mission of women to serve in the domestic
sphere, the scarcity of labor in the colonies opened new social opportunities. Quite a few women, either by necessity or choice, went into
gainful occupations. In her role as a paid midwife, for example, Martha
Ballard delivered almost 800 babies. In the towns, women commonly
served as tavern hostesses and shopkeepers, but some women also
worked as doctors, printers, upholsterers, painters, silversmiths, and
shipwrights. They often, but not always, were widows who carried on
their husbands' trades. Some women in the South managed plantations.

The acute shortage of women in the early years of colonial settlement
made them more highly valued than in Europe, and the Puritan emphasis on well-ordered family life led to laws protecting wives from physical
abuse and allowing for divorces. In addition, colonial laws gave wives
greater control over property that they contributed to a marriage or that
was left after a husband's death. But the central notion of female subor-
dination and domesticity remained firmly entrenched in the New

World. As a Massachusetts boy maintained in 1662, the superior aspect of life was "masculine and eternal; the feminine inferior and mortal."

SOCIETY AND ECONOMY IN THE SOUTHERN COLONIES

CROPS AND LAND The southern colonies had one unique advantage—the climate, which enabled them to grow exotic staples (market crops) prized by the mother country. In Virginia by 1619, tobacco production had reached 20,000 pounds, and by 1688, it was up to 18 million pounds. Smoking had become the rage among Europeans, and Virginia planters took full advantage of the situation. As one of them stressed, "all our riches for the present do consist in tobacco." Tobacco, however, was only one of many cash crops being grown in the southern colonies. After 1690 rice became the staple in South Carolina. The southern woods also provided harvests of lumber and naval stores (tar, pitch, and turpentine). From their early leadership in the latter trade North Carolinians would later derive the nickname of Tar Heels.

In 1614 each of the Virginia Company's colonists received three acres, and this marked the beginning of a "headright" policy that provided every settler in the colony with a plot of land. When Virginia became a royal colony in 1624, the headright system continued to apply, administered by the governor and his council. Lord Baltimore adopted the same practice in Maryland, and successive proprietors in the other southern and middle colonies offered variations on the plan.

If one distinctive feature of the South's staple economy was a good market in England, another was a trend toward large-scale production. Those who planted tobacco discovered that it quickly exhausted the soil, thereby giving an advantage to the planter who had extra fields to rotate in beans and corn or to leave fallow. With the increase of the tobacco crop, moreover, a fall in prices meant that economies of scale might come into play—the large planter with lower cost per unit might still make a profit. Gradually he would extend his holdings along the riverfronts, and thereby secure the advantage of direct access to the oceangoing vessels that moved freely up and down the waterways of the Chesapeake. So easy was the access in fact that the Chesapeake colonies never required a city of any size as a center of commerce.

The plantation economy depended upon manual labor, and voluntary indentured servitude accounted for probably half the arrivals of white settlers in all the colonies outside New England. The name derived from the indenture, or contract, by which a person could agree to labor in return for transportation to the New World. Not all went voluntarily. The London underworld developed a flourishing trade in "kids" and "spirits" who were enticed or "spirited" into servitude. One servant recalled how he and others were "stolen in Ireland" by English soldiers. Taken from their beds during the night "against their Consents," they were whisked away to a waiting ship, "weeping and crying." On occasion orphans were bound off to the New World, and from time to time the mother country sent convicts into colonial servitude, the first as early as 1617. Once the indenture had run its course, usually after four to seven years, the servant claimed the freedom dues set by law—some money, tools, clothing, food—and often took up landowning.

SLAVERY   Slavery, long a dying institution in Europe, evolved in the Chesapeake after 1619, when a Dutch vessel dropped off twenty Africans in Jamestown. Some of the first were treated as indentured servants, with a limited term. Court records indicate that black and white servants occasionally escaped together. A Virginia court, for instance, declared that six white servants and a "negro Servant" who had run away from their masters be given "thirty-nine lashes well layed on." Those African servants who worked out their term of indenture gained freedom and a fifty-acre parcel of land. They themselves sometimes acquired slaves and white indentured servants. But gradually, with rationalizations based on color difference or heathenism, the practice of perpetual black slavery became the custom and the law of the land.

As colonists developed staple crops, the demand for slaves grew, and as readily available lands diminished, Virginians were less eager to bring in indentured servants who would lay claim to land at the end of their service. Though British North America brought less than 5 percent of the total slave imports to the Western Hemisphere during the more than three centuries of that squalid traffic—400,000 out of some 9,500,000—it offered slaves better chances for survival, if few for human fulfillment. The natural increase of black immigrants in America

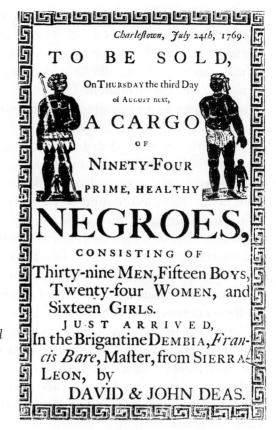

Advertisement for the sale of slaves—men, boys, women, and girls.

approximated that of whites by the end of the colonial period, and over 20 percent of the American population was black. In South Carolina blacks were in the majority.

AFRICAN ROOTS   Slaves are so often lumped together as a social group that their great ethnic diversity is overlooked. They came from lands as remote from each other as Angola and Senegal, the west coast of Africa, and the area around the hump in between, and they spoke Mandingo, Ibo, Kongo, and countless other tongues. Still, the many peoples of Africa did share similar kinship and political systems. Not unlike native American cultures, African societies were often matrilineal. Property and political status descended through the mother rather than the father. When a couple married, the wife did not leave her family; the husband left his family to join that of his bride.

West African tribes were organized hierarchically. Priests and the nobility lorded over the masses of farmers and craftspeople. Below the masses were the slaves, typically war captives, criminals, or debtors. African slaves, however, did have certain rights. They could marry, be educated, and have children. Their servitude was not permanent, nor were children automatically slaves by virtue of their parentage, as would be the case in North America.

West Africans were predominantly agricultural people. Their economy centered on hunting, fishing, planting, and animal husbandry. Men and women typically worked alongside one another in the fields. Religious belief served as the spine of West African life. All tribal groups believed in a supreme Creator of the world and an array of lesser gods tied to specific natural forces such as rain, fertility, and animal life. These gods directly intervened in daily life. West Africans were pantheistic in that they believed that spirits resided in trees, rocks, and streams. Those who died were also subjects of reverence because they served as mediators between the living and the gods.

Herded up by ruthless traders, frequently branded with a company label, Africans were packed together in slave ships and subjected to a four- to six-week Atlantic passage so brutal that one in seven captives died en route. Once in America they were thrown indiscriminately together and treated like work animals. More than a few "saltwater" slaves rebelled against their new masters, resisting work orders, sabotaging crops and tools, or running away to the frontier. In a few cases slaves organized rebellions that were ruthlessly suppressed. "You would be surprised at their perseverance," noted one white planter. "They often die

Neck and wrist irons used to subdue slaves during the passage from Africa.

The survival of African culture among American slaves is evident in this late-eighteenth-century painting of a South Carolina plantation. The musical instruments, pottery, and clothing are of African origin, probably Yoruba.

before they can be conquered." Those still alive when recaptured frequently faced ghastly retribution. After capturing slaves who participated in the Stono uprising in South Carolina in 1739, enraged planters "Cutt off their heads and set them up at every Mile Post."

With the odds so heavily stacked against resistance, most slaves resigned themselves to the overwhelming authority of the "peculiar institution." Yet in the process of being forced into lives of bondage, diverse blacks from diverse homelands forged a new identity as African Americans, while at the same time leaving entwined in the fabric of American culture more strands of African heritage than historians and anthropologists can ever disentangle. Among them were new words that entered the language, such as goober, yam, banana, and the names of the Coosaw, Peedee, and Wando Rivers.

More important were African influences in music, folklore, and religious practices. On one level slaves used songs, stories, and sermons to distract them from their toil; on another level these conveyed coded messages of distaste for masters or overseers. Slave religion, a unique blend of African and Christian beliefs, was frequently practiced in secret. Its fundamental theme was deliverance: God, they believed, would eventually free them from slavery and open up the gates to the promised land. As one popular slave spiritual said:

> And it won't be long. And it won't be long,
> And it won't be long, Poor sinner suffer here.
> We'll soon be free.
> The Lord will call us home.

The planters, however, sought to strip slave religion of its liberationist hopes. They insisted that being "born again" had no effect upon their workers' status as slaves. In 1667 the Virginia legislature declared that "the conferring of baptism does not alter the condition of the person as to his bondage or freedom."

Africans also brought with them to America powerful kinship ties. Although most colonies outlawed slave marriages, many masters realized that slaves would work harder and more reliably if allowed to form families. True, many couples were broken up when one partner was sold, but slave culture was remarkable for its powerful domestic ties. It was also remarkable for developing sex roles distinct from white society. Most slave women were by necessity field workers as well as wives and mothers responsible for household affairs. They worked in close proximity to black men, and in the process were treated more equally than most of their white counterparts.

Slavery and the growth of a multiracial South had economic, political, and cultural effects far into the future, and set America on the way to tragic conflicts. Questions about the beginnings of slavery still have a bearing on the present. Did a deep-rooted color prejudice lead to slavery, for instance, or did the existence of slavery produce the prejudice? Clearly, slavery evolved because of the desire for a supply of controlled labor, and the English fell in with a trade established by the Portuguese and Spanish more than a century before—the very word "Negro" is Spanish for "black." But while the English settlers often enslaved Indian captives, they did not enslave white Europeans captured in wartime. Color was the crucial difference, or at least the crucial rationalization.

One historian has marshaled evidence that the seeds of slavery were already planted in Elizabethan attitudes. The English associated the color black with darkness and evil; they stamped the different appearance, behavior, and customs of Africans as representing "savagery." At the very least such perceptions could soothe the consciences of those who traded in human flesh. On the other hand most of the qualities imputed to blacks to justify slavery were the same qualities that the English assigned to their own poor to explain their status: their alleged bent for laziness, improvidence, treachery, and stupidity, among other shortcomings. Similar traits, moreover, were imputed by ancient Jews to the Canaanites and by the Mediterranean peoples of a later date to the Slavic captives sold among them. The names Canaanite and Slav both became synonymous with slavery—the latter lingers in our very word for it. Such expressions would seem to be the product of power relationships and not the other way around. Dominant peoples repeatedly assign ugly traits to those they bring into subjection.

THE GENTRY   By the early eighteenth century, Virginia and South Carolina were moving into the golden age of the tidewater gentry, leaving the more isolated and rustic colony of North Carolina as "a valley of humiliation between two mountains of conceit." The stately country seats in the Georgian, or "colonial," style began to emerge along the banks of the great rivers.

The new aristocracy patterned its provincial lifestyle after that of the English country gentleman. The great houses became centers of sumptuous living, and the planters relished their dominance over the region's social life. William Byrd remembered Virginia as a "place free from those 3 great Scourges of Mankind, Priests, Lawyers, and Physicians." In their zest for the good life the planters kept in touch with the latest refinements of London style and fashion, living on credit extended for the next year's crop and the years' beyond that, to such a degree that in the late colonial period Thomas Jefferson called the Chesapeake gentry "a species of property annexed to certain English mercantile houses." Dependence on outside capital remained a chronic southern problem lasting far beyond the colonial period.

RELIGION   Although Americans during the seventeenth century took religion more seriously than at any time since, many of the colonists were not active communicants. One estimate holds that the proportion of church members to residents in the southern colonies was less than one in fifteen. There the tone of religious belief and practice was quite different from that in Puritan New England or Quaker Pennsylvania. Anglicanism predominated in the region, and it proved especially popular among the large landholders. As in England, colonial Anglicans were more conservative, rational, and formal in their forms of worship than their Puritan, Quaker, or Baptist counterparts. Anglicans tended to stress collective rituals over personal religious experience. Through most of the seventeenth century the Church of England was established (tax supported) only in Virginia and Maryland, but by the early eighteenth century it had become the established church throughout the South.

In the new environment, the Anglican church evolved into something quite unlike the state church of England. The scattered population and the absence of bishops in America made centralized control difficult. In practice therefore, if not in theory, the Anglican churches became as independent of any hierarchy as the Puritan congregations of New England. In Virginia ministerial salaries depended on the taxes paid in the parish, and after 1662 salaries fluctuated with the price of tobacco. Standards were often lax, and the Anglican clergy around the Chesapeake became notorious for its "sporting parsons," addicted to fox-hunting, gambling, drunkenness, and worse. Few among the conscientious and upright Anglican ministers preached fire and brimstone sermons. Their congregations showed little toleration for being chastised from the pulpit. One minister lamented that the powerful planters removed any preacher who "had the courage and resolution to preach against any Vices taken into favor by the leading Men of his Parish."

SOCIETY AND ECONOMY IN NEW ENGLAND

TOWNSHIPS   By contrast to the seaboard planters who transformed the English manor into the southern plantation, the Puritans transformed the English village into the New England town, although there were many varieties. Land policy in New England had a stronger social and religious purpose than elsewhere. The headright system of the Chesapeake never took root in New England. There were cases of large individual grants, but the standard practice was one of township grants to organized groups. A group of settlers, often gathered already into a congregation, would petition the General Court for a town, then divide the parcel according to a rough principle of equity—those who invested more or had larger families or greater status might receive more land—retaining some pasture and woodland in common and holding some for later arrivals. In some early cases the towns arranged each settler's land in separate strips after the medieval practice, but with time land was commonly divided into separate farms to which landholders would move, away from the central village.

ENTERPRISE   New England farmers and their families led hard lives. Simply clearing the glacier-scoured soil of rocks might require sixty days of strenuous labor per acre. The growing season was short, and the harsh climate precluded any exotic staples. The crops and livestock were those familiar to the English countryside: wheat, barley, oats, some cattle, swine, and sheep.

With virgin forests ready for conversion into masts, lumber, and ships, and abundant fishing grounds that stretched northward to Newfoundland, it is little wonder that New Englanders turned to the sea for livelihood. New England's proximity to waters frequented by cod, mackerel, halibut, and other varieties of fish made it America's most important maritime center. Whales, too, abounded in New England waters and supplied oil for lighting and lubrication, as well as ambergris, a secretion used in perfumes.

New England's fisheries, unlike its farms, supplied a staple of export to Europe, while lesser grades of fish went to the West Indies as food for slaves. Fisheries encouraged the development of shipbuilding, and experience at seafaring spurred commerce. This in turn led to wider contacts in the Atlantic world and a degree of materialism and cosmopolitanism that clashed with the Puritan credo of plain living and high thinking. In 1714 an anxious Puritan deplored the "great extravagance that people are fallen into, far beyond their circumstances, in their purchases, buildings, families, expenses, apparel, generally in the whole way of living."

TRADE   But such laments failed to stop the material growth of the New England colonies. By the end of the seventeenth century, America had become part of a great North Atlantic commercial network, trading

not only with the British Isles and the British West Indies, but also—
and often illegally—with Spain, France, Portugal, Holland, and their
colonies. Since they lacked the means to produce goods themselves,
the colonists had to import manufactured goods from Britain and Europe. Their central economic problem was to find the means of paying
for these imports—the eternal problem of the balance of trade.

The mechanism of trade in New England and the middle colonies
differed from that in the South in two respects: the northern colonies
were at a disadvantage in their lack of staples (valuable commodities) to
exchange for English goods, but the abundance of their own shipping
and mercantile enterprise worked in their favor. After 1660, in order to
protect English agriculture and fisheries, the English government raised
prohibitive duties (taxes) against certain major imports from the northern colonies: fish, flour, wheat, and meat, while leaving the door open
to timber, furs, and whale oil. As a consequence, in the early eighteenth
century New York and New England bought more from England than
they sold there, incurring an unfavorable trade balance.

The northern colonies met the problem in two ways: they used their
own ships and merchants, thus avoiding the "invisible" charges for trade

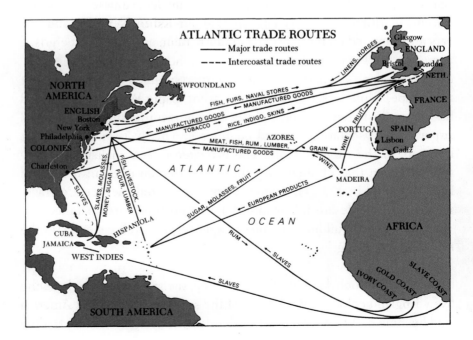

and transport; and they found other markets for the staples excluded from England, thus acquiring goods or bullion to pay for imports from the mother country. American lumber and fish therefore went to southern Europe, Madeira, and the Azores for money or in exchange for wine; lumber, rum, and provisions went to Newfoundland; and all of these and more went to the West Indies, which became the most important outlet of all. American merchants could sell fish, flour, corn, pork, beef, and horses to West Indian planters who specialized in sugarcane. In return they got money, sugar, molasses, rum, indigo, and other products, much of which went eventually to England. This gave rise to the famous "triangular trade" (more a descriptive convenience than a rigid pattern) in which New Englanders shipped rum to the west coast of Africa and bartered for slaves, took the slaves on the "Middle Passage" to the West Indies, and returned home with various commodities including molasses, from which they manufactured rum. In another version they shipped provisions to the West Indies, carried sugar and molasses to England, and returned with manufactured goods from Europe.

The generally unfavorable balance of trade left the colonies with a chronic shortage of hard money, which drifted away to pay for imports and invisible charges. Various expedients met the currency shortage. Most of the colonies at one time or another issued bills of credit, on promise of payment in hard currency later (hence the dollar "bill"), and most set up land banks that issued paper money for loans to farmers on the security of their lands, which were mortgaged to the banks. Colonial farmers, recognizing that an inflation of paper money led to an inflation of crop prices, asked for more and more paper. Thus began in colonial politics what was to become a recurrent problem in later times, the issue of currency inflation. Wherever the issue arose, debtors commonly favored growth in the money supply, which would make it easier for them to settle accounts, whereas creditors favored a limited money supply, which would increase the value of their capital.

RELIGION   It has been said that in New England one was never far from the smell of fish and brimstone. The Puritans for many years had a bad press. The picture of the dour Puritan, hostile to all pleasures, rings false. Puritans, especially those of the upper class, wore colorful clothing, enjoyed secular music, and drank rum. "Drink is in itself a good creature of God," said the Reverend Increase Mather, ". . . but the abuse of drink is from Satan." If found incapacitated by reason of strong drink, one was subject to arrest. A Salem man, for example, was tried for staggering into a house where he "eased his stomak in the Chimney." Repeated offenders were forced to wear the letter "D" in public.

Moderation in all things except piety was the Puritan guideline. This was true for sexual activity as well. Contrary to prevailing images of the Puritans as prudes, they were quite open in recognizing natural human desires. One minister emphasized that "the Use of the Marriage Bed" is "founded in man's Nature." Therefore, any unwillingness to engage in sexual intercourse on the part of husband or wife "Denies all reliefe in Wedlock unto Human necessity: and sends it for supply unto Beastiality . . ." Churches occasionally expelled members for failing to satisfy their partner's sexual needs. To be sure, sexual activity outside the bounds of marriage was strictly forbidden but, like most prohibitions, it seemed to provoke transgression. New England court records bulge with cases of adultery and fornication. In part the abundance of sexual offenses reflected the disproportionate number of men in the colonies. Many were unable to find a wife and were therefore tempted to satisfy their sexual desires outside of marriage.

The Puritans who settled Massachusetts, unlike the Separatists of Plymouth, proposed only to form a purified version of the Anglican church. They believed that they could remain loyal to the Church of England, the unity of church and state, and the principle of compulsory uniformity. But their remoteness from England led them very quickly to a congregational form of church government identical with that of the Pilgrim Separatists.

Certain aspects of the Puritan faith were pregnant with meaning for the future. In the Puritan version of Calvin's theology, God had voluntarily entered into a covenant, or contract, with people through which his creatures could secure salvation. By analogy, therefore, an assembly of true Christians could enter into a church covenant, a voluntary union for the common worship of God. From this it was a fairly short step to the idea of a voluntary union for purposes of government.

The covenant theory contained certain kernels of democracy in both church and state, but democracy was no part of Puritan political thought, which like so much else in Puritan belief began with original sin. Innate human depravity made governments necessary. "If people be governors," asked the Reverend John Cotton, "who shall be governed?" The Puritan was dedicated to seeking not the will of the people but the will of God. The ultimate source of authority resided in the Bible, but the Bible had to be known by right reason, which was best applied by those trained to the purpose. Hence, most Puritans deferred to an intellectual elite for a true knowledge of providential design. Church and state were but two aspects of the same unity, the purpose of which was to carry out God's will on earth. The New England way might thus be summarized in one historian's phrase as a kind of "dictatorship of the regenerate," or of those who had undergone the conversion experience required for church membership.

The church exercised a pervasive influence over the life of the town, but unlike the Church of England it technically had no political power. While Puritan New England has often been called a theocracy, the church in theory was entirely separated from the state—except that town residents were taxed for its support. And if not all inhabitants were church members, they were to be present for church services. So complete was the apparent consensus of church member and nonmember alike that the closely knit communities of New England have been called peaceable kingdoms. Life in the small rural townships was intimate and essentially cooperative. Studies of Andover, Dedham, and Plymouth, Massachusetts, among other towns, suggest that, at least in the seventeenth century, family ties grew stronger and village life more cohesive than in the homeland.

DIVERSITY AND SOCIAL STRAINS   Such harmony, however, was frequently short-lived. Increasing diversity and powerful disruptive forces combined to erode the idyllic consensual society envisioned by the founding settlers. Despite long-enduring myths, New England towns were not always pious, harmonious, static, and self-sufficient rural utopias populated by praying Puritans. Many communities were founded as centers of fishing, trade, and commerce rather than farming, religion, and morality, and the animating concerns of residents in such towns tended to be more entrepreneurial than spiritual. Interestingly enough, however, in Massachusetts seaport towns such as Gloucester and Marblehead, founded by contentious English immigrants on the make, community life grew more cohesive, settled, and religious in the midst of economic growth.

Nevertheless, among most of the godly communities in the backwoods, social strains and worldly pursuits increased as time passed, a consequence primarily of population pressure on the land and rising disparities of wealth. Initially, among the first settlers, fathers exercised strong patriarchal authority over their sons through their control of the land. They kept the sons in town, not letting them set up their own households or get title to their farmlands until they reached middle age. In New England as elsewhere the tendency was to subdivide the land among all the children. But by the eighteenth century, with land scarcer, the younger sons were either getting control of property early or else moving on. Often the younger male children were forced, with family help and blessings, to seek land elsewhere or find new kinds of work in the commercial cities along the coast or inland rivers. With the growing pressure on land in the settled regions, poverty and social tension increased in what had once seemed a country of unlimited opportunity.

Sectarian disputes and religious indifference were also on the rise in many communities. The emphasis on a direct accountability to God, which lay at the base of all Protestant theology, caused a persistent tension and led believers to challenge authority in the name of private conscience. Massachusetts repressed such heresy in the 1630s, but it resurfaced during the 1650s among Quakers and Baptists, and in 1659–1660 the colony hanged four Quakers who persisted in returning after they were expelled. These acts caused such revulsion—and an investigation by the crown—that they were not repeated, although heretics continued to face harassment and persecution.

More damaging to the Puritan utopia was the increasing pluralism and worldliness of New England, which placed growing strains on church discipline. More and more children of the "visible saints" found themselves unable to testify that they had received the gift of God's grace. In 1662 an assembly of ministers at Boston accepted the "Half-Way Covenant," whereby baptized children of church members could be admitted to a "half-way" membership. Their own children could be baptized, but such "half-way" members could neither vote nor take communion. A further blow to Puritan convention and control came with the Massachusetts royal charter of 1691, which required toleration of dissenters and based the right to vote on property rather than on church membership.

NEW ENGLAND WITCHCRAFT   The strains accompanying Massachusetts's transition from Puritan utopia to royal colony reached an unhappy climax in the witchcraft hysteria at Salem Village (later Danvers) in 1692. Belief in witchcraft pervaded European and New England society in the seventeenth century. Indeed, prior to the dramatic episode in Salem, almost 300 New Englanders (mostly lower-class, middle-aged, marginal women—spinsters or widows) had been accused as witches, and more than thirty hanged.

Still, the Salem outbreak exceeded all precedents in its scope and intensity. The general upheaval in the colony's political, economic, social, and religious life was compounded in that locale by a conflict of values between a community rooted in the subsistence farm economy and the thriving port of Salem proper. Seething insecurities and family conflicts within the community apparently made many residents receptive to accusations by adolescent girls that they had been bewitched.

The episode began when a few teenage girls became entranced listeners to voodoo stories told by Tituba, a West Indian slave, and began acting strangely—shouting, barking, groveling and twitching for no apparent reason. The town doctor concluded that they had been bewitched, and the girls pointed to Tituba and two white women as the culprits. Soon town dwellers were seized with panic as word spread that the devil was in their midst, wreaking havoc. At a hearing before the magistrates the "afflicted" girls rolled on the floor in convulsive fits as the three women were questioned by the magistrates. In the midst of this hysterical carnival, Tituba shocked her listeners by not only confessing to the charge but also divulging that many others in the community were performing the devil's work.

With that, the crazed girls began pointing accusing fingers at dozens of residents, including several of the most respected members of the community. Within a few months the Salem jail overflowed with townspeople—men, women, and children—accused of practicing witchcraft. That the accusing girls were so readily believed illustrates how overwrought the community had become. Before the hysteria ran its course ten months later, nineteen people (including some men) had been hanged, one man—stubborn Giles Corey—pressed to death by heavy stones, and more than 100 others jailed.

But as the net of accusation spread wider, extending far beyond the confines of Salem, colonial leaders began to worry that the witch-hunts

Four women being hanged as witches in seventeenth-century England. At Salem, nineteen people were hanged for witchcraft.

were out of control. When the afflicted girls charged Samuel Willard, the distinguished pastor of Boston's First Church and president of Harvard College, the stunned magistrates had seen enough. Shortly thereafter, the governor intervened when his own wife was accused of serving the devil. He disbanded the special court and ordered the remaining suspects released. A year after it had begun, the fratricidal event was finally over. Nearly everybody responsible for the Salem executions later recanted, and nothing quite like it happened in the colonies again.

What explains the witchcraft hysteria at Salem? Some have argued that it may have represented nothing more than a contagious exercise in adolescent imagination intended to enliven the dreary routine of everyday life. Yet it was adults who pressed the formal charges against the accused and provided most of the testimony. This has led some scholars to speculate that long-festering local feuds and property disputes may have triggered the prosecutions. One of the leaders of the young girls, for instance, was twelve-year-old Ann Putnam, whose older male kinfolk pressed many of the complaints. The Putnam clan were landowners whose power was declining, and their frenetic pursuit of witches might have served as a psychic weapon to restore their prestige.

More recently, historians have focused on the most salient fact about the accused witches. Almost all of them were women. Many of the accused women, it turns out, had in some way defied the traditional roles assigned to females. Some had engaged in business transactions outside the home, others did not attend church; some were sour curmudgeons. Most of them were middle-aged or older, beyond child-bearing age, and without sons or brothers. They thus stood to inherit property and live as independent women. The notion of autonomous spinsters flew in the face of prevailing social conventions.

Whatever the precise cause, there is little doubt that the witchcraft hysteria reflected the peculiar social dynamics of the Salem community. Late in 1692, as the hysteria in Salem subsided, several of the afflicted girls were traveling through nearby Ipswich when they encountered an old woman resting on a bridge. "A witch!" they shouted and began writhing as if possessed. But the people of Ipswich were unimpressed. Passersby showed no interest in the theatrical girls. Unable to generate either sympathy or curiosity, the girls picked themselves up and continued on their way.

SOCIETY AND ECONOMY IN THE MIDDLE COLONIES

AN ECONOMIC MIX   Both geographically and culturally the middle colonies stood between New England and the South, blending their own influences with elements derived from the older regions on either side. In so doing they more completely reflected the diversity of colonial life and more fully foreshadowed the pluralism of the later American nation than the regions on either side. Their crops were those of New England but more bountiful, owing to better land and a longer growing season, and they developed surpluses of foodstuffs for export to the plantations of the South and the West Indies: wheat, barley, and livestock. Three great rivers—the Hudson, Delaware, and Susquehanna—and their tributaries gave the middle colonies a unique access to their backcountry and to the fur trade of the interior, where New York and Pennsylvania long enjoyed friendly relations with the Indians. As a consequence the region's commerce rivaled that of New England, and indeed Philadelphia in time supplanted Boston as the largest city in the colonies.

Land policies followed the headright system of the South. In New York the early royal governors carried forward, in practice if not in name, the Dutch device of the patroonship, granting to influential favorites vast estates on Long Island and up the Hudson and Mohawk valleys. These realms most nearly approached the Old World manor, self-contained domains farmed by tenants who paid fees to use the landlords' mills, warehouses, smokehouses, and wharves. But with free land elsewhere, New York's population languished, and the new waves of immigrants sought the promised land of Pennsylvania.

AN ETHNIC MIX   In the makeup of their population the middle colonies stood apart from both the mostly English Puritan settlements and the biracial plantation colonies to the south. In New York and New Jersey, for instance, Dutch culture and language lingered for some time, along with the Dutch Reformed church. Up and down the Delaware River the few Swedes and Finns, the first settlers, were overwhelmed by the influx of English and Welsh Quakers, followed in turn by the Germans and Scotch-Irish.

The Germans came mainly from the Rhineland. Penn's brochures on the bounties of Pennsylvania circulated in German translation, and his promise of religious freedom brought an excited response from persecuted sects, especially the Mennonites, whose beliefs resembled those of the Quakers. They were but the vanguard of a swelling migration in the eighteenth century that included Lutherans, Reformed Calvinists, Moravians, Dunkers, and others, a large proportion of whom paid their way as indentured servants or "redemptioners," as they were commonly called. West of Philadelphia these thrifty farmers and artisans created a belt of settlement in which the "Pennsylvania Dutch" (a corruption of "Deutsch," meaning German) predominated.

The Scotch-Irish began to arrive later and moved still farther out in the backcountry. "Scotch-Irish" is an enduring misnomer for Ulster Scots, Presbyterians transplanted from Scotland to confiscated lands in northern Ireland to give that country a more Protestant tone. The Ulster plantation dated from 1607–1609, the years when Jamestown was fighting for survival. A century later the Ulster Scots, mostly Presbyterians, were on the move again, in flight from economic disaster and Anglican persecution. This time they looked mainly to Pennsylvania

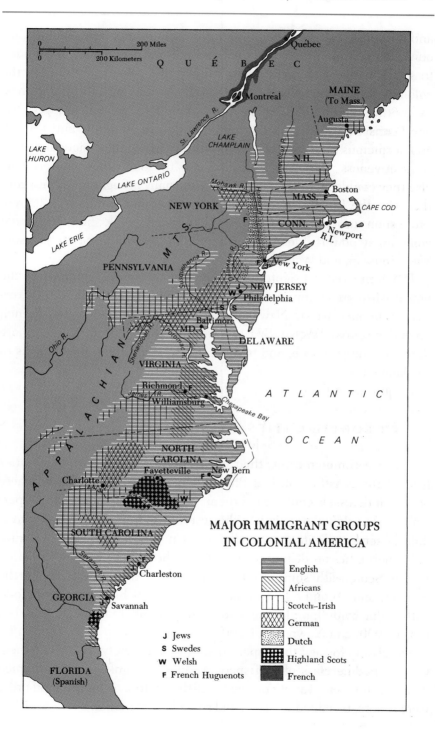

MAJOR IMMIGRANT GROUPS
IN COLONIAL AMERICA

English
Africans
Scotch–Irish
German
Dutch
Highland Scots
French

J Jews
S Swedes
W Welsh
F French Huguenots

and the fertile valleys stretching southwestward into Virginia and Carolina. Unlike the more communal and pastoral Germans, they tended to settle in the wilderness areas, usually the western portions of the colonies, where they cleared the land, built rude log cabins, and lived by hunting and scratch farming. These "bold and indigent strangers," as one Pennsylvania official described them, were virulently anti-English and suspicious of all governments. Renowned for their piety and their acquisitiveness, they were said to keep "the Sabbath and everything else they could lay their hands on." This usually brought them into conflict with the Indians, toward whom they harbored an abiding hatred. From such rugged, hardheaded, and hardfisted people, however, would come many powerful leaders, such as John Calhoun, Andrew Jackson, Sam Houston, and Woodrow Wilson.

The Germans and Scotch-Irish became the most numerous of the non-English groups in the colonies, but others also enriched the diversity of population in New York and the Quaker colonies: French Huguenots, Irish, Welsh, Swiss, Jews, and others. By 1790 little more than half the populace, and perhaps fewer, could trace their origins to England.

COLONIAL CITIES

Since commerce was their chief reason for being, colonial cities hugged the coastline or, like Philadelphia, sprang up on rivers where oceangoing vessels could reach them. Never holding more than 10 percent of the colonial population, they exerted an influence in commerce, politics, and civilization generally out of proportion to their size. Five major port cities outdistanced the rest. By the end of the colonial period Philadelphia, with some 30,000 people, was the largest city in the colonies and second only to London in the British Empire; New York, with about 25,000, ranked second; Boston numbered 16,000; Charleston, 12,000; and Newport, 11,000.

Merchants formed the upper crust of urban society, and below them came a middle class of craftspeople, retailers, innkeepers, and small jobbers who met a variety of needs. At the bottom of the pecking order were sailors, unskilled workers, and some artisans. Such class stratification in the cities became more pronounced during the eighteenth century and after.

Problems created by urban growth are nothing new. Colonial cities had traffic that required not only paved streets and lighting but regulations to protect children and animals in the streets from reckless riders. Other regulations restrained citizens from creating public nuisances by tossing their garbage into the streets. Devastating fires led to preventive standards in building codes, restrictions on burning rubbish, and the organization of volunteer and, finally, professional fire companies. Crime and violence made necessary more police protection. And in cities the poor became more visible than in the countryside. Colonists brought with them the English principle of public responsibility for the needy. The number of Boston's poor receiving public assistance rose from 500 in 1700 to 4,000 in 1736; New York's rose from 250 in 1698 to 5,000 in the 1770s. Most of it went to "outdoor" relief in the form of money, food, clothing, and fuel, but almshouses also appeared in colonial cities.

THE URBAN WEB   Communication within and between cities was difficult at first. On land people traveled initially by horse or by foot, and there was not a single hard-surfaced road during the entire colonial period, aside from city streets. Postal service through the seventeenth century was almost nonexistent—people entrusted letters to travelers or sea captains. During the eighteenth century, however, a postal system was established and eventually extended the length of the Atlantic seaboard.

More reliable deliveries gave rise to newspapers in the eighteenth century. By 1745 twenty-two colonial newspapers had been started. An important landmark in the progress of freedom of the press was John Peter Zenger's trial for seditious libel for publishing criticisms of New York's governor in his paper, the New York *Weekly Journal*. Imprisoned for ten months and brought to trial in 1735, he was charged with fostering "an ill opinion of the government." The jury's function was only to determine whether the defendant had published the opinion, but the defense attorney startled the court with his claim that Zenger had published the truth—which the judge ruled an unacceptable defense. The jury, however, agreed with the assertion and found the editor not guilty.

The libel law remained standing as before, but editors thereafter were emboldened to criticize officials more freely.

THE ENLIGHTENMENT

In the world of ideas a new fashion dazzled minds: the Enlightenment. During the seventeenth century Europe experienced a scientific revolution in which the prevailing notion of an earth-centered universe was overthrown by the new sun-centered system of Polish astronomer Nicolaus Copernicus. The revolution climaxed in 1687 when England's Sir Isaac Newton set forth his theory of gravitation. Newton had, in short, hit upon the design of a mechanistic universe moving in accordance with natural laws that could be grasped by human reason and explained by mathematics.

By analogy from Newton's view of the world as a machine, one could reason that natural laws governed all things—the orbits of the planets and also the orbits of human relations: politics, economics, and society. Reason could make people aware, for instance, that the natural law of supply and demand governed economics or that natural rights to life, liberty, and property determined the limits and functions of government.

Much of enlightened thought could be reconciled with established beliefs—the idea of natural law existed in Christian theology, and religious people could reason that the worldview of Copernicus and Newton simply showed forth the glory of God. Puritan leaders accepted Newtonian science from the start. Yet Deists carried the idea to its ultimate conclusion, reducing God to the position of a remote Creator, a master clockmaker who planned the universe and set it in motion. Evil in the world, one might reason further, resulted not from original sin so much as from an imperfect understanding of the laws of nature. People, the English philosopher John Locke argued in his *Essay on Human Understanding* (1690), reflected the impact of their environment, the human mind being a blank tablet at birth that gained knowledge through experience. Corrupt society therefore might corrupt the mind. The way to improve both society and human nature was by the application and improvement of Reason—which was the highest Virtue (enlightened thinkers often capitalized both words).

THE AMERICAN ENLIGHTENMENT   However interpreted, such ideas profoundly affected the climate of thought in the eighteenth century. As a Connecticut minister recognized in 1788, "The present age is an enlightened one." The premises of Newtonian science and the Enlightenment, moreover, fitted the American experience. In the New World people no longer moved in the worn grooves of tradition that defined the roles of priest or peasant or noble. Much of their experience had already been with observation, experiment, and the need to think anew. America was therefore receptive to the new science. Anybody who pretended to a degree of learning revealed a curiosity about natural philosophy, and some carried it to considerable depth.

Benjamin Franklin epitomized the Enlightenment more than any other single person. Franklin rose from the ranks of the common folk and never lost the common touch, a gift that accounted for his success as a publisher. Born in Boston in 1706, Franklin was the son of a candle and soap maker. Apprenticed to his older brother, a printer, Franklin left home at the age of seventeen and relocated to Philadelphia. There, before he was twenty-four, he owned a print shop where he edited and published the *Pennsylvania Gazette*. When he was twenty-seven he brought out *Poor Richard's Almanac*, full of homely maxims on success and happiness. Before he retired from business at the age of forty-two, Franklin, among other achievements, had founded a library, set up a fire company, helped start the academy that became the University of

Benjamin Franklin (1767).

Pennsylvania, and organized a debating club that grew into the American Philosophical Society. After his early retirement he intended to devote himself to public affairs and the sciences.

The course of events allowed Franklin less and less time for science, but that remained his passion. His speculations extended widely to the fields of medicine, meteorology, geology, astronomy, and physics. He invented the Franklin stove, the lightning rod, and a glass harmonica for which Mozart and Beethoven composed. The triumph of this untutored genius further confirmed the Enlightenment trust in the powers of Nature.

EDUCATION IN THE COLONIES   The heights of abstract reasoning, of course, were remote from the everyday concerns of most colonists. For the colonists at large, education in the traditional ideas and manners of society—even literacy itself—remained primarily the responsibility of family and church, and one not always accepted.

Conditions in New England proved most favorable for the establishment of schools. The Puritan emphasis on Scripture reading, which all Protestants shared in some degree, implied an obligation to ensure literacy. In 1647 Massachusetts Bay required every town of fifty or more families to set up a grammar school (a Latin school that could prepare a student for college). Although the act was widely evaded, it set an example that the rest of New England emulated.

In Pennsylvania the Quakers never heeded William Penn's instructions to establish public schools, but did respect the usefulness of education and financed a number of private schools teaching practical as well as academic subjects. In the southern colonies efforts to establish schools were hampered by the more scattered populations, and in parts of the backcountry by indifference and neglect. Some of the wealthiest planters and merchants of the tidewater sent their children to England or hired tutors, who in some cases would also serve the children of neighbors. In some places wealthy patrons or the people collectively managed to raise some kind of support for secondary academies.

THE GREAT AWAKENING

As a consequence of the new currents of learning and the Enlightenment, however, many people seemed to be drifting away from the old moorings of piety. Intellectually the educated classes were attracted to Deism and skepticism. And, so it was thought, if the Lord had allowed great Puritan and Quaker merchants of Boston and Philadelphia to prosper, the haunting fear arose that the devil had lured them into the vain pursuit of worldly gain. Meanwhile, out along the fringes of settlement there grew up a great backwater of the unchurched, people who had no minister to preach or administer sacraments or perform marriages, who fell, according to some, into a primitive and sinful life, little different from the "heathens" who lurked in the woods. An Anglican divine called the backcountry preachers in the Carolinas "ignorant wretches, who cannot write" and compared a Baptist communion service to "A Gang of frantic Lunatics broke out of Bedlam." By the 1730s the sense of falling away from religious orthodoxy had prepared the time for a revival of faith, the Great Awakening, a wave of evangelism that within a few years swept the colonies from one end to the other, America's first mass movement.

EDWARDS AND WHITEFIELD   In 1734–1735 a remarkable spiritual revival occurred in the congregation of Jonathan Edwards, a Congregationalist minister in Northampton, Massachusetts. One of America's most brilliant philosophers and theologians, Edwards entered Yale in 1716 at age thirteen and graduated valedictorian four years later. While a college student, he developed a mystical religious strain. "God's excellency, his wisdom, his purity and love," he wrote, "seemed to appear in everything; in the sun, moon and stars; in the clouds, and blue sky; in the grass, flowers, trees; in the water, and all nature; which used greatly to fix my mind."

In 1726 Edwards took charge of the Congregational church in Northampton and found the congregation's spirituality at low ebb. "Licentiousness for some years greatly prevailed among the youth of the town: there were many of them much addicted to night walking and frequenting the tavern, and lewd practices wherein some by their example exceedingly corrupted others." He was convinced that Christians had become too preoccupied with making and spending money and that religion had become too intellectual and in the process had lost its animating force. "Our people," he said, "do not so much need to have their heads stored as to have their hearts touched." He added that he considered it a "reasonable thing to endeavor to fright persons away from hell."

His own vivid descriptions of the torments of hell and the delights of heaven helped rekindle spiritual fervor among his congregants. By 1735 he could report that "the town seemed to be full of the presence of God; it never was so full of love, nor of joy."

About the same time, William Tennent set up a "Log College" in Pennsylvania for the education of ministers to serve the Scotch-Irish Presbyterians around Philadelphia. The Log College specialized in turning out zealots who scorned complacency and proclaimed the need for revival. Among the most successful was Tennent's son Gilbert. Critics scorned these backwoods revivalists, branding them "half educated enthusiasts," but two of these rustic preachers later became presidents of Princeton.

The true catalyst of the Great Awakening, however, was a twenty-seven-year-old English minister, George Whitefield, whose reputation as a spellbinding evangelist in the Wesleyan revivals then underway in England preceded him to the colonies. Congregations were lifeless, he claimed, "because dead men preach to them." Too many ministers were "slothful shepherds and dumb dogs." To restore the fires of religious fervor to American congregations, Whitefield reawakened the notion of individual salvation. In the autumn of 1739 he arrived in Philadelphia, and late in that year preached to crowds of as many as 6,000 around Philadelphia. After visiting in Georgia, he made a triumphal procession northward to New England, drawing great crowds and releasing "Gales of Heavenly Wind" that dispersed sparks throughout the colonies.

Young and magnetic, possessed of a golden voice and a squinting left eye, Whitefield enthralled audiences with his unparalleled eloquence. Even the skeptical Benjamin Franklin, who went to see the show in Philadelphia, found himself so carried away that he emptied his pockets into the collection plate—perhaps the ultimate tribute to Whitefield's persuasiveness. The English revivalist stressed the need for individuals to experience a "new birth"—the need for a sudden and emotional moment of conversion and salvation—and the dangers of an unconverted ministry that had not experienced such rebirth. By the end of his sermon, one listener reported, the entire congregation was "in utmost Confusion, some crying out, some laughing, and Bliss still roaring to them to come to Christ, they answering, *I will, I will, I'm coming, I'm coming.*"

Jonathan Edwards heard Whitefield preach and was so moved that he wept through most of the sermon. Thereafter he spread his own revival gospel. The Awakening in New England reached its peak in 1741, when Edwards delivered his most famous sermon at Enfield, Massachusetts. Entitled "Sinners in the Hands of an Angry God," it represented a devout appeal to repentance. Edwards reminded the congregation of the reality of hell, the omnipotence of God's vision, and the certainty of his judgment. "The bow of God's wrath is bent," he declared, "and the arrow made ready on the string, and justice bends the arrow at your heart, and strains the bow, and it is nothing but the mere pleasure of God, and that of an angry God, without any promise or obligation at all, that keeps the arrow one moment from being made drunk with your blood." In a compelling metaphor, Edwards warned that God "holds you over the pit of hell, much as one holds a spider, or some loathsome insect, over the fire, abhors you, and is dreadfully provoked . . . he looks upon you as worthy of nothing else, but to be cast into the fire." But for all the terror of his theme, Edwards did not rant or engage in theatrics. Instead he delivered the carefully reasoned sermon in a soft, solemn voice and a calm manner. When he finished he had to wait several minutes for the congregation to quiet down before leading them in a closing hymn.

The message and technique of Edwards and Whitefield were infectious, and imitators sprang up everywhere. Once unleashed, however, spiritual enthusiasm was hard to control, and in many ways the Awakening backfired on those who had intended it to bolster church discipline and social order. Some of the revivalists began to court those at the bottom of the social scale—laborers, seamen, servants, and farmers. The Reverend James Davenport, for instance, a fiery New England Congregationalist, set about shouting, raging, and stomping on the devil and beseeching his listeners to renounce the established clergy and become the agents of their own salvation. The churched and unchurched flocked to hear his mesmerizing sermons. Seized by the terror and ecstasy, they groveled on the floor or lay unconscious on the benches, to the chagrin of more decorous churchgoers. One never knew, the more traditional clergymen warned, whence came these enthusiasms—perhaps they were delusions sent by the devil to discredit the true faith. The radical revivalists, said one worried conservative, were breeding "anarchy, levelling, and dissolution."

PIETY AND REASON   Whatever their motive or method, the revivalists succeeded in awakening the piety of many Americans. Between 1740 and 1742 some 25,000–50,000 New Englanders, out of a total population of 300,000, joined churches. The Awakening spawned a proliferation of new religious groups and sects that helped undermine the notion of state-supported churches. Everywhere the revivals brought splits, especially in the more Calvinistic churches. Traditional clergymen found their position undermined as church members chose sides and either dismissed their ministers or deserted them. Many of the revivalists, or "New Lights," went over to the Baptists, and others flocked to Presbyterian or, later, Methodist groups, which in turn divided and subdivided into new sects.

By the middle of the eighteenth century, New England Puritanism had finally fragmented. The precarious balance in which the founders had held the elements of piety and reason was shattered, and more and more Baptists, Presbyterians, Anglicans, and other denominations began establishing footholds in formerly Congregationalist Puritan communities. But the revival tradition paradoxically scored its most lasting victories along the chaotic frontiers of the middle and southern colonies. In the more sedate churches of Boston, moreover, Enlightened rationalism got the upper hand in a reaction against the excesses of revival emotion. Bostonian ministers like Charles Chauncey and Jonathan Mayhew assumed the lead in preaching a doctrine of calm rationality. Reassessing Calvinist theology, they found it too forbidding and irrational that people could be forever damned by predestination. The rationality of Newton and Locke, the idea of natural law, crept more and more into their sermons, and they embarked on the road to Unitarianism and Universalism.

In reaction to taunts that the "born-again" ministers lacked learning, the Awakening gave rise to the denominational colleges that became so characteristic of American higher education. The three colleges already in existence had originated earlier from religious motives: Harvard, founded in 1636, because the Puritans dreaded "to leave an illiterate ministry to the church when our present ministers shall lie in the dust"; the College of William and Mary, in 1693, to strengthen the Anglican ministry; and Yale College, in 1701, set up to serve the Puritans of Connecticut, who felt that Harvard was drifting from the strictest orthodoxy. The Presbyterian College of New Jersey, later Princeton University, was founded in 1746 as successor to William Tennent's Log

College. In close succession came King's College (1754) in New York, later Columbia University, an Anglican institution; the College of Rhode Island (1764), later Brown University, Baptist; Queen's College (1766), later Rutgers, Dutch Reformed; and Congregationalist Dartmouth (1769), the outgrowth of an earlier school for Indians. Among the colonial colleges only the University of Pennsylvania, founded as the Philadelphia Academy in 1754, arose from a secular impulse.

The Great Awakening, like the Enlightenment, set in motion currents that still flow in American life. It implanted permanently in American culture evangelical principles and methods. Moreover, by weakening the status of the old-fashioned clergy and encouraging believers to exercise their own judgment, Awakeners thereby weakened habits of deference generally. The proliferation of denominations heightened the need for toleration of dissent. But in some respects the counterpoint between the Awakening and the Enlightenment, between the principles of piety and reason, led by different roads to similar ends. Both emphasized the power and right of individual choice and popular resistance to established authority, and both aroused millennial hopes that America would become the promised land in which people might approach the perfection of piety or reason, if not of both. Such hopes had both social and political, as well as religious, implications. As the eighteenth century advanced, fewer and fewer people were willing to defer to the ruling social and political elite, and many such rebellious, if pious, folk would be transformed into Revolutionaries.

MAKING CONNECTIONS

- This chapter contains hints of tensions in colonial Virginia society; in the next chapter, these tensions will come to a head with Bacon's Rebellion.

- During the imperial crisis of the 1760s and 1770s the ideas of the Great Awakening and especially the Enlightenment helped shape the American response to British actions and thereby contributed to a revolutionary mentality.

FURTHER READING

The diversity of colonial societies may be seen in Jack P. Greene's *Pursuits of Happiness: The Social Development of the Early Modern British Colonies and the Formation of American Culture* (1988)* and in David Hacketts Fischer's *Albion's Seed: Four British Folkways in America* (1989).* Gary B. Nash examines early race relations in *Red, White, and Black* (2nd ed., 1982).* Also see Jack P. Greene's *Imperatives, Behaviors, and Identities: Essays in Early American Cultural History* (1992).*

Until recently Puritan communities received the bulk of scholarly attention. John Frederick Martin's *Profits in the Wilderness: Entrepreneurship and the Founding of New England Towns in the Seventeenth Century* (1991) indicates that economic concerns rather than spiritual motives were driving forces in many New England towns. Of the more recent works, see also Janice Knight's *Orthodoxies in Massachusetts: Rereading American Puritanism* (1994), and Stephen Innes's *Creating the Commonwealth: The Economic Culture of Puritan New England* (1995).

Discussions of women in the New England colonies can be found in Laurel Ulrich's *Good Wives* (1982),* Joy Buel and Richard Buel's *The Way of Duty* (1984),* and Carol Karlsen's *The Devil in the Shape of a Woman: Witchcraft in Colonial New England* (1987).* Bernard Rosenthal challenges many myths concerning the Salem witch trials in *Salem Story: Reading the Witch Trials of 1692* (1993).

Later generations of these colonists are described in Michael Zuckerman's *Peaceable Kingdoms: Massachusetts Towns in the Eighteenth Century* (1970), Robert A. Gross's *The Minutemen and Their World* (1976),* and Richard L. Bushman's *From Puritan to Yankee: Character and Social Order in Connecticut* (1976).*

For the social history of the southern colonies, see Allen Kulikoff's *Tobacco and Slaves: The Development of Southern Cultures in the Chesapeake Colonies, 1680–1800* (1986) and *Colonial Chesapeake Society* (1988), edited by Lois Green Carr et al.

The best southern social history is intertwined with analysis of the origins of slavery. Begin with Edmund S. Morgan's *American Slavery,*

*These books are available in paperback editions.

American Freedom: The Ordeal of Colonial Virginia (1975),* which examines Virginia's social structure, environment, and labor patterns in a biracial context. More specific on the racial nature of the origins of slavery is Winthrop D. Jordan's *White over Black: American Attitudes toward the Negro* (1986).* On the interaction of the cultures of blacks and whites, see Mechal Sobel's *The World They Made Together: Black and White Values in Eighteenth-Century Virginia* (1987). Black viewpoints are presented in two books on Virginia: Gerald W. Mullin's *Flight and Rebellion: Slave Resistance in Eighteenth Century Virginia* (1972)* and Timothy H. Breen and Stephen Innes's *"Myne Owne Ground": Race and Freedom on Virginia's Eastern Shore, 1640–1676* (1980).* David W. Galenson's *White Servitude in Colonial America* (1981) looks at the indentured labor force.

For the role of Indians and settlers in shaping the New World's ecology, see William Cronon's fine work *Changes in the Land* (1983)* and Albert E. Cowdrey's *This Land, This South* (1983). Henry F. May's *The Enlightenment in America* (1976) examines intellectual trends in eighteenth-century America.

A concise introduction to the events and repercussions of the Great Awakening is J. M. Bumsted and John E. Van de Wetering's *What Must I Do to Be Saved?* (1976), but see also Patricia U. Bonomi's *Under the Cope of Heaven* (1986). The political impact of the new religious enthusiasm is shown in Rhys Isaac's *The Transformation of Virginia, 1740–1790* (1982).*

*These books are available in paperback editions.

3 ∾ THE IMPERIAL PERSPECTIVE

CHAPTER ORGANIZER

This chapter focuses on:

- England's changing policies in the political and economic administration of the colonies

- how colonial governments themselves were structured

- the relations between English colonists and their neighbors in North America: the French and the Indians

For the better part of the seventeenth century England remained too distracted by the struggle between Parliament and the Stuart kings to perfect either a systematic colonial policy or effective agencies of imperial control. The English Civil War, which lasted from 1642 to 1649, was followed by Oliver Cromwell's Puritan Commonwealth and Protectorate, during which the colonies were given a respite from royal control. After the Restoration of Charles II and the Stuart dynasty in 1660, the British government slowly developed a plan of colonial administration. But by the end of the century it still lacked coherence and efficiency, leaving Americans accustomed to rather loose colonial reins.

ENGLISH ADMINISTRATION OF THE COLONIES

THE MERCANTILE SYSTEM   If the English government showed little passion for colonial administration, it had a lively interest in colonial trade, which had fallen largely to Dutch shipping during the English Civil War. To win back this trade, Cromwell, in 1651, convinced Parliament to adopt a Navigation Act which required that all goods imported into England or the colonies must arrive on English ships, and that the majority of each crew must be English.

On economic policy, if nothing else, Restoration England under Charles II took its cue from the mercantile system Cromwell had instituted. Mercantilism became in the seventeenth and eighteenth centuries the operative economic theory of all major European powers. It was based on a premise quite alien to modern economic theory. Mercantilism assumed that economies could not grow by themselves. A nation could gain wealth only at the expense of another country—by seizing its bullion and dominating its trade.

In a world of national rivalries, the reasoning went, power and wealth went hand in hand. To be strong a state must be wealthy. Mercantilists assumed that the world's wealth, as reflected in the total stock of gold and silver, remained essentially fixed. All that changed was a nation's share of that stock, which it could increase only at the expense of its rivals. This meant limiting foreign imports and preserving a favorable balance of trade. To accomplish this the state should encourage manufacturers, providing subsidies and monopolies if need be, to develop and protect its own shipping, and exploit colonies as sources of raw materials and markets for its own finished goods.

The Navigation Act of 1660 added a new twist to Cromwell's act of 1651. Ships' crews now had to be not half but three-quarters English, and certain articles not produced by the mother country were to be shipped from the colonies only to England or other English colonies. The list included tobacco, cotton, indigo dye, and sugar. Later, rice, naval stores, masts, copper, and furs were added. Not only did England (and the colonies) become the sole outlet for these colonial exports, but three years later the Navigation Act of 1663 sought to make England the funnel through which all colonial imports had to be routed. The act was sometimes called the Staple Act because it made England the staple market (or trade center) for goods sent to the colonies. Virtually all ships carrying goods from Europe to America had to dock in England, be offloaded, and pay a duty before proceeding. A third major act rounded out the trade system. The Navigation Act of 1673 (sometimes called the Plantation Duty Act) required that every captain loading enumerated articles in the colonies pay a duty or tax on the item.

ENFORCING THE NAVIGATION ACTS   The Navigation Acts supplied a convenient rationale for a colonial system to serve the economic needs of the mother country. Their enforcement in far-flung colonies, however, was another matter. During the reign of Charles II a bureaucracy of colonial administrators emerged, but it took shape slowly and in fact was never fully developed. In 1675 Charles II designated certain privy councilors the Lords of Trade and Plantations, a name reflecting the overall importance of economic factors. The Lords of Trade were to make the colonies abide by the mercantile system and to make them more profitable to the crown. To these ends they served as the clearinghouse for all colonial affairs, building up a staff of colonial experts. They also named colonial governors, wrote or reviewed the governors' instructions, and handled all reports and correspondence dealing with colonial affairs.

Between 1673 and 1679, British collectors of customs duties arrived in all the colonies, and with them appeared the first seeds of colonial resentment. New England's expanding commercial interests counseled prudence and accommodation, but the Puritan leaders harbored a persistent distrust of Stuart intentions. Consequently, the Bay Colony not only ignored royal wishes; it tolerated violations of the Navigation Acts. This led the Lords of Trade to begin legal proceedings against the colonial charter in 1678. The issue remained in legal snarls for another six years, but eventually, in 1684, the Lords of Trade won a court decision annulling the Massachusetts charter. The Puritan utopia was fast becoming a lost cause.

THE DOMINION OF NEW ENGLAND   Temporarily, the Massachusetts Bay government was placed in the hands of a special royal commission. Then in 1685 Charles II died, to be succeeded by his brother, the duke of York, as James II, the first Catholic sovereign since the death of Queen Mary in 1558. Plans long maturing in the Lords of Trade for a general reorganization of colonial government coincided with the autocratic notions of James II, who asserted his prerogatives more forcefully than his brother. The new king therefore readily approved a proposal to create a Dominion of New England and to place under its jurisdiction all colonies south through New Jersey. Something of the sort might have been in store for Pennsylvania and the southern colonies as well if the reign of James II had lasted longer. In that case the English colonies might have found themselves on the same tight leash as the colonies of Spain or France.

The Dominion was to have a government named by royal authority, a governor and council who would rule without any colonial assembly. The royal governor, Sir Edmond Andros, appeared in Boston in 1686 to establish his rule, which he soon extended over Connecticut and Rhode Island, and in 1688 over New York and East and West Jersey. Andros was a soldier, accustomed to taking—and giving—orders. He seems to have been honest, efficient, and loyal to the crown, but tactless in circumstances that called for the utmost diplomacy—the uprooting of long-established institutions in the face of popular hostility.

A rising resentment greeted his measures, especially in Massachusetts. Andros now levied taxes without consent of the General Court, and when residents protested against taxation without representation, he imprisoned or fined a number of them. Andros suppressed town governments, enforced the trade laws, and clamped down on smuggling. Most ominous of all, he and his lieutenants took over one of Boston's Puritan churches for Anglican worship. Puritan leaders believed, with good reason, that he proposed to break their power and authority.

But the Dominion was scarcely established before word arrived of the Glorious Revolution of 1688–1689. James II, like Andros in New England, had aroused resentment in England by his arbitrary measures and, what was more, by openly parading his Catholic faith. His second wife bore him a son, who was sure to be reared a Catholic, and this put the opposition on notice that James's system would survive him. In 1688, parliamentary leaders, their patience exhausted, invited James's Protestant daughter Mary and her husband, the Dutch leader, William of Orange, to assume the throne as joint monarchs. James II, his support dwindling, fled to France.

THE GLORIOUS REVOLUTION IN AMERICA   When news reached Boston that William and Mary had landed in England, Boston staged its own Glorious Revolution, as bloodless as that in England. Andros and his councilors were arrested, and Massachusetts reverted to its former government, as did the other colonies that had been absorbed into the Dominion. All were permitted to retain their former status except Massachusetts and Plymouth, which, after some delay, were united under a new charter in 1691 as the royal colony of Massachusetts Bay.

The Glorious Revolution had significant long-term effects on American history. The Bill of Rights and Toleration Act, passed in England in 1689, limited the powers of rulers and affirmed a degree of freedom of worship for Christians. These acts influenced attitudes and the course of events in the colonies. And what was more significant for the future, the overthrow of James II set a precedent for revolution against the monarch. In defense of that action the English philosopher John Locke published his *Two Treatises on Government* (1690), which had an enormous impact on political thought in the colonies. While the *First Treatise* refuted theories of the divine right of kings, the more important *Second Treatise* set forth Locke's contract theory of government, which argued that people were endowed with natural rights to life, liberty, and property. When rulers violated these rights, the people had the right—in extreme cases—to overthrow the monarch and change their government.

In the American experience colonial governments had actually grown out of contractual arrangements such as Locke described. A good example would be the Mayflower Compact. The royal charters themselves also constituted a sort of contract between the crown and the settlers. Such precedents made Locke's writings especially appealing to colonial readers, and his philosophy probably had more influence in America than in England.

AN EMERGING COLONIAL SYSTEM   The accession of William and Mary to the English throne provoked a refinement of the Navigation Acts and the administrative system for regulating the American colonies. In 1696 two developments created at last the structure for a coherent colonial system. First, the Navigation Act of 1696 required colonial governors to enforce the Navigation Acts, allowed customs officials to use "writs of assistance" (general search warrants that did not have to specify the place to be searched), and ordered that accused violators be tried in Admiralty Courts, because colonial juries habitually refused to convict their peers. Admiralty cases were decided by judges whom the governors appointed.

Second, also in 1696, William III created the Board of Trade to take the place of the Lords of Trade and Plantations. Colonial officials were required to report to the board, which continued through the remainder of the colonial period to make policy. Intended to ensure that the colonies served the mother country's economy, the board oversaw the enforcement of the Navigation Acts, and recommended ways to limit manufacturing in the colonies and to encourage their production of raw materials.

From 1696 to 1725 the Board of Trade met regularly and worked vigorously toward subjecting the colonies to a more efficient royal control. After 1725, however, its energies and activities waned. The Board of Trade declined during the reign of the Hanoverian monarchs, George I (1714–1727) and George II (1727–1760), German princes who became English kings by virtue of their descent from James I. Under these monarchs, the cabinet (a kind of executive committee in the Privy Council) emerged as the central agency of administration. Robert Walpole, as first minister (1721–1742), deliberately followed a lenient policy toward the colonies, a policy which the philosopher Edmund Burke later called "a wise and salutary neglect." The board became chiefly an agency of political patronage, studded with officials who took an interest mainly in their salaries.

THE HABIT OF SELF-GOVERNMENT

Government within the colonies, like colonial policy, evolved essentially without plan. In broad outline the governor, council, and assembly in each colony corresponded to the king, lords, and commons of the mother country. At the outset, all the colonies except Georgia had begun as projects of trading companies or feudal proprietors holding charters from the crown, but eight colonies eventually relinquished or forfeited their charters and became royal provinces. Connecticut and

Rhode Island were the last of the corporate colonies; they elected their own governors to the end of the colonial period. In the corporate and proprietary colonies, and in Massachusetts, the charter served as a rough equivalent to a written constitution. Rhode Island and Connecticut in fact kept their charters as state constitutions after independence. Over the years certain anomalies appeared as colonial governments diverged from trends in England. On the one hand the governors retained powers and prerogatives that the king had lost in the course of the seventeenth century. On the other hand the assemblies acquired powers, particularly with respect to appointments, that Parliament had yet to gain.

POWERS OF THE GOVERNORS   The crown never vetoed acts of Parliament after 1707, but the colonial governors still held an absolute veto over the assemblies, and the crown could disallow (in effect, veto) colonial legislation on advice of the Board of Trade. With respect to the assembly, the governor still had the power to determine when and where it would meet, to prorogue (adjourn or recess) sessions, and to dissolve the assembly for new elections or to postpone elections indefinitely. The crown, however, had pledged to summon Parliament every three years and call elections at least every seven, and could not prorogue sessions. The royal or proprietary governor, moreover, nominated for life appointment the members of his council (except in Massachusetts, where they were chosen by the lower house), and the council functioned as both the upper house of the legislature and the highest court of appeal within the colony.

    With respect to the judiciary, in all but the charter colonies the governor still held the prerogative of creating courts and of naming and dismissing judges, powers explicitly denied the king in England. The assemblies, however, generally made good their claim that courts should be created only by legislative authority, although the crown repeatedly disallowed acts to grant judges life tenure in order to make them more independent.

    As chief executive the governor could appoint and remove officials, command the militia and naval forces, grant pardons, and, as his commission often put it, "execute everything which doth and of right ought to belong to the governor"—which might cover a multitude of powers. In these respects his authority resembled the crown's, for the king still exercised executive authority and had the power generally to name all administrative officials. This often served as a powerful means of royal influence in Parliament, since the king could appoint members or their friends to lucrative offices. And while the arrangement might seem to another age a breeding ground for corruption or tyranny, it was often viewed in the eighteenth century as a stabilizing influence, especially by the king's friends. But it was an influence less and less available to the governors. On the one hand colonial assemblies nibbled away at their power of appointment; on the other hand the authorities in England increasingly drew the control of colonial patronage into their own hands.

POWERS OF THE ASSEMBLIES Unlike the governor and council, appointed by either king or proprietor, the colonial assembly was elected. Whether called the House of Burgesses (Virginia), or Delegates (Maryland), or Representatives (Massachusetts), or simply "assembly," the lower houses were chosen by popular vote in counties or towns or, in South Carolina, parishes. Religious tests for voting were abandoned during the seventeenth century, and the chief restriction left was a property qualification, based on the notion that only men who held a "stake in society" could vote responsibly. Yet the property qualifications generally set low hurdles in the way of potential voters. Property holding was widespread, and a greater proportion of the population could vote in the colonies than anywhere else in the world of the eighteenth century. Women, Indians, and blacks were excluded—few then questioned this—and continued to be excluded for the most part into the twentieth century.

Colonial politics of the eighteenth century mirrored English politics of the seventeenth. In one case there had been a tug of war between king and Parliament, ending with the Parliament's supremacy, confirmed by the Glorious Revolution. In the other case colonial governors were still trying to wield prerogatives which the king had lost in England. The assemblies knew this; they also knew all the arguments for the "rights" and "liberties" of the people and their legislative bodies. A further anomaly in the situation was the undefined relationship of the colonies to Parliament. The colonies had been created by royal authority, yet Parliament on occasion passed laws which applied to the colonies and were tacitly accepted by the colonies.

By the early eighteenth century the assemblies, like Parliament, held two important strands of power. First, they held the power of the purse string in their right to vote on taxes and expenditures. Second, they held the power to initiate legislation and not merely, as in the early history of some colonies, the right to act on proposals from the governor and council. They used these powers to pull other strands of power into their hands when the chance presented itself. Governors were held on a tight leash by the assembly's control of political salaries, which were voted annually and sometimes not at all.

Throughout the eighteenth century the assemblies expanded their power and influence, sometimes in conflict with the governors and sometimes in harmony with them. Often in the course of routine business, the assemblies passed laws and set precedents the collective significance of which neither they nor the imperial authorities fully recognized. Once established, however, these laws and practices became fixed principles, parts of the "constitution" of the colonies. Self-government in the colonies became first a habit, then a "right."

TROUBLED NEIGHBORS

Self-government was not the only institution that began as a habit during the colonial period. The claims of white settlers on Indian lands had their roots in the first English settlements, where relations between the colonists and Indians were at times cooperative and at times viciously hostile. Indian-white relations transformed the human and ecological landscape of colonial North America, roiled colonial politics, and disrupted or destroyed the fabric of Indian culture. Relations between European settlers and North American Indians were themselves agitated by the fluctuating balance of power in Europe. The French and the English each sought to use Indians to their advantage in fighting one another for control of New World territory.

DISPLACING THE INDIANS The English invasion of North America would have been a different story, maybe a shorter and simpler story, had the English encountered greater Indian resistance. Instead, in the coastal regions they found scattered and mutually hostile tribes whom they subjected to a policy of divide and conquer. Some, perhaps most,

The Puritans and their Indian allies, the Narragansetts, mount a ferocious attack on the Pequots at Mystic, Connecticut (1637).

of the Indians guessed at the settlers' purpose quickly, like those, Powhatan told John Smith, "who do inform me your coming is not for trade, but to invade my people and possess my country." Whether tempted by trade goods or the promise of alliances, or intimidated by a show of force, most of the native Americans let matters drift until the English were too entrenched to be pushed back into the sea.

During the first half of the seventeenth century the most severe tests of the colonists' will to prevail came with the Virginia troubles of 1622 and 1644 and Connecticut's Pequot War of 1637. In both colonies Indian leaders engaged in last-chance efforts to save their lands; in both they failed. For the Pequots the result was virtual extermination—Puritans killed Pequots with such savagery that they offended their allies, the Narragansetts, who had never seen such total war. In Virginia, according to a census taken in 1669, only eleven of twenty-eight tribes described by John Smith in 1608 and only about 2,000 of some 30,000 Indians remained in the colony. Indian resistance had been broken for the time.

Then in the mid-1670s both New England and Virginia went through another time of troubles: an Indian war in New England, and in Virginia a civil war masquerading as an Indian war. For a long time in New England the Indian fur trade had contributed to peaceful relations, but the growth of settlement and the decline of the animal population were reducing the eastern tribes to relative poverty. Colonial governments encroached repeatedly, forcing Indians to acknowledge English laws and customs, including Puritan codes of behavior, and to permit English arbitration of disputes. On occasion colonial justice imposed fines, whippings, and worse. At the same time Puritan missionaries reached out to the tribes and one, John Eliot, translated the Bible into the Algonquian language. By 1675 several thousand converts had settled in special "praying Indian" towns.

The spark that set New England ablaze was struck by the murder of Sassamon, a "praying Indian" who had attended Harvard, later strayed from the faith while serving King Philip of the Wampanoag tribe, and then returned to the Christian fold. When Plymouth tried and executed three Wampanoags for the murder of Sassamon, King Philip's tribesmen attacked.

Thus began "King Philip's War," which the land-hungry leaders of Connecticut and Massachusetts quickly enlarged by assaulting the peaceful Narragansetts at their chief refuge in Rhode Island—a massacre the Rhode Island authorities were helpless to prevent. From June to December 1675, Indian attacks ravaged the interior of Massachusetts and Plymouth, and guerrilla war continued through 1676. At one point Indians burned a town within twenty miles of Boston. Finally, depleted supplies and the casualty toll wore down Indian resistance. In August 1676 Philip himself was tracked down and killed. Sporadic fighting continued until 1678 in New Hampshire and Maine. Indians who survived the slaughter had to submit to colonial authority and accept confinement to ever-dwindling plots of land.

BACON'S REBELLION   The news from New England heightened tensions among settlers strung out into the interior of Virginia, and contributed to the tangled events thereafter known as Bacon's Rebellion.

Depressed tobacco prices, rising taxes, and crowds of freed servants lusting for Indian lands provided the fuel for the rebellion. The discontent turned to violence in 1675 when a petty squabble between a frontier planter and the Doeg Indians on the Potomac led to the murder of the planter's herdsman, and in turn retaliation by frontier militiamen who killed ten or more Doegs and, by mistake, fourteen Susquehannocks. Soon a force of Virginia and Maryland militiamen laid siege to the Susquehannocks and murdered in cold blood five chieftains who came out for a parley. The enraged Indian survivors then took their revenge on frontier settlements. Scattered attacks continued on down to the James, where Nathaniel Bacon's overseer was killed.

In 1676 Nathaniel Bacon defied Governor William Berkeley's authority by assuming command of a group of frontier vigilantes. The tall, slender, black-haired, twenty-nine-year-old Bacon, a graduate of Cambridge University, had been in Virginia only two years, but he had been well set up by an English father relieved to get his vain, ambitious, and hot-tempered son out of the country. Later historians would praise Bacon as "The Torchbearer of the Revolution" and leader of the first struggle of common man versus aristocrat, of frontier versus tidewater. In part this was true. The rebellion was largely a battle of servants, small farmers, and even slaves against the wealthy planters and political leaders of Virginia. But Bacon was also the spoiled son of a rich squire, with a talent for trouble and an enthusiasm for punitive expeditions against peaceful Indians.

Bacon was early in the line of one lamentable American tradition. Indians, he declared, were "all alike," in that they were "wolves, tigers, and bears" who preyed upon "our harmless and innocent lambs," and therefore were fair game. After threatening to kill the governor and the assembly if they tried to intervene, Bacon began preparing for a total war against all Indians. To prevent any governmental interference, he ordered the governor arrested. Berkeley's forces resisted—but only feebly—and Bacon's men burned Jamestown in 1676. But Bacon could not savor the victory long; he fell ill and died of swamp fever a month later.

Governor Berkeley quickly regained control and subdued the leaderless rebels. In the process he hanged twenty-three and confiscated several estates. When his men captured one of Bacon's closest lieutenants, Berkeley gleefully exclaimed: "I am more glad to see you than any man in Virginia. Mr. Drummond, you shall be hanged in half an hour." For such severity the king recalled Berkeley to England and a royal commission made treaties of pacification with the remaining Indians, some of whose descendants still live on tiny reservations guaranteed them in 1677. The fighting opened new lands to the colonists and confirmed the power of an inner group of established landholders who sat on the Virginia council.

SPANISH AMERICA IN DECLINE   By the start of the eighteenth century, the Spanish ruled over a huge colonial empire spanning North America. Yet in fact their settlements in the borderlands north of Mexico were a colossal failure when compared to the colonies of the other European powers. In 1821, when Mexico declared its independence without firing a shot and the Spanish withdrew from North America, the most populated Hispanic settlement, Santa Fe, had only 6,000 residents. The next two largest, San Antonio and St. Augustine, totaled only 1,500 each.

The Spanish failed to create thriving North American colonies for several reasons. Perhaps the most obvious was that the region lacked the gold and silver as well as the large native populations that attracted Spanish priorities to Mexico and Peru. In addition, the Spanish were distracted by their need to control the perennial unrest in Mexico among the natives and *mestizos* (people of mixed Indian and European ancestry). Moreover, those Spaniards who led the colonization effort in the borderlands were so preoccupied with military and religious exploitation that they never devoted enough attention to the factors necessary for producing viable settlements with self-sustaining economies. Only rarely, for example, did the Spanish send many women to their colonies in North America. Even more important, they never understood that the main factor in creating successful communities was a thriving market economy. Instead they concentrated on building missions and forts and looking—in vain—for gold. Where the French and the English built their Indian policies around trading relationships (including firearms), Spain emphasized conversion to Catholicism and stubbornly adhered to an outdated mercantilism that forbade manufacturing within the colonies and strictly limited trade with the natives.

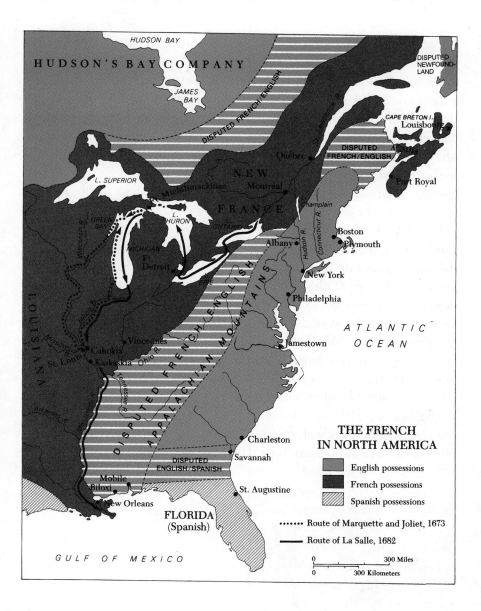

HUDSON BAY

HUDSON'S BAY COMPANY

JAMES
BAY

DISPUTED
NEWFOUND-
LAND

DISPUTED FRENCH/ENGLISH

CAPE BRETON I.
Louisbourg

St. Lawrence R.

Québec

DISPUTED
FRENCH/ENGLISH

ACADIA

Port Royal

L. SUPERIOR

N E W

Michilimackinac

Montréal

F R A N C E

GREEN
BAY

L.
HURON

ONTARIO

Champlain

Wisconsin R.

L.
MICHIGAN

Hudson R.

Connecticut R.

Boston
Plymouth

Albany

Ft.
Detroit

Erie

New York

Philadelphia

A T L A N T I C
O C E A N

L O U I S I A N A

Missouri R.

Vincennes

Cahokia

St. Louis

Kaskaskia

Ohio R.

Tennessee R.

Jamestown

A P P A L A C H I A N   M O U N T A I N S

D I S P U T E D   F R E N C H / E N G L I S H

Arkansas R.

Mississippi R.

Charleston

Savannah

DISPUTED
ENGLISH/SPANISH

Mobile

Biloxi

New Orleans

St. Augustine

FLORIDA
(Spanish)

GULF   OF   MEXICO

THE FRENCH
IN NORTH AMERICA

English possessions

French possessions

Spanish possessions

•••••• Route of Marquette and Joliet, 1673

——— Route of La Salle, 1682

0   300 Miles
0   300 Kilometers

NEW FRANCE AND LOUISIANA Permanent French settlement in the New World began soon after the Jamestown landing, far away in Québec at Port Royal, Acadia (later Nova Scotia). While Acadia remained a remote outpost, New France expanded well beyond Québec, from which Samuel de Champlain pushed his explorations into the Great Lakes as far as Lake Huron, and southward to the lake that still bears his name. There, in 1609, he joined a band of Huron and Ottawa allies in a fateful encounter, fired his gun into the ranks of their Iroquois foes, and thereby kindled a hatred which pursued New France to the end. Shortly afterward the Iroquois had a more friendly meeting with Henry Hudson near Albany, and soon acquired firearms from Dutch, and later English, traders. Thenceforth the Iroquois stood as a buffer against any French designs to move toward the English of the middle colonies, and as a constant menace on the flank of the French waterways to the interior.

From the Great Lakes French explorers moved southward. In 1673 Louis Joliet and Père Marquette, a Jesuit priest, ventured into Lake Michigan, and then journeyed down the Mississippi. Satisfied that the great river flowed to the Gulf of Mexico, they turned back for fear of meeting with Spaniards. Nine years later, in 1682, the daring explorer La Salle went all the way to the Gulf and named the country Louisiana after King Louis XIV. Actual settlement of the Louisiana country occurred later, when the French built several fortified towns, the most important of which was New Orleans, founded in 1718.

The French thus enjoyed access to the great water routes which led to the heartland of the continent. In the Illinois region scattered settlers began farming the fertile soil and courageous priests established missions at places such as Terre Haute ("high land") and Des Moines

An Iroquois warrior in an eighteenth-century French etching.

("some monks"). In the dense woods around the Great Lakes rugged French Canadians became adept trappers and traders. Unlike their English counterparts, many of these hardy *coureurs de bois* (runners of the woods) shed their Old World culture and adopted Indian ways of dress and living. Many of them married Indian women.

Yet French involvement in North America never approached that of the British. In part this was because the French-held areas were less enticing than the English seaboard settlements. Few Frenchmen were willing to challenge the interior's rugged terrain, fierce winters, and hostile Indians. In addition, the French government impeded colonization by refusing to allow French Protestants (Huguenots) to migrate. New France was to remain Roman Catholic. It also remained largely a howling wilderness, home to a mobile population of traders, trappers, missionaries—and, mainly, Indians. In 1750, when the English colonies numbered about 1.5 million, the French population was no more than 80,000.

In some ways, however, the French had the edge on the British. Their relatively small numbers forced the French to develop cooperative relationships with the Indians. Unlike the English settlers, the French established trading outposts rather than farms, mostly along the St. Lawrence River, on lands not claimed by Indians. Thus they did not have to confront initial hostility. In addition, the French served as effective mediators between rival Great Lakes tribes. This diplomatic role gave them much more local authority and influence than their English counterparts along the Atlantic coast, who disdained such mediation. The heavily outnumbered and disproportionately male French settlers sought to integrate themselves with Indian culture rather than to displace it and encouraged the Indians to embrace Catholicism and hate the English. This more fraternal bond between the French and the Indians proved to be a source of strength in the wars with the English that enabled New France to survive until 1760, despite the lopsided disparity in numbers between the two colonial powers.

In addition, French Jesuit missionaries were far better financed and educated, as well as more organized and tenacious, than their English Protestant counterparts. The French also offered European goods in return for furs, encroached far less upon Indian lands, and so won allies against the English, who came to possess the land. French governors could mobilize for action without any worry about quarreling assemblies or ethnic and religious diversity. The British may have had the greater number of colonists, but their separate colonies often worked at cross purposes. The middle colonies, for instance, protected by the Iroquois buffer, could afford to ignore the French threat—for a time at least. Whenever conflict threatened, colonial assemblies seized the opportunity to extract new concessions from their governors. Colonial merchants, who built up a trade supplying foodstuffs to the French, persisted in smuggling supplies even in wartime.

THE COLONIAL WARS

For most of the seventeenth century the French and British empires developed in relative isolation from each other, and for most of that century the homelands remained at peace. After the Restoration, Charles II and James II pursued a policy of friendship with Louis XIV. The Glorious Revolution of 1688, however, abruptly reversed English diplomacy. William III, the new British king from the Dutch Republic, had fought a running conflict against the ambitions of Louis XIV in the Netherlands and the German Palatinate. His ascent to the throne brought England almost immediately into a Grand Coalition against Louis in the War of the League of Augsburg, known in the colonies simply as King William's War (1689–1697).

This was the first of four great European and intercolonial wars over the next sixty-four years. The other three were: the War of the Spanish Succession (Queen Anne's War, 1701–1713); the War of the Austrian Succession (King George's War, 1744–1748); and the Seven Years' War (the French and Indian War, which lasted nine years in America, 1754–1763). In all except the last, the battles in America were but a sideshow to greater battles in Europe, where British policy aimed to keep a balance of power against the French. The alliances shifted from one fight to the next, but Britain and France were pitted against each other every time.

So for much of the century after the great Indian conflicts of 1676, the colonies were embroiled in wars and rumors of wars. The effect on much of the population was devastating. The New England colonies, especially Massachusetts, suffered probably more than the rest, for they were closest to the centers of French population. The casualty rate for Massachusetts men exceeded that suffered by the Union in the

Civil War. One result of such carnage was that Boston's population stagnated through the eighteenth century while Philadelphia and New York continued to grow, and the city had to struggle to support a large population of widows and orphans. Eventually, the economic impact of the four wars left increasing numbers of poor people in New England, and many of them would participate in the popular unrest leading to the revolutionary movement.

THE FRENCH AND INDIAN WAR   Of the four major wars involving the European powers and their New World colonies, the climactic conflict between Britain and France in North America was the French and Indian War. It began in 1754 after enterprising Virginians crossed the Appalachians into the upper Ohio Valley in order to trade with Indians and survey 200,000 acres granted them by King George. This infuriated the French, who saw such activity as a threat to their holdings, and they set about building a string of forts in the disputed area.

When news of these developments reached Williamsburg, the governor sent an emissary to warn off the French. An ambitious young officer in the Virginia militia, Major George Washington, volunteered for the mission. With a few companions, he made his way to Fort LeBoeuf and returned with a polite but firm French refusal. The governor then sent a small force to erect a fort at the strategic fork where the Allegheny and Monongahela Rivers meet to form the great Ohio. No sooner was it started than a larger French force appeared, ousted the Virginians, and proceeded to build Fort Duquesne on the same strategic site. Meanwhile Washington had been organizing a force of volunteers, and in the spring of 1754 he set out with an advance guard and a few Indian allies. Their clash with a French detachment marked the first bloodshed of a long—and finally decisive—war that reached far beyond America. Washington fell back with his prisoners and hastily constructed a stockade, Fort Necessity, which soon fell under siege by a larger French force. On July 4, 1754, Washington surrendered and was permitted to withdraw with his survivors.

Back in London, the Board of Trade already had taken notice of the growing conflict in the backwoods and had called a meeting in Albany, New York, of commissioners from all the colonies as far south as Maryland to confer on precautions. The Albany Congress, which met during the summer of 1754, accomplished little. It is remembered mainly for

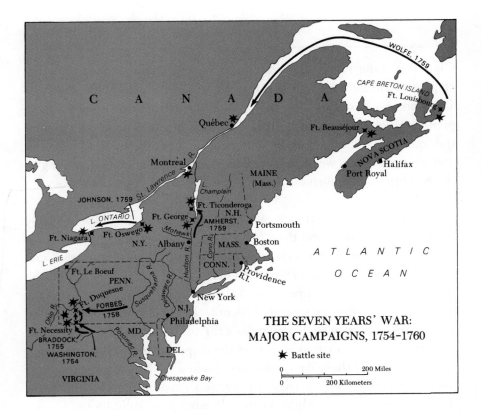

the Plan of Union worked out by a committee under Benjamin Franklin. The plan called for a chief executive, appointed and supported by
the crown, and a supreme assembly called the Grand Council, with
forty-eight members chosen by the colonial assemblies. This federal
body would oversee matters of defense, Indian relations, and trade and
settlement in the West, and would levy taxes to support its programs. It
must have been a good plan, Franklin reasoned, since the assemblies
thought it gave too much power to the crown and the crown thought
it gave too much to the colonies. At any rate the assemblies either
rejected or ignored the plan.

In London the government decided to force a showdown with the
French in America, but things went badly at first. In 1755 the British
fleet failed to halt the landing of French reinforcements in Canada, but
scored one success in Nova Scotia with the capture of a fort. The
British buttressed their hold on the area by expelling most of its French
population. Some 5,000–7,000 Acadians who refused to take an oath of
allegiance were scattered through the colonies from Maine to Georgia.
Impoverished and homeless, many of them desperately found their way

to French Louisiana, where they became the "Cajuns" (a corruption of "Acadians") whose descendants still preserve elements of the French language along the remote bayous and in many urban centers.

A WORLD WAR   For two years war raged along the American-Canadian frontier without becoming the cause of war in Europe. In 1756, however, the colonial war merged with what became the Seven Years' War in Europe. There, Empress Maria Theresa of Austria, still brooding over the loss of territory in the last conflict, staged a diplomatic revolution by bringing Austria's old enemy, France, as well as Russia, into an alliance against Frederick the Great of Prussia. Britain, ever mindful of the European balance of power, now deserted Austria to ally with Frederick. The onset of war brought into office a new British government with the popular, eloquent William Pitt as war minister. Pitt's ability and assurance ("I know that I can save England and no one else can") instilled confidence at home and abroad. Pitt committed his main forces to the war for overseas empire while providing subsidies to Frederick, who was desperately fighting off attacks from three sides.

Soon the force of British sea power began to cut off French reinforcements and supplies to the New World—and the trading goods with which they bought Indian allies. Pitt improved the British forces, gave command to young men of ability, and carried the battle to the enemy. In 1758 the tide began to turn. Fort Louisbourg fell to the British. A new expedition marched against Fort Duquesne, and the outnumbered French chose discretion as the better part of valor, burned the fort and fled the scene. On the site arose the British Fort Pitt, and later, the city of Pittsburgh.

In 1759 following the capture of Fort Niagara, which virtually cut the French lifeline to the interior, the decisive battle occurred at Québec. Commanding the British expedition up the St. Lawrence was General James Wolfe, a dedicated professional soldier who, at the age of thirty-three, had already spent more than half his life in military service. For two months Wolfe probed the defenses of Québec, seemingly impregnable on its fortified heights and manned by alert forces under General Louis Joseph de Montcalm. Finally Wolfe's troops found a path up the cliffs behind Québec. During the night of September 12–13, they scrambled up the sheer walls and emerged on the Plains of Abraham, athwart the main roads to the city. There, in a battle more like conventional European warfare than a frontier skirmish, the British forces allowed the French to advance within close range and then loosed two devastating volleys that ended French power in North America for all time. News of the victory was clouded by the word of Wolfe's—and Montcalm's—death in the battle.

The war dragged on until 1763, but the rest was a process of mopping up. In the South, where little significant action had occurred, the Cherokee nation flared into belated hostility, but a force of British regulars and provincials broke Cherokee resistance in 1761. In the North, just as peace was signed, an Ottawa chief, Pontiac, attempted to unify all the Indians of the frontier and launched a series of attacks that were not finally suppressed until 1764, after the backwoods had been ablaze for ten years.

Just six weeks after the capture of Montréal in 1760, King George II died and his grandson ascended to the throne as George III. The new king resolved to take a more active role than his Hanoverian predecessors. He yearned for peace, which entailed forcing Pitt out of office. Pitt had wanted to carry the fight to the enemy by declaring war on Spain before the French could bring that other Bourbon monarchy into the conflict. He was forestalled, but Spain belatedly entered in 1761. During the next year the Spanish met the same fate as the French: in 1762 British forces took Manila in the Philippines and Havana in Cuba.

THE PEACE OF PARIS   The war culminated in the Peace of Paris of 1763. It ended French power in North America and all but eliminated it in India. In America, Britain took all of France's North American possessions east of the Mississippi River, several islands in the West Indies, and all of Spanish Florida. The English split Spanish Florida into two administrative districts, West Florida and East Florida, separated by the Appalachicola and Chattahoochee Rivers. The English invited the Spanish settlers to remain and practice their Catholic religion, but few accepted the offer. The Spanish king ordered them to evacuate the colony and provided free transportation to Spanish possessions in the Caribbean. Within a year most of the Spaniards sold their property at bargain prices to English speculators and began an exodus to Cuba and Mexico.

NORTH AMERICA, 1763

England

Spain

— Proclamation Line of 1763

0   1000 Miles

0   1000 Kilometers

RUSSIANS

UNEXPLORED

HUDSON BAY

HUDSON'S BAY COMPANY

NEWFOUND-LAND

OREGON
Disputed by
Russia and Spain

ST. PIERRE
& MIQUELON
(France)

NOVA
SCOTIA

LOUISIANA

QUEBEC

INDIAN RESERVE

NEW ENGLAND

PACIFIC OCEAN

THE THIRTEEN COLONIES

VIRGINIA

CAROLINAS

ATLANTIC OCEAN

N E W

Mississippi

WEST
FLORIDA

EAST FLORIDA

GULF OF MEXICO

CUBA

HISPANIOLA

S P A I N

BRITISH
HONDURAS

HAITI
(France)

CARIBBEAN SEA

NEW GRANADA

In compensation for the loss of Florida, Spain received Louisiana from France. Unlike the Spanish in Florida, however, few of the French settlers left Louisiana after 1763. The French government encouraged them to stay and work with their new Spanish governors to create a bulwark against further English expansion. Instead, the French colonists revolted against their Spanish rulers in 1768. The Spanish governor and his small contingent of soldiers fled the region. Fearful of irritating their ally, French officials refused to reestablish their claim to the colony. A year later Spanish forces reasserted their control over the recalcitrant colony and arrested the rebel leaders. Spain would hold title to Louisiana for nearly four decades, but would never succeed in erasing the region's French roots. The French-born settlers always outnumbered the Spanish.

The loss of Louisiana left France with no territory on the continent of North America. British power reigned supreme over North America east of the Mississippi. But a fatal irony would pursue the British victory.

In gaining Canada the British government put in motion a train of events that would end twenty years later with the loss of all the rest of British North America. France, humiliated in 1763, thirsted for revenge. In London, Benjamin Franklin, agent for the colony of Pennsylvania from 1764 to 1775, found the French minister inordinately curious about America and suspected him of wanting to ignite the coals of controversy. Less than three years after Franklin left London, and only fifteen years after the conquest of New France, he would be in Paris arranging an alliance on behalf of Britain's rebellious colonists.

MAKING CONNECTIONS

- Although the British victory in the French and Indian War brought the colonies and England closer together in some ways, it was also an important factor in the approach of the American Revolution, as demonstrated in Chapter 4.

- One of the great struggles of the Revolution would be transforming the British colonies described in this chapter into the American states in Chapter 5.

FURTHER READING

The economics motivating colonial policies are covered in John J. McCusker and Russell R. Menard's *The Economy of British America, 1607–1789* (1985).* The effect of imperial policies on colonial politics is covered in Alison G. Olson's *Anglo-American Politics, 1600–1775*

*These books are available in paperback editions.

(1973), which traces the rise of party-like factions on the provincial level. The Andros crisis and related topics are treated in David S. Lovejoy's *The Glorious Revolution in America* (1972) and Jack M. Sosin's *English America and the Revolution of 1688* (1982).

Historians of early Indian wars have taken several different approaches to the topic. Richard Slotkin's *Regeneration through Violence* (1973)* links the colonists' treatment of Indians with later national character traits. Alden T. Vaughan defends the treatment of Indians by the Puritans in *New England Frontier: Puritans and Indians, 1620–1675* (1965).* Francis Jennings counters this thesis in *The Invasion of America* (1975).* See also Jennings's *The Ambiguous Iroquois Empire* (1984) and *Empire of Fortune: Crowns, Colonies and Tribes in the Seven Years War in America* (1988). Gregory Evans Dowd describes the unification efforts of Indians east of the Mississippi in *A Spirited Resistance: The North American Indian Struggle for Unity, 1745–1815* (1992). Fred Anderson's *A People's Army* (1984)* is a social history of the Seven Years' War.

*These books are available in paperback editions.

4 ∞ FROM EMPIRE TO INDEPENDENCE

CHAPTER ORGANIZER

This chapter focuses on:

- the changes in British colonial policy after 1763

- how the Whig ideology shaped the colonial response to changes in British policy

- the role of revolutionary leaders, including Samuel Adams, John Dickinson, Thomas Paine, and Thomas Jefferson

THE HERITAGE OF WAR

Seldom if ever since the days of Queen Elizabeth had England thrilled with such pride as in the closing years of the Great War for Empire. The victories of 1759 had delivered Canada and India to British control. In 1760 the young, vigorous George III ascended to the throne and confirmed once again the Hanoverian succession. And in 1763 the Peace of Paris confirmed the possession of a great new empire. The end of the French imperial domain in North America opened the prospect of future development of the sprawling region between the Appalachian Mountains and the Mississippi River and from the Gulf of Mexico to Hudson's Bay.

The American colonists shared in the euphoria of victory, but the moment of celebration served to mask festering resentments and new problems. Underneath the pride in the growing British Empire a sense of an American nationalism was maturing. For over a generation the colonists had essentially been allowed to govern themselves and were beginning to think and speak of themselves more as Americans than as English or British. With a great new land to exploit, they could look to the future with confidence.

The colonists had a new sense of importance after starting and fighting a vast world war with such success. Some harbored resentment, justified or not, at the haughty air of British soldiers and slights received at their hands, and many in the early stages of the war lost their awe of British soldiers, who were at such a loss in frontier fighting. One Massachusetts soldier expressed some puzzlement that he should be expected to "stand still and be shot at" in the field rather than take cover. Many colonists were dismayed by the extremely sharp social distinctions between officers and men in the British army. The provincials, by contrast, presumed that by volunteering they had formed a contract with a particular American officer from their community.

In the aftermath of victory the British ministry faced a burden of new problems. How should they manage the defense and governance of the new possessions? What should be done with the western lands? How were they to pay an unprecedented debt built up during the war and bear the new burdens of greater administration and more far-flung defense? And—the thorniest problem of all, as it turned out—what role should the colonies play in all this? The problems were of a magnitude and complexity to challenge men of the greatest statesmanship and vision, but those qualities were rare among the ministers of George III. They were perhaps even more lacking in the king himself, who was justly described by his father as "half-witted."

In the British politics of the day nearly everybody called himself a Whig, even King George. "Whig" had been the name given to those who opposed James II, led the Glorious Revolution of 1688, and secured the Protestant Hanoverian succession in 1714. The Whigs were the champions of liberty and parliamentary supremacy, but with the passage of time Whiggism had drifted into complacency and leadership settled upon an aristocratic elite of the Whig gentry. This dominant group of landholding families focused on the pursuit of personal power and local

George III, at age thirty-three, the young king of a victorious empire.

questions. In the absence of party organization, parliamentary politics hinged on factions bound together by personal loyalties, family connections, local interests, and on the pursuit of royal patronage. Throughout the 1760s the king turned first to one and then to another prime minister, and the government grew more and more unstable just as the new problems of empire required forceful solutions. Colonial policy remained marginal to the chief concerns of British politics. The result was first inconsistency and vacillation, followed by stubborn inflexibility.

WESTERN LANDS

No sooner was peace arranged in 1763 than events thrust the problem of America's western lands upon the British government in an acute form. The Indians of the Ohio region, unable to believe that their French friends were helpless and fearing the arrival of English settlers, grew restless and receptive to the warnings of Pontiac, chief of the Ottawa. In 1763, the western tribes joined Pontiac's attempt to reopen frontier warfare, and within a few months wiped out every British post in the Ohio region except Detroit and Fort Pitt.

To secure peace, the ministers in London reasoned, further settlement of the western lands could wait until another day. The immediate need was to stop Pontiac's warriors and pacify the Indians. The king signed the Royal Proclamation of 1763, which drew an imaginary line along the crest of the Appalachians beyond which settlers were forbidden to go and colonial governors were forbidden to authorize surveys or issue land grants. It also established the new British colonies of Quebec and East and West Florida, the last two consisting mainly of small settlements at St. Marks and St. Augustine respectively, peopled mainly by British garrisons.

But Pontiac did not agree to peace until 1766, and Britain's Proclamation Line did not long remain intact. During the turbulent decade that followed, hardy pioneers pushed on over the ridges. By 1770 the town of Pittsburgh had twenty log houses, and a small village had appeared on the site of Wheeling. Four years later Daniel Boone and a party of settlers cut the Wilderness Road through the Cumberland Gap in southwestern Virginia to the Kentucky River.

GRENVILLE AND THE STAMP ACT

As the Proclamation of 1763 was being drafted, a new ministry in London began to grapple with the problems of imperial finances. The new chief minister, George Grenville, first lord of the Treasury, was much like the king: industrious, honest, meticulous, and obtuse. Grenville assumed the need for redcoats to defend the frontier, although the colonies had been left mostly to their own devices before 1754. He also wanted to keep a large army in America to avoid a rapid demobilization that would force many influential officers to retire and thereby provoke political criticism at home. But on top of an already staggering debt he faced sharply rising costs for American defense.

Because there was a heavy tax burden at home and a much lighter one in the colonies, Grenville reasoned that the Americans were obligated to share the cost of their own defense. He also learned that the American customs service was amazingly inefficient. Evasion and corruption were rampant. Grenville thus issued stern orders to colonial officials and dispatched the navy to patrol the coasts. Parliament agreed to set up a new maritime or vice-admiralty court in Halifax with jurisdiction over all the colonies. This court would have no juries of colonists sympathetic to smugglers. Judges would be appointed by the

Crown, and they would serve without juries. The old habits of salutary neglect in the enforcement of the Navigation Acts were coming to an end, causing no little annoyance to American shippers.

In 1764 Grenville also put through the Sugar Act, which cut the duty in half. This, he believed, would reduce the temptation to smuggle or to bribe customs officers. In addition the Sugar Act levied new duties on imports into the colonies of foreign textiles, wines, coffee, indigo, and sugar. The act, Grenville estimated, would bring in enough revenue to help defray "the necessary expenses of defending, protecting, and securing" the colonies. For the first time Parliament had adopted duties frankly designed to raise revenues in the colonies rather than just to regulate trade.

Another measure in Grenville's new colonial program that had an important impact on the colonies was the Currency Act of 1764. The colonies faced a chronic shortage of hard money, which kept going out to pay debts in England. To meet the shortage they issued their own paper money. British creditors, however, feared payment in such a depreciated currency. To alleviate their fears, Parliament in 1751 had forbidden the New England colonies to make their currency legal tender. Now Grenville extended the prohibition to all the colonies. The value of existing paper money soon plummeted, since nobody was obligated to accept it in payment of debts, even in the colonies. The deflationary impact of the Currency Act, combined with new duties and stricter enforcement, delivered a severe shock to a colonial economy already suffering a postwar slump.

THE STAMP ACT   Grenville's new design entailed one more key provision. Because the Sugar Act would defray only part of the cost of maintaining the 10,000 British troops to be stationed along the western frontier, he proposed another measure to raise money in America, a stamp tax. Enacted on February 13, 1765, the Stamp Act created revenue stamps that were to be attached to printed matter and legal documents of all kinds: newspapers, pamphlets, almanacs, bonds, leases, deeds, licenses, insurance policies, ship clearances, college diplomas, even dice and playing cards. The requirement would go into effect on November 1, 1765.

In March 1765 Grenville put through the final measure of his new program, the Quartering Act. It required the colonies to supply British troops with provisions and to provide them barracks or submit to their use of inns and vacant buildings. It applied to all colonies, but affected mainly New York, headquarters of the British forces.

THE IDEOLOGICAL RESPONSE   The cumulative effect of Grenville's measures raised colonial suspicions to a fever pitch. Unwittingly this plodding minister of a plodding king had stirred up a storm of protest and set in motion a profound exploration of English traditions and imperial relations. By this time the radical ideas of the so-called "Real Whig" minority in England slowly began to take hold in the colonies. These ideas derived from various sources but above all from the writings of John Locke, which justified the struggle by Parliament to preserve life, liberty, and property against royal tyranny.

Colonial critics of British policy also knew from their religious heritage and by what Patrick Henry called "the lamp of experience" that human nature is corruptible and lusts after power. The safeguard against abuses, in the view of those who called themselves "Real Whigs," was not to rely on human goodness but to check power with power so as to preserve individual liberty. The British Constitution had embodied these principles in a mixed government of kings, lords, and commons, each serving as a check on the others.

But in 1764 and 1765 many colonists insisted that the separation of powers was not working. Grenville had loosed upon them the very engines of tyranny from which Parliament had rescued England in the seventeenth century, and by imposition of that very Parliament! A standing army encouraged despots, and now, with the French gone and Pontiac subdued, several thousand British soldiers remained in the colonies: to protect the colonists or to subdue them? It was beginning to seem clear that it was the latter. Among fundamental English rights were trial by jury and the presumption of innocence, but vice-admiralty courts excluded juries and put the burden of proof on the defendant. Most important, the English had the right to be taxed only by their elected representatives. Parliament claimed that privilege in England, and the colonial assemblies had long exercised it in America. Now, with the Stamp Act, Parliament was out to usurp the assemblies' power of the purse strings.

In a flood of colonial pamphlets, speeches, and resolutions, debate on the Stamp Tax turned mainly on the point expressed in a slogan familiar to all Americans: "no taxation without representation." Grenville had one of his subordinates prepare an answer, which developed the ingenious theory of "virtual representation." If the colonies had no vote in Parliament, neither did most Englishmen who lived in boroughs that had developed since the last apportionment. Large cities, such as Manchester and Birmingham, had arisen that had no right to elect a member, while old boroughs with little or no population still returned members. Nevertheless, according to this theory, each member of Parliament represented the interests of the whole country and indeed the whole empire. To the colonists, however, virtual representation was nonsense, justified neither by logic nor by their own experience.

PROTEST IN THE COLONIES   The Stamp Act became the chief target of colonial protest: the Sugar Act affected mainly New England, but the Stamp Act burdened all colonists who did any kind of business. And it affected most of all the articulate elements in the community: merchants, planters, lawyers, printer-editors—all strategically placed to influence opinion.

Through the spring and summer of 1765 popular resentment against Grenville boiled over. The *Boston Gazette* directed a threatening couplet at the British minister:

> To make us all Slaves, now you've lost Sir! the Hope,
> You've but to go hang yourself.—We'll find the Rope.

Such anger found outlets in mass meetings, parades, bonfires, and other demonstrations. To be sure, only a minority engaged in such public protests. They included farmers, laborers, dock workers, and seamen. North Carolina's royal governor reported the mobs to be composed of "gentlemen and planters." Calling themselves Sons of Liberty, they met underneath "Liberty Trees"—in Boston a great elm, in Charleston a live oak. One day in mid-August, nearly three months before the effective date of the Stamp Act, an effigy of Boston's stamp agent swung from the Liberty Tree. In the evening a mob carried it through the streets, destroyed the stamp office, and used the wood to burn the effigy. Somewhat later another mob sacked the home of the lieutenant-governor and the local customs officer. The Boston stamp agent, thoroughly shaken, resigned his commission, and stamp agents

In protest of the Stamp Act, which was to take effect the next day, the Pennsylvania Journal *appeared with the skull and crossbones on its masthead.*

throughout the colonies felt impelled to follow his example. Loyalists deplored such riotous violence, arguing that the rebels were behaving more tyrannically than the British.

The widespread protests encouraged colonial unity, as colonists discovered that they had more in common with each other than with London. In May 1765, long before the mobs went into action, the Virginia House of Burgesses had struck the first blow against the Stamp Act in the Virginia Resolves, a series of resolutions inspired by young Patrick Henry's "torrents of sublime eloquence." Virginians, the burgesses declared, were entitled to all English rights, and the English could be taxed only by their own representatives. Virginians, moreover, had always been governed by laws passed with their own consent. Newspapers spread the resolutions throughout the colonies, along with even more radical statements that were kept out of the final version, and other assemblies hastened to copy Virginia's example. On June 8, 1765, the Massachusetts House of Representatives issued a circular letter inviting the various assemblies to send delegates to confer in New York on appeals for relief from the king and Parliament.

Nine responded, and on October 7 the Stamp Act Congress of twenty-seven delegates convened and issued expressions of colonial sentiment: a Declaration of the Rights and Grievances of the Colonies, a petition to the king for relief, and a petition to Parliament for repeal of the Stamp Act. The delegates argued that Parliament might have powers to legislate for the regulation of colonial trade, but it had no right to levy taxes, which were a gift granted by the people through their representatives.

By November 1, its effective date, the Stamp Act was a dead letter. Business went on without the stamps. Newspapers appeared with the skull and crossbones in the corner where the stamp belonged. Colonial rebels were beginning to sense their power. After passage of the Sugar Act a movement had begun to boycott British goods. Now colonists adopted non-importation agreements to exert pressure on British merchants. Americans knew they had become a major market for British products. By shutting off imports they could exercise real leverage. Sage and sassafras took the place of tea, and homespun garments became the fashion as symbols of colonial defiance.

REPEAL OF THE ACT   The storm had scarcely broken before Grenville's ministry was out of office, dismissed not because of the colonial turmoil but because of tensions with the king over the distribution of lucrative government offices. In 1765 the king installed a new minister, the marquis of Rockingham, leader of the "Rockingham Whigs," who sympathized with the colonists' views. Rockingham resolved to end the quarrel by repealing the Stamp Act, but he needed to move carefully in order to win a majority. Simple repeal was politically impossible without some affirmation of parliamentary authority over the colonies. When Parliament assembled early in 1766, William Pitt demanded that the Stamp Act be repealed "absolutely, totally, and immediately," but urged that Britain's authority over the colonies "be asserted in as strong terms as possible," except on the point of taxation. Rockingham steered a cautious course and seized upon the widespread but false impression that Pitt accepted the principle of "external" taxes or duties on trade but rejected "internal" taxes, such as the stamp tax, within the colonies.

In March 1766 Parliament passed the repeal, but at the same time passed the Declaratory Act, which asserted the full power of Parliament to make laws binding the colonies "in all cases whatsoever." It was a cunning evasion that made no concession with regard to taxes, but made no mention of them either. It left intact in the minds of many members the impression that a distinction had been drawn between "external" taxes on trade and "internal" taxes within the colonies, an impression that would have fateful consequences for the future. For the moment, however, the Declaratory Act seemed little more than a face-saving gesture. Amid the rejoicing and relief on both sides of the Atlantic there were no omens that the quarrel would be reopened within a year. To be sure, the Sugar Act remained on the books, but Rockingham reduced the molasses tax from three pence to one pence a gallon, less than the cost of a bribe.

FANNING THE FLAMES

Meanwhile, the king continued to have his ministers play musical chairs. Rockingham fell because he lost the confidence of the king, and his own administration suffered a paralyzing fragmentation. The king invited Pitt to form a ministry including the major factions of Parliament. Soon thereafter, however, William Pitt slipped over the fine line between genius and madness, and he resigned in 1768. For a time in 1767 the guiding force in the ministry was Charles Townshend, chancellor of the Exchequer, whose "abilities were superior to those of all men," according to Horace Walpole, "and his judgment below that of any man." The witty but erratic Townshend took advantage of Pitt's absence to reopen the question of colonial taxation and seized upon the notion that "external" taxes were tolerable to the colonies—not that he believed it for a moment.

THE TOWNSHEND ACTS In May and June 1767 Townshend put his plan through the House of Commons, and in September he died, leaving a bitter legacy: the Townshend Acts. Their first objective was to bring the New York assembly to its senses. That body had defied the Quartering Act and refused to provide billets or supplies for the king's troops. Parliament, at Townshend's behest, suspended all acts of the New York assembly until it yielded. New York finally caved in, inadvertently confirming the British suspicion that too much indulgence had encouraged colonial bad manners. Townshend followed up with the Revenue Act of 1767, which levied duties ("external taxes") on colonial imports of glass, lead, paints, paper, and tea. Next, he set up a Board of Customs Commissioners at Boston, the colonial headquarters of smuggling. Finally, he reorganized the vice-admiralty courts, providing four in the continental colonies—at Halifax, Boston, Philadelphia, and Charleston.

The Townshend duties did increase government revenues, but the intangible costs were greater. The duties taxed goods exported from England, indirectly hurting British manufacturers, and had to be collected in colonial ports, increasing collection costs. More important, the new taxes accelerated colonial resistance. The Revenue Act of 1767 posed a more severe threat to colonial assemblies than Grenville's taxes, for Townshend proposed to apply the revenues to pay the salaries of governors and other officers and release them from financial dependence on the assemblies.

DICKINSON'S *LETTERS*   The Townshend Acts provoked the colonists to resist, to boycott British goods, to wear homespun, to develop their own manufactures. Once again the colonial press spewed out expressions of protest, most notably the essays of John Dickinson, a Philadelphia lawyer who hoped to resolve the dispute by persuasion. Late in 1767 his twelve *Letters of a Pennsylvania Farmer* (as he chose to style himself) began to appear in the *Pennsylvania Chronicle,* from which they were copied in other papers and in pamphlet form. He argued that Parliament might regulate commerce and collect duties incidental to that purpose, but it had no right to levy taxes for revenue, whether they were internal or external. Dickinson used moderate language throughout. The colonists, he declared, should "speak at the same time the language of affliction and veneration" toward the mother country.

SAMUEL ADAMS AND THE SONS OF LIBERTY   But the affliction grew and the veneration waned. British ministers could neither conciliate moderates like Dickinson nor cope with firebrands like Boston's Samuel Adams, who was now emerging as the supreme genius of revolutionary agitation. Born in 1722, Adams, the son of moderately well off and sternly pious parents, graduated from Harvard and soon thereafter inherited the family brewery, which he proceeded to manage into bankruptcy. His distant cousin John Adams described Sam as a "universal good character," a "plain, simple, decent citizen, of middling stature, dress, and manners," who prided himself on his frugality and his distaste for ceremony and display. Politics, not profits, excited his passion, and he spent most of his time at midcentury and after debating political issues with sailors, roustabouts, and stevedores at local taverns. Adams insisted that Parliament had no right to legislate at all for the colonies, that Massachusetts must return to the spirit of its Puritan founders and defend itself from a new conspiracy against its liberties.

While other men tended their private affairs, Adams whipped up the Sons of Liberty, writing incendiary newspaper articles and letters, and organizing protests in the Boston pubs, town meeting, and the provincial assembly. A Tory opponent begrudgingly acknowledged Adams's intense commitment, noting that he "eats little, drinks little, thinks much, and is most decisive and indefatigable in the pursuit of his objects." The royal governor called him "the most dangerous man in Massachusetts." Early in 1768 Adams and James Otis formulated another Massachusetts Circular Letter, which the assembly dispatched to the other colonies. The letter restated the illegality of parliamentary taxation, warned that the new duties would be used to pay colonial officials, and invited the other colonies to join in a boycott of British goods.

In mid-May 1769 the Virginia assembly passed a new set of resolves reasserting its exclusive right to tax Virginians and calling upon the colonies to unite in protest. Virginia's governor promptly dissolved the assembly, but the members met independently, and adopted a new set of non-importation agreements. Once again, as with the Virginia Resolves against the Stamp Act, most of the other assemblies followed suit. One South Carolina planter urged his fellows: "Let us then, AT LAST, follow the example of our brother sufferers in the Northern Colonies, and encourage the making of our own manufactures. . . . Let us, Brother Planters, wear our old clothes as they will ever hang on us."

THE BOSTON MASSACRE   In Boston roving gangs enforced the boycott, intimidating Tory merchants and their customers. This led the governor to appeal for military support, and two British regiments sailed from Halifax. The presence of soldiers in Boston had been a constant provocation, and now tensions heightened, as surly crowds frequently heckled the "lobster backs." On March 5, 1770, in the square before the customs house, a mob of toughs began heaving taunts, snowballs, and oyster shells at the British sentry, whose call for help brought reinforcements. Then somebody rang the town firebell, drawing a larger

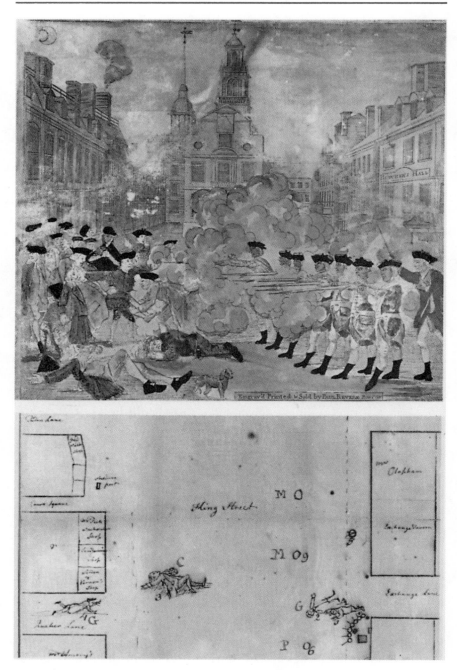

Paul Revere's partisan engraving of the Boston Massacre (top). *Revere drew a plan of the Massacre* (bottom) *for use at the trial of the British soldiers. It shows the places where four of the dead fell.*

crowd to the scene. At their head, or so the story goes, was Crispus Attucks, a runaway mulatto slave who had worked for some years on ships out of Boston. The riotous crowd began striking at the troops with sticks, and finally knocked one soldier down. He rose to his feet and fired into the crowd. Others fired too, and when the smoke cleared, five people lay dead or dying and eight more were wounded.

The cause of colonial resistance now had its first martyrs, and the first to die was Crispus Attucks. Governor Thomas Hutchinson, at the insistence of a mass meeting in Faneuil Hall, moved the soldiers out of town to avoid another incident. The troops involved in the shooting were indicted for murder but were defended by John Adams, who portrayed them as the victims of circumstance, provoked, he said, by a "motley rabble of saucy boys, negroes and mulattoes, Irish teagues and outlandish Jack tars." All were acquitted except two, who were convicted of manslaughter and branded on the thumb.

News of the Boston Massacre sent shock waves through the colonies. The incident, remembered one Bostonian, "created a resentment which emboldened the timid" and "determined the wavering." But late in April 1770 news arrived that Parliament had repealed all the Townshend duties save one. The cabinet, by a fateful vote of five to four, had advised keeping the tea tax as a token of parliamentary authority. Colonial diehards insisted that pressure should be kept on British merchants until Parliament gave in altogether, but the non-importation movement soon faded. Parliament, after all, had given up the substance of the taxes, with one exception, and much of the colonists' tea was smuggled in from Holland anyway.

For two years thereafter discontent simmered down and suspicions began to fade on both sides of the ocean. The Stamp Act was gone, as were all the Townshend duties except that on tea. Yet most of the hated innovations remained in effect: the Sugar Act, the Currency Act, the Quartering Act, the vice-admiralty courts, the Board of Customs Commissioners. The redcoats had left Boston but they remained nearby, and the British navy still patrolled the coast. Each remained a source of irritation and the cause of occasional incidents. There was still tinder awaiting a spark, and colonial patriots were primed to resist new tyrannies. As Sam Adams stressed, "Where there is a Spark of patriotick fire, we will enkindle it."

DISCONTENT ON THE FRONTIER

Many colonists showed no interest in the disputes over British regulatory policies raging along the seaboard. Parts of the backcountry had stirred with quarrels that had nothing to do with the Stamp and Townshend Acts. Rival land claims to the east of Lake Champlain pitted New York against New Hampshire, and the Green Mountain Boys led by Ethan Allen against both. Eventually the residents of the area would simply create their own state of Vermont in 1777, although not recognized as a member of the Union until 1791. In Pennsylvania a group of frontier ruffians took the law into their own hands. Outraged at the lack of frontier protection provided by the Quaker-influenced assembly during Pontiac's rebellion, a group called the "Paxton Boys" took revenge by massacring peaceful Conestoga Indians in Lancaster County, then threatened the so-called Moravian Indians, a group of Moravian converts near Bethlehem. When the Moravian Indians took refuge in Philadelphia, some 1,500 Paxton Boys marched on the capital, where Benjamin Franklin talked them into returning home by promising that more protection would be forthcoming.

Farther south, South Carolina frontier folk voiced similar complaints about the lack of settled government and the need for protection against horse thieves, cattle rustlers, and Indians. They organized societies called "Regulators" to administer vigilante justice in the region and refused to pay taxes until they gained effective government. In 1769 the assembly finally set up six new circuit courts in the region and revised the taxes, but still did not respond to the backcountry's demand for representation in the legislature.

In North Carolina the protest was less over the lack of government than over the abuses and extortion inflicted by government appointees from the eastern part of the colony. Farmers felt especially oppressed at the government's refusal either to issue paper money or to accept produce in payment of taxes, and in 1766 they organized to resist. Efforts of these "Regulators" to stop seizures of property and other court proceedings led to more disorders and a new law that made the rioters guilty of treason. In the spring of 1771 the royal governor and 1,200 militiamen defeated some 2,000 ill-organized Regulators in the Battle of Alamance. The pitched battle illustrated the growing tensions between backcountry settlers and the wealthy planters in the eastern part of the colony, tensions that would erupt again during and after the Revolution.

These internal disputes and revolts within the colonies illustrate the fractious diversity of opinion and outlook evident among Americans on the eve of the Revolution. Colonists were of many minds about many things, including British rule. The disputatious frontier in colonial America also helped convince British authorities that the colonies were inherently unstable. The colonies required even more keen oversight and needed to be managed with firmness, even to the extent of using military force to ensure civil stability.

A WORSENING CRISIS

Two events in June 1772 shattered the period of calm in the quarrels with the mother country. Near Providence, Rhode Island, a British schooner, the *Gaspee,* patrolling for smugglers, accidentally ran aground. Under cover of darkness a crowd from the town boarded the ship, removed the crew, and set fire to the vessel. A commission of inquiry was formed with authority to hold suspects, but no witnesses could be found. Four days after the burning, Massachusetts' governor, Thomas Hutchinson, told the provincial assembly that his salary thenceforth would come out of the customs revenues. Superior Court judges would be paid from the same source and would thereby no longer be dependent on the assembly for their income. The assembly feared that this portended "a despotic administration of government."

To keep the pot simmering, in November 1772 Sam Adams convinced the Boston Town Meeting to form a Committee of Correspondence, which issued a statement of rights and grievances and invited other towns to do the same. Committees of Correspondence sprang up across Massachusetts and spread into other colonies. In March 1773 the Virginia assembly proposed the formation of such committees on an intercolonial basis, and a network of the committees spread across the colonies, keeping in touch, mobilizing public opinion, and keeping colonial resentments at a simmer. In unwitting tribute to their effectiveness, a loyalist called the committees "the foulest, subtlest, and most venomous serpent ever issued from the egg of sedition."

Americans throwing the Cargoes of the Tea Ships into the River, at Boston, 1773.

THE BOSTON TEA PARTY   Lord North, who had replaced Townshend as chancellor of the Exchequer, soon brought colonial resentment from a simmer to a boil. In May 1773 he contrived a scheme to bail out the foundering East India Company. The company had in its British warehouses some 17 million pounds of unsold tea. Under the Tea Act of 1773 the government would refund the British duty of twelve pence per pound on all tea shipped to the colonies and collect only the existing three pence duty payable at the colonial port. By this arrangement colonists could get tea more cheaply than the English could, for less even than the black market Dutch tea. North, however, miscalculated in assuming that price alone would govern colonial reaction. And he erred even worse by permitting the East India Company to serve retailers directly through its own agents or consignees, bypassing the colonial wholesalers who had handled it before. Once that kind of monopoly was established, colonial merchants began to wonder, how soon would the precedent apply to other commodities?

The Committees of Correspondence, backed by colonial merchants, alerted people to the new danger. The government, they reported, was trying to purchase their loyalty and passivity with cheap tea. Before the end of the year, large shipments of tea went out to major colonial ports. In New York and Philadelphia popular hostility forced company agents to resign. When no one received the tea, it went back to England. In Charleston it was unloaded into warehouses—and later sold to finance the Revolution. In Boston, however, Governor Hutchinson and Sam Adams resolved upon a test of will. The ships' captains, alarmed by the radical opposition, proposed to turn back, but Hutchinson refused permission until the tea was landed and the duty paid. On December 16, 1773, a group of colonial patriots disguised themselves as Mohawk Indians, boarded the three ships, and threw the 342 chests of tea overboard—cheered on by a crowd along the shore. Like those who had burned the *Gaspee,* they remained parties unknown—except to hundreds of Bostonians. One participant later testified that Sam Adams and John Hancock were there. "Sam Adams is in his glory," Governor Hutchinson muttered, and indeed he was.

Given a more tactful response from London, the Boston Tea Party might easily have undermined the radicals' credibility. Many people, especially merchants, abhorred the wanton destruction of property. A town meeting in Bristol, Massachusetts, condemned the action, and Benjamin Franklin called on his native city to pay for the spoiled tea. British authorities, however, had reached the end of their patience. They were now convinced that the very existence of the empire was at stake. The rebels in Boston were provoking what could become a widespread effort to evade royal authority and imperial regulations. A firm response was required. "The colonists must either submit or triumph," George III wrote to Lord North, and North hastened to make the king's judgment a self-fulfilling prophecy.

THE COERCIVE ACTS   In April 1774 Parliament enacted four harsh measures designed by North to discipline Boston. The Boston Port Act closed the port from June 1, 1774, until the lost tea was paid for. An Act for the Impartial Administration of Justice let the governor transfer to England the trial of any official accused of committing an offense in the line of duty—no more redcoats would be tried on technicalities. A new Quartering Act directed local authorities to provide lodging for British soldiers, in private homes if necessary. Finally, the Massachusetts Government Act made the colony's council and law-enforcement officers all appointive, rather than elected; sheriffs would select jurors and no town meeting could be held without the governor's consent, except for the annual election of town officers. In May, General Thomas Gage re-

The Able Doctor, or America Swallowing the Bitter Draught. *This 1774 engraving shows Lord North, with the Boston Port Act in his pocket, pouring tea down America's throat. America spits it back.*

placed Hutchinson as governor and assumed command of British forces.

Designed to isolate Boston and make an example of the colony, the actions instead cemented colonial unity and emboldened resistance. "Your scheme yields no revenue," Edmund Burke warned North in Parliament; "it yields nothing but discontent, disorder, disobedience. . . ." At last, it seemed to the colonists, their worst fears were confirmed. If these "Intolerable Acts," as the colonists labeled the Coercive Acts, were not resisted, they would eventually be applied to the other colonies. Further confirmation of British designs came with news of the Quebec Act, passed in June 1774. It set up an unrepresentative government in the Canadian colony under an appointed governor and council and gave a privileged position to the Catholic church. The measure was actually designed to deal with the peculiar milieu of a British colony peopled mainly by French settlers unused to representative assemblies, but it seemed merely another indicator of tyrannical designs for the rest of the colonies. In addition, colonists pointed out that they had lost many lives in an effort to liberate the trans-Appalachian West from the control of French Catholics. Now the British seemed to be protecting papists at the expense of their own colonists. What was more, the act placed within the boundaries of Quebec the western lands north of the Ohio River, lands that Pennsylvania, Virginia, and Connecticut had long claimed.

Meanwhile, colonists rallied to the cause of besieged Boston, taking up collections and sending provisions. When the Virginia assembly met in May 1774, a young member of the Committee of Correspondence, Thomas Jefferson, proposed to set aside June 1, the effective date of the Boston Port Act, as a day of fasting and prayer in Virginia. The irate colonial governor thereupon dissolved the assembly, whose members retired to a nearby tavern and drew up a resolution for a "Continental Congress" to make representations on behalf of all the colonies. Similar calls were coming from Providence, New York, Philadelphia, and elsewhere, and in June the Massachusetts assembly suggested a September meeting at Philadelphia. Shortly before George Washington left to represent Virginia at the meeting, he wrote to a friend that "the crisis is arrived when we must assert our rights, or submit to every imposition, that can be heaped upon us, till custom and use shall make us as tame and abject slaves, as the blacks we rule over with such arbitrary sway."

THE CONTINENTAL CONGRESS   On September 5, 1774, the First Continental Congress assembled in Philadelphia. The fifty-five delegates, elected by provincial congresses or irregular conventions, represented twelve continental colonies, all but Georgia, Quebec, Nova Scotia, and the Floridas. Peyton Randolph of Virginia was elected president and Charles Thomson, "the Sam Adams of Philadelphia," became secretary, but not a member. The Congress agreed to vote by colonies, although Patrick Henry urged the members to vote as individuals on the grounds that they were not Virginians or New Yorkers, but Americans. In effect the delegates functioned as a congress of ambassadors, gathered to join forces on common policies and neither to govern nor to rebel but to adopt and issue a series of resolutions and protests.

The Congress endorsed the radical Suffolk Resolves, resolutions that declared the Intolerable Acts null and void, urged Massachusetts to arm for defense, and called for economic sanctions against British commerce. The Congress also adopted a Declaration of American Rights, which conceded only Parliament's right to regulate commerce and those matters that were strictly imperial affairs. It denied Parliament's authority with respect to internal colonial affairs and proclaimed the right of each assembly to determine the need for troops within its own province. In addition, the Congress sent the king a petition for relief and issued addresses to the people of Great Britain and the colonies.

Finally, the Congress adopted the Continental Association of 1774, which recommended that every county, town, and city form committees to enforce a boycott on all British goods. These committees would become the organizational and communications network for the Revolutionary movement, connecting every locality to the leadership. The Continental Association also included provisions for the non-importation of British goods (implemented in December 1774) and the non-exportation of American goods to Britain (to be implemented in September 1775 unless colonial grievances were addressed).

In taking its stand Congress had adopted what later would be called the dominion theory of the British Empire, a theory long implicit in the assemblies' claim to independent authority but more recently formulated in two widely circulated pamphlets by James Wilson of Pennsylvania and Thomas Jefferson of Virginia. Each had argued that the colonies were not subject to Parliament but merely to the crown; each colony, like England itself, was a separate realm. Another congress was called for May 1775.

In London the king fumed. In late 1774 he wrote his prime minister that the "New England colonies are in a state of rebellion," and "blows must decide whether they are to be subject to this country or independent." British critics of the American actions reminded the colonists that Parliament had absolute sovereignty. Power could not be shared. Parliament could not relinquish its claim to authority in part without abandoning it altogether. Few members of Parliament were ready to comprehend, much less accept, the Congress's "liberal and expanded thought," as Jefferson called it. In the House of Commons, Edmund Burke, in a brilliant speech on conciliation, urged merely an acceptance of the American view on taxation as consonant with English principles. The real question, he argued, was "not whether you have the right to render your people miserable; but whether it is not your interest to make them happy."

But Parliament rejected the notion of compromise. Instead, it declared Massachusetts in rebellion, forbade the New England colonies to trade with any nation outside the empire, and excluded New Englanders from the North Atlantic fisheries. Lord North's Conciliatory Resolution, adopted February 27, 1775, was as far as they would go. Under its terms, Parliament would levy taxes only to regulate trade and would grant to each colony the duties collected within its boundaries, provided the colonies would contribute voluntarily to a quota for defense of the empire. It was a formula, Burke said, not for peace but for new quarrels.

SHIFTING AUTHORITY

Events were already moving beyond conciliation. All through late 1774 and early 1775, the patriot defenders of American rights were seizing the initiative. The uncertain and unorganized Loyalists (or Tories), if they did not submit to non-importation agreements, found themselves confronted with tar and feathers. The Continental Congress urged each colony to mobilize its militia. The militia, as much a social as a military organization in the past, now took to serious drill in formations, tactics, and marksmanship, and organized special units of Minute Men ready for quick mobilization. Everywhere royal and proprietary officials were losing control as provincial congresses assumed authority and colonial militias organized and gathered arms and gunpowder. Still, British military officials remained smugly confident. Major John Pitcairn wrote home from Boston in March: "I am satisfied that one active campaign, a smart action, and burning two or three of their towns, will set everything to rights."

LEXINGTON AND CONCORD   Pitcairn soon had his chance. On April 14, 1775, Governor Gage received orders to suppress the "open rebellion," even at the risk of conflict. Leaders of the Massachusetts Provincial Congress, whom Gage was directed to arrest, were mostly beyond his reach, but he decided to seize Sam Adams and John Hancock in Lexington and destroy the militia's supply depot at Concord, about twenty miles away from his Boston headquarters. On the night of April 18, Lieutenant-Colonel Francis Smith and Major Pitcairn gathered 700 men on Boston Common and set out on a soggy route across the Cambridge marsh to Concord by way of Lexington. But local patriots got wind of the plan, and Boston's Committee of Safety sent silver-

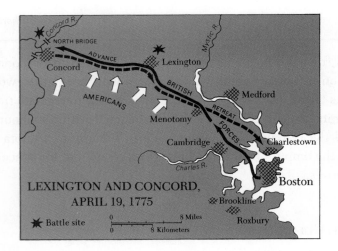

LEXINGTON AND CONCORD,
APRIL 19, 1775

★ Battle site

0   8 Miles
0   8 Kilometers

smith Paul Revere and tanner William Dawes by separate routes on their famous ride to spread the alarm. Revere reached Lexington about midnight and alerted Hancock and Adams. Joined by Dawes and Dr. Samuel Prescott, who had been visiting in Lexington, he rode on toward Concord. A British patrol intercepted the trio, but Prescott slipped through with the warning.

At dawn on April 19 the British advance guard found Captain John Parker and about seventy Minute Men lined up on the dewy Lexington village green. Parker apparently intended only a silent protest, but Pitcairn rode onto the green, swung his sword, and brusquely yelled, "Disperse, you damned rebels! You dogs, run!" The Americans already had begun backing away when someone fired a single pistol shot, whereupon the British soldiers loosed a volley into the Minute Men, and then charged them with bayonets, leaving eight dead and ten wounded.

The British officers hastily reformed their men and proceeded to Concord. There the Americans had already carried off most of their valuable supplies, but the British destroyed what they could. In the meantime American patriots were swarming over the countryside, eager to wreak vengeance on the hated British troops. At Concord's North Bridge the growing American forces inflicted fourteen casualties on a British platoon, and about noon the exhausted redcoats began marching back to Boston.

By then, however, the road back had turned into a gauntlet of death as the embattled farmers from "every Middlesex village and farm" sniped at the redcoats from behind stone walls, trees, barns, and farmhouses, all the way back to Charlestown peninsula. By nightfall the red-coat survivors were safe under the protection of the fleet and army at Boston, having suffered over 250 killed or wounded; the Americans lost 93. A British official reported to London that the rebels, though untrained, had earned his respect: "Whoever looks upon them as an irregular mob will find himself much mistaken."

THE SPREADING CONFLICT   The war had started. When the Second Continental Congress convened at Philadelphia on May 10, 1775, British-held Boston was under siege by the Massachusetts militia. On the very day that Congress met, a force of "Green Mountain Boys" under Ethan Allen of Vermont and Massachusetts volunteers under Benedict Arnold of Connecticut captured strategic Fort Ticonderoga in New York. In a prodigious feat of daring energy, the Americans then managed to transport 60 captured British cannon down rivers and over ridges to support the siege of Boston.

The Continental Congress, with no legal authority and no resources, thus met amid reports of spreading warfare and had little choice but to assume the role of a revolutionary government. The Congress accepted a request that it "adopt" the motley army gathered around Boston and on June 15 named George Washington to be general and commander-in-chief of a Continental army. He accepted on the condition that he receive no pay. The Congress fastened on Washington because his service in the Seven Years' War made him one of the most experienced officers in America. The fact that he was from populous and influential Virginia heightened his qualifications. To support the enterprise Congress resorted to a familiar colonial expedient, paper money, and voted to issue $2 million with the colonies pledged to redemption in proportion to their population.

On June 17, the very day that Washington was commissioned, the colonial rebels and British troops engaged in their first major fight, the Battle of Bunker Hill. While the Congress deliberated, both American and British forces in and around Boston had increased in strength. Militiamen from Rhode Island, Connecticut, and New Hampshire joined in the siege. British reinforcements included three major-generals—Sir William Howe, Sir Henry Clinton, and John Burgoyne. On the day before the battle Americans began to fortify the high ground of Charlestown peninsula, overlooking Boston. Breed's Hill was the battle location, nearer to Boston than Bunker Hill, the site first chosen (and the source of the battle's erroneous name).

The rebels were spoiling for a fight. As Joseph Warren, a dapper Boston physician put it, "The British say we won't fight; by heavens, I hope I shall die up to my knees in blood!" He soon got his wish. With civilians looking on from rooftops and church steeples, Gage ordered a conventional frontal assault in the blistering heat, with 2,200 British troops moving in tight formation through tall grass. Numerous fences obstructed the assault and broke up the uniform lines. The Americans, pounded by naval guns, watched from behind hastily built earthworks as the waves of brightly uniformed British troops advanced up the hill. Ordered not to fire until they could "see the whites of their eyes," the militiamen waited until the attackers came within fifteen to twenty paces, then loosed a shattering volley. Through the cloud of oily smoke, the Americans could see fallen bodies "as thick as sheep in a fold." The militiamen cheered as they watched the greatest soldiers in the world retreating in panic.

Within a half hour, however, the British had reformed and attacked again. Another sheet of flame and lead greeted them, and the vaunted redcoats retreated a second time. Still, the proud British generals were determined not to be humiliated by such ragtag rustics. On the third attempt, when the colonials began to run out of gunpowder, and were forced to throw stones, a bayonet charge ousted them. The British took the high ground, but at the cost of 1,054 casualties. Colonial losses were about 400. "A dear bought victory," recorded General Clinton; "another such would have ruined us."

The Battle of Bunker Hill had two profound effects. First, the high number of British casualties made the English generals more cautious in subsequent encounters with the Continental army. Second, Congress recommended after the battle that all able-bodied men enlist in the militia. This tended to divide the male population into Patriot and Loyalist camps. A middle ground was no longer tenable.

While Boston remained under siege, the Continental Congress held to the dimming hope of a possible compromise. On July 5 and 6, 1775, the delegates issued two major documents: an appeal to the king, thereafter known as the Olive Branch Petition, and a Declaration of the Causes and Necessity of Taking Up Arms. The Olive Branch Petition, written by John Dickinson, professed continued loyalty to George III and begged him to restrain further hostilities pending a reconciliation. The Declaration, also largely Dickinson's work, traced the history of the controversy, denounced the British for the unprovoked assault at Lexington, and rejected independence but affirmed the colonists' purpose to fight for their rights rather than submit to slavery. "Our cause is just," he declared. "Our Union is perfect." Such impassioned rhetoric failed to impress the outraged king. On August 22 George III ordered the army at Boston to regard the colonists "as open and avowed enemies." The next day he issued a proclamation of rebellion.

As the fighting spread north into Canada and south into Virginia and the Carolinas, the Continental Congress assumed the functions of government. In July 1775 it appointed commissioners to negotiate peace treaties with Indian tribes and organized a Post Office Department with Benjamin Franklin as postmaster-general. In October it authorized formation of a navy, in November a marine corps. A committee began to explore the possibility of foreign aid. But the delegates continued to hold back from the seeming abyss of formal independence. Yet through late 1775 and early 1776 word came of one British action after another that proclaimed rebellion and war. In December 1775 Parliament declared the colonies closed to all commerce, and the king began hiring German mercenaries. Eventually almost 30,000 Germans served, about 17,000 of them from the region of Hesse-Kassel, and "Hessian" became the epithet applied to them all.

When Washington arrived outside of Boston to take charge of the American forces after the Battle of Bunker Hill, the military situation was stalemated, and so it remained through the winter, until early March 1776. At that time American forces occupied Dorchester Heights to the south of Boston, bringing the city under threat of bombardment with cannon and mortars. General William Howe, who had long since replaced Gage as British commander, reasoned that discretion was the better part of valor, and he retreated with his forces by water to Halifax, Nova Scotia. The last British troops, along with fearful American Loyalists, embarked from Boston on March 17, 1776. By that time British power had collapsed nearly everywhere, and the British faced not the suppression of a rebellion but the reconquest of a continent.

COMMON SENSE In early 1776 Thomas Paine's pamphlet *Common Sense* was published anonymously in Philadelphia, transforming the revolutionary controversy. Born of Quaker parents, Paine had distinguished himself in England chiefly as a drifter, a failure in marriage and business. At age thirty-seven he sailed for America with a letter of introduction from Benjamin Franklin and the purpose of setting up a school for young ladies. When that did not work out, he moved into the political controversy as a freelance writer and, with *Common Sense,* proved himself the consummate revolutionary rhetorician. Until his pamphlet appeared the squabble had been mainly with Parliament, but Paine directly attacked allegiance to the monarchy, the last frayed connection to Britain. The common sense of the matter, to Paine, was that King George III and his advisers bore the responsibility for the malevolence toward the colonies. Americans should consult their own interests, abandon George III, and declare their independence: "The blood of the slain, the weeping voice of nature cries, 'TIS TIME TO PART."

INDEPENDENCE

Within three months, more than 100,000 copies of Paine's pamphlet were in circulation, an enormous number for the time. "*Common Sense* is working a powerful change in the minds of men," George Washington noted. One by one the provincial governments authorized their delegates in the Continental Congress to take the final step. On

The Continental Congress votes Independence, July 2, 1776.

June 7, 1776, Richard Henry Lee of Virginia moved a resolution "that these United Colonies are, and of right ought to be, free and independent states." Sam Adams immediately endorsed the idea: "We have no other alternative than independence, or the most ignominious and appalling servitude." But others balked. South Carolina and Pennsylvania initially opposed severing ties with England. After feverish lobbying by radical patriots, however, the dissenters changed their mind, and the resolution passed on July 2, a date that "will be the most memorable epoch in the history of America," John Adams wrote to his wife, Abigail. Reluctant American revolutionaries might "stamp and foam and curse," he added, "but all in vain. The decree has gone forth." The memorable date, however, became July 4, 1776, when Congress adopted the Declaration of Independence.

JEFFERSON'S DECLARATION   John Adams, a member of the committee appointed to draft the official declaration, coaxed a reluctant Thomas Jefferson to draft the document. "I am obnoxious, suspected, and unpopular," Adams explained: "You are much the otherwise." Jefferson's summary of the prevailing political sentiment was an eloquent restatement of John Locke's contract theory of government. In Jefferson's words, governments derived "their just Powers from the consent of the people," who were entitled to "alter or abolish" governments that denied their "unalienable rights" to "Life, Liberty, and the pursuit of Happiness." The appeal was no longer simply to "the rights of Englishmen" but to the broader "laws of Nature and Nature's God." Yet at the same time the Declaration implicitly supported the theory that the British Empire was a federation united only through the crown. Parliament, which had no proper authority over the colonies, was never mentioned by name. The enemy was a king who had "combined with others to subject us to a jurisdiction foreign to our constitution, and unacknowledged by our laws." The document set forth "a history of repeated injuries and usurpations, all having in direct object the establishment of an absolute Tyranny over these States." The "Representatives of the United States of America," therefore, declared the thirteen "United Colonies" to be "Free and Independent States."

"WE ALWAYS HAD GOVERNED OURSELVES"   So it had come to this, thirteen years after Britain had won domination of all of North

Thomas Jefferson's draft of the Declaration of Independence.

America. Historians have advanced numerous explanations of the revolutionary controversy: trade regulation, the restrictions on western lands, the tax controversy, the debts to British merchants, the fear of an Anglican bishop, the growth of a national consciousness, the lack of representation in Parliament, ideologies of Whiggery and the Enlightenment, the evangelistic impulse, Scottish moral philosophy, the abrupt shift from a mercantile to an "imperial" policy after 1763, class conflict, revolutionary conspiracy.

Individually and collectively they are subject to challenge, but each contributed something to collective colonial grievances that rose to a climax in a gigantic failure of British statesmanship. A conflict between British sovereignty and American rights had come to a point of confrontation that adroit statesmanship might have avoided, sidestepped, or outflanked. Irresolution and vacillation in the British ministry finally gave way to the stubborn determination to force an issue long permitted to drift. The colonists saw these developments as the conspiracy of a corrupted oligarchy—and finally, they decided, of a despotic king—to impose an "absolute Tyranny."

Perhaps the last word on how the Revolution came about should belong to an obscure participant, Levi Preston, a Minute Man from Danvers, Massachusetts. Asked sixty-seven years after Lexington and Concord about British oppressions, he responded, as his young interviewer reported later: " 'What were they? Oppressions? I didn't feel them.' " When asked about the hated Stamp Act, he claimed that he " 'never saw one of those stamps,' " and was " 'certain I never paid a penny for one of them.' " Nor had he ever heard of John Locke or his theories. " 'We read only the Bible, the Catechism, Watts's Psalms and Hymns, and the Almanack.' " When his exasperated interviewer asked why, then, did he support the Revolution, Preston replied: " 'Young man, what we meant in going for those redcoats was this: we always had governed ourselves, and we always meant to. They didn't mean we should.' "

MAKING CONNECTIONS

- The American revolutionary rhetoric was important not only for fighting the American Revolution; it also provided the framework for the creation of new American governments. This will be discussed in the next two chapters.

- The section titled "Discontent on the Frontier" shows the tension between people in the more urban eastern areas of several states and those on the western frontier. These same tensions will reappear in several future chapters—for example, in the Federalist/Anti-Federalist debate over ratification of the Constitution (in Chapter 6).

FURTHER READING

For a narrative survey of the events leading to the Revolution, see Edward Countryman's *The American Revolution* (1985).* For the perspective of Great Britain on the imperial conflict, see Ian Christie, *Crisis of Empire* (1966).

The intellectual foundations for revolt are traced in Bernard Bailyn's *The Ideological Origins of the American Revolution* (1967),* and in John Phillip Reid's *Constitutional History of the American Revolution: The Authority of Rights* (1987). To understand how these views were connected to organized protest, see Pauline Maier's *From Resistance to Revolution: Colonial Radicals and the Development of American Opposition to Great Britain, 1765–1776* (1972).

Profiles of the Revolutionary generation can be found in Pauline Maier's *The Old Revolutionaries: Political Lives in the Age of Samuel Adams* (1980).* Several books deal with specific events in the chain of crisis. Oliver M. Dickerson's *The Navigation Acts and the American Revolution* (1951) stresses the change from trade regulation to taxation in 1764. Edmund S. Morgan and Helen M. Morgan's *The Stamp Act Crisis* (rev. ed., 1962)* gives the colonial perspective on that crucial event. Also valuable are Hiller B. Zobel's *The Boston Massacre* (1970), Benjamin W. Labaree's *The Boston Tea Party* (1964), and David Ammerman's *In the Common Cause* (1974), on the Coercive Acts.

*These books are available in paperback editions.

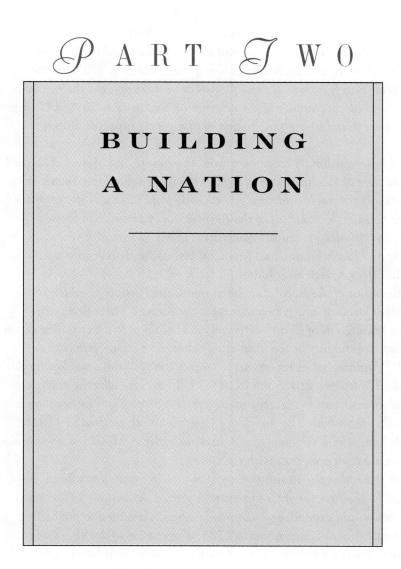

PART TWO

BUILDING
A NATION

The signing of the Declaration of Independence generated great excitement among the rebellious colonists. Yet a stern reality tempered their celebrations. It was one thing for Patriot leaders to declare American independence from British authority; it was quite another to win it on the battlefield. Barely a third of the colonists actively supported the revolution. The political stability of the new nation was uncertain. And George Washington found himself in command of a poorly supplied, untested army.

Yet the Revolutionary movement would persevere and prevail. The skill and fortitude of Washington and his lieutenants enabled the Americans to exploit their geographic advantages. Equally important was the intervention of the French on behalf of the Revolutionary cause. The Franco-American Alliance proved to be decisive. After eight years of sporadic fighting and heavy human and financial losses, the British gave up the fight and their American colonies.

In the midst of the Revolutionary turmoil, the Patriots faced the daunting task of forming new governments for themselves. Their deeply engrained resentment of British imperial rule led them to decentralize power and place sovereignty in the individual states. As Thomas Jefferson declared, "Virginia, Sir, is my country." John Adams felt the same loyalty for his native Massachusetts. Such local ties help explain why the colonists focused their attention on creating new state constitutions rather than a national government. The Articles of Confederation, ratified in 1781, provided only the semblance of national authority. All final power to make and execute laws remained with the states.

After the end of the Revolutionary War in 1783, the flimsy bonds authorized by the Articles of Confederation proved inadequate to the needs of the new—and expanding—nation. This realization led to the calling of the Constitutional Convention in 1787. The process of drafting and ratifying the new constitution spawned a debate about the relative significance of national power, local control, and individual freedom that has provided the central theme of American political thought ever since.

The American Revolution, however, involved much more than the apportionment of political power. It also unleashed social forces and posed social questions that would help to reshape the very fabric of American culture. What would be the role of women, blacks, and Native Americans in the new republic? How would the contrasting economies of the various regions of the new United States be developed? Who would control and *facilitate access to the vast territories to the west of the original thirteen states? How would the new Republic relate to the other nations of the world?*

These complex and controversial questions helped foster the creation of the first national political parties in the United States. During the 1790s, Federalists led by Alexander Hamilton and Democrat-Republicans led by Thomas Jefferson and James Madison engaged in a heated debate about the political and economic future of the new nation. With Jefferson's election as president in 1800, the Republicans gained the upper hand in national politics for the next quarter century. In the process they presided over a maturing American society that aggressively expanded westward at the expense of the Native Americans, ambivalently embraced industrial development, fitfully engaged in a second war with Great Britain, and ominously witnessed a growing sectional controversy over slavery.

5 THE AMERICAN REVOLUTION

Few foreign observers thought the upstart American revolutionaries could win a war against the world's greatest empire, yet that is what happened. The Americans lost most of the battles in the revolutionary war, but eventually forced the British to sue for peace and grant their independence. The surprising result testified to the tenacity of the patriots, to the importance of the French alliance, and to the peculiar difficulties facing the British as they tried to conduct a demanding campaign thousands of miles from home.

Like all major military events, the Revolution had profound and unexpected consequences affecting political, economic, and social life. It not only secured American independence, generated a new sense of nationalism, and created a unique system of self-governance; it also began a process of societal definition and change that has yet to run its course. The turmoil of the Revolution upset traditional class and social relationships and helped transform the lives of people who have long been relegated to the periphery of historical concern—blacks, women, and Indians. In important ways, then, the Revolution was much more than simply a war for independence. It was an engine for political experimentation and social change.

1776: WASHINGTON'S NARROW ESCAPE

On July 2, 1776, the day that Congress voted independence, British redcoats landed on Staten Island. They were the vanguard of a gigantic effort to reconquer America and the first elements of an enormous force that gathered around New York Harbor over the next month. By mid-August General William Howe, with the support of a fleet under his older brother, had some 32,000 men at his disposal, including 9,000 German "Hessians"—the biggest single force ever mustered by the British in the eighteenth century. Washington had expected the move and transferred most of his men from Boston, but could muster only about 19,000 Continental soldiers and militiamen. Such a force could not defend New York, but Congress wanted it held. This forced Washington to expose his men to entrapments from which they escaped more by luck and Howe's caution than by any strategic genius of the American commander. Washington was still learning his trade, and the New York campaign afforded some costly lessons.

FIGHTING IN NEW YORK AND NEW JERSEY   The first conflicts took place on Long Island. By invading and occupying New York, the British sought to sever New England from the rest of the rebellious colonies. In late August Howe inflicted heavy losses and forced Washington to evacuate Long Island to reunite his dangerously divided forces. A timely rainstorm kept the British fleet out of the East River and made possible a nighttime withdrawal to Manhattan.

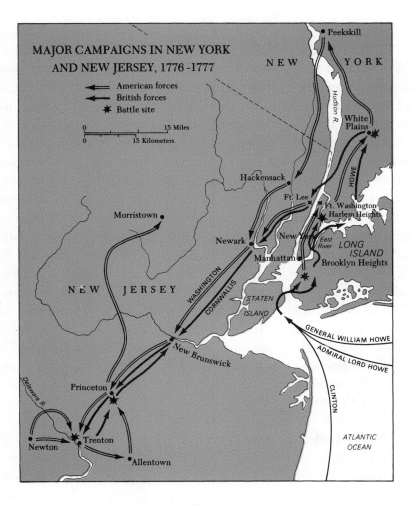

MAJOR CAMPAIGNS IN NEW YORK
AND NEW JERSEY, 1776-1777

⟵ American forces
⟵ British forces
★ Battle site

0 ——————— 15 Miles
0 ——————— 15 Kilometers

NEW   YORK

Peekskill

Hudson R.

White
Plains

HOWE

Hackensack

Ft. Lee
Ft. Washington
Harlem Heights

Morristown

Newark   New York
East
River   LONG
ISLAND
Manhattan   Brooklyn Heights

NEW   JERSEY

WASHINGTON
CORNWALLIS

STATEN
ISLAND

New Brunswick

GENERAL WILLIAM HOWE
ADMIRAL LORD HOWE

Princeton

CLINTON

Delaware R.

Trenton
Newton   ATLANTIC
OCEAN
Allentown

After their success on Long Island, the brothers Howe offered pardons to those revolutionaries who returned to British allegiance and made vague promises of fair treatment—but only after all "extralegal" congresses and conventions were dissolved. Had Howe moved quickly, he could have trapped Washington's army in lower Manhattan. But the main American force of 6,000 men was able to withdraw northward to the mainland and retreat slowly across New Jersey and over the Delaware River into Pennsylvania. In the retreating army marched a volunteer from England, Thomas Paine. Having opened an eventful year with his inspiring pamphlet *Common Sense,* he now composed *The American Crisis,* in which he exhorted Americans to fight on with the immortal line "These are the times that try men's souls." The eloquent pamphlet, ordered read in the revolutionary army camps, helped restore shaken morale—as events would soon do more decisively.

General Howe, firmly—and comfortably—based in New York (which the British held throughout the war), followed conventional practice and settled down with his army to wait out the winter. But Washington was not yet ready to hibernate; instead he seized the initiative. On Christmas night 1776, he slipped across the icy Delaware River with 2,400 men. Near dawn at Trenton the Americans surprised a garrison of 1,500 Hessians (German mercenaries) still befuddled from too much holiday rum. The daring raid was a total rout from which only 500 royal soldiers escaped death or capture. Washington's men suffered but six casualties, one of whom was Lieutenant James Monroe, the future president. At nearby Princeton, on January 3, the Americans repelled three regiments of redcoats before taking refuge in winter quarters at Morristown, in the hills of northern New Jersey. The campaigns of 1776 had ended, after repeated American defeats, with two minor, but uplifting victories. Howe had missed his great chance, indeed several chances, to bring the rebellion to a speedy end. Grumbled one British officer, the Americans had "become a formidable enemy," even though they had yet to win a full-scale conventional battle.

AMERICAN SOCIETY AT WAR

DIVIDED LOYALTIES   After the British occupied New York, many civilians had assumed that the rebellion was collapsing, and thousands hastened to sign an oath of allegiance to the crown. But the events at Trenton and Princeton reversed the outlook. With the British withdrawal, New Jersey quickly reverted to insurgent control. Yet many colonists remained Tory in outlook. During or after the war roughly 100,000 of them, or more than 3 percent of the total population, left America. Opinion concerning the Revolution divided in three ways: Patriots or Whigs (as the revolutionaries called themselves), Tories (as Patriots called the Loyalists, recalling the die-hard royalists in England), and an indifferent middle group swayed by the better organized and more energetic radicals.

American Tories were concentrated mainly in the seaport cities, but they came from all walks of life. Almost all governors, judges, and other royal officials were loyal to Britain; most Anglican ministers also preferred the mother country; colonial merchants might be tugged one way

"One of those ubiquitous American frontiersmen-turned-soldier," second from right. Sketches of the American militia by a French soldier at Yorktown.

or the other, depending on how much they had benefited or suffered from mercantilist regulation; the great planters were swayed one way by dependence on British bounties, another by their debts to British merchants. In the backcountry of New York and the Carolinas many humble folk rallied to the crown. Where planter aristocrats tended to be Whig, as in North Carolina, backcountry farmers (many of them recently Regulators) leaned to the Tories.

The Revolution has ever since seemed to have been a fight between the Americans and the British, but the War for Independence was also very much a civil war that divided families and communities. The fratricidal hatred that often goes with civil war gave rise to bloodcurdling atrocities in the backcountries of New York and Pennsylvania, and in Georgia, where Tory Rangers and their Indian allies went marauding against frontier Whigs. Whigs responded in kind against the Loyalists.

Because Patriot militias quickly returned whenever the British left an area, any Loyalists in the region faced a difficult choice: either accompany the British and leave behind their property or stay behind and face the wrath of the Patriots. In addition, the British policy of offering slaves their freedom in exchange for their loyalty and even arming many of them to fight against the Americans alienated large numbers of neutral or even Tory planters.

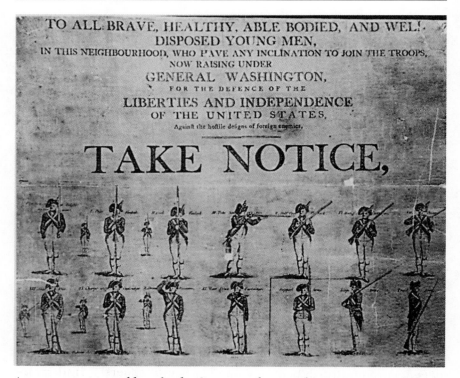

A poster recruiting soldiers for the Continental army. The Congress appealed to those interested in "viewing the different parts of this beautiful continent, in the honourable and truly respectable character of a soldier," and then returning home "with his pockets FULL of money and his head COVERED with laurels."

The Patriot militia kept springing to life whenever the redcoats appeared nearby, and all adult white males, with few exceptions, were obligated under state law to serve when called. With time, even the most apathetic would be pressed into a commitment, if only to turn out for drill. And sooner or later nearly every colonial county experienced military action that would call for armed resistance. The war itself, then, whether through British or Loyalist behavior or the call of the militia, mobilized the apathetic into at least the appearance of support for the American cause. Once made, this commitment was seldom reversed.

MILITIA AND ARMY   American militiamen served two purposes. They were a home guard, defending their own community, and they also helped augment the Continental army. In the backcountry, the militia engaged in the kind of fighting that had become habitual when they were colonists. Dressed in hunting shirts and armed with muskets with long, grooved barrels, they preferred to ambush their opponents or engage them in hand-to-hand combat rather than fight in traditional formations. They also tended to kill unnecessarily and to torture prisoners. To repel an attack, the militia somehow materialized; the danger past, it evaporated, for there were chores to do at home. They "come in, you cannot tell how," George Washington said in exasperation, "go, you cannot tell when, and act you cannot tell where, consume your provisions, exhaust your stores, and leave you at last at a critical moment." Often the green troops would panic in a formal line of battle, and they were therefore usually placed in the front ranks in the hope that they would get off a shot or two before they fled. As General Nathanael Greene pointed out, the untested militiamen were hard pressed to "stand the shocking scenes of war, to march over dead men, to hear without concern the groans of the wounded."

The Continental Army, by contrast, was on the whole better trained and motivated. As one British officer commented, the American forces displayed "a sort of implacable ardor and revenge, which happily are a good deal unknown in the prosecution of war in general." True, many American troops were attracted by bounties of land or cash, and some deserted, but most of those who persevered were animated by genuine patriotic fervor and a thirst for adventure that enabled them to survive the horrors of combat and camp life. Unlike the full-time professional soldiers in the British army, Washington's army, which fluctuated in size from 5,000 to 20,000, was populated mostly by citizen-soldiers, poor native-born Americans or immigrants who had been indentured servants or convicts. Line regiments were organized state by state, and the states were supposed to keep them filled with volunteers, or conscripts if need be, but Washington could never be sure that his requisitions would be met.

PROBLEMS OF FINANCE AND SUPPLY The Congress struggled to provide the army with adequate supplies. None of the states contributed more than a part of its share, and Congress reluctantly let army agents take supplies directly from farmers in return for certificates promising future payment. To pay for the war, Congress printed nearly $250 million in paper money, and the states issued about another $200 million. With goods scarce, prices in terms of paper dollars, or "Continentals," rose sharply. During the winter of 1777–1778 Washington's men would suffer terribly, less because of actual shortages than because farmers preferred to sell their produce for British gold and silver.

Amid the harsh winter at Morristown (1776–1777) Washington's army nearly disintegrated as enlistments expired and deserters fled the hardships of camp. Only about 1,000 soldiers stuck it out. With the spring thaw, however, recruits began arriving to claim the bounty of $20 and 100 acres of land offered by Congress to those who would enlist for three years or for the duration of the conflict, if less. With some 9,000 regular troops, Washington began sparring and feinting with Howe in northern New Jersey. Howe had been making other plans, however, and so had other British officers.

BEHIND THE LINES   Civilians saw their lives profoundly changed by the revolutionary war. British forces occupied the major cities (Boston, New York, Philadelphia, Savannah, Charleston), towns and villages were destroyed, crops and livestock confiscated, families disrupted, husbands and fathers killed or maimed. As in all wars, the families of soldiers suffered terrible anxiety and hardship. Sarah Hodgkins, a twenty-five-year-old mother of two living in Ipswich, Massachusetts, had a third child after her husband left to serve with the American forces after the battle of Lexington. In a letter to her husband, she expressed her loneliness: "I have got a Sweet Babe almost six months old but have got no father for it." She was understandably upset when her husband agreed to reenlist for three more years of service, but placed her trust in God. As she wrote her husband, "all I can do for you is commit you to God . . . for God is able to preserve us as ever and he will do it if we trust in him aright."

Not all civilians were so pious or patriotic. The inflationary spiral generated by a scarcity of consumer goods and the supplies needed for the military effort created new opportunities for quick profits and entrepreneurial chicanery. Many Americans saw in the Revolution a means of self-aggrandizement rather than self-sacrifice. Robert Morris, a prominent Philadelphia merchant who became treasurer of the Congress upon the condition that he could continue his private ventures, told a colleague that "there never has been so fair an opportunity for making a large fortune since I have been conversant in the world."

Throughout the war years George Washington complained that "speculation, peculation, and an insatiable thirst for riches seems to have got the better of every other of Men." Traders from Spain, France, and Holland replaced Great Britain as the source of consumer goods, and affluent Americans quickly abandoned notions of patriotic austerity.

The poor suffered most amid the disruptions and skyrocketing prices created by the war. A bushel of wheat that sold for less than a dollar in 1777 brought $80 two years later. Many consumers appealed to authorities to institute price controls so they could afford basic necessities. Others took more direct action. In Boston a throng of women paraded a merchant accused of hoarding through the streets while "a large concourse of men stood amazed." The shoemakers and leather tanners of Philadelphia expressed the frustrations of many among the "laboring poor" when they declared in 1779 that their efforts had always brought them a "bare living profit," regardless of "however industrious and attentive to business, however frugal in manner of living" they had been. Nevertheless, they had been "contented to live decently without acquiring wealth" because "our professions rendered us as useful and necessary members of the community." But they now saw themselves as victims of gouging merchants and retailers. No longer willing to defer quietly to such discrimination, they grabbed the opportunity afforded by the revolutionary crisis to claim new economic and political rights.

To revolutionary leaders such as John Adams, the "democratical" demands put forward by the laboring classes were as odious as British regulatory measures. The specter of unlearned mechanics and laborers exercising political power horrified him. The American people, he and others insisted, must accept social inequality as a fact of human existence and defer to the leadership of their betters. The "one thing" absolutely required of a new republic was "a decency, and respect, and veneration introduced for persons of authority."

1777: SETBACKS FOR THE BRITISH

Indecision, overconfidence, and poor communications plagued British planning for the campaigns of 1777. The profoundly confident General "Gentleman Johnny" Burgoyne, a charming mixture of poet, gambler, lover, and warrior, proposed to bisect the colonies. His men

CANADA

Quebec

Montreal

ST. LEGER

St. Lawrence R.

BURGOYNE

Richelieu R.

MAINE
(Mass.)

LAKE
CHAMPLAIN

LAKE
ONTARIO

Ft. Oswego

N. Y.

Crown Point

Ft. Ticonderoga

VT.

N.H.

Connecticut R.

GATES

LAKE
GEORGE

Ft. Stanwix

ST. LEGER

Oriskany

Mohawk R.

Saratoga

ARNOLD

Freeman's Farm

Albany

Bennington

MASS.

Boston

Kingston

Hudson R.

CONN.

R.I.

PENN.

Susquehanna R.

Delaware R.

WASHINGTON

LONG ISLAND

New York

Princeton

Valley Forge
(WINTER QUARTERS)

Trenton

Germantown

Brandywine

Philadelphia

Wilmington

N.J.

HOWE

MD.

DEL.

HOWE

ATLANTIC OCEAN

CHESAPEAKE BAY

VA.

MAJOR CAMPAIGNS OF 1777:
Saratoga and Philadelphia

⬅ American forces

⬅ British forces

✳ Battle site

| 0 | | 100 Miles |
| 0 | | 100 Kilometers |

would advance southward from Quebec to the Hudson River while another force moved eastward from Oswego down the Mohawk Valley. Howe had proposed a similar plan, combined with an attack on New England. Had he stuck to it, he might have cut the colonies in two and delivered them a disheartening blow. But he changed his mind and decided to move against the Patriot capital, Philadelphia, expecting that the Pennsylvania Tories would then rally to the crown and secure the colony.

Howe's plan succeeded, up to a point. Washington sensed Howe's purpose and withdrew most of his men from New Jersey to meet the new threat. At Brandywine Creek, south of Philadelphia, Howe pushed Washington's forces back on September 11, and eight days later the British occupied Philadelphia. But they found fewer Tories there than expected. Washington counterattacked against a British encampment at Germantown on October 4, but reinforcements from Philadelphia under General Lord Cornwallis arrived in time to repulse the Americans. Washington then retired into winter quarters at Valley Forge while Howe and his men remained in the relative comfort of Philadelphia, twenty miles away. To the north, meanwhile, Burgoyne was stumbling into disaster.

SARATOGA   After concluding his marching orders by declaring "This Army must not Retreat," Burgoyne moved southward toward Lake Champlain in 1777 with about 7,000 men, his mistress, and a baggage train that included some thirty carts filled with his personal trappings and a large supply of champagne. A powerful force on paper, the expedition was in fact much too cumbersome to be effective in the dense forests and rugged terrain of upstate New York. When they met the more mobile and seasoned Americans, the British suffered two serious reversals.

At Oriskany, New York, on August 6, 1777, a band of militia thwarted an ambush by Tories and Indians, and gained time for Benedict Arnold to bring a thousand Continentals to the relief of Fort Stanwix. The Indians, convinced they faced an even greater force than they actually did, deserted, and the Mohawk Valley was secured for the Patriot forces. To the east, at Bennington, Vermont (August 16), a body of New England militia repulsed a British foraging party with heavy losses. American reinforcements continued to gather, and after two sharp clashes, Burgoyne pulled back to Saratoga, where American forces under General Horatio Gates surrounded him. On October 17, 1777, Burgoyne, resplendent in his scarlet, gold, and white uniform, surrendered to the plain, blue-coated Gates. Most of Burgoyne's 5,700 soldiers were imprisoned in Virginia, but "Gentleman Johnny" himself was permitted to go home, where he received an icy reception. The victory at Saratoga proved critically important to the American cause.

ALLIANCE WITH FRANCE   On December 2, 1777, news of the American triumph at Saratoga reached London; two days later it reached Paris, where it was celebrated almost as if it were a French victory. Its impact on the French made Saratoga a decisive turning point of the war. In 1776 the French had taken their first step toward aiding the colonists by sending fourteen ships with war supplies to America; most of the Continental army's powder in the first years of the war came from this source. After Saratoga, the French saw their chance to strike a sharper blow at their hated enemy and entered into serious negotiations with the Americans.

On February 6, 1778, France and America signed two treaties: a Treaty of Amity and Commerce, in which France recognized the United States and offered trade concessions, including important privileges to American shipping, and a Treaty of Alliance. Under the latter both agreed, first, that if France entered the war, both countries would fight until American independence was won; second, that neither would conclude a "truce or peace" without the consent of the other; and third, that each guaranteed the other's possessions in America "from the present time and forever against all other powers." France further bound itself to seek neither Canada nor other British possessions on the mainland of North America.

By June 1778 British vessels had fired on French ships, and the two nations were at war. In 1779, after extracting promises from the French to help it regain territories taken by the British in the previous war, including Gibraltar, Spain entered the war as an ally of France, but not of the United States. The following year Britain declared war on the Dutch, who persisted in a profitable trade with the French and Americans. The embattled farmers at Concord had indeed fired the "shot heard round the world." Like Washington's encounter with the French in

1754, it was the start of another world war, and the fighting now spread to the Mediterranean, Africa, India, the West Indies, and the high seas.

1778: BOTH SIDES REGROUP

After Saratoga, Lord North, the British Prime Minister, knew that winning the war was unlikely, but the king refused to let him either resign or make peace. On March 16, 1778, the House of Commons adopted a program that in effect granted all the American demands prior to independence. Parliament repealed the Townshend tea duty, the Massachusetts Government Act, and the Prohibitory Act, which had closed the colonies to commerce. It then dispatched a peace commission, but its members did not reach Philadelphia until after Congress had ratified the French treaties. The Congress refused to begin any negotiations until independence was recognized or British forces withdrawn, neither of which the commissioners could promise.

Unbeknownst to the British commissioners, the crown had already authorized the evacuation of British troops from Philadelphia, a withdrawal that further weakened what little bargaining power they had. Af-

The British Lion Engaging Four Powers. *The American Revolution sparked a world war, as the British cartoon suggests: "Behold the Dutch and Spanish Currs, / Perfidious Gallus in his Spurs, / And Rattlesnake, with head upright, / The British Lion join to fight; / He scorns the Bark, the Hiss, the Crow, / That he's a Lion soon they'll know."*

ter Saratoga, General Howe had resigned his command and Sir Henry Clinton had replaced him, with orders to pull out of Philadelphia, and if necessary, New York, but to keep Newport, Rhode Island. In short, he was to take a defensive stance except in the South, where the government believed a latent Tory sentiment in the backcountry needed only a visible British presence for its release. The ministry was right, up to a point, but the pro-British sentiment turned out once again, as in other theaters of war, to be weaker than it seemed.

For Washington's army, bivouacked at Valley Forge, near Philadelphia, the winter of 1777–1778 had been a season of suffering far worse than the previous winter at Morristown. The American force, encamped in lice-infested log huts, endured cold, hunger, and disease. Many deserted or resigned their commissions, leading Washington to warn Congress that unless substantial supplies were forthcoming, the army "must inevitably be reduced to one or other of these three things: starve, dissolve, or disperse."

As winter drew to an end, the army's morale gained strength from congressional promises of extra pay and bonuses after the war and from news of the French alliance. As General Clinton's forces withdrew eastward toward New York, Washington pursued them across New Jersey. On June 28, 1778, he engaged the British in an indecisive battle at Monmouth Court House. Clinton's forces then slipped away into New York while Washington took up a position at White Plains, north of the city. From that time on, the northern theater, scene of the major campaigns and battles in the first years of the war, settled into a long stalemate, interrupted by minor and mostly inconclusive engagements.

ACTIONS ON THE FRONTIER   The one major American success of 1778 occurred far from the New Jersey battlefields. Out to the west, the British at Forts Niagara and Detroit had incited frontier Tories and Indians to raid western settlements and had offered to pay for American scalps. To end such attacks, young George Rogers Clark took 175 frontiersmen and a flotilla of flatboats down the Ohio River in early 1778. They marched through the woods, and on the evening of July 4 surprised the British at Kaskaskia. At the end of the year, Clark marched his men (almost half French volunteers) through icy rivers and flooded prairies, sometimes in water neck deep, and captured an astonished British garrison at Vincennes.

WESTERN CAMPAIGNS, 1776–1779

◄══ American forces   △ Cherokee settlements
◄━━ British forces
✳ Battle site   ▨ Tory-Seneca raids (1778)

0 _____ 200 Miles
0 _____ 200 Kilometers

While Clark's captives traveled eastward, Tories and Iroquois Indians in western Pennsylvania continued to terrorize frontier settlements through the summer of 1778. Led by the charismatic Mohawk Joseph Brant, the Iroquois killed hundreds of militiamen along the Pennsylvania frontier. In response Washington dispatched an expedition of 4,000 men to the area. At Newton (now Elmira) the American force met and defeated the only serious opposition on August 29, 1779, and proceeded to carry out Washington's instruction that the Iroquois country be not "merely overrun but destroyed."

The American troops devastated about forty Seneca and Cayuga villages together with their orchards and food stores. So ruthless and complete was the destruction that large numbers of the Indians were thrown completely upon their British allies for scant supplies from Fort Niagara. The action broke the power of the Iroquois federation for all time, but it did not completely pacify the frontier. Sporadic encounters with various tribes of the region continued to the end of the war.

The Mohawk leader Thayendanegea (Joseph Brant), who fought against the Americans in the Revolution. Portrait painted by Gilbert Stuart in 1786.

In the Kentucky territory, Daniel Boone and his small band of settlers risked constant attack from the Shawnees and their British and Tory allies. During the Revolution, they survived frequent ambushes, at least seven skirmishes, and three pitched battles. In 1778 Boone and some thirty men, aided by their wives and children, held off an assault by more than 400 Indians at Boonesborough. Thereafter, Boone himself was twice shot and twice captured. Indians killed two of his sons, a brother, and two brothers-in-law. His daughter was captured and another brother was wounded four times. Despite such ferocious fighting and dangerous circumstances, the white settlers refused to leave Kentucky.

By thus weakening the major Indian tribes along the frontier, the American Revolution, among its other results, cleared the way for rapid settlement of the trans-Appalachian West.

THE WAR IN THE SOUTH

At the end of 1778 the focus of British military action shifted suddenly to the south. The whole region from Virginia southward had been free from major action since 1776. Now the British would test King

MAJOR CAMPAIGNS IN THE SOUTH,
1778 — 1781

YORKTOWN, 1781

American forces
British forces
Battle site

George's belief that a sleeping Tory power in the South needed only the presence of a few redcoats to awaken it.

From the point of view of British imperial goals, the southern colonies were ultimately more important than the northern ones because they produced valuable staple crops such as tobacco, indigo, and naval stores. The war in the Carolinas eventually involved not only opposing British and American armies, but also degenerated into brutal guerrilla-style civil conflicts between local Loyalists and local Patriots. The result of such infighting was chaos.

At this point, Congress, against Washington's advice, turned to the victor of Saratoga, Horatio Gates, to take command and sent him south. Meanwhile, the British commander, Charles Lord Cornwallis, dispatched with one of three columns to subdue the Carolina interior, surprised Gates's force at Camden, South Carolina, and routed his new army. The Patriots retreated all the way to Hillsborough, North Carolina, 160 miles away.

THE CAROLINAS   In November 1778 British forces took Savannah, Georgia and drove toward Charleston, South Carolina, plundering plantation houses along the way. Outside Charleston the British encamped and awaited additional naval and land forces sent by Clinton from New York and New Jersey. In 1780 the British launched a massive assault against the Patriot defenders, and on May 12 General Benjamin Lincoln surrendered the city and its 5,500 defenders. This was the single greatest American loss of the war. Cornwallis had South Carolina just about under British control, but his cavalry leaders Banastre Tarleton and Patrick Ferguson, who mobilized Tory militiamen, overreached themselves in their effort to subdue the Whigs. "Tarleton's Quarter" became bywords for savagery, because "Bloody Tarleton" ordered rebels killed after they surrendered. Ferguson sealed his own doom when he threatened to march over the mountains and hang the revolutionary leaders there. Instead the feisty "overmountain men" went after Ferguson. Allied with other backcountry Whigs, they caught him and his Tories on Kings Mountain along the border between North and South Carolina. There, on October 7, 1780, they devastated his force. By then feelings were so strong that American irregulars continued firing on Tories trying to surrender and later slaughtered Tory prisoners. Kings Mountain was the turning point of the war in the South. By proving that the British were not invincible, it emboldened small farmers to join guerrilla bands under partisan leaders like Francis Marion, "the Swamp Fox," and Thomas Sumter, "the Gamecock."

While the overmountain men were closing on Ferguson, Congress had chosen a new commander for the southern theater, General Nathanael Greene, the "fighting Quaker" of Rhode Island. A man of infinite patience, skilled at managing men and saving supplies, careful to avoid needless risks, he was well suited to a war of attrition against the British forces. He was also a selfless patriot who sold his own lands in order to provide supplies for his army. Greene shrewdly lured Cornwallis and his troops into chasing the Americans across the Carolinas, thus taxing British energies and supplies. Greene finally offered battle near Guilford Courthouse on March 15, 1781. After inflicting heavy losses,

Greene prudently withdrew to fight another day, and Cornwallis was left in possession of the field, but at a cost of nearly 100 men killed and more than 400 wounded. In London, when the word arrived, a parliamentary leader moaned, "Another such victory and we are undone."

Cornwallis marched off toward the coast at Wilmington to lick his wounds and take on new supplies. Greene then resolved to go back into South Carolina in the hope of drawing Cornwallis after him or forcing the British to give up the state. There he joined forces with the guerrillas already active on the scene, and in a series of brilliant actions kept losing battles while winning the war: "We fight, get beat, rise, and fight again," he said. By September 1781 he had narrowed British control in the Deep South to Charleston and Savannah, although for more than a year longer Whigs and Tories slashed at each other "with savage fury" in the backcountry, where there was "nothing but murder and devastation in every quarter," Greene said.

Meanwhile Cornwallis had headed north away from Greene, reasoning that Virginia must be eliminated as a source of reinforcement before the Carolinas could be subdued. In 1781 Cornwallis met up with Benedict Arnold, now a British general, who was engaged in a war of maneuver against American forces. Arnold, until September 1780, had been American commander at West Point. Overweening in ambition, lacking in moral scruples, and a reckless spender, he nursed a grudge over an official reprimand for his extravagances as commander of reoccupied Philadelphia. Traitors have a price, and Arnold soon found his. He crassly plotted to sell out the West Point garrison to the British, even suggesting how they might capture Washington himself. The American seizure of the British go-between, Major John André, ended Arnold's plot. Forewarned that his plan had been discovered, Arnold joined the British in New York; the Americans hanged André as a spy.

YORKTOWN   When Cornwallis linked up with Arnold at Petersburg, Virginia, their combined forces rose to 7,200, far more than the small American force they faced. The arrival of American reinforcements led Cornwallis to pick Yorktown as a defensible site. There appeared to be little reason to worry about a siege, since Washington's main land force seemed preoccupied with attacking New York and the British navy controlled American waters.

To be sure, there was a small American navy, but it was no match for the British fleet. Most celebrated were the exploits of Captain John Paul Jones, who sailed east across the Atlantic in 1778 and gave the British navy some bad moments in its home waters. Off England's coast on September 23, 1779, Jones won a desperate battle with a British frigate, which he captured and occupied before his own ship sank. This was the occasion for his stirring and oft-repeated response to a British demand for surrender: "I have not yet begun to fight."

Such heroics were little more than nuisances to the British, but at a critical point, thanks to the French navy, the British lost control of the Chesapeake waters. Indeed, it is impossible to imagine an American victory in the Revolution without the assistance of the French. As long as the British navy maintained supremacy at sea, the Americans could not hope to force a settlement to their advantage. For three years Washington had waited to get some military benefit from the French alliance. In 1780 the French finally landed a force of about 6,000 at Newport, but the French army under the comte de Rochambeau sat there for a year, blockaded by the British fleet.

Then, in 1781, the elements for combined action suddenly fell into place. As Cornwallis moved into Virginia in May, Washington persuaded Rochambeau to join forces for an attack on New York. The two armies linked up in July, but before they could strike at New York, word came from the West Indies that Admiral De Grasse was bound for the Chesapeake with his entire French fleet and some 3,000 soldiers. Washington and the combined American-French forces immediately set out toward Yorktown.

On August 30 De Grasse's fleet reached Yorktown, where his troops joined the American force already watching Cornwallis. On September 6, the day after a British fleet appeared, De Grasse gave battle and forced the British to give up the effort to relieve Cornwallis, whose fate was quickly sealed. De Grasse then sent ships up the Chesapeake to ferry down Washington's 16,000 American and French forces, double the size of Cornwallis's army.

The siege began on September 28. At one point during the attack, Washington and his staff came under fire as they observed the action. A worried aide suggested to the commanding general that perhaps he should "step back a little." Washington tersely replied: "Colonel Cobb, if you are afraid, you have the liberty to step back."

This French engraving shows Lord Cornwallis handing over his sword in surrender at Yorktown, October 19, 1781.

On October 14 two major outposts guarding the left of the British line fell to French and American attackers, the latter led by Washington's aide Alexander Hamilton. A British counterattack on October 16 failed to retake them. Later that day a squall forced Cornwallis to abandon a desperate plan to escape across the York River. On October 17, 1781, four years to the day after Saratoga, a red-coated drummer boy climbed atop the British parapet and began beating the call for a truce. Cornwallis sued for peace, and on October 19 the British force of almost 8,000 marched out, their colors cased, to the tune of "The World Turned Upside Down." Cornwallis himself claimed to be too "ill" to appear.

NEGOTIATIONS

Whatever lingering hopes of victory the British may have harbored vanished at Yorktown. "Oh God, it's all over," Lord North groaned at news of the surrender. On February 27, 1782, the House of Commons voted against continuing the war and on March 5 authorized the crown

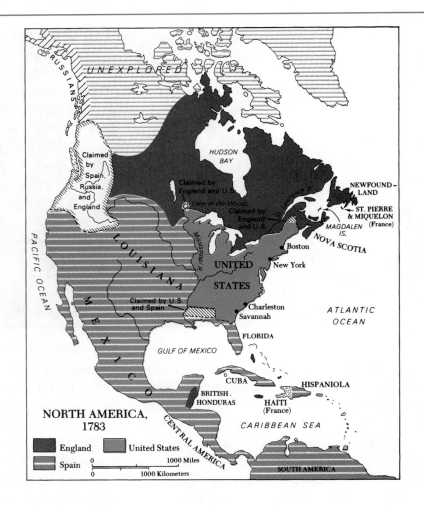

NORTH AMERICA, 1783

England
Spain
United States

0   1000 Miles
0   1000 Kilometers

to make peace. On March 20 Lord North resigned. The new ministry included old friends of the Americans headed by the duke of Rockingham, who had brought about repeal of the Stamp Act. The new colonial minister, Lord Shelburne, became chief minister after Rockingham's death in September and directed the Paris negotiations with American commissioners appointed by the Continental Congress.

The American peace commissioners in Paris were John Adams, John Jay, minister to Spain, Benjamin Franklin, and Henry Laurens from South Carolina. Their difficult task was immediately complicated by the French commitment to Spain. Spain and the United States were both allied with France, but not with each other. America was bound by its alliance to fight on until the French made peace, and the French were bound to help the Spanish recover Gibraltar from England. Unable to deliver Gibraltar, or so the tough-minded Jay reasoned, the French might try to bargain off American land west of the Appalachians in its place. Fearful that the French were angling for a separate peace with the British, Jay persuaded Franklin to play the same game. Ignoring their instructions to consult fully with the French, they agreed to further talks with the British. On November 30, 1782, the talks produced a preliminary treaty with Great Britain. If it violated the spirit of the alliance, it did not violate the strict letter of the treaty with France, for the French minister was notified the day before it was signed, and final agreement still depended on a Franco-British settlement.

THE PEACE OF PARIS   Early in 1783 France and Spain gave up on Gibraltar and reached an armistice with Britain. The Peace of Paris was finally signed on September 3, 1783. In accord with the bargain already struck, Great Britain recognized the independence of the United States and agreed to a Mississippi River boundary to the west. Both the northern and southern borders left ambiguities that would require further definition. Florida, as it turned out, passed back to Spain. The British further granted Americans the "liberty" of fishing off Newfoundland and in the Gulf of St. Lawrence, and the right to dry their catches on the unsettled coasts of Canada. On the matter of pre-revolutionary debts, the best the British could get was a promise that British merchants should "meet with no legal impediment" in seeking to collect them. And on the tender point of Loyalists whose property had been confiscated, the negotiators agreed that Congress would "earnestly recommend" to the states the restoration of confiscated property. Each of the last two points was little more than a face-saving gesture for the British.

THE POLITICAL REVOLUTION

REPUBLICAN IDEOLOGY   The Americans had won their War for Independence. Had they undergone a political revolution as well? John Adams offered one answer: "The Revolution was effected before the war commenced. The Revolution was in the minds and hearts of the people. . . . This radical change in the principles, opinions, sentiments, and affections of the people, was the real American Revolution." Yet Adams's observation ignores the fact that the Revolutionary War itself served as the catalyst for a prolonged internal debate about what new forms of government would best serve an independent republic. The conventional British model of mixed government sought to balance the monarchy, aristocracy, and the common people and thereby protect individual liberty. Because of the more fluid and democratic nature of their new society, however, Americans knew that they must develop new political assumptions and institutions. They had no monarchy or aristocracy. Yet how could sovereignty reside in the common people? How could Americans ensure the survival and effectiveness of a republican form of government, long assumed to be the most fragile? The war thus provoked a spate of state constitution-making that remains unique in human history.

A struggle for traditional English rights had become a fight for independence in which those rights found expression in governments that were new, yet deeply rooted in the colonial experience and in the prevailing viewpoints of Whiggery and the Enlightenment. Such ideas as the contract theory of government, the sovereignty of the people, the separation of powers, and natural rights found their way quickly, almost automatically, into the new frames of government that were devised while the fight went on—amid other urgent business.

The very idea of republican government—a balanced polity animated by civic virtue—was a far more radical departure in that day than it would seem to later generations. Through the lens of republican thinking, Americans began to see themselves in a new light, no longer as the rustic provincials in a backwater of European culture but rather as the embodiment of the classical republican virtue so long praised by philosophers and so necessary to the success of a republican form of government. As free citizens of a republic, Americans would cast off the aristocratic corruptions of the Old World and usher in a new reign of individual liberty and public virtue. The new American republic, in other words, would endure as long as the majority of the people were virtuous and willingly placed the good of society above the self-interests of individuals. Herein lay the hope and the danger of the new American experiment in popular government: even as leaders enthusiastically fashioned new state constitutions, they feared that their experiments in republicanism would fail because of a lack of civic virtue.

NEW STATE CONSTITUTIONS   Most of the political experimentation between 1776 and 1787 occurred at the state level. Innovations
devised in the state constitutional conventions created the core principle of the American political system: representative government defined in written constitutions in which the people are sovereign and
delegate limited authority to the government. In addition, the states initiated bills of rights guaranteeing particular individual rights, and fashioned procedures for constitutional conventions that have also remained an essential part of the American political system. In sum, the
innovations at the state level during the Revolution created a reservoir
of ideas and experience that formed the basis for the creation of the
federal constitution in 1787.

At the onset of the fighting every colony experienced the departure of
governors and other officials and usually the expulsion of Loyalists from
the assemblies, which then assumed power as provincial "congresses"
or "conventions." But they were acting as revolutionary bodies without
any legal basis for the exercise of authority. In two of the states this presented little difficulty. Connecticut and Rhode Island, which had been
virtually little republics as corporate colonies, simply purged their charters of any reference to colonial ties. Massachusetts followed their example until 1780.

In the other states the prevailing notions of social contract and popular sovereignty led to written constitutions that specified the framework
and powers of government. One of the lessons of the Revolution, it
seemed, had been that the vague body of law and precedent that made
up the unwritten British constitution was unreliable. Constitution-
making began even before independence. In May 1776 Congress advised the colonies to set up new governments "under the authority of
the people."

The first state constitutions varied mainly in detail. They formed governments much like the colonial administrations, with elected governors and senates instead of appointed governors and councils. Generally they embodied, sometimes explicitly, a separation of powers as a
safeguard against abuses. Most of them also included a bill of rights
that protected the time-honored rights of petition, freedom of speech,
trial by jury, freedom from self-incrimination, and the like. Most tended
to limit the powers of governors and increase the powers of the legislatures, which had led the people in their quarrels with the colonial gov-

ernors. Pennsylvania went so far as to eliminate the governor and upper house of the legislature altogether. It had a twelve-man executive council and operated until 1790 with a unicameral legislature limited only by a house of "censors," who reviewed its work every five years.

THE ARTICLES OF CONFEDERATION   The central government, like the state governments, grew out of an extralegal revolutionary body. The Continental Congress exercised governmental powers without any constitutional sanction before 1781. Plans for a permanent frame of government were started very early, however, when on July 12, 1776, a committee headed by John Dickinson produced a draft constitution, the "Articles of Confederation and Perpetual Union." For more than a year Congress debated the articles in between more urgent matters and finally adopted them in November 1777, subject to ratification by all the states.

When the Articles of Confederation took effect in 1781, they did little more than legalize the status quo. Congress had a multitude of responsibilities but little authority to carry them out. The Congress was intended not as a legislature, nor as a sovereign entity unto itself, but as a collective substitute for the monarch. In essence, it was to be a plural executive rather than a parliamentary body. It had full power over foreign affairs and questions of war and peace; it could decide disputes between the states; it had authority over coinage, postal service, and Indian affairs, and responsibility for the government of the western territories. But it had no power to enforce its resolutions and ordinances upon either states or individuals. It also had no power to levy taxes, but had to rely on requisitions, which state legislatures could ignore at their will.

The states, after their battles with Parliament, were in no mood for a strong central government. The Congress in fact had less power than the colonists had once accepted in Parliament, since it could not regulate interstate and foreign commerce. For certain important acts, moreover, a "special majority" was required. Nine states had to approve measures dealing with war, privateering, treaties, coinage, finances, or the army and navy. Amendments to the articles required unanimous ratification by the states. The Confederation had neither an executive nor a judicial branch; there was no administrative head of government (only the president of the Congress, chosen annually) and no federal courts.

Yet for all its weaknesses the Confederation government represented the most appropriate structure for the new nation. After all, the Revolution on the battlefields had yet to be won, and the statesmen did not have the luxury of engaging in prolonged and perhaps fratricidal debates over the distribution of power that proposals for other systems would have provoked. There would be time later for modifications.

THE SOCIAL REVOLUTION

Americans formed a consensus on the general frame of government—the forms grew so naturally out of the experience and the ideas of the colonial period. On other issues raised by the Revolution, however, there was sharp disagreement. Just as the Great Awakening had created unforeseen social effects, the revolutionary turmoil allowed outlets for long-festering frustrations among the lower ranks. What did the Revolution mean to those workers, servants, farmers, and freedmen who participated in the Stamp Act demonstrations, supported the boycotts, idolized Tom Paine, and fought with Washington and Greene?

Many laboring folk hoped that the Revolution would remove, not reinforce, the traditional political and social advantages exercised by colonial elites. The more conservative Patriots would have been content to replace royal officials with the rich, the well-born, and the able, and let it go at that. But more radical elements, in the apt phrase of one historian, raised the question not only of home rule, but of who shall rule at home.

EQUALITY AND ITS LIMITS This spirit of equality weakened old habits of deference. A prominent Virginian told of being in a tavern when a group of rough farmers entered, spitting and pulling off their muddy boots without regard to the sensibilities of the gentlemen present: "The spirit of independence was converted into equality," he wrote, "and every one who bore arms, esteems himself upon a footing with his neighbors. . . . No doubt each of these men considers himself, in every respect, my equal." No doubt each did.

Participation in the army or militia activated people who had before taken little interest in politics. The large number of new political opportunities afforded by the creation of new state governments thus led more ordinary citizens into participation than ever before. The social base of the new legislatures was much broader than that of the old assemblies.

Men fighting for their liberty found it difficult to justify the denial to other white men of the rights of suffrage and representation. The property qualifications for voting, which already admitted an overwhelming majority of white males, were lowered still further in some states. In Pennsylvania, Delaware, North Carolina, Georgia, and Vermont, any male taxpayer could vote, although officeholders had to meet higher property requirements. In the state legislatures, new men often replaced older men, some of whom had been Loyalists. More often than not the newcomers were men of lesser property and little education. Some states concentrated much power in a legislature chosen by a wide suffrage, but not even Pennsylvania, which adopted the most radical state constitution, went quite so far as universal manhood suffrage. Others, like New York and Maryland, took a more conservative stance and instituted stiff property requirements for voting.

New developments in land tenure that grew out of the Revolution extended the democratic trends of suffrage requirements. Confiscations during the war resulted in the seizure of Tory estates by all the state legislatures. These lands, however, were of small consequence in comparison to the unsettled lands that had formerly been at the disposal of crown and proprietors. Now in the hands of state assemblies, much of this land went as bonuses to veterans of the war. Western lands, formerly closed by the Proclamation of 1763 and the Quebec Act of 1774, were soon thrown open for settlers.

THE PARADOX OF SLAVERY   The revolutionary generation of leaders was the first to confront the issue of slavery and to consider abolishing it. The principles of liberty and equality so crucial to the rebellion had clear implications for America's enslaved blacks. Jefferson's draft of the Declaration had indicted the king for having violated the "most sacred rights of life and liberty of a distant people" by encouraging the slave trade in the colonies, but he deleted the clause "in complaisance to South Carolina and Georgia." The clause was in fact inaccurate in completely ignoring the implication of American slaveholders and slave traders in the traffic. After independence, all the states except Georgia stopped the importation of slaves, although South Carolina later reopened it.

Black soldiers or sailors were present at most of the major battles, from Lexington to Yorktown; most were on the Loyalist side. Slaves who served in the cause of independence got their freedom and in some cases land bounties. But the British army, which freed probably tens of thousands of slaves during the war, was a greater instrument of emancipation than the American forces. Most of the newly freed blacks found their way to Canada or to British colonies in the Caribbean. American Whigs showed no mercy to blacks who were caught aiding or abetting the British cause. A Charleston mob hanged and then burned Thomas Jeremiah, a free black man who was convicted of telling slaves that the British "were come to help the poor Negroes." White Loyalists who were caught stirring up slave militancy were tarred and feathered.

In the northern states, which had fewer slaves than the southern, the doctrines of liberty led swiftly to emancipation for all either during the fighting or shortly afterward. South of Pennsylvania the potential consequences of emancipation were so staggering—South Carolina had a black majority—that whites refused to extend the principle of liberty to their slaves. Yet even there slaveholders like Washington, Jefferson, Patrick Henry, and others were troubled. On the slavery issue Jefferson sounded a note of foreboding in his *Notes on Virginia* (1785): "Indeed I tremble for my country when I reflect that God is just; that his justice cannot sleep forever." But he, like many other white southerners, was riding the tiger and did not know how to dismount. Antislavery sentiment in the southern states went only so far as to relax the manumission laws under which the owners might voluntarily free their slaves. Some 10,000 slaves in Virginia were manumitted during the 1780s. A much smaller number would be shipped back to Africa during the early nineteenth century. By the outbreak of the Civil War in 1861, approximately half of the blacks living in Maryland were free.

Slaves, especially in the upper South, also earned freedom through their own actions during the Revolutionary era, frequently by running away. They often gravitated to the growing number of African-American communities. Because of emancipation laws in the northern states, and with the formation of free black neighborhoods in the North and in several southern cities, runaways found refuges and the opportunities for new lives. Many of these free blacks used the egalitarian rhetoric spawned by the Revolution to speak out against the evils of slavery. It is estimated that 55,000 slaves fled to freedom during the Revolution.

Elizabeth Freeman, born in Africa around 1742, was sold as a slave to a Massachusetts family. She won her freedom by claiming in court that the "inherent liberty" of all applied to slaves as well.

THE STATUS OF WOMEN   The logic of liberty applied to the status of women as much as to that of slaves. Women had remained essentially confined to the domestic sphere during the eighteenth century. They could not vote or preach or hold office. Few had access to formal education. Although women could own property and execute contracts, in several colonies they could not legally own even their own clothes, and they had no legal rights over their children. Divorces were extremely difficult to obtain.

Initially, women predicted that the Revolution would do little to improve their social status. Soon after the fighting started, Margaret Livingston of New York wrote her sister that "our Sex are doomed to be obedient in every stage of life so that we shant be gainers by this contest." Yet the revolutionary ferment offered women new opportunities and engendered in many a new outlook. The war also drew women at least temporarily into new roles. They plowed fields and melted down pots and pans to make shot. Women also served the armies in various ways, such as handling supplies and serving as spies or couriers. Wives often followed their husbands to camp, where they nursed the wounded and sick, cooked and washed for the able, and frequently buried the dead. On occasion women took their places in the firing line.

To be sure, most women retained the circumscribed domestic outlook that had long been their fate. But a few free-spirited reformers argued that only educated and independent mothers could raise children fit for republican citizenship. Some demanded equal treatment. In an essay entitled "On the Equality of the Sexes," written in 1779 and published in 1790, Judith Sargent Murray of Gloucester, Massachusetts, stressed the importance of mutuality in marriage: "Mutual esteem, mutual friendship, mutual confidence, begirt about by mutual forbearance." Murray and others insisted that women were perfectly capable of excelling outside the domestic sphere.

Early in the struggle, on March 31, 1776, Abigail Adams, one of the most learned, spirited, and principled women of the time, wrote her husband, John: "In the new Code of Laws which I suppose it will be necessary for you to make I desire you would remember the Ladies. . . . Do not put such unlimited power into the hands of the Husbands." Since men were "Naturally Tyrannical," she stressed, "why then, not put it out of the power of the vicious and the Lawless to use us with cruelty and indignity. . . ." Otherwise, "the Ladies" would "foment a Rebellion, and will not hold ourselves bound by any Laws in which we have no voice, or Representation."

Husband John expressed surprise that women might be discontented, but he clearly knew the privileges enjoyed by males and was determined to retain them: "Depend upon it, we know better than to repeal our Masculine systems." The supposedly more liberal Thomas Jefferson was of one mind with John Adams on this matter. When asked about women's voting rights, he replied that "the tender breasts of ladies were not formed for political convulsion."

Abigail Adams, in a portrait by Gilbert Stuart. She advised her husband, John: "Do not put such unlimited power into the hands of the Husbands."

The legal status of women thus did not benefit dramatically from the equalitarian doctrine unleashed by the Revolution. True, in Pennsylvania and parts of New England, divorces were somewhat easier to obtain after the Revolution. One Connecticut woman, for instance, brought suit against her husband on the grounds that he had "rendered her life miserable by frequent beating with brutal violence, almost constant intoxication and lascivious conduct with several lewd women." But married women in most of the new states still forfeited control of their own property to their husbands, and women gained no political rights. Under the 1776 New Jersey constitution, which neglected to specify an exclusively male franchise because the delegates apparently took the distinction for granted, women who met the property qualifications for voting exercised the right until denied access early in the nineteenth century.

FREEDOM OF RELIGION   The Revolution also set in motion a transition from the toleration of religious dissent to a complete freedom of religion in the separation of church and state. The Anglican church, established as the state religion in five colonies and parts of two others, was especially vulnerable because of its association with the crown and because dissenters outnumbered Anglicans in most states except Virginia. And all but Virginia removed tax support for the church before the fighting was over. In 1776, the Virginia Declaration of Rights guaranteed the free exercise of religion, and in 1786 the Virginia Statute of Religious Freedom (written by Thomas Jefferson) declared that "no man shall be compelled to frequent or support any religious worship, place or ministry whatsoever," that none should in any way suffer for his religious opinions and beliefs, "but that all men shall be free to profess and by argument to maintain, their opinions in matters of religion." These statutes and the revolutionary ideology that spawned them helped shape the course that religion would take in the new United States: pluralistic and voluntary rather than monolithic and state supported.

New England, with its Puritan heritage, was in less haste to end state tax support for the Congregational church, although the rules were already being relaxed enough by the 1720s to let Quakers and Baptists assign their tax support to their own churches. New Hampshire finally discontinued tax support for its churches in 1817, Connecticut in

The Congregational church developed a national body in the early nineteenth century, and Lemuel Haynes, depicted here, was its first black preacher.

1818, Maine in 1820, and Massachusetts in 1833. Certain religious requirements for officeholding lingered here and there on the law books: Massachusetts and Maryland required a declaration of Christian faith; Delaware had a Trinitarian test; New Jersey and the Carolinas held that officeholders must be Protestants. But in most cases these requirements disappeared before many more years.

In churches as well as in government, the Revolution set off a period of constitution-making, as some of the first national church bodies emerged. In 1784 the Methodists, who at first were an offshoot of the Anglicans, came together in a general conference at Baltimore. The Anglican church, rechristened Episcopal, gathered in a series of meetings which by 1789 had united the various dioceses in a federal union; in 1789 the Presbyterians also held their first general assembly in Philadelphia. The following year, 1790, the Catholic church had its first bishop in the United States when John Carroll was named bishop of Baltimore. Other churches would follow in the process of organizing on a national basis.

EMERGENCE OF AN AMERICAN CULTURE

The Revolution generated a budding sense of common nationality. The Revolution taught many Americans to think "continentally," as Alexander Hamilton put it. As early as the Stamp Act Congress of 1765, Christopher Gadsden, leader of the Charleston radicals, had said: "There ought to be no New England man, no New Yorker, known on the Continent; but all of us Americans." In the first Continental Congress Patrick Henry asserted that such a sense of national identity had come to pass: "The distinctions between Virginians, Pennsylvanians, New Yorkers, and New Englanders are no more. I am not a Virginian but an American." Henry claimed too much. Before long he and others would reassert state loyalties, but for now an American spirit was in the air.

ARTS IN THE NEW NATION   The Revolution provided the first generation of native artists with inspirational subjects. It also filled them with high expectations that individual freedom would release creative energies and vitalize both commerce and the arts.

Ironically, the best American painters of the time spent all or most of the Revolution in England, studying with Benjamin West of Pennsylvania and John Singleton Copley of Massachusetts, both of whom had set up shop in London before the outbreak of hostilities. Even John Trumbull, who had served in the siege of Boston and the Saratoga campaign, somehow managed a visit to London during the war before returning. Later he highlighted patriotic themes in numerous canvases celebrating scenes from the Revolution. Similarly, Charles Willson Peale, who fought at Trenton and Princeton and survived the winter at Valley Forge, produced a virtual portrait gallery of Revolutionary War figures. Over twenty-three years he painted George Washington seven times from life and produced in all sixty portraits of the general.

EDUCATION   The most lasting cultural effect of postwar nationalism may well have been its mark on education. The colonies had founded a total of nine colleges, but after the Revolution eight more sprang up in the 1780s and six more in the 1790s. Several of the revolutionary state constitutions provided for state universities. Georgia's was the first chartered, in 1785, but the University of North Carolina (chartered in 1789) was the first to open, in 1795.

Even more important, the Revolution provided the initial impetus for state-supported public school systems. Many of the founders believed that the survival of the new nation depended upon instilling in the public an appreciation for the fragility of republican government and its utter dependence on private and civic virtue. They viewed public schools as the best agencies for such moral and civic development. In such schools, as Pennsylvania's Benjamin Rush maintained, American children would not only become literate but would also learn to choose the public good over all private interests and concerns.

Jefferson agreed that public education would serve as the very "keystone of our arch of government," and in 1779 he introduced his "Bill for the More General Diffusion of Knowledge" into the Virginia assembly. It included an elaborate plan for the state to fund elementary schools for all free persons, and higher education for the talented, up through a state university. Several years later Samuel Adams proposed the same in Massachusetts. Yet almost every one of these schemes for public schools came to naught. Wealthy critics opposed spending tax money on schools that would mingle their sons "in a vulgar and suspicious communion" with the masses. The spread of public schools would have to wait for a more democratic climate.

Perhaps the single most influential educational tool enhancing a sense of nationalism after the Revolution was Noah Webster's elementary spelling book published first in 1783. A native of Hartford, Connecticut, Webster was teaching at Goshen, New York, when he compiled his "Blue Back Speller." By 1890 more than 60 million copies had been printed, and the book continued to sell well into the twentieth century.

MISSION   In a special sense American nationalism embodied an idea of mission. Many people, at least since the time of the Pilgrims, had thought America to be singled out for a special identity, a special mission. John Winthrop had referred to the Puritan commonwealth as representing a "city upon a hill," and to Jonathan Edwards, God had singled out America as "the glorious renovator of the world." Still later John Adams proclaimed the opening of America "a grand scheme and design in Providence for the illumination and the emancipation of the slavish part of mankind all over the earth." This sense of mission was neither limited to New England nor rooted solely in Calvinism. From the democratic rhetoric of Jefferson, to the pragmatism of Washington, to heady toasts bellowed in South Carolina taverns, Americans everywhere articulated a special American leadership role in human history. The mission was now a call to lead the way toward liberty and equality. Meanwhile, however, Americans had to come to grips with more immediate problems created by their new nationhood. The Philadelphia patriot, doctor, and scientist, Benjamin Rush, issued a prophetic statement in 1787: "The American war is over: but this is far from being the case with the American revolution. On the contrary, but the first act of the great drama is closed."

MAKING CONNECTIONS

- The American Revolution was the starting point for the foreign policy of the United States. Many of the specific foreign concerns discussed in Chapters 7 and 8 sprang from issues directly relating to the Revolution.

- Much of what became Jacksonian Democracy (introduced in Chapter 9) can be traced to social and political movements associated with the American Revolution.

- The Articles of Confederation, the document that established the first national government for the United States, saw the new nation through the Revolution; but within a few years the Articles were discarded in favor of a new government, set forth in the Constitution.

FURTHER READING

The Revolutionary War is the subject of Robert Middlekauff's *The Glorious Cause: The American Revolution, 1763–1789* (1982).*

On the social history of the Revolutionary War see Charles Royster's *A Revolutionary People at War* (1979),* Lawrence D. Cress's *Citizens in Arms* (1982), and E. Wayne Carp's *To Starve the Army at Pleasure* (1984).

Why some Americans remained loyal to the crown is the subject of Robert M. Calhoon's *The Loyalists in Revolutionary America, 1760–1781* (1973),* and Mary Beth Norton's *The British-Americans* (1972).*

One of the few community-level studies of revolutionary change is Robert A. Gross's *The Minutemen and Their World* (1976). Mary Beth Norton's *Liberty's Daughters* (1980)* and Linda K. Kerber's *Women of the Republic* (1980)* document the role women played in securing independence. Joy D. Buel and Richard Buel's *The Way of Duty* (1984)* shows the impact of the Revolution on one New England family.

*These books are available in paperback editions.

6 SHAPING A FEDERAL UNION

CHAPTER ORGANIZER

This chapter focuses on:

• the achievements and weaknesses of the Confederation government

• the issues involved in writing the Constitution

• the debate over ratifying the Constitution

THE CONFEDERATION

In an address to fellow graduates at the Harvard commencement in 1787, young John Quincy Adams lamented "this critical period" when the country was struggling to establish itself as a new nation. Historians thereafter used his phrase to designate the years when the United States operated under the Articles of Confederation, 1781 to 1787. The temptation for many has been to focus on the weaknesses of the Confederation and neglect the nation's major achievements during the so-called "critical period."

The Congress of the Confederation, to be sure, had little governmental authority. It could only request money from the states; it could make treaties with foreign countries but could not enforce them; it could borrow money but lacked the means to ensure repayment. The Congress was virtually helpless to cope with the postwar problems of diplomacy and economic depression, problems that would have challenged the resources of a much stronger government. It was not easy to find men of stature to serve in such a body, and often hard to gather a quorum of those who did. Yet in spite of its handicaps the Confederation Congress somehow managed to keep afloat and to lay important foundations for the future. It concluded the Peace of Paris in 1783, created the first executive departments, and formulated principles of land distribution and territorial government that guided expansion all the way to the Pacific coast.

Throughout most of the War for Independence the Congress remained distrustful of executive power. It assigned administrative duties to its committees and thereby imposed a painful burden on conscientious members. At one time or another John Adams, for instance, served on some eighty committees.

In 1781, however, anticipating ratification of the Articles of Confederation, Congress began to set up three departments: Foreign Affairs, Finance, and War. Each was to have a single head responsible to Congress. Given time and stability, Congress and the department heads might have evolved something like the parliamentary cabinet system. As it turned out, these agencies were the forerunners of the government departments to be established under the Constitution.

FINANCE   As yet, however, there was neither president nor prime minister, only the presiding officer of Congress and its secretary, Charles Thomson, who served continuously from 1774 to 1789. The closest thing to an executive head of the Confederation was Robert Morris, who as superintendent of finance in the final years of the war became the most influential figure in the government. He wanted to make both himself and the Confederation more powerful. He envisioned a coherent program of taxation and debt management to make the government financially stable.

As the foundation of his plan, Morris secured in 1781 a congressional charter for the Bank of North America, which would hold government deposits, lend money to the government, and issue bank notes that would provide a stable currency. But his program depended ultimately on a secure income for the Confederation government, and it proved impossible to win the unanimous approval of the states for the necessary amendments to the Articles of Confederation. Local interests and the fear of a central authority—a fear strengthened by the recent quarrels with king and Parliament—hobbled action. As a consequence, the Confederation never did put its finances in order. The Continental currency quickly proved worthless, and it was never redeemed. The debt, domestic and foreign, grew from $11 million to $28 million as Congress paid off citizens' and soldiers' claims. Each year Congress ran a deficit on its operating expenses.

LAND POLICY   The one source from which Congress might hope ultimately to draw an independent income was the sale of western lands, but throughout the Confederation period that income remained more a fleeting promise than an accomplished fact. The Confederation nevertheless dealt more effectively with the western lands than with anything else. There Congress had direct authority, at least on paper. Thinly populated by Indians, French settlers, and a growing number of American squatters, the region north of the Ohio River had long been the site of overlapping claims by colonies and speculators. In 1784 Virginia completed its cession of lands north of the Ohio, and by 1786 all states had abandoned their claims in the area except for a 120-mile strip along Lake Erie, which Connecticut held until 1800 as its "Western Reserve."

As early as 1779 Congress had decided not to treat the western lands as colonies. The delegates resolved instead that western lands ceded by the states "shall be . . . formed into distinct Republican states," equal in all respects to other states. Between 1784 and 1787 policies for western development emerged in three major ordinances of the Confederation Congress. These documents, which rank among its greatest achievements—and among the most important in American history—set precedents that the United States would follow in its future expansion. Thomas Jefferson's inclination was to grant self-government to western territories at an early stage, when settlers would meet and choose their own officials. Under Jefferson's ordinance of 1784, when a territory's population equaled that of the smallest existing state, it would achieve full statehood.

In the Land Ordinance of 1785 the delegates outlined a plan of surveys and sales that eventually stamped a rectangular pattern on much of the nation's surface. Wherever Indian titles had been extinguished, the

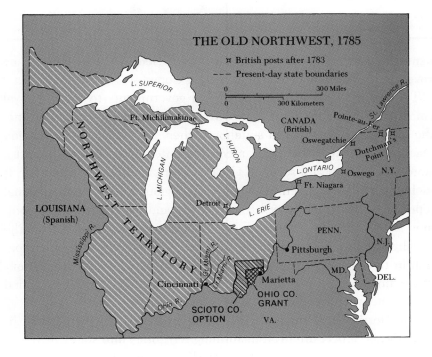

THE OLD NORTHWEST, 1785

¤ British posts after 1783
--- Present-day state boundaries

Northwest was to be surveyed into townships six miles square along east-west and north-south lines. Each township in turn was divided into thirty-six lots (or sections), each one mile square (or 640 acres). The 640-acre sections were to be auctioned for no less than $1 per acre or $640 total. Such terms favored land speculators, of course, since few common folk had that much money or were able to work that much land. In later years new land laws would make smaller lots available at lower prices, but in 1785 Congress confronted an empty treasury. In each township, however, Congress did reserve the income from the sixteenth section for the support of schools—a significant departure at a time when public schools were rare.

Spurred by the plans for land sales and settlement, Congress drafted a more specific frame of territorial government to replace Jefferson's ordinance of 1784. The new plan backed off from the commitment to early self-government. Because of the trouble that might be expected from squatters who were clamoring for free land, the Northwest Ordinance of 1787 required a period of colonial tutelage. At first the territory fell subject to a governor, a secretary, and three judges, all chosen by Congress. When any territory in the Northwest region had 5,000 free male adults it could choose an assembly, and Congress would name a governing council from names proposed by the assembly. The governor would have a veto and so would Congress.

The resemblance of these territorial governments to the old royal colonies is clear, but there were two significant differences. For one, the Ordinance anticipated statehood when any territory's population reached 60,000. At that point a convention could be called to draft a state constitution and apply to Congress for statehood. For another, it included a bill of rights that guaranteed religious freedom, proportional representation, trial by jury, habeas corpus, and the application of common law. Finally, the Ordinance excluded slavery permanently from the Northwest. This proved a fateful decision. As the progress of emancipation in the existing states gradually freed all slaves above the Mason-Dixon line, the Ohio River boundary of the Old Northwest extended the line between freedom and slavery all the way to the Mississippi.

The Northwest Ordinance had an importance larger than establishing a formal procedure for transforming territories into states. It represented a sharp break with the imperialistic assumption behind European expansion into the Western Hemisphere. The new states were to be admitted as equals into the American republic.

The lands south of the Ohio River followed a different process of development. Title to the western lands remained with Georgia, North Carolina, and Virginia for the time being, but settlement proceeded at a far more rapid pace during and after the Revolution, despite the Indians' fierce resentment of encroachments on their hunting grounds. Substantial population centers grew up in Kentucky and along the Watauga, Holston, and Cumberland Rivers, as far west as Nashborough (Nashville).

The white settlers trampled Indian lands. The Iroquois and Cherokees, badly battered during the Revolution, were in no position to resist encroachments. During the mid-1780s the Iroquois were forced to cede land in western New York and Pennsylvania, and the Cherokees gave up all claims in South Carolina, much of western North Carolina, and large portions of present-day Kentucky and Tennessee. At the same time, the major Ohio tribes dropped their claim to most of Ohio, except for a chunk bordering the western part of Lake Erie. The Creeks, pressed by Georgia to cede portions of their lands in 1784–1785, went to war in the summer of 1786 with covert aid from Spanish Florida. When Spanish support lapsed, however, the Creek chief struck a bargain in 1791 that gave the Creeks favorable trade arrangements with the United States but did not restore the lost lands.

TRADE AND THE ECONOMY   In its economic life, as in planning westward expansion, the young nation dealt vigorously with the difficult wartime problems. Congress had little to do with achievements in the economy, but neither could it bear the blame for an acute economic contraction between 1770 and 1790, the result primarily of the war and separation from the British Empire. Although farmers enmeshed in local markets maintained their livelihood during the revolutionary era, commercial agriculture dependent upon trade with foreign markets suffered a severe downturn. In New England and much of the backcountry, fighting seldom interrupted the tempo of farming, and the producers of foodstuffs for local markets especially benefited from rising prices and wartime demands. The southern tidewater suffered a loss of slave labor, much of it carried off by the British. Chesapeake planters also lost their lucrative foreign markets. Tobacco was especially hard hit. The British decision to close its West Indian colonies to American trade devastated what had been a thriving trade in timber, wheat, and other foodstuffs. Returns from indigo and naval stores declined with the loss of British bounties for those products.

Merchants suffered far more wrenching adjustments during the Revolution than farmers. Cut out of the British mercantile system, they had to find new outlets for their trade. Circumstances that impoverished some enriched those who financed privateers, supplied the armies on both sides, and hoarded precious goods while demand and prices soared. By the end of the war a strong sentiment for free trade had developed in both Britain and America. In the memorable year 1776, the Scottish economist Adam Smith published *The Wealth of Nations,* a classic manifesto against mercantilism. Some British statesmen embraced the new gospel of free trade, but the public and Parliament still clung to mercantilism for many years to come.

British trade with the United States resumed after 1783. American ships were allowed to deliver American products and return to the United States with British goods, but they could not carry British goods anywhere else. The pent-up demand for familiar goods created a vigorous market in exports to America, fueled by British credits and the hard money that had come into the new nation from foreign aid, the expenditures of foreign armies, or wartime trade and privateering. The result was a quick cycle of postwar boom and bust, a buying spree followed by a money shortage and economic troubles that lasted several years.

In colonial days the chronic trade deficit with Britain had been offset by the influx of coins from trade with the West Indies. Now American ships found themselves legally excluded from the British West Indies. But the islands still demanded wheat, fish, lumber, and other products from the mainland, and American shippers had not lost their talent for smuggling; by 1787 their seaports were flourishing more than ever. By 1790 American commerce and exports had far outrun the trade of the colonies. American merchants had more ships than before the war. Farm exports were twice what they had been. Although most of the exports were the products of American forests, fields, and fisheries, during and after the war more workers had turned to small-scale manufacturing—shoes, textiles, soap—mainly for domestic markets.

DIPLOMACY The achievements of the flourishing young nation are more visible in hindsight than they were at the time. Until 1787 the shortcomings and failures of the Confederation government remained far more apparent—and the advocates of a stronger central government were extremely vocal on the subject. In diplomacy, there remained the nagging problems of relations with Great Britain and Spain, both of which still kept military posts on American soil and conspired with Indians and white settlers in the West. The British, despite the peace treaty of 1783, held on to a string of forts along the northern frontier. From these they kept a hand in the fur trade and a degree of influence with the Indian tribes, whom they were suspected of stirring up to make sporadic attacks on American settlers.

Another major irritant was the confiscation of Loyalist property. The peace treaty had obligated Congress to stop confiscations, to guarantee immunity to Loyalists for twelve months during which they could return and wind up their affairs, and to recommend that the states return confiscated property. Persecutions, even lynchings, of Loyalists still occurred until after the end of the war. Some Loyalists returned unmolested, however, and once again took up their lives in their former homes. By the end of 1787, moreover, all the states had rescinded those laws discriminating against former Tories that were in conflict with the peace treaty.

The British refused even to dispatch an ambassador to the new nation before 1791. As early as 1785, however, the United States took the initiative by sending over John Adams as ambassador to Great Britain. He spent three years in futile efforts to settle disputes over the forts, debts, property rights of Loyalists, and trade concessions in the British West Indies.

With Spain the chief issues were the southern boundary and the right to navigate the Mississippi. According to the preliminary treaty with Britain, the United States claimed as its traditional boundary a line running eastward from the mouth of the Yazoo River. The American treaty with Britain had also specified the right to navigate the Mississippi River to its mouth, but the river was entirely within Spanish Louisiana in its lower reaches. The right to navigation assumed importance because of the growing settlements in Kentucky and Tennessee, but in 1784 Louisiana's Spanish governor closed the river to American commerce. He also began to intrigue with the Creeks, Choctaws, Chickasaws, and other Indians of the Southwest against the American settlers and with the Americans against the United States. In 1785 the Spanish government sent an ambassador to the United States, who entered into long but fruitless negotiations with John Jay, the secretary for foreign affairs. The issue of American access to the lower Mississippi remained unsettled for nearly another decade.

THE CONFEDERATION'S PROBLEMS   The problems of trans-Appalachian settlers, however, were of remote interest to most Americans. Of greater concern were protection for infant American industries and the currency shortage. Mechanics (skilled workers who made, used, or repaired tools and machines) and artisans who were developing exports ranging from crude iron nails to the fine silver bowls of Paul Revere were frustrated by British policies excluding them from British markets. In retaliation, they sought from the states tariffs against foreign goods that competed with theirs. The country would be on its way to economic independence, they argued, if only the money that flowed into the country were invested in domestic manufactures instead of being paid out for foreign goods. Nearly all the states gave some preference to American goods, but the lack of consistency in their laws put them at cross purposes, and so urban mechanics along with merchants were drawn into the movement demanding a stronger central government in the interest of uniform regulation.

The shortage of cash and other economic difficulties gave rise to more immediate demands for paper currency as legal tender, for postponement of tax and debt payments, and for laws to "stay" the foreclosure of mortgages. Farmers, who had profited during the war, found themselves squeezed by depressed crop prices and mounting debts while merchants sorted out and opened up their new trade routes. Creditors demanded hard money, but it was in short supply—and paper money was both scarce and virtually worthless after the depreciation of the Continental currency. The result was an outcry among debtor groups for relief, and around 1785 the demand for new paper money became the most divisive issue in state politics. In 1785–1786 seven states issued paper money. In spite of the cries of calamity at the time, the money served positively as a means of credit to hard-pressed farmers through state loans on farm mortgages. It was variously used to fund state debts and to pay off the claims of veterans.

SHAYS'S REBELLION But many Americans—especially bankers and merchants—were horrified by such inflationary policies. Developments in Massachusetts provided the final proof (some said) that the country was poised on the brink of anarchy: Shays's Rebellion. After 1780 Massachusetts had remained in the grip of a rigidly conservative regime. Ever higher poll and land taxes were levied to pay off a heavy debt, held mainly by wealthy creditors in Boston, and the taxes fell most heavily upon beleaguered farmers and the poor in general. When the legislature adjourned in 1786 without providing either paper money or any other relief from taxes and debts, three western counties erupted into spontaneous revolt. Armed bands closed the courts and prevented foreclosures, and a ragtag "army" of some 1,200 disgruntled farmers led by Captain Daniel Shays, a destitute farmer and "brave and good" war veteran, advanced upon the federal arsenal at Springfield in 1787.

A small militia force, however, scattered Shays's men with a single volley that left four dead. General Benjamin Lincoln, arriving soon after with reinforcements from Boston, routed the remaining Shaysites. The rebels nevertheless had a victory of sorts. The new state legislature included members sympathetic to the agricultural crisis. They omitted direct taxes the following year, lowered court fees, and exempted clothing, household goods, and tools from the debt process. But a more important consequence was the impetus the rebellion gave to conservatism and nationalism.

Rumors, at times deliberately inflated, greatly exaggerated the extent of this pathetic rebellion of desperate men. Stories accusing them of seeking to pillage the wealthy horrified those whom New York's John Jay called the "better kind of people." The uprising seemed to provide an ominous example of possible greater turmoil. "There are combustibles in every State," George Washington wrote, "which a spark might set fire to." Panic set in among the republic's elite. New York's Gouverneur Morris was typically blunt: "The mob begin to think and reason. Poor reptiles! They bask in the sun and ere noon they will bite, depend upon it. The gentry begin to fear this." In a letter to Thomas Jefferson, Abigail Adams was equally anxious. She tarred the Shaysites as "Ignorant, wrestless, desperadoes, without conscience or principles . . . mobbish insurgents [who] are for sapping the foundation" of the struggling young government.

Jefferson disagreed. If Adams and others were overly critical of Shays's Rebellion, Jefferson was, if anything, too complacent. From his post in Paris, where one of history's great civil bloodbaths would soon occur, he wrote to a friend back home: "The tree of liberty must be refreshed from time to time with the blood of patriots and tyrants." Abigail Adams was so infuriated by Jefferson's position that she stopped corresponding with him for months.

CALLS FOR A STRONGER GOVERNMENT   Shays's Rebellion convinced many political leaders that the Articles of Confederation were incapable of providing an effective basis for the new republican government. Advocates of a stronger central authority already had gained momentum from the adversities of the times. Self-interest frequently led bankers, merchants, and mechanics to promote a stronger central government. At the same time many public-spirited men saw it as the only alternative to anarchy. Gradually people were losing the ingrained fear of a tyrannical central authority as they saw evidence that tyranny might come from other quarters, including the common people themselves.

By the mid-1780s, in fact, several prominent political spokesmen had become convinced that the new state governments were being run by uneducated entrepreneurs pursuing selfish economic and petty political interests. Men of humble origins and parochial points of view were allegedly displacing the "wise and virtuous" from seats of power. Such inexperienced and frequently uncouth lawmakers were passing an avalanche of legislation merely to serve particular interest groups and constituents rather than the general welfare. They were printing excessive amounts of paper money and passing "stay" laws preventing judicial action against debtors.

Such developments led many of the revolutionary leaders to revise their assessment of American character. "We have, probably," concluded George Washington in 1786, "had too good an opinion of human nature in forming our confederation." The following year James Madison reported to Jefferson that America was displaying "symptoms . . . truly alarming, which have tainted the faith of most orthodox republicans." People were stretching the meaning of liberty far beyond what he and others had envisioned. He found a "spirit of *locality*" rampant in the state legislatures that was destroying the "aggregate interests of the community." Even worse, he saw people taking the law and other people's property into their own hands. Such developments led Madison and others to revise their assumptions about the degree of republican virtue evident in the American people. At any given time, they decided, only a distinct minority could be relied upon to set aside their private interests in favor of the common good. Madison and these so-called Federalists concluded that the new republic must now depend for its success on the constant virtue of the few rather than the public-spiritedness of the many.

For these reasons, well before the Shaysite rebellion in New England, nationalists were demanding a convention to revise the Articles of Confederation. Noah Webster, of dictionary fame, moaned in 1785 that "Our pretended union is but a name, and our confederation a cobweb." Animated by similar concerns, commissioners from Virginia and Maryland had met at Mount Vernon in 1785 on Washington's invitation to promote economic development and to settle outstanding questions about the navigation of the Potomac and Chesapeake Bay. The delegates agreed on interstate cooperation, and at Madison's suggestion invited all thirteen states to send delegates for a general discussion of commercial problems. Representatives from only five appeared at the Annapolis Convention in 1786. Apparent failure soon turned into success, however, when the alert New York delegate, Alexander Hamilton, presented a resolution for still another convention in Philadelphia to consider all measures necessary "to render the constitution of the Federal Government adequate to the exigencies of the Union."

ADOPTING THE CONSTITUTION

THE CONSTITUTIONAL CONVENTION   After stalling for several months, Congress, in February 1787, passed a resolution endorsing a convention "for the sole and express purpose of revising the Articles of Confederation." By then five states had already named delegates; before the meeting six more states had acted. Rhode Island kept aloof throughout, leading critics to label it "Rogue Island." Twenty-nine delegates began work in Philadelphia on May 25. Altogether seventy-three men were elected by the state legislatures, fifty-five attended at one time or another, and after four months thirty-nine signed the Constitution they had drafted.

The document's durability and flexibility testify to the remarkable quality of the men who made it. Thomas Jefferson, who was still serving abroad as minister to France, later referred to the convention as "an assembly of demigods." The delegates were surprisingly young—forty-two was the average age. Only two were small farmers. Most were planters, merchants, lawyers, judges, bankers—many of them widely read in history, law, and political philosophy, familiar with the writings of Locke and Montesquieu, and at the same time practical men of experience, tested in the fires of the Revolution. Twenty-one had worn uniforms in the conflict, seven had been state governors, most of them had served in the Continental Congress and eight had signed the Declaration of Independence. "Experience must be our only guide," insisted Pennsylvania's John Dickinson. "Reason may mislead us."

The magisterial Washington served as presiding officer but participated little in the debates. Eighty-one-year-old Benjamin Franklin, the oldest and most infirm delegate, also said little from the floor but did provide a wealth of experience, wit, and common sense. More active in the debates were the thirty-six-year-old James Madison, the ablest political philosopher in the group; Massachusetts's lanky, dapper Elbridge Gerry, a Harvard graduate and merchant who earned the nickname "Old Grumbletonian" because, as John Adams once said, he "opposed

James Madison was only thirty-six when he assumed a major role in the drafting of the Constitution. This miniature is by Charles Willson Peale (c. 1783).

everything he did not propose"; George Mason, the prickly author of the Virginia Bill of Rights and a planter and slaveholder who was burdened by gout, chronic indigestion, and a deep-rooted suspicion of all government; the witty, eloquent, and arrogant New York aristocrat, Gouverneur Morris; Marylander Luther Martin, the ardent spokesman for states' rights, whose speeches were made livelier by his frequent drunkenness; Scots-born James Wilson of Pennsylvania, one of the shrewdest lawyers in the new nation and next in importance at the convention only to Washington and Madison; and Roger Sherman of Connecticut, a self-trained lawyer adept at negotiating compromises. John Adams, like Jefferson, was serving abroad. Also conspicuously absent during most of the convention was thirty-two-year-old Alexander Hamilton, the staunch nationalist who regretfully went home when the two other New York delegates walked out because of their states'-rights principles.

The delegates spent four sweltering months fighting flies, the humidity, and each other. They worked earnestly and with a sense of urgency, five to six hours a day, six days a week, hammering out the compromises embedded in the Constitution. Their differences on political philosophy for the most part fell within a narrow range. On certain fundamentals they generally agreed: that government derived its just powers from the consent of the people, but that society must be protected from the tyranny of the majority; that the people at large must have a voice in their government, but that checks and balances must be provided to keep any one group from dominating power; that a stronger central authority was essential, but that all power was subject to abuse. They assumed with Madison that if people "were angels, no government would be necessary." Even the best of people were naturally selfish, they believed, and therefore government could not be founded upon a trust in goodwill and virtue. Yet by carefully checking power with countervailing power, the Founding Fathers hoped to devise institutions that could somehow constrain individual sinfulness and channel individual self-interest on behalf of the public good.

THE VIRGINIA AND NEW JERSEY PLANS At the outset the delegates decided to meet behind closed doors in order to discourage outside pressures and theatrical speeches to the galleries. The secrecy of the proceedings was remarkably well kept, and knowledge of the debates comes mainly from Madison's extensive notes. Small of stature—barely over five feet tall—and frail in health, Madison was a shy, studious bachelor descended from wealthy slave-owning Virginia planters. Crowds made him nervous, and he hated to use his high-pitched voice in public, much less in open debate.

But the Princeton graduate who had found the practice of law too "coarse and dry" possessed a keen, agile mind with a voracious appetite for learning. He proved to be the energizing force at the convention, persuading others by the convincing eloquence of his arguments. "Every person seems to acknowledge his greatness," wrote one delegate. Another commented that he possessed a "calm expression, blue eyes—and looked like a thinking man." Madison arrived in Philadelphia with trunks full of books and a head full of ideas, and he set about drafting the proposals that came to be called the "Virginia Plan," presented on May 29.

The Virginia plan called for separate legislative, executive, and judicial branches, and a truly national government whose laws would be binding upon individual citizens as well as upon states. Congress would be divided into two houses, a lower house to be chosen by popular vote and an upper house to be chosen by the lower house from nominees of the state legislatures. Congress could disallow state laws under the plan and would itself define the extent of its and the states' authority.

On June 15 William Paterson submitted the "New Jersey Plan," which kept the existing equal representation of states in a unicameral Congress, but gave the Congress power to levy taxes, regulate commerce, and name a plural executive (with no veto) and a Supreme Court. The different plans presented the convention with two major issues: whether to amend the Articles of Confederation or draft an entirely new document, and whether to apportion congressional representation by population or by states.

On the first point the Convention voted to work toward a national government as envisioned by the Virginians. Regarding the powers of this government there was little disagreement except in detail. Experience with the Articles had persuaded the delegates that an effective central government, as distinguished from a confederation, needed the power to levy taxes, to regulate commerce, to raise an army and navy, and to make laws binding upon individual citizens. The lessons of the 1780s suggested to them, moreover, that in the interest of order and uniformity the states must be denied certain powers: to issue money, to void contracts, to make treaties or wage war, to levy tariffs or export duties.

But furious disagreements then arose. The first clash in the Convention involved the issue of representation, and it was solved by the "Great Compromise," sometimes called the "Connecticut Compromise," offered by Roger Sherman. The more populous states won apportionment by population in the House of Representatives; the states that sought to protect state power won equality in the Senate, but with the vote there by individuals and not by states.

An equally contentious struggle ensued between northern and southern delegates over slavery, an omen of future sectional controversies. Slavery, Madison's secretary noted, was a "distracting question" rather than a compelling moral dilemma for most of the delegates. Few if any of the framers even considered the possibility of abolishing slavery in those states—mostly southern—where it was still legal. In this respect they reflected the prevailing attitudes of their time. Most agreed with South Carolina's canny John Rutledge, described by the French minister as "the proudest and most imperious man in the United States," when he asserted: "Religion and humanity [have] nothing to do with this [slavery] question. Interest alone is the governing principle of nations."

The interest of southern delegates, with slaves so numerous in their states, dictated that slaves be counted as part of the population in determining the number of representatives. Northerners were willing to have slaves counted in deciding each state's share of direct taxes but not for purposes of representation. The delegates, with little dissent, agreed in a compromise to count three-fifths of the slaves as a basis for apportioning both representatives and direct taxes.

A more sensitive issue involved an effort to prevent the new central government from stopping the Atlantic slave trade. Some state governments had already outlawed the practice, and several delegates demanded that the national government do the same. Southern delegates quickly protested. Eventually a compromise was reached whereby the delegates established a time limit after which the slave trade would be prohibited. Congress could not prohibit the traffic until 1808, but it could levy a tax of $10 a head on all imported slaves. In drafting both provisions, a sense of delicacy—and hypocrisy—dictated the use of euphemisms. The Constitution thus spoke of "free persons" and "all other persons," of persons "held to Service of Labor." The odious word "slavery" did not appear in the Constitution until the Thirteenth Amendment (1865) abolished the "peculiar institution" by name.

If the delegates found the slavery issue distracting, they considered irrelevant any discussion of the legal or political role of women under the new Constitution. The Revolutionary rhetoric of liberty prompted a few women to demand political equality. "The men say we have no business" with politics, Eliza Wilkinson of South Carolina observed, "but I won't have it thought that because we are the weaker sex as to bodily strength we are capable of nothing more than domestic concerns. They won't even allow us liberty of thought, and that is all I want." Her complaint, however, fell on deaf ears. There was never any formal discussion of women's rights at the Convention. The new nationalism still defined politics and government as outside the realm of female endeavor.

THE SEPARATION OF POWERS   The details of governmental structure, while causing disagreement, caused far less trouble than the basic issues pitting the large against the small states and the northern against the southern states. Existing state constitutions, several of which already separated powers among legislative, executive, and judicial branches, set an example that reinforced the Convention's resolve to disperse power with checks and balances. Some delegates displayed a thumping disdain for any democratizing of the political system. Hamilton called the people "a great beast," and Massachusetts's Elbridge Gerry asserted that most of the nation's problems "flow from an excess of democracy."

Roger Sherman likewise insisted that the people "should have as little to do as may be about the Government."

These elitist views were incorporated into the Constitution's mixed legislative system, which acknowledged the "genius of the people," as George Mason phrased it, but allowed direct popular choice of just one chamber of the Congress. The lower house was designed to be closest to the voters, who elected it every two years. The House of Representatives would be, according to Mason, "the grand repository of the democratic principle of the Government." Its members should "sympathize with their constituents, should think as they think, & feel as they feel; and for these purposes should even be residents among them." The upper house, or Senate, was elected by state legislatures rather than directly by the voters. Staggered six-year terms prevented the choice of a majority in any given year, and thereby further isolated senators from the passing fancies of public passion.

The decision that a single person be made the chief executive caused the delegates "considerable pause," according to Madison. George Mason protested that this would create a "fetus of monarchy." Indeed, the president was to be an almost monarchical figure. Although subject to election every four years, the chief executive would wield powers that would exceed those of the British king. This was the sharpest departure from the recent experience in state government, where the office of governor had commonly been diluted because of the recent memory of struggles with the colonial executives. The president could veto acts of Congress, subject to being overridden by a two-thirds vote in each house, was commander-in-chief of the armed forces, and was responsible for the execution of the laws. The chief executive could make treaties with the advice and consent of two-thirds of the Senate and appoint diplomats, judges, and other officers with the consent of a Senate majority.

But the president's powers were limited in certain key areas. The chief executive could neither declare war nor make peace; those powers were reserved for Congress. In addition the Constitution required that the president report annually on the state of the nation. Unlike the British king, moreover, the president could be removed. "Shall any man be above Justice?" asked George Mason. "Above all, shall that man be above it who can commit the most extensive injustice?" No, answered the delegates, and they built into the Constitution the machinery for removing the president. The House could impeach (indict) the chief executive—and other civil officers—on charges of treason, bribery, or "other high crimes and misdemeanors"; the president could then be removed by the Senate with a two-thirds vote to convict. The presiding officer at the trial of a president would be the chief justice, since the usual presiding officer of the Senate (the vice president) would have a personal stake in the outcome.

The convention's nationalists—men like Madison, James Wilson, and Hamilton—wanted to strengthen the independence of the executive by entrusting the choice to popular election. At least in this instance, the nationalists, often accused of being the aristocratic party, favored a bold new exercise in democracy. But an elected executive was still too far beyond the American experience. Besides, a national election would have created enormous problems of organization and voter qualification. Wilson suggested instead that the people of each state choose presidential electors equal to the number of their senators and representatives. Others proposed that the legislators make the choice. Finally, the convention voted to let the legislature decide the method in each state. Before long nearly all the states were choosing their electors by popular vote, and the electors were acting as agents of party will, casting their votes as they had pledged before the election. This method diverged from the original expectation that the electors would deliberate and make their own choices.

On the third branch of government, the judiciary, there was surprisingly little debate. Both the Virginia and New Jersey plans had called for a Supreme Court, which the Constitution established, providing specifically for a chief justice of the United States and leaving up to Congress the number of other justices. The only major dispute centered on courts "inferior" to the Supreme Court, and that too was left up to Congress. Although the Constitution nowhere authorized the courts to declare laws void when they conflicted with the Constitution, the power of judicial review was implied and was soon exercised in cases involving both state and federal laws. Article VI declared the federal constitution, federal laws, and treaties to be the "supreme law of the land," state laws or constitutions to the contrary notwithstanding.

While the Constitution extended vast new powers to the national government, the delegates' mistrust of unchecked power is apparent in repeated examples of countervailing forces: the separation of the three branches of government, the president's veto, the congressional power of impeachment and removal, the Senate's power over treaties and appointments, the courts' implied right of judicial review. In addition the new frame of government specifically forbade Congress to pass ex post facto laws (laws adopted after the event to make past deeds criminal). It also reserved to the states large areas of sovereignty—a reservation soon made explicit by the Tenth Amendment. By dividing sovereignty between the people and the government, the framers of the Constitution provided a distinctive contribution to political theory. That is, by vesting ultimate authority in the people, they divided sovereignty *within* the government. This constituted a dramatic break with the colonial tradition. The British had always insisted that the sovereignty of the king-in-Parliament was indivisible.

The most glaring defect of the Articles of Confederation, the rule of unanimity that defeated every effort to amend them, led the delegates to provide a less forbidding though still difficult method of amending the new Constitution. Amendments could be proposed either by two-thirds vote of each house or by a national convention specially called by two-thirds of the state legislatures. Amendments could be ratified by approval of three-fourths of the states acting through their legislatures or through special conventions. The national convention has never been used, however, and state conventions have been called only once—to ratify the repeal of the Eighteenth Amendment, which had enacted Prohibition.

THE FIGHT FOR RATIFICATION   The final article of the Constitution provided that it would become effective upon ratification by nine states (not quite the three-fourths majority required for amendment). The Congress submitted the Convention's work to the states on September 28, 1787. In the ensuing political debate advocates of the new Constitution, who might properly have been called Nationalists because they preferred a strong central government, assumed the more reassuring name of Federalists. Opponents, who favored a more decentralized federal system, became anti-Federalists.

The Federalists were not only better prepared but better organized, and on the whole they represented the more articulate elements in the community. The Federalists were usually clustered in or near cities and tended to be more cosmopolitan, urbane, and well educated. Anti-

Signing the Constitution, September 17, 1787. *Thomas Pritchard Rossiter's painting shows George Washington presiding over what Thomas Jefferson called "an assembly of demi-gods."*

Federalists tended to be small farmers and frontiersmen who saw little to gain from the promotion of interstate commerce and much to lose from prohibitions on paper money and "stay" laws preventing the seizure of property for nonpayment of debts. Many of them also feared that an expansive land policy was likely to favor speculators.

Historians have long debated what motivated the advocates of the new Constitution. In 1913 Charles A. Beard advanced the controversial thesis in his book, *An Economic Interpretation of the Constitution*, that the Philadelphia Convention was made up of men who had a selfish economic interest in the outcome. They held large amounts of depreciated government securities and otherwise stood to gain from the power and stability of the new central government. In his view, then, the Constitution was essentially an economic document reflecting the self-interest of a powerful minority.

Beard's thesis provided a useful antidote to unquestioning hero worship, and it still contains a germ of truth, but he rested his argument too heavily on the claim that material self-interest predominated in the Convention. Most of the delegates, according to evidence unavailable to Beard, had no compelling economic interests at stake. Many prominent nationalists, including the "Father of the Constitution," James Madison himself, had no western lands or bonds. Some opponents of the Constitution, on the other hand, held large blocks of bonds and securities. Economic interests certainly figured in the process of constitution-making, but they functioned in a complex interplay of state, sectional, group, and individual interests that turned largely on how well people had fared under the Confederation.

But exaggerating the influence of selfish economic interests in shaping the Constitution obscures an important point. The most notable circumstance of the times was that, unlike so many later revolutions, the American Revolution led not to general chaos and class strife but to a remarkably orderly process of constitution-making. From the 1760s through the 1780s there occurred a prolonged debate over the fundamental issues of government, which in its scope and depth—and in the durability of its outcome—is without parallel.

THE FEDERALIST   Among the supreme legacies of that debate was a collection of essays called *The Federalist,* originally published in New York newspapers between October 1787 and July 1788. Initiated by Alexander Hamilton, the eighty-five articles published under the name "Publius" included about thirty by James Madison, nearly fifty by Hamilton, and five by John Jay. Written in support of ratification, the essays defended the principle of a supreme national authority, but at the same time sought to reassure doubters that there was little reason to fear tyranny by the new government.

In perhaps the most famous single essay, Number Ten, Madison argued that the country's very size and diversity would make it impossible for any single faction to form a majority that could dominate the government. This contradicted prevailing notions of republican government. Republics, the conventional wisdom of the times insisted, could work only in small, homogeneous countries like Switzerland and the Netherlands. In larger countries republican government would descend into anarchy and tyranny through the influence of factions. Quite the contrary, Madison argued. A republic with a balanced federal government could survive in a large and diverse country better than in a smaller country. "Extend the sphere," he wrote, "and you take in a greater variety of parties and interests; you make it less probable that a majority of the whole will have a common motive to invade the rights of other citizens."

The Federalists did try to cultivate a belief that the new union would contribute to prosperity, in part to link their movement with the economic recovery already under way. The anti-Federalists, however, highlighted the dangers of power. They noted the absence of a Bill of Rights protecting individuals and states, and they found the ratification process highly irregular, which it was—indeed, illegal under the Articles of Confederation. Patrick Henry "smelt a rat" from the beginning. Not only did he refuse to attend the Constitutional Convention, he demanded later (unsuccessfully) that it be investigated as a conspiracy. Maryland's Luther Martin, who had walked out of the Constitutional Convention, urged his state not to ratify by rejecting "those chains which are forged for it." The anti-Federalist leaders such as Martin, Patrick Henry and Richard Henry Lee of Virginia, George Clinton of New York, Sam Adams and Elbridge Gerry of Massachusetts were often men whose careers and reputations had been established well before the Revolution. The Federalist leaders, on the other hand, were more likely to be younger men whose careers had begun in the Revolution and who had been "nationalized" in the fires of battle—men like Hamilton, Madison, and Jay.

The two groups disagreed, however, more over means than ends. Both sides for the most part agreed that a stronger national authority was needed, and that it required an independent income to function properly. Both were convinced that the people must erect safeguards against tyranny, even the tyranny of the majority. Once the new government had become an accomplished fact, few diehards were left who wanted to undo the work of the Philadelphia Convention.

THE DECISION OF THE STATES   Ratification of the new federal constitution gained momentum before the end of 1787, and several of the smaller states were among the first to act, apparently satisfied that they had gained all the safeguards they could hope for in equality of representation in the Senate. New Hampshire was the ninth to ratify, on June 21, 1788, and the Constitution could then be put into effect, but the union could hardly succeed without the approval of Virginia, the most populous state, or New York, with the third highest population, which occupied a key position geographically.

There was strong opposition in both states. In Virginia Patrick Henry became the chief spokesman of backcountry farmers who feared the powers of the new government, but wavering delegates were won over by a proposal that the convention should recommend a Bill of Rights. Virginia's convention ratified on June 25, 1788. In New York, Hamilton and the other Federalists delayed a vote in the hope that action by Virginia would persuade the delegates that the new framework would go into effect with or without New York. On July 26, 1788, they carried the day by the closest margin thus far, 30 to 27. North Carolina and Rhode Island remained the only holdouts, and the former stubbornly withheld action until November 1789, when amendments comprising a Bill of Rights were actually submitted by Congress. Rhode Island, true to form, continued to hold out and did not relent until May 29, 1790, by the closest margin of all—two votes.

Upon notification that New Hampshire had become the ninth state to ratify, the Confederation Congress began to draft plans for an orderly transfer of power. On September 13, 1788, it selected New York City as the seat of the new government and fixed the date for elections. On October 10, 1788, the Confederation Congress transacted its last business and passed into history. "Our constitution is in actual operation," the elderly Ben Franklin wrote to a friend; "everything appears to promise that it will last; but in this world nothing is certain but death and taxes." George Washington was even more uncertain about the future under the new plan of government. He had told a fellow delegate as the convention adjourned: "I do not expect the Constitution to last for more than twenty years."

RATIFICATION OF THE CONSTITUTION

Order of Ratification	State	Date of Ratification
1	Delaware	December 7, 1787
2	Pennsylvania	December 12, 1787
3	New Jersey	December 18, 1787
4	Georgia	January 2, 1788
5	Connecticut	January 9, 1788
6	Massachusetts	February 7, 1788
7	Maryland	April 28, 1788
8	South Carolina	May 23, 1788
9	New Hampshire	June 21, 1788
10	Virginia	June 25, 1788
11	New York	July 26, 1788
12	North Carolina	November 21, 1789
13	Rhode Island	May 29, 1790

"A MORE PERFECT UNION"

The Constitution has lasted much longer, of course, and in the process it has provided a model of republican government whose features have been repeatedly borrowed by other nations through the years. Yet what makes the American Constitution so distinctive is not its specific provisions but its remarkable harmony with the particular "genius of the people" it governs. The Constitution has been neither a static abstraction nor a "machine that would go of itself," as the poet James Russell Lowell would later assert. Instead it has provided a flexible system of government that presidents, legislators, judges, and the people have modified to accord with a fallible human nature and changing social, economic, and political circumstances. In this sense the Founding Fathers not only created "a more perfect Union" in 1787; they engineered a form of government whose resilience has enabled later generations to continue to perfect their republican experiment. But the Framers of the Constitution failed in one significant respect. In skirting the issue of slavery so as to cement the new union, they unknowingly allowed tensions over the "peculiar institution" to reach the point where there would be no political solution—only civil war.

MAKING CONNECTIONS

- The Founding Fathers might have created "a more perfect Union," but from time to time Americans have debated the nature of the national government, its relation to the people and the states, and so forth. Examples include the Kentucky and Virginia Resolutions (Chapter 7), the Hartford Convention (Chapter 8), and the Nullification Crisis (Chapter 10).

- Slavery, viewed by the delegates to the Constitutional Convention as little more than a "distracting question," soon became a major political problem—especially after the Missouri Compromise (in Chapter 9).

FURTHER READING

A good overview of the Confederation period is Richard B. Morris's *The Forging of the Union, 1781–1789* (1987). Relevant chapters of Gordon S. Wood's *The Creation of the American Republic, 1776–1787* (1969)* trace the changing contours of political philosophy during these years. The behavior of Congress is the subject of Jack N. Rakove's *The Beginnings of National Politics* (1979).*

David P. Szatmary's *Shays's Rebellion* (1980) covers that fateful incident. For a fine account of cultural change during the period, see Joseph J. Ellis's *After the Revolution: Profiles of American Culture* (1979).*

Excellent studies of the origins and context of the Constitution include Edmund S. Morgan's *Inventing the People* (1988), Michael Kammen's *Sovereignty and Liberty* (1988), and Forrest McDonald's *Novus Ordo Seclorum: The Intellectual Origins of the Constitution* (1985). On the Constitutional Convention, see Christopher Collier and James Lincoln Collier's *Decision in Philadelphia* (1986).

Bruce Ackerman's *We the People: Foundations* (1990) examines Federalist political principles. See also Richard B. Morris's *Witness at the Creation: Hamilton, Madison, Jay, and the Constitution* (1985) and James MacGregor Burns and Stewart Burns's *A People's Charter: The Pursuit of Rights in America* (1990).

*These books are available in paperback editions.

7 ⌘ THE FEDERALISTS:
WASHINGTON AND ADAMS

CHAPTER ORGANIZER

This chapter focuses on:

- the early operation of the new government

- Alexander Hamilton's Federalist program

- the beginnings of the first party system (Federalists and Republicans)

- the elements of Federalist foreign policy

A NEW NATION

The framers of the Constitution sought to create a new federal government capable of administering a rapidly expanding territory and population. In 1789 the United States and the western territories covered an area from the Atlantic Ocean to the Mississippi River and included almost 4 million people. This vast area harbored distinct regional differences. New England remained a region of small farms and bustling seaports, but it was on the verge of developing a small-scale manufacturing sector. The Middle States boasted the most well-balanced economy, the largest cities, and the most diverse collection of ethnic and religious groups. The South was a more ethnically homogeneous agricultural region that was increasingly dependent on slave labor. By 1790 the southern states were exporting as much tobacco as they had been before the Revolution, and new farm commodities such as grains, indigo, and hemp helped diversify the economy. Most important, however, was the surge in cotton production. Between 1790 and 1815 the annual production of cotton rose from less than 3 million pounds to 93 million pounds.

The United States in 1790 was predominantly a rural society. Eighty percent of households were involved in agricultural production. Only a few cities had more than 5,000 people. The first national census, taken in 1790, reported that there were 750,000 African Americans, almost one-fifth of the population. Most of them lived in the five southernmost states. Less than 10 percent of the blacks lived outside the South. Most African Americans, of course, were slaves, but there were many free blacks as a result of the revolutionary turmoil. In fact, the proportion of free blacks to slaves was never higher than in 1790.

The 1790 census did not even include the many Indians still living east of the Mississippi River. Most Americans still viewed the Native Americans as those peoples whom the Declaration of Independence dismissed as "merciless Indian savages." It is estimated that there were over eighty tribes numbering perhaps as many as 150,000 persons in 1790. In the Old Northwest along the Great Lakes, the British continued to arm the Indians and encouraged them to resist American encroachments. Between 1784 and 1790, Indians killed or captured some 1,500 settlers in Kentucky alone. Such bloodshed generated a ferocious reaction. "The people of Kentucky," observed an official frustrated by his inability to negotiate a treaty between whites and Indians, "will carry on private expeditions against the Indians and kill them whenever they meet them, and I do not believe there is a jury in all Kentucky that will punish a man for it." In the South the five most powerful tribes—the Cherokees, Chickasaws, Choctaws, Creeks, and Seminoles—numbered between 50,000 and 100,000. They steadfastly refused to recognize American authority and used Spanish-supplied weapons to thwart white settlement.

Only about 125,000 whites and blacks lived west of the Appalachians in 1790. But that was soon to change. The great theme of nineteenth-century American history would be the ceaseless stream of migrants flowing westward from the Atlantic seaboard. By foot, horse, boat, and wagon, pioneers and adventurers headed west. "A rage for emigrating to the western country prevails," noted New Yorker John Jay in 1785, "and thousands have already fixed their habitations in that wilderness. . . . The seeds of a great people are daily planting beyond the mountains." Kentucky, still a part of Virginia but destined for statehood in 1792, harbored 75,000 settlers in 1790. In 1776 there had been only 150 pioneers.

Rapid population growth, cheap land, and new economic opportunities fueled this phenomenon. Although immigrants contributed significantly to the rising numbers, the extraordinary growth rate resulted primarily from natural increase. The average white woman gave birth to eight children, and the white population doubled approximately once every twenty-two years. This made for a very young population on average. In 1790 almost half of all white Americans were under the age of sixteen.

A NEW GOVERNMENT   The men who drafted the Constitution and helped to gain its ratification were justifiably proud of their achievement. But they knew that many questions were left unanswered. And they feared that putting the new form of government into practice would pose unexpected challenges. The new Congress of the United States opened with a whimper rather than a bang. On March 4, 1789, the appointed date of its first session in bustling New York City, only eight senators and thirteen representatives took their seats. A month passed before both chambers gathered a quorum. Only then could the temporary presiding officer of the Senate count the ballots and certify the foregone conclusion that George Washington, with sixty-nine votes, was the unanimous choice of the electoral college for president. John Adams, with thirty-four votes, the second-highest number, became vice-president.

Washington's journey from Mount Vernon, Virginia, to New York, where he was inaugurated on April 30, turned into a triumphal procession that confirmed the universal confidence he commanded. But the fifty-seven-year-old Washington, tall and imposing, grown gray-haired, partly deaf, and almost toothless, himself confessed to feeling like "a culprit who is going to his place of execution," burdened with dread that so much was expected of him: "I face an ocean of difficulties." An

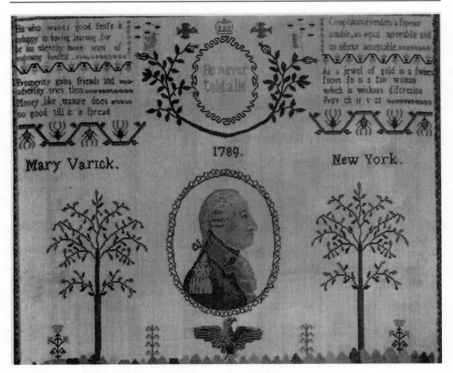

Mary Varick's sampler celebrates George Washington's inauguration as president of the United States in 1789.

awkward speaker, he shook visibly as he read his inaugural address. The new nation of 4 million Americans, however, required not brilliant oratory but firm leadership, and Washington possessed that in abundance.

GOVERNMENTAL STRUCTURE   The president and the Congress had to create a government anew. Washington inherited but the shadow of a bureaucracy: a foreign office with John Jay at its head and two clerks; a Treasury Board with little or no treasury; a 300-pound secretary of war, Henry Knox, with a lightweight army of 672 officers and men, and no navy at all; a heavy federal debt and almost no federal revenue.

During the summer of 1789 Congress created executive departments corresponding in each case to those already formed under the Confederation. To head the Department of State Washington named Thomas Jefferson, recently back from his mission to France. Leadership of the Department of the Treasury went to Washington's wartime aide Alexander Hamilton, who had since become a prominent lawyer in New York.

Tall, graceful Edmund Randolph, former governor of Virginia and owner of a 7,000-acre, debt-ridden plantation worked by 200 slaves, assumed the new position of attorney-general.

Almost from the beginning Washington routinely called these men to sit as a group for discussion and advice on policy matters. This was the origin of the president's cabinet, an advisory body for which the Constitution made no formal provision—except insofar as it provided for the heads of departments. The office of vice-president also took on what would become its typical character. "The Vice-Presidency," John Adams wrote his wife, Abigail, was the most "insignificant office . . . ever . . . contrived."

As the first chief justice of the Supreme Court, Washington named New Yorker John Jay, who served until 1795. Born in New York City in 1745, Jay graduated from King's College (now Columbia University) in 1764. His distinction as a lawyer led New York to send him as its representative to the First and Second Continental Congresses. After serving as president of the Continental Congress in 1779, Jay became the American minister in Spain. While in Europe he helped John Adams and Benjamin Franklin negotiate the Treaty of Paris in 1783. After the Revolution Jay served as secretary of foreign affairs. He then joined Madison and Hamilton as co-author of *The Federalist* and became one of the most effective champions of the Constitution.

THE BILL OF RIGHTS   In the new House of Representatives, James Madison made a Bill of Rights one of the first items of business. The lack of protection for individual rights had been one of the anti-Federalists' major objections to the Constitution. During the ratification debate, Madison and other Federalists had argued that the Constitution needed no enumeration of specific "rights" because, as Madison said, "everything not granted is reserved." He later said that the proposals for a Bill of Rights were "unnecessary and dangerous." He feared that any list of rights would be incomplete. Madison and other Federalists also worried that specifying such rights might imply the existence of a parallel set of powers never meant to be delegated to the central government. Or, as Alexander Hamilton phrased it in the eighty-fourth paper of *The Federalist,* "Why declare things should not be done which there is no power to do?"

But public anxiety about individual rights persisted, so in May 1789

Madison reluctantly drew the first eight amendments from the Virginia Bill of Rights, which George Mason had written in 1776. These all provided safeguards for certain fundamental individual rights: freedom of religion, press, speech, and assembly; the right to keep and bear firearms; the right to refuse to house soldiers in private homes; protection from unreasonable searches and seizures; the right to refuse to testify against oneself; the right to a speedy public trial before an impartial jury and to have legal counsel present; and protection against cruel and unusual punishment. The Ninth and Tenth Amendments declared that the enumeration of rights in the Constitution "shall not be construed to deny or disparage others retained by the people" and that "powers not delegated to the United States by the Constitution . . . are reserved to the States respectively, or to the people." The states voted separately on each proposed amendment, and the Bill of Rights became effective December 15, 1791.

Madison viewed the Bill of Rights as "the most dramatic single gesture of conciliation that could be offered the remaining opponents of the government." Those "opponents" included prominent statesmen such as Virginians George Mason and Richard Henry Lee as well as artisans, small traders, and backcountry farmers who expressed a profound egalitarianism. These "poor and middling" folk were skeptical that even the "best men" were capable of subordinating self-interest to the good of the Republic. Said one semiliterate Maine democrat: "I never wish to be in the power of any Sett of Men let them be never so good, but hope to be left in the hands of my Country." He and other anti-Federalists argued that no country could be founded on the premise that its leaders would possess an extraordinary degree of civic virtue. All people were prone to corruption. No one could be trusted. Therefore, a Bill of Rights was necessary to protect the liberties of all against the encroachments of a few. The Bill of Rights provided no rights or legal protection to African Americans.

HAMILTON'S VISION OF AMERICA

Revenue was the new federal government's most critical need, and Congress quickly enacted a tariff (a tax on imports) intended to raise revenue and protect America's new manufacturers from foreign competition by raising prices on imported goods. Tariffs and tonnage duties resulted in higher prices on goods bought by Americans, most of whom were tied to the farm economy. This raised a basic and perennial question: should these rural consumers be forced to subsidize the nation's infant manufacturing sector?

The tariff launched the effort to get the country on a sound financial basis. In finance, with all its broad implications for policy in general, it was thirty-four-year-old Alexander Hamilton who seized the initiative. The first secretary of the treasury was the protégé of the president. Born out of wedlock on a Caribbean island, deserted by a ne'er-do-well Scottish father, Hamilton was left an orphan at thirteen by the death of his mother. With the help of friends and relatives, he found his way at seventeen to New York, attended King's College (later Columbia University), entered the revolutionary agitations as speaker and pamphleteer, and joined the army, where he attracted Washington's attention. Hamilton distinguished himself at the siege of Yorktown, and he remained a frustrated military genius, hungry for greater glory on the field of battle. He studied law, passed the bar examination, established a legal practice in New York, and became a self-made aristocrat, serving as collector of revenues and member of the Confederation Congress. An early convert to nationalism, he played a crucial part in promoting the Constitutional Convention and defending its work in the *The Federalist.*

The new government needed all of Hamilton's ambition and brilliance. In a series of classic reports submitted to Congress in 1790 and 1791, he outlined his program for government finances and the economic development of the United States. The reports were soon adopted, with some alterations in detail but little in substance. Less well-received was the last of the series, the Report on Manufactures, which outlined a neomercantilist program of protective tariffs and other governmental aid to business.

ESTABLISHING THE PUBLIC CREDIT   The First Report on the Public Credit made two key recommendations: first, funding of the federal debt at face value, which meant that those citizens holding government securities could exchange them for new interest-bearing bonds of the same face value; and second, the federal government's assumption of state debts from the Revolution to the amount of $21 million. The funding scheme was controversial because many farmers and soldiers in need of immediate money had sold their securities for a fraction of their value to speculators. Spokesmen for these Americans argued that they should be reimbursed for their losses; otherwise, the speculators would gain a windfall. Hamilton sternly resisted. The speculators, he argued, had "paid what the commodity was worth in the market, and took the risks." Therefore, they should reap the benefits. In fact, Hamilton insisted, the government should do all it could to win over the financial community because it represented the bedrock of a successful nation.

Hamilton's report echoed the one Robert Morris had urged upon the Confederation a decade before, one that Hamilton had strongly endorsed at the time. As Hamilton had written Morris in 1781, a "national debt, if it is not excessive, will be to us a great national blessing." Payment of the national debt, both felt, would be not only a point of national honor and sound finance, ensuring the country's credit for the future; it would also be an occasion to assert a national taxing power and thus instill respect for the authority of the national government.

It was on this point, however, that Madison, who had been Hamilton's close ally in the movement for a stronger government, broke with him. Their disagreement carried ominous overtones of sectionalism. Madison did not question that the debt should be paid, but was troubled that speculators and "stock-jobbers" would become the chief beneficiaries. Also disturbing was the fact that northerners held most of the debt. Madison's opposition touched off a vigorous debate that deadlocked the whole question of debt funding and assumption through much of 1790.

The stalemate finally ended when Hamilton, Jefferson, and Madison reached an understanding. In return for northern votes in favor of locating the permanent national capital on the Potomac, Madison pledged to seek enough southern votes to pass the assumption bill, with the further arrangement that those states with smaller debts would get in effect outright grants from the federal government to equalize the difference. These arrangements secured enough votes to carry Hamilton's funding and assumption plans. The capital would be moved to Philadelphia for ten years, after which it would be settled at a new federal city on the Potomac, the site to be chosen by the president. In August 1790 Congress finally passed the legislation for Hamilton's plan.

A NATIONAL BANK   Through this vast program of funding and assumption, Hamilton had called up from nowhere, as if by magic, a great sum of capital. As he put it in his original report, a national debt "answers most of the purposes of money." Transfers of government bonds, once the debt was properly funded, would be equivalent to monetary payments. This feature of the program was especially important in a country that had, from the first settlements, suffered a shortage of hard money.

Having established the public credit, Hamilton moved on to a related measure essential to his vision of national greatness. He called for a national bank, which by issuance of banknotes (paper money) might provide a uniform currency as well as a source of capital for the developing economy. Government bonds held by the bank would back up the currency. The national bank, chartered by Congress, would remain under governmental surveillance, but private investors would supply four-fifths of the $10 million capital and name twenty of the twenty-five directors; the government would purchase the other fifth of the capital and name five directors. Government bonds would be received in payment for three-fourths of the stock in the bank, and the other fourth would be payable in gold and silver.

Once again Madison rose to lead the opposition, arguing that he could find no basis in the Constitution for such a bank. That was enough to raise in President Washington's mind serious doubts as to the constitutionality of the measure, which Congress passed over Madison's objections. Before signing the bill into law, therefore, the president sought the advice of his cabinet and found an equal division of opinion. This resulted in the first great debate on constitutional interpretation. Should there be a strict or a broad construction of the document? Were the powers of Congress only those explicitly stated in the Constitution or were others implied? The argument turned chiefly on Article I, Section 8, which authorized Congress to "make all laws which shall be necessary and proper for carrying into execution the foregoing Powers."

Such language left room for disagreement and led to a confrontation between Jefferson and Hamilton. Jefferson pointed to the Tenth Amendment, which reserved to the states and the people powers not delegated to Congress. A bank might be a convenient aid to Congress in collecting taxes and regulating the currency, but it was not, as Article I,

Section 8, specified, *necessary.* Hamilton insisted that the power to charter corporations was included in the sovereignty of any government, whether or not expressly stated. The president accepted Hamilton's argument and signed the bill. By doing so, in Jefferson's words, he opened up "a boundless field of power," which in coming years would lead to a further broadening of implied powers with the approval of the Supreme Court.

ENCOURAGING MANUFACTURES   Hamilton's imagination and his ambitions for the new country were not yet exhausted. At the end of 1790, he submitted a Second Report on Public Credit, which included a proposal for an excise tax on alcoholic beverages to aid in raising revenue to cover the nation's debts. Six weeks later, the secretary proposed a national mint—which was established in 1792. And finally, on December 5, 1791, as the culmination of his basic reports, the Report on Manufactures proposed an extensive program of government aid to the development of manufacturing enterprises.

In the Report on Manufactures, Hamilton argued for the active encouragement of manufacturing to provide productive uses for the new capital he had created by his funding, assumption, and banking schemes. Multiple advantages would flow from the development of manufactures: the diversification of labor in a country given over too exclusively to farming; greater use of machinery; work for those not ordinarily employed, such as women and children; the promotion of immigration; a greater scope for the diversity of talents in business; and a better domestic market for agricultural products.

To secure his ends Hamilton advocated protective tariffs, "which in some cases might be put so high as to keep out foreign products altogether; restraints on the export of raw materials; bounties and premiums to encourage certain industries; inducements to inventions and discoveries; and finally, the encouragement of internal improvements in transportation, the development of roads, canals, and navigable streams."

Some of his tariff proposals were enacted in 1792. Otherwise the program was filed away—but not forgotten. It provided an arsenal of arguments for the manufacturing sector in years to come. Hamilton denied that his scheme favored the northern states. If, as seemed likely, the northern and middle states should become the chief sites for manufacturing, he claimed, they would create robust markets for agricultural products, some of which the southern states were peculiarly qualified to produce. The nation as a whole would benefit, he argued, as commerce between North and South increased, supplanting the trade across the Atlantic.

HAMILTON'S ACHIEVEMENT   Largely because of the skillful Hamilton, the Treasury Department began retiring the Revolutionary War debt, enhanced the value of a "Continental" dollar, secured the government's credit, and attracted foreign investment capital. Prosperity, so elusive in the 1780s, began to flourish once again, although President Washington cautioned against attributing "to the Government what is due only to the goodness of Providence."

Yet suspicions lingered that Hamilton had designed his program to promote a particular class and sectional interest, and some even thought a personal interest. Such charges were largely without foundation. There is no reason to believe that Hamilton's conscious aim was to benefit either a section or a class at the expense of the country. He was inclined toward a truly nationalist outlook, and he focused his energies on the rising power of commercial capitalism. Tying the government closely to the rich and the well-born, Hamilton believed, promoted the government's financial stability and guarded the public order against the potential turbulence that always haunted him.

But many Americans then and since have interpreted such views as elitist and self-serving. To be sure, Hamilton never understood the people of the small villages and farms, the people of the frontier. They were foreign to his world, despite his own humble beginnings. And they, along with the planters of the South, would be at best only indirect beneficiaries of his programs. There were, in short, vast numbers of people who saw little gain from the Hamiltonian program and thus were drawn into opposition. Indeed, Jefferson claimed that he and Hamilton were "pitted against each other every day in the cabinet like two fighting-cocks."

THE REPUBLICAN ALTERNATIVE

In this split over the Hamiltonian program lay the seeds of the first national political parties. Hamilton emerged as the embodiment of the party known as the Federalists; Madison and Jefferson assumed the leadership of those who took the name Republicans and thereby implied that the Federalists really aimed at a monarchy. Parties were slow in developing, or at least in being acknowledged as legitimate. All the political philosophers of the age deplored the spirit of party, or faction. The concept of a loyal opposition, of a two-party system as a positive good, was yet to be formulated. Parties, or "factions," were bodies of men bent upon self-aggrandizement through the favor of the government. They smelled of corruption. As Jefferson once remarked, "If I could not go to heaven but with a party I would not go there at all."

Neither side in the disagreement over national policy deliberately set out to create a party system. But there were important differences of both philosophy and self-interest that simply would not dissolve, and the strongly partisan and often malicious newspapers of the day ensured that such differences were repeatedly accented for the reading public.

The crux of the debate centered on the relative power of the federal government and the states. At the outset Madison assumed leadership of Hamilton's opponents in the Congress, and he argued that Hamilton was trampling upon states' rights in forging a consolidated central government. After the compromise on the funding of state debts, Jefferson joined Madison in ever more resolute opposition to Hamilton's policies. They opposed his move to place an excise tax on whiskey, which would especially burden the trans-Appalachian farmers, whose grain was the source of that liquid; his proposal for a national bank; and his report on manufactures. Against the last two both men raised constitutional objections. As these differences developed, the personal hostility between Jefferson and Hamilton festered, much to the distress of President Washington. In the process, Jefferson, the temperamentally shy and retiring secretary of state, emerged as the leader of the opposition to Hamilton's policies within the administration, while Madison continued to direct the opposition in Congress.

JEFFERSON'S AGRARIAN VIEW   Thomas Jefferson, twelve years Hamilton's senior, was in most respects his opposite. In contrast to the self-made Hamilton, Jefferson was to the manor born, son of a successful surveyor and land speculator. Displaying little of Hamilton's ordered intensity, Jefferson instead conveyed an aristocratic carelessness and a

*Thomas Jefferson. A portrait by Charles
Willson Peale (1791).*

breadth of cultivated interests that ranged perhaps more widely in science, the arts, and the humanities than those of any contemporary,
even Franklin. Jefferson read or spoke seven languages. He was an architect of some distinction (Monticello, the Virginia Capitol, and the
University of Virginia are monuments to his talent), a man who understood mathematics and engineering, an inventor, an agronomist. In his
Notes on Virginia (1785) he displayed a knowledge of geography, pale-
ontology, zoology, botany, and archeology. He collected paintings and
sculpture, knew music and practiced the violin, although some said
only Patrick Henry played it worse.

Philosophically, Hamilton and Jefferson had contrasting visions of
the character of the Union in the first generation under the Constitution, and their opposite views defined certain fundamental issues of
American life that still echo two centuries later. Hamilton foresaw a di-
versified capitalistic economy, agriculture balanced by commerce and
industry, and was thus the better prophet. Jefferson feared the growth
of crowded cities divided into a capitalistic aristocracy on the one hand
and a deprived working class on the other. Hamilton feared anarchy and
loved order; Jefferson feared tyranny and loved liberty.

Where Hamilton wanted a strong central government run by a
wealthy elite actively encouraging capitalistic enterprise, Jefferson desired a decentralized agrarian republic. "I am not a friend to a very ener-

getic government," he once stressed; nor was he a friend of the financial and commercial elite. Jefferson's ideal republic was to remain one in which small farmers predominated: "Those who labor in the earth," he wrote, "are the chosen people of God, if ever he had a chosen people, whose breasts He has made His peculiar deposit for genuine and substantial virtue." Jefferson did not oppose all forms of manufacturing. What he feared was that the unlimited expansion of commerce and industry would produce a class of propertyless wage laborers who were dependent on others for their livelihood and therefore subject to political manipulation and economic exploitation.

Jefferson, who spent several years in France, was the enlightened *philosophe,* the natural radical and reformer who attacked the aristocratic relics of entail and primogeniture in Virginia, opposed an established church, proposed an elaborate plan for public schools, prepared a more humane criminal code, and was instrumental in eliminating slavery from the Old Northwest, although he kept the slaves he had inherited. On his tomb were finally recorded his proudest achievements: author of the Declaration of Independence and the Virginia Statute of Religious Freedom, and founder of the University of Virginia.

CRISES FOREIGN AND DOMESTIC

As the disputes between Jefferson and Hamilton intensified, Washington proved ever more adept at transcending party differences and holding things together with his unmatched prestige. In 1792 he won unanimous reelection, and no sooner had his second term begun than problems of foreign relations leapt to center stage, brought there by the consequences of the French Revolution, which had begun during the first months of Washington's presidency. Americans supported the popular revolt against the French monarchy, up to a point. By the spring of 1792, though, the hopeful experiment in liberty, equality, and fraternity had turned into a monster that plunged France into war with Austria and Prussia and began devouring its own children along with its enemies in the Terror of 1793–1794.

After the execution of King Louis XVI in 1793, Great Britain joined with the monarchies of Spain and Holland in a war against the French Republic. For the next twenty-two years Britain and France were at war, with only a brief respite, until the final defeat of the French forces under Napoleon in 1815. The war presented Washington, just beginning his second term, with an awkward problem. By the treaty of 1778 the United States was a perpetual ally of France, obligated to defend her possessions in the West Indies.

But Americans wanted no part of the war. They were determined to maintain their lucrative trade with both sides of the European conflict. Of course, the combatants resented and resisted America's profitable neutrality. For their part, Hamilton and Jefferson found in the neutrality policy one issue on which they could agree. Where they differed was in how best to implement the policy. On April 22, 1793, President Washington issued a neutrality proclamation that simply declared the United States "friendly and impartial toward the belligerent powers."

CITIZEN GENÊT   At the same time, Washington accepted Jefferson's argument that the United States should recognize the new French government (becoming the first country to do so) and receive its new ambassador, Edmond Charles Genêt. Early in 1793 Genêt landed at Charleston, South Carolina, and made his way northward to New York. Along the way he brazenly began engaging in quite un-neutral activities. He outfitted privateers for use against the British royal navy and intrigued with frontiersmen and land speculators to launch an attack on Spanish Florida and Louisiana in retaliation for Spain's opposition to the French Revolution.

Genêt quickly became an embarrassment even to his Republican friends. "His conduct has been that of a madman," Madison charged. The cabinet finally agreed unanimously that he had to go, and Washington demanded his recall. Genêt's foolishness and the growing excesses of the French radicals were fast cooling American support for their revolution. To Hamilton's followers it began to resemble their worst nightmares of democratic anarchy and infidelity. The French made it hard even for Republicans to retain sympathy, but Jefferson and others swallowed hard and made excuses. Nor did the British make it easy for Federalists to rally to their side. Near the end of 1793 they announced Orders in Council under which they seized the cargoes of American ships with provisions for or produce from French islands in the Caribbean.

Despite the offenses by both sides, the French and British causes polarized American opinion and the two parties. In the contest, it seemed, one had to be either a Republican and support liberty, reason, and France or a Federalist and support order, religious faith, and Britain. And the division gave rise to some curious loyalties: slave-holding planters cheered Jacobin radicals who dispossessed their aristocratic counterparts in France, while Massachusetts shippers, who still profited from the British trade, kept quiet about British seizures of American ships. Boston, once a hotbed of revolution, became a bastion of Federalism.

JAY'S TREATY   Early in 1794 Republican leaders in Congress were gaining support for commercial retaliation to bring the British to their senses, when the British gave Washington a timely opening for a settlement. They repealed the Orders under which American ships were being seized, and on April 16, 1794, Washington named Chief Justice John Jay as a special envoy to Great Britain. Jay left with instructions to settle all major issues: to get the British out of their posts along the western frontier and to win reparations for the losses of American shippers, compensation for slaves carried away in 1783, and a commercial treaty that would legalize American commerce with the British West Indies.

The pro-British Jay, however, had little leverage with which to wring concessions from the British, and after seven months of negotiations he won only two pledges: the British promised to evacuate the northwest posts by 1796 and to pay damages for the seizures of American ships and cargoes in 1793–1794. In exchange for these gains, Jay conceded the British definition of neutral rights. He accepted the principles that provisions could not go in neutral ships to enemy ports, and that trade with enemy colonies prohibited in peacetime could not be opened in wartime (the "Rule of 1756"). Britain gained most-favored-nation treatment in American commerce and a promise that French privateers would not be outfitted in American ports. Jay also conceded that the long-standing American debts to British merchants would be adjudicated and paid by the American government. Perhaps most important, he failed to gain access for American shippers to the British West Indies.

Public outrage greeted the terms of the treaty. Even Federalist shippers, ready for settlement on almost any terms, criticized Jay's failure to open up the British West Indies to American commerce. But much of the outcry came from disappointed Republican partisans who sought an escalation of conflict with hated England. Jay remarked that he could travel across the country by the light of his burning effigies. Yet the Senate debated the treaty in secret, and in the end moderation prevailed. Without a single vote to spare, Jay's Treaty won the necessary two-thirds majority on June 24, 1795. Washington hesitated but finally signed the treaty as the best he was likely to get and out of fear that refusal would throw the United States into the role of a French satellite.

THE FRONTIER STIRS   Other events also had an important bearing on Jay's Treaty, adding force to the importance of its settlement of the Canadian frontier. While Jay was haggling in London, frontier conflict with Indians was moving toward a temporary resolution. Washington had named General Wayne, known as "Mad Anthony," to head an expedition into the Northwest Territory, and in the fall of 1793 he marched into Indian country with some 2,600 men. On August 4, 1794, Indians representing eight tribes, led by the Miami and reinforced by some Canadian militia, attacked Wayne's force at the Battle of Fallen Timbers. The Americans repulsed them with heavy Indian losses, after which American detachments destroyed their fields and villages. Dispersed and decimated, the Indians finally agreed to the Treaty of Greenville, signed in 1795. In the treaty, at the cost of a $10,000 annuity, the United States bought from twelve tribes the rights to the southeastern quarter of the Northwest Territory (now Ohio and Indiana) and enclaves at the sites of Vincennes, Detroit, and Chicago.

THE WHISKEY REBELLION   Wayne's forces were still mopping up after the Battle of Fallen Timbers when the administration decided on another show of strength in the backcountry against the so-called Whiskey Rebellion. Hamilton's excise tax on strong drink, levied in 1791, had angered frontier farmers because it taxed their staple crop. Their grain was more easily transported to market in concentrated liquid form than in bulk. A pack horse, for example, could carry two bushels of unprocessed rye, but it could carry two barrels of whiskey representing twenty-four bushels of rye. Frontiersmen considered the tax another part of Hamilton's scheme to pick the pockets of the poor to enrich privileged speculators. All through the backcountry, from Georgia to Pennsylvania and beyond, the tax provoked resistance and evasion. In the summer of 1794 the rumblings of discontent broke into open rebellion in Pennsylvania's four western counties, where vigilantes, mostly of Scottish or Irish descent, organized to terrorize revenuers and taxpayers. One group, disguised as women, assaulted a revenue collector, cropped his hair, coated him with tar and feathers, and stole his horse. Other rebels robbed the mails, stopped court proceedings, and threatened an assault on Pittsburgh. On August 7, 1794, President Washington issued a proclamation ordering the rebels to disperse and go home, and calling out militiamen from Virginia, Maryland, Pennsylvania, and New Jersey. Getting no response from the "Whiskey Boys," he issued a proclamation for suppression of the rebellion.

Under the command of Virginia's governor, General Henry (Light-Horse Harry) Lee, 13,000 men, a force larger than any Washington had ever commanded in the Revolution, marched out from Harrisburg across the Alleghenies with Hamilton in their midst, itching to smite the insurgents. But the rebels vaporized like corn mash when heated. By dint of great effort and much marching, the troops finally rounded up twenty barefoot, ragged prisoners, whom they paraded down Market Street in Philadelphia and clapped into prison. Some of the soldiers regretted not having cornered the rebels. As one of the militiamen explained, "We all lament that so few of the insurgents fell—such disorders can only be cured by copious bleedings." There was, in fact, little bleeding of any kind. One of the captured rebels died in prison. Two were convicted of treason and sentenced to be hanged, but Washington pardoned them on the grounds that one was a "simpleton" and the other "insane." The government had made its point in defense of the rule of law and federal authority. It thereby gained "reputation and strength," according to Hamilton, by suppressing a rebellion that, in Jefferson's words, "could never be found." But this came at the cost of creating or confirming new numbers of Republicans, who scored heavily in the next Pennsylvania elections.

PINCKNEY'S TREATY   While these stirring events were transpiring in the Keystone State, Spain was suffering some setbacks to its schemes to consolidate its control over Florida and the Louisiana territory. Spain had refused to recognize the legitimacy of America's southern boundary established by the Treaty of Paris in 1783, and its agents thereafter sought to thwart American expansion southward. Spanish intrigues

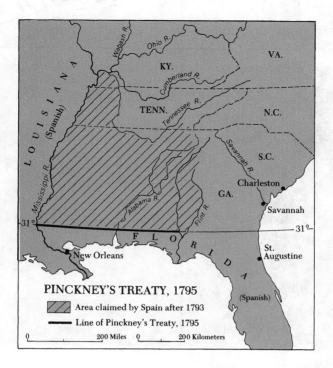

PINCKNEY'S TREATY, 1795

///// Area claimed by Spain after 1793
── Line of Pinckney's Treaty, 1795

0 ⎯⎯⎯ 200 Miles   0 ⎯⎯⎯ 200 Kilometers

among the Creeks, Choctaws, Chickasaws, and Cherokees were keeping up the same turmoil the British fomented along the Ohio.

But for reasons growing out of the shifting balance of power in Europe, Spain decided in the mid-1790s to end its designs on America. This change of heart resulted in Pinckney's Treaty (1795), by which United States Minister Thomas Pinckney won acceptance of an American boundary at the thirty-first parallel; free navigation of the Mississippi; the right to deposit goods at New Orleans without having to pay customs duties for a period of three years (with promise of renewal); a commission to settle American claims against Spain; and a promise on each side to refrain from inciting Indian attacks on the other. Ratification of the Pinckney Treaty ran into no opposition. Indeed, it was immensely popular, especially among westerners eager to use the Mississippi River to transport their crops to market.

Now that Jay and Pinckney had settled matters with Britain and Spain, and General Wayne in the Northwest had ended organized Indian resistance, a renewed surge of settlers headed for the West. New lands, ceded by the Indians in the Treaty of Greenville, revealed Congress once again divided on land policy. There were two basic viewpoints on the matter, one that the public domain should serve mainly as a source of revenue, the other that it was more important to accommo-

A newly cleared American farm.

date settlers with low prices, even free land, and get the country settled. In the long run policy would evolve from the first toward the second viewpoint, but for the time being the government's need for revenue took priority.

Opinions on land policy, like other issues, separated Federalists from Republicans. Federalists involved in speculation might prefer lower land prices, but the more influential Federalists like Hamilton and Jay preferred to build the population of the eastern states first, lest the East lose political influence and a labor force important to the future growth of manufactures. Men of their persuasion favored high land prices to enrich the treasury, and the sale of relatively large parcels of land to speculators rather than small tracts to actual settlers. Jefferson and Madison were reluctantly prepared to go along with such a land policy for the sake of reducing the national debt, but Jefferson yearned for a plan by which the lands could be more readily settled. In any case, he suggested, frontiersmen would do as they had done before: "They will settle the lands in spite of everybody." The Daniel Boones of the West, always moving out beyond the settlers and surveyors, were already proving him right.

The Federalist land policy prevailed in the Land Act of 1796, which retained the 640-acre minimum size mandated by the Northwest Ordinance of 1787 while doubling the price per acre to $2 and requiring that the full amount be paid within a year. This was well beyond the means of most settlers and even many speculators. As a result, by 1800 government land offices had sold fewer than 50,000 acres. Continuing demands for cheaper land led to the Land Act of 1800, which reduced the minimum sale to 320 acres and spread the payments over four years. Thus with a down payment of $160 one could get a farm. The Land Act of 1804 further reduced the minimum parcel to 160 acres, which became the traditional homestead, and the price per acre went down to $1.64.

WASHINGTON'S FAREWELL   By 1796 President Washington had decided that two terms in office were enough. Tired of the political quarrels and the venom of the partisan press, he was ready to retire to Mount Vernon. He would leave behind a formidable record of achievement: the organization of a national government with demonstrated power, establishment of the national credit, the settlement of territory previously held by Britain and Spain, stabilization of the northwestern frontier, and the admission of three new states: Vermont (1791), Kentucky (1792), and Tennessee (1796). With the help of Jay and especially Hamilton, Washington set about preparing a valedictory address, using a draft prepared by Madison four years before.

Washington's Farewell Address focused on domestic policy and particularly on the need for unity among Americans in backing their new government. Washington decried the "baneful effects" of sectionalism and partisanship, while acknowledging a body of opinion that parties were "useful checks upon the administration of the government, and serve to keep alive the spirit of liberty."

In foreign relations, he asserted, America should show "good faith and justice toward all nations" and avoid either "an habitual hatred or an habitual fondness" for other countries. The United States should also "steer clear of permanent alliances with any portion of the foreign world." This statement drew little notice at the time, but it proved to be profoundly important in affecting American attitudes toward foreign policy for generations thereafter. Later spokesmen for an isolationist policy would distort Washington's position by claiming that he had opposed any "entangling alliances." On the contrary, Washington was not preaching isolationism; he was instead warning against any further permanent arrangements like the one with France, still technically in effect. Washington recognized that "we may safely trust to temporary alliances for extraordinary emergencies." Washington's warning against permanent foreign entanglements thereafter served as a fundamental principle in American foreign policy until the early twentieth century.

THE ADAMS YEARS

With Washington out of the race, the United States in 1796 held its first partisan election for president. The logical choice of the Federalists would have been Washington's protégé Hamilton, the chief architect of their programs. But like many a later presidential candidate, Hamilton was not "available," however willing. His policies had left scars and made enemies. Nor did he suffer fools gladly, a common affliction of Federalist leaders, including the man on whom the choice fell. In Philadelphia a caucus of Federalist congressmen chose John Adams as heir apparent, with Thomas Pinckney of South Carolina, fresh from his triumph in Spain, as nominee for vice-president. As expected, the Republicans drafted Jefferson and added geographical balance to the ticket with Aaron Burr of New York.

The rising strength of the Republicans, largely due to the smoldering resentment toward Jay's Treaty, very nearly swept Jefferson into office, and perhaps would have but for the public appeals of the French ambassador for Jefferson's election—an action that backfired. The Federalists won a majority among the electors, but Alexander Hamilton hatched an impulsive scheme that very nearly threw the election away after all. Between Hamilton and Adams there had been no love lost since the Revolution. As Abigail Adams warned her husband, Hamilton "is a man ambitious as Julius Caesar, a subtle intriguer. His abilities would make him dangerous if he was to espouse a wrong side, his thirst for fame is insatiable. I ever kept my Eye on him." Abigail was typically observant, for Hamilton indeed was plotting to thwart Adams's bid for the presidency. Thomas Pinckney, Hamilton thought, would be easier to influence than the strong-minded Adams. He therefore sought to have South Carolina Federalists withhold a few votes from Adams and bring Pinckney in first. The Carolinians cooperated, but New Englanders got wind of the scheme and dropped Pinckney. The upshot of

The Providential Detection. *An anti-Republican cartoon shows the American eagle arriving just in time to stop Thomas Jefferson from burning the Constitution on the "Altar to Gallic Despotism."*

Hamilton's intrigue was to cut Pinckney out of both offices and elect Jefferson as vice-president with sixty-eight votes, second to Adams's seventy-one.

Adams had behind him a distinguished career as a Massachusetts lawyer, a leader in the revolutionary movement and the Continental Congress, a diplomat in France, Holland, and Britain, and as vice-president. His political philosophy fell somewhere between Jefferson's and Hamilton's. He shared neither the one's faith in the common people nor the other's fondness for an aristocracy of "paper wealth." He favored the classic republican balance of aristocratic, democratic, and monarchical elements in government. A man of powerful intellect, forthright convictions, and uncontrollable vanity, Adams was always haunted by the feeling that he was never properly appreciated—and he may have been right. On the overriding issue of his administration, war and peace, he kept his head when others about him were losing theirs—probably at the cost of his reelection.

WAR WITH FRANCE   Adams inherited from Washington his divided cabinet—there was as yet no precedent for changing personnel with each new administration. Adams also inherited a menacing quarrel with France, a by-product of Jay's Treaty. When Jay accepted the British position that food supplies and naval stores—as well as war matériel—bound for enemy ports were contraband subject to seizure, the French reasoned that American cargoes in the British trade were subject to the same interpretation. The French loosed their corsairs with even more devastating effect than the British had in 1793–1794. By the time of Adams's inauguration in 1797, the French had plundered some 300 American ships and had broken diplomatic relations with the United States.

Adams immediately acted to restore relations in the face of an outcry for war from the "High Federalists," including Secretary of State Timothy Pickering. Hamilton, however, agreed with Adams on this point and approved his last-ditch effort for a settlement. In 1797 Charles C. Pinckney sailed for Paris with John Marshall (a Virginia Federalist) and Elbridge Gerry (a Massachusetts Republican) for further negotiations. After long, nagging delays, the three commissioners were accosted by three French counterparts (whom Adams labeled X, Y, and Z in his report to Congress), agents of Foreign Minister Talleyrand, a past master of the diplomatic shakedown. The three French diplomats delicately let it be known that negotiations could begin only if there were a loan to France of $12 million, a bribe of $250,000 to the five directors then heading the government, and suitable apologies for remarks recently made in Adams's message to Congress.

Such bribes were common eighteenth-century diplomatic practice—Washington himself had bribed a Creek chieftain, and ransomed American sailors from Algerian pirates at a cost of $100,000 each—but Talleyrand's price was high merely for a promise to negotiate. The answer, according to the commissioners' report, was "no, no, not a sixpence." When the XYZ Affair broke in Congress and the public press, this was translated into the more stirring slogan "Millions for defense but not one cent for tribute." Expressions of hostility toward France rose to a crescendo—even the most partisan Republicans were hard put to make any more excuses—and many of them joined a chorus for war. An undeclared naval war in fact raged from 1798 to 1800, but Adams resisted a formal declaration of war. Congress, however, authorized the capture of

A cartoon indicating the anti-French feeling generated by the XYZ Affair. The three American ministers at left reject the "Paris Monster's" demand for money.

armed French ships, suspended commerce with France, and renounced the alliance of 1778, which was already bankrupt.

Adams used the French crisis to strengthen American defenses. An American navy had ceased to exist at the end of the Revolution, but after Algerian pirates began to prey on American merchant vessels in the Mediterranean, Congress, in 1794, authorized the arming of six ships. Three of these—the *Constitution,* the *United States,* and the *Constellation,* were eventually completed in 1797. In 1798 Congress created a Department of the Navy, and by the end of 1799 the number of naval ships had increased to thirty-three. By then American ships had captured eight French vessels and provided secure passage for American commerce.

While the naval war went on, a new army was established in 1798 as a 10,000-man force to serve three years. Adams called Washington from retirement to be its commander, agreeing to the General's condition that he name his three chief subordinates. Washington sent in the names of Hamilton, Charles C. Pinckney, and Henry Knox. In the revolutionary army the three had ranked in precisely the opposite order, but Washington insisted that Hamilton be his second in command. Adams relented, but resented the slight to his authority as commander-in-chief. The rift among the Federalists themselves thus widened further. Because of Washington's age, the choice meant that if the army ever took the field, Hamilton would be in command. But recruitment went slowly until late in 1799, by which time all fear of French invasion had been dispelled. Hamilton continued to dream of imperial glory, though, planning the seizure of Louisiana and the Floridas to keep them out of French hands, and even the invasion of South America, but these hopes remained Hamilton's dreams.

By the fall of 1798, even before the naval war was fully under way, Talleyrand began to make peace overtures. Adams named three peace commissioners, who arrived in Paris to find themselves confronting a new government under First Consul Napoleon Bonaparte. They sought two objectives: $20 million to pay for the American ships seized by the French, and the formal cancellation of the 1778 Treaty of Alliance. By the Convention of 1800, ratified in 1801, the French agreed only to terminate the alliance and the quasi-war.

THE WAR AT HOME   The real purpose of the French crisis all along, the more ardent Republicans suspected, was to create an excuse to put down domestic political opposition. The Alien and Sedition Acts of 1798 lent credence to their suspicions. These four measures, passed amid the wave of patriotic war fever, limited freedom of speech and the press and the liberty of aliens. Proposed by Federalists in Congress, the legislation did not originate with Adams but had his blessing. Three of the four acts reflected native hostility to foreigners, especially the French and Irish, a large number of whom had become active Republicans and were suspected of revolutionary intent.

The Naturalization Act changed from five to fourteen years the residence requirement for citizenship. The Alien Act empowered the president to expel "dangerous" aliens at his discretion. The Alien Enemy Act authorized the president in time of declared war to expel or imprison enemy aliens at will. Finally, the Sedition Act defined as a high misdemeanor any conspiracy against legal measures of the government, including interference with federal officers and insurrection or riot. What is more, the law forbade writing, publishing, or speaking anything of "a false, scandalous and malicious" nature against the government or any of its officers.

The purpose of such laws was transparently partisan, designed to punish Republicans. To be sure, zealous Republican journalists were resorting to scandalous lies and misrepresentations. Just a few months before the new legislation took effect, for instance, a Republican editor characterized the president as the "old, querulous, bald, blind, crippled, toothless Adams." Such intemperate language was hardly grounds for clamping down on free speech, but it was a time when both sides seemed afflicted with paranoia. Of the ten convictions under the act, all were directed at Republicans, and some for trivial matters. In the very first case a man was fined $100 for wishing out loud that the wad of a salute cannon might hit President Adams in his rear. The few convictions under the act only created martyrs to the cause of freedom of speech and the press, and exposed the vindictiveness of Federalist judges.

To offset the Alien and Sedition Acts, Jefferson and Madison brought forth drafts of what came to be known as the Kentucky and Virginia Resolutions. These passed the legislatures of the two states in late 1798. The resolutions, much alike in their arguments, denounced the Alien and Sedition Acts as unconstitutional and advanced the state-compact theory. Since the Constitution arose as a compact among the states, the resolutions argued, it followed logically that the states retained the right to say when Congress had exceeded its powers. The states could "interpose" their judgment on acts of Congress and "nullify" them if necessary.

The doctrines of interposition and nullification, revised and edited by later theorists, were destined to be used for causes unforeseen by the authors of the Kentucky and Virginia Resolutions. At the time, it seems, both Jefferson and Madison intended the resolutions to serve chiefly as propaganda, the opening guns in the political campaign of 1800. Neither Kentucky nor Virginia took steps to nullify or interpose its authority against enforcement of the Alien and Sedition Acts. Instead, both called upon the other states to help them win a repeal in Congress. Jefferson counseled against any thought of violence, which was "not the kind of opposition the American people will permit." Alluding to the Federalists and a tax they had enacted in 1798 on houses, land, and slaves, he assured a fellow Virginian that "the reign of witches" would soon end, that it would be discredited by the arrival of the tax collector more than anything else. As Jefferson realized, the Alien and Sedition

Acts touched comparatively few individuals, but the tax reached every property holder in the country. In eastern Pennsylvania the general discontent with the tax reached the stage of armed resistance and provoked Adams to dispatch army regulars and militia to enforce the law.

REPUBLICAN VICTORY   Thus as the presidential election of 1800 approached, grievances were mounting against Federalist policies: taxation to support an army that had little to do but chase Pennsylvania farmers, the Alien and Sedition Acts, the lingering fears of "monarchism," the hostilities aroused by Hamilton's programs, the suppression of the Whiskey Rebellion, and Jay's Treaty. When Adams decided for peace in 1800, he probably doomed his one chance for reelection. Only a wave of patriotic war fever with a united party behind him could have gained him victory at the polls. His decision gained him much goodwill among the people at large, but left the Hamiltonians unreconciled and his party divided.

In 1800 the Federalists summoned enough unity to name Adams as their candidate. But the Hamiltonians continued to snipe at the president and his policies, and soon after his renomination Adams removed two of them from his cabinet. Hamilton struck back with a pamphlet questioning Adams's fitness to be president, citing his "disgusting egotism." Intended for private distribution among Federalist leaders, the pamphlet reached the hands of Aaron Burr, who put it in circulation.

Jefferson and Burr, as the Republican candidates, once again represented the alliance of Virginia and New York. Jefferson, perhaps even more than Adams, became the target of abuse. Unscrupulous opponents labeled him an atheist and a supporter of the excesses of the French Revolution. His election, people were told, would bring "dwellings in flames, hoary hairs bathed in blood, female chastity violated . . . children writhing on the pike and halberd." Jefferson kept quiet, refused to answer the attacks, and directed the campaign by mail from his home at Monticello. He was portrayed as the farmers' friend, the champion of states' rights, frugal government, liberty, and peace.

Adams proved more popular than his party, whose candidates generally fared worse than the president, but the Republicans edged him out by seventy-three electoral votes to sixty-five. The decisive states were New York and South Carolina, either of which might have given the victory to Adams. But in New York Burr's organization won control of the

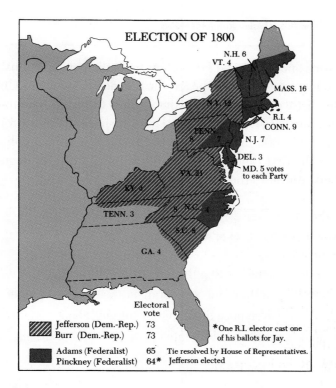

ELECTION OF 1800

N.H. 6
VT. 4
MASS. 16
N.Y. 12
R.I. 4
CONN. 9
PENN.
8   7
N.J. 7
DEL. 3
MD. 5 votes
to each Party
VA. 21
KY. 4
N.C. 4
TENN. 3
S.C. 8
GA. 4

Electoral
vote
Jefferson (Dem.-Rep.) 73
Burr (Dem.-Rep.) 73

Adams (Federalist) 65
Pinckney (Federalist) 64*

*One R.I. elector cast one
of his ballots for Jay.

Tie resolved by House of Representatives.
Jefferson elected

legislature, which cast the electoral votes. In South Carolina, Charles Pinckney won over the legislature by well-placed promises of Republican patronage. Still, the result was not final, for Jefferson and Burr had tied with seventy-three votes each, and the choice of the president was thrown into the House of Representatives, where Federalist diehards tried vainly to give the election to Burr. This was too much for Hamilton, who opposed Jefferson but held a much lower opinion of Burr. Eventually the deadlock was broken when a confidant of Jefferson assured a Federalist congressman from Delaware that Jefferson would refrain from wholesale removals of Federalists and uphold the new fiscal system. The representative resolved to vote for Jefferson, and several other Federalists agreed simply to cast blank ballots, permitting Jefferson to win without any of them actually having to vote for him.

Before the Federalists relinquished power to the Jeffersonian Republicans on March 4, 1801, their "lame duck" Congress passed the Judiciary Act of 1801. Intended to ensure Federalist control of the judicial system, this act provided that the next vacancy on the Supreme Court should not be filled, created sixteen Circuit Courts with a new judge for each, and increased the number of attorneys, clerks, and marshals. Before he left office Adams named John Marshall to the vacant office of

Chief Justice and appointed Federalists to all the new positions, including forty-two justices of the peace for the new District of Columbia. The Federalists, defeated and destined never to regain national power, had in the words of Jefferson "retired into the judiciary as a stronghold." The election of 1800 marked a turning point in American political history. It was the first time that one political party, however ungracefully, relinquished power to the opposition party.

MAKING CONNECTIONS

- Thomas Jefferson's Republican philosophy offered a strong alternative to Hamilton's Federalism. As the next chapter shows, however, once the Republicans got into power, they adopted a number of Federalist principles and positions.

- The Bank of the United States and the protective tariff continued to be controversial. The Bank was renewed for another twenty years in 1816, the same year in which the first truly protective tariff was passed (Chapter 9), but in the 1830s the Bank was eliminated, and the tariff became a major source of sectional conflict (Chapter 10).

- The foreign policy crises with England and France described in this chapter will lead to the War of 1812, discussed in Chapter 8.

FURTHER READING

Stanley Elkins and Eric McKitrick's *The Age of Federalism* (1993)* traces the persistence and transformation of ideas first fostered during the revolutionary crisis. John F. Hoadley's *Origins of American Political Parties, 1789–1803* (1986) is superb.

*These books are available in paperback editions.

For a female perspective on pre- and post-revolutionary America, see Phyllis Lee Levin's *Abigail Adams* (1991)* and Edith B. Gelles's *Portia: The World of Abigail Adams* (1992).* The Republican viewpoint is the subject of Lance Banning's *The Jeffersonian Persuasion: Evolution of a Party Ideology* (1978).*

Federalist foreign policy is explored in Felix Gilbert's *To the Farewell Address: Ideas of Early American Foreign Policy* (1961).*

For specific domestic issues, see Thomas Slaughter's *The Whiskey Rebellion* (1986) and Harry Ammon's *The Genêt Mission* (1973).* Patricia Watlington's *The Partisan Spirit* (1972) examines the Kentucky Resolutions. The treatment of Indians in the Old Northwest is explored in Richard H. Kohn's *Eagle and Sword: The Federalists and the Creation of the Military Establishment in America, 1783–1802* (1975). For the Alien and Sedition Acts, consult Leonard W. Levy's *Legacy of Suppression: Freedom of Speech and Press in Early American History* (1960).

The African-American experience in the Revolutionary era is detailed in Mechal Sobel's *The World They Made Together: Black and White Values in Eighteenth-Century Virginia* (1988) and Gary B. Nash's *Forging Freedom: The Formation of Philadelphia's Black Community, 1720–1840* (1988).

*These books are available in paperback editions.

8 ⟡ REPUBLICANISM:
JEFFERSON AND MADISON

CHAPTER ORGANIZER

This chapter focuses on:

- the domestic policies of the Republicans in power

- political divisions in the early republic

- the causes and effects of the War of 1812

JEFFERSON IN POWER

On March 4, 1801, the soft-spoken, brilliant, and charming Thomas Jefferson became the first president to be inaugurated in the new federal city, Washington, District of Columbia. The city was then an array of undistinguished buildings around two centers, Capitol Hill and the Executive Mansion. Between them lay a swampy wilderness full of stumps and mudholes. The Congress, having met in eight different towns since 1774, had at last found a permanent home, but as yet enjoyed few amenities. There were two places of amusement, one a racetrack, the other a theater filled with "tobacco smoke, whiskey breaths, and other stenches." Practically deserted much of the year, the town came to life only when Congress assembled.

A watercolor of the president's house during Jefferson's term in office. Jefferson called it "big enough for two emperors, one pope, and the grand lama in the bargain."

Jefferson's inauguration befitted the surroundings. Tall and thin, with ill-fitting clothes, chiseled features, red hair, and a ruddy complexion, the new president left his lodgings and walked two blocks to the unfinished Capitol, entered the Senate chamber, took the oath from the recently appointed Chief Justice John Marshall, read his address in a barely audible voice, and returned to his boardinghouse for dinner. A tone of simplicity and conciliation ran through Jefferson's inaugural address. "We are all Republicans—we are all Federalists," he assured the nation. He then presented a ringing affirmation of republican government: "I know, indeed, that some honest men fear that a republican government cannot be strong; that this government is not strong enough. I believe this, on the contrary, the strongest government on earth. I believe it is the only one where every man . . . would meet invasions of the public order as his own personal concern."

The deliberate display of republican simplicity at Jefferson's inauguration set the style of his administration. He took pains to avoid the monarchical trappings of his Federalist predecessors. Presidential messages went to Congress in writing lest they resemble the parliamentary speech from the throne. The practice also allowed Jefferson, a notoriously bad public speaker, to exploit his considerable skill as a writer. Jefferson, a widower, discarded the coach and six in which Washington and Adams had traveled to state occasions and rode about the city on horseback, often by himself. He also continued to attire himself in plain clothes. A Federalist senator, upon entering the White House, mistook Jefferson for "a servant." White House dinners were held around a circular table, so that none should take precedence. "When brought together in society, all are perfectly equal," Jefferson maintained. This infuriated several European diplomats accustomed to aristocratic formalities, and they boycotted White House affairs. But Jefferson had by no means ceased to be the Virginia gentleman, nor had he abandoned elegant manners or the good life. The cuisine of his French chef and the wines for his frequent dinners strained his budget to the point that he had to borrow money, and he left office with a debt that was to pursue him the rest of his life.

Jefferson liked to think of his election as the "Revolution of 1800," but the margin had been close and the policies that he followed were more conciliatory than revolutionary. Perhaps the most revolutionary aspect of Jefferson's presidency was the orderly transfer of power in 1801, an uncommon event in the world of that day. Jefferson placed in policy-making positions men of his own party, and was the first president to pursue the role of party leader, cultivating congressional support at his dinner parties and otherwise. In the cabinet the leading fixtures were Secretary of State James Madison, a longtime neighbor and political ally, and Swiss-born Secretary of the Treasury Albert Gallatin, a Pennsylvania Republican whose financial skills had won him the respect of Federalists. In an effort to cultivate Federalist New England, Jefferson chose men from that region for the positions of attorney-general, secretary of war, and postmaster-general.

In lesser offices, however, Jefferson resisted the wholesale removal of Federalists, preferring to wait until vacancies appeared. But pressure from Republicans often forced him to yield and remove Federalists, trying as best he could to assign some other than partisan causes for the removals. In one area, however, he managed to remove the offices rather than the appointees. In 1802 Congress repealed the Judiciary Act of 1801, and so abolished the circuit judgeships and other offices to which Adams had made his "midnight appointments." A new judiciary act restored to six the number of Supreme Court justices and set up six circuit courts, each headed by a justice.

MARBURY V. MADISON Adams's "midnight appointments" sparked the important case of *Marbury v. Madison* (1803), the first in which the

Supreme Court asserted its right to declare an act of Congress unconstitutional. The case involved the appointment of one William Marbury as justice of the peace in the District of Columbia. Marbury's official letter of appointment, or commission, signed by President Adams two days before he left office, remained undelivered when Madison became secretary of state, and Jefferson directed him to withhold it. Marbury then sued for a court order (a writ of mandamus) directing Madison to deliver his commission. John Marshall, Jefferson's distant Virginia cousin with the gravelly voice, crystalline logic, and staunch Federalist views, wrote the Court's opinion. He held that Marbury deserved his commission, but he then denied that the Court had jurisdiction in the case. Section 13 of the Judiciary Act of 1789, which gave the Court original jurisdiction in mandamus proceedings, was unconstitutional, Marshall and the court ruled, because the Constitution specified that the Court should have original jurisdiction only in cases involving ambassadors or states. The Court, therefore, could issue no order in the case. With one bold stroke Marshall thus had chastised the Jeffersonians while avoiding an awkward confrontation with an administration that might have defied his order. At the same time, he established the precedent that the Court could declare a federal law invalid on the grounds that it violated provisions of the Constitution.

DOMESTIC REFORMS   Jefferson's first term was a succession of triumphs in both domestic and foreign affairs. He did not set out to discard Hamilton's program. Under Treasury Secretary Gallatin's tutoring, he learned to accept the national bank as an essential convenience. It was too late, of course, to undo Hamilton's funding and debt assumption operations, but none too soon, in the opinion of both Jefferson and Gallatin, to begin retiring the resultant federal debt. In 1802 Jefferson won the repeal of the whiskey tax and other Federalist excises, much to the relief of backwoods distillers, drinkers, and grain farmers.

Without the excise taxes, frugality was all the more necessary to a government dependent for revenue chiefly on tariffs and the sale of western lands. Happily for Gallatin's treasury, both flourished. The European war brought a continually increasing traffic to American shipping and revenues to the Treasury. At the same time settlers flocked to the western lands, which were coming more and more within their reach. The admission of Ohio in 1803 increased the number of states to seventeen.

Cincinnati in 1800, twelve years after its founding. Though its population was only about 750, its inhabitants were already promoting Cincinnati as "the metropolis of the north-western territory."

By the "wise and frugal government" promised in the inaugural, Jefferson and Gallatin reasoned, the United States could live within its income, like a prudent farmer. The basic formula was simple: cut back expenses on the military. A standing army was a menace to a free society anyway. It therefore should be kept to a minimum, with defense left to the militia. The navy, which the Federalists had already reduced after the quasi-war with France, ought to be reduced further. Coastal defense, Jefferson argued, should rely on fortifications and a "mosquito fleet" of small gunboats.

In 1807 Jefferson crowned his reforms by signing an act that outlawed the foreign slave trade as of January 1, 1808, the earliest date possible under the Constitution. At the time, South Carolina was the only state that still permitted the trade, but for years to come an illegal traffic in African slaves would continue. By one informal estimate perhaps 300,000 slaves were smuggled into southern states between 1808 and 1861.

THE BARBARY PIRATES   Issues of foreign relations intruded on Jefferson early in his term, when events in the Mediterranean gave him second thoughts about the need for a navy. On the Barbary Coast of North Africa, the rulers of Morocco, Algeria, Tunis, and Tripoli (now part of Libya) had for years practiced piracy and extortion. After the Revolution, American shipping in the Mediterranean became fair game, no longer protected by British payments of tribute. The new American government paid protection money too, first to Morocco in 1786, then to the others in the 1790s. In 1801, however, the pasha of Tripoli upped his demands and declared war on the United States. Jefferson thereupon sent warships to blockade Tripoli. A wearisome war dragged on until 1805, punctuated in 1804 by the notable exploit of Lieutenant Stephen Decatur, who slipped into Tripoli harbor by night and set fire to the frigate *Philadelphia,* which had been captured (along with its crew) after it ran aground. In 1805 the pasha settled for $60,000 ransom and released the *Philadelphia's* crew (mostly British subjects), whom he had held hostage for more than a year. It was still tribute, but less than the $300,000 the pasha had demanded, and much less than the cost of the war.

THE LOUISIANA PURCHASE   It was an inglorious end to a shabby affair, but well before it was over, events elsewhere had conspired to produce the greatest single achievement of the Jefferson administration. The Louisiana Purchase of 1803 more than doubled the territory of the United States by bringing into its borders the entire Mississippi Valley west of the river itself. The French had settled Louisiana in the early eighteenth century, but after their defeat by England in the Seven Years' War, they had ceded the Louisiana territory to Spain. Soon after taking power in France in 1799, however, Napoleon Bonaparte forced the Spanish to return the territory and expressed his intention of creating a North American empire. When word of the deal reached Washington in 1801, Jefferson hastened Robert R. Livingston, the new minister to France, on his way to Paris. Spain in control of the Mississippi outlet was bad enough, but Napoleon in control could only mean serious trouble. Jefferson wrote Livingston: "The day that France takes possession of New Orleans . . . we must marry ourselves to the British fleet and nation," a sobering prospect for Jefferson.

Livingston had instructions to talk the French out of it, if it was not too late, and a series of long and frustrating negotiations dragged out into 1803. In April Napoleon's minister, Talleyrand, suddenly asked if the United States would like to buy the whole of Louisiana. Livingston, once he could regain his composure, snapped up the offer. Having failed to conquer the sugar-rich island of Santo Domingo, and eager to renew his struggle against England, Napoleon had apparently decided simply to cut his losses in the New World, turn a quick profit, please the Americans, and go back to reshaping the map of Europe.

By the treaty of cession, dated April 30, 1803, the United States paid about $15 million for the huge territory. In defining the boundaries of Louisiana, the treaty was vague. Its language could be stretched to provide a tenuous claim on Texas and a much stronger claim on West Florida, from Baton Rouge on the Mississippi past Mobile to the Perdido River on the east. When Livingston asked about the boundaries, Talleyrand responded: "I can give you no direction. You have made a noble bargain for yourselves, and I suppose you will make the most of it."

The turn of events had indeed presented Jefferson with a noble bargain, a great new "empire of liberty," but also with a constitutional dilemma. Nowhere did the Constitution mention the purchase of territory. By a strict construction, which Jefferson had professed, no such power existed. Jefferson at first thought to resolve the matter by amendment, but his advisers argued against delay lest Napoleon change his mind. The power to purchase territory, they reasoned, resided in the power to make treaties. Jefferson relented, trusting, he said, "that the good sense of our country will correct the evil of loose construction when it shall produce ill effects." New England Federalists boggled at the prospect of new states that would probably strengthen the Jeffersonian party, and in a reversal that foreshadowed many future reversals on constitutional issues, Federalists found themselves arguing strict construction of the Constitution while Republicans brushed aside such scruples.

The Senate ratified the treaty by an overwhelming vote of 26 to 6, and on December 20, 1803, American representatives took formal possession of Louisiana. The Spanish kept West Florida, but within a decade it would be ripe for the plucking. American settlers in 1810 staged a rebellion in Baton Rouge and proclaimed the Republic of West Florida, which was quickly annexed and occupied by the United States as far eastward as the Pearl River. In 1812 the state of Louisiana absorbed the region. The following year, with Spain itself a battlefield for French and British forces, American troops took over the rest of West Florida, now the Gulf coast of Mississippi and Alabama. The United States had truly made the most of a shrewd bargain.

EXPLORING THE CONTINENT An amateur scientist long before he was president, Jefferson had nourished an active curiosity about the vast Louisiana country. In 1803 he asked Congress for money to send

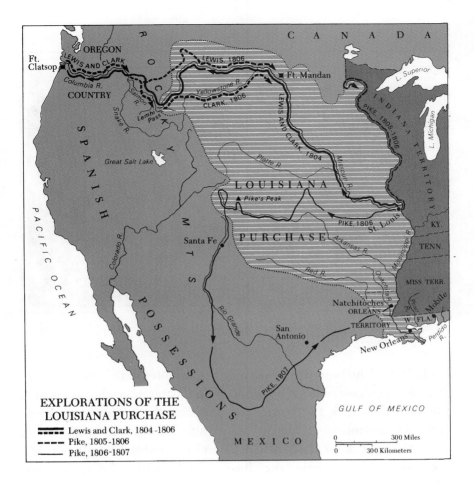

an expedition to explore the far northwest, beyond the Mississippi, in what was still foreign territory. Congress approved and Jefferson assigned as commanders Meriwether Lewis, the president's private secretary, and another Virginian, William Clark, the much younger brother of the Revolutionary hero George Rogers Clark.

In 1804 the "Corps of Discovery," numbering nearly fifty, set out from St. Louis to ascend the Missouri River. Forced to live off the land, they quickly adapted themselves to a new environment. Local Indians introduced them to clothes made from deer hides and to new hunting techniques. Six months later, near the Mandan Sioux villages in what is now North Dakota, they built a fort and wintered there in relative comfort, sending back a barge loaded with plant and animal specimens such as the prairie dog, previously unknown to science, and the magpie, previously unknown in America. In the spring they added to the main party a French guide and his remarkable Shoshone wife, Sacajawea ("Canoe

"Treed" by a grizzly bear, from a book of engravings (c. 1812) of the Lewis and Clark expedition.

Launcher"), who proved an enormous help as interpreter among the Indians of the region, and set out once again upstream. At the head of the Missouri they took the north fork, thenceforth the Jefferson River, crossed the Continental Divide, braved attacks by grizzly bears, and in dugout canoes descended the Snake and Columbia Rivers to the Pacific. The following spring they headed back east by almost the same route, and after a swing through the Yellowstone country, returned to St. Louis in 1806, having been gone nearly two and a half years. No longer was the Far West unknown country. Their reports of friendly Indians and abundant pelts attracted traders and trappers to the region and also gave the United States a claim to the Oregon country by right of discovery and exploration.

POLITICAL SCHEMES   Jefferson's policies, including the Louisiana Purchase, brought him almost solid support in the South and West. Even New Englanders were moving to his side. By 1809 even John Quincy Adams, the son of the second president, would become a Republican. Diehard Federalists read the handwriting on the wall. The acquisition of a vast new empire in the west would reduce New England to insignificance in political affairs, and along with it the Federalist cause. Under the leadership of Senator Timothy Pickering, a group of bitter Massachusetts Federalists called the Essex Junto considered seceding from the Union, an idea that would simmer in New England for another decade.

Soon these New Englanders hatched a scheme to link New York with their secessionist fantasy. They contacted Vice-President Aaron Burr, who had long been on the outs with the Jeffersonians and who was, as ever, ready for conspiracies. Their plan depended on Burr's election as governor of New York, but in April 1804 Burr was overwhelmed by the regular Republican candidate. The extreme Federalists, it turned out, could not even hold members of their own party to their disunionist plan. Hamilton bitterly opposed the conspiracy, noting that Burr was "a dangerous man, and one who ought not to be trusted with the reins of government." When Hamilton's remarks appeared in the press, Burr's demand for an explanation led in 1804 to a duel in which Burr shot Hamilton through the heart. Hamilton went to his death, as his son had done in a similar affair the previous year, determined not to fire at his opponent. Burr had no such scruples. The death of Hamilton ended both Pickering's scheme and Burr's political career—but not his intrigues.

Meanwhile the presidential campaign of 1804 began when a Republican congressional caucus renominated Jefferson. Opposed by the Federalist Charles C. Pinckney, Jefferson won 162 of 176 electoral votes. He proudly noted in his second inaugural address that he had carried out the general policies announced in the first: "The suppression of unnecessary offices, of useless establishments and expenses, enabled us to discontinue our internal taxes. . . . What farmer, what mechanic, what laborer ever sees a tax-gatherer of the United States?"

DIVISIONS IN THE REPUBLICAN PARTY

RANDOLPH AND THE *TERTIUM QUID*   "Never was there an administration more brilliant than that of Mr. Jefferson up to this period," asserted John Randolph of Roanoke after the 1804 election. "We were indeed in the full tide of successful experiment." But freed from a strong opposition—Federalists made up only a quarter of the new Congress— the majority began to lose its cohesion. Cracks appeared in the Republican façade, signs of major fissures that would finally split the party. Ironically, John Randolph, a Jeffersonian mainstay in the first term, became the most conspicuous of the dissidents. A brilliant, witty, but erratic and unyielding Virginia planter-philosopher, subject to fits of insanity in his later years, he was a powerful combination of principle, intelligence, wit, arrogance, and rancor. Famous for his venomous assaults delivered in a shrill soprano voice, the Virginia congressman flourished best in opposition. He once dismissed a rival as "a man of splendid abilities but utterly corrupt. Like a rotten mackerel by moonlight, he shines and stinks." Few of Randolph's colleagues had the stomach for his tongue-lashings.

Randolph became the crusty spokesman for a shifting group of "Old Republicans," whose adherence to party principles had rendered them more Jeffersonian than Jefferson himself. Their philosopher was John Taylor of Caroline, a Virginia planter-pamphleteer whose fine-spun theories reflected the continuing fear on the part of many that the national government was growing in power and scope at the expense of individual liberty and states' rights. Taylor's ideas had little effect at the time but delighted secessionists of later years. Neither Randolph nor Taylor could accept Jefferson's pragmatic gift for adjusting principle to circumstance, and they steadfastly defended states' rights against the intrusions of federal power. Said Randolph: "Asking one of the States to surrender part of her sovereignty is like asking a lady to surrender part of her chastity."

Randolph broke with Jefferson in 1806, when the president sought an appropriation of $2 million for a thinly disguised bribe to win French influence in persuading Spain to give up the Floridas. "I found I might co-operate or be an honest man—I have therefore opposed and will oppose them," Randolph pledged. Thereafter he resisted Jefferson's initiatives almost out of reflex. Randolph and his colleagues were sometimes called "Quids," or the *Tertium Quid* (the "third something"), and their dissents gave rise to talk of a third party, neither Republican nor Federalist. But they never got together, and their failure would typify the experience of almost all third-party movements thereafter.

THE BURR CONSPIRACY   If feisty John Randolph was sincerely committed to principle, opportunistic Aaron Burr was sincerely committed to himself. Born of a distinguished line of Puritans, including grandfather Jonathan Edwards, he cast off the family Calvinism to pursue money, power, and women. Burr was small and slight, with finely cut features and remarkably dark, piercing eyes. Rarely without a fine cigar or a grasping vision, he was a talented, witty, and charming man who was rumored to be the richest lawyer in New York. He boasted of never having lost a case. Sheer brilliance and shrewdness carried him to the vice-presidency, and he might have become heir apparent to Jefferson, but a taste for intrigue was the tragic flaw in his character. Caught up in the dubious schemes of Federalist diehards in 1800 and again in 1804, he ended his political career once and for all when he killed Hamilton. Indicted in New York and New Jersey for murder and heavily in debt, the vice-president fled first to Spanish-held Florida. Once the furor subsided, he boldly returned to Washington in November to preside over the Senate. As long as he stayed out of New York and New Jersey, he was safe. Groused one senator: "We are indeed fallen on evil times."

But Burr focused his attention less on the Senate than on a cockeyed scheme to carve out a personal empire for himself in the West. The so-called Burr Conspiracy originated when Burr met with General James Wilkinson, an old friend with a tainted Revolutionary War record who was a spy for the Spanish and had a penchant for easy money, a taste for rum, and an eye for intrigue. Just what he and Burr were up to probably will never be known. The most likely explanation is that they sought to organize a secession of Louisiana and set up an independent republic. Earlier Burr had solicited British support for his scheme to separate "the western part of the United States in its whole extent."

Whatever the goal, Burr succeeded in having Wilkinson appointed governor of the Louisiana Territory. In the summer of 1805 Burr himself sailed downriver from Pittsburgh on a lavishly outfitted flatboat, leaving behind a wake of rumors. By the summer of 1806 he was in Lexington, Kentucky, recruiting adventurers. Meanwhile, rumors began to reach Jefferson, and in November 1806, so did a letter from General Wilkinson warning of "a deep, dark, wicked, and wide-spread conspiracy." Wilkinson had apparently developed cold feet and now feigned ignorance of the whole affair.

In 1807, as Burr neared Natchez with his motley crew, he learned that Wilkinson had betrayed him and that Jefferson had ordered his arrest. He cut out cross-country for Pensacola, disguised as a boatman, but was caught in Alabama and taken off to Richmond, Virginia, for a trial which, like the conspiracy, had a stellar cast. Charged with treason by the grand jury, Burr was brought for trial before Chief Justice Marshall.

Events then revealed both Marshall and Jefferson at their partisan worst. Jefferson, determined to get a conviction at any cost, published relevant affidavits in advance and promised pardons to conspirators who helped to convict Burr. The Federalist Marshall in turn was so indiscreet as to attend a dinner given by the defense counsel at which Burr himself was present.

The case established two major constitutional precedents. First, on the grounds of executive privilege, Jefferson ignored a subpoena requiring him to appear in court with certain papers. He believed that the independence of the executive branch would be compromised if the president were subject to a court writ. The second major precedent was the rigid definition of treason. On this Marshall adopted the strictest of constructions. Treason under the Constitution, he concluded, consisted of "levying war against the United States or adhering to their enemies" and required "two witnesses to the same overt act" for conviction. Since the prosecution failed to produce two witnesses to an overt act of treason by Burr, the jury found him not guilty.

Whether or not Burr escaped his just deserts, Marshall's strict construction of the Constitution protected the United States, as the authors of the Constitution clearly intended, against the capricious judgments of "treason" that governments through the centuries have used to terrorize dissenters. As to Burr, with further charges pending, he skipped bail and took refuge in France, but returned unmolested in 1812 to practice law in New York. He survived to a virile old age. At age eighty, shortly before his death, he was divorced on grounds of adultery.

WAR IN EUROPE

Oppositionists of whatever stripe were more an annoyance than a threat to Jefferson. The more intractable problems of his second term involved the renewal of the European war in 1803, which helped resolve the problem of Louisiana but put more strains on Jefferson's desire to avoid "entangling alliances" and the quarrels of Europe. In 1805 Napoleon's smashing defeat of Russian and Austrian forces made him the master of western Europe. The same year, the British defeat of the French and Spanish fleets in the Battle of Trafalgar secured Britain's control of the seas. The war resolved itself into a battle of elephant and whale, Napoleon dominant on land, the British dominant on the water, neither able to strike a decisive blow at the other, and neither restrained by an appreciation of neutral rights or international law.

HARASSMENT BY BRITAIN AND FRANCE   For two years after the renewal of hostilities, American shippers reaped the benefits, taking over trade with the French and Spanish West Indies. But in the case of the *Essex* (1805), a British court ruled that the practice of shipping French and Spanish goods through American ports while on their way elsewhere did not neutralize enemy goods. Such a practice violated the British rule of 1756, under which trade closed in time of peace remained closed in time of war. Goods shipped in violation of the rule, the British held, could be seized at any point under the doctrine of continuous voyage. After 1807 British interference with American shipping increased, not just to keep supplies from Napoleon's continent but also to hobble competition with British merchant ships.

In a series of Orders of Council adopted in 1806 and 1807, the British ministry set up a paper blockade of Europe. Vessels headed for continental ports had to get licenses and accept British inspection or be liable to seizure. Napoleon retaliated with his "Continental System," proclaimed in the Berlin Decree of 1806 and the Milan Decree of 1807. In the first he declared a blockade of the British Isles, and in the second he ruled that neutral ships that complied with British regulations were subject to seizure when they reached continental ports. The situation presented American shippers with a dilemma. If they complied with the demands of one side they were subject to seizure by the other.

It was humiliating, but the prospects for profits were so great that shippers ran the risk. Seamen faced a more dangerous risk: a renewal of the practice of impressment. The use of press gangs to kidnap men in British (and colonial) ports was a long-standing method of recruitment for the British navy. The seizure of British subjects from American vessels became a new source of recruits, justified on the principle that British subjects remained British subjects for life: "Once an Englishman, always an Englishman."

In the summer of 1807, the British *Leopard* accosted an American naval vessel, the *Chesapeake,* just outside territorial waters off Norfolk. After the *Chesapeake*'s captain refused to be searched, the *Leopard* opened fire, killing three and wounding eighteen. The *Chesapeake,* caught unready for battle, was forced to strike its colors in surrender. A British search party seized four men, one of whom was later hanged for desertion from the British navy. Soon after the *Chesapeake* limped back into Norfolk, a Washington newspaper editorialized: "We have never, on any occasion, witnessed such a thirst for revenge. . . ." Public wrath was so aroused that Jefferson could have had war on the spot. But like Adams before him, he resisted the war fever and suffered politically as a result. One Federalist called Jefferson a "dish of skim milk curdling at the head of our nation."

THE EMBARGO   Jefferson resolved to channel public indignation into an effort at "peaceable coercion." In December 1807, in response to his request, Congress passed the Embargo Act, which stopped all export of American goods and prohibited American ships from clearing for foreign ports. It also effectively ended imports, since it was unprofitable for foreign ships to return from America empty. The constitutional basis of the embargo was the power to regulate commerce, which in this case Republicans interpreted broadly as the power to prohibit commerce.

Jefferson's embargo, however, failed from the beginning, for the public was unwilling to make the necessary sacrifices. Trade remained profitable despite the risks, and violating the embargo was almost laughably easy. Neither France nor Great Britain was significantly hurt by Jefferson's policy.

But Jefferson was. The embargo revived the languishing Federalist party in New England, which renewed the charge that Jefferson was in league with the French. The embargo, one New Englander said, was "like cutting one's throat to cure the nosebleed." At the same time, agriculture in the South and West suffered for want of outlets for grain, cotton, and tobacco. After fifteen months of ineffectiveness, Jefferson finally accepted failure and on March 1, 1809, repealed the embargo shortly before he relinquished the "splendid misery" of the presidency. In the election of 1808 the succession passed to another Virginian, Secretary of State James Madison.

THE DRIFT TO WAR   Madison was entangled in foreign affairs from the beginning. Still insisting on neutral rights and freedom of the seas, he pursued Jefferson's policy of "peaceful coercion" by different but

Preparation for War to Defend Commerce. *In 1806 and 1807 American ship-ping was caught in the crossfire of war between Britain and France.*

equally ineffective means. In place of the embargo Congress had sub-stituted the Non-Intercourse Act, which reopened trade with all coun-tries except France and Great Britain and authorized the president to reopen trade with whichever nation gave up its restrictions. Non-intercourse proved as ineffective as the embargo. In the vain search for an alternative, Congress on May 1, 1810, reversed its ground and adopted a measure introduced by Nathaniel Macon of North Carolina, Macon's Bill Number 2, which reopened trade with the warring powers but provided that if either dropped its restrictions non-intercourse would be restored with the other.

Napoleon's foreign minister, the duc de Cadore, then informed the American minister in Paris that he had withdrawn the Berlin and Milan Decrees, but the carefully worded Cadore letter had strings attached:

revocation of the decrees depended on withdrawal of the British Orders in Council. The strings were plain to see, but either Madison misunderstood or, more likely, went along in hope of putting pressure on the British. In response to the Cadore letter, he restored non-intercourse with the British. London refused to give in, but Madison clung to his policy despite Napoleon's continued seizure of American ships. The seemingly hopeless effort did indeed finally work. With more time, patience, or a transatlantic cable, Madison's policy would have been vindicated without resort to war. On June 16, 1812, the British foreign minister, facing economic crisis, revoked the Orders in Council. Britain preferred not to risk war with the United States on top of its war with Napoleon. But it was too late. On June 1 Madison had asked for war, and by mid-June the Congress concurred.

THE WAR OF 1812

CAUSES   The main cause of the war—the demand for neutral rights—seems clear enough. Neutral rights dominated Madison's war message and provided the salient reason for mounting public hostility toward the British. Yet the geographical distribution of the congressional vote for war raised a troubling question. Most votes for war came from the farm regions that stretched from Pennsylvania southward and westward. The maritime states of New York and New England, the region that bore the brunt of British attacks on American trade, voted against the declaration of war. One explanation for this seeming anomaly is simple enough. The farming regions suffered damage to their markets for grain, cotton, and tobacco, while New England shippers made profits in spite of British restrictions.

Other plausible explanations for the sectional vote, however, include frontier Indian attacks that were blamed on the British, western land hunger, and the desire for territory in British Canada and Spanish Florida. The constant pressure to open new lands repeatedly forced or persuaded Indians to sign treaties they did not always understand, causing stronger resentment among tribes that were losing more and more of their lands. It was an old story, dating from the Jamestown settlement, but one that took a new turn with the rise of a powerful Shawnee leader, Tecumseh.

THE WAR OF 1812:
Major Northern Campaigns
⟵⟵⟵ American forces   ⟵⟵⟵ British forces
★ Battle site

LAKE SUPERIOR

Ft. Michilimakinac

LAKE MICHIGAN

LAKE HURON

MICHIGAN
TERRITORY

Ft. Dearborn

Detroit

The Thames

York
(Toronto)

LAKE ONTARIO

Ft. Niagara
Queenstown Heights
RENSSELAER
OCT. 1812

CANADA

Quebec

Montreal

PREVOST,
AUG.-SEPT.
1814

Plattsburgh
Lake
Champlain

VT.

N.H.

N.Y.

MASS.

CONN.

Hudson R.

LAKE ERIE

Presque Isle
(Erie)

PERRY,
SEPT. 1813

Put-in-Bay

HARRISON
OCT. 1813

HULL AUG. 1812

Maumee R.

Wabash R.

INDIANA
TERRITORY

OHIO

Ohio R.

Pittsburgh

PENN.

Susquehanna R.

N.J.

MD. Baltimore
Ft. McHenry
Washington D.C.

DEL.

Potomac R.

Chesapeake
Bay

ROSS,
AUG. 1814

BRITISH BLOCKADE

KY.

VIRGINIA

0   200 Miles
0   200 Kilometers

According to General William Henry Harrison, governor of the Indiana Territory, Tecumseh was "one of those uncommon geniuses, which spring up occasionally to produce revolutions and overturn the order of things." Tecumseh recognized the consequences of Indian disunity and set out to form a confederation of tribes to defend Indian hunting grounds, insisting that no land cession was valid without the consent of all tribes, since they held the land in common. By 1811 Tecumseh had matured his plans and headed south from the Indiana Territory to win the Creeks, Cherokees, Choctaws, and Chickasaws to his cause. His speeches were filled with emotion and anger. "The white race is a wicked race," he declared. "They seize your land; they corrupt your women." Only by driving them out "upon a trail of blood" would the Indians survive.

Governor Harrison gathered a force near Tecumseh's capital on the Tippecanoe River while the leader was away. The Indians took the bait and attacked Harrison's encampment, although Tecumseh had warned against any fighting in his absence. The Shawnees lost a bloody engagement that left about a quarter of Harrison's men dead or wounded. Harrison then burned the Shawnee town and destroyed all its supplies.

Tecumseh, the Shawnee leader who tried to unite the tribes in defense of their lands. He was killed in 1813 at the Battle of the Thames.

Tecumseh's dreams of an Indian confederacy went up in smoke, and he fled to British protection in Canada.

The Battle of Tippecanoe reinforced suspicions that the British were inciting the Indians. To eliminate the Indian menace, frontier settlers reasoned, they needed to remove its foreign support. Conquest of Canada would thus accomplish a twofold purpose. It would end British influence among the Indians and open a new empire for land-hungry Americans. It was also the only place, in case of war, where the British were vulnerable to American attack. East Florida, still under the Spanish flag, posed a similar threat, since Spain was either too weak or unwilling to prevent sporadic Indian attacks across the frontier. The British were also suspected of smuggling through Florida and intriguing with the Indians on the southwest border.

Such concerns helped generate a war fever. In the Congress that assembled in 1811, a number of new, young members from southern and western districts began to clamor for war in defense of "national honor." Among them were Henry Clay of Kentucky, who became Speaker of the House, Richard M. Johnson, also of Kentucky, Felix Grundy of Tennessee, and John C. Calhoun of South Carolina. John Randolph of Roanoke christened these "new boys" the "War Hawks." After they entered the House, Randolph said, "We have heard but one word—like the whippoor-will, but one eternal monotonous tone—Canada! Canada! Canada!"

PREPARATIONS   As it turned out, the War Hawks would get neither Canada nor Florida. For in 1812 James Madison had carried into war a country that was ill prepared both financially and militarily. The year before, despite earnest pleas from Treasury Secretary Gallatin, Congress had let the twenty-year charter of the Bank of the United States expire. A combination of strict-constructionist Republicans and Anglophobes, who feared the large British interest in the bank, caused its demise. Meanwhile, trade had collapsed and tariff revenues had declined. Loans were needed for about two-thirds of the war costs, but Northeast opponents of the war were reluctant to lend money.

The military situation was almost as bad. War had been likely for nearly a decade, but Republican budgetary constraints had prevented preparations. When the war began the army numbered only 6,700 men, ill-trained, poorly equipped, and led by aging officers. One young Virginia officer named Winfield Scott, destined for military distinction, commented that most of the veteran commanders "had very generally slunk into either sloth, ignorance, or habits of intemperate drinking." The navy, on the other hand, was in comparatively good shape, with able officers and trained men whose seamanship had been tested in the fighting against France and Tripoli. Its ships were well outfitted and seaworthy—all sixteen of them. In the first year of the war the navy produced the only American victories in isolated duels with British vessels, but their effect was mainly an occasional lift to morale. Within a year the British had blockaded the coast, except for New England, where they hoped to cultivate antiwar feeling, and most of the little American fleet was bottled up in port.

THE WAR IN THE NORTH   The only place where the United States could effectively strike at the British was Canada. Madison's best hope was a quick attack on Quebec or Montreal to cut Canada's lifeline, the St. Lawrence River. Instead of striking directly at the lifeline, however, the administration opted for a three-pronged drive against Canada: along the Lake Champlain route toward Montreal, with General Henry Dearborn in command; along the Niagara River, with forces under General Stephen Van Rensselaer; and into Upper Canada (north of Lake Erie) from Detroit, where General William Hull and some 2,000 men arrived in early July 1812. In Detroit, the sickly and senile Hull procrastinated, while his position worsened and the news arrived that an American fort isolated at the head of Lake Huron had surrendered in mid-July. The British commander cleverly played upon Hull's worst fears. Gathering what redcoats he could to parade in view of Detroit's defenders, he announced that thousands of Indian allies were at the rear and that once fighting began he would be unable to control them. Fearing massacre, Hull, without consulting his officers and without a shot being fired, surrendered his entire force in August.

Along the Niagara front, General Van Rensselaer was more aggressive than Hull. On October 13 an advance party of 600 Americans crossed the Niagara River and worked their way up the bluffs on the Canadian side to occupy Queenstown Heights. The stage was set for a major victory, but the New York militia refused to reinforce Van Rensselaer's men, claiming that their military service did not obligate them to leave the country. They complacently remained on the New York side and watched their outnumbered countrymen fall to a superior force across the river.

On the third front, the old invasion route via Lake Champlain, the trumpet once more gave an uncertain sound. On November 19, 1812, the incompetent General Dearborn led his army north from Plattsburgh toward Montreal. He marched them up to the border, where the militia once again stood on its alleged constitutional rights and refused to cross, and then marched them down again.

Madison's navy secretary now pushed vigorously for American control of inland waters. At Presque Isle (Erie), Pennsylvania, twenty-eight-year-old Commodore Oliver H. Perry, already a fourteen-year veteran who had seen action against Tripoli, was busy building ships from green timbers. By the end of the summer Perry set out in search of the British, whom he found at Lake Erie's Put-in Bay on September 10, 1813. After completing the preparations for battle, Perry told an aide: "This is the most important day of my life."

It was indeed. Two British warships used their superior weapons to pummel the *Lawrence,* Perry's flagship, at long distance. Blood flowed on the deck so freely that the sailors slipped and fell as they wrestled with the cannon. After four hours of intense shelling, none of the *Lawrence*'s guns was left working and 80 percent of the crew were dead or wounded. The British expected the Americans to turn tail, but Perry refused to quit. He transferred to another vessel, carried the battle to the enemy, and finally accepted surrender of the entire British squadron. Hatless, begrimed, and bloodied, Perry sent General William Henry Harrison the long-awaited message: "We have met the enemy nd they are ours."

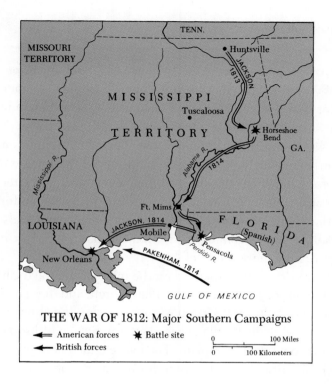

THE WAR OF 1812: Major Southern Campaigns

◄═ American forces   ✳ Battle site
◄— British forces

0   100 Miles
0   100 Kilometers

More good news followed. At the Battle of the Thames (October 5), in Canadian territory east of Detroit, General Harrison eliminated British power in Upper Canada and released the Northwest from any further threat. In the course of the battle, Tecumseh fell, and his persistent dream of Indian unity died with him.

THE WAR IN THE SOUTH   In the Southwest, too, the war flared up in 1813. On August 30 the Creeks attacked Fort Mims, on the Alabama River above Mobile, killing almost half the people in the fort. The news found Andrew Jackson home in bed in Nashville, recovering from a street brawl with Thomas Hart Benton, later a senator from Missouri. As major-general of the Tennessee militia, Jackson summoned about 2,000 volunteers and set out on a campaign that utterly crushed Creek resistance. The decisive battle occurred on March 27, 1814, at the Horseshoe Bend of the Tallapoosa River, in the heart of the upper Creek country. In the Treaty of Fort Jackson, signed that August, the Indians ceded two-thirds of their lands to the United States, including part of Georgia and most of Alabama.

Four days after the Battle of Horseshoe Bend, Napoleon's empire collapsed. Now free to deal with America, the British developed a three-fold plan of operations for 1814. They would launch a two-pronged invasion of America via Niagara and Lake Champlain to increase the clamor for peace in the Northeast, extend the naval blockade to New England, subjecting coastal towns to raids, and seize New Orleans to cut the Mississippi River, lifeline of the West. Uncertainties about the peace settlement in Europe, however, prevented the release of British veterans for a full-scale assault upon the New World. And after a generation of conflict, war weariness countered the British thirst for revenge against the former colonials. British plans were stymied also by the more resolute young commanders Madison had placed in charge of strategic areas by the summer of 1814.

The main British effort focused on the invasion via Lake Champlain. A land assault might have taken Plattsburgh and forced American troops out of their protected positions nearby, but England's army bogged down while its flotilla engaged an American naval squadron in a deadly battle on Lake Champlain. The battle ended in September 1814 with the entire British flotilla either destroyed or captured.

FIGHTING IN THE CHESAPEAKE   Meanwhile, however, American forces suffered the most humiliating experience of the war, the capture and burning of Washington, D.C. With attention focused on the Canadian front, the Chesapeake Bay offered the British a number of inviting targets, including Baltimore, now the fourth-largest city in America. On the evening of August 24, 1814, the British marched unopposed into Washington, where British officers ate a meal in the White House intended for President and Mrs. Madison, who had hastily joined the other refugees in Virginia. The British then burned the White House, the Capitol, and all other government buildings except the Patent Office. A tornado the next day compounded the damage, but a violent thunderstorm dampened both the fires and the enthusiasm of the British forces, who left to prepare a new assault on Baltimore. One English newspaper editor expressed shameful regret at the army's actions: "The Cossacks spared Paris, but we spared not the Capital of America!"

The attack on Baltimore was a different story. With some 13,000 men, chiefly militia, American forces fortified the heights behind the city. About 1,000 men held Fort McHenry, on an island in the harbor. The British landed at North Point, where an advance group of American

The Taking of the City of Washington in America. *An English cartoon depicts the taking of Washington, D.C., on August 24, 1814.*

militia inflicted severe casualties. When the British finally came into sight of the city on September 13, they halted in the face of American defenses. All through the following night the British fleet bombarded Fort McHenry to no avail, and the invaders abandoned the attack on the city as too costly to risk. Francis Scott Key, a Washington lawyer, watched the siege from a vessel in the harbor. The sight of the flag still in place at dawn inspired him to draft the verses of "The Star-Spangled Banner." Later revised and set to the tune of an English drinking song, it was immediately popular and eventually became the national anthem.

THE BATTLE OF NEW ORLEANS   The British failure at Baltimore followed by three days their failure on Lake Champlain, and their offensive against New Orleans had yet to run its course. Along the Gulf coast General Andrew Jackson had been busy shoring up the defenses of Mobile and New Orleans. In late 1814, without authorization, he invaded Spanish Florida and took Pensacola, ending British intrigues there. Back in Louisiana by the end of November, he began to erect defenses on the approaches to New Orleans. But the British fleet, with some 7,500 European veterans under General Sir Edwin Pakenham, cautiously took up positions on a level plain near the Mississippi just south of New Orleans.

Pakenham's painfully careful approach—he waited until all his artillery was available—gave Jackson time to build earthworks bolstered by cotton bales. It was an almost invulnerable position, but Pakenham, contemptuous of Jackson's motley array of frontier militiamen, Creole aristocrats, free blacks, and pirates, ordered a frontal assault at dawn on January 8, 1815. His redcoats emerged out of the morning fog and ran into a murderous hail of artillery shells and deadly rifle fire. Before the British withdrew about 2,000 had been killed or wounded, including Pakenham himself, whose body, pickled in a barrel of rum, was returned to the ship where his wife awaited news of the battle.

The Battle of New Orleans occurred after a peace treaty had already been signed. But this is not to say that it was an anticlimax or that it had no effect on the outcome of the war, for the treaty was yet to be ratified and the British might have exploited to advantage the possession of New Orleans had they won it. The battle assured ratification of the treaty as it stood, and both governments acted quickly.

THE TREATY OF GHENT AND THE HARTFORD CONVENTION
Peace efforts had begun in 1812, even before hostilities commenced, but negotiations bogged down after the fighting started. The British were stalling, awaiting news of smashing victories to strengthen their hand. Word of the American victory on Lake Champlain weakened the British resolve. Their will to fight was further eroded by a continuing power struggle in Europe, by the eagerness of British merchants to renew trade with America, and by the war weariness of a tax-burdened public. The British finally decided that the war was not worth the cost. Envoys from both sides eventually agreed to end the fighting, return prisoners, restore previous boundaries, and to settle nothing else. The Treaty of Ghent was signed on Christmas Eve, 1814.

While the diplomats converged on a peace settlement, an entirely different kind of meeting took place in Hartford, Connecticut. An ill-fated affair, the Hartford Convention represented the climax of New

England's disaffection with "Mr. Madison's war." New England had managed to keep aloof from the war and extract a profit from illegal trading and privateering. After the fall of Napoleon, however, the British extended their blockade to New England, occupied part of Maine, and conducted several raids along the coast. Even Boston seemed threatened. Instead of rallying to the American flag, however, Federalists in the Massachusetts legislature voted on October 5, 1814, to convene a meeting of New England states to plan independent action.

On December 15 the Hartford Convention assembled with delegates chosen by the legislatures of Massachusetts, Rhode Island, and Connecticut, two delegates from Vermont and one from New Hampshire: twenty-two in all. The convention included an extreme faction, Timothy Pickering's "Essex Junto," who were prepared to secede from the Union, but it was controlled by a more moderate group led by Harrison Gray Otis, who sought only a protest against the war in language reminiscent of Madison's Virginia Resolutions of 1798. As the ultimate remedy for their grievances they proposed seven constitutional amendments designed to limit Republican influence, including the requirement of a two-thirds vote to declare war or admit new states, a prohibition on embargoes lasting more than sixty days, a one-term limit for the presidency, and a ban on successive presidents from the same state.

Their call for a later convention in Boston carried the unmistakable threat of secession if the demands were ignored. Yet the threat quickly evaporated. When messengers from Hartford reached Washington, they found the battered capital celebrating the good news from Ghent and New Orleans. The consequence was a fatal blow to the Federalist party, which never recovered from the stigma of disloyalty and narrow provincialism stamped on it by the Hartford Convention.

THE WAR'S AFTERMATH   For all the ineptitude with which the War of 1812 was fought, it generated an intense patriotic feeling. Despite the standoff with which it ended at Ghent, the American public felt victorious, thanks to Andrew Jackson and his men at New Orleans as well as the heroic exploits of American frigates in their duels with British ships. Remembered too were the vivid words of the dying Captain James Lawrence on the *Chesapeake:* "Don't give up the ship." Under

We Owe Allegiance to No Crown. *The War of 1812 generated a new feeling of nationalism.*

Republican leadership the nation had survived a "Second War of Independence" against the greatest military power on earth and emerged with new symbols of nationhood and a new gallery of heroes.

The war revealed America's need for a more efficient system of internal transportation—roads, bridges, canals. Even more important, the conflict launched the United States toward economic independence, as the interruption of trade encouraged the birth of American manufactures. This was a profound development, for the emergence of an American factory system would generate far-reaching social effects as well as economic growth. After forty years of independence, it dawned on the world that the new republic might not only survive but flourish.

As if to underline the point, Congress authorized a quick and decisive blow at the Barbary pirates. During the War of 1812 the dey of Algiers had renewed his plundering of American ships, claiming that he was getting too little tribute. On March 3, 1815, little more than two weeks after the Senate ratified the Peace of Ghent, Congress authorized a naval expedition against the Mediterranean pirates. On May 10

Captain Stephen Decatur sailed from New York with ten vessels. He first seized two Algerian ships and then sailed boldly into the harbor of Algiers. On June 30, 1815, the dey agreed to cease molesting American ships and to return all American prisoners. Decatur then forced similar concessions from Tunis and Tripoli. Piracy against American vessels was over.

One of the strangest results of the War of 1812 was a reversal of roles by the Republicans and Federalists. Out of the wartime experience the Republicans had learned some lessons in nationalism. The necessities of war had "Federalized" Madison, or "re-Federalized" the father of the Constitution. Perhaps, he reasoned, a peacetime army and navy would not be so bad after all. He also had come to see the value of a national bank and of higher tariffs to protect infant American industries from foreign competition. But while Madison was embracing such nationalistic measures, the Federalists were borrowing the Jeffersonian theory of states' rights and strict construction. It was the first great reversal of roles in constitutional interpretation. It would not be the last.

MAKING CONNECTIONS

- Jefferson's embargo and the War of 1812 encouraged the beginnings of manufacturing in the United States, an important subject in Chapter 11.

- The Federalist party collapsed because of its opposition to the War of 1812. But as the next chapter shows, Republicans did not prosper as much as might have been expected in the absence of political opposition.

- The American success in the War of 1812 (a moral victory at best) led to a tremendous sense of national pride and unity, a spirit analyzed in the next chapter.

FURTHER READING

Marshall Smelser's *The Democratic Republic, 1801–1815* (1968)*
presents an overview of the Republican administration. The standard
biography of Jefferson is the multivolume work by Dumas Malone, *Jefferson and His Time* (6 vols, 1948–1981).* A one-volume biography
which emphasizes Jefferson's public, political life is Noble Cunningham, Jr.'s *In Pursuit of Reason: The Life of Thomas Jefferson* (1987). On
the life of Jefferson's friend and successor see Drew R. McCoy's *The
Last of the Fathers: James Madison and the Republican Legacy* (1989).

The concept of judicial review and the courts can be studied in
Richard E. Ellis's *The Jeffersonian Crisis* (1971). For the Louisiana Purchase, consult Alexander De Conde's *This Affair of Louisiana* (1976). A
detailed account of the explorations of Lewis and Clark may be found
in David Lavender's *The Way to the Western Sea: Lewis and Clark Across
the Continent* (1988).

Burton Spivak's *Jefferson's English Crisis: Commerce, the Embargo,
and the Republican Revolution* (1979) discusses Anglo-American relations during Jefferson's administration; Clifford L. Egan's *Neither Peace
nor War* (1983) covers Franco-American relations. A review of the
events that brought on war in 1812 is presented in Robert A. Rutland's
*Madison's Alternatives: The Jeffersonian Republicans and the Coming of
War, 1805–1812* (1975).

*These books are available in paperback editions.

Chapter 6

9 NATIONALISM AND SECTIONALISM

CHAPTER ORGANIZER

This chapter focuses on:

monroe

• the elements of the "Era of Good Feelings"

• how economic policies, diplomacy, and judicial decisions reflected the nationalism of these years

• the various issues that promoted sectionalism

• the fate of the Republican party after the collapse of the Federalists

---

ECONOMIC NATIONALISM

When did the United States become a nation? There is no easy answer to the question, for a sense of nationhood develops gradually and is always subject to cross currents of localism, sectionalism, and class interest. Colonial Americans identified more closely with the local community and at most the province in which they resided than with any larger idea of empire or nation. The Revolution gave rise to a sense of nationhood, but Jefferson's "Revolution of 1800" revealed the countervailing forces of local and state interest. Jefferson himself, for instance, always spoke of Virginia as "my country."

Immediately after the War of 1812, however, Americans experienced a new surge of nationalism. An unusual economic prosperity after the war generated a sense of well-being and enhanced the prestige of the national government. The idea spread that the country needed a more balanced economy of farming, commerce, and manufacturing and a more muscular military. President Madison, in his first annual message to Congress after the war, recommended several steps toward these ends: better fortifications, a standing army and a strong navy, a new national bank, effective protection of the new infant industries, a system of canals and roads for commercial and military use, and to top it off, a great national university. "The Republicans have out-Federalized Federalism," one observer remarked.

THE BANK OF THE UNITED STATES The trinity of economic nationalism—proposals for a second national bank, protective tariffs, and internal improvements—inspired the greatest controversies of the time. After the national bank expired in 1811, the country had fallen into a financial muddle. State-chartered banks mushroomed with little or no control, and their banknotes (paper money) flooded the channels of commerce with money of uncertain value. Because hard money had been so short during the war, many state banks had suspended specie (gold or silver) payments in redemption of their notes, thereby further depressing their value. And this was the money on which Americans depended.

To remedy this situation, in 1816 Congress adopted over the protest of Old Republicans a provision for a new Bank of the United States. It was located in Philadelphia and modeled after Hamilton's bank. Once again the charter ran for twenty years, once again the government owned a fifth of the stock and named five of the twenty-five directors, and again the bank served as the depository for government funds. Its banknotes were accepted in payments to the government. In return for its privileges the bank had to keep the government's funds without charge, lend the government $5 million on demand, and pay the government a cash bonus of $1.5 million.

The colorful and bitter debate on the bank set the pattern of regional alignment for most other economic issues. Missouri senator Thomas

Hart Benton predicted that the currency-short western towns would be at the mercy of such a centralized eastern bank. "They may be devoured by it any moment! They are in the jaws of the monster! A lump of butter in the mouth of a dog! One gulp, one swallow, and all is gone!"

The debate was also noteworthy because of the leading roles played by the great triumvirate of John C. Calhoun of South Carolina, Henry Clay of Kentucky, and Daniel Webster of New Hampshire, later of Massachusetts. Calhoun, still in his youthful phase as a War Hawk nationalist, introduced the measure and pushed it through, justifying its constitutionality by citing the congressional power to regulate the currency. Clay, who had earlier opposed Hamilton's bank, now asserted that new circumstances had made the bank indispensable. Webster, on the other hand, led the opposition of the New England Federalists, who did not want Philadelphia to displace Boston as the nation's banking center. Later, after he moved from New Hampshire to Massachusetts, Webster would return to Congress as the champion of a much stronger national power, while events would carry Calhoun in the other direction.

A PROTECTIVE TARIFF   The shift of capital from commerce to manufactures, begun during Jefferson's embargo of 1807, had accelerated during the war. Peace in 1815 brought a sudden renewal of cheap

The Union Manufactories of Maryland in Patapsco Falls, Baltimore County, c. 1815. *A textile mill begun during the embargo of 1807; by 1825 the Union Manufactories would employ over 600 people.*

British imports and provoked a movement for the protection of young American industries. The self-interest of the manufacturers, who as yet had little political impact, was reinforced by a patriotic desire for economic independence from Britain.

The Tariff of 1816, the first intended more for the protection of industry against foreign competition than for revenue, easily passed Congress. The South and New England registered a majority of their votes against the bill, while the middle states and Old Northwest cast only five negative votes altogether. Led by Calhoun, the minority of southerners who voted for the tariff had hoped that the South might itself become a manufacturing center. But within a few years New England moved ahead of the South, and Calhoun turned against protection. The tariff then became a sectional issue, with manufacturers and food growers favoring higher tariffs, while planters and shipping interests favored lower duties.

INTERNAL IMPROVEMENTS   The third major economic issue of the time involved internal improvements: the building of roads and the development of water transportation. The war had highlighted the shortcomings of existing arteries. Troop movements through the western wilderness had proved very difficult, and settlers found that unless they located near navigable waters, they were cut off from trade and limited to a frontier subsistence.

The federal government had entered the field of internal improvements under Jefferson, who went along with some hesitation. In 1803,

THE NATIONAL ROAD, 1811-1838

=== Built 1811-1818

— Built 1825-1838

0   100 Miles

0   100 Kilometers

when Ohio became a state, Congress decreed that 5 percent of the proceeds from state land sales would go to building a National Road from
the Atlantic coast into Ohio and beyond as the territory developed. In
1806 Jefferson authorized a survey, and construction of the National
Road began in 1811.

Originally called the Cumberland Road, it was the first federally financed interstate road network. By 1818 the road ran from Cumberland, Maryland, to Wheeling on the Ohio River. Construction stopped
temporarily during the business panic of 1819, but by 1838 the road extended all the way to Vandalia, Illinois. By reducing transportation costs
and opening up new markets, the National Road and privately financed
turnpikes helped accelerate the commercialization of agriculture.

In 1817 Calhoun put through the House a bill to place in a fund for
internal improvements the $1.5 million bonus the Bank of the United
States had paid for its charter, as well as all future dividends on the government's bank stock. Once again opposition centered in New England
and the South, regions that expected to gain least. Support came largely
from the West, which badly needed good roads. On his last day in office
Madison, bothered by its constitutionality, vetoed the bill. Internal improvements remained for another hundred years, with few exceptions,
the responsibility of states and private enterprise.

"GOOD FEELINGS"

JAMES MONROE   As Madison approached the end of a turbulent
tenure he, like Jefferson, turned to a fellow Virginian, another secretary
of state, as his successor: James Monroe. At the outbreak of the Revolution, Monroe was just beginning college at William and Mary. He
joined the army at age sixteen, was wounded at Trenton, and was a lieutenant-colonel when the war ended. Later he studied law with Jefferson
and absorbed Jeffersonian principles.

Monroe never displayed the depth in scholarship or political theory
of his Republican predecessors, but what he lacked in intellect he made
up in dedication to public service. His soul, Jefferson said, if turned inside out would be found spotless. Monroe served in the Virginia assembly, as governor, in the Confederation Congress and United States Senate, and as minister to Paris, London, and Madrid. Under Madison he

had been secretary of state and twice had doubled as secretary of war. In the 1816 presidential election he overwhelmed his Federalist opponent, Rufus King of New York. Tall, rawboned Monroe, with his powdered wig, cocked hat, and knee breeches, was the last of the revolutionary generation to serve in the White House and the last president to dress in the old style.

Firmly grounded in Republican principles, Monroe was never able to keep up with the onrush of the new nationalism. He accepted as accomplished fact the bank and the protective tariff, but during his tenure there was no further extension of economic nationalism. Indeed, there was a minor setback. He permitted the National (or Cumberland) Road to be carried forward, but in his veto of the Cumberland Road Bill (1822), he denied the authority of Congress to collect tolls for its repair and maintenance. Like Jefferson and Madison, he also urged a constitutional amendment to remove all doubt about federal authority in the field of internal improvements.

Whatever his limitations, Monroe surrounded himself with some of the ablest young Republican leaders: John Quincy Adams became secretary of state, William Crawford of Georgia continued as secretary of the treasury, and John C. Calhoun headed the War Department. The new administration took power with America at peace and the economy flourishing. Soon after his 1817 inauguration, Monroe embarked on a goodwill tour of New England. In Boston, lately a hotbed of wartime dissent, a Federalist paper commented on the president's visit under the heading "Era of Good Feelings." The label became a popular catchphrase for Monroe's administration, and one that historians seized upon later. Like many a maxim, it conveys just enough truth to be sadly misleading. The collapse of the Federalist party did not mean that the Republicans grew more unified. They continued to suffer from rancorous internal tensions. Moreover, the social order began to show signs of increasing stratification as the nation experienced dramatic economic growth and rapid westward migration. Finally, a resurgence of sectionalism erupted just as the postwar prosperity collapsed in the Panic of 1819.

For two years, however, general harmony reigned, and even when the country's troubles revived, little of the blame fell on Monroe. In 1820 he was reelected without opposition, indeed without even a formal nomination. The Federalists were too weak to put up a candidate, and the Republicans did not bother to call a caucus. Monroe won all the electoral votes except for three abstentions and one vote from New Hampshire for John Quincy Adams.

IMPROVING RELATIONS WITH BRITAIN   Adding to the prevailing contentment after the war was a growing rapprochement with England. American shippers resumed trade with Britain in 1815. The Peace of Ghent had left unsettled a number of minor disputes, but in the sequel two important compacts—the Rush-Bagot Agreement of 1817 and the Convention of 1818—removed several potential causes of irritation. In the first, resulting from an exchange of notes between Acting Secretary of State Richard Rush and British Minister Charles Bagot, the threat of naval competition on the Great Lakes vanished with an arrangement to limit forces there to several revenue cutters. Although the exchange made no reference to the land boundary between the United States and Canada, its spirit gave rise to the tradition of an unfortified border, the longest in the world.

The Convention of 1818 covered three major points. The northern limit of the Louisiana Purchase was settled by extending the national boundary along the Forty-ninth Parallel west from Lake of the Woods to the crest of the Rocky Mountains. West of that point the Oregon country would be open to joint U.S.-British occupation, but the boundary remained unsettled. The right of Americans to fish off Newfoundland and Labrador, granted in 1783, was acknowledged once again. The chief remaining problem was Britain's continuing exclusion of American ships from the West Indies in order to reserve that lucrative trade for British ships. The rapprochement with Britain therefore fell short of perfection.

JACKSON TAKES FLORIDA   The year 1819 was one of the more fateful in American history, a time when a whole sequence of developments came into focus. Controversial efforts to expand American territory, a sharp financial panic, a tense debate over the extension of slavery, and several landmark Supreme Court cases combined to bring an unsettling end to the "Era of Good Feelings."

The aggressive new nationalism reached a climax with the acquisition of Florida. Spanish sovereignty over Florida was more a technicality than an actuality. The thinly held province had been a thorn in the

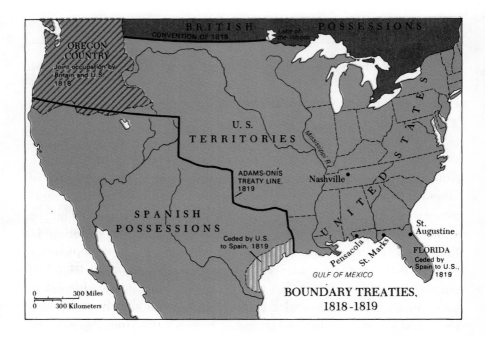

side of the United States during the recent war, a center of British intrigue, a haven for Creek refugees who were beginning to take the name Seminole ("runaway" or "separatist"), and a harbor for runaway slaves and criminals.

Spain, once the dominant power of the Americas, was now a nation in rapid decline, suffering from both internal and colonial revolt, and unable to enforce its obligations under the Pinckney Treaty of 1795 to pacify the frontiers. In 1816 American forces clashed with a group of escaped slaves who had taken over a British fort on the Appalachicola River. Seminoles were soon fighting white settlers in the area, and in 1817 Secretary of War Calhoun authorized a campaign against the Seminoles, summoning General Andrew Jackson from Nashville to take command. Jackson's orders allowed him to pursue the offenders into Spanish territory, but not to attack any Spanish post. A man of Jackson's tenacity naturally felt hobbled by such a restriction, since when it came to Spaniards or Indians, no white Tennessean—certainly not Andrew Jackson—was likely to bother with technicalities. Jackson pushed eastward through Florida, reinforced by Tennessee volunteers and a party of friendly Creeks, taking a Spanish post and skirmishing with the Seminoles. Jackson hanged two of their leaders without a trial. For two British intriguers in the area, he convened a court-martial, during which it was revealed that they had befriended the Seminoles and had offered them military training. Jackson had one hanged and the other shot. The Florida panhandle was in American hands by the end of May 1818.

News of Jackson's exploits aroused anger in Madrid and concern in Washington. Spain demanded the return of its territory, reparations, and the punishment of Jackson, but Spain's impotence was plain for all to see. Monroe's cabinet at first prepared to disavow Jackson's action, especially his direct attack on Spanish posts. Calhoun, as secretary of war, wanted to discipline Jackson for disregard of orders—a stand that later caused bad blood between the two men—but privately confessed a certain pleasure at the outcome. In any case a man as popular as Jackson was almost invulnerable. And he had one important friend in Washington, Secretary of State John Quincy Adams, who realized that Jackson had strengthened his hand in negotiations already under way with the Spanish minister. American forces withdrew from Florida, but negotiations resumed with the knowledge that the United States could retake Florida at any time.

With Florida's fate a foregone conclusion, Adams cast his eye on a larger purpose, a final definition of the western boundary of the Louisiana Purchase and—his boldest stroke—extension of a boundary to the Pacific coast. In lengthy negotiations Adams gradually gave ground on claims to Texas, but stuck to his demand for a transcontinental line. Agreement finally came early in 1819. Spain ceded all of Florida to the United States in return for American assumption of private claims against Spain up to $5 million. The western boundary of the Louisiana Purchase would run along the Sabine River and then in stairstep fashion up to the Red River, along the Red, and up to the Arkansas River. From the source of the Arkansas it would go north to the Forty-second Parallel and thence west to the Pacific coast. Florida became a territory, and its first governor was briefly Andrew Jackson. In 1845 Florida finally achieved statehood.

SPECULATION AND SLAVERY

THE PANIC OF 1819 Adams's Transcontinental Treaty was a triumph of foreign policy and the climactic event of America's postwar nationalism. Even before it was signed in early 1819, however, two thunderclaps signaled the end of the brief "Era of Good Feelings" and gave warning of stormy weather ahead: the financial Panic of 1819 and the controversy over statehood for Missouri. The panic resulted from a sudden collapse of cotton prices in the English market, as British manufacturers turned away from American sources to cheaper East Indian cotton. The price collapse set off a decline in the demand for other American goods and suddenly revealed the fragility of the prosperity that had begun after the War of 1812.

Since 1815 much of the economic boom had been built on a shaky foundation. Businessmen, bankers, farmers, and land jobbers had caused a volatile expansion of credit, succumbing to the contagion of get-rich-quick fever that was sweeping the country. Even the directors of the Second Bank of the United States (B.U.S.) engaged in the same reckless extension of loans that state banks had pursued. In 1819, just as alert businessmen began to take alarm, a case of extensive fraud and embezzlement in the Baltimore branch came to light. The disclosure led to the resignation of the B.U.S. director. His replacement, Langdon Cheves, former congressman from South Carolina, established a sounder policy.

Cheves reduced salaries and other costs, postponed dividends, restrained the extension of credit, and presented for redemption the state banknotes that came in, thereby forcing the state-chartered banks to keep specie reserves. Cheves rescued the B.U.S. from near-ruin, but only by putting heavy pressure on state banks. The state banks in turn put pressure on their debtors, who found it harder to renew old loans or get new ones. In 1823, his job completed, Cheves relinquished his position to Nicholas Biddle of Philadelphia. The Cheves policies were the result rather than the cause of the Panic, but hard-pressed debtors found it all the more difficult to meet their obligations. Hard times lasted about three years, and in the popular mind the bank deserved much of the blame. The Panic passed, but resentment of the national bank lingered, and it never fully regained the confidence of the South and the West.

THE MISSOURI COMPROMISE   Just as the Panic was breaking over the country, another cloud appeared on the horizon, the onset of a sectional controversy over slavery. By 1819 the country had an equal number of slave and free states, eleven of each. The line between them was

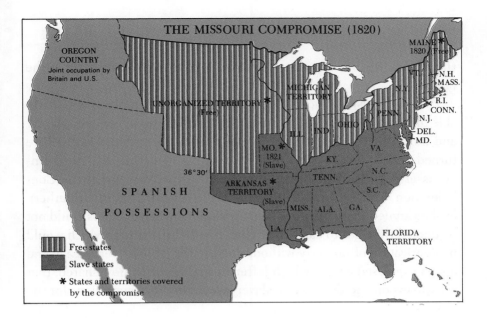

THE MISSOURI COMPROMISE (1820)

OREGON
COUNTRY
Joint occupation by
Britain and U.S.

UNORGANIZED TERRITORY *
(Free)

36°30'

SPANISH

POSSESSIONS

MICHIGAN
TERRITORY

MO. *
1821
(Slave)

ARKANSAS *
TERRITORY
(Slave)

ILL. | IND. | OHIO

KY.

TENN.

MISS. | ALA. | GA.

LA.

VA.

N.C.

S.C.

MAINE *
1820 / Free

VT. — N.H.
— MASS.
N.Y. — R.I.
CONN.
PENN. — N.J.
— DEL.
— MD.

FLORIDA
TERRITORY

Free states

Slave states

* States and territories covered
by the compromise

defined by the southern and western boundaries of Pennsylvania and
the Ohio River. Although slavery lingered in some places north of the
line, it was on the way to extinction there. Beyond the Mississippi, however, no move had been made to extend the dividing line across the
Louisiana Purchase territory, where slavery had existed from the days
when France and Spain had colonized the area. At the time the Missouri Territory embraced all of the Louisiana Purchase except the state
of Louisiana (1812) and the Arkansas Territory (1819). In the westward
rush of population, the old French town of St. Louis became the funnel
through which settlers pushed on beyond the Mississippi. These were
largely settlers from the South who brought their slaves with them.

In early 1819, the House of Representatives was asked to approve
legislation enabling Missouri to draft a state constitution, its population
having passed the minimum of 60,000. At that point Representative
James Tallmadge, Jr., a New York congressman, introduced a resolution
prohibiting the further introduction of slaves into Missouri, which had
some 10,000, and providing freedom at age twenty-five for those born
after the territory's admission as a state. After brief but fiery exchanges,
the House passed the amendment on an almost strictly sectional vote
and the Senate rejected it by a similar tally, but with several northerners
joining in the opposition. With population at the time growing faster in
the North, a political balance between the two sections could be held
only in the Senate. In the House, slave states had 81 votes while free

states had 105; a balance was unlikely to be restored ever again in the House.

The Congressional debate over slaves in the territories was remarkable for the absence of moral argument, although repugnance to slavery and moral guilt about it were never far from the surface. The debate turned instead on the constitutional issue. Congress, several northerners asserted, was empowered to forbid slavery in Missouri as the Confederation Congress had done in the Northwest Territory. Southern leaders argued that under the Fifth Amendment, slaveholders could not be denied the right to carry their chattel into the territory, which would be deprivation of property without due process of law. Henry Clay and others expressed a view, which Jefferson and Madison now shared, that the expansion and dispersal of slavery would improve conditions for the slaves.

Maine's application for statehood made it easier to arrive at an agreement. Since colonial times Maine had been the northern province of Massachusetts. The Senate linked its request for separate statehood with Missouri's and voted to admit Maine as a free state and Missouri as a slave state, thus maintaining the balance in the Senate. An Illinois senator further extended the compromise by an amendment to exclude slavery from the rest of the Louisiana Purchase north of 36°30', Missouri's southern border. Slavery thus would continue in the Arkansas Territory and in Missouri, and be excluded from the remainder of the area. Since most considered this the Great American Desert, unlikely ever to be settled, the arrangement seemed to be a victory for the slave states. On August 10, 1821, President Monroe proclaimed the admission of Missouri as the twenty-fourth state. For the time the controversy was settled. "But this momentous question," the aging Thomas Jefferson wrote to a friend after the first compromise, "like a firebell in the night awakened and filled me with terror. I considered it at once as the knell of the Union."

JUDICIAL NATIONALISM

JOHN MARSHALL, CHIEF JUSTICE Meanwhile, nationalism still flourished in the Supreme Court, where Chief Justice John Marshall preserved Hamiltonian Federalism for yet another generation. Marshall, a veteran of the Revolution, was among those who had been forever nationalized by the experience. In later years he said: "I was confirmed in the habit of considering America as my country and Congress as my government." Never a judge before he became chief justice in 1801, he established the power of the Supreme Court by his force of mind and determination. During Marshall's early years on the Court (altogether he served thirty-four years) he affirmed the principle of judicial review of legislative acts. In *Marbury v. Madison* (1803) and *Fletcher v. Peck* (1810) the Court first struck down a federal law and then a state law as unconstitutional.

In the fateful year 1819 Marshall and the Court made two more decisions of major importance in checking the power of the states and expanding the power of the federal government: *Dartmouth College v. Woodward*, and *McCulloch v. Maryland*. The Dartmouth College case involved an attempt by the New Hampshire legislature to alter a charter granted the college by King George III in 1769, under which the governing body of trustees became a self-perpetuating board. In 1816 the state's Republican legislature, irritated by this residue of monarchical rule as well as by the fact that Federalists dominated the board of trustees, placed Dartmouth under the control of a new board named by the governor. The original trustees sued, lost in the state courts, but with Daniel Webster as their counsel gained a hearing before the Supreme Court. The charter, declared Marshall in speaking for the Court, was a valid contract that the legislature had violated, an act expressly forbidden by the Constitution. This decision implied a new and enlarged definition of *contract* that seemed to put private corporations beyond the reach of the states that chartered them. "If business is to prosper," Marshall explained, "men must have the assurance that contracts will be enforced."

Marshall's single most important interpretation of the constitutional system appeared in *McCulloch v. Maryland*. In the unanimous decision the Court upheld the "implied powers" of Congress to charter the Bank of the United States and denied the state of Maryland's attempt to tax the bank. In a lengthy opinion Marshall rejected Maryland's argument that the federal government was the creature of sovereign states. Instead, he insisted, it arose directly from the people acting through the conventions that ratified the Constitution. While sovereignty was divided between the states and the national government, the latter, "though limited in its powers, is supreme within its sphere of action."

Deck Life on the *Paragon*, 1811–1812. *The* Paragon, *"a whole floating town,"
was the third steamboat operated on the Hudson by Robert Fulton and Robert R.
Livingston. Fulton said the Paragon "beats everything on the globe, for made as
you and I are we cannot tell what is in the moon."*

The state's effort to tax the bank conflicted with the supreme law of
the land. One great principle that "entirely pervades the constitution,"
Marshall wrote, was "that the constitution and the laws made in pursuance thereof are supreme: that they control the constitution and laws
of the respective states, and cannot be controlled by them." The state
tax therefore was unconstitutional for "the power to tax involves the
power to destroy"—which was precisely what the legislatures of Maryland and several other states had in mind with respect to the bank.

Marshall's last great decision, *Gibbons v. Ogden* (1824), established
national supremacy in regulating interstate commerce. In 1808 the
New York legislature granted Aaron Ogden the exclusive ferry rights
across the Hudson between New York and New Jersey. A competitor,
Thomas Gibbons, protested the state's right to grant such a monopoly.

On behalf of a unanimous Court, Marshall ruled that the state's action conflicted with the federal Coasting Act, under which Gibbons operated. Congressional power to regulate commerce, the Court said, "like all others vested in Congress, is complete in itself, may be exercised to its utmost extent, and acknowledges no limitations other than are prescribed in the constitution." In striking down the monopoly created by the state, the nationalist Marshall had opened the way to extensive development of steamboat navigation and, soon afterward, steam railroads. Such judicial nationalism provided an important support for economic expansion.

NATIONALIST DIPLOMACY

THE NORTHWEST   In foreign affairs, too, nationalism continued to be an effective force. Within two years after final approval of Adams's Transcontinental Treaty, the secretary of state was able to draw another important transcontinental line. In 1819 Spain had abandoned its claim to the Oregon country above the Forty-second Parallel. Russia, however, had claims along the Pacific coast as well, including trading outposts from Alaska as far south as California. In 1823 Secretary of State Adams contested "the right of Russia to any territorial establishment on this continent." The American government, he informed the Russian minister, assumed the principle "that the American continents are no longer subjects for any new European colonial establishments." The upshot of his protest was a treaty signed in 1824 whereby Russia, which had more pressing concerns in Europe, accepted the line of 54°40′as the southern boundary of its claim. The Oregon Territory, to the south of the line, remained subject to joint occupation by the United States and Great Britain under their agreement of 1818.

THE MONROE DOCTRINE   Adams's disapproval of further colonization also had clear implications for Latin America. One consequence of the Napoleonic wars and French occupation of Spain and Portugal had been a series of wars of liberation in Latin America. Within little more than a decade after the flag of rebellion was first raised in 1811, Spain had lost almost its entire empire in the Americas. All that was left were the islands of Cuba, Puerto Rico, and Santo Domingo.

That Spain could not regain her empire seems clear enough in retrospect. The British navy would not permit it because Britain's trade with the area was too important. For a time after Napoleon's defeat, however, European rulers were determined to restore monarchical "legitimacy" everywhere. In 1822, when the allies met in the Congress of Verona, they authorized France to suppress the constitutionalist movement in Spain and restore the authority of the monarchy. In 1823 French troops crossed the Spanish border, put down the rebels, and restored King Ferdinand VII to absolute authority. Rumors began to circulate that France would also try to restore Ferdinand's "legitimate" power over Spain's American empire. Monroe and Secretary of War Calhoun were alarmed at the possibility, although John Quincy Adams took the more realistic view that such action was unlikely. British Foreign Minister George Canning was also worried about French and Spanish intentions, and he urged Anglo-American protection of Latin America. Monroe at first agreed, with the support of his sage advisers Jefferson and Madison.

Adams, however, urged upon Monroe and the cabinet the independent course of proclaiming a unilateral policy against the restoration of Spain's colonies. "It would be more candid," Adams said, "as well as more dignified, to avow our principles explicitly to Russia and France, than to come in as a cock-boat in the wake of the British man-of-war." Adams knew that the British navy would stop any action by a European power in Latin America. The British wanted, moreover, the United States to agree not to acquire any more Spanish territory, including Cuba, Texas, or California, and Adams preferred to avoid such a commitment.

Monroe incorporated the substance of Adams's views in his annual message to Congress on December 2, 1823. The Monroe Doctrine, as it was later called, comprised four major points: (1) that "the American continents . . . are henceforth not to be considered as subjects for future colonization by any European powers"; (2) the political system of European powers was different from that of the United States, which would "consider any attempt on their part to extend their system to any portion of this hemisphere as dangerous to our peace and safety"; (3) the United States would not interfere with existing European colonies; and (4) the United States would keep out of the internal affairs of European nations and their wars.

At the time the statement drew little attention either in the United States or abroad. Over the years, however, the Monroe Doctrine, not even so called until 1852, became one of the cherished principles of American foreign policy. But for the time being it slipped into obscurity for want of any occasion to invoke it. In spite of Adams's affirmation, the United States came in as a cock-boat in the wake of the British man-of-war after all, for the effectiveness of the doctrine depended on British naval supremacy. The doctrine had no standing in international law. It was merely a statement of intent by an American president to the Congress and did not even draw enough interest at the time for the European powers to renounce it.

ONE-PARTY POLITICS

Almost from the start of Monroe's second term the jockeying for the presidential succession in 1824 had begun. Three members of Monroe's cabinet were active candidates: Secretary of War John Calhoun, Secretary of the Treasury William Crawford, and Secretary of State John Quincy Adams. Henry Clay, longtime Speaker of the House, also thirsted after the office. And on the fringes of the Washington scene a new force appeared in the person of Andrew Jackson, the scourge of the British, Spaniards, and Seminoles, who was elected a senator from Tennessee in 1823. All were Republicans, for again no Federalist stood a chance, but they were competing in a new political world, complicated by the crosscurrents of nationalism and sectionalism. With only one party there was in effect no party, for there existed no generally accepted method for choosing a "regular" candidate.

State legislatures were free to nominate candidates. Tennessee and Pennsylvania supported Jackson, and Calhoun agreed to serve as his running mate. (The 1824 election was the first to feature paired presidential and vice-presidential candidates.) Kentucky named Clay, Massachusetts named Adams, and the amiable, hulking Crawford was selected by a poorly attended congressional caucus. Of the four candidates, only two had clearly defined programs, and the outcome was an early lesson in the danger of being committed on the issues too soon. Crawford's friends emphasized his devotion to states' rights and strict construction.

Clay, on the contrary, took his stand for the "American System": he favored the national bank, the protective tariff, and a national program of internal improvements to bind the country together and build its economy. Adams was close to Clay, openly dedicated to internal improvements but less strongly committed to the tariff. Jackson, where issues were concerned, carefully avoided commitment. His managers hoped that, by being all things to all voters, Jackson could capitalize on his popularity as the hero of New Orleans.

THE "CORRUPT BARGAIN" The outcome turned on personalities and sectional allegiance more than on issues. Adams, the only northern candidate, carried New England, the former bastion of Federalism, and won most of New York's electoral votes. Clay took Kentucky, Ohio, and Missouri, while Crawford carried Virginia, Georgia, and Delaware. Jackson swept the Southeast, plus Illinois and Indiana, and with Calhoun's support the Carolinas, Pennsylvania, Maryland, and New Jersey.

The result in 1824 was inconclusive in both the electoral vote and the popular vote. In the electoral college Jackson had 99, Adams 84, Crawford 41, and Clay 37; in the popular vote the proportion ran about the same. Whatever might have been said about the outcome, it was a defeat for Clay's American System: New England and New York opposed him on internal improvements, the South and Southwest on the protective tariff. Sectionalism had defeated the national program, yet the advocate of the American System now assumed the role of president-maker, since the election was thrown into the House of Representatives, where Speaker Clay's influence was decisive. Clay had little trouble in choosing, since he regarded Jackson as unfit for the office. "I cannot believe," he muttered, "that killing 2,500 Englishmen at New Orleans qualifies for the various, difficult and complicated duties of the Chief Magistracy." He eventually threw his support to Adams. The final vote in the House, which was by state, carried Adams to victory with thirteen votes to Jackson's seven and Crawford's four.

It was a costly victory, for it united Adams's foes and crippled his administration before it got under way. There is no evidence that Adams entered into any bargain with Clay to win his support, but the charge was widely believed after Adams made Clay his secretary of state, the office from which three successive presidents had risen. A campaign to elect Jackson next time was launched almost immediately after the

1824 decisions. "The people have been cheated," Jackson growled. The Crawford people, including Martin Van Buren, the "Little Magician" of New York politics, soon moved into the Jackson camp.

JOHN QUINCY ADAMS'S PRESIDENCY   Short, plump, peppery John Quincy Adams was one of the ablest men, hardest workers, and finest intellects ever to enter the White House, but he lacked the common touch and the politician's gift for maneuver. He refused to play the game of patronage, believing that the presidency should be above partisan politics. His first annual message to Congress provided a grandiose blueprint for national development, set forth in such a blunt way that it became a political disaster. In the boldness and magnitude of its conception, the Adams plan outdid both Hamilton and Clay. The central government, the president asserted, should promote internal improvements, set up a national university, finance scientific explorations, build astronomical observatories, and create a new Department of the Interior.

To refrain from using broad federal powers, Adams maintained, "would be treachery to the most sacred of trusts." Officers of the government should not be "palsied by the will of our constituents." Such provocative language obscured whatever grandeur of conception the message to Congress had. For a minority president to demean the sovereignty of the voter was tactless enough, but for the son of John Adams to cite the example "of the nations of Europe and of their rulers" was downright suicidal. At one fell swoop he had revived all the Republican suspicions of the Adamses.

Adams's presidential message hastened the emergence of a new party system. The minority who cast their lot with Adams and Clay were turning into National-Republicans; the opposition, the growing party of Jacksonians, were the Democratic-Republicans, who would eventually drop the name Republican and become Democrats.

Adams's headstrong plunge into nationalism and his refusal to play the game of politics condemned his administration to utter frustration. Congress ignored his domestic proposals, and in foreign affairs the triumphs he had scored as secretary of state had no sequels. The climactic effort to discredit Adams came on the tariff issue. The Panic of 1819 had provoked calls for a higher tariff in 1820, but the effort failed by one vote in the Senate. In 1824 the advocates of protection renewed the effort, with greater success. The Tariff of 1824 favored the Middle

Atlantic and New England manufacturers with higher duties on woolens, cotton, iron, and other finished goods. Clay's Kentucky won a tariff on hemp, a fiber used for making rope, and a tariff on raw wool brought the wool-growing interests to the support of the measure. Additional revenues were provided by duties on sugar, molasses, coffee, and salt.

Three years later Jackson's supporters sought to advance their candidate through an awkward scheme hatched by John Calhoun. The plan was to present a bill with such outrageously high tariffs on raw materials that the eastern manufacturers would join the commercial interests there, and, with the votes of the agricultural South and Southwest, combine to defeat the measure. In the process Jackson men in the Northeast could take credit for supporting the tariff, and Jackson men, wherever it fitted their interests, could take credit for opposing it—while Jackson himself remained in the background. Virginia's John Randolph saw through the ruse. The bill, he asserted, "referred to manufactures of no sort of kind, but the manufacture of a President of the United States."

The complicated scheme helped elect Jackson, but in the process Calhoun was hoist on his own petard. His tariff bill, to his chagrin, passed, thanks to the growing strength of manufacturing interests in New England and to several crucial amendments that exempted certain raw materials. Daniel Webster, now a senator from Massachusetts, explained that he was ready to deny all he had said before against the tariff because New England had built up her manufactures on the understanding that the protective tariff was a settled policy.

When the bill passed on May 11, 1828, it was Calhoun's turn to explain his newfound opposition to the gospel of protection, and nothing so well illustrates the flexibility of constitutional principles as the switch in positions by Webster and Calhoun. Back in South Carolina, Calhoun prepared the *South Carolina Exposition and Protest* (1828), which was issued anonymously along with a series of resolutions by the state legislature. In that document Calhoun set forth the right of a state to nullify an act of Congress that it found unconstitutional.

JACKSON SWEEPS IN   Thus far the stage was set for the election of 1828, which might more truly be called a revolution than that of 1800. But if the issues of the day had anything to do with the election, they

Jackson is to be President, and you will be HANGED. *This anti-Jackson cartoon, published during the 1828 campaign, shows him as a frontier ruffian.*

were hardly visible in the campaign, in which politicians on both sides reached depths of scurrilousness that had not been plumbed since 1800. Jackson was denounced as a hot-tempered and ignorant barbarian, a participant in repeated duels and frontier brawls, a man whose fame rested on his reputation as a killer, and a man whom Thomas Jefferson himself had pronounced unfit because of his rash personality. In addition to that, his enemies dredged up the old story that Jackson had lived in adultery with his wife, Rachel, before they had been legally married. In fact they had been married for two years in the mistaken belief that her divorce from a former husband was final. Anxiety over this humiliation and her probable reception in Washington may have contributed to an illness from which Rachel died before her husband took office, a tragedy for which Jackson could never forgive his enemies.

The Jacksonians, however, were not averse to mudslinging. They got in their licks against Adams, condemning him as a man corrupted by foreigners in the courts of Europe. They called him a gambler and a spendthrift for having bought a billiard table and a chess set for the White House, and a puritanical hypocrite for despising the common people and warning Congress to ignore the will of its constituents. Adams had finally reached the presidency, the Jacksonians claimed, by a corrupt bargain with Henry Clay.

In the campaign of 1828 Jackson held most of the advantages. As a military hero he had some claim on patriotism. As a son of the West he was almost unbeatable there. As a planter and slaveholder he had the trust of southern planters. Debtors and local bankers who hated the national bank turned to Jackson. In addition, his vagueness on the issues protected him from attack by various interest groups. Not least of all, Jackson benefited from a spirit of democracy in which the common folk were no longer satisfied to look to their betters for leadership, as they had done in the past. It had become politically fatal to be labeled an aristocrat.

Since the Revolution and especially since 1800, more and more states had been granting the vote to taxpaying white males. The traditional story of the broadening franchise has been that a surge of Jacksonian Democracy came out of the West like a great wave, supported mainly by small farmers, leading the way for the East. But there were other forces working in the older states toward a wider franchise: the revolutionary doctrine of equality and the feeling on the parts of the workers, artisans, and small merchants of the towns, as well as small farmers and landed grandees, that a democratic ballot provided a means to combat the rising commercial and manufacturing interests. After 1815 the new states of the West entered the Union with either white manhood suffrage or a low taxpaying requirement, and older states such as Connecticut (1818), Massachusetts (1821), and New York (1821) all abolished their property requirements.

Jackson embodied the ideal of this new, more democratic political world. A tall, sinewy frontiersman born into poverty in South Carolina, Jackson had scrambled his way up by will and tenacity. He grew to be proud, gritty, short-tempered, and a good hater. During the Revolution, when he was a young boy, his mother died, two of his brothers were killed by redcoats, and Jackson himself was wounded by a British officer's saber. He would carry this scar for life, along with the conviction that it was not enough for a man to be right; he had to be tough as well. His toughness inspired his soldiers to nickname him "Old Hickory." During a duel with a man reputed to be the best shot in Tennessee, Jackson nevertheless let his opponent fire first. For his gallantry he received a bullet wedged next to his heart. But he straightened himself, patiently took aim, and killed his aghast foe. "I should have hit him," Jackson claimed, "if he had shot me through the brain."

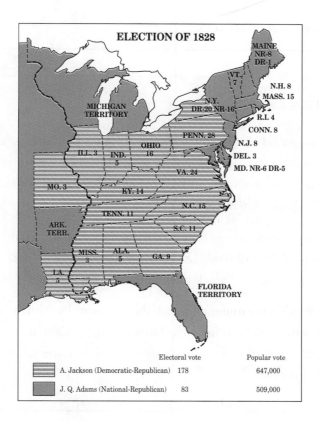

ELECTION OF 1828

	Electoral vote	Popular vote
A. Jackson (Democratic-Republican)	178	647,000
J. Q. Adams (National-Republican)	83	509,000

As a fighter, horse trader, land speculator, and frontier lawyer, Jackson symbolized the rugged new western temperament. A fellow law student described him as a "most roaring, rollicking, game-cocking, horse-racing, card-playing, mischievous fellow." One of his campaign slogans announced: "Adams can write, Jackson can fight." He could write, too, but he once said that he had no respect for a man who could think of only one way to spell a word.

The 1828 returns revealed that Jackson had won by a comfortable margin. The electoral vote was 178 to 83. Adams won all of New England, except for one of Maine's nine electoral votes, and a scattering of votes in New York and Maryland. All the rest belonged to Jackson. A new, convulsive era in American politics was about to begin.

MAKING CONNECTIONS

- Thomas Jefferson referred to the Missouri Compromise as "a firebell in the night." He was right. The controversy over the expansion of slavery, introduced here, will reappear in Chapter 13's discussion of Texas and the Mexican War.

- John Quincy Adams's National-Republicans, who could trace some of their ideology back to the Federalists, will be at the core of the Whig coalition that opposes Jackson in Chapter 10.

- Several of the issues on which the nation united during the "Era of Good Feelings"—the Bank and the protective tariff, for example—will become much more divisive, as discussed in the next chapter.

FURTHER READING

The standard overview of the Era of Good Feelings remains George Dangerfield's *The Awakening of American Nationalism, 1815–1828* (1965).*

For discussions of the American System, see Bray Hammond's *Banks and Politics in America from the Revolution to the Civil War* (1957) and George R. Taylor's *The Transportation Revolution, 1815–1860* (1951). For an overview of all the economic trends of the period, see Douglas C. North's *The Economic Growth of the United States, 1790–1860* (1961).*

On diplomatic relations during James Monroe's presidency, see William Earl Weeks's *John Quincy Adams and American Global Empire* (1992). For relations after 1812, see Ernest R. May's *The Making of the Monroe Doctrine* (1975).

*These books are available in paperback editions.

PART THREE

AN EXPANSIVE NATION

The election of Andrew Jackson signaled a new era in American history. By 1828 the United States was no longer an infant nation hugging the Atlantic coast. The maturing republic now included twenty-four states and almost thirteen million people. Many Americans were on the move during the early nineteenth century. Millions of them formed a relentless migratory stream that spilled over the Appalachian mountains, spanned the Mississippi River, and in the 1840s reached the Pacific Ocean. Wagons, canals, flatboats, steamboats, and eventually railroads transported the settlers westward.

The feverish expansion of the United States into new western territories brought Americans into conflict with Native Americans, Mexicans, and the British. Only a few people, however, expressed moral reservations about displacing others. Most Americans believed it was the "manifest destiny" of the United States to spread across the entire continent—at whatever cost and at whomever's expense. Americans generally felt that they enjoyed the blessing of Providence in their efforts to consolidate the entire continent under their control.

While most Americans during the Jacksonian era continued to earn their living from the soil, textile mills and manufacturing plants began to dot the landscape and transform the nature of work and the pace of life. By mid-century the United States was emerging as one of the world's major industrial powers. In addition, the lure of cheap land and plentiful jobs, as well as the promise of political equality and religious freedom, attracted hundreds of thousands of immigrants from Europe. These newcomers, mostly from Germany and Ireland, faced ethnic prejudices, religious persecution, and language barriers that made assimilation into American culture all the more difficult.

All these developments gave to American life in the second quarter of the nineteenth century its dynamic and fluid quality. The United States, said the philosopher-poet Ralph Waldo Emerson, was "a country of beginnings, of projects, of designs, of expectations." A restless optimism seemed to characterize the period. People of lowly social status who heretofore had accepted their lot in life now strove to climb the social ladder and enter the political arena. The patrician republicanism espoused by Jefferson and Madison gave way to the frontier democracy promoted by the Jacksonians. Americans were no longer content to be governed by a small, benevolent aristocracy of talent and wealth. They began to demand—and obtain—government of, by, and for the people.

The fertile economic environment during the antebellum era helped foster the egalitarian idea that individuals (except African Americans, Native Americans, and women) should have an equal opportunity to better themselves and should be granted political rights and privileges. In America, observed a journalist in 1844, "One has as good a chance as another according to his talents, prudence, and personal exertions."

The exuberant individualism embodied in such mythic expressions of economic equality and political democracy spilled over into the cultural arena during the Jacksonian era. The so-called Romantic movement applied democratic ideals to philosophy, religion, literature, and the fine arts. In New England, Ralph Waldo Emerson, Henry David Thoreau, and Margaret Fuller joined other Transcendentalists in espousing a radical individualism. Other reformers were motivated more by a sense of spiritual mission than democratic individualism. In striving to enhance personal morality and the general welfare, mostly middle-class reformers sought to introduce public-supported schools, abolish slavery, promote temperance in the use of alcoholic beverages, and improve the lot of the disabled, insane, and imprisoned. Their efforts helped ameliorate some of the problems created by the frenetic pace of economic growth and territorial expansion. But the reformers made little headway against slavery. It would take a brutal civil war to dislodge America's "peculiar institution."

10 THE JACKSONIAN IMPULSE

CHAPTER ORGANIZER

This chapter focuses on:

- the social and political context of the Jackson/Van Buren administrations

- Andrew Jackson's attitudes and actions concerning the tariff (and nullification), Indian policy, and the Bank

- the rise of a new party system (Democrats and Whigs)

SETTING THE STAGE

The election of Andrew Jackson initiated a new era in American politics and social development. He was the first president not to come from a prominent colonial family. As a self-made soldier-politician-land speculator from the backcountry, he symbolized a sea change in the social temper. The nation he prepared to govern was vastly different from that led by Washington and Jefferson. In 1828 the United States boasted twenty-four states and nearly 13 million people, many of them recent arrivals from Germany and Ireland. An incredible surge in foreign demand for cotton and other goods, along with British investment in American enterprises, helped fuel a transportation revolution and an economic boom. Textile factories sprouted like mushrooms across the New England countryside, their ravenous spinning looms fed by cotton grown in the newly cultivated lands of Alabama and Mississippi. This fluid new economic environment fostered a mad scramble for material gain and political advantage. People of all ranks and backgrounds raced to acquire wealth and thereby gain social status and prestige. "The desire to grow suddenly rich has seized on all classes," exclaimed a character in one of James Fenimore Cooper's novels.

The Jacksonians sought to democratize economic opportunity and political participation. As Jackson frequently declared, the majority, the "great body of the people," would genuinely rule. Yet to call the Jacksonian era the "age of the common man," as many historians have done, is misleading. While political participation increased during the Jacksonian era, most of the common folk remained *common* folk. The period never produced true economic and social equality. Power and privilege, for the most part, remained in the hands of an "uncommon" elite. Jacksonians in power proved to be as opportunistic and manipulative as the patricians they displaced. And they never embraced the principle of material equality. "Distinctions in society will always exist under every just government," Andrew Jackson observed. "Equality of talents, or education, or of wealth cannot be produced by human institutions." He and other Jacksonians wanted people to have an equal chance to compete in the economic marketplace and political arena, but they never sanctioned equality of results. "True republicanism," one commentator declared, "requires that every man shall have an equal chance—that every man shall be free to become as unequal as he can." But in the afterglow of Jackson's election victory, few observers troubled with such distinctions. It was time to celebrate the commoner's ascension to the presidency.

INAUGURATION   On Inauguration Day, March 4, 1829, the new president, a sixty-two-year-old widower, plagued by a persistent cough and severe headaches, delivered his address in a voice so low that few in the crowd of 15,000 spectators could hear it. It mattered little, for Jackson's advisers had eliminated anything that might give offense. On the major issues of the tariff, internal improvements, and the Bank of the United States, the new president remained vague. Only a few points foreshadowed policies that he would pursue: he favored retire-

All Creation Going to the White House. *The scene following Jackson's inauguration as president, according to satirist Robert Cruikshank.*

ment of the national debt, a proper regard for states' rights, a "just" policy toward Indians, and rotation in federal office holders, which he pronounced "a leading principle in the republican creed"—a principle his enemies would dub the "spoils system."

After his speech Jackson mounted his horse and rode off to the White House, where he hosted a reception for all who chose to come. The boisterous party exhibited the turmoil that seemed always to surround Jackson. A huge crowd pushed into the White House, surged through the rooms, jostled the waiters, broke dishes, leaped onto the furniture—all in an effort to shake the president's hand or at least get a glimpse of him. To Supreme Court Justice Story, "the reign of 'King Mob' seemed triumphant."

APPOINTMENTS AND POLITICAL RIVALRIES Jackson believed that government workers who stayed too long in office became corrupted by a sense of power. So he set about replacing Adams's appointees with his own supporters. But his use of the "spoils system" has been exaggerated. During his first year in office Jackson replaced only about 9 percent of the appointed officials in the federal government, and during his entire term fewer than 20 percent.

Cartoon depicting Jackson as a demon dangling political plums before office seekers.

Jackson's administration was from the outset a house divided between the partisans of Secretary of State Martin Van Buren of New York and Vice-President Calhoun of South Carolina. Much of the political history of the next few years would turn upon the rivalry between the two, as each man jockeyed for position as Jackson's heir apparent. Van Buren held most of the advantages, foremost among them his skill at timing and tactics. As John Randolph put it, Van Buren always "rowed to his objective with muffled oars." Jackson, new to political administration, leaned heavily on him for advice and for help in soothing the ruffled feathers of rejected office seekers.

But Calhoun could not be taken lightly. He, too, expected to be Jackson's successor. A man of towering intellect, humorless outlook, and apostolic zeal, he possessed a demonic sense of duty and a brilliant interest in ideas. "There is no *relaxation* with him," a frazzled friend once wrote. Perhaps Henry Clay described Calhoun best: "tall, careworn, with furrowed brow, haggard and intensely gazing, looking as if he were dissecting the last abstraction which sprung from a metaphysician's brain." Since returning from Washington to his plantation in South Carolina in 1825, Calhoun had nurtured his crops and his ardent love for his native region. Now, as vice-president, he was determined to defend southern interests against the advance of northern industrialism and abolitionism.

THE EATON AFFAIR   In his battle for political power with Calhoun, Van Buren had luck as well as political skill on his side. Fate had quickly handed him a trump card: the succulent scandal of the Peggy Eaton affair. Peggy Eaton was a vivacious Irish widow whose husband supposedly had committed suicide upon learning of her affair with Tennessee Senator John Eaton. Her marriage to Eaton, three months before he entered Jackson's cabinet as secretary of war, had scarcely made a virtuous woman of her in the eyes of the proper ladies of Washington. Floride Calhoun, the vice-president's wife, pointedly snubbed her, and other cabinet wives followed suit.

Peggy's plight reminded Jackson of the gossip that had pursued his wife, Rachel, and he pronounced Peggy "chaste as a virgin." But the cabinet members were unable to cure their wives of what Van Buren dubbed "the Eaton Malaria." Van Buren, however, was a widower, and therefore free to lavish on poor Peggy all the attention that Jackson thought was her due. Mrs. Eaton herself finally wilted under the chill and withdrew from society. The outraged Jackson came to link Calhoun with what he called a conspiracy against her and drew even closer to Van Buren.

INTERNAL IMPROVEMENTS   During the chilly winter of 1829–1830, Van Buren prepared some additional blows to Calhoun. It was easy to bring Jackson into opposition to internal improvements and thus to federal programs with which Calhoun had long been identified. In 1830 the Maysville Road Bill, passed by Congress, offered Jackson a happy chance for a dual thrust at both Calhoun and Clay. The bill authorized the government to buy stock in a road from Maysville to Clay's hometown of Lexington. The road lay entirely within the state of Kentucky, and though part of a larger scheme to link up with the National Road via Cincinnati, it could be viewed as a purely local undertaking. On that ground Jackson vetoed the bill, prompting widespread popular acclaim. Yet while Jackson continued to oppose federal aid to local projects, he supported projects such as the National Road, as well as road building in the territories, and rivers and harbors bills, the "pork barrels" from which every congressman tried to pluck a morsel for his district. Even so, Jackson's attitude toward the Maysville Road set an important precedent, on the eve of the railroad age, for limiting federal initiative in internal improvements. Railroads would be built altogether by state and private capital at least until 1850.

NULLIFICATION

CALHOUN'S THEORY   There is a fine irony to Calhoun's plight in the Jackson administration, for Calhoun was now in midpassage from his early phase as a War Hawk nationalist to his later phase as a states'-rights sectionalist—and open to thrusts on both flanks. Conditions in his home state had brought on this change. Suffering from agricultural depression, South Carolina lost almost 70,000 people to emigration during the 1820s, and would lose nearly twice that number in the 1830s. Most South Carolinians blamed the protective tariff, which tended to raise the prices of manufactured goods and, insofar as it discouraged the sale of foreign goods in the United States, reduced the ability of British and French traders to acquire the American money

John C. Calhoun.

with which to buy American cotton. This worsened problems of low cotton prices and exhausted lands. The South Carolinians' malaise was compounded by the increasing criticism of slavery. Hardly had the country emerged from the Missouri controversy when the city of Charleston was thrown into panic by the thwarted Denmark Vesey slave insurrection of 1822.

The unexpected passage of the Tariff of 1828, called the Tariff of Abominations by its critics, left Calhoun no choice but to join the opposition or give up his home base. Calhoun's *South Carolina Exposition and Protest* (1828), written in opposition to that tariff, contained a fine-spun theory of nullification that stopped just short of justifying secession from the Union. The unsigned statement accompanied resolutions of the South Carolina legislature protesting the tariff. Calhoun, however, had not entirely abandoned his earlier nationalism. He wanted to preserve the Union by protecting the minority rights that the agricultural and slaveholding South claimed. The fine balance he struck between states' rights and central authority was actually not far removed from Jackson's own philosophy, but growing tension between the two men would complicate the issue. Jackson, in addition, was determined to draw the line at any defiance of federal law.

THE WEBSTER-HAYNE DEBATE   South Carolina had proclaimed its dislike for the tariff, but had postponed any action against its enforcement, awaiting with hope the election of 1828 in which Calhoun was the Jacksonian candidate for vice-president. The state anticipated a new tariff policy from the Jackson administration. There the issue stood until 1830, when the great Webster-Hayne debate sharpened the lines between states' rights and the Union. The immediate occasion for the debate, however, was the question of public lands.

The federal government still owned immense tracts of land, and the issue of their disposition elbowed its way again onto the center stage of sectional debate. Late in 1829 a Connecticut senator, fearing the continued drain of able-bodied folk from New England, sought to restrict land sales in the West. When his resolution came before the Senate in 1830, Missouri's Thomas Hart Benton, who for years had been calling for lower land prices, denounced it as a sectional attack designed to impede the settlement of the West so that the East might maintain its supply of cheap factory labor.

Robert Y. Hayne of South Carolina took Benton's side. Hayne saw in the public-lands issue a chance to strengthen the alliance of South and West reflected in Jackson's election. Perhaps by endorsing a policy of cheap lands in the West the southerners could win western support for lower tariffs. The government, said Hayne, endangered the Union by imposing a hardship upon one section to the benefit of another. The use of public lands as a source of revenue to the central government would create "a fund for corruption—fatal to the sovereignty and independence of the states."

At this point Daniel Webster of Massachusetts rose to offer a dramatic defense of the East. Possessed of a thunderous voice and a theatrical flair, Webster was widely recognized as the nation's foremost orator and lawyer. His striking physical presence enhanced his rhetorical skills. Webster had the torso of a bull, and his huge head, with its jet-black hair, domed forehead, craggy brows overhanging deep-set eyes, and a mastiff's mouth, commanded attention. With the gallery hushed, the "God-like Daniel" began by denying that the East had ever sought to restrict development of the West. He then rebuked those southerners who "habitually speak of the Union in terms of indifference, or even of disparagement." Federal money derived from land sales, Webster argued, was not a source of corruption but a source of improvement. At this point the issue of western lands vanished from sight. Webster had adroitly shifted the ground of debate and lured Hayne into defending states' rights and upholding the doctrine of nullification instead of pursuing coalition with the West.

Hayne took the bait. Young, handsome, and himself an accomplished speaker, Hayne launched into a defense of Calhoun's *South Carolina Exposition,* arguing that the union was a compact of the states, and the federal government could not be the judge of its own powers, else its powers would be unlimited. Rather, the states remained free to judge when the national government had overstepped the bounds of its constitutional authority. The right of state "interposition" to thwart an unjust federal statute was as "full and complete as it was before the Constitution was formed."

In rebuttal to the state-compact theory, Webster defined a nationalistic view of the Constitution. From the beginning, he asserted, the American Revolution had been a crusade of the united colonies rather than of each separately. True sovereignty resided in the people as a whole, for whom both federal and state governments acted as agents in their respective spheres. If a single state could nullify a law of the general government, then the Union would be a "rope of sand," a practical absurdity. Instead the Constitution had created a Supreme Court with the final jurisdiction on all questions of constitutionality. A state could neither nullify a federal law nor secede from the Union. The practical outcome of nullification would be a confrontation leading to civil war.

Those sitting in the Senate galleries and much of the country at large thrilled to Webster's eloquence. His closing statement has become justly famous: "Liberty and Union, now and forever, one and inseparable." In the practical world of coalition politics, Webster also had the better of the argument, for the Union and majority rule meant more to westerners, including Jackson, than the abstractions of state sovereignty and nullification. As for the public lands, the disputed resolution was soon defeated anyway. And whatever one might argue about the origins of the Union, its evolution would more and more validate Webster's position.

THE RIFT WITH CALHOUN   As yet, however, the enigmatic Jackson had not spoken out on the issue. Jackson, like Calhoun, was a slaveholder, albeit a westerner, and might be expected to sympathize with South Carolina, his native state. Soon all doubt was removed, at least on the point of nullification. On April 13, 1830, the Jefferson Day Dinner, honoring the birthday of the former president, was held in Washington. Jackson and Van Buren agreed that the president should present a toast that would indicate his opposition to nullification. When his turn came, Jackson rose, stood erect as a poplar, raised his glass, pointedly stared at Calhoun, and announced: "Our Union—it must be preserved!" Calhoun, who followed, trembled so that he spilled some of the amber fluid from his glass, but tried quickly to retrieve the situation with a toast to "The Union, next to our liberty most dear!" But Jackson had set off a bombshell that exploded the plans of the states'-righters.

Nearly a month afterward the final nail was driven into the coffin of Calhoun's presidential ambitions. On May 12, 1830, Jackson saw a letter confirming reports that in 1818 Calhoun, as secretary of war, had proposed to discipline Jackson for his reckless behavior during the Florida invasion. This discovery provoked a tense correspondence between President Jackson and Calhoun, and ended with a curt note from the president cutting it off. "Understanding you now," Jackson wrote, "no further communication with you on this subject is necessary."

The growing rift prompted Jackson to remove all Calhoun partisans from the cabinet. He then named Van Buren minister to London, pending Senate approval. In the fall of 1831 Jackson announced his readiness for one more term, with the idea of returning Van Buren from London in time for the New Yorker to succeed him as president in 1836. But in 1832, when the Senate reconvened, Van Buren's enemies opposed his appointment as minister, and gave Calhoun, as vice-president, a chance to reject the nomination by a tie-breaking vote. "It will kill him [Van Buren], sir, kill him dead," Calhoun told Senator Thomas Hart Benton. Benton disagreed: "You have broken a minister, and elected a Vice-President." So, it turned out, he had. Calhoun's vote against Van Buren aroused popular sympathy for the New Yorker, who would soon be nominated to succeed Calhoun as vice-president.

His own presidential hopes blasted, Calhoun eagerly became the public leader of the nullificationists. These South Carolinians believed that, despite reductions supported by Jackson, tariff rates remained too high. By the end of 1831 Jackson was calling for further reductions to take the wind out of the nullificationists' sails, and the tariff of 1832 did cut revenues another $5 million, but mainly on unprotected items. Average tariff rates were about 25 percent, but rates on cottons, woolens, and iron remained up around 50 percent. South Carolinians labeled such high rates an "abomination."

THE SOUTH CAROLINA ORDINANCE   In the South Carolina state elections of 1832, the advocates of nullification took the initiative in organization and agitation. A special legislative session called for the election of a state convention, which assembled at Columbia a month later and overwhelmingly adopted a nullification ordinance. This ordinance repudiated the tariff acts of 1828 and 1832 as unconstitutional and forbade collection of the duties in the state after February 1, 1833. The legislature also chose Robert Hayne as governor and elected Calhoun to succeed him as senator. Calhoun promptly resigned as vice-president in order to defend nullification on the Senate floor.

In the crisis South Carolina found itself standing alone. The Georgia legislature dismissed nullification as "rash and revolutionary." Alabama pronounced it "unsound in theory and dangerous in practice"; Mississippi stood "firmly resolved" to put down nullification. Jackson's response was measured and firm, but not rash—at least not in public. In private he threatened to hang Calhoun and all other traitors—and later expressed regret that he had failed to hang at least Calhoun. In his annual message on December 4, 1832, Jackson announced his firm intention to enforce the tariff, but once again urged Congress to lower the rates. On December 10 he followed up with his Nullification Proclamation, a document that characterized that doctrine as an "impractical absurdity." Jackson appealed to the people of his native state not to follow false leaders: "The laws of the United States must be executed. . . . Those who told you that you might peaceably prevent their execution, deceived you. . . . Their object is disunion. But be not deceived by names. Disunion by armed force is treason."

CLAY'S COMPROMISE Jackson sent General Winfield Scott to Charleston Harbor with reinforcements of federal soldiers. "In 40 days," the president announced, "I can have within the limits of South Carolina 50,000 men." A ship of war and seven revenue cutters appeared in the harbor, ready to enforce the tariff before ships had a chance to unload their cargoes. The nullifiers mobilized the state militia while unionists in the state organized a volunteer force. In 1833 the president requested from Congress a "Force Bill" authorizing him to use the army to compel compliance with federal law in South Carolina. At the same time he endorsed a bill in Congress that would have lowered duties to a maximum of 20 percent within two years.

When the Force Bill was introduced, Calhoun immediately rose in opposition, denying that either he or his state favored disunion. Indeed, Calhoun personally opposed the idea of secession. He did not want the South to leave the Union; he wanted the region to regain its political dominance of the Union. His comments to the Senate, wrote the future president, John Tyler of Virginia, were "warm—impassioned—burning." Passage of the bill eventually came to depend on the support of Henry Clay, who finally yielded to those urging him to save the day. On February 12, 1833, he introduced a plan to reduce the tariff gradually until 1842, by which time no rate would be more than 20 percent. South Carolina would have preferred a greater reduction, but Clay's plan got the nullifiers out of the corner into which they had painted themselves.

On March 1, 1833, the compromise tariff and the Force Bill passed

Congress, and the next day Jackson signed both. The South Carolina convention then met and rescinded its nullification ordinance. In a face-saving gesture, it then nullified the Force Bill, for which Jackson no longer had any need. Both sides were able to claim victory. The president had upheld the supremacy of the Union, and South Carolina had secured a reduction of the tariff. Calhoun, worn out by the controversy, returned to his plantation. "The struggle, so far from being over," he ominously wrote, "is not more than fairly commenced."

INDIAN POLICY

During the 1820s and 1830s the United States was fast becoming a multicultural nation of many peoples from many different countries. As economic growth reinforced the institution of slavery and accelerated westward expansion, policy makers struggled to preserve white racial homogeneity and cultural hegemony. "Next to the case of the black race within our bosom," declared former president James Madison, "that of the red [race]on our borders is the problem most baffling to the policy of our country." Andrew Jackson, however, saw nothing baffling about Indian policy. His attitude toward Indians was the typically western one, that they were barbaric impediments to white social progress. By the time of his election in 1828 he was convinced that a "just, humane, liberal policy toward Indians" dictated moving them onto the plains west of the Mississippi, an area fit mainly for horned toads and rattlesnakes. Congress agreed, and in 1830 it approved the Indian Removal Act. Thereafter some ninety-four removal treaties were negotiated, and in 1835 Jackson announced that the policy had been carried out or was in process of completion for all but a handful of Indians.

Most of the northern tribes were too weak to resist the offers of Indian commissioners who, if necessary, used bribery and alcohol to woo the chiefs. If sometimes the tribes rebelled, there was, on the whole, remarkably little resistance. In Illinois and Wisconsin Territory an armed clash known as the Black Hawk War sprang up in 1832, when the Sauk and Fox under Chief Black Hawk sought to reoccupy some lands they had abandoned in the previous year. Facing famine and hostile Sioux west of the Mississippi River, they were simply seeking a place to get in a corn crop. The Illinois militia mobilized to expel them, chased them into Wisconsin Territory, and massacred women and children as they tried to escape across the Mississippi. When Black Hawk surrendered he confessed that his "heart is dead, and no longer beats quick in his bosom. He is now a prisoner to the white men; they will do with him as they wish. But he can stand torture and is not afraid of death. He is no coward. Black Hawk is an Indian." The Black Hawk War came to be remembered later, however, less because of the atrocities inflicted on the Indians than because the participants included two native Kentuckians later to be pitted against each other: Lieutenant Jefferson Davis of the regular army and Captain Abraham Lincoln of the Illinois volunteers.

In the South two proud Indian nations, the Seminoles and Cherokees, also put up a stubborn resistance. The Seminoles were in fact a group of different tribes that had gravitated to Florida in the eighteenth century. They fought a protracted guerrilla war in the Everglades from 1835 to 1842, but most of the vigor went out of their resistance after 1837, when their leader, Osceola, was seized by treachery under a flag of truce, imprisoned, and left to die. After 1842 only a few hundred Seminoles remained, hiding out in the swamps. Most of the rest had been banished to the West.

THE TRAIL OF TEARS   The Cherokees had by the end of the eighteenth century fallen back into the mountains of northern Georgia and western North Carolina, onto land guaranteed to them in 1791 by treaty with the United States. In 1827 the Cherokees, relying on their treaty rights, adopted a constitution in which they said pointedly that they were not subject to any other state or nation. The next year Georgia responded with a law stipulating that after June 1, 1830, the authority of state law would extend over the Cherokees living within the boundaries of the state.

The discovery of gold in 1829 whetted the whites' appetite for Cherokee lands and brought bands of rough prospectors into the country. The Cherokees sought relief in the Supreme Court, but in *Cherokee Nation v. Georgia* (1831) John Marshall ruled that the Court lacked jurisdiction because the Cherokees were a "domestic dependent nation" rather than a foreign state in the meaning of the Constitution. Marshall added, however, that the Cherokees had "an unquestionable right" to their lands until they wished to cede them to the United States.

The first issue of the Cherokee Phoenix *published the Constitution of the Cherokee nation, which embraced "the lands solemnly guaranteed and reserved forever to the Cherokee Nation by the Treaties concluded with the United States."*

In 1830 a Georgia law had required whites in the Cherokee territory to get licenses authorizing their residence there, and to take an oath of allegiance to the state. Two New England missionaries among the Indians refused and were sentenced to four years at hard labor. On appeal, their case reached the Supreme Court as *Worcester v. Georgia* (1832), and the court held that the Cherokee nation was "a distinct political community" within which Georgia law had no force. The Georgia law was therefore unconstitutional. Now Georgia faced down the Supreme Court with the tacit consent of the president. Jackson is supposed to have said privately: "Marshall has made his decision, now let him enforce it!" Whether or not he put it so bluntly, Jackson did nothing to implement the decision. In the circumstances there was nothing for the Cherokees to do but give in and sign a treaty, which they did in 1835. They gave up their lands in the Southeast in exchange for lands in the Indian Territory west of Arkansas, $5 million from the federal government, and expenses for transportation.

By 1838 15,000 Cherokees had departed on the thousand-mile "Trail of Tears" westward, following the Choctaws, Chickasaws, Creeks, and

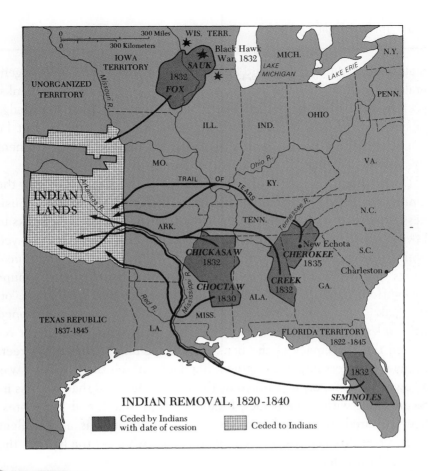

Seminoles. It was a grueling journey marked by the cruelty and neglect of soldiers and private contractors, and scorn and pilferage by whites along the way. Four thousand Cherokees did not survive the trip. A few never left their homeland. They held out in their native mountains and acquired title to lands in North Carolina; thenceforth they were the "Eastern Band" of Cherokees.

THE BANK CONTROVERSY

THE BANK'S OPPONENTS The overriding national issue in the presidential campaign of 1832 was neither Jackson's Indian policy nor South Carolina's obsession with nullification. It was the question of rechartering the Bank of the United States, whose legal mandate would soon lapse. Jackson had absorbed the West's hostility toward the bank after the Panic of 1819, and he insisted that it was unconstitutional no matter what Marshall had said in *McCulloch v. Maryland*. Banks in general had fed a speculative mania, and Jackson, suspicious of all banks, preferred a hard-money policy. The general had no informed knowledge of banking; he was in fact blissfully ignorant of the subject. But he felt strongly that such a central bank was wrong, and his government "would never recharter that monster of corruption."

Under the management of Nicholas Biddle, the Second Bank of the United States had prospered and grown. The bank had facilitated business expansion and supplied a stable currency by forcing state banks to keep a specie reserve (gold or silver) behind their notes. But arrayed against the bank were powerful enemies: some of the state and local banks that had been forced to reduce their note issues, debtor groups that suffered from the reduction, and businessmen and speculators "on the make" who wanted easier credit. States'-rights groups questioned the bank's constitutionality. Financiers on New York's Wall Street resented the supremacy of the bank on Philadelphia's Chestnut Street. Many westerners and workingmen, like Jackson, felt that the bank was a powerful monopoly controlled by the wealthy few and that this was irreconcilable with a democracy. Biddle, born to wealth and social prestige, cultured, witty, and supremely self-confident, was an excellent banker but also a convenient symbol for those who saw the bank as the friend of capitalists.

BIDDLE'S RECHARTER EFFORT The bank's twenty-year charter would run through 1836, but Biddle could not afford the uncertainty of waiting until then for a renewal. He pondered whether to force the issue of recharter before the election of 1832 or after. On this point leaders of the National-Republicans, especially Clay and Webster, argued that the time to move was before the election. Clay, already the candidate of the National-Republicans, proposed to make the bank the central issue of the presidential election. Friends of the bank held a majority in Congress, and Jackson would risk loss of support in the election if he vetoed renewal. But they failed to grasp the depth of popular prejudice against the bank, and thereby they succeeded mainly in handing Jackson a charged issue on the eve of the election.

Both houses passed the recharter by comfortable margins, but without the two-thirds majority needed to override a veto. On July 10, 1832, Jackson vetoed the bill, sending it back to Congress with a ringing denunciation of monopoly and special privilege. The bill, he argued, demonstrated that many "of our rich men have not been content with equal protection and equal benefits, but have besought us to make them richer by act of Congress." An effort to overrule the veto failed in the Senate, where the vote of twenty-two to nineteen for the bank fell far short of the needed two-thirds majority. The stage was set for a nationwide financial crisis. "This worthy President," fumed Biddle, "thinks that because he has scalped Indians and imprisoned judges, he is to have his way with the Bank. He is mistaken."

CAMPAIGN INNOVATIONS   The presidential campaign, as usual, began early, the nominations having been made before the bank veto, two in fact before the end of 1831. For the first time a third party entered the field. The Anti-Masonic party was, like the bank, the object of strong emotions then sweeping the new democracy. The group had grown out of popular hostility toward the Masonic order, a fraternal organization whose members were suspected of having kidnapped and murdered a New Yorker for revealing the "secrets" of his lodge. Opposition to a fraternal order was hardly the foundation on which to build a

George Caleb Bingham's Verdict of the People *depicts the increasingly democratic politics of the early to middle nineteenth century.*

lasting national political organization, but the Anti-Masonic party had three important "firsts" to its credit: in addition to being the first third party, it was the first party to hold a national nominating convention and the first to announce a platform, all of which it accomplished in 1831 when it nominated William Wirt of Maryland for president.

The major parties followed its example by holding national conventions of their own. In 1831 National-Republican party delegates assembled in Baltimore to nominate Henry Clay for president. Jackson endorsed the idea of a nominating convention for the Democratic party (the name "Republican" was now formally dropped) to demonstrate popular support for its candidates. To that purpose the convention adopted the two-thirds rule for nomination (which prevailed until 1936), and then named Martin Van Buren as Jackson's running mate. The Democrats, unlike the other two parties, adopted no formal platform at their first convention, and relied substantially on hoopla and the president's personal popularity to carry their cause.

The outcome was an overwhelming endorsement of Jackson in the electoral college by 219 votes to 49 for Clay, and a less overwhelming but solid victory in the popular vote, 688,000 to 530,000. William Wirt carried only Vermont. South Carolina, preparing for nullification and unable to stomach either Jackson or Clay, delivered its eleven votes to the governor of Virginia.

REMOVAL OF GOVERNMENT DEPOSITS   Jackson viewed the election as a mandate to proceed further against the B.U.S., and he now resolved to remove all government deposits and distribute them to state banks. When Secretary of the Treasury McLane opposed removal of the government deposits and suggested a new and modified version of the bank, Jackson shook up his cabinet. He kicked McLane upstairs to head the State Department and replaced him with William J. Duane of Philadelphia. But by some oversight Jackson failed to explore Duane's views fully or advise him of his own expectations. Duane was antibank, but he was consistent in his convictions. Dubious about banks in general, he saw no merit in removing deposits from the central bank for deposit in countless state banks. Jackson might well have listened to Duane's warnings that such action would lead to speculative inflation, but the old general's combative instincts were too much aroused. He summarily dismissed Duane and moved Attorney-General Roger Taney

The Downfall of Mother Bank. *In this pro-Jackson cartoon, the bank crumbles and Jackson's opponents flee in the face of the heroic president's removal of government deposits.*

to the Treasury, where the new secretary gladly complied with the president's wishes, which corresponded to his own views.

Taney continued to draw on governmental accounts with Biddle's bank and to deposit all new governmental receipts in state banks. By the end of 1833 there were twenty-three state banks that had the benefit of governmental deposits, "pet banks" as they came to be called. Jackson's headlong plunge into finance, it soon turned out, backfired. As so often happens with complex public issues, dissatisfaction had become focused on a symbol. In this case the symbol was the "Monster of Chestnut Street," which had been all along the one institution able to maintain some degree of order in the financial world. Jackson's action initially provoked a contraction of credit by Biddle's bank in order to shore up its defenses against the loss of deposits. By 1834 the tightness of credit was creating widespread complaints of business distress.

The contraction resulting from the bank war quickly gave way, however, to a speculative binge encouraged by the deposit of government funds in the pet banks. With the restraint of Biddle's bank removed, the state banks unleashed their wildcat tendencies, issuing banknotes without keeping sufficient gold reserves on hand. (The term "wildcat," used in this sense, originated in Michigan, where one of the fly-by-night banks featured a panther, or wildcat, on its worthless notes.) New banks mushroomed, blissfully printing banknotes to lend to speculators. Sales of public lands rose from 4 million acres in 1834 to 15 million in 1835 and to 20 million in 1836. At the same time the states plunged heavily into debt to finance the building of roads and canals, inspired by the success of New York's Erie Canal. By 1837 total state indebtedness had soared to $170 million, a very large sum for this time.

FISCAL MEASURES   Still the federal surplus continued to mount as the widespread speculation in public lands continued, and this set off an intense debate over how to deal with the growing federal surplus. Many westerners proposed simply to lower the price of land; southerners preferred to lower the tariff—but such action would now upset the compromise achieved in the Tariff of 1833. Finally, in 1836, a compromise allowed the government to distribute most of the surplus as loans to the states. To satisfy Jackson's concerns the funds were technically "deposits," but they were never demanded back. Distribution was to be in proportion to each state's representation in Congress.

About a month after passage of this Distribution Act, Jackson's treasury secretary issued the Specie Circular of July 11, 1836. With that document the president belatedly applied his hard-money convictions to the sale of public lands. According to his order, the government after August 15 would accept only gold and silver in payment for lands. Doing so would supposedly "repress frauds," withhold support "from monopoly of the public lands in the hands of speculators and capitalists," and discourage the "ruinous extension" of banknotes and credit.

Irony dogged Jackson to the end on this matter. Since few actual settlers could get their hands on hard money, they were now left all the more at the mercy of speculators for land purchases. Both the distribution and the Specie Circular put many state banks in a precarious plight. The distribution reduced their deposits, or at least threw things into disarray by shifting them from bank to bank, and the increased demand for specie put an added strain on the supply of gold and silver. The distribution of the federal surplus to the state governments entailed the removal of large deposits from state banks. In turn, the state banks had to call in many of their loans in order to accumulate enough money to make the transfer of federal funds to the state governments. This caused greater dismay among the already chaotic state banking community. At the same time, the new requirement that only hard money be accepted for federal land purchases put an added strain on the local supplies of gold and silver.

BOOM AND BUST   But the boom and bust of the 1830s had causes larger even than Andrew Jackson, causes that were beyond his control. The inflation of mid-decade was rooted not solely in a sudden expansion of banknotes, as it seemed at the time, but also in an increase of gold and silver flowing in from England and France, and especially from Mexico, for investment and for the purchase of American cotton and other products.

Contrary to appearances, therefore, the specie reserves in American banks actually kept pace with the increase of banknotes, despite reckless behavior by some banks. But by 1836 a tighter economy caused a decline in British investments abroad and in British demand for American cotton, just when the new western lands were creating a rapid increase in cotton supply. Fortunately for Jackson, the Panic of 1837 did not ease until he was out of the White House and safely back at the Hermitage, his plantation near Nashville. His successor would serve as the scapegoat.

VAN BUREN AND THE NEW PARTY SYSTEM

THE WHIG COALITION   Before the economic crash, however, the Jacksonian Democrats reaped a political bonanza. Jackson had downed the dual monsters of nullification and the bank, and the people loved him for it. By 1834, however, his opponents began to pull together a new coalition of diverse elements united chiefly by their hostility to Jackson. The imperious demeanor of that champion of democracy had given rise to the name of "King Andrew I." His followers therefore were "Tories," supporters of the king, and his opponents "Whigs," a name that linked them to the patriots of the American Revolution. This diverse coalition clustered around its center, the National-Republican party of John Quincy Adams, Clay, and Webster. Into the combination streamed remnants of the Anti-Masons and Democrats who, for one reason or another, were alienated by Jackson's stands on the bank, Indian removal, hard money, or internal improvements. Of the forty-one Democrats in Congress who had voted to recharter the bank, twenty-eight had joined the Whigs by 1836.

Whiggery always had about it an atmosphere of social conservatism and superiority. The core Whigs were the supporters of Henry Clay, men whose vision was quickened by the vistas of his "American System." In the South the Whigs enjoyed the support of the urban banking and commercial interests, as well as their planter associates, owners of most of the slaves in the region. In the West, farmers who valued internal improvements joined the Whig ranks. Most states'-rights supporters eventually dropped away, and by the early 1840s the Whigs were becoming the party of nationalism, even in the South. Unlike the Democrats, who attracted Catholic immigrants from Germany and Ireland, Whig voters tended to be native-born and British-American evangelical Protestants—Presbyterians, Baptists, and Congregationalists—who were active in promoting social reforms such as abolitionism and temperance. Throughout their two decades of strength the Whigs were a national party, strong both north and south, and a cohesive force for Union.

THE ELECTION OF 1836   By the presidential election of 1836 a new two-party system was emerging out of the Jackson and anti-Jackson forces, a system that would remain in fairly even balance for twenty years. In 1835, eighteen months before the election, the Democrats held their second national convention and nominated Jackson's hand-picked successor, Vice-President Martin Van Buren. The Whig coalition, united chiefly in its opposition to Jackson, held no convention but adopted a strategy of multiple candidacies, hoping to throw the election into the House of Representatives. The result was a free-for-all reminiscent of 1824, except that this time one candidate stood apart from the rest. It was Van Buren against the field. The Whigs put up three favorite sons: Daniel Webster, named by the Massachusetts legislature; Hugh Lawson White, chosen by anti-Jackson Democrats in the Tennessee legislature; and William Henry Harrison of Indiana, nominated by a predominantly Anti-Masonic convention in Harrisburg, Pennsylvania. In the popular vote Van Buren outdistanced the entire Whig field, with

765,000 votes to 740,000 votes for the Whigs, most of which were cast for Harrison.

Martin Van Buren, the eighth president, was the first of Dutch ancestry and, at the age of fifty-five, the first born under the Stars and Stripes. Son of a tavernkeeper in Kinderhook, New York, he had been schooled in a local academy, read law, and entered politics. Although he kept up a limited legal practice, he had been primarily a professional politician, so skilled in the arts of organization and manipulation that he was dubbed the "Little Magician." In 1824 he supported Crawford, then switched to Jackson in 1828, but continued to look to the Old Republicans of Virginia as the southern anchor of his support. After a brief tenure as governor of New York, Van Buren resigned to join the cabinet and, because of Jackson's support, became minister to London and then vice-president. Short and trim, Van Buren was also called the "Red Fox" for his long reddish sideburns, dominant forehead, and long, striking nose. His elegant attire, engaging personality, and constant political scheming gave further credence to his nicknames.

THE PANIC OF 1837   Van Buren owed much of his political success to having been in the right place at the right time. But once he had climbed to the top of the greased pole, luck suddenly deserted him. Van Buren had inherited Jackson's favor and a good part of his following, but he also inherited a financial panic. An already precarious economy was tipped over into crisis by depression in England, which resulted in a drop in the price of cotton from 17 1/2 cents to 13 1/2 cents a pound, and caused English banks and investors to contract their activities in the New World and refuse extensions of loans. This was a particularly hard blow, since much of America's economic expansion depended on European—and mainly English—capital. As creditors hastened to foreclose, the inflationary spiral went into reverse. States curtailed ambitious plans for roads and canals, and in many cases felt impelled to repudiate their debts. In the crunch a good many of the wildcat banks succumbed, and the government itself lost some $9 million it had deposited in pet banks.

The working classes, as always, were particularly hard hit during the economic slump, and they largely had to fend for themselves. By the fall of 1837 a third of the work force was jobless. Those still fortunate

The Times. *This anti-Jacksonian cartoon depicts the effects of the depression of 1837: a panic at the bank, beggars in the street.*

enough to have jobs saw their wages cut by 30–50 percent within two years. At the same time, prices for food and clothing skyrocketed. As winter approached in late 1837, a journalist reported that in New York City there were 200,000 people "in utter and hopeless distress with no means of surviving the winter but those provided by charity." Indeed, there was no government aid, only that provided by churches and voluntary societies.

Van Buren's advisers and supporters were inclined to blame speculators and bankers for the hard times. At the same time they expected the evildoers to get what they deserved in a healthy shakeout that would bring the economy back to stability. Van Buren did not believe that he or the government had any responsibility to rescue hard-pressed farmers or businessmen, or to provide public welfare. But he did feel obliged to keep the government itself in a healthy financial situation. To that end he called a special session of Congress in 1837, which quickly voted to postpone indefinitely the distribution of the surplus because of a probable upcoming deficit, and also approved an issue of Treasury notes to cover immediate expenses.

AN INDEPENDENT TREASURY   Van Buren proposed that the government cease risking its deposits in shaky banks and set up an independent treasury. Under this plan the government would keep its funds in its own vaults and do business entirely in hard money. Van Buren observed that the republic's founders had "wisely judged that the less government interfered with private pursuits the better for the general prosperity." Webster's response typified the Whig reaction: "I feel . . . as if this could not be America when I see schemes of public policy proposed, having for their object the convenience of Government only, and leaving the people to shift for themselves." The Whiggish approach, presumably, would have been some kind of Hamiltonian program of government promotion of economic development, perhaps in the form of tariff or currency legislation. Good Jacksonians disapproved of such programs, at least when they were run from Washington.

Van Buren's Independent Treasury Act encountered stiff opposition from a combination of Whigs and conservative Democrats who feared deflation, and it took the "Red Fox" several years of maneuvering to get what he wanted. Calhoun signaled a return to the Democratic fold, after several years of flirting with the Whigs, when he came out for the independent treasury. Van Buren gained western support for the plan by backing a more liberal land policy. Congress finally passed the Independent Treasury Act on July 4, 1840. Although the Whigs repealed it in 1841, it would be restored in 1846.

The protracted hassle over the treasury was only one of several issues that kept Washington preoccupied through the Van Buren years. Petitions asking Congress to abolish slavery and the slave trade in the District of Columbia provoked tumultuous debate, especially in the House of Representatives. A dispute over the Maine boundary kept British-American animosity at a simmer. But basic to the spreading malaise of the time was the depressed condition of the economy, which lasted through Van Buren's entire term. Fairly or not, the administration became the target of growing discontent. The president won renomination easily enough, but the general election was another matter.

THE "LOG CABIN AND HARD CIDER" CAMPAIGN   The Whigs got an early start on their campaign when they met at Harrisburg, Pennsylvania, on December 4, 1839, to choose a candidate. Henry Clay, the warm and personable legislative veteran who coupled the ideas of a visionary with shrewd political savvy, expected 1840 to be his year. He was wrong. Although he led on the first ballot, the convention preferred a Whiggish Jackson, as it were, a military hero who could enter the race with few known political convictions or enemies. So the delegates turned to William Henry Harrison, victor at the battle of Tippecanoe against the Shawnees in 1811, while governor of the Indiana territory, and briefly a congressman and a senator from Ohio. To rally their states'-rights wing, the Whigs chose for vice-president John Tyler of Virginia, Clay's close friend.

The Whigs had no platform. That would have risked dividing a coalition united chiefly by opposition to the Democrats. But they had a slogan, "Tippecanoe and Tyler too," that went trippingly on the tongue. And they soon had a rousing campaign theme, which a Democratic paper unwittingly supplied them when it declared sardonically "that upon condition of his receiving a pension of $2,000 and a barrel of cider, General Harrison would no doubt consent to withdraw his pretensions, and spend his days in a log cabin on the banks of the Ohio." The Whigs seized upon the cider and log cabin symbols to depict Harrison as a simple man sprung from the people. Actually, he sprang from one of the first families of Virginia, was a college graduate, and lived in a commodious Ohio farmhouse.

The campaign produced the largest turnout of any election up to that time and left one lasting heritage in the American language, a usage now virtually worldwide. The expression "O.K." was picked up as an abbreviation for "Old Kinderhook," an affectionate name for Van Buren, whose supporters organized "O.K. Clubs" during the campaign. But the president was anything but O.K. to the Whigs. To them he symbolized the economic slump as well as aristocratic snobbery. "Van! Van! Is a Used-up Man!" went one of their campaign slogans, and down he went by the thumping margin of 234 electoral votes to 60.

ASSESSING THE JACKSON YEARS

The Jacksonian impulse had permanently altered American politics. Long-standing ambivalence about political parties had been purged in the fires of political conflict, and mass political parties had

Andrew Jackson in 1845. Jackson died shortly after this daguerreotype was taken.

arrived to stay. They were now widely justified as a positive good. By 1840 both parties were tightly organized down to the precinct level, and the proportion of adult white males who voted in the presidential election nearly tripled, from 27 percent in 1824 to 78 percent in 1840. That much is beyond dispute, but the phenomenon of Jackson, the great symbol for an age, has inspired conflicts of interpretation as spirited as those among his supporters and opponents at the time. Was he the leader of a vast democratic movement that welled up in the West and mobilized a farmer-laborer alliance to sweep the "Monster" bank into the dustbin of history? Or was he essentially a frontier tycoon, an opportunist for whom the ideal of democracy provided effective political rhetoric?

Whatever else Jackson and his supporters had in mind, they followed an ideal of republican virtue, of returning to the Jeffersonian vision of the Old Republic in which government would leave people largely to their own devices. In the Jacksonian view the alliance of government and business always invited special favors and provided an eternal source of corruption. The central bank epitomized such evil. Good governmental policy, at the national level in particular, refrained from granting special privileges and let free competition regulate the economy.

In the bustling world of the nineteenth century, however, the idea of a return to agrarian simplicity represented a futile exercise in nostalgia. Instead, Jackson's laissez-faire policies actually opened the way for a host of aspiring entrepreneurs eager to replace the established economic elite with a new order of free enterprise capitalism. And in fact there was no great conflict in the Jacksonian mentality between the farmer or planter who delved in the soil and the independent speculator and entrepreneur who won his way by other means. Jackson himself was all these things. The Jacksonian mentality could not foresee the degree to which, in a growing country, unrestrained enterprise could lead to new economic combinations, centers of gigantic power largely independent of governmental regulation. But history is forever producing unintended consequences. Here the ultimate irony would be that the laissez-faire rationale for republican simplicity eventually became the justification for the growth of unregulated centers of economic power far greater than any ever wielded by Biddle's bank.

MAKING CONNECTIONS

- This chapter analyzes the political side of "Jacksonian Democracy." Chapter 11 concludes with an assessment of the accuracy of that term from social and economic perspectives.

- John C. Calhoun, Henry Clay, and Daniel Webster, three of the statesmen described in this chapter, continued for many years to be the major spokesmen for their positions. The last great debate for the three, over the Compromise of 1850, is discussed in Chapter 15.

FURTHER READING

A survey of events covered in the chapter can be found in Harry L. Watson's *Liberty and Power: The Politics of Jacksonian America* (1990).* An introduction to the development of political parties of the 1830s can

*These books are available in paperback editions.

be found in Richard P. McCormick's *The Second Party System* (1966).*
For an outstanding analysis of women in New York City during the Jacksonian period, see Christine Stansell's *City of Women* (1986).* In
Chants Democratic (1984),* Sean Wilentz analyzes the social basis of
working-class politics.

The political philosophies of those who came to oppose Jackson are
treated in Daniel W. Howe's *The Political Culture of American Whigs*
(1979).

An outstanding book on the nullification issue is William W.
Freehling's *Prelude to Civil War: The Nullification Controversy in South
Carolina, 1816–1836* (1966).* John M. Belohlavek's *"Let the Eagle
Soar!": The Foreign Policy of Andrew Jackson* (1985) is a thorough study
of Jacksonian diplomacy. Ronald N. Satz's *American Indian Policy in the
Jacksonian Era* (1974) surveys that tragedy. The question of rising in-
equality in American cities is treated in Edward Pessen's *Riches, Class,
and Power before the Civil War* (1973).

*These books are available in paperback editions.

11 ~ THE DYNAMICS OF GROWTH

AGRICULTURE AND THE NATIONAL ECONOMY

During the decades following the end of the War of 1812, the American economy grew at a pace that generated profound social and political changes. The first stage of industrialization brought with it an expansive commercial and urban outlook that by the end of the century would supplant the agrarian philosophy espoused by Thomas Jefferson and many others. "We are greatly, I was about to say fearfully, growing," John C. Calhoun told his congressional colleagues in 1816, and many other statesmen shared his ambivalent outlook. Would the Republic retain its virtue and cohesion amid the turmoil of commercial development? But in the brief period of good feelings after the War of 1812, such a troublesome question was easily brushed aside. Economic opportunities seemed available to free Americans everywhere, and nowhere more than in Calhoun's native South Carolina. The reason was cotton, the profitable new staple crop of the South, which was spreading from South Carolina and Georgia into the new lands of Mississippi and Alabama.

COTTON Cotton had been in use from ancient times, but the proliferation of English textile mills during the late eighteenth century created a rapidly growing market for the fluffy staple. For many years cotton had remained rare and expensive because of the need for hand labor to separate the lint from the tenacious green seeds of most varieties. But that problem was solved in 1793 when Eli Whitney, a Yale graduate who went south to teach, devised a mechanism for removing the sticky seeds. The cotton gin enabled a person to separate fifty times as much cotton as could be done by hand.

By inventing the cotton gin, Whitney had unwittingly begun a revolution. Cotton production soared during the first half of the nineteenth century, and planters had found a new and profitable use for slavery. Indeed thereafter slavery became almost synonymous with the Cotton Kingdom in the popular view. Planters and their slaves migrated westward into Kentucky, Tennessee, Alabama, Mississippi, Louisiana, and Texas, and the cotton culture became a way of life that tied the Old Southwest to the coastal Southeast in a common interest.

Not the least of the cotton gin's revolutionary consequences was that cotton became a major export commodity for the United States. After Napoleon's defeat in 1815, European demand for cotton skyrocketed. From 1815 to 1819 American cotton exports averaged 39 percent of the value of all exports, and from the mid-1830s to 1860 they accounted for more than half the total. For the national economy as a whole during the first half of the century, cotton precipitated a phenomenal expansion. The South supplied the North both raw materials and markets for manufactures. Income from the North's role in handling the cotton trade then provided surpluses for capital investment.

FARMING THE WEST The westward flow of planters and their slaves to Alabama and Mississippi during these flush times mirrored another migration through the Ohio Valley and the Great Lakes region, where the Indians had been steadily pushed westward. "Old America seems to be breaking up and moving westward," an English traveler observed in

Farm Residence, Putnam County, Illinois. Through the early decades of the nineteenth century migrants transformed midwestern plains to farmland.

1817. Family groups, stages, light wagons, riders on horseback made up "a scene of bustle and business, extending over three hundred miles, which is truly wonderful." By 1860 more than half the nation's expanded population resided in trans-Appalachia, and the restless movement had long since spilled across the Mississippi and touched the shores of the Pacific.

North of the expanding cotton belt in the Gulf states, the fertile woodland soils, riverside bottom lands, and black loam of the prairies drew farmers from the rocky land of New England and the leached, exhausted soils of the Southeast. The development of effective iron plows greatly eased the grueling job of breaking the soil. In 1819 a New York farmer developed an improved iron plow with parts that could be replaced separately without buying a whole new plow. Demand for plows grew so fast that the manufacturer could not supply the need. Further improvements would follow, including John Deere's steel plow (1837), which was better suited for breaking up the rock-hard soil of the Great Plains.

A new land law of 1820 reduced the minimum price per acre and the minimum plot from 160 to 80 acres. The settler could now buy a place for as little as $100, and over the years the proliferation of state banks made it possible to continue buying on credit. Even that was not enough for westerners who began a long—and eventually victorious—

agitation for further relaxation of the land laws. They favored preemption, the right of squatters to purchase land at the minimum price, and graduation, the progressive reduction of the price on lands that did not sell.

Congress eventually responded with two acts. Under the Preemption Act of 1830, squatters could stake out claims ahead of the land surveys and later get 160 acres at the minimum price of $1.25 per acre. In effect the law recognized a practice enforced more often than not by frontier vigilantes. Under the Graduation Act of 1854, prices of unsold lands were to go down in stages until the lands could sell for 12 1/2 cents per acre after thirty years.

TRANSPORTATION AND THE NATIONAL ECONOMY

NEW ROADS   Transportation improvements helped spur the development of a national market. In 1795 the Wilderness Road, which followed the trail blazed by Daniel Boone twenty years before, was opened to wagon traffic, thereby easing the route through the Cumberland Gap in Kentucky. In the Deep South there were no such major highways. South Carolinians and Georgians pushed westward on whatever trails or rutted roads had appeared.

To the northeast public demand for graded and paved roads packed with crushed stones gathered momentum after completion of the Philadelphia-Lancaster Turnpike in 1794 (the term derives from a pole or pike at the tollgate, turned to admit the traffic). By 1821 there were some 4,000 miles of turnpikes, mainly connecting eastern cities, but western traffic could move along the Frederick Pike to Cumberland and thence along the National Road, completed to Wheeling on the Ohio in 1818, and to Vandalia, Illinois, by about mid-century.

WATER TRANSPORT   Once turnpike travelers had reached the Ohio River, they could float westward in comparative comfort. At Pittsburgh, Wheeling, and other points, the emigrants could buy flatboats. At the destination the boat could be used again or sold for lumber. In the early 1820s an estimated 3,000 flatboats went down the Ohio every year, and

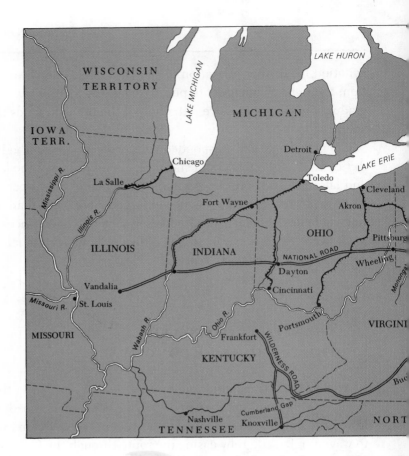

for many years thereafter the flatboat remained the chief means for conveying heavy traffic downstream.

By the early 1820s the turnpike boom was giving way to new developments in water transportation: the river steamboat and the canal barge, which carried bulk commodities far more cheaply than did Conestoga wagons on the National Road. The first commercially successful steamboat appeared when Robert Fulton and Robert R. Livingston sent the *Clermont* up the Hudson to Albany in 1807. After that the use of steamboats spread rapidly to other eastern and western rivers.

By 1836, 361 steamboats navigated the western waters. During the next decade the shallow-draft, steam-powered ships that traveled *on* rather than *in* the water were said to be "so built that when the river is low and the sandbars come out for air, the first mate can tap a keg of beer and run the boat four miles on the suds." These boats ventured into far reaches of the Mississippi Valley, up such rivers as the Wabash, the Monongahela, the Cumberland, the Tennessee, the Missouri, and the Arkansas.

St. Lawrence R.

KE ONTARIO

MAINE

VT.

N.H.

NEW YORK

ERIE CANAL

Syracuse

uffalo MOHAWK & GENESEE
TURNPIKE

Troy

Albany

Lowell

MASS.

Northampton

Boston

Kingston

Hudson R.

R.I.

DELAWARE &
HUDSON CANAL

CONN.

New Haven

PENN.

Susquehanna R.

DELAWARE &
RARITAN CANAL

New York

STATE CANAL

Harrisburg

New Brunswick

BES ROAD

Lancaster

Trenton

Del. R.

Philadelphia

Baltimore

NEW
JERSEY

mberland

MD.

Washington

DELAWARE

Potomac R.

Richmond

James R.

chburg

Portsmouth

CHESAPEAKE BAY

AROLINA

TRANSPORTATION WEST, about 1840

⊔⊔⊔⊔⊔ Canals   ▬▬ Roads

Navigable rivers

0   200 Miles

0   200 Kilometers

The durable flatboat still carried to market most of the western wheat, corn, flour, meal, port, whiskey, soap and candles (the by-products of slaughterhouses), lead from Missouri, copper from Michigan, lumber from the Rockies, and ironwork from Pittsburgh. But the steamboat, by bringing cheaper and faster two-way traffic to the Mississippi Valley, created a continental market and an agricultural empire that became the new breadbasket of America. Along with the new farmers came promoters, speculators, retailers, and land-boomers. Villages at strategic trading points along the streams evolved into centers of commerce and urban life. The port of New Orleans grew in the 1830s and 1840s to lead all others in exports.

But by then the Erie Canal was drawing eastward much of the trade that once went down to the Gulf. In 1817 the New York legislature endorsed Governor De Witt Clinton's dream of a canal connecting the Hudson River with Lake Erie and authorized construction. Eight years later, in 1825, the canal was open for its entire 350 miles from Albany to Buffalo; branches soon put most of the state within reach of the canal.

The speedy success of the New York system inspired a mania for canals that lasted more than a decade and resulted in the completion of about 3,000 miles of waterways by 1837. But no canal ever matched the spectacular success of the Erie. It rendered the entire Great Lakes region an economic tributary to New York City, and had major economic and political consequences tying together the West and East while further isolating the Deep South. With the addition of new canals spanning Ohio and Indiana from north to south, much of the upper Ohio Valley was also drawn within New York's economic sphere.

RAILROADS   The Panic of 1837 and the subsequent depression cooled the canal fever. Some states that had borrowed heavily to finance canals were forced to repudiate their debts. Meanwhile, a new and more versatile form of transportation was gaining on the canal: the railroad. In 1825, the year the Erie Canal was completed, the world's first commercial steam railway began operations in England, and soon the port cities of Baltimore, Charleston, and Boston were alive with schemes to penetrate the hinterlands by rail.

By 1840 American railroads, with a total of 3,328 miles, had outdistanced the canals by just two miles. Over the next twenty years, though, railroads grew nearly tenfold to cover 30,626 miles; more than two-thirds of this total was built in the 1850s. But it was still not until the eve of the Civil War that railroads surpassed canals in total haulage: in 1859 they carried a little over 2 billion tons compared to 1.6 billion on canals.

Travel on the early railroads tested the courage of passengers. Wood was used for fuel, and the sparks often caused fires along the way or damaged passengers' clothing. An English traveler, Harriet Martineau, reported seeing a lady's shawl ignited on one trip. She discovered in her own gown thirteen holes "and in my veil, with which I saved my eyes, more than could be counted." Invention of the "spark arrester" and the use of coal for fuel alleviated but never eliminated the hazard. Different track widths often forced passengers to change trains until a standard gauge became national in 1882. Land travel, whether by stagecoach or train, was a jerky, bumpy, wearying ordeal.

Water travel, where available, offered far more comfort, but railroads gained supremacy over other forms of transport because of their economy, speed, and reliability. Early trains averaged ten miles an hour, dou-

WANTED!
3,000 LABORERS
On the 12th Division of the
ILLINOIS CENTRAL RAILROAD
Wages, $1.25 per Day.

Fare, from New-York, only - - $4½

**By Railroad and Steamboat, to the work in the
State of Illinois.**

Constant employment for two years or more
given. Good board can be obtained at two
dollars per week.
This is a rare chance for persons to go
West, being sure of permanent employment
in a healthy climate, where land can be
bought cheap, and for fertility is not surpassed
in any part of the Union.
Men with families preferred.

Advertisement (1853) for laborers on the Illinois Central Railroad, "a rare chance for persons to go West, . . . sure of permanent employment in a healthy climate, where land can be bought cheap, and for fertility is not surpassed in any part of the Union."

bling the speed of stagecoaches. Railroads provided indirect benefits by encouraging frontier settlement and boosting farming. During the antebellum period, the reduced shipping costs provided by the railroads aided the expansion of farming more than manufacturing, since manufacturers in the Northeast, especially New England, had better access to water transportation. The railroads' demand for iron and equipment of various kinds, however, did provide an enormous market for the industries that made these capital goods. And the ability of railroads to operate year round in all kinds of weather gave them an advantage in carrying finished goods, too.

But the epic railroad boom had negative effects as well. By opening up new possibilities for quick and often shady profits, it helped to corrupt political life, and by opening up access to the trans-Appalachian west, it helped accelerate the decline of Indian culture. In addition, the railroad dramatically quickened the tempo and mobility of life. The noted writer Nathaniel Hawthorne spoke for many sensitive Americans when he charged that the locomotive "comes down upon you like fate, swift and inevitable." With its unsettling whistle it brought "the noisy world into the midst of our slumbrous peace."

OCEAN TRANSPORT   For oceangoing traffic, the start of service on regular schedules was the most important change of the early 1800s. In the first week of 1818 ships of the New York–based Black Ball Line inaugurated a weekly transatlantic packet service between New York and Liverpool. With the business recovery in 1822 the packet business grew in a rush. By 1845 some fifty-two transatlantic lines ran square-riggers on schedule from New York, with three regular sailings per week. Many others ran in the coastwise trade, to Charleston, Savannah, New Orleans, and elsewhere.

The same year, 1845, witnessed a great innovation with the launching of the first clipper ship, the *Rainbow*. Built for speed, the sleek clippers were the nineteenth-century equivalent of the supersonic jetliner. They doubled the speed of the older merchant vessels, and trading companies rushed to purchase them. Long and lean, with taller masts and more sails, they cut dashing figures during their brief but colorful career, which lasted less than two decades. What provoked the clipper boom was the lure of Chinese tea, a drink long coveted in America but in scarce supply. The tea leaves were a perishable commodity that had to reach market quickly, and the new clippers made this possible. Even more important, the discovery of California gold in 1848 lured thousands of prospectors and entrepreneurs from the Atlantic seaboard. These new settlers generated an urgent demand for goods, and the clippers met the need. In 1854 the *Flying Cloud* took eighty-nine days and eight hours to get from New York to San Francisco, a speed that took steamships several decades to equal. But clippers, while fast, lacked ample cargo space, and after the Civil War they would give way to the larger steamship.

THE ROLE OF GOVERNMENT   The massive internal improvements of the antebellum era were the product of both state government and private initiatives, sometimes undertaken jointly and sometimes separately. After the Panic of 1837, however, the states left railroad development mainly to private corporations, the source of most investment capital. Still, several southern and western states built their own lines, and most states granted generous tax concessions.

The federal government helped too, despite the constitutional scruples of some against direct involvement in internal improvements. The government bought stock in turnpike and canal companies, and after the success of the Erie, extended land grants to several western states for the support of canal projects. Congress provided for railroad surveys by government engineers, granted tracts of land, and reduced the tariff duties on iron used in railroad construction.

THE GROWTH OF INDUSTRY

While the South and West developed the agricultural basis for a national economy, the Northeast was laying the foundation for an industrial revolution. Technology in the form of the cotton gin, the harvester, and improvements in transportation had quickened agricultural development and to some extent decided its direction. But technology altered the economic landscape even more profoundly by giving rise to the factory system.

EARLY TEXTILE MANUFACTURES   At the end of the colonial period manufacturing remained in the household or handicraft stage of development, or at most the "putting-out" stage, in which the merchant capitalist would distribute raw material (say, leather patterns for shoes) to be worked up at a laborer's home, then collected and sold. Farm families had to produce much of what they needed in the way of crude implements, shoes, and clothing. The transition from such production to the factory was slow, but one for which a base had been laid before 1815.

In the eighteenth century Great Britain had jumped out to a long head start in industrial production. Britain led the way in the development of iron smelting by coke (refined coal), the invention of the steam engine in 1705 and its improvement by James Watt in 1765, and a series of inventions that mechanized textile production. Britain also carefully guarded its hard-won secrets, forbidding the export of machines or descriptions of them, even preventing informed mechanics from leav-

New England Factory Village, 1830. *Mills and factories gradually transformed the New England landscape in the early nineteenth century.*

ing the country. But the secrets could not be kept. In 1789 Samuel Slater arrived in Rhode Island from England with the plan of a textile water frame in his head. He contracted with an enterprising merchant-manufacturer to build a mill in Pawtucket, and in this little mill, completed in 1790, nine children turned out a satisfactory cotton yarn.

Still, the beginnings of an American textile industry were slow and faltering until Jefferson's embargo in 1807 and the War of 1812 restricted imports and encouraged New England merchant capitalists to switch their resources into manufacturing. New England, it happened, had one distinct advantage in that its ample waterpower stood near the coast, where water transportation was also readily available. In 1813 a group of wealthy merchants known as the Boston Associates formed the Boston Manufacturing Company. At Waltham, Massachusetts, they built the first factory in which the processes of spinning and weaving by power machinery were brought under one roof, mechanizing every process from raw material to finished cloth. By 1815 New England textile mills numbered in the hundreds. The foundations of textile manufacture were laid, and they spurred the growth of garment trades and a machine-tool industry to build and service the mills.

TECHNOLOGY IN AMERICA   Meanwhile, American ingenuity was adding other bases for industrial growth. In 1804 Oliver Evans developed a high-pressure steam engine adapted to a variety of uses in ships and factories. Among the other outstanding American originals was Cyrus Hall McCormick of Virginia. McCormick invented a primitive grain reaper in 1834, a development as significant to the agricultural economy of the Old Northwest as the cotton gin was to the South. After tinkering with his machine for almost a decade, McCormick applied for a patent in 1841. Six years later he moved to Chicago and built a manufacturing plant for his reapers and mowers. Within a few years he had sold thousands of new machines, transforming the scale of American agriculture. With a hand-operated sickle a farmer could harvest a half acre of wheat a day; with a McCormick reaper two people could work twelve acres a day. McCormick's success attracted other manufacturers and inventors, and soon there were mechanical threshers to separate the grains of wheat from the straw. Farming remained, as it still is, a precarious vocation, subject to the whims of climate, the assault of insects, and the fluctuations of foreign markets, but by the 1850s it had become a major commercial activity. As the volume of agricultural products soared, prices dropped, income rose, and the standard of living for many farm families in the Old Northwest improved.

A spate of inventions in the 1840s generated profound changes in American life. In 1844 Charles Goodyear patented a process for vulcanizing rubber, which made it stronger and more elastic and in the process created the fabric for rainproof coats. In the same year the first intercity telegraph message was transmitted from Baltimore to Washington on the device Samuel F. Morse had invented back in 1832. The telegraph was slow to catch on at first, but seventeen years after that demonstration, with the completion of connections to San Francisco, an entire continent had been wired for instant communication. In 1846 Elias Howe invented the sewing machine, soon improved by Allen B. Wilson and Isaac Merritt Singer. The sewing machine, incidentally, was one invention that slowed the progress of the factory. Since it was adapted to use in the home, it gave the "putting-out" system a new lease on life in the clothing industry.

It is hard to exaggerate the importance of science and technology in changing the ways people lived by midcentury. To cite but a few examples: improved transportation and a spreading market economy combined with innovations in canning and refrigeration to provide people a more healthful and varied diet. Fruit and vegetables, heretofore available only during harvest season, could be shipped during much of the year. Scientific breeding of cattle helped make meat and milk more abundant.

Technological advances also helped improve living conditions: houses were larger, better heated, and better illuminated. Although working-class residences remained spartan, with few creature comforts, the affluent were able to afford indoor plumbing, central heating, gas lighting, bathtubs, iceboxes, and sewing machines. Even the lower classes were able to afford new coal-burning, cast-iron cooking stoves that facilitated more varied meals and improved heating. The first sewer systems began to help rid city streets of human and animal waste, while underground water lines enabled fire companies to use hydrants rather than bucket brigades. Machine-made clothes fit better and were cheaper than homespun; newspapers and magazines were more abundant and affordable, as were clocks and watches.

THE LOWELL SYSTEM   Before the 1850s the factory system still had not become widespread. Handicraft and domestic production (putting-out) remained common, and as late as 1860 the United States was still preponderantly rural and agricultural. But modern industrialism made significant inroads, especially in New England. At Lowell, Massachusetts, along the Merrimack River, the Merrimack Manufacturing Company in 1822 developed a new plant similar to the Waltham mill. Lowell grew dramatically, and it soon provided the model for other mill towns in Massachusetts, New Hampshire, and Maine.

The chief features of the "Lowell System" were a large capital investment, the concentration of all processes in one plant under unified management, and specialization in a relatively coarse cloth requiring minimum skill by the workers. In the public mind, however, the system then and afterward was associated above all with the conscious attempt by the founders to establish an industrial center compatible with republican virtues. Jefferson and others had early on characterized urban-industrial development as being incompatible with a republican form

The cotton mills at Lowell, Massachusetts, 1852.

of government rooted in self-reliant agrarianism, and early industrial developers were quite sensitive to such concerns.

As a consequence, Lowell's founders insisted that they could design model factory centers and communities that would enhance rather than corrupt the social fabric. The drab, crowded, and wretched life of English mill villages would be avoided by locating American mills in the countryside and then establishing an ambitious program of paternal supervision for the workers. The operatives were mostly young women from New England farm families who were increasingly without gainful employment and faced diminishing prospects for finding a husband. With so many men migrating westward, New England had been left with a surplus of women. Moreover, much of the household production previously carried out by daughters had given way to "store-bought" goods. Many women workers were also drawn to the mills by the chance to escape the routine of farm life and to earn money to help the family or improve their own circumstances. As one female mill worker explained, she was working because of "a father's debts . . . to be paid, an aged mother to be supported, a brother's ambition to be aided." Another stressed in a letter to her parents the greater excitement and fellowship afforded by life in Lowell: "You may think me unkind but how can you blame me for wanting to stay here. I have but one life to live and I want to enjoy myself as well as I can."

Single girls began flocking toward Lowell. To reassure concerned parents, the mill owners promised to provide the "Lowell girls" with good wages, tolerable work, comfortable housing, moral discipline, and a variety of educational and cultural opportunities. Such a carefully planned and supervised factory system would thereby bring together the benefits of both industrial capitalism and republican simplicity. Kentucky statesman Henry Clay asserted that the Lowell experiment "will tell whether the manufacturing system is compatible with the social virtues."

Initially visitors to Lowell praised the well-designed mills. The laborers appeared "healthy and happy." One appreciative worker, in fact, described the new community as demonstrating that "corporations should have souls, and should exercise a paternal influence over the lives of their operatives." Lowell was certainly paternalistic: the women workers lived in dormitories staffed by matronly supervisors, church attendance was mandatory, and temperance regulations and curfews were rigidly enforced. Despite the twelve-hour days and seventy-hour weeks, one woman operative described Lowell's community life as approaching "almost Arcadian simplicity." But like Arcadia, Lowell soon lost its innocence as it experienced mushrooming growth. By 1840 Lowell had thirty-two mills and factories in operation, and the blissful rural town had become a bustling, grimy, bleak industrial city.

Other factory centers began sprouting up across New England, displacing forests and farms and engulfing villages, filling the air with smoke, noise, and stench. As early as 1832, the writer Washington Irving lamented that the "march of mechanical invention is driving everything poetical before it." Between 1820 and 1840 the number of Americans engaged in manufactures increased eightfold, and the number of city dwellers more than doubled.

Such booming growth transformed the experiment in industrial republicanism. By 1846 a concerned worker told those young farm women thinking about taking a job in a factory that they would do well not to leave their "homes in the country. It will be better for you to stay at home on your fathers' farms than to run the risk of being ruined in a manufacturing village."

During the 1830s, as prices and wages dropped, relations between workers and managers rapidly deteriorated. A new generation of owners and foremen stressed efficiency and profit margins over community values. The machines and their operatives were worked at a faster pace, and workers organized strikes to protest deteriorating conditions. Visitors now noted the growing similarity between Lowell and the dismal factory towns of England immortalized in Charles Dickens's writings.

The "Lowell girls" drew attention less because they were typical than because they were special. An increasingly common pattern for industry was the family system, sometimes called the Rhode Island or Fall River system, which prevailed in textile manufactures outside of northern New England. Factories that relied on waterpower often rose in unpopulated areas, and part of their construction included tenements or mill villages that increasingly housed newly arrived foreign immigrants. Whole families might be hired, the men for heavy labor, the women and children for the lighter work. This system also promoted paternalism. Employers dominated the life of the mill villages, often setting rules of good behavior. Wages under the system are hard to establish, for employers often paid in goods from the company store. Working hours often ran from sunup to sunset, and longer in winter—a sixty-eight- to seventy-two-hour week. Such hours were common on the farms of the time, but in factories the work was more intense and offered no seasonal letup. The labor of children, a necessity for most rural families, excited little censure from communities still close to the soil.

INDUSTRY AND CITIES In 1855 a journalist exclaimed that "the great phenomenon of the Age is the growth of cities." Using the census definition of "urban" as places with 8,000 inhabitants or more, the proportion of urban population grew from 3.3 percent in 1790 to 16.1 percent in 1860. New York outpaced all its competitors and the nation as a whole in its population growth. By 1860 it was the first American city to boast a population of more than a million, largely because of its superior harbor and its unique access to commerce afforded by the Erie Canal.

Pittsburgh, at the head of the Ohio River, was already a center of iron production by 1800, and Cincinnati, at the mouth of the Little Miami, soon surpassed all other centers of meatpacking, with pork a specialty. Louisville, because it stood at the falls of the Ohio, became an important trade center. On the Great Lakes the leading cities also stood at important breaking points in water transportation: Buffalo, Cleveland, Detroit, Chicago, and Milwaukee. Chicago was especially well located to become a hub of both water and rail transportation on into the trans-Mississippi West. During the 1830s St. Louis tripled in size mainly because most of the trans-Mississippi grain and fur trade was funneled down the Missouri River. By 1860 St. Louis and Chicago were positioned to challenge Boston and Baltimore for third and fourth places.

IMMIGRATION

Amid all the new economic growth, one condition of American life carried over beyond the mid-nineteenth century: land remained plentiful and relatively cheap, while labor was scarce and relatively dear. A decline in the birth rate coinciding with the onset of industry and urbanization reinforced this condition. The United States in the nineteenth century remained a strong magnet to immigrants, offering them chances to take up farms in the country or jobs in the cities. Glowing reports from early arrivals who made good also reinforced romantic views of American economic opportunity and political and religious freedom. A German immigrant in Missouri wrote home applauding the "absence of overbearing soldiers, haughty clergymen, and inquisitive tax collectors."

During the forty years from the outbreak of the Revolution until the end of the War of 1812, immigration had slowed to a trickle. The wars of the French Revolution and Napoleon restricted travel from Europe until 1815. Within a few years, however, packet lines had begun to cross the north Atlantic, and competing shippers who needed westbound payloads kept the transatlantic fares as low as $30 per person. The years from 1845 to 1854 saw the greatest proportionate influx of immigrants in American history, 2.4 million, or about 14.5 percent of the total population in 1845.

During the early 1800s most European immigrants entered the United States through the Port of New York. Ships would discharge passengers at wharves, and the newcomers would immediately have to fend for themselves in their alien environment. Before long thieves, thugs, and wily con men began preying upon the new arrivals. The infectious diseases that many of the immigrants brought with them also aroused popular concern. By 1855 the problems associated with the immigrants' arrival in America provoked the New York state legislature to lease Castle Garden, at the southern tip of Manhattan, for use as an immigration receiving center. Inside the depot, clerks would record the names, nationalities, and destinations of the new arrivals, physicians would give them a cursory physical exam, and labor bureau representatives would assist them in seeking jobs.

THE IRISH   In 1860 America's population was 31 million, with more than one of every eight foreign born. The largest groups among them were 1.6 million Irish, 1.2 million Germans, and 588,000 British (mostly English). The Irish had a long-standing reason for migrating from their country: resentment of British rule, British landlords, British Protestantism, and British taxes. But what caused so many Irish to flee their homeland in the nineteenth century was the onset of a prolonged depression that brought immense social hardship. The most densely populated country in Europe, Ireland was so ravaged by the economic collapse that in rural areas the average age at death declined to nineteen. By the 1830s the number of Irish migrants to America was growing quickly, and after an epidemic of potato rot in 1845 brought a famine to rural Ireland that killed upwards of a million peasants, the flow of Irish immigrants to Canada and the United States rose to a flood.

In 1847 Irish arrivals numbered above 100,000, and they stayed above that level for eight years, reaching a peak of 221,000 in 1851. By 1850 the Irish constituted 43 percent of the foreign-born population in the United States. Unlike the German immigrants, who were predominantly male, the Irish newcomers were more evenly apportioned by sex; in fact a slight majority of them were women, most of them single young adults. Most of the Irish arrivals had been tenant farmers, but their rural sufferings left them little taste for farm work and little money to buy land in America. Great numbers of the men hired on with construction gangs building the canals and railways—about 3,000 set to work on the Erie Canal as early as 1818. Others worked in iron foundries, steel mills, warehouses, and shipyards. Many Irish women found jobs as domestic servants, laundresses, or textile mill workers in New England. In 1845, the Irish constituted only 8 percent of the work force in the Lowell mills; by 1860 they made up 50 percent. Although there were substantial Irish communities in New Orleans, Vicksburg, and Memphis, relatively few immigrants during the Jacksonian era

In 1847, nearly 214,000 Irish emigrated to the United States and Canada aboard ships of the White Star Line and other companies. Thirty percent of these immigrants died on board, despite company promises of "unusually spacious, well-lighted, ventilated, and warmed" steerage accommodations.

found their way into the South, where land was expensive and industries scarce. The widespread use of slaves also left few opportunities in the region for manual laborers.

Too poor to move inland, most of the destitute Irish congregated in the eastern cities, in or near their port of entry. By the 1850s the Irish made up over half the populations of Boston and of New York City, and they were almost as prominent in Philadelphia. They clustered in murky slums and around Catholic churches, both of which became familiar features of the urban scene. Irish newcomers crowded into filthy, poorly ventilated tenements, plagued by high rates of crime, infectious disease, prostitution, alcoholism, and infant mortality. The archbishop of New York City at midcentury described the Irish as "the poorest and most wretched population that can be found in the world."

But many enterprising Irish immigrants seized opportunities in their new environment to forge remarkable success stories. Twenty years after arriving in New York, Alexander T. Stewart became the owner of America's largest department store and thereafter accumulated vast real estate holdings in Manhattan. Michael Cudahy, who began work in a Milwaukee meatpacking business at age fourteen, became head of the Cudahy Packing Company and developed the process for the summer curing of meats under refrigeration. Dublin-born Victor Herbert emerged as one of America's most revered composers, and Irish dancers and playwrights came to dominate the American stage. Irishmen were equally successful in the boxing arena and on the baseball diamond.

These accomplishments did little to quell the acute anti-Irish sentiments prevalent in nineteenth-century America. Irish immigrants confronted demeaning stereotypes and intense anti-Catholic prejudices. It was commonly assumed that the Irish were ignorant, filthy, clannish folk incapable of assimilation. George Templeton Strong, a prominent New York civic leader, expressed the contempt felt by many of his peers toward the Irish when he said: "Our Celtic fellow citizens are almost as remote from us in temperament and constitution as the Chinese." Even Theodore Parker, the esteemed minister and social reformer, dismissed the Irish as "the worst people in Europe to make colonists of." Many employers felt the same way, and "No Irish Need Apply" signs sprouted in every eastern city. But the Irish could be equally contemptuous of other groups, such as free blacks who competed with them for low-status jobs. In 1850 the *New York Tribune* expressed consternation at the fact that the Irish, having themselves escaped from "a galling, degrading bondage" in their homeland, typically voted against any proposal for equal rights for the Negro. For their part, many blacks viewed the Irish with equal disdain.

Experienced at organized resistance to rent and tax collectors in their homeland, the Irish, after becoming naturalized citizens, formed powerful blocs of voters and found their way into American politics more quickly than any other immigrant group. Drawn mainly to the party of Jackson, they set a crucial pattern of identification with the Democrats that other ethnic groups by and large followed. In Jackson the Irish immigrants found a hero. Himself the son of Irish colonists, he was also popular for having defeated the hated British at New Orleans. In addition, the Irish loathing of aristocracy, which they associated with British rule, attracted them to the party claiming to represent "the common man."

Although property requirements initially kept most Irish-Americans from voting, a New York state law extended the franchise in 1821, and five years later the state removed the property qualification altogether. The following year masses of Irish voters made the difference in the election between Jackson and John Quincy Adams. One newspaper expressed alarm at this new force in politics: "Every thing in the shape of an Irishman was drummed to the polls and their votes made to pass. . . . It was emphatically an Irish triumph. The foreigners have carried the day." Although women, blacks, and Indians still could not vote, the Irish newcomers were able to use the franchise to exert a remarkable political influence.

Perhaps the greatest collective achievement of the Irish immigrants was stimulating the growth of the Catholic Church in the United States. "In this country," wrote an Irish teacher in 1840, "the idea of Catholicity and Ireland is so blended in the minds of the American people, as to be in a manner inseparable." Years of persecution had instilled in Irish Catholics a fierce loyalty to the doctrines of the church, leading one Irish-American to proclaim that religion "overrides all other sovereigns, and has the supreme authority over all the affairs of the world." Such passionate attachment to Catholicism generated both community cohesion among Irish-Americans and fears of Romanism among American Protestants.

THE GERMANS AND OTHERS   During the eighteenth century, Germans had responded to William Penn's offer of free religious expression and cheap, fertile land by coming in large numbers to America. As a consequence, when a new wave of German migration formed in the 1830s, there were still large German enclaves in Pennsylvania and Ohio who had preserved their language and cultures, and in the Old World style had clustered in agricultural villages. The new German migration took on a markedly different cast. It peaked in 1854, just a few years after the crest of Irish arrivals, when 215,000 Germans disembarked in American ports. These immigrants included a large number of learned, cultured professional people—doctors, lawyers, teachers, engineers—some of them refugees from the failed German revolutions of 1830 and 1848. In addition to an array of political opinions ranging from laissez-faire conservatism to Marxism, the Germans at midcentury and after also brought with them a variety of religious preferences. A third of the new arrivals were Catholic, most were Protestants (usually Lutherans), and a significant number were Jewish, freethinking atheists, or agnostics.

Unlike the Irish, the Germans included fair numbers of independent farmers, skilled workers, and shopkeepers who arrived with some means to get themselves established in skilled labor or on the land. More so than the Irish, they migrated in families and groups rather than as individuals, and this clannish quality helped them sustain elements of German language and culture in their New World environment. Among those who prospered in America were Ferdinand Schmacher, who began peddling oatmeal in glass jars in Ohio and eventually formed the Quaker Oats Company; Heinrich Steinweg, a piano-maker from Lower Saxony, who in America changed his name to Steinway and became famous for the quality of his pianos; and Levi Strauss, a Jewish tailor who followed the gold rushers to California and began making long-wearing work pants that later were dubbed blue jeans or Levi's. Major centers of German settlement developed in Missouri and southwestern Illinois (around St. Louis), in Texas (near San Antonio), in Ohio, and in Wisconsin (especially around Milwaukee). The larger German communities developed traditions of bounteous food, beer, and music along with German *Turnvereine* (gymnastic societies), sharpshooter clubs, fire engine companies, and kindergartens.

Among the British immigrants too were large numbers of professionals, independent farmers, and skilled workers. Two other groups that began to arrive in some number during the 1840s and 1850s were but the vanguard of greater numbers to come later. Annual arrivals from

Scandinavia, most of them religious dissenters, did not exceed 1,000 until 1843, but by 1860 a total of 72,600 Scandinavians lived in America. The Norwegians and Swedes gravitated usually in family groups to Wisconsin and Minnesota, where the climate and woodlands reminded them of home.

By the 1850s the sudden development of California after the discovery of gold attracted Chinese who, like the Irish in the East, did the heavy work of construction. Infinitesimal in numbers until 1854, the Chinese in America numbered 35,500 by 1860. Most of the Chinese immigrants came from Kwangtung (Guangdong)* province, a region noted for its political turmoil, social violence, and economic hardships. The migrants to the United States were mostly married, illiterate men desperate for work. Single women did not travel abroad, and married women usually stayed behind to raise their children. During the mid-nineteenth century, a laborer in south China might earn five dollars a month; in California, he could work for a railroad or a mine and make six times as much. After three or four years of such work, an immigrant could return to China with his savings and become a "big, very big gentleman."

Contrary to popular myth, the Chinese laborers in the United States were not "coolies." Technically, "coolies" were unfree workers who were kidnapped or pressed into service by force and shipped to foreign countries such as Peru and Cuba. The Chinese workers who arrived in the United States did so voluntarily. Some borrowed funds from friends or relatives for their passage; most used the services of brokers who charged a commission to be paid back with interest with their American wages.

NATIVISM   America had always been a land of immigrants, but the welcome accorded them had often been less than cordial. For many natives these waves of strangers in the land posed a threat of unknown tongues, mysterious customs, and, perhaps worst, feared religions. The flood of Irish and German Catholics aroused Protestant hostility to "popery." A militant Protestantism growing out of the early nineteenth-

*The Wade-Giles transliterations are used in this text with the Pinyin transliterations, adopted by the Chinese government after Mao Tse-tung's (Mao Zedong's) death in 1976, given in parentheses.

century revivals heated up the climate of suspicion. There were fears of radicalism among the Germans and of voting blocs among the Irish, but above all hovered the menace of unfamiliar religious practices. Catholic authoritarianism was widely perceived as a threat to hard-won liberties, religious and political.

By the 1830s nativism was conspicuously on the rise. In 1834 a series of anti-Catholic sermons by the leading New England minister of the era, revivalist and later abolitionist Lyman Beecher, aroused feelings to the extent that a mob attacked and burned a convent in Charlestown, Massachusetts. In 1844 armed clashes between Protestants and Catholics in Philadelphia ended with about twenty killed and one hundred injured. Sporadically, the nativist spirit took organized form in groups that proved their patriotism by hating foreigners and Catholics.

In 1854 delegates from thirteen states gathered to form the American Party, which had the trappings of a secret fraternal order. Members pledged never to vote for any foreign-born or Catholic candidate. When asked about the organization, they were to say "I know nothing," and in popular parlance the American party thus became the Know-Nothing party. For a season it seemed that the American Party might achieve major-party status. In state and local campaigns during 1854 the Know-Nothings carried one election after another. In November they swept the Massachusetts legislature, winning all but two seats in the lower house. That fall they elected more than forty congressmen. For a while they threatened to control New England, New York, and Maryland, and showed strength elsewhere, but the movement subsided when slavery became the focal issue of the 1850s (it would be exploited again by the new Republican party).

The Know-Nothings demanded the exclusion of immigrants and Catholics from public office and extension of the period for naturalization from five to twenty-one years, but the party never gathered the political strength to effect such legislation. Nor did Congress act during the period to restrict immigration in any way.

IMMIGRANT LABOR   After 1840 waves of immigration became critical to the dynamics of growth. The increase in population contributed to economic growth and to demand, whether the newcomer took up farming or settled in a city. By meeting the demand for cheap, unskilled labor, immigrants made a twofold contribution: they moved into jobs vacated or bypassed by those who went into the factories, and they themselves made up a pool of labor from which in time factory workers were drawn.

In New England the large numbers of Irish workers, accustomed to hard treatment and willing to work for what natives considered low wages, spelled the end of the "Lowell girls." By 1860 immigrants made up more than half the labor force in New England mills. Even so, their pay was generally higher than that of the women and children who worked to supplement family incomes. The flood of immigration never rose fast enough to stop the long-term rise in wages. Factory labor thus continued to draw people from the countryside. Work in the cities offered higher real wages than work on the farm. Labor costs encouraged factory owners to seek ever more efficient machines in order to increase production without hiring more workers. In addition, the owners' desire to control the upward pressure on wage rates accelerated the emphasis on mass production. By stressing high production and low prices, owners made it easier for workers to buy the items they made. Artisans who emphasized quality and craftsmanship for a custom trade found it hard to meet such competitive conditions. Many artisans in fact found that their skills were going out of style. Some took work as craftsmen in factories, while others went into small-scale manufacturing or shopkeeping, and some bought homesteads to practice their crafts in the West.

ORGANIZED LABOR

EARLY UNIONS   Few workers of the period belonged to unions, but in the 1820s and 1830s a growing fear that they were losing status led artisans of the major cities into intense activity in labor politics and unions. After the Revolution organizations of journeymen carpenters, masons, shipfitters, tailors, printers, and cordwainers (as shoemakers were called) became concerned with wages, hours, and working conditions and began to back up their demands with such devices as the strike and the closed shop (a requirement that all workers in a company be union members). These organizations were local, often largely social in purpose, and frequently lasted only for the duration of a dispute.

Early labor unions faced serious legal obstacles, including prosecution as unlawful conspiracies. In 1806, for instance, Philadelphia shoemakers were found "guilty of a combination to raise their wages." The decision broke the union, and such precedents were used for many years to thwart labor organizations until the Massachusetts Supreme Court made a landmark ruling in the case of *Commonwealth v. Hunt* (1842). In this case the court ruled that forming a trade union was not in itself illegal, nor was a demand that employers hire only members of the union.

Until the 1820s labor organizations took the form of local trade unions, confined to one city and one craft. During the ten years from 1827 to 1837 organization on a larger scale began to take hold. In 1834 the National Trades' Union was set up in the effort to combine the local organizations. At the same time national craft unions were established by the shoemakers, printers, carpenters, and weavers, but all the national groups and most of the local ones vanished in the economic collapse of 1837.

LABOR POLITICS   With the removal nearly everywhere of property qualifications for voting, labor politics flourished briefly in the 1830s. Working Men's parties appeared in New York, Boston, Philadelphia, and about fifteen states. The Working Men's parties admitted many who were not workers by any strict definition, and their leaders were mainly reformers and small businessmen. These labor parties faded quickly for a variety of reasons: the inexperience of labor politicians that left the parties prey to manipulation by political professionals; the fact that some of their causes were also espoused by the major parties; and their vulnerability to attack on grounds of extreme radicalism. In addition, they often splintered into warring factions, which limited their effectiveness.

Once the parties had faded, however, many of their supporters found their way into a radical wing of the Jacksonian Democrats, which became the Equal Rights party. In 1835 party members acquired the name "Locofocos" when their opponents from New York City's regular Democratic organization, Tammany Hall, turned off the gas lights at one of their meetings, and the Equal Rights supporters produced candles, lighting them with the new friction matches known as Locofocos. The Locofocos soon faded as a separate group but endured as a radical faction within the Democratic party.

Though the labor parties elected few candidates, they did succeed in drawing notice to their demands, many of which attracted the support of middle-class reformers. Above all they called for free public education and the abolition of imprisonment for debt, causes that won widespread popular support. The labor parties and unions also actively promoted the ten-hour day. In 1836 President Jackson established the ten-hour day at the Philadelphia Navy Yard in response to a strike, and in 1840 President Van Buren extended the limit to all government offices and projects. In private jobs the ten-hour day became increasingly common, although by no means universal, before 1860.

THE REVIVAL OF UNIONS After the Panic of 1837 the nascent labor movement went into decline, but began to revive with improved business conditions in the early 1840s. Still, the unions of the time remained local, weak, and given to sporadic activity. Often they came and went with a single strike. The greatest single labor dispute before the Civil War came on February 22, 1860, when shoemakers at Lynn and Natick, Massachusetts, walked out for higher wages. Before the strike ended it had spread through New England, involving perhaps twenty-five towns and 20,000 workers. It stood out also because it was a strike the workers won. Most of the employers agreed to wage increases, and some also agreed to recognize the union as a bargaining agent.

This reflected the growing tendency of workers to view their unions as permanent. Workers sought union recognition and regular collective bargaining agreements. They also shared a growing sense of solidarity. In 1852 the National Typographical Union revived the effort to organize skilled crafts on a national scale. Others followed, and by 1860 about twenty such organizations had appeared, although none was strong enough as yet to do much more than hold national conventions and pass resolutions.

JACKSONIAN INEQUALITY

During the years before the Civil War, the United States had begun to develop a distinctive working class, and the gap between rich and poor visibly widened. But the American myth of "rags to riches" endured. The legend had just enough basis in fact to make it plausible. John Jacob Astor, the wealthiest man in America, worth more than $20

million at his death in 1848, came of humble if not exactly destitute origins. But his and similar cases were more exceptional than common.
Those who started with the handicap of poverty and ignorance seldom
made it to the top. In 1828 the top 1 percent of New York's families
(owning $34,000 or more) held 40 percent of the wealth, and the top
4 percent held 76 percent. Similar circumstances prevailed in Philadelphia, Boston, and other cities.

A supreme irony of the times was that the so-called "age of the common man," the "age of Jacksonian Democracy," seems actually to have
been an age of increasing social stratification. Years before, in the late
eighteenth century, slavery aside, American society probably approached
equality more closely than any other population of its size anywhere else
in the world. During the last half of the 1700s, social mobility was higher
than either before or since. By the time popular egalitarianism caught up
with reality, reality was moving back toward greater inequality.

Why this happened is difficult to say, except that the boundless
wealth of the untapped frontier narrowed as the land was occupied and
claims on various opportunities were staked out. Such developments
took place in New England towns even before the end of the seventeenth century. But despite growing social distinctions, it seems likely
that the white population of America, at least, was better off than the
general run of European peoples. New frontiers, geographical and technological, raised the level of material well-being for all.

MAKING CONNECTIONS

- Eli Whitney's invention of the cotton gin had a profound effect on southern economic and social development. Chapter 14 describes the economy and society of the Old South in greater detail.

- The westward migration traced in this chapter will increase tremendously in the 1840s, a trend discussed in Chapter 13.

- As this chapter demonstrates, the birth and expansion of railroads in the first half of the nineteenth century was an important part of "The Dynamics of Growth." Chapter 15 shows how a proposal for the first transcontinental railroad had an unexpected side effect: it intensified the debate over the spread of slavery westward.

FURTHER READING

On economic development in the nation's early decades, see Stuart W. Bruchey's *Enterprise: The Dynamic Economy of a Free People* (1990).

The resilient classic on transportation and economic growth is George R. Taylor's *The Transportation Revolution, 1815–1861* (1951). Concurrent with transportation innovations was industrial growth. Thomas C. Cochran's *Frontiers of Change: Early Industrialism in America* (1981) is a useful survey. For introductions to urbanization, see Sam Bass Warner, Jr.'s *The Urban Wilderness* (1972).*

*These books are available in paperback editions.

12 ∽ AN AMERICAN RENAISSANCE: RELIGION, ROMANTICISM, AND REFORM

CHAPTER ORGANIZER

This chapter focuses on:

- the rise of new religious movements

- the development of a distinctive American literary culture

- the variety of social reform movements

RATIONAL RELIGION

American thought and culture in the early nineteenth century remained rooted in Puritan piety and Enlightenment rationalism. Those ideas, most vividly set forth in Jefferson's Declaration of Independence, had in turn a universal application. America, it was widely believed, had a mission to stand as an example to the world, much as John Winthrop's "city upon a hill" had once stood as an example to errant humanity. The concept of America's unique mission still carried spiritual overtones, for the religious fervor quickened in the Great Awakening had reinforced the idea of providential national destiny. In turn the sense of high calling infused the national character with an element of perfectionism— and an element of impatience when reality fell short of expectations. The combination brought major reforms and advances in human rights. It also brought disappointments that could fester into cynicism and alienation.

DEISM   The currents of the Enlightenment and the Great Awakening, now mingling, now parting, flowed on into the nineteenth century and in different ways eroded the remnants of Calvinist orthodoxy. As time passed, the orthodox image of a just but stern God promising predestined hellfire and damnation gave way to a more optimistic religious outlook. Enlightenment rationalism increasingly stressed mankind's inherent goodness rather than depravity, and it encouraged a belief in social progress and the promise of individual perfectibility.

Many leaders of the Revolutionary War era, such as Jefferson and Franklin, became deists, even while nominally attached to churches. Deism, which arose in eighteenth-century Europe, simply carried the logic of Sir Isaac Newton's image of the world as a smoothly operating machine to its logical conclusion. The God of the deist had planned the universe, built it, set it in motion, and then left it to its own devices. By the use of reason people might grasp the natural laws governing the universe.

Orthodox believers could hardly distinguish such doctrine from atheism, but Enlightenment rationalism soon began to make deep inroads into American Protestantism. The old Congregational churches around Boston proved most vulnerable. A strain of rationalism had run through Puritan belief in its stress on literacy and the need for "right reason" to interpret the Scriptures. Moreover, Boston's progress—some would say degeneration—from Puritanism to prosperity had persuaded many rising families that they were anything but sinners in the hands of an angry God. Drawn toward more consoling and less strenuous doctrines, some went back to the traditional rites of the Episcopal church. Others simply dropped or qualified their adherence to Calvinist theology while remaining in the Congregational churches.

UNITARIANISM AND UNIVERSALISM   By the end of the eighteenth century many New Englanders were drifting into Unitarianism, a belief emphasizing the oneness and benevolence of God, the inherent goodness of humankind, and the primacy of the individual's reason and con-science over established creeds and Scriptural literalism. Humans were not inherently depraved, Unitarianism stressed; people were capable of doing tremendous good and all were eligible for salvation. Boston was very much the center of the movement, and its notion of "rational religion" flourished chiefly within Congregational churches until controversy began to smoke Unitarians out. During the early nineteenth century, more and more of these "liberal" churches accepted the name of Unitarian.

Boston's revered Unitarian minister William Ellery Channing emerged as the chief spokesman for the liberal position. "I am surer that my rational nature is from God," he said, "than that any book is an expression of his will." The American Unitarian Association, formed in 1826, included 125 churches (all but five of them in Massachusetts). Among them were twenty of the twenty-five oldest Calvinist churches in the United States. That same year, when the Presbyterian minister Lyman Beecher moved to Boston, he lamented: "All the literary men of Massachusetts were Unitarian; all the trustees and professors of Harvard College were Unitarian, all the elite of wealth and fashion crowded Unitarian churches."

A parallel movement, Universalism, attracted a different social group: wage laborers and people of more humble means. Universalists stressed the salvation of all men and women, not just the predestined elect of the Calvinist doctrine. God, they taught, was too merciful to condemn anyone to eternal punishment; eventually all souls would come into harmony with God. "Thus, the Unitarians and Universalists were in fundamental agreement," wrote one historian of religion, "the Universalists holding that God was too good to damn man; the Unitarians insisting that man was too good to be damned."

THE SECOND GREAT AWAKENING

For all the impact of rationalism, Americans remained a profoundly religious people—as they have ever since. There was, the perceptive French visitor Alexis de Tocqueville observed in the 1830s, "no country in the world where the Christian religion retains a greater influence over the souls of men than in America." Around 1800 fears that secularism was indeed taking root sparked a revival that soon grew into a Second Awakening.

FRONTIER REVIVALS   In its frontier phase, the Second Awakening, like the first, generated great excitement and strange manifestations. It gave birth, moreover, to a new ritual, the camp meeting, in which the fires of faith were repeatedly rekindled. Missionaries found ready audiences among lonely frontier folk hungry for spiritual meaning and a sense of community.

The Baptists embraced a simplicity of doctrine and organization that appealed especially to the common people of the frontier. Their theology was grounded in the authority of the Bible and the recognition of a person's innate depravity. But they replaced the Calvinist notion of predestination with the concept of universal redemption and highlighted the ritual of adult baptism. They also explicitly stressed the equality of all men and women before God, regardless of wealth, social standing, or educational training. Since each congregation was its own highest authority, a frontier group could form a church and call a minister on their own. Sometimes whole congregations moved across the mountains as a body. As one historian and future president, Theodore Roosevelt, later described it: "Baptist preachers lived and worked exactly as their flocks. . . . They cleared the ground, split rails, planted corn, and raised hogs on equal terms with their parishioners."

But the Methodists, who shared with the Baptists an emphasis on salvation by free will but established a much more centralized organization, may have had the most effective recruiting method of all: the circuit rider who sought out people in the most remote areas with the message of salvation as a gift free for the taking. The system began with Francis Asbury, an aggressive, fervent, and tireless British-born revivalist who scoured the trans-Appalachian frontier for lost souls, preaching some 25,000 sermons while defying hostile Indians and suffering through harsh winters. "When he came to America," a biographer wrote, "he rented no house, he hired no lodgings, he made no arrangements to board anywhere, but simply set out on the Long Road, and was traveling forty-five years later when death caught up with him." Asbury's mobile evangelism perfectly suited the frontier environment and the new democratic age.

While Methodist preachers address the crowd at this revivalist camp meeting, a man in the foreground is overcome with religious ecstasy.

Peter Cartwright emerged as the most successful Methodist "circuit rider," and this sturdy, fearless preacher grew justly famous for his highly charged sermons. He recalled stopping at a decaying Baptist church in frontier Kentucky: "While I was preaching, the power of God fell on the assembly, and there was an awful shaking among the dry bones. Several fell to the floor and cried for mercy. . . . I believe if I had opened the doors of the Church then, all of them would have joined the Methodist Church." Cartwright typified the Methodist disdain for an educated clergy, at one point arguing that it was "the illiterate Methodist preachers [who]actually set the world on fire." He may have been right, for by the 1840s the Methodists had grown into the largest Protestant denomination in the country.

The Great Revival spread quickly through the West and into more settled regions back east. Camp meetings were held typically in late summer or fall, when farm work slackened. People converged from far and wide, camping in wagons, tents, or crude shacks. Mass excitement swept up even the most skeptical onlookers, and infusions of the spirit provoked participants to strange manifestations. Some went into cataleptic trances; others contracted the "jerks," laughed the "holy laugh," babbled in unknown tongues, or got down on all fours and barked like dogs to "tree the Devil."

But dwelling on the bizarre aspects of the camp meetings distorts a social institution that offered a meaningful outlet to an isolated people.

This was especially true for women, for whom the camp meetings provided an alternative to the rigors and isolation of frontier domesticity. Camp meetings also brought a more settled community life through the churches they spawned, and they helped spread a more democratic faith among the frontier people.

FINNEY AND THE "BURNED-OVER DISTRICT" Regions swept by such revival fevers have been compared to forests devastated by fire. In the single year 1830–31 alone, the number of churches in New England grew by one-third. Lyman Beecher called the awakening of 1831 "the greatest work of God, and the greatest revival of religion, that the world has ever seen." Western New York from Lake Ontario to the Adirondacks and including Rochester experienced such intense levels of evangelical activity that it was labeled the "Burned-Over District."

The most successful evangelist in the region was a lawyer named Charles Grandison Finney. In 1839 he preached for six months in Rochester and helped generate 100,000 conversions. He arrived at his intense religious convictions through a circuitous route. Raised in the backwoods of New York, he never heard the name of God mentioned in his home except in profanity. He left home to study law and then began his legal practice in Adams, New York. While visiting the local Presbyterian church, he scoffed when he heard the parishioners praying for revival. This led several young adults in the congregation, including the woman he would marry, to begin praying for him. Finney's conscience began to gnaw at him. He could not eat or sleep. Finally, one evening in 1821, he fled to the woods on the edge of town and a "mighty baptism of the Holy Ghost overwhelmed him." The spirit went through him in "waves of liquid love," he remembered, and the next day he announced a new profession as a revivalist. In 1823 Finney was ordained and for the next decade he subjected the Burned-Over District to yet another scorching. Finney claimed to have converted "the great mass of the most influential people" in the community.

Finney became the greatest single exemplar of evangelical Protestantism, and, some would argue, the very inventor of professional revivalism. He wrestled with an age-old question that had plagued Protestantism: what role can the individual play in earning salvation? Orthodox Calvinists had long argued that people could neither earn nor choose salvation on their own accord. Grace was a gift of God, a predetermined decision incapable of human understanding or control. In contrast, Finney insisted that the only thing preventing conversion was the individual. And what most often discouraged individual conversion was the terrifying loneliness of the decision. To combat such discomfort and bolster the courage of the ambivalent, Finney transformed revivals into collective conversion experiences in which spectacular public events displaced private communion and the unregenerate were brought into intense and public contact with praying Christians. Group prayer generated a sense of trust and common purpose among the community of strangers. The saving of souls did not have to wait for a miracle, he argued, nor did it depend upon narrow doctrinal discussions; it could result from careful planning, advertising, showmanship, and, above all, emotion. He sought to arouse excitement, not for its own sake but to rivet attention on the Word. "New measures are necessary from time to time to awaken attention and bring the gospel to bear on the public mind." To those who challenged such calculated use of emotion Finney had a frank answer: "The results justify my methods."

Untrained in theology, Finney read the Bible and worked out his own theology of free will that was anything but Calvinist in its emphasis on the individual's ability to choose salvation. His gospel also combined faith and good works; one led to the other. "All sin consists in selfishness," he declared, "and all holiness or virtue, in disinterested benevolence." Regeneration therefore produced "a change from selfishness to benevolence, from having a supreme regard to one's own interest to an absorbing and controlling choice of the happiness and glory of God's Kingdom."

In 1835 Finney took the chair of theology at the new Oberlin College, founded by pious New Englanders in Ohio's Western Reserve. Later he served as its president. From the start Oberlin radiated a spirit of reform predicated on faith; it was the first college in America to admit women and blacks, and it was a hotbed of antislavery activity. Finney himself, however, held that people must be reformed from within, and he cautioned against relying primarily on political action for moral ends.

THE MORMONS   In addition to providing the scene of revivals, the Burned-Over District gave rise to several new religious departures, of which the most important was the Church of Jesus Christ of Latter Day

Saints, or the Mormons. The founder, Joseph Smith, Jr., was the fourth child of wandering parents who finally settled in the village of Palmyra, New York. In 1820 young Smith (then fourteen) had a vision of "two Personages, whose brightness and glory defy all description." They identified themselves as the Savior and God the Father and cautioned him that all existing religious beliefs were false. About three years later, Smith claimed, an angel named Moroni led him to a hill where he found the Book of Mormon, a lost section of the Bible. It told the story of ancient Hebrews who had inhabited the New World and to whom Jesus had made an appearance.

On the basis of this revelation, Smith began forming his own church in 1830, and after a few years he was gathering converts by the thousands. Mostly poor farmers, these religious seekers found in Mormonism the promise of a pure kingdom of Christ in America and an alternative to the social turmoil and the degrading materialism of the era. From the outset the Mormon saints upset the "gentiles" with their close-knit sense of community and their assurance of righteousness. Mormons rejected the notion of original sin staining the human race. They professed an optimistic creed stressing human goodness and the virtues of common folk.

In their search for a refuge from persecution, the Mormons moved from New York to Ohio, then to several places in Missouri, and finally in 1839 to Nauvoo, Illinois, where they settled for some five years. Nauvoo became a bustling city of 12,000 people, and Joseph Smith, "the Prophet," became the community's leading entrepreneur: he owned the hotel and general store, served as mayor and lieutenant general of the Nauvoo Legion, the city's 2,000-man militia, and was trustee for the church. At Nauvoo he codified the theocratic church organization, combining a hierarchical structure with the Protestant idea of the priesthood of all (male) believers.

The charismatic Smith also practiced "plural marriage," much to the dismay of his first wife, Emma, who never accepted his argument that God sanctioned polygamy. In 1844 a crisis arose when dissidents accused Smith of justifying polygamy. The upshot was a schism in the church, a gathering movement among non-Mormons in the neighboring counties to attack Nauvoo, and the arrest of Smith and his brother Hyrum. On June 27, 1844, an anti-Mormon lynch mob stormed the feebly defended Nauvoo jail and shot both Joseph and Hyrum Smith.

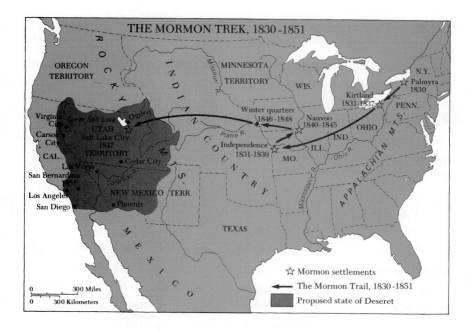

THE MORMON TREK, 1830-1851

OREGON TERRITORY

MINNESOTA TERRITORY

WIS.

N.Y.

Palmyra 1830

Kirtland 1831-1837

PENN.

Winter quarters 1846-1848

Nauvoo 1840-1845

OHIO

Virginia City

Great Salt Lake

Ogden

UTAH

Carson City

Salt Lake City 1847

TERRITORY

Platte R.

Independence 1831-1839

IND.

ILL.

Ohio R.

MO.

CAL.

Cedar City

San Bernardino 1851

Las Vegas

NEW MEXICO TERR.

Colorado R.

Mississippi R.

APPALACHIAN MTS.

Los Angeles

San Diego

Phoenix

TEXAS

MEXICO

0   300 Miles
0   300 Kilometers

☆ Mormon settlements

← The Mormon Trail, 1830-1851

Proposed state of Deseret

In Brigham Young, successor to Joseph Smith, the Mormons found a leader who was strong-minded, intelligent, and decisive. He was also prolific, eventually marrying sixteen women and fathering fifty-seven children. After the murder of the founder, Young patched up an unsure peace with the neighbors by promising to leave Illinois. Before that year was out Young had chosen a new destination, sight unseen, from promotional literature on the West. It lay near the Great Salt Lake in Utah, guarded by mountains to the east and north, deserts to the west and south, yet itself fed by mountain streams of melted snow. Despite its isolation, moreover, it was close enough to the Oregon Trail for the saints to prosper by trade with passing gentiles.

Brigham Young trusted God, but made careful preparations—no wandering in the wilderness for the Mormon Moses. As a result, the epic Mormon trek was better organized and less arduous than most of the overland migrations of the time. By the fall of 1846 all 15,000 of the migrants had reached winter quarters on the Missouri River, where they paused until the first bands set out the next spring for the Promised Land. The first arrivals at Salt Lake in July 1847 found only "a broad and barren plain hemmed in by mountains . . . the paradise of the lizard, the cricket and the rattlesnake." But by the end of 1848 the Mormons had developed an efficient irrigation system and over the next decade, by cooperative labor, they brought about a spectacular greening of the desert. They organized at first their own State of Deseret (meaning "land of the honey bee," according to Young), but their independence was short-lived. Congress incorporated the Utah Territory, including the Mormon's Salt Lake settlement, into the United States in 1849. Nevertheless, with Brigham Young named the territorial governor, the new arrangement afforded the Mormons almost the same control.

ROMANTICISM IN AMERICA

The revival of piety during the early 1800s represented a widespread tendency in the western world to accentuate the stirrings of the spirit over the dry logic of reason. Another great victory of heart over head was the romantic movement in thought, literature, and the arts. By the 1780s a revolt was brewing in Europe against the well-ordered world of the Enlightened thinkers. Were there not, many wondered, more things in this world than reason and logic could box up and explain: moods, impressions, feelings; mysterious, unknown, and half-seen things? Americans took readily to the romantics' emphasis on individual freedom and the inspiring beauties of Nature.

Rose above

TRANSCENDENTALISM   The most intense expression of such thought in America was the Transcendentalist movement of New England, which drew its name from its emphasis on that realm of thought that transcended (or rose above) the limits of reason. American Transcendentalism was largely inspired by European thinkers such as Immanuel Kant and Samuel Taylor Coleridge, but it was rooted in New England Puritanism, to which it owed a pervasive moralism. It also had a close affinity with the Quaker doctrine of the inner light. The inner light, a gift from God's grace, was transformed by Transcendentalists into intuition, a faculty of the mind.

In 1836 an informal discussion group soon named the Transcendental Club began to meet in Boston and Concord. It drew at different times clergymen such as Theodore Parker and George Ripley; philosophical writers such as Henry David Thoreau, Bronson Alcott, and Orestes Brownson; and learned women like Margaret Fuller and Elizabeth and Sophia Peabody. Fuller edited the group's quarterly review, *The Dial* (1840–1844), before the duty fell to Ralph Waldo Emerson, soon to become the acknowledged high priest of transcendentalism.

Ralph Waldo Emerson, author of Nature, America's "intellectual Declaration of Independence."

EMERSON AND THOREAU   More than any other person, Emerson spread the Transcendentalist gospel. Sprung from a line of New England ministers, he set out to be a Unitarian parson, then quit the "cold and cheerless" denomination before he was thirty because of growing doubts about its vitality. After travel to Europe, where he met England's great literary romantics, Emerson settled in Concord to take up the life of an essayist, poet, and popular speaker on the lecture circuit, preaching the good news of optimism, self-reliance, and the individual's unlimited potential. Having found reason "cold as a cucumber" and having discovered that the "ideal is truer than the actual," he was determined to *transcend* the limitations of inherited conventions and of Lockean rationalism in order to penetrate the inner recesses of the self. As he once suggested, Transcendentalism meant "a little beyond" the rational world.

Emerson's young friend and Concord neighbor, Henry David Thoreau, practiced the introspective self-reliance that Emerson preached. "I like people who can do things," Emerson stressed, and Thoreau, fourteen years his junior, could do many things well—carpentry, masonry, painting, surveying, sailing, and gardening. Thoreau, Emerson noted, was "as ugly as sin, long-nosed, queer-mouthed" and possessed of "uncouth and somewhat rustic manners." But he displayed a sense of uncompromising integrity, outdoor vigor, and tart individuality that Emerson found

Henry David Thoreau, author of the American classics Walden *and* "Civil Disobedience."

captivating. Short and sinewy, Thoreau was an acknowledged master of the woodland arts and a probing thinker.

He was also a thoroughgoing individualist. "If a man does not keep pace with his companion," Thoreau wrote, "perhaps it is because he hears a different drummer." After graduating from Harvard, Thoreau settled down in Concord to eke out a living as a part-time surveyor and pencil-maker. But he yearned to be a writer and a philosophical naturalist, and he made almost daily escapes to the woods and fields to drink in the beauties of nature and reflect upon the mysteries of life. The contemporary scramble for wealth disgusted rather than tempted him. It too often corrupted the pursuit of happiness and led people to work too hard. "The mass of men," he wrote, "lead lives of quiet desperation."

Determined himself to practice "plain living and high thinking," Thoreau boarded with the Emersons for a time and then embarked on an experiment in self-reliant simplicity. On July 4, 1845, he took to the woods to live in a cabin he had built on Emerson's land beside Walden Pond. He wanted to see how far he could free himself from the complexities and hypocrisies of modern commercial life, and to devote his time to reflection and writing. His purpose was not to lead a hermit's life. He frequently walked the mile or so to town to dine with his friends, and he often welcomed guests at his cabin. "I went to the woods because I wished to live deliberately," he wrote in *Walden, or Life in the Woods* (1854), ". . . and not, when I came to die, discover that I had not lived."

While Thoreau was at Walden Pond, the Mexican War erupted. Believing it a corrupt attempt to advance the cause of slavery, he refused to pay his state poll tax as a gesture of opposition, for which he was put in jail (only for one night; an aunt paid the tax). Out of the incident grew the classic essay "Civil Disobedience" (1849), which was later to influence the passive-resistance movements of Mahatma Gandhi in India and Martin Luther King, Jr., in the American South. "If the law is of such a nature that it requires you to be an agent of unjustice to another," Thoreau wrote, "then, I say, break the law. Let your life be a counter friction to stop the machine."

The broadening ripples of influence more than a century after Thoreau's death show the impact a contemplative individual can have on the larger world of action. Although both he and Emerson lent their voices to worthy causes, they both shied away from organized reform or political activities. They prized their individual freedom and distrusted all institutions—even those promoting causes they deemed worthy. They primarily supplied the force of an animating idea: people must follow their consciences. In doing so they and other Transcendentalists inspired reform movements and were the quickening force for a generation of writers that produced the first great classic age of American literature.

THE FLOWERING OF AMERICAN LITERATURE

Ever since gaining independence, the United States had suffered from a cultural inferiority complex. The Old World continued to set the standards in philosophy, literature, and the fine arts. As a British critic sneered in 1819, the "Americans have no national literature." That may have been true, but during the Jacksonian era and after, American culture began to flower. Two New York writers, Washington Irving and

James Fenimore Cooper, and four New England poets, Henry Wadsworth Longfellow, John Greenleaf Whittier, Oliver Wendell Holmes, Sr., and James Russell Lowell, began to achieve international distinction.

DICKINSON   A fifth poet, Emily Dickinson, the most original of the writers who contributed to the "New England Renaissance," lived as a recluse in Amherst, Massachusetts. Only two of her almost 1,800 poems had been published (anonymously) before her death in 1886, and the full corpus of her work remained unknown for years thereafter. Yet she possessed an imaginative power and inventive genius superior to her more famous male peers. Born in Amherst in 1830, the child of a prominent, stern father and gentle mother, she received a first-rate secondary education and then attended the new Mount Holyoke Female Seminary. Neither she nor her sister married, and they both lived out their lives in their parents' home.

Perhaps it was Emily's severe eye trouble during the 1860s that induced her solitary withdrawal from the larger society; perhaps it was the aching despair generated by her unrequited love for a married minister. Whatever the reason, her intense isolation led her to write about her own shifting psychic state. Her themes were elemental: life, death, fear, loneliness, Nature, and, above all, God, a "Force illegible," a "distant, stately lover."

HAWTHORNE   Nathaniel Hawthorne, the supreme artist of the New England group of fiction writers, never shared the sunny optimism of his Transcendentalist neighbors or their perfectionist belief in reform. A sometime resident of Concord, but a native and longtime inhabitant of coastal Salem, he was haunted by the knowledge of evil bequeathed to him by his Puritan forebears—one of whom had been a judge at the Salem witchcraft trials. After graduating from Bowdoin, he worked for some time in obscurity in Salem, gradually began to sell a few stories, and finally earned a degree of fame with his collection of *Twice-Told Tales* (1837). In these, as in most of his later work, he presented powerful moral allegories. His central themes explored evil and its consequences: pride and selfishness, secret guilt, selfish egotism, the impossibility of rooting sin out of the human soul. His greatest novel, *The Scarlet Letter* (1850), explicitly pondered such burdens, focusing on the guilt felt by a woman and a minister who had committed adultery.

POE   Edgar Allan Poe, born in Boston and reared in Virginia, was arguably America's most inventive genius in the first half of the century, and many Europeans considered him the most important American writer of the time. As a poet he strove to design verses that would display the classic virtues of restraint, discipline, and unity. "The Raven" is a masterful example of his preoccupation with form as well as his interest in probing the dark recesses of the human soul. The tormented, hard-drinking, quarrelsome Poe was also a master of Gothic horror in the short story and the inventor of the detective story. He judged prose by its ability to provoke emotional tension, and since he considered fear to be the most powerful emotion, he focused his efforts on making the grotesque and supernatural seem disturbingly real to his readers. Anyone who has read the "Tell-Tale Heart" or "The Pit and the Pendulum" can testify to his success.

MELVILLE   Although today considered one of America's greatest novelists, Herman Melville during his later years saw his literary reputation evaporate. Born in New York in 1819, he had only two years of formal schooling before he was forced to drop out because of his father's death. He then worked on a farm, as a bank messenger, and as a store clerk before shipping out as a seaman at age twenty. Some time later, after eighteen months aboard a whaler, he wound up in the South Seas and jumped ship with a companion. After a month spent with a friendly tribe in the valley of the Typees, he signed onto an Australian whaler, jumped ship again in Tahiti, was jailed for mutiny, obtained his release by signing on as a harpooner, and after landing in Hawaii, he finally returned to Boston as a seaman aboard a frigate of the U.S. navy. An embroidered account of his exotic adventures, in *Typee* (1846), became an instant popular success, which he repeated in *Omoo* (1847), based on his stay in Tahiti.

Melville then produced a masterpiece in *Moby-Dick* (1851), a novel rich in action as well as symbolism. The story of Captain Ahab and his obsessive quest for the white whale that had caused the loss of his leg, *Moby-Dick* was aimed at two audiences. On one level it was a ripping good yarn of adventure on the high seas. But Ahab's single-minded mission to slay the evildoer turned the captain himself into a destructive monster who sacrificed his ship, his crew, and himself to his folly, leaving as the one survivor the narrator of the story. Unhappily, neither the

Walt Whitman.

larger reading public nor many of the critics at the time accepted the novel on either level, and after the Civil War Melville's career wound down into futility.

WHITMAN   The most provocative American writer during the antebellum period was Walt Whitman, a remarkably vibrant personality who disdained inherited social conventions and artistic traditions. There was something elemental in Whitman's character, something bountiful and generous and compelling—even his faults and inconsistencies were ample. Born on a Long Island farm, he moved with his family to Brooklyn and from the age of twelve worked mainly as a handyman and journalist, frequently taking the ferry across the river to booming, bustling Manhattan. The city fascinated him, and he gorged himself on the urban spectacle—shipyards, crowds, factories, shop windows.

From such material Whitman drew his editorial opinions and poetic inspiration, but he remained relatively obscure until the first edition of *Leaves of Grass* (1855) caught the eye and aroused the ire of readers. Emerson found it "the most extraordinary piece of wit and wisdom that America has yet contributed," but more conventional critics shuddered at Whitman's explicit sexual references and groused at his indifference to rhyme and meter as well as his buoyant egotism. The jaunty Whitman, however, refused to conform to genteel notions of art, and he spent most of his career working on his gargantuan collection of poems, *Leaves of Grass,* enlarging and reshaping it in successive editions. He identified the growth of the book with the growth of the country, which he celebrated in all its variety.

THE POPULAR PRESS   The flowering of American literature came at a time of massive expansion in the popular press. In 1847 Richard Hoe of New York invented the Hoe Rotary Press, which printed 20,000 sheets an hour. Like many technological advances, this was a mixed blessing. The high cost of such a press made it harder for someone of small means to break into publishing. On the other hand it expedited production of cheap "penny" newspapers as well as magazines and books—which were often cheap in more ways than one.

The *New York Sun,* in 1833 the first successful penny daily, and others like it often ignored the merely important in favor of scandals and sensations, true or false. James Gordon Bennett, a native of Scotland, perfected this style in the *New York Herald,* which he founded in 1835. His innovations drew readers by the thousands: the first Wall Street column, the first society page (which satirized the well-to-do until it proved more gainful to show readers their names in print), pictorial news, telegraphic news, and great initiative in getting scoops. Eventually, however, the *Herald* suffered from dwelling so much on crime, sex, and depravity in general.

The chief beneficiary of a rising revulsion against the gutter press was the *New York Tribune,* founded as a Whig party organ in 1841. Horace Greeley, who became the most important journalist of the era, announced that it would be a cheap but decent paper avoiding the "matters which have been allowed to disgrace the columns of our leading Penny Papers." And despite occasional lapses, Greeley's "Great Moral Organ" typically amused its readers with wholesome human-interest stories. For a generation it was probably the most influential paper in the country. By 1860 its weekly edition had a national circulation of 200,000. The number of newspapers around the country grew from about 1,200 in 1833 to about 3,000 in 1860.

The boom in periodicals gave rise to more journals directed to specialized audiences. Worthy of mention, among others, are such magazines as *Godey's Lady's Book* (1830–1898), *The Southern Literary*

Messenger (1834–1864), *Hunt's Merchants' Magazine* (1839–1870), *DeBow's Commercial Review of the South and West* (1846–1880), and *The American Farmer* (1819–1897), the first important agricultural journal. The new methods of production and distribution boosted the book market as well. The publisher Samuel Goodrich estimated gross sales of books in America at $2 million in 1820, $12 million in 1850, and nearly $20 million in 1860. From 1820 to 1850, he estimated, books by American authors doubled their share of the market from about a third to about two-thirds.

EDUCATION

EARLY PUBLIC SCHOOLS   Literacy in Jacksonian America was surprisingly widespread, given the condition of public education. In 1840, according to census data, some 78 percent of the total population and 91 percent of the white population could read and write. Since the colonial period, in fact, Americans had enjoyed the highest literacy rate in the Western world. Most children learned their letters from church or private schools, formal tutors, or from their families.

By the 1830s the demand for public schools was rising fast. Reformers argued that popular government depended upon a literate and informed electorate. With the lowering of barriers to the ballot box, the argument carried all the more force. Workers wanted free schools to give their children an equal chance. Education, it was also argued, would be a means of social reform by improving manners and lessening crime and poverty.

Horace Mann of Massachusetts stood out in the early drive for statewide school systems. Trained as a lawyer, he shepherded through the legislature in 1837 a bill that created a state board of education, which he then served as secretary. Mann went on to sponsor many reforms in Massachusetts, including the first state-supported training for teachers, a state association of teachers, and a minimum school year of six months. Mann defended the school system as the way to social stability and equal economic opportunity. "Education then, beyond all other devices of human origin, is a great equalizer of the conditions of men—the balance wheel of the social machinery."

While the North made great strides in public education by 1850, the educational pattern in the South continued to reflect the region's aristocratic pretensions and rural isolation: the South had a higher percentage of college students than any other region, but a lower percentage of public school students. And the South had some 500,000 white illiterates, more than half the total number in the country.

Public school teachers were at first mostly men, often young men who did not regard teaching as a career but as a means of support while preparing for a career as a lawyer or preacher, or as part-time work during slack seasons on the farm. With the encouragement of educational reformers, however, teaching was beginning to be regarded as a profession. As the schools multiplied and the school term lengthened, women increasingly entered the field.

Most students going beyond the elementary grades went to private academies, often subsidized by church and public funds. Such schools, begun in colonial days, multiplied until there were more than 6,000 of them in 1850. Public high schools became well established in school systems only after the Civil War; in 1860 there were barely 300 in the whole country.

POPULAR EDUCATION   Beyond the schools there grew up many societies and institutes to inform the general public: mechanics' and workingmen's "institutes," "young men's associations," "debating societies," "literary societies," and such. Outstanding in the field was the Franklin Institute, founded at Philadelphia in 1824 to inform the public mainly in the fields of science and industry. Similar institutes were sponsored by major philanthropists such as Francis Cabot Lowell in Boston, George Peabody in Baltimore, and Peter Cooper in New York. Some cities offered evening classes to those who could not attend day schools. The most widespread and effective means of popular education, however, was the lyceum movement, which aimed to diffuse knowledge through public lectures. Professional agencies provided speakers and performers of all kinds, in literature, science, music, humor, travel, and other fields.

Akin to the lyceum movement and ultimately reaching more people was the movement for public libraries. Benjamin Franklin's Philadelphia Library Company (1731) had given impulse to the growth of subscription or association libraries. In 1803 Salisbury, Connecticut, opened a free library for children and in 1833 Peterborough, New Hampshire, established a tax-supported library open to all. The opening of the Boston Public Library in 1851 was a turning point. By 1860 there were approximately 10,000 public libraries (not all completely free) housing some 8 million volumes.

HIGHER EDUCATION   The postrevolutionary proliferation of colleges continued after 1800 with the spread of small church schools and state universities. Nine colleges had been founded in the colonial period, all of which survived; but not many of the fifty that sprang up between 1776 and 1800 lasted. Among those that did were Hampden-Sydney, Bowdoin, and Middlebury, all of which went on to long and fruitful careers. Of the seventy-eight colleges and universities in 1840, fully thirty-five had been founded after 1830, almost all as church schools. A postrevolutionary movement for state universities flourished in those southern states that had had no colonial university. Federal policy abetted the spread of universities into the West. When Congress granted statehood to Ohio in 1803, it set aside two townships for the support of a state university and kept up that policy in other new states.

The coexistence of state and religious schools, however, generated conflicts over funding and curriculum. Beset by the need for funds, as colleges usually were, denominational schools often competed with tax-supported schools. Regarding curricula, the Second Awakening led many of the church schools to emphasize theology at the expense of science and the humanities. On the other hand, America's development required broader access to education and programs geared to vocations. The University of Virginia, "Mr. Jefferson's University," founded in 1819 within sight of Monticello, introduced in 1826 a curriculum that reflected Jefferson's view that education ought to combine pure knowledge with "all the branches of science useful *to us,* and *at this day.*" The model influenced the other new state universities of the South and West.

American colleges and universities during the nineteenth century were tiny when compared to today's institutions of higher learning. Most enrolled a hundred students or less, and the largest rarely had more than 600. Virtually all of these students were men. Elementary education for girls was generally accepted, but training beyond that

level was not. Many men and women thought higher education unsuited to women's destiny in life. Some, such as Abigail Adams, argued
that education would produce better wives and mothers, but few were
ready to demand equality on principle. Progress began with the academies, some of which taught boys and girls alike. Good "female seminaries" like those founded by Emma Willard at Troy, New York (1824), and
Mary Lyon at Mount Holyoke, Massachusetts (1836), prepared the way
for women's colleges.

The work in female seminaries usually differed from the courses in
men's schools, giving more attention to the social amenities and such
"embellishments" as music and art. Vassar, opened at Poughkeepsie, New
York, in 1865, is usually credited with being the first women's college to
give priority to conventional academic standards. Oberlin College in
Ohio, founded in 1833, opened as both a biracial and a coeducational
institution. Its first women students were admitted in 1837. In general,
the West gave the greatest impetus to coeducation, with state universities in the lead. But once admitted, women students remained in a subordinate status. At Oberlin, for instance, they were expected to clean
male students' rooms and were not allowed to speak in class or recite at
graduation exercises. Coeducation did not mean equality.

SOME MOVEMENTS FOR REFORM

Emerson spoke for his generation, as he so often did, when he
asked: "What is man born for, but to be a Reformer, a Remaker of what
man has made?" The urge to eradicate evil from nineteenth-century
America had its roots in the widespread sense of mission, which in turn
drew upon rising faith in the perfectibility of humankind. Belief in perfectibility had both evangelical and liberal bases. Transcendentalism,
the spirit of which infected even those unfamiliar with its philosophical
roots, offered a romantic faith in the individual and the belief that human intuition led to right thinking.

Such a perfectionist bent found outlet in diverse reform movements
and activities during the Jacksonian era. Few areas of life escaped the
concerns of the reformers, however trivial or weighty: observance of the
Sabbath, dueling, crime and punishment, the hours and conditions of
work, poverty, vice, care of the handicapped, pacifism, foreign missions,

temperance, women's rights, the abolition of slavery. Some crusaders challenged a host of evils; others focused on pet causes. One Massachusetts reformer, for example, insisted that "a vegetable diet lies at the basis of all reforms." The greatest dietary reformer of the age, however, was Sylvester Graham, who started as a temperance speaker in 1830 and moved on to champion a natural diet of grains, vegetables, and fruits, and abstinence from alcohol, coffee, tea, tobacco, and many foods. The Graham cracker is one of the movement's legacies.

TEMPERANCE   The temperance crusade was perhaps the most widespread of all. The census of 1810 reported some 14,000 distilleries producing 25 million gallons of spirits each year. With a hard-drinking population of just over 7 million, the "alcoholic republic" was producing well over three gallons per year for every man, woman, and child, not counting beer, wine, and cider. And the census takers no doubt missed a few stills. William Cobbett, an English reformer who traveled in the United States, noted in 1819 that one could "go into hardly any man's house without being asked to drink wine or spirits, even *in the morning*."

The temperance movement rested on a number of arguments. First and foremost was the religious demand that "soldiers of the cross" lead blameless lives. Others stressed the economic implications of sottish workers. The dynamic new economy, with factories and railroads moving on strict schedules, made tippling by the labor force a far greater problem than it had been in a simple agrarian economy. Humanitarians emphasized the relations between drinking and poverty. Much of the movement's propaganda focused on the sufferings of innocent mothers and children. "Drink," said a pamphlet from the Sons of Temperance, "is the prolific source (directly or indirectly) of nearly all the ills that afflict the human family."

In 1826 a group of Boston ministers organized the American Society for the Promotion of Temperance. The society pursued its objectives through lecturers, press campaigns, a prize essay contest, and the formation of local and state societies. A favorite device was to ask each person who took the pledge to put by his signature a T for Total Abstinence. With that a new word entered the language: "teetotaler."

In 1833 the society called a national convention in Philadelphia, where the American Temperance Union was formed. The convention,

The Way of Good & Evil. *Intemperance was one of the steps on the way of evil, leading to "everlasting punishment."*

however, revealed internal tensions: Was the goal moderation or total abstinence, and if the latter, abstinence merely from ardent spirits or also from wine, cider, and beer? Should the movement work by persuasion or by legislation? Like nearly every movement of the day, temperance had a wing of perfectionists who rejected all compromises with Demon Rum, and they passed a resolution that the liquor traffic was morally wrong and ought to be prohibited by law. The union, at its spring convention in 1836, called for abstinence from all alcoholic beverages—a costly victory that caused moderates to abstain from the movement instead. Still, between 1830 and 1860 the temperance agitation drastically reduced Americans' per-capita consumption of alcohol.

PRISONS AND ASYLUMS   The sublime optimism of the Jacksonian age, the belief that people are innately good and capable of improvement, brought major changes in the treatment of prisoners, the handicapped, and dependent children. Public institutions arose dedicated to the treatment and cure of social ills. If removed from society, it was believed, the needy and deviant could be made whole again. Unhappily, this ideal kept running up against the dictates of convenience and economy. The institutions had a way of turning into breeding grounds of brutality and neglect.

In the colonial period prisons were usually places for brief confinement before punishment, which was either death or some kind of pain or humiliation: whipping, mutilation, confinement in stocks, branding, and the like. A new attitude began to emerge after the Revolution, and gradually the idea of the penitentiary developed. It would be a place where the guilty experienced penitence and underwent rehabilitation, not just punishment.

An early model of the new system, widely copied, was the Auburn Penitentiary, commissioned by New York in 1816. The prisoners at Auburn had separate cells and gathered for meals and group labor. Discipline was severe. The men were marched out in lockstep and never put face to face or allowed to talk. But prisoners were at least reasonably secure from abuse by other prisoners. The system, its advocates argued, had a beneficial effect on the prisoners and saved money, since the workshops supplied prison needs and produced goods for sale at a profit. By 1840 there were twelve prisons of the Auburn type in the United States.

The reform impulse naturally found another outlet in the care of the insane. The Philadelphia Hospital (1752), one of the first in the country, had a provision in its charter that it should care for "lunaticks," but before 1800 few hospitals provided care for the mentally ill. There were in fact few hospitals of any kind. The insane were usually confined at home with hired keepers or in jails and almshouses. After 1815, however, public asylums that housed the disturbed separately from criminals began to appear. Early efforts led to such optimism that a committee reported to the Massachusetts legislature in 1832 that with the right treatment "insanity yields with more readiness than ordinary diseases." These high expectations gradually faded with experience.

The most important figure in arousing the public conscience to the plight of these unfortunates was Dorothea Lynde Dix. A pious, withdrawn, frail, almost saintly Boston schoolteacher, she was called upon to instruct a Sunday-school class at the East Cambridge House of Cor-

Dorothea Dix.

rection in 1841. She found there a roomful of insane persons completely neglected, fed slop, and left without heat on a cold March day. In a report to the state legislature in 1843, Dix told of persons confined "in *cages, closets, cellars, stalls, pens! Chained, naked, beaten with rods, and lashed into obedience!*" Wardens charged Dix with "slanderous lies," but she won the support of leading reformers as well as a large state appropriation for improving the treatment of the insane. From Massachusetts she carried her campaign throughout the country and abroad. By 1860 she had convinced twenty states to heed her advice and adopt similar programs to improve the conditions in prisons and asylums.

WOMEN'S RIGHTS While Dorothea Dix stood out as an example of the opportunity reform gave middle-class women to enter public life, Catharine Beecher, a founder of women's schools in Connecticut and Ohio, published a guide prescribing the domestic sphere for women. A *Treatise on Domestic Economy* (1841) became the leading handbook of what historians have labeled the "cult of domesticity." While Beecher upheld high standards in women's education, she also accepted the prevailing view that the "woman's sphere" was the home and argued that young women should be trained in the domestic arts of housework and childrearing.

The official status of women during this period remained much as it had been in the colonial era. Legally, a woman was unable to vote, and, after marriage, denied legal control of her property and even of her children. A wife could not make a will, sign a contract, or bring suit in court without her husband's permission. Her legal status was thus like that of a minor, a slave, or a free black. Gradually, however, more and more women began to complain about their status. The organized movement for women's rights had its origins in 1840, when the American antislavery movement split over the question of women's right to participate. American women decided then that they needed to organize on behalf of their own emancipation too.

In 1848 two prominent moral reformers and advocates of women's rights, Lucretia Mott, a fifty-five-year-old Philadelphia Quaker, and Elizabeth Cady Stanton, a thirty-two-year-old graduate of Troy Seminary who refused to be merely "a household drudge," decided to call a convention to discuss "the social, civil, and religious condition and rights of women." The hastily organized Seneca Falls Convention, the first of its kind, issued on July 19, 1848, the Declaration of Sentiments, mainly the work of Mrs. Stanton, who also was the wife of a prominent abolitionist and mother of seven. In a clever paraphrase of Jefferson's Declaration, the document proclaimed the self-evident truth that "all men and women are created equal," and the attendant resolutions said that all laws placing woman "in a position inferior to that of men, are contrary to the great precept of nature, and therefore of no force or authority." Such language was too strong for most of the thousand delegates, and only about a third of them signed it. Ruffled male editors lampooned the women activists as being "love-starved spinsters" and "petticoat rebels." Yet the Seneca Falls gathering represented an important first step in the evolving campaign for women's rights.

From 1850 until the Civil War the women's-rights leaders held annual conventions and carried on a program of organizing, lecturing, and petitioning. The movement had to struggle in the face of meager funds and antifeminist women and men. The movement owed its success to the work of a few undaunted women who refused to be overawed by the odds against them. Susan B. Anthony, an ardent Quaker already active in temperance and antislavery groups, joined the crusade in the 1850s.

Elizabeth Cady Stanton (left) and Susan B. Anthony. Mrs. Stanton "forged the thunderbolts and Miss Anthony hurled them."

At age seventeen she had angrily noted, "What an absurd notion that women have not intellectual and moral faculties sufficient for anything else but domestic concerns!"

Unlike Stanton and Mott, Anthony was unmarried and therefore able to devote most of her attention to the women's crusade. As one observer put it, Mrs. Stanton "forged the thunderbolts and Miss Anthony hurled them." Both were young when the movement started and both lived into the twentieth century, focusing after the Civil War on demands for women's suffrage. While women did not win voting rights until much later, there were some legal gains. The state of Mississippi, seldom regarded as a hotbed of reform, was the first to grant married women control over their property in 1839; by the 1860s eleven more states had such laws.

Still, the only jobs open to educated women in any numbers were nursing and teaching, both of which extended the domestic roles of health care and nurturing into the world outside the home. Both brought relatively lower status and pay than "man's work" despite the skills, training, and responsibility involved. Yet if women could be teachers, Susan Anthony asked, why not lawyers or doctors or ministers or intellectuals? Why not indeed, replied a small band of hardy women who did carve out professional careers. Harriet Hunt of Boston was a teacher who, after nursing her sister through a serious illness, set up shop in 1835 as a self-taught physician and persisted in medical practice although twice rejected by Harvard Medical School. Voted into Geneva Medical College in western New York as a joke, Elizabeth Blackwell of Ohio had the last laugh when she finished at the head of her class in 1849. She founded the New York Infirmary for Women and Children and later had a long career as a professor of gynecology in the London School of Medicine for Women.

An intellectual prodigy among women of the time—the derisory term was "bluestocking"—was Margaret Fuller. A precocious child, she was force-fed education by a father who began teaching her Latin when she was six. (She would later claim that "I find no intellect comparable to my own" in America.) As a young adult she moved confidently in the literary circles of Boston and Concord, edited *The Dial* for two years, and became literary editor and critic for Horace Greeley's *New York Tribune*. From 1839 to 1844 she conducted "conversations" with the cultivated ladies of Boston. From this classroom-salon emerged many of the ideas that went into her pathbreaking book, *Woman in the Nineteenth Century* (1845), a plea for the removal of all intellectual and economic disadvantages. Minds and souls were neither masculine nor feminine, she argued. Genius had no sex. "What woman needs," Fuller contended, "is not as a woman to act or rule, but as a nature to grow, as an intellect to discern, as a soul to live freely and unimpeded, to unfold such powers as were given her when we left our common home."

UTOPIAN COMMUNITIES The pervasive climate of reform during the Jacksonian era and after also provoked a quest for utopia. "We are all a little mad here with numberless projects of social reform," Emerson wrote in 1840. Everyone, it seemed "has a draft of a new community in his pocket." Plans for new communities had long been an American passion, at least since the Puritans set out to build a Wilderness Zion. The visionary communes of the nineteenth century often had purely economic and social objectives, but those that were rooted in religion proved most durable.

Over a hundred utopian communities sprang up between 1800 and 1900. Among the most durable were the Shakers, officially the United Society of Believers in Christ's Second Appearing, founded by Ann Lee Stanley (Mother Ann), who reached New York state with eight followers in 1774. Believing religious fervor a sign of inspiration from the Holy Ghost, they had strange fits in which they saw visions and prophesied.

These manifestations later evolved into a ritual dance—hence the name Shakers. Mother Ann claimed that God was genderless and that she was the female incarnation, as Jesus had been the male. She preached celibacy to prepare Shakers for the perfection that was promised them. The church would first gather in the elect, and eventually in the spirit world convert and save all humankind.

Mother Ann died in 1784, but the group found new leaders. From the first community at Mount Lebanon, New York, the movement spread to new colonies in New England, and soon afterward into Ohio and Kentucky. By 1830 about twenty groups were flourishing. In Shaker communities all property was held in common, and strict celibacy was practiced. Men and women not only slept separately but also worked and ate separately. Governance of the colonies was concentrated in the hands of select elders chosen by the ministry. To outsiders this might seem almost despotic, but the Shakers emphasized equality of labor and reward, and members were free to leave at will. The superbly managed Shaker farms yielded a surplus for the market. They were among the leading sources of garden seed and medicinal herbs, and many of their manufactures, including clothing, household items, and especially furniture, were prized for their simple beauty. By the mid-twentieth century, however, few members remained alive; the Shakers had reached the peak of activity in the years 1830–1860.

John Humphrey Noyes, founder of the Oneida Community, was the son of a Vermont congressman. Educated at Dartmouth and then Yale Divinity School, he discovered true religion at one of Charles G. Finney's revivals and entered the ministry. He was forced out, however, when he concluded that with true conversion came perfection and a complete release from sin. In 1836 he gathered a group of a dozen or so "Perfectionists" around his home in Putney, Vermont. Ten years later Noyes announced a new doctrine of "complex marriage," which meant that every man in the community was married to every woman and vice versa. "In a holy community," he claimed, "there is no more reason why sexual intercourse should be restrained by law, than why eating and drinking should be." To outsiders such theology smacked of "free love," and Noyes was arrested. He fled to New York and in 1848 established the Oneida Community, which numbered more than 200 by 1851.

The communal group shared alike in the food, clothing, and shelter produced by their hard work. They eked out a living with farming and logging until the mid-1850s, when the inventor of a new steel trap joined the community. Oneida traps were soon known as the best money could buy. The community then branched out into sewing silk, canning fruits, and making silver tableware.

Meanwhile, the community also carefully regulated its social life. Women enjoyed the same rights as men, and children were raised by the community as a whole, placed in a common nursery, supplied with toys and affection, and allowed to sleep until they awoke themselves. At age fourteen boys and girls were trained in sexual activity by elderly women. No one was forced to have sexual relations, but Noyes encouraged wide circulation in order to enhance community ties. In addition he insisted that only those who had embraced Christ as their Savior could participate. "Holiness," he stressed, "must go before free love."

Noyes also practiced eugenics, pairing up "superior" mates in order to produce brighter and healthier offspring. (He named himself the most qualified male in nine instances, even though he was by then in his sixties.) For well over a generation the passionate community prospered. In 1879, however, it faced a crisis when Noyes fled to Canada to avoid prosecution for adultery. The members then abandoned complex marriage, and in 1881 decided to convert into a joint-stock company, the Oneida Community, Ltd, which remains today a thriving flatware company.

In contrast to these religious communities, Robert Owen's New Harmony was based on a secular principle. A British capitalist who worried about the social effects of the factory system, Owen bought the town of Harmony, Indiana, from a group of communalists known as Rappites and promptly christened it New Harmony. In 1825 a varied group of about 900 colonists gathered in New Harmony and established a cooperative community based on the principles of Enlightenment rationalism and symmetry. Separate residences were to be built for the married, unmarried, and children. A complete school system, including nursery and university, was to be built along with a library, lecture halls, laboratories, and gymnasium. The high proportion of learned participants generated a certain intellectual electricity about the place. There were frequent lectures and social gatherings with music and dancing.

For a time it looked like a brilliant success, but New Harmony soon fell into discord. Leaders complained of "grumbling, carping, and murmuring" members, and others who had the "disease of laziness." The problem, it seems, was one common to most reform groups. Every idealist wanted his own patented plan put into practice. In 1827 Owen returned from a visit to England to find New Harmony insolvent. The following year he dissolved the project and sold or leased the lands on good terms, in many cases to the settlers.

Brook Farm was the most celebrated of all the utopian communities, because it had the support of Emerson, Fuller, and countless other well-known literary figures of New England. George Ripley, a Unitarian minister and Transcendentalist, conceived of Brook Farm as a kind of early-day "think tank," combining high thinking and plain living. Nathaniel Hawthorne, a member, later memorialized its failure in his novel *The Blithedale Romance* (1852). He joined the community full of excitement at the prospect of living among articulate and interesting co-workers but soon grew tired of his assignment—shoveling manure—and he left the community after less than a year's residence. Soon after Hawthorne left Brook Farm he wrote that his life there was "an unnatural and unsuitable, and therefore an unreal one." But his disillusionment was exceptional rather than representative. Most Brook Farmers found considerable fulfillment in the new community. Said one: "We were happy, contented, well-off and care-free; doing a great work in the world, enthusiastic and faithful, we enjoyed every moment of every day." The place survived financially, however, mainly because of an excellent community school that drew tuition-paying students from outside. But when a new central building burned down on the day of its dedication in 1846, the community spirit expired in the embers.

Like Brook Farm, most of the utopian communities were short-lived. Such experiments, performed in relative isolation, had little effect on the larger society. Yet they did express the deeply ingrained desire for perfectionism inherent in the American character, a desire that would continue to spawn such noble, if frequently naïve, experiments thereafter.

Among all the targets of reformers' wrath, however, one great evil would finally take precedence over the others—human bondage. The paradox of American slavery coupled with American freedom, of "the world's fairest hope linked with man's foulest crime," in Herman Melville's words, would inspire the climactic crusade of the age, abolitionism, one that would ultimately move to the center of the political stage and sweep the nation into an epic—and tragic—struggle.

MAKING CONNECTIONS

- The antislavery campaign, especially its abolitionist aspect, was related to the reform movements in this chapter. It is discussed following the section on slavery in Chapter 14.

- Chapter 16 shows how the Civil War had a significant impact on the status of women in American society, a continuation of a theme discussed here.

FURTHER READING

Few single-volume works cover the diversity of early American reform and culture. A good start is Ronald G. Walter's *American Reformers, 1815–1860* (1978).* Sydney E. Ahlstrom's *A Religious History of the American People* (1972) provides a solid survey of antebellum religious movements and developments. Revivalist religion is discussed in John B. Boles's *The Great Revival* (1972). Donald G. Mathews, in *Religion in the Old South* (1977), assesses the evangelical temperament. For splinter sects, the scholarship is most voluminous on the Mormons. See Klaus J. Hansen's *Mormonism and the American Experience* (1981).

The best introductions to Transcendentalist thought remain Paul Boller's *American Transcendentalism, 1830–1860* (1974)* and Anne Rose's *Transcendentalism as a Social Movement* (1981).* A solid introduction to antebellum newspapers is Frank L. Mott's *American Journalism* (3rd ed., 1962). A different aspect of the nineteenth-century intellectual community is described in Robert V. Bruce's *The Launching of Modern American Science, 1846–1876* (1987).

Several good works describe various aspects of the antebellum reform movement. For temperance, see W. J. Rorabaugh's *The Alcoholic Republic: An American Tradition* (1979)* and Barbara Leslie Epstein's

* These books are available in paperback editions.

The Politics of Domesticity: Women, Evangelism, and Temperance in Nineteenth-Century America (1981).* On prison reform and other humanitarian projects, see Charles Rosenberg's *The Care of Strangers: The Rise of America's Hospital System* (1987). Lawrence A. Cremin's *American Education: The National Experience, 1783–1876* (1980) traces early school reform.

The literature on women's history is both voluminous and diverse. See Nancy F. Cott's *The Bonds of Womanhood: "Women's Sphere" in New England, 1780–1835* (1977).* Changing ideals of the family in the nineteenth century are described in Steven Mintz and Susan Kellog's *Domestic Revolutions: A Social History of American Family Life* (1988).

Michael Fellman's *The Unbounded Frame: Freedom and Community in Nineteenth Century Utopianism* (1973) surveys the utopian movements.

* These books are available in paperback editions.

13 ∞ MANIFEST DESTINY

CHAPTER ORGANIZER

This chapter focuses on:

- national politics in the 1840s

- the factors leading to westward migrations and the conditions faced by western settlers

- the causes, course, and consequences of the Mexican War

THE WESTERING IMPULSE

During the 1840s the westering impulse, the quest for a better chance and more living room, continued to excite the American imagination. "If hell lay to the west," one pioneer declared, "Americans would cross heaven to get there." That may or may not have been true, but millions of Americans were willing to cross the Mississippi River and experience unrelenting hardships in order to conquer new frontiers and express their "providential destiny" to subdue the entire continent. By 1860 some 4.3 million people had settled in the trans-Mississippi West.

Of course, most of these settlers and adventurers wanted to exploit the many economic opportunities afforded by the new lands. Trappers and farmers, miners and merchants, hunters, ranchers, teachers, domestics, and prostitutes, among others, headed west seeking their fortune. Others sought religious freedom or new converts to Christianity. Whatever the reason, they formed an unceasing migratory stream flowing across the Great Plains and the Rocky Mountains. The Indian and Mexican inhabitants of the region soon found themselves swept aside by successive waves of American settlers. In 1858 President James Buchanan could report that the nation was bound east and west "by a chain of Americans which can never be broken."

THE TYLER YEARS When William Henry Harrison took office in 1841, elected like Jackson mainly on the strength of his military record and his lack of a public stand on major issues, the Whig leaders expected him to be a tool in the hands of Webster and Clay. Webster became secretary of state, and while Clay preferred to stay in the Senate, his friends filled the cabinet. Harrison served the shortest term of any president—after the longest inaugural address. At the inauguration, held on a chilling rainy day, he caught cold. The pleadings of office seekers in the following month filled his days and sapped his strength. On April 4, 1841, exactly one month after the inauguration, Harrison died of pneumonia.

John Tyler, the first vice-president to succeed on the death of a president, served practically all of Harrison's term. At age fifty-one the thin, fragile Virginia slaveholder was the youngest president to date. He already had a long career behind him as legislator, governor, congressman, and senator, and his positions on all the important issues had been forcefully stated and were widely known. Although a Whig, he favored a strict construction of the Constitution and was a stubborn defender of states' rights. When someone asked if he were a "nationalist," Tyler retorted that he had "no such word in my political vocabulary." Consequently, he ardently opposed Clay's American System—protective tariffs, a national bank, internal improvements at national expense. Once a Democrat, he had broken with the party over Jackson's denial of a state's right to nullify a federal law and Jackson's imperious use of executive authority. Thus Tyler, the states'-rights Whig, had been chosen to "balance" the ticket by the party leaders in 1840; no one expected that he would actually wield power. Acid-tongued John Quincy Adams said Tyler's proper title should be "vice-president acting as president." Other critics called the new president "His Accidency."

DOMESTIC AFFAIRS   Given more finesse on Clay's part, he might have bridged the policy divisions over financial issues between himself and Tyler. But for once, driven by disappointment and ambition, the "Great Compromiser" lost his instinct for compromise. When Congress met in special session in 1841, Clay introduced a series of resolutions designed to supply the platform that the party had evaded in the previous election. The chief points were repeal of the Independent Treasury, establishment of a third Bank of the United States, distribution to the states of proceeds from public land sales, and a higher tariff. Clay then set out to push his program through Congress. "Tyler dares not resist me. I will drive him before me," Clay predicted.

Tyler, it turned out, was not easily driven. Although he agreed to allow the repeal of the Independent Treasury and signed a higher tariff bill in 1842, Tyler vetoed Clay's bill for a new national bank. This provoked his entire cabinet, with the exception of Webster, to resign in an unprecedented action. Tyler replaced the defectors with anti-Jackson Democrats like himself who had become Whigs. Clay's leadership of the Whig party was now established beyond question, and Tyler had become a president without a party.

FOREIGN AFFAIRS   In foreign relations, meanwhile, developments of immense significance were taking place. A major issue between Britain and the United States involved the suppression of the African slave trade, which both countries had outlawed in 1808. In 1841 the British prime minister asserted the right to patrol off the coast of Africa and search vessels flying the American flag to see if they carried slaves. But the American government remembered the impressments and seizures during the Napoleonic Wars and refused to accept such intrusions. Relations were further strained late in 1841 when American slaves on the *Creole,* bound from Hampton Roads to New Orleans, mutinied and sailed into Nassau, where the British set them free. Secretary of State Webster demanded that the slaves be returned as American property, but the British refused.

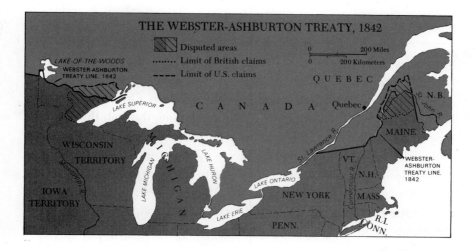

THE WEBSTER-ASHBURTON TREATY, 1842

Disputed areas
.... Limit of British claims
---- Limit of U.S. claims

0   200 Miles
0   200 Kilometers

Fortunately at this point a new British ministry decided to accept Webster's overtures for negotiations and sent Lord Ashburton to Washington. Ashburton was widely known to be friendly to Americans, and the talks proceeded smoothly. The negotiations settled the Maine boundary as well as other border disputes by accepting the existing line between the Connecticut and St. Lawrence Rivers, and by compromising on the line between Lake Superior and the Lake-of-the-Woods. The Webster-Ashburton Treaty (1842) also provided for joint patrols off Africa to suppress the slave trade.

MOVING WEST

In the 1840s the American people were no more stirred by the quarrels of Tyler and Clay over such issues as banking, tariffs, and distribution, important as they were, than students of history would be at a later date. What stirred the blood was the mounting evidence that more and more pioneers were hurdling the barriers of the "Great American Desert" and the Rocky Mountains, reaching out toward the Pacific coast. In 1845 editor John Louis O'Sullivan labeled this bumptious spirit of expansion. "Our manifest destiny," he wrote, "is to overspread the continent allotted by Providence for the free development of our yearly multiplying millions." At its best, this much-trumpeted notion of "Manifest Destiny" offered a moral justification for American expansion, a prescription for what an enlarged United States could and should be. At its worst, it was a cluster of flimsy rationalizations for naked greed and imperial ambition.

Most of the western pioneers during the second quarter of the nineteenth century were American-born whites from the upper South and Midwest. A few free blacks joined in the migration. One settler remembered seeing "a Negro woman . . . tramping along through the heat and dust, carrying a cast iron black stove on her head, with her provisions and a blanket piled on top . . . bravely pushing on for California." Although some emigrants traveled by sea to California, most went overland. Between 1841 and 1867, some 350,000 men, women, and children made the arduous trek to California or Oregon, while hundreds of thousands of others settled along the way in Colorado, Texas, Arkansas, and other areas.

THE INDIAN AND SPANISH FRONTIER

As they crossed the Mississippi River and made their way westward, American pioneers entered not only a new environment but a new culture as well. The Great Plains and the Far West were already occupied by Indians and Mexicans, peoples who had lived in the region for centuries and had established their own distinctive customs and ways of life. Now they were joined by Americans of diverse ethnic origin and religious persuasion. It made for a volatile mix.

WESTERN INDIANS   Historians estimate that over 325,000 Indians inhabited the Southwest, the Great Plains, California, and the Pacific Northwest in 1840, when the great migration of white settlers began to pour into the region. These Native Americans were divided into more than 200 different tribes, each with its own language, religion, economic base, kinship practices, and system of governance. Some were primarily farmers who tended peach orchards or raised corn and beans in the fertile river valleys. Others were nomadic hunters who preyed upon game animals as well as other Indians.

Some twenty-three tribes resided in the Great Plains, a vast grassland stretching from the Mississippi River west to the Rocky Mountains and from Canada to Mexico. This region had been virtually devoid of a human presence until the Spaniards arrived and introduced the horse and gun in the late sixteenth century. Prior to the advent of horses, Indians relied upon dogs as their beast of burden—other than women, who carried whatever the dogs could not. A horse could carry seven times as much weight as a dog. Even more important, a horse dramatically increased the mobility and hunting ability of the Plains Indians. Indians from the Midwest were able to leave their villages and follow the great buffalo herds. The buffalo offered Indians virtually a self-sufficient livelihood. They used the meat for food and transformed the skins into clothing, bedding, and tipi coverings. The bones and horns served as tools and utensils. Even buffalo manure could be dried and used for fuel.

Plains Indians such as the Arapaho, Blackfoot, Cheyenne, Kiowa, and Sioux were horse-borne nomads; they moved across the grasslands with the buffalo herds, carrying their tipis with them. About fifteen feet in diameter, a tipi was a remarkably efficient and mobile dwelling. It typically consisted of a network of poles covered by buffalo hides tied in place and staked to the ground. A smoke flap at the top enabled the residents to build fires inside. Three beds were usually placed inside, along with firewood and other articles of equipment.

Disputes over buffalo and hunting grounds provoked clashes between rival tribes, which help explain the cult of the warrior among the Plains Indians. Scalping or killing an enemy would earn praise from elders and feathers for their ceremonial headdresses. The most revered chiefs were allowed to wear eagle-feather warbonnets. Yet chiefs exercised only modest authority over their followers. As Chief Low Horn, a Blackfoot, explained, the chiefs "could not restrain their young men . . . their young men were wild, and ambitious, in their turn to be braves and chiefs."

Several quite different Indian tribes lived to the south and west of the Plains Indians. In the arid region including what is today Arizona, New Mexico, and southern Utah were the peaceful Pueblo tribes—Acoma, Hopi, Laguna, Taos, Zia, Zuni. They were sophisticated farmers who lived in adobe villages along rivers that they used to irrigate their crops of corn, beans, and squash. The word *pueblo* comes from the Spanish term for "village." Their rivals were the Apache and Navajo, warlike hunters who roamed the countryside in small bands and preyed upon the Pueblos. They, in turn, were periodically harassed by their powerful enemies, the Comanches.

To the north, in the Great Basin between the Rocky Mountains and the Sierra Nevada range, Indians such as the Paiutes and Gosiutes struggled to survive in the harsh, arid region of what is today Nevada, Utah, and eastern California. They traveled in family groups and subsisted on berries, pine nuts, insects, and rodents. West of the mountains, along the California coast, the Indians lived in small villages. They gathered wild plants and acorns and were quite adept at fishing in the rivers and bays. More than 100,000 Indians lived in coastal California in the 1840s.

The Indian tribes living along the northwest Pacific Coast—the Nisqually, Spokane, Yakima, Chinook, Klamath, and Nez Percé (pierced noses)—enjoyed the most abundant natural resources and the most temperate climate. The ocean and rivers provided abundant seafood—whales, seals, salmon, crabs. The lush forests just east of the coast harbored game, berries, and nuts. And the majestic stands of fir, redwood, and cedar offered wood for cooking and shelter.

All these Indian tribes eventually felt the unrelenting pressure of white expansion. Because Indian life on the plains depended on the buffalo, the influx of white settlers posed a direct threat to their cultural survival. In an 1846 petition to President Polk, the Sioux protested that "for several years past the Emigrants going over the Mountains from the United States, have been the cause that Buffalo in great measure left our hunting grounds, thereby causing us to go into the Country of Our Enemies to hunt, exposing our lives daily for the necessary subsistence of our wives and children and getting killed on several occasions." But the federal government turned a deaf ear to such pleas for assistance. It continued to build a string of frontier forts to protect the advancing settlers, and it sought to use treaties to gain control of new lands. When officials of the Indian Bureau could not coerce, cajole, or confuse Indian leaders into selling title to their tribal lands, fighting ensued. And after the discovery of gold in California in 1848, the tidal wave of white expansion flowed all the way to the west coast.

THE SPANISH WEST   As American settlers moved westward they also encountered Spanish-speaking peoples. Many whites were as contemptuous of these people as they were of Indians. Senator Lewis Cass, the expansionist from Michigan, expressed the sentiment of many Americans during a debate over the annexation of New Mexico. "We do not want the people of Mexico," he declared, "either as citizens or as subjects. All we want is a portion of territory . . . with a population, which would soon recede, or identify itself with ours." He viewed Mexicans as ignorant, indolent, and conniving. The vast majority of the Spanish-speaking people in what is today called the American Southwest resided in New Mexico. Most of these were of mixed Indian and Spanish blood and were usually poor ranch hands or small farmers and herders.

The Spanish had been less successful in colonizing Arizona and Texas than in New Mexico and Florida. The Yuma and Apache Indians in Arizona and the Comanches and Apaches in Texas thwarted efforts to establish Catholic missions. After years of fruitless missionary efforts among the Pueblo Indians, one Spaniard complained that "most" of them "have never forsaken idolatry, and they appear to be Christians more by force than to be Indians who are reduced to the Holy Faith." In eastern Texas during the first half of the eighteenth century, French traders from Louisiana undermined the authority and influence of the Spanish missions. The French furnished the Indians with guns, ammunition, and promises of protection. "We do not have a single gun," lamented one Franciscan friar, "while we see the French giving hundreds of arms to the Indians." Several of the Texas missions were abandoned and reestablished near San Antonio in 1731. By 1750 the

Church interior, Las Trampas, New Mexico, constructed around 1760.

Pawnees, Wichitas, Comanches, and Apaches were using Spanish horses and French rifles to raid Spanish settlements in Texas. One Spanish commander reported that "the enemy is so superior . . . in firearms as well as in numbers, that our destruction seems probable." Such conditions help explain why Texas was one of the most sparsely populated provinces on the northern frontier of New Spain. By 1790, the Hispanic population in Texas numbered only 2,510 while in New Mexico it exceeded 20,000.

THE MEXICAN REVOLUTION   In 1807 French forces occupied Spain and imprisoned the king. This created both consternation and confusion throughout Spain's colonial possessions, including Mexico. Miguel Hidalgo y Costilla, a *creole* (European born in the New World) Mexican priest, took advantage of the fluid situation to organize a revolt of Indians and *mestizos* (people of mixed Indian and white ancestry) against Spanish rule. But the poorly organized uprising failed miserably. In 1811 Spanish troops captured Hidalgo and executed him. Other Mexicans, however, continued to yearn for independence. In 1820, a revolt by liberals in Spain greatly weakened the authority of the monarch, and Mexican *creoles* seized the opportunity to again liberate themselves from Spanish authority. By then, the Spanish forces in Mexico had lost much of their cohesion and dedication. Facing a growing revolt, the last Spanish officials withdrew from Mexico in 1821, and it became an independent nation.

Mexican independence unleashed tremors throughout the Southwest. In New Mexico and Arizona, American fur traders streamed into the region and developed a lucrative commerce in beaver pelts. Soon thereafter, wagon trains carrying American settlers began to make their way along the Santa Fe Trail. In California, American entrepreneurs also flooded into the now-Mexican province and soon became a powerful force for change. By 1848 Americans made up half of the non-Indian population. In Texas, American adventurers decided to promote their own independence from a newly independent—and chaotic—Mexican government. Suddenly, it seemed, the Southwest was a ripe new frontier for American exploitation and settlement.

SPANNING THE ROCKIES   One of the first targets of this spirit of "manifest destiny" was Santa Fe, a remote outpost of the Spanish em-

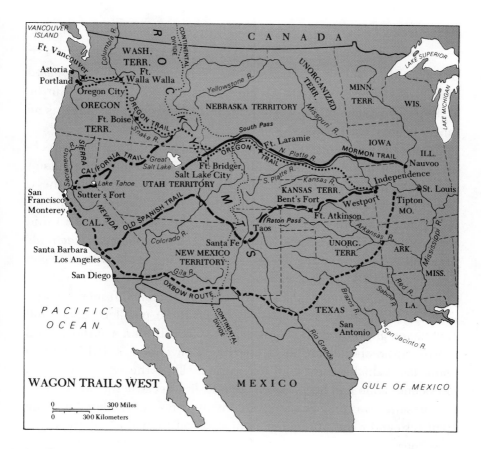

WAGON TRAILS WEST

0   300 Miles

0   300 Kilometers

pire founded in the seventeenth century, the capital and trading center for a population of perhaps 60,000 Mexicans and Indians in New Mexico. In 1821 Mexico, newly independent from Spain, let it be known that American traders were welcome in Santa Fe. Word spread quickly and eastern merchants began making the long wagon train journey west along the Santa Fe Trail. The trade never involved more than one or two hundred merchants, but it was a profitable enterprise in which American goods were traded for Mexican gold, silver, and furs. But the Santa Fe traders had pioneered more than a new trail. They showed that heavy wagons could cross the plains and penetrate the mountains, and they developed the technique of organized caravans for mutual protection.

The more important avenue for the fur trade, however, was the Missouri River with its many tributaries. The heyday of the mountain fur trade began in 1822 when a Missouri businessman sent his first trading party to the upper Missouri. By the mid-1820s there developed the "rendezvous system," in which trappers, traders, and Indians from all over the Rocky Mountain country gathered annually at some designated place, usually in or near the Grand Tetons, in order to trade. But by 1840 the great days of the western fur trade were over. The streams no longer teemed with beavers.

During the 1820s and 1830s the fur trade had sired a uniquely reckless breed of "mountain men" who deserted civilization for the pursuit of the beaver and reverted to a primitive existence in the wilderness, sometimes in splendid isolation, sometimes in the shelter of primitive forts, and sometimes among the Indians. They were the first to find their way around in the Rocky Mountains, and they pioneered the trails over which settlers by the 1840s were beginning to flood the Oregon Country and trickle across the border into California.

Beyond the mountains the Oregon country stretched from the Forty-second Parallel north to 54°40′. Between these parallels, Spain and Russia had given up their claims, leaving Great Britain and the United States as the only claimants. Under the Convention of 1818 the two countries had agreed to "joint occupation." Until the 1830s, however, joint occupation had been a legal technicality, because the only American presence was the occasional mountain man who wandered into the Pacific slope or the infrequent trading vessel from Boston, Salem, or New York.

But word of Oregon's fertile soil, temperate climate, and magnificent forests gradually spread, largely through the efforts of Methodist missionaries recently settled there. This enticed adventurous Americans, and by the late 1830s, a trickle of emigrants began flowing along the Oregon Trail. Soon "Oregon Fever" spread like a contagion. By 1843 the movement began to assume the proportions of mass migrations. That year about a thousand overlanders followed the trail westward from Independence, Missouri, along the Platte River into Wyoming, through South Pass down to Fort Bridger (abode of a celebrated mountain man, Jim Bridger), then down the Snake River to the Columbia and along the Columbia to their goal in the fertile Willamette Valley. By 1845 there were about 5,000 settlers in the region.

EYEING CALIFORNIA   California was also becoming an alluring attraction for new settlers and entrepreneurs. It first felt the influence of European culture in 1769, when Spain grew concerned about Russian fur traders moving south along the Pacific coast from their base in

Alaska. To thwart Russian intentions, Spain sent a naval expedition to explore and settle the region. The Spanish discovered San Francisco Bay and constructed presidios (military garrisons) at San Diego and Monterey. Even more importantly, Franciscan friars led by Junipero Serra established a mission at San Diego.

Over the next fifty years Franciscans built twenty more missions, spaced a day's journey apart along the coast from San Diego to San Francisco. There they converted Indians to their faith and established thriving agricultural estates. As in Mexico, the Spanish monarchy awarded huge land grants in California to a few ex-soldiers and colonists, who turned the grants into profitable cattle ranches. The Indians were left with the least valuable land, and most of them subsisted as farmers or artisans serving the missions. By 1803, 40 percent of California's Indian population had embraced Catholicism. Friars encouraged the piety and diligence of these "Mission Indians" with whippings, causing some to flee the jurisdiction of the church. Within three decades infectious diseases transmitted by European settlers decimated the Indian population, leaving only a third as many by 1833 as in 1803.

For all of its rich natural resources, California remained thinly populated by Indians and mission friars well into the nineteenth century. It was a simple, almost feudal, agrarian society, without schools, industry, or defenses. In 1821, when Mexico wrested its independence from Spain, Californians took comfort in the fact that Mexico City was so far away that it would exercise little effective control over its farthest state. During the next two decades, Californians, including many recent American arrivals, staged ten revolts against the governors dispatched to lord over them.

Yet Mexican rule did produce a dramatic change in California history. In 1824, Mexico passed a colonization act that granted hundreds of huge "rancho" estates to Mexican settlers. With free labor extracted from Indians, who were treated like slaves, these *rancheros* lived a life of self-indulgent luxury and ease, gambling, horse-racing, bull-baiting, and dancing. They soon cast covetous eyes on the vast estates controlled by the Franciscan missions, and in 1833–1834, they convinced the Mexican government to confiscate the California missions, exile the Franciscan friars, release the Indians from church control, and make the mission lands available to new settlement. Within a few years some 700 huge new rancho grants of 4,500 to 50,000 acres were issued along the coast from San Diego to San Francisco. Organized like feudal estates, these California ranches resembled southern plantations, but the death rate for Indian workers was twice as high as that of slaves in the Deep South.

Few accounts of life in California, however, took note of the brutalities inflicted on the Indians. Instead they portrayed the region as a proverbial land of milk and honey, ripe for development. Such a natural paradise could not long remain a secret, and Americans had already been visiting the Pacific coast in search of profits and land. By the late 1820s American trappers wandered in from time to time, and American ships began to enter the "hide and tallow" trade. The *rancheros* produced cowhide and beef tallow in large quantity, and both products enjoyed a brisk demand, cowhides mainly for shoes and the tallow chiefly for candles.

By the mid-1830s shippers began setting up agents on the scene to buy the hides and store them until a company ship arrived. One of these agents, John A. Sutter, had tried the Santa Fe trade first, then found his way to California. At the juncture of the Sacramento and American Rivers (later the site of Sacramento) he built an enormous enclosure that guarded an entire village of settlers and shops. Completed in 1843, the enclosure became the mecca for Americans bent on settling the Sacramento country. It stood at the end of what became the most traveled route through the Sierras, the California Trail, which forked off from the Oregon Trail and led through the mountains near Lake Tahoe. By 1846 there were perhaps 800 Americans in California, along with some 8,000–12,000 Californios of Spanish descent.

LIFE ON THE OVERLAND TRAIL   The settlers bound for Oregon and California traveled mostly in family groups, and they came from all over the United States. They usually left Missouri in late spring, completing the grueling 2,000-mile trek in six months. Traveling in ox-drawn, canvas-covered wagons nicknamed "prairie schooners," they jostled their way across dusty or muddy trails and traversed rugged mountains at the rate of about twelve to fifteen miles per day. The first wagon trains departed in 1841. By 1845 some 5,000 made the arduous journey annually. The discovery of gold in California in 1848 brought some 30,000 pioneers along the Oregon Trail in 1849. By 1850, the peak year of travel along the trail, the number had risen to 55,000.

Contrary to popular myth, the Indians rarely attacked wagon trains. Less than 4 percent of the fatalities associated with the overland trail experience resulted from Indian raids. More often, the Indians either allowed the settlers to pass through their tribal lands unmolested or demanded payment. The Sioux were especially shrewd toll keepers, who "in every case get the best of the bargain," observed one overlander. Many wagon trains never encountered a single Indian, and others received generous aid from Indians who served as guides, advisers, or traders. The Indians, one woman pioneer noted, "proved better than represented." To be sure, as the number of pioneers increased dramatically during the 1850s, tensions between overlanders and Indians increased, but never to the degree portrayed in Western novels and films.

Still, the journey west was incredibly difficult. Few who embarked on their western quest were adequately prepared for the ordeals they were to face. The carcasses of mules, oxen, and wagons from previous groups signaled the travails they would endure. Cholera claimed many lives. On average there was one grave every eighty yards along the trail between the Missouri River and the Willamette Valley. Some 20,000 pioneers died in all.

The never-ending routine of necessary chores and grinding physical labor took its toll on once-buoyant spirits. This was especially true for women, whose labors went on day and night. Uprooting their families and journeying west placed a heavy burden on wives and mothers, especially those accustomed to the comforts of middle-class domesticity. The hardships of trail life shattered the conventional notion of the settled home as the family's moral center and nursery. The diary of one woman settler records with great poignancy the trail's wearying regimen: "I have done a washing. Stewed apples, made pies and a rice pudding, and mended our wagon cover. Rather tired." The next day brought more of the same: "Baked biscuits, stewed berries, fried meat, boiled and mashed potatoes, and made tea for supper, afterward baked bread. Thus you see I have not much rest." Another woman complained that, unlike the men, who smoked and talked together after supper, "we *have no time for sociability.*" All was "hurry scurry." There "is no rest in such a journey."

Initially, the pioneers along the Overland Trail adopted the same division of labor used back East. Women cooked, washed, sewed, and monitored the children while men drove the wagons, tended the horses and cattle, and handled the heavy labor. But the unique demands of the trail soon dissolved such neat distinctions and posed new tasks. Women found themselves gathering buffalo dung for fuel, pitching in to help liberate a wagon mired in mud, helping to construct an impromptu bridge, or performing a variety of other unladylike activities. Yet only rarely did men assume conventional female roles. Most of the older women strove to keep distinct the traditional boundaries between men's and women's work, and quarrels frequently erupted. One woman reported that there was "not a little fighting" in their group, "invariably the outcome of disputes over divisions of labor."

Hard labor understandably provoked tensions within families and powerful yearnings for home. Many a tired pioneer could identify with the following comment in a girl's journal: "Poor Ma said only this morning, 'Oh, I wish we had never started.' She looks so sorrowful and dejected." Another woman wondered "what had possessed my husband, anyway, that he should have thought of bringing us away out through this God forsaken country." Some turned back, but most continued on. And once in Oregon or California they set about establishing stable communities. Noted one settler:

> Friday, October 27—Arrived at Oregon City at the falls of the Willamette.
> Saturday, October 28—Went to work.

JOHN FRÉMONT   Despite the hardships and dangers of the overland crossing, the Far West remained an irresistible attraction. The premier press agent for California, and the Far West generally, was John Charles Frémont, "the Pathfinder." Frémont, born in Savannah, Georgia, and raised in the South, became the consummate explorer and romantic adventurer. Possessed of boundless energy and reckless courage, a relentless love of the outdoors and an exuberant, charismatic personality, he inspired both respect and awe. His densely curled black beard, high forehead, commanding nose, and piercing blue eyes added to his dash and bounce.

Frémont was commissioned a second lieutenant in the United States Topographical Corps in 1838. In 1842 he mapped the Oregon Trail beyond South Pass—and met Christopher "Kit" Carson, one of the most knowledgeable of the mountain men. Carson became Frémont's frequent associate and the most famous frontiersman after Daniel Boone. In 1843–1844 Frémont, typically clad in deerskin shirt, blue army trousers, and moccasins, moved on to Oregon, then made a heroic sweep down the eastern slopes of the Sierras, headed southward through the central valley of California, bypassed the mountains in the south, and returned via Great Salt Lake. His reports on both expeditions, published together in 1845, gained a wide circulation and helped excite the interest of easterners.

Meanwhile, rumors flourished that the British and French were scheming to grab California, though neither government had such intentions. Political conditions in Mexico left the remote territory in near anarchy much of the time, as governors came and went in rapid succession. Amid the chaos a substantial number of Californians reasoned that they would be better off if they cut ties to Mexico altogether. Some favored an independent state, perhaps under French or British protection. A larger group admired the balance of central and local authority in the United States and felt their interests might best be served by American annexation. By the time the Americans were ready to fire the spark of rebellion in California, there was little will in Mexico to resist.

ANNEXING TEXAS

AMERICAN SETTLEMENTS   America's lust for land was most clearly at work in the most accessible of all the Mexican borderlands, Texas. More Americans resided there than in all the other coveted regions combined. During the 1820s Texas was rapidly turning into an American province, for Mexico in 1823 began welcoming American settlers into the region as a means of stabilizing the border.

First and foremost among the promoters of Anglo-American settlement was Stephen F. Austin, a Missouri resident who gained from Mexico a huge land grant originally given to his father by Spanish authorities. Before Spain finally granted Mexican independence, he had started a colony on the lower Brazos River, and by 1824 more than 2,000 hardy souls had settled on his lands. Most of the newcomers were southern farmers drawn to rich new cotton lands selling for only a few cents an acre. As a young woman settler recalled, "I was a young thing then, but 5 months married, my husband . . . failed in Tennessee. . . . I ready to go anywhere . . . freely consented. . . . Texas fever rose then . . . there we must go. There without much reflection, we did go." By 1830 the coastal region of eastern Texas had approximately 20,000 white settlers and 1,000 black slaves brought in to work the cotton. The newcomers quickly outnumbered the 5,000 Mexicans in the area, and showed little interest in Catholicism or other aspects of Mexican culture.

At that point the Mexican government grew alarmed at the flood of strangers threatening to engulf the province, and it forbade further immigration. Mexican troops moved to the frontier to enforce the law. But illegal American immigrants crossed the long border as easily as illegal Mexican immigrants would later cross over in the other direction. By 1835 the American population had mushroomed to around 30,000, about ten times the number of Mexicans in Texas. Friction mounted in 1832 and 1833 as Americans organized conventions to demand greater representation and power from the Mexican government. Instead of granting the request, General Santa Anna, who had seized power in Mexico, dissolved the national congress late in 1834, abolished the federal system, and became dictator. Texans rose in rebellion, summoned a convention, and pledged to fight for the old Mexican constitution. On March 2, 1836, however, as Santa Anna approached with an army of conquest, the Texans declared their independence.

INDEPENDENCE FROM MEXICO   The Mexican army delivered its first blow at San Antonio, where it assaulted a small garrison of 188 Texans and American volunteers holed up in an abandoned mission, the Alamo. Among the most celebrated of the volunteers was Davy Crockett, the Tennessee frontiersman and soldier who had fought Indians under Andrew Jackson and then served as a congressman. He was indeed a colorful character, full of spunk and brag, and thoroughly expert at killing with his trusty rifle, "Old Betsy." As he once told his men, "Pierce the heart of the enemy as you would a feller that spit in your face, knocked down your wife, burnt up your houses, and called your dog a skunk! Cram his pesky carcass full of thunder and lightning like a stuffed sassidge . . . and bite his nose off into the bargain."

On February 23, 1836, Santa Anna demanded that the 185 defenders surrender, only to be answered with a cannon shot. The 4,000 Mexicans then launched a series of frontal assaults. For twelve days they were repulsed and suffered fearful losses. At one point, during a lull in the fighting, Colonel William B. Travis, the garrison commander from South Carolina, drew a line on the ground with his sword as he described their hopeless plight. "Those prepared to give their lives in freedom's cause," he said in a trembling voice, "come over to me." Every man crossed the line. The notorious slave smuggler, Indian fighter, and inventor of the Bowie knife, Colonel James Bowie, stricken with pneumonia, asked that his cot be carried over the line.

In the chilly predawn hours of March 6, the defenders of the Alamo were awakened by the sound of Mexican bugles playing the dreaded "Deguello" ("no mercy to the defenders"). Soon thereafter Santa Anna's men attacked from every side. They were twice repulsed, but on the third try, as the defenders ran low on ammunition, the Mexicans broke through the battered north wall and swarmed through the breach. Colonel Travis was killed by a bullet in the forehead. Davy Crockett and the other frontiersmen used their muskets as clubs, but they too were slain. Jim Bowie, his pistols emptied, his famous knife bloodied, and his body riddled by bullets, lay dead on his cot. Santa Anna ordered the wounded Americans put to death and their bodies burned with the rest. All but one of the defenders was killed. The survivor, a Mexican, persuaded his captors that he had been forced to fight against his will. It was a complete victory, but a costly one. The defenders of the Alamo gave their lives at the cost of 1,544 Mexicans, and their heroic stand inspired the rest of Texas to fanatical resistance.

The commander-in-chief of the gathering Texas forces was Sam Houston, a flamboyant Tennessee frontiersman who had learned war under the tutelage of Andrew Jackson at Horseshoe Bend, had later represented the Nashville district in Congress, and had moved to Texas in 1833, only three years before. After the Mexican victory at the Alamo, Houston beat a strategic retreat eastward, gathering reinforcements as he went, including volunteers from the United States. Just west of the San Jacinto River he finally paused near the site of the city that later bore his name, and on April 21, 1836, surprised a Mexican encampment there. The 800 Texans and American volunteers charged,

Sam Houston.

yelling "Remember the Alamo," and overwhelmed the Mexican force within fifteen minutes. They killed 630 while losing only 9, and they took Santa Anna prisoner. The Mexican dictator bought his freedom by signing a treaty recognizing Texan independence. The Mexican Congress repudiated the treaty, but the war was at an end.

THE MOVE FOR ANNEXATION   Residents of the Lone Star Republic then drafted a constitution, made Houston their first president, and voted almost unanimously for annexation to the United States as soon as the opportunity arose. Houston's old friend Jackson was still the American president, but even Old Hickory could be discreet when delicacy demanded it. The addition of a new slave state at a time when Congress was beset with abolitionist petitions threatened to cause a serious sectional quarrel that might endanger Van Buren's election. Worse than that, it raised the specter of war with Mexico. Consequently, Jackson delayed recognition of the Texas Republic until his last day in office, and his successor, Van Buren, shied away from the issue of annexation during his entire term as president.

Rebuffed in Washington, Texans turned their thoughts to creating a separate country. Under President Mirabeau Bonaparte Lamar, elected in 1838, they began to talk of expanding to the Pacific as a new nation that would rival the United States. France and Britain extended recognition to the new nation of Texas and began to develop trade relations. Texas supplied them with an independent source of cotton, new markets, and promised also to become an obstacle to American expansion. The British, who had abolished slavery in their empire in 1833, hoped Texans might embrace abolition in exchange for British protection against any Mexican effort to reassert its sovereignty over Texas.

Many Texans, however, had never abandoned their hopes of annexation. Reports of growing British influence created anxieties in the United States government and among southern slaveholders, who became the chief advocates of annexation. The United States began secret negotiations with Texas in 1843, and in April John C. Calhoun, the new secretary of state, completed a treaty that went to the Senate for ratification.

Calhoun chose this moment also to send the British minister a letter instructing him on the blessings of slavery and stating that annexation of Texas was needed to foil the British abolitionists. Publication of the note fostered the claim that annexation was planned less in the national interest than to promote the expansion of slavery. It was so worded, one editor wrote Jackson, as to "drive off every northern man from the support of the measure." Sectional division, plus fear of a war with Mexico, contributed to the Senate's overwhelming rejection of the treaty. Solid Whig opposition contributed more than anything else to its defeat.

POLK'S PRESIDENCY

THE ELECTION OF 1844 Prudent leaders in both political parties had hoped to keep the divisive issue of Texas out of the 1844 campaign. Clay and Van Buren, the leading candidates, both wrote letters opposing annexation because it would risk civil war. Whig party leaders showed no qualms about Clay's stance. The convention nominated him unanimously, and the Whig platform omitted any reference to Texas.

The Democratic convention was a different story. Van Buren's southern supporters, including Jackson, abandoned him because of his opposition to Texas annexation. With the convention deadlocked, expansionist forces nominated James K. Polk of Tennessee. The party platform took an unequivocal stand favoring expansion, and to win support in the North and West as well as the South it called for "the re-occupation of Oregon and the re-annexation of Texas."

The combination of southern and western expansionism constituted a winning strategy so popular that Clay began to hedge his statement on Texas. While he still believed the integrity of the Union to be the chief consideration, he had "no personal objection to the annexation of Texas" if it could be achieved "without dishonor, without war, with the common consent of the Union, and upon just and fair terms." His explanation seemed clear enough, but prudence was no match for spread-eagle oratory and the emotional pull of Manifest Destiny. Clay's stand turned more votes to the Liberty party, an antislavery party begun by a group of abolitionists in 1840. In the western counties of New York the Liberty party drew enough votes away from the Whigs to give the state to Polk. Had he carried New York, Clay would have won the election by seven electoral votes. Polk won a narrow plurality of 38,000 popular votes nationwide but a clear majority of the electoral college, 170 to 105. At forty-nine Polk was the youngest president up to that time.

Born near Charlotte, North Carolina, Polk moved to Tennessee as a young man. After studying mathematics and classics at the University of North Carolina, he became a successful lawyer and planter, entered politics early, served fourteen years in Congress (four as Speaker of the House) and two as governor of Tennessee. Young Hickory, as his partisans liked to call him, was a short, slender man with a shock of long, grizzled hair, probing gray eyes, and a seemingly permanent grimace on his face. He had none of Jackson's charisma, but shared Jackson's strong prejudices and his stubborn determination. Polk had a penchant for hard work and eighteen-hour days, which destroyed his health during four years in the White House. Single-mindedly committed to the tasks at hand, Polk was a poor diplomat but a formidable leader.

POLK'S PROGRAM In domestic affairs "Young Hickory" Polk adhered to the principles of the old hero, but he and the new Jacksonians subtly reflected the growing influence of the slave-holding South within the party. Abolitionism, Polk warned, could bring the dissolution of the Union, but his proslavery stance further fragmented public opinion. Antislavery northerners had already begun to drift away from the Democratic party, which was perceived to represent the slave-holding interest.

Polk's major objectives were reduction of the tariff, reestablishment of the Independent Treasury, settlement of the Oregon question, and the acquisition of California. He got them all. The Walker Tariff of 1846, in keeping with Democratic tradition, lowered the tariff, and in the same year Polk persuaded Congress to restore the Independent Treasury, which the Whigs had eliminated. Twice Polk vetoed internal improvement bills.

But Polk's chief concern remained geographic expansion. He privately vowed to acquire California and New Mexico as well, preferably by purchase. The acquisition of Texas was already under way before Polk took office. President Tyler, taking Polk's election as a mandate to act, had asked Congress to accomplish annexation by joint resolution, which required only a simple majority in each house and avoided the two-thirds Senate vote needed to ratify a treaty. Congress had read the election returns too, and after a bitter debate over slavery, the resolution passed by votes of 27 to 25 in the Senate and 120 to 98 in the House. Tyler signed the resolution on March 1, 1845, offering to admit Texas to statehood. Texas voters ratified the action in October, and the new state formally entered the Union on December 29, 1845.

OREGON   Meanwhile, the Oregon issue heated up as expansionists aggressively insisted that Polk abandon previous offers to settle on the Forty-ninth Parallel and stand by the platform pledge to take all of Oregon. Some expansionists were prepared to risk war with Britain, even while relations with Mexico were simultaneously moving toward the breaking point. "Fifty-four forty or fight," they insisted. "All of Oregon or none." In his inaugural address Polk declared the American title to Oregon "clear and unquestionable," but privately he favored a prudent compromise. The British, however, refused his offer to extend the boundary along the Forty-ninth Parallel. Polk then withdrew the offer and renewed his claim to all of Oregon. In the annual message to Congress at the end of 1845, he asked for permission to give Britain a year's notice that joint occupation would be ended. After a long and bitter debate Congress adopted the resolution.

Fortunately for Polk the British government had no enthusiasm for war over that remote wilderness at the cost of profitable trade relations with the United States. In early June 1846 the British government submitted a draft treaty to extend the border along the Forty-ninth Parallel and through the main channel south of Vancouver Island. On June 18 the Senate ratified the treaty. Most of the country was satisfied. Southerners cared less about Oregon than Texas, and northern business interests valued British trade more than they valued Oregon. Besides, the country was already at war with Mexico.

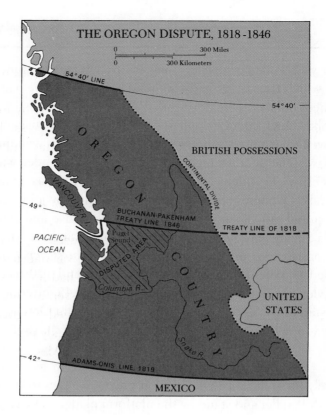

THE OREGON DISPUTE, 1818-1846

54°40' LINE

54°40'

BRITISH POSSESSIONS

OREGON

CONTINENTAL DIVIDE

VANCOUVER I.

49°

BUCHANAN-PAKENHAM
TREATY LINE 1846

TREATY LINE OF 1818

PACIFIC
OCEAN

Puget
Sound

DISPUTED AREA

Columbia R.

COUNTRY

UNITED
STATES

Snake R.

42°

ADAMS-ONIS LINE, 1819

MEXICO

THE MEXICAN WAR

THE OUTBREAK OF WAR   Relations with Mexico had gone from bad to worse. On March 6, 1845, two days after Polk took office, the Mexican ambassador broke off relations and left for home to protest the annexation of Texas. When an effort at negotiation failed, Polk focused his efforts on unilateral initiatives. Already his secretary of war was egging on American intrigues in California, telling the American consul in Monterey that "if the people should desire to unite their destiny with ours, they would be received as brethren."

Meanwhile, Polk ordered American troops under General Zachary Taylor to take up positions along the Rio Grande in the new state of Texas. These positions lay in territory that was doubly disputed: Mexico recognized neither the American annexation of Texas nor the Rio Grande boundary. Polk's intention was clear: he wanted to goad the Mexicans into a conflict in order to secure Texas and obtain California and New Mexico. As Ulysses S. Grant, then a young officer serving under Taylor, later admitted, "We were sent to provoke a fight, but it was essential that Mexico commence it."

Polk resolved that he could achieve his purposes only by force, and he won the cabinet's approval of a war message to Congress. That very evening, May 9, the news arrived that Mexicans had attacked American soldiers north of the Rio Grande. Eleven Americans were killed, five wounded, and the remainder taken prisoner. Polk's provocative scheme had worked. "Hostilities may now be considered as commenced," wrote General Taylor.

In his war message Polk seized the high ground, declaring that the war was a response to aggression, a recognition that war had been forced upon the United States. "The cup of forbearance had been exhausted" before the incident; now, he said, Mexico "has passed the boundary of the United States, has invaded our territory, and shed American blood upon the American soil." The House and Senate quickly passed the war resolution, and Polk signed the declaration of war on May 13, 1846.

OPPOSITION TO THE WAR   In the Mississippi Valley, where expansion fever ran high, the war was immensely popular. Likewise in New York, novelist Herman Melville reported that "people here are all in a state of delirium. . . . A military ardor pervades all ranks." Whig opinion, however, ranged from lukewarm to hostile. John Quincy Adams, who voted against participation, called it "a most unrighteous war." An obscure one-term congressman from Illinois named Abraham Lincoln, upon taking his seat in 1847, began introducing "spot resolutions," calling on Polk to name the spot where American blood had been shed on American soil, implying that the troops may in fact have been in Mexico when fired upon. Once again, as in 1812, New England was a hotbed of opposition, largely in the belief that this war was the work of "Land-Jobbers and Slave-Jobbers." Some New Englanders were ready to separate from the slave states, and the Massachusetts legislature formally pronounced the conflict a war of conquest.

PREPARING FOR BATTLE   Both the United States and Mexico approached the war ill prepared. The American military was especially small and inexperienced. At the outset of war the regular army numbered barely over 7,000, in contrast to the Mexican force of 32,000. Many of the Mexicans, however, were pressed into service or recruited from prisons and thus made less than enthusiastic fighters. Before the war ended the American force grew to 104,000, of whom about 31,000 were regular army troops and marines. The rest were six- and twelve-month volunteers.

Among the volunteers were sons of Henry Clay and Daniel Webster, but most came from coarser backgrounds. Volunteer militia companies, often filled with frontier toughs, made up as raunchy a crew as ever graced the American military—lacking uniforms, standard equipment, and discipline alike. Repeatedly, despite the best efforts of the commanding generals, these undisciplined forces ran out of control in plunder, rape, and murder. Nevertheless, these rough-and-tumble Americans consistently defeated larger Mexican forces, which had their own problems with training, discipline, and munitions. Mexican artillery pieces were generally obsolete, and the powder was so faulty that American soldiers could often dodge cannonballs that fell short and bounced ineffectively along the ground.

The United States entered the war without even a tentative plan of action. One had to be worked out hastily, and politics complicated the task. What Polk wanted, Thomas Hart Benton wrote later, was "a small war, just large enough to require a treaty of peace, and not large enough to make military reputations, dangerous for the presidency." Winfield Scott, general-in-chief of the army, was both a Whig and politically ambitious. Polk nevertheless named him to take charge of the Rio Grande front, but when Scott quarreled with Polk's secretary of war, the exasperated president withdrew the appointment.

There now seemed a better choice. Zachary Taylor's men had scored two victories over Mexican forces north of the Rio Grande, and on May 18, 1846, they crossed over and occupied Matamoros, which a demoralized and bloodied Mexican army had abandoned. These quick victories brought Taylor instant popularity, and the president responded willingly to the demand that he be made overall commander for the conquest of Mexico. "Old Rough and Ready" Taylor, a bowlegged, squat, burly, and none-too-handsome man of sixty-one, seemed unlikely stuff from which to fashion a hero, but he had achieved Polk's main objective, the conquest of Mexico's northern provinces. Taylor became an immediate folk hero to his troops and to Americans back home, so much so that Polk began to see him as a political threat.

ANNEXATION OF CALIFORNIA   Polk had long coveted the valuable Mexican territory along the Pacific coast and had first tried buying it, but to no avail. He then sought to engineer a Texas-style revolt against Mexican rule among the thousand or so American settlers in California. To that purpose, near the end of 1845, John C. Frémont brought out a band of sixty frontiersmen, including Kit Carson, ostensibly on another exploration of California and Oregon. In 1846 Frémont and his men moved into the Sacramento Valley. Americans in the area fell upon Sonoma on June 14, proclaimed the independent "Republic of California," and hoisted the hastily designed Bear Flag, a California grizzly and star painted on white cloth—a version of which became the state flag.

By the end of June Frémont had endorsed the Bear Flag Republic and set out for Monterey. Before he arrived, the commander of the Pacific Fleet, having heard of the outbreak of hostilities, sent a party ashore to raise the American flag and proclaim California a part of the United States. The Republic of California had lasted less than a month, and most Californians of whatever origin welcomed a change that promised order instead of the confusion of the unruly Bear Flaggers. Sporadic clashes with Mexicans continued until 1847, when they finally capitulated. That same month, Colonel Stephen Kearny and 300 soldiers, having earlier captured Santa Fe, ousted the Mexican forces from southern California and occupied Los Angeles.

TAYLOR'S BATTLES   Both California and New Mexico had been taken before General Zachary Taylor fought his first major battle in northern Mexico. Having waited for more men and munitions, Taylor finally headed southward (in September 1846) toward the heart of Mexico. His first goal was the fortified city of Monterrey, which he took after a five-day siege. Polk, however, was growing increasingly unhappy with Taylor's popularity and with what he considered to be Taylor's excessive passivity.

But Polk's grand strategy was itself flawed. Having never seen the Mexican desert, he wrongly assumed that Taylor's men could live off the country and need not depend on resupply. Polk therefore misunderstood the general's reluctance to strike out across several hundred miles of barren land in front of Mexico City. On another point the president was simply duped. The old dictator Santa Anna, forced out in 1844, got

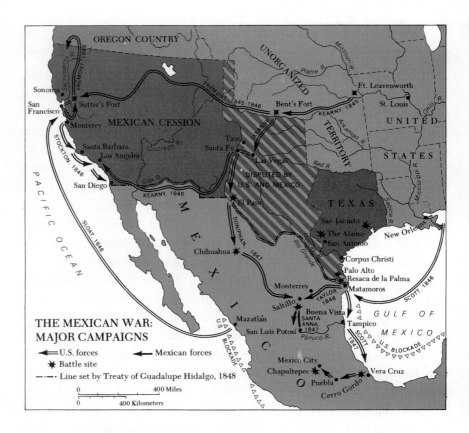

THE MEXICAN WAR:
MAJOR CAMPAIGNS

◀— U.S. forces   ◀— Mexican forces
✶ Battle site
–·–·– Line set by Treaty of Guadalupe Hidalgo, 1848

0   400 Miles
0   400 Kilometers

word to Polk from his exile in Cuba that in return for the right consider-
ations he could bring about a settlement of the war. Polk in turn assured
the Mexican leader that Washington would pay well for any territory
taken through such a settlement. In 1846, after another overturn in the
Mexican government, American forces allowed Santa Anna to return to
his homeland. Soon he was again in command of the Mexican army and
then was named president once more. But instead of carrying out his
pledge to Polk to negotiate an end to the war, Santa Anna prepared to
fight Taylor's army. Polk's intrigue had put the ablest Mexican general
back in command of the enemy army.

In October 1846, Polk and his cabinet decided on a move against
Mexico City from the south by way of Vera Cruz, which left Taylor's
forces idle. Polk would have preferred a Democratic general to lead the
new offensive, but for want of a better choice, he named Winfield Scott
to the field command. Taylor, miffed at his reduction to a minor role
and harboring a "violent disregard" for Scott's abilities, disobeyed orders
and took the offensive himself.

Near the hacienda of Buena Vista, Santa Anna's large but ill-trained army met Taylor's untested volunteers. The Mexican general invited the vastly outnumbered Americans to surrender. "Tell him to go to hell," Taylor replied. In the hard-fought Battle of Buena Vista (February 22–23, 1847), Taylor saw his son-in-law, Colonel Jefferson Davis, the future president of the Confederacy, lead a regiment that broke up a Mexican cavalry charge. Neither side could claim victory on the strength of the outcome, but Taylor was convinced that only his lack of trained regular troops prevented him from striking a decisive blow. At one point as he watched a Kentucky regiment in action, he exclaimed: "Hurrah for Old Kentuck! That's the way to do it. Give them hell, damn them." Buena Vista was the last major action on the northern front, and Taylor was granted leave to return home.

SCOTT'S TRIUMPH   Meanwhile, the long-planned southern assault on the enemy capital had begun on March 9, 1847, when Scott's army landed on the beaches south of Vera Cruz. It was the first major amphibious operation by American military forces, and was carried out without loss. The Mexican commander at Vera Cruz surrendered on March 27 after a week-long siege. Scott and some 14,000 soldiers then retraced the 260-mile route to Mexico City taken by Cortés more than 300 years before. Santa Anna tried to set a trap for the Americans at the mountain pass of Cerro Gordo, but Scott's men did the trapping, taking more than 3,000 prisoners, large quantities of equipment and provisions, and the Mexican president's personal effects.

Thereafter Scott waited until reinforcements and new supplies arrived from the coast. After three months, with his numbers almost doubled, Scott and his army set out on August 7 through the mountain passes into the valley of Mexico, cutting his supply line to the coast. Scott directed a brilliant flanking operation around the lakes and marshes guarding the eastern approaches to Mexico City, then another around the Mexican defenses at San Antonio. On September 13, 1847, American forces entered Mexico City. At the National Palace a battalion of marines ran up the flag and occupied the "halls of Montezuma."

THE TREATY OF GUADALUPE HIDALGO   After the fall of the capital, Santa Anna resigned and a month later fled the country. By the treaty of Guadalupe Hidalgo, signed on February 2, 1848, Mexico gave up all claims to Texas above the Rio Grande and ceded California and New Mexico to the United States. In return the United States agreed to pay Mexico $15 million and assume the claims of American citizens against Mexico up to a total of $3 1/4 million.

A growing movement to annex all of Mexico had impelled Polk to hold out for more. But as Polk confided in his diary, rejecting the treaty would be too risky. If he rejected a treaty made in accord with his own original terms in order to gain more territory, "the probability is that Congress would not grant either men or money to prosecute the war." In that case he might eventually have to withdraw the army and lose everything. The treaty went to the Senate, which ratified it on March 10, 1848. By the end of July the last remaining American soldiers had boarded ship in Vera Cruz.

THE WAR'S LEGACIES   The seventeen-month-long war had cost the United States 1,721 killed, 4,102 wounded, and far more—11,155— dead of disease. The military and naval expenditures had been $98 million. For this price, and payments made under the treaty, the United States acquired more than 500,000 square miles of territory (more than a million counting Texas), including the great Pacific harbors of San Diego, Monterey, and San Francisco, with uncounted millions in mineral wealth. Except for a small addition by the Gadsden Purchase in 1853, these annexations rounded out the continental United States. Several important "firsts" are associated with the Mexican War: the first successful offensive war, the first major amphibious operation, and the nation's first war covered by correspondents. It was also the first significant combat experience for a group of junior officers who would later serve as leading generals during the Civil War: Robert E. Lee, Ulysses S. Grant, Thomas "Stonewall" Jackson, George B. McClellan, George Pickett, Braxton Bragg, George Meade, and others.

Initially, the victory in Mexico provoked a surge of national pride. American triumphs "must elevate the *true* self-respect of the American people," Walt Whitman exclaimed. Others were not so sure. Ralph Waldo Emerson rejected war "as a means of achieving America's destiny," but then accepted such forceful annexations of new territory with the explanation that "most of the great results of history are brought about by discreditable means." As the years passed the Mexican War somehow never became entrenched in the national legends. It was increasingly seen as a war of conquest provoked by a president bent on expansion. For a brief season, however, the glory of conquest did shed luster on the names of Zachary Taylor and Winfield Scott. Despite Polk's best efforts, he had manufactured the next, and last, two Whig candidates for president. One of them, Taylor, would replace him in the White House, with the storm of sectional conflict already on the horizon.

MAKING CONNECTIONS

- This chapter opens with the brief administration of William Henry Harrison, the first Whig president. The collapse of the Whig party is detailed in Chapter 15.

- The West developed quickly after the expansionist policies of the 1840s. Chapter 18 takes the story to the 1890s.

- This chapter ends with the observation of "the storm of sectional conflict already on the horizon." Chapter 15's discussion of "The Crisis of Union" traces the relationship between the Mexican War and the Civil War more explicitly.

FURTHER READING

For background on Whig programs and ideas, see William R. Brock's *Parties and Political Conscience* (1979). A probing treatment of expansionist ideology is Thomas R. Hietala's *Manifest Design: Anxious Aggrandizement in Late Jacksonian America* (1985). John D. Unruh's *The Plains Across: The Overland Emigrants and the TransMississippi West, 1840–1860* (1979),* and John Mack Faragher's *Women and Men on the Overland Trail* (1979)* narrate well the story of pioneer movement.

*These books are available in paperback editions.

California was the promised land for many, and several scholars have concentrated on that area. Kevin Starr's *Americans and the California Dream, 1850–1915* (1973)* is a fine introduction. A focused treatment of the Oregon migration is Malcolm Clark, Jr.'s, *Eden Seekers: The Settlement of Oregon, 1812–1862* (1982).

The controversy over the annexation of Texas is analyzed in David M. Pletcher's *The Diplomacy of Annexation: Texas, Oregon, and the Mexican War* (1973).* Gene M. Brack's *Mexico Views Manifest Destiny, 1821–1846* (1975) takes Mexico's viewpoint on American designs on the West. A survey of the military conflict is provided in K. Jack Bauer's *The Mexican War, 1846–1848* (1974).

*These books are available in paperback editions.

PART FOUR

A HOUSE
DIVIDED

Of all the regions of the United States during the first half of the nineteenth century, the South was the most distinctive. Southern society remained fundamentally rural and agricultural long after the rest of the nation embraced the urban-industrial revolution. By 1860 a southern white was only one third as likely as a northern white to look at a non-farm job, live in a city, or be foreign born. Likewise, the southern elite's tenacious effort to preserve and expand the institution of slavery muted social reform impulses in the South and ignited a prolonged political controversy that would end in civil war.

The relentless settlement of the western territories set in motion a feverish competition between North and South for political influence in the burgeoning West. Would the new states in the West be "slave" or "free"? The issue of allowing slavery into the new territories involved more than humanitarian concern for the plight of enslaved blacks. By the 1840s, North and South had developed quite different economic interests. The North wanted high tariffs on imported products to "protect" its infant industries from foreign competition. Southerners, on the other hand, favored free trade because they wanted to import British goods in exchange for the cotton they provided British textile mills.

A series of ingenious political compromises glossed over the fundamental differences between the sections during the first half of the nineteenth century. But abolitionists refused to give up their crusade against slavery. Moreover, a new generation of national political leaders emerged in the 1850s, men from both North and South who were less willing to seek political compromises. The continuing debate over allowing slavery into the new western territories kept sectional tensions at a fever pitch. By the time Abraham Lincoln was elected in 1860, many Americans had decided that the nation could not survive half-slave and half-free; something had to give.

In a desperate effort to preserve the institution of slavery, eleven southern states seceded from the Union and created a separate Confederate nation. This, in turn, prompted northerners such as Lincoln to support a civil war to preserve the Union. No one realized in 1861 how prolonged and costly the war between the states would become. Over 600,000 soldiers and sailors died of wounds or disease. The colossal carnage caused even the most seasoned observers to blanch in disbelief. As President Lincoln confessed in his second inaugural address, no one expected the war to become so "fundamental and astonishing."

Nor did people envision how sweeping the war's effects would be on the future of the nation. The northern victory in 1865 restored the Union and in the process helped to accelerate America's transformation into a modern nation-state. National power and a national consciousness began to displace the sectional emphases of the antebellum era. A Republican-led Congress pushed through legislation to foster industrial and commercial development and western expansion. In the process, the United States began to leave behind the Jeffersonian dream of a decentralized agrarian republic.

The Civil War also ended slavery. Yet the actual status of the three million freed blacks remained precarious. How would they fare in a society built upon slavery? In 1865 the daughter of a Georgia planter expressed her concern about such issues when she wrote in her diary that "there are sad changes in store for both races. I wonder the Yankees do not shudder to behold their work" ahead in trying to "reconstruct" the defeated South.

The former slaves found themselves legally free, but most were without property, homes, education, or training. Although the Fourteenth Amendment (1867) set forth guarantees for the civil rights of African Americans and the Fifteenth Amendment (1870) provided that black males could vote, local white authorities found shrewd—and often violent—ways to avoid the spirit and letter of these new laws.

The restoration of the former Confederate states to the Union did not come easily. Much bitterness and resistance remained among the vanquished. Although Confederate leaders were initially disenfranchised, they continued to exercise considerable authority in political and economic matters. Indeed, in 1877, when the last federal troops were removed from the occupied South, former Confederates declared themselves "redeemed" from the stain of occupation. By the end of the nineteenth century, most states of the former Confederacy had devised a complex system of legal discrimination based on race that recreated many aspects of slavery.

14 ∾ THE OLD SOUTH:
AN AMERICAN TRAGEDY

CHAPTER ORGANIZER

This chapter focuses on:

- industry and agriculture in the Old South

- southern society, black and white

- the antislavery movement and southern reactions to it

MYTH, REALITY, AND THE OLD SOUTH

SOUTHERN MYTHOLOGY Southerners, a North Carolina editor once wrote, are "a mythological people, created half out of dream and half out of slander, who live in a still legendary land." Indeed, most Americans, including southerners, carry in their minds a cluster of myths about the South. But the main burden of southern mythology is carried in those especially pernicious images of the Old South set during the nineteenth-century sectional conflict: the idealized picture of a kindly old "massa" with his mint julep on the white-columned porch, happy "darkies" singing in fields perpetually in harvest, coquettish belles wooed by slender gallants underneath the moonlight and magnolias.

There are other elements in the traditional myth. Off in the piney woods and erosion-gutted clay hills, away from the plantation elite, dwelt a depraved group known as the poor white trash. Somewhere in the myth the respectable small farmer so often praised by Jefferson and Jackson was lost from sight. He was absent too from the image of the Benighted South, in which the plantation myth simply appeared in reverse, as a pattern of corrupt opulence resting on human exploitation. Gentle old "massa" became the arrogant, haughty, imperious potentate, the very embodiment of sin, the central target of antislavery attack. He kept a slave mistress, and he bred his slaves like cattle and sold them "down the river" to certain death in the sugar mills, separating families if that suited his purpose, while southern white women suffered in silence the guilty knowledge of their men's infidelity. The "happy darkies" in this picture became an oppressed people longing for freedom, the victims of countless atrocities, forever seeking a chance to follow the North Star to freedom. The masses of the white folks were, once again, poor whites, relegated to ignorance and degeneracy by the slavocracy.

THE SOUTHERN CONDITION   Of course these pictures are overdrawn stereotypes, but myths die hard, partly because they have roots in reality. Efforts to get at what really set the Old South apart generally turn on two lines of thought: the impact of environment (geography and

A slave family in the cotton fields near Savannah, Georgia.

climate) and the effects of human decisions and actions. The South's warm, humid climate fostered the growing of staple crops, and thus the plantation system and black slavery. These developments in turn brought sectional conflict and civil war.

But while geography was and is a key determinant of southern life, explanations that involve human action are more persuasive. In the 1830s many observers located the origins of southern distinctiveness in the institution of slavery. The resolve of whites to maintain such a system in turn led to a sense of racial unity that muted class conflict among whites. Yet the biracial character of the population influenced other aspects of life. In shaping patterns of speech and folklore, of music and literature, black southerners immeasurably influenced and enriched the region's culture.

The South differed from other sections too in its high proportion of native population, both white and black. Despite a great diversity of origins in the colonial population, the South drew few immigrants after the Revolution. One reason was that the main shipping lines went to northern ports; another, that the prospect of competing with slave labor was unattractive to immigrants. After the Missouri Controversy of 1819–1821 the South became more and more a conscious minority, its population growth lagging behind that of other sections, its "peculiar institution" of slavery more and more an isolated and odious anachronism.

The South also differed in its architecture, its peculiar work ethic, and its men's penchant for fighting, for guns, and for the military, and its country-gentleman ideal. The preponderance of farming remained a distinctive characteristic, whether pictured as the Jeffersonian yeoman living by the sweat of his brow or the lordly planter dispatching his slave gangs. But in the end what made the South distinctive was the popular assumption that it *was* distinctive.

AGRICULTURAL DIVERSITY   The focus in popular myth on King Cotton and the other cash crops such as rice and sugarcane has obscured the degree to which the South fed itself from its own fields. The upper South in many areas practiced general farming in much the same way as the Old Northwest. Cyrus McCormick first tested his harvester in the wheatfields of Virginia. Corn grew everywhere, but went less into the market than into local consumption, as feed and fodder, as hoecake and grits. On many farms and plantations the rhythms of the growing season permitted the labor force to alternate attention between the staples and the food crops. Livestock added to the diversity of the farm economy. In 1860 the South had half the nation's cattle, over 60 percent of the swine, nearly 45 percent of the horses, 52 percent of the oxen, nearly 90 percent of the mules, and nearly a third of the sheep, the last mostly in the upper South.

Yet the picture was hardly one of unbroken prosperity. The South's staple crops quickly exhausted the soil, and open-row crops such as tobacco, cotton, and corn left the bare ground in between subject to erosion. By 1860 much of eastern Virginia had abandoned tobacco and in some places had turned to growing wheat for the northern market. The older farming lands had trouble competing with the newer soils farther west, but soon western lands too began to show wear and tear. So the Southeast and then the Old Southwest faced a growing sense of economic crisis as the nineteenth century advanced.

MANUFACTURING AND TRADE   By 1840 many thoughtful southerners reasoned that by staking everything on agriculture the region had wasted chances in manufacturing and trade. After the War of 1812, as cotton growing swept everything before it, the South became increasingly dependent on northern manufacturing and trade. Cotton and tobacco were exported mainly in northern vessels. Southerners also relied on connections in the North for imported goods. The South became, economically if not formally, a kind of colonial dependency of the North.

The Tredegar Iron Works in Richmond, Virginia.

There were two major explanations generally put forward at the time for the lag in southern industrial development. First, blacks were presumed unsuited to factory work, perhaps because they supposedly could not adjust to the discipline of work by the clock. Second, the ruling orders of the Old South were said to have developed a lordly disdain for commercial activity, because a certain aristocratic prestige derived from owning land and slaves, and from conspicuous consumption. But any argument that black labor was incompatible with industry simply flew in the face of the evidence, since factory owners bought or hired slave operatives for just about every kind of manufacture.

Nor should one take at face value the legendary indifference of aristocratic planters to profits and losses. More often than not the successful planter was a driving entrepreneur bent on maximizing profits. While the profitability of slavery has been a long-standing subject of controversy, in recent years economic historians, applying new statistical tools, have concluded that slaves on the average supplied a hefty 10 percent return on their cost. By a strictly hardnosed and hardheaded calculation, investment in slaves and cotton lands was the most profitable investment available at the time in the South.

The notion that the South was economically backward emerged from the sectional quarrels of the times, in which southerners took a poorer-than-thou attitude, so to speak, in order to bolster their claims of northern exploitation. Antislavery elements also contributed to this notion by way of arguing the failure of a slave economy. It was true that in any economic comparison of the South with the North, the South usually came off second best. But in comparison with the rest of the world, the South as a whole was quite well off.

If an understanding of the Old South must begin with a knowledge of social myths, it must end with a sense of tragedy. White southerners had won short-term gains at the cost of both lagging development and moral isolation in the eyes of the world. The concentration on land and slaves, as well as the paucity of cities and immigrants, deprived the South of the dynamic bases of innovation. The slaveholding South hitched its wagon not to a star, but to the growing world (largely British) demand for cotton. During the late 1850s, it seemed that prosperity would never end. The South, "safely entrenched behind her cotton bags . . . can defy the world—for the civilized world depends on the cotton of the South," boasted a Vicksburg newspaper in 1860. "No power on earth dares to make war upon it," added a South Carolinian. "Cotton is king." The only perceived threat to King Cotton was the growing anti-slavery sentiment in the North. The unperceived threat was an imminent slackening of the cotton market. The hey-day of expansion in British textiles ended by 1860, but by then the Deep South was locked into cotton production for generations to come.

WHITE SOCIETY IN THE SOUTH

THE PLANTERS   Although great plantations were relatively few in number, they set the tone of economic and social life in the South. What distinguished the plantation from the farm, in addition to its size, was the use of a large labor force managed by overseers to grow primarily staple crops (cotton, rice, tobacco, and sugarcane) for profit. A clear-cut distinction between management and labor set the planter apart from the small slaveholder, who often worked side by side with slaves at the same tasks.

If, to be called a planter, one had to own 20 slaves, the South in 1860 numbered only 46,274 planters. Fewer than 8,000 owned 50 or more slaves, and the owners of over 100 numbered 2,292. The census listed only 11 with 500 and just one with as many as 1,000 slaves. Yet this privileged elite tended to think of its class interest as synonymous with the interest of the entire South, and to perceive themselves as community leaders in much the fashion of the English gentry. The planter group, making up only 4 percent of the adult white males in the South, owned more than half the slaves, produced most of the cotton and tobacco and all of the sugar and rice. In a white population numbering just over 8 million in 1860, the total number of slaveholders was only 383,637. But assuming that each family numbered five people, the whites with some proprietary interest in slavery came to 1.9 million, or roughly one-fourth of the South's white population. While the preponderance of southern whites belonged to the small-farmer class, the presumptions of the planters were seldom challenged. In part, such deference reflected the desire of many small farmers to become planters themselves.

Some planters did live in splendor, with the wealth and leisure to cultivate the arts of hospitality, good manners, learning, and politics. More often the scene was less charming. Some of the mansions on closer inspection turned out to be modest houses with false fronts. The planter commonly had less leisure than legend would suggest, for he in fact managed a large enterprise.

THE PLANTATION MISTRESS   The mistress of the plantation, like the master, seldom led a life of idle leisure. She supervised the domestic household in the same way the planter took care of the business, to see after food, linens, housecleaning, the care of the sick, and a hundred other details. The insightful Mary Boykin Chesnut, wife of a South Carolina planter, complained in her illuminating diary that "there is no slave like a wife."

The wives of all but the most wealthy planters were expected to supervise the domestic household activities and manage the slaves. One of the most frustrating realities for the plantation mistress was the lack of personal freedom and leisure occasioned by the complex demands of her "separate sphere" of genteel domesticity. White women living within a slave-owning culture also confronted a double standard in terms of moral and sexual behavior. While they were expected to be models of Christian piety and sexual discretion, their husbands, brothers, and sons enjoyed greater latitude. "God forgive us," Mary Chesnut wrote, "but ours is a monstrous system. Like the patriarchs of old, our men live all in one house with their wives and their concubines; and the mulattos one sees in every family partly resemble the white children. Any lady is ready to tell you who is the father of all the mulatto children in everybody's household but her own. Those, she seems to think, drop from the clouds."

Such a double standard both illustrated and reinforced the arrogant authoritarianism displayed by many male planters. Chesnut said that her father-in-law lorded over his plantation household. He was "as absolute a tyrant as the Czar of Russia . . . or the Sultan of Turkey." Yet for all of their complaints and burdens, few plantation mistresses criticized the prevailing social order and racist climate.

THE MIDDLE CLASS   Overseers on the largest plantations generally came from the middle class of small farmers or skilled workers, or were younger sons of planters. Most wanted to become slaveholders themselves, and sometimes rose to that status, but others were constantly on the move in search of better positions. Occasionally there were black overseers, but the highest management position to which a slave could aspire was usually that of "driver" or leader, placed in charge of a small group of slaves with the duty of getting them to work without creating dissension.

The most numerous white southerners were the yeoman farm families, who lived in modest two-room cabins rather than columned mansions. They raised a few hogs and chickens, grew some corn and cotton, and traded with neighbors more than with stores. The men in the family focused their energies on outdoor labors. Women also worked in the fields during harvest time, but most of their days were spent attending to domestic chores. As a Tennessee farmer explained, he and his father "did all kinds of farm work [while] my mother cooked, sewed, spun thread, wove clothes, and clothed the family of eleven children." Many of these "middling" farmers owned a handful of slaves, but most owned none. The most prosperous of these farm families generally lived in the mountain-sheltered valleys from the Shenandoah of Virginia down to northern Alabama, areas with rich soil but without ready access to markets, and so less suitable for staple crops or slave labor. But most of the South's small farms were located in the midst of the plantation economy.

In North Carolina in 1860, for instance, 70 percent of the farmers held less than 100 acres, and they were scattered throughout the state. These and other southern farmers were typically mobile folk, willing to pull up stakes and move west or southwest in pursuit of better land. They tended to be fiercely independent and suspicious of government authority, and they overwhelmingly identified with the party of Andrew Jackson and the spiritual fervor of evangelical Protestantism. Even though only a minority of the middle-class farmers owned slaves, most of them supported the slave system. They feared that the slaves, if freed, would compete with them for land, and they also enjoyed the status that racially based slavery afforded them. Such sentiments pervaded the border states as well as the deep South. Kentucky, for example, held a popular referendum on the issue of slavery in 1849, and the voters, most of whom owned no slaves, resoundingly endorsed the "peculiar institution."

THE "POOR WHITES" But outside observers often had trouble telling yeomen apart from the true "poor whites," a degraded class crowded off into the hills, hollows, and least desirable lands. Stereotyped views of southern society had prepared many travelers to see only planters and "poor whites," and many a small farmer living in rude comfort, his wealth concealed in cattle and swine off foraging in the woods, was mistaken for "white trash." The latter were characterized by a pronounced lankness and sallowness; the men were given over to hunting and fishing, to hound dogs and moonshine whiskey. As one English traveler observed, they were "the most degraded race of human beings claiming an Anglo-Saxon origin that can be found on the face of the earth."

Speculation had it that the "poor whites" were descended from indentured servants or convicts transported to the colonies. But the problem was less heredity than environment, the consequence of a trilogy of "lazy diseases": hookworm, malaria, and pellagra, all of which produced an overpowering lethargy. Many poor Southerners—white and black— displayed a morbid craving to chew clay, from which they got the name "dirt eaters"; the cause was a dietary deficiency, although a folklore grew up about the nutritional and medicinal qualities of certain clays. Around 1900 modern medicine discovered the causes and cures for these diseases. By 1930 they had practically disappeared, taking with them many stereotypes of poor whites.

BLACK SOCIETY IN THE SOUTH

"FREE PERSONS OF COLOR" In the Old South, "free persons of color" occupied an uncertain status, balanced somewhere between slavery and freedom, subject to legal restrictions not imposed on whites. In the seventeenth century a few blacks had been freed on the same basis as indentured servants. Over the years some slaves were able to purchase their freedom, while some gained freedom as a reward for service in American wars. Others were simply freed by conscientious masters, either in their wills, as in the case of George Washington, or during their lifetimes, as in the case of John Randolph.

The free persons of color included a large number of mulattoes, people of mixed white and black ancestry. In urban centers like Charleston and especially New Orleans, "colored" society became virtually a third caste, a new people who occupied a status somewhere between black and white. Some of them built substantial fortunes and even became slaveholders. In Louisiana a mulatto bought an estate with ninety-one slaves for $250,000.

William Ellison, a freed slave of partial white ancestry who lived in Stateburg, South Carolina, prospered as a cotton-gin maker. In 1816, at the age of twenty-six, he purchased his own freedom from his white master (who may have been his father). By the start of the Civil War he had become the wealthiest free black in South Carolina, owner of a thriving business, an 800-acre plantation, and some sixty slaves. He was so indifferent to the plight of his fellows of African descent that he commonly sold his slaves' female babies because he believed they were unprofitable in his business. Like other successful mulattoes, Ellison distanced himself from the slaves and displayed a snobbish preoccupation with gradations of color. As a member of Charleston's "brown aristocracy," he looked down upon black people. During the Civil War Ellison supported the Confederacy.

But such cases were rare. Black slaveholders were a tiny minority. The 1830 census revealed that only 3,775 free blacks, about 2 percent of the total free black population, owned 12,760 slaves. Although most of these black slave owners were in the South, some also lived in Rhode Island, Connecticut, Illinois, New Jersey, New York, and the border states. Many blacks owned slaves for humanitarian purposes. One minister, for instance, bought slaves and then enabled them to purchase their freedom from him on easy terms. Most often, black slaveholders were free blacks who bought their own family members with the express purpose of later freeing them. But some blacks engaged in slavery for purely selfish rather than humanitarian reasons. Like their white counterparts, they participated in slave auctions and advertised for the return of runaways.

Free blacks were often skilled artisans (blacksmiths, carpenters, cobblers), farmers, or common laborers. The increase in their numbers slowed as legislatures put more and more restrictions on the right to free slaves, but by 1860 there were 262,000 free blacks in the slave

The offices of Price, Birch & Co., dealers in slaves, Alexandria, Virginia.

states, a little over half the national total of 488,000. They were most numerous in the upper South.

THE TRADE IN SLAVES   The slaves languished at the bottom of the social hierarchy. From the first census in 1790 to the eighth in 1860, their numbers had grown from 698,000 to almost 4 million. The rise in the slave population occurred mainly through a natural increase, the rate of which was very close to that of whites at the time. When the African slave trade was outlawed in 1808, it seemed to many a step toward the extinction of slavery, but the expansion of the cotton belt, with its voracious appetite for workers, soon increased the demand for slaves. And shutting off the import of slaves only added to the value of those already present. Prices for prime fieldhands ranged between $300 and $400 in the 1790s, up to $1,000–$1,300 in the 1830s, peaked just before the onset of depression in 1837, and rose again in the great prosperity of the 1850s to $1,500–$2,000. Slaves with special skills cost even more.

The rise in slave value tempered some of the harsher features of the peculiar institution. "Massa was purty good," one ex-slave recalled later. "He treated us jus' 'bout like you would a good mule." Some owners hired wage laborers, often Irish immigrants, for ditching and other dangerous work rather than risk the lives of the more valuable slaves.

The end of the foreign slave trade gave rise to a flourishing domestic trade, with slaves moving mainly from the used-up lands of the Southeast into the booming new country of the Old Southwest. Many slaves moved south and west with their owners, but there also developed an organized business with brokers, slave pens, and auctioneers. Every town of any size had public auctioneers and dealers willing to buy and sell slaves—along with other merchandise—or handle sales on a commission. The worst aspect of the slave trade was its breakup of families. Many such sales are matters of record, and although the total number is controversial, it took only a few to have a damaging effect on the morale of all.

PLANTATION SLAVERY   More than half of all slaves in 1860 worked on plantations, and most of those were fieldhands. The preferred jobs were those of household servants and skilled workers, including blacksmiths, carpenters, and coopers. Fieldhands were usually housed in simple one- or two-room wooden shacks with dirt floors, some without windows. Based on detailed records from eleven plantations in the lower South, scholars have calculated that more then half of all slave babies died in the first year of life, a mortality rate more then twice that of white infants.

To some extent, chiefly in the rice and tobacco belts, work was parceled out by the task. But more commonly fieldhands worked long hours from dawn to dusk, or "from kin [see]to kaint." The slave codes adopted in each state concerned themselves mainly with the owner's interests and subjected the slaves not only to his governance but to surveillance by patrols of county militiamen, who struck fear into the slave quarters by abusing slaves found at large. Evidence suggests that a majority of both planters and small farmers used the whip, which the slave codes authorized. The difference between a good owner and a bad one, according to one ex-slave, was the difference between one who did not "whip too much" and one who "whipped till he bloodied you and blistered you."

A slave's ultimate recourse was rebellion or flight, but most recog-

Sale of Slaves and Stock.

The Negroes and Stock listed below, are a Prime Lot, and belong to the ESTATE OF THE LATE LUTHER McGOWAN, and will be sold on Monday, Sept. 22nd, 1852, at the Fair Grounds, in Savannah, Georgia, at 1:00 P. M. The Negroes will be taken to the grounds two days previous to the Sale, so that they may be inspected by prospective buyers.

On account of the low prices listed below, they will be sold for cash only, and must be taken into custody within two hours after sale.

No.	Name.	Age	Remarks.	Price.
1	Lunesta	27	Prime Rice Planter,	$1,275.00
2	Violet	16	Housework and Nursemaid,	900.00
3	Lizzie	30	Rice, Unsound,	300.00
4	Minda	27	Cotton, Prime Woman,	1,200.00
5	Adam	28	Cotton, Prime Young Man,	1,100.00
6	Abel	41	Rice Hand, Eyesight Poor,	675.00
7	Tanney	22	Prime Cotton Hand,	950.00
8	Flementina	39	Good Cook, Stiff Knee,	400.00
9	Lanney	34	Prime Cottom Man,	1,000.00
10	Sally	10	Handy in Kitchen,	675.00
11	Maccabey	35	Prime Man, Fair Carpenter,	980.00
12	Dorcas Judy	25	Seamstress, Handy in House,	800.00
13	Happy	60	Blacksmith,	575.00
14	Mowden	15	Prime Cotton Boy,	700.00
15	Bills	21	Handy with Mules,	900.00
16	Theopolis	39	Rice Hand, Gets Fits,	575.00
17	Coolidge	29	Rice Hand and Blacksmith,	1,275.00
18	Bessie	69	Infirm, Sews,	250.00
19	Infant	1	Strong Likely Boy	400.00
20	Samson	41	Prime Man, Good with Stock,	975.00
21	Callie May	27	Prime Woman, Rice,	1,000.00
22	Honey	14	Prime Girl, Hearing Poor,	850.00
23	Angelina	16	Prime Girl, House or Field,	1,000.00
24	Virgil	21	Prime Field Hand,	1,100.00
25	Tom	40	Rice Hand, Lame Leg,	750.00
26	Noble	11	Handy Boy,	900.00
27	Judge Lesh	55	Prime Blacksmith,	800.00
28	Booster	43	Fair Mason, Unsound,	600.00
29	Big Kate	37	Housekeeper and Nurse,	950.00
30	Melie Ann	19	Housework, Smart Yellow Girl,	1,250.00
31	Deacon	26	Prime Rice Hand,	1,000.00
32	Coming	19	Prime Cotton Hand,	1,000.00
33	Mabel	47	Prime Cotton Hand,	800.00
34	Uncle Tim	60	Fair Hand with Mules,	600.00
35	Abe	27	Prime Cotton Hand,	1,000.00
36	Tennes	29	Prime Rice Hand and Coachman,	1,250.00

There will also be offered at this sale, twenty head of Horses and Mules with harness, along with thirty head of Prime Cattle. Slaves will be sold separate, or in lots, as best suits the purchaser. Sale will be held rain or shine.

Announcement of a "Sale of Slaves and Stock," with prices, and the implication that families may be broken up.

Jack (Driver), Guinea. Plantation of B.F. Taylor, Esq. Columbus, S.C. 1850.

nized the futility of such measures, with whites wielding most of the power and weapons. Female slaves rarely saw escape as an option, concerned as they were with pregnancies and child-raising responsibilities. "Slavery is terrible for men; but it is far more terrible for women," declared Harriet Jacobs, a North Carolina slave. In the nineteenth century only three slave insurrections drew much notice, and two of those were betrayed before they got under way. Only the Nat Turner insurrection of 1831 in rural Virginia got beyond the planning stage. Turner, a black overseer, was also a religious exhorter who professed a divine mission in leading the movement. The revolt began when a small group killed Turner's master's family and set off down the road repeating the process at other farmhouses, where other slaves joined in. Before it ended at least fifty-five whites had been killed. Eventually trials resulted in seventeen hangings and seven deportations. The Virginia militia, for its part, killed large numbers of slaves indiscriminately in the process of putting down the rebels.

There were very few Nat Turners, however. Slaves more often retaliated against oppression by malingering or by outright sabotage, though there were constraints even on such protests. Slaves would likely eat better on a prosperous plantation than on one they had reduced to poverty, and the shrewdest slaveholders knew that they would more likely benefit by holding out rewards than by inflicting pain. Plantations based on the profit motive fostered between slaves and owners mutual dependency as well as natural antagonism. And in an agrarian society where personal relations counted for much, blacks could win concessions that moderated the harshness of slavery, permitting them a certain degree of individual and community development.

FORGING THE SLAVE COMMUNITY   To generalize about slavery is to miss elements of diversity from place to place and from time to time. The experience could be as varied as people are. Slaves were victims, but to stop with so obvious a perception would be to miss an important story of endurance and achievement. If ever there was a melting pot in American history, the most effective may have been that in which Africans from a variety of ethnic, linguistic, and tribal origins fused into a new community and a new culture as African Americans.

Members of the slave community were bound together in helping and protecting one another, which in turn created a sense of cohesion and pride. Slave culture incorporated many African customs, especially in areas where whites were few. Among the Gullah blacks of the South Carolina and Georgia coast, a researcher found as late as the 1940s, more than 4,000 words still in use from the languages of twenty-one African tribes. Elements of African cultures not only have survived but have interacted with other cultures with which they came in contact.

SLAVE RELIGION AND FOLKLORE   Among the most important manifestations of slave culture was its religion, a mixture of African and Christian elements. Most Africans brought with them a concept of a Creator, or Supreme God, whom they could recognize in Jehovah, and lesser gods whom they might identify with Christ, the Holy Ghost, and the saints, thereby reconciling their earlier beliefs with the new Christian religion. Alongside the church they also retained African beliefs in spirits, magic spells and herbs, and conjuring (the practice of healing and warding off evil spirits). Belief in magic is in fact a common human response to conditions of danger or helplessness.

Slaves, however, found greater comfort in the church. There they could find both balm for the soul and release for their emotions, and they brought with them from Africa a demonstrative spirituality. Masters sought to instill lessons of Christian humility and obedience, but blacks could identify their plight with that of the Israelites in Egypt. And the ultimate hope of a better world gave solace in this one. Some owners openly encouraged religious meetings among their slaves, but those who were denied the open use of "praise houses" held "bush meetings" in secret. The preachers and exhorters who sprang up in the slave world commonly won the acceptance of the owners, if only because efforts to get rid of them proved futile. The peculiar cadences of their exhortations, chants, and spirituals have produced music of great rhythmic complexity, forms of dance and body language, and folk tales.

THE SLAVE FAMILY   Slave marriages had no legal status, but slave-owners generally seem to have accepted marriage as a stabilizing influence on the plantation. Sometimes they performed marriages themselves or had a minister celebrate a formal wedding with all the trimmings. But whatever the formalities, the norm for the slave community as for the white was the nuclear unit of parents and children, with the father regarded as head of the family. Slaves also displayed a lively awareness of the extended family of cousins. Most slave children

Several generations of a family raised in slavery. Plantation of J. J. Smith, Beaufort, South Carolina, 1862.

were socialized into their culture through the nuclear family, which afforded some degree of independence from white influence.

Slaves were not always allowed to realize this norm. In some cases the matter of family arrangements was ignored or left entirely up to the slaves on the assumption that black females were simply promiscuous—a convenient rationalization for sexual exploitation, to which the presence of many mulattoes attested. The census of 1860 reported 412,000 persons of mixed ancestry in the United States, or about 10 percent of the African-American population, probably a drastic undercount. Planters and their sons often took sexual advantage of female slaves. They sometimes clumsily defended such abuse on the ground that the practice protected the chastity of white women.

THE CULTURE OF THE SOUTHERN FRONTIER

There were substantial social and cultural differences within the South during the three decades before the Civil War. The antebellum southern frontier, for example, was a quite different region from the more settled areas in the states along the Atlantic seaboard. Of all the many frontiers that have combined to produce a distinctive American culture, the Old Southwest is perhaps the least well known and studied. It included the states and territories west of the Georgia-Alabama border—Alabama, Mississippi, Louisiana, Texas, and Arkansas—as well as the frontier areas in Tennessee, Kentucky, and Florida.

Largely unsettled until the 1820s, this region bridged the South and the West, exhibiting characteristics of both areas. Raw and dynamic, filled with dangers, uncertainties, and opportunities, it served as a powerful magnet, luring thousands of settlers from Virginia and the Carolinas when the seaboard economy faltered during the 1820s and 1830s. The agricultural economy of the upper South suffered from depressed commodity prices and soil exhaustion. Large farm families, especially, struggled to provide each child with sufficient land and resources to subsist and maintain the family legacy. As the international market for cotton soared in the early nineteenth century, the sons of seaboard planters began heading to the Southwest, eager to exploit a splendid new "land of promise." By the 1830s, most cotton production was occurring in the lower South. The migrating southerners carved out farms, built churches, raised towns, and eventually brought culture and order to a raw frontier. As they took up new lives and occupations, these southern pioneers transplanted many practices and institutions from the coastal states. But they also fashioned a distinctly new set of cultural values and social customs.

THE DECISION TO MIGRATE Young white men aspiring to be planters, usually in their twenties, responded to the siren call of fertile soil in the Southwest. Several factors prompted their decision to move. The dwindling economic opportunities available in the Carolinas and Virginia and restrictive kinship ties played a major role. As one young pioneer explained, he did not want to "creep and crawl in North Carolina like a poor sloth" when he could amass a fortune in the Southwest. Fathers were living longer; the best lands were already occupied and often exhausted of nutrients; the professions were overpopulated.

Like their northern counterparts, restless sons of the southern planter and professional elite wanted to make it on their own, to be "self-made men," economically self-reliant and socially independent. To them, speculative profit-seeking was more enticing than family stability. They refused to be "kept back" from economic gain and social status by the "prejudices" of the old men governing their families. A North Carolinian expected to "rise and soar like an eagle" in the Southwest because he would be freed from the strictures of his family circle. Many sons of seaboard planters also believed that they could prove their masculinity more readily on the southwestern frontier than in the more settled society along the Atlantic coast. A South Carolinian longed to prove his mettle on the frontier's "busy battle ground—to meet opposition—to trample it underfoot. I feel that the West is the land for me."

Women were underrepresented among migrants to the Old Southwest. Most dreaded the thought of taking up life on a disease-ridden, violent, and primitive frontier. The new region did not offer them independence or adventure. They would remain part of a patriarchal culture in either area. And their never-ending routine of domestic tasks would only increase in the frontier environment. In general, women regretted more than men the loss of kinship ties that migration would entail. To them a stable family life was more important than the prospect of material gain. As a Carolina woman prepared to depart for Alabama, she confided to a friend that "you *cannot* imagine the state of despair that I am in." Another said that "my heart bleeds within me" at the thought of the "many tender cords [of kinship]that are now severed forever." Others feared that life on the frontier would produce a "dissipation" of morals. They heard vivid stories of frontier lawlessness, drunkenness, gambling, and miscegenation.

Slaves had many of the same reservations about moving west. Almost a million captive African Americans joined in the migration to the Southwest during the antebellum era, most of them making the journey in the 1830s. Like white women, they feared the harsh working conditions and torpid heat and humidity of the Southwest. They also were despondent at the breaking up of their family ties. As Frederick Douglass observed, the "removal" of a slave to the Southwest was considered a form of psychological "death." Departures were seared with emotional anguish. When a young slave girl left Virginia for the Southwest, her mother ran after the wagon, eventually fell down and rolled "over on de groun' jes' acryin'." She never saw her daughter again.

JOURNEY AND SETTLEMENT   Most of the migrants to the Southwest headed for the fertile lands of Alabama, Mississippi, and central Tennessee. The typical trek was about 500 miles long. Along rough roads and trails, the pioneers averaged about fifteen miles per day, occasionally staying overnight in taverns, more often camping in the open air amid panthers, bears, and wolves. At times the route was clogged with people. One traveler said that often he would see "an uninterrupted line of walkers, wagons, and carriages." For slaves the journey was especially dangerous. Most traveled on foot, tied or chained together. Many drowned while fording rivers; others contracted mortal illnesses along the way.

Once in the Southwest the pioneers bought land that had been appropriated from the Indians. Parcels of 640 acres sold for as little as two dollars an acre. Land in Alabama's black belt (named for the color of the soil) brought higher prices. As cotton prices soared in the 1830s, aspiring planters bought as much land and as many slaves as possible. As a result, the average size of farms and plantations in the Southwest was larger than that in the Carolinas and Virginia. For many, it seems, the new region lived up to its images as a land of fertile possibilities. One recent arrival pronounced Alamaba to be "a glorious farming country." Another expressed his delight that he was finally on his own. "I never felt more independent & cheerful in my life."

But the Southwest was not utopia. The region was much more un-healthy than the Carolina Piedmont. The hot climate, contaminated water, and poor sanitation combined to unleash an epidemic of diseases on the new settlers. Malaria was especially endemic to the region. Women and slaves also found their harsh new surroundings uninviting. Life in tents and rude log cabins made many newcomers yearn for the material comforts they had left behind. A male settler reported that "all the men is very well pleased but the women is not very satisfied." The physical and social isolation on the frontier was a disheartening new re-ality. People usually settled far from relatives. The kinship networks that had provided them with practical assistance and emotional fulfillment disintegrated. After starting a homestead in Alabama, Mary Drake re-gretted the loss of her "large and respectable circle of relations" in North Carolina. Many decided to return home or move farther west.

A MASCULINE CULTURE   The southern frontier environment pro-voked important changes in sex roles, and relations between men and women became even more inequitable. Frontier life lent itself to the psychology of "manly independence" that many male pioneers eagerly sought. Young adult males indulged themselves in activities that would have generated disapproval in the more settled seaboard society. They drank, gambled, fought, and indulged their sexual desires. According to one disheartened observer, the typical young male settler, his "desires and appetites . . . unrestrained," became an embarrassment and source of sorrow to his family back east.

Alcohol consumption hit new heights along the southwestern fron-tier. Most plantations had their own stills to manufacture whiskey, and alcoholism ravaged frontier families. Masculine violence was also com-monplace. A Virginian who settled in Mississippi fought in fourteen duels and killed ten men in the process. The frequency of fights, stab-bings, shootings, and murders shocked visitors. Equally disturbing was the propensity of white men to take sexual advantage of slave women. An Alabama woman married to a lawyer-politican was outraged by the "beastly passions" of the white men who fathered slave children and then sold them like livestock. She also recorded in her diary instances of men regularly beating their wives with whips and drinking to excess. Wives, it seems, had little choice but to endure such mistreatment be-cause, as one woman wrote about a friend whose husband abused her, she was "wholly dependent upon his care."

CELIA   Occasionally a single historical incident can illustrate the larger web of laws and customs within a society. Such is the case with the story of a teenaged slave girl named Celia. Robert Newsom migrated from Virginia to the Old Southwest in the early 1820s and eventually established a prosperous 800-acre homestead. He owned a half dozen slaves, including Celia. Newsom told his family that he had bought her to serve as a domestic servant. But immediately after purchasing Celia, while driving her back to his farm, Newsom raped her. For the next five years Newsom treated Celia as his mistress. During that time she gave birth to two children, presumably his offspring. In a fit of tortured generosity, Newsom built Celia a separate, comfortable brick cabin fifty yards from the main house. But the anguish and humiliation she suffered took its toll. When Celia privately appealed to Newsom's two grown daughters to intervene on her behalf and put a stop to their father's sexual advances, they turned a deaf ear.

Desperate for relief from her tormentor, Celia resolved in 1855 to resist his next assault, with words if possible, with a club if necessary. Soon thereafter, Newsom again entered her cabin, ignored her impassioned appeal, and kept advancing until she struck him on the head. As he fell to the floor, she clubbed him to death. As she later explained, "the Devil got into me, and I struck him with the stick until he was dead." Celia then burned the body, pulverized the bones, and convinced one of Newsom's grandsons to help her discard the ashes. She eventually was accused of the crime and confessed. Her attorneys, all of them slaveowners, argued that the right of white women to defend their sexual honor against assault should be extended to slaves as well. The judge and jury, however, disagreed, and Celia was hanged.

ANTISLAVERY MOVEMENTS

EARLY OPPOSITION TO SLAVERY   Scattered criticism of slavery developed in the North and the South in the decades after the Revolution, but the emancipation movement accelerated with the formation of the American Colonization Society in 1817. The society proposed to resettle freed slaves in Africa. Its supporters included such prominent figures as James Madison, James Monroe, Henry Clay, John Marshall, and Daniel Webster, and it appealed to diverse opinions. Some backed it as an antislavery group, while others saw it as a way to bolster slavery by getting rid of potentially troublesome free Negroes. Articulate elements of the free black community denounced it from the start. A group of free blacks in Philadelphia, for example, stressed in 1817 that they had "no wish to separate from our present homes for any purpose whatever." America, they insisted, was now their native land.

Nevertheless, in 1821 agents of the society acquired from local chieftains in West Africa a parcel of land that became the nucleus of a new country. In 1822 the first freed slaves arrived there, and twenty-five years later the society relinquished control to the independent republic of Liberia. But given its uncertain purpose, the colonization movement received only meager support from either antislavery or proslavery elements. By 1860 only about 15,000 blacks had migrated to Africa, approximately 12,000 with the help of the Colonization Society. The number was infinitesimal compared to the number of slave births.

FROM GRADUALISM TO ABOLITIONISM   Meanwhile, in the early 1830s the antislavery movement took a new departure. Three dramatic events marked its transition from favoring gradualism to demanding the immediate end of slavery. In 1829 a pamphlet appeared in Boston: *Walker's Appeal . . . to the Colored Citizens of the World*. Its author, David Walker, born a free black in North Carolina, sold secondhand clothes in Boston. In the pamphlet Walker preached insurrection and violence as a proper response to the wrongs that blacks suffered. He warned whites: "We must and shall be free . . . in spite of you. . . . And woe, woe, will it be to you if we have to obtain our freedom by fighting." Over the next few years Walker circulated the pamphlet widely among blacks and white sympathizers. Southerners demanded his arrest, but Massachusetts officials replied that he had broken no law.

Two other major events followed in close sequence during 1831. On January 1, William Lloyd Garrison began publication in Boston of a new antislavery newspaper, *The Liberator*. Garrison, who rose from poverty in Newburyport, Massachusetts, had been apprenticed to a newspaperman and had edited a number of antislavery papers, but he grew impatient with the prevailing strategy of moderation. In the first issue of his new paper he renounced "the popular but pernicious doctrine of gradual emancipation" and vowed: "I *will be* as harsh as truth, and as uncompromising as justice. On this subject, I do not wish to think, to speak, or write, with moderation."

Garrison's combative language provoked outraged retorts from slave-holders, who publicized the paper more than his own supporters did. In the South, literate blacks would more likely encounter Garrison's ideas being criticized in the local papers than in the few copies of *The Liberator* that found their way to them. Slaveholders' outrage mounted higher after the Nat Turner insurrection in August 1831. Garrison, they assumed, bore a large part of the responsibility for the affair, but there is no evidence that Nat Turner had ever heard of him, and Garrison said that he had not a single subscriber in the South at the time. What is more, however violent his language, Garrison was a pacifist, opposed to the use of physical violence.

THE AMERICAN ANTI-SLAVERY SOCIETY   In 1832 Garrison and his followers set up the New England Anti-Slavery Society. A year later two wealthy New York merchants, Arthur and Lewis Tappan, founded a similar group in their state and then took the lead in starting a national society with the help of Garrison and others. They hoped to build on the publicity gained by the British antislavery movement, which in 1833 had induced Parliament to end slavery, with compensation to slaveholders, throughout the British Empire.

The American Anti-Slavery Society conceded the right of each state to legislate its domestic institutions, but set a goal of convincing fellow citizens "that Slaveholding is a heinous crime in the sight of God, and that the duty, safety, and best interests of all concerned, require its *immediate abandonment, without expatriation.*" The society went beyond the issue of emancipation to argue that blacks should "share an equality with the whites, of civil and religious privileges." The group issued a barrage of propaganda for its cause, including periodicals, tracts, agents, lecturers, organizers, and fund-raisers.

THE MOVEMENT SPLITS   As the antislavery movement spread, debates over tactics intensified. The Garrisonians, mainly New Englanders, were radicals who felt that American society had been corrupted from top to bottom and needed universal reform. Garrison embraced just about every important reform movement of the day: antislavery, temperance, pacifism, and women's rights. Deeply affected by the perfectionism of the times, he refused to compromise principle for expediency, to sacrifice one reform for another. Abolition was not enough. He opposed colonization of freed slaves and stood for equal rights. He broke with the organized church, which to his mind was in league with slavery. The federal government was all the more so. The Constitution, he said, was "a covenant with death and an agreement with hell." Garrison therefore refused to vote. He was, however, prepared to collaborate with those who did or with those who disagreed with him on other matters.

Other reformers saw American society as fundamentally sound and concentrated their attention on purging it of slavery. Most of these abolitionists were evangelical Christians, and they promoted pragmatic political organization as the best instrument of reform. Garrison struck them as an impractical fanatic—as he was.

A showdown came in 1840 on the issue of women's rights. Women had joined the abolition movement from the start, but quietly and largely in groups without men. The activities of the Grimké sisters brought the issue of women's rights to center stage. Sarah and Angelina Grimké, daughters of a prominent slave-owning family in South Carolina, had broken with their parents and moved north to embrace Quakerism, antislavery, and feminism. They set out speaking to women in New England and slowly widened their audiences to "promiscuous assemblies" of both men and women.

Such unseemly behavior inspired male leaders to chastise the Grimké sisters and other women activists for engaging in "unfeminine" activity. The chairman of the Connecticut Anti-Slavery Society declared: "No woman will speak or vote where I am a moderator. It is enough for women to rule at home." He refused to "submit to PETTI-COAT GOVERNMENT." Catharine Beecher reminded the activist sisters that women occupied "a subordinate relation in society to the other sex" and should therefore limit their activities to the "domestic and social circle." Angelina Grimké stoutly rejected such conventional arguments. "It is a woman's right," she insisted, "to have a voice in all laws and regulations by which she is to be governed, whether in church or in state."

This debate over the role of women in the antislavery movement crackled and simmered until it finally exploded in 1840. At the American Anti-Slavery Society's annual meeting the Garrisonians insisted on the right of women to participate equally in the organization, and they carried their point. They did not commit the group to women's rights in any other way, however. Contrary opinion, mainly from the Tappans' New York group, ranged from outright antifeminism to simple fear of scattering shots on too many reforms. The New Yorkers broke away to form the American and Foreign Anti-Slavery Society.

BLACK ANTISLAVERY   White male antislavery activists also balked at granting full recognition to black abolitionists of either sex. Often blindly patronizing, white leaders expected free blacks to take a back seat in the movement. Not all blacks were easily put down, and most became exasperated at whites' tendency to value purity over results, to strike a moral posture at the expense of action. But despite the invitation to form separate black groups, black leaders were active in the white societies from the beginning. Three attended the organizational meeting of the American Anti-Slavery Society in 1833, and some became outstanding agents for the movement, notably the former slaves who could speak from firsthand experience.

Among the black abolitionists one of the most effective was Sojourner Truth. Born in New York State in 1797, Isabella Baumfree renamed herself in 1843 after experiencing a mystical conversation with God, who told her "to travel up and down the land" preaching the sins of slavery. She did just that, crisscrossing the country during the 1840s and 1850s, exhorting audiences to support abolitionism and women's rights. Having been a slave until she fled to freedom in 1827, Sojourner Truth was able to speak with added conviction and knowledge about the evils of the "peculiar institution" and the inequality of women. As she told a gathering of the Ohio Women's Rights Convention in 1851, "I have plowed, and planted, and gathered into barns, and no man could head me—and ar'n't I a woman? I have borne thirteen children, and seen 'em mos' all sold off into slavery, and when I cried out with a mother's grief, none but Jesus heard—and ar'n't I a woman?"

Through such compelling testimony, Sojourner Truth demonstrated the powerful intersection of abolitionism and women's rights agitation, and in the process she displayed and tapped the distinctive energies that women brought to reformist causes. "If the first woman God ever made was strong enough to turn the world upside down all alone," she concluded her address to the Ohio gathering, "these women together ought to be able to turn it back, and get it right side up again!"

An equally gifted black abolitionist was Frederick Douglass of Maryland. Blessed with an imposing frame and a simple eloquence, he became the best-known black man in America. "I appear before the

Frederick Douglass (left) *and Sojourner Truth* (right) *were both leading aboli-tionists.*

immense assembly this evening as a thief and a robber," he told a Mass-achusetts group in 1842. "I stole this head, these limbs, this body from my master, and ran off with them." Fearful of capture after publishing his *Narrative of the Life of Frederick Douglass* (1845), he left for an ex-tended lecture tour of the British Isles and returned two years later with enough money to purchase his freedom. He then started an abolitionist newspaper for blacks, the *North Star*, in Rochester, New York.

Douglass's *Narrative* was the best known among a hundred or more such accounts. Escapees often made it out on their own—Douglass borrowed a pass from a free black seaman—but many were aided by the Underground Railroad, which grew in legend into a vast system to con-ceal runaways and spirit them to freedom, often over the Canadian bor-der. Actually, there seems to have been more spontaneity than system about the matter, and blacks contributed more than was credited in the legend. Experience had conditioned escapees to distrust whites. One escapee recalled later: "We did not dare ask [for food], except when we found a slave's or a free colored person's house remote from any other, and then we were never refused, if they had food to give." A few in-trepid black refugees actually ventured back into slave states to organize escapes. Harriet Tubman, the most celebrated liberator, went back nineteen times.

REACTIONS TO ANTISLAVERY   Even the road north, many blacks found to their dismay, did not lead to the Promised Land. North of slavery, they encountered much of the discrimination and segregation that freed slaves would later encounter in the southern states. When Prudence Crandall of Connecticut admitted a black girl to her private school in 1833, she lost most of her white pupils. She held out in the face of insults, vandalism, and a law that made her action illegal, but closed the school after eighteen months and left the state. Garrison, Douglass, and other abolitionists had to face down hostile crowds who disliked blacks or found antislavery agitation bad for business. In 1837 an Illinois mob killed the antislavery editor Elijah P. Lovejoy, giving the movement a martyr to both abolition and freedom of the press.

In the 1830s abolitionism took a political turn, focusing at first on Congress. One shrewd strategy was to deluge Congress with petitions calling for the abolition of slavery in the nation's capital, the District of Columbia. Most such petitions were presented by former President John Quincy Adams, elected to the House from Massachusetts in 1830. In 1836, however, the House adopted a rule to lay abolition petitions automatically on the table, in effect ignoring them. Adams, "Old Man Eloquent," stubbornly fought this "gag rule" as a violation of the First Amendment and hounded its supporters until the gag rule was finally repealed in 1844.

Meanwhile, in 1840, the year of the schism in the antislavery movement, a small group of abolitionists called a convention in Albany, New York, and launched the Liberty party, with James G. Birney, one-time slaveholder from Alabama and Kentucky, as its candidate for president. In the 1840 election Birney polled only 7,000 votes, but in 1844 his total rose to 60,000, and from that time forth an antislavery party contested every national election until Abraham Lincoln won the presidency in 1860.

THE DEFENSE OF SLAVERY   Birney was but one among a number of southerners propelled north during the 1830s by the South's growing hostility to emancipationist ideas. Antislavery in the upper South had its last stand in 1831–1832, when the Virginia legislature debated a plan of gradual emancipation and colonization, then rejected it by a vote of 73 to 58. Thereafter, southern partisans worked out an elaborate intellectual defense of slavery, presenting it as a positive good.

The biblical argument in favor of slavery became one of the most powerful. The evangelical churches, which had widely condemned slavery at one time, gradually turned proslavery, at least in the South. Ministers of all denominations joined in the argument. Had not the patriarchs of the Old Testament held bondsmen? Had not Saint Paul advised servants to obey their masters and told a fugitive servant to return to his master? And had not Jesus remained silent on the subject, at least so far as the Gospels reported his words? In 1843–1844 disputes over slavery split two great denominations along sectional lines and led to the formation of the Southern Baptist Convention and the Methodist Episcopal Church, South. Presbyterians, the only other major denomination to split, did not divide until the Civil War.

Another, and more fundamental, feature of the proslavery argument developed a theory of the intrinsic inferiority of blacks. Other arguments took a more "practical" view of slavery. Not only was slavery profitable, it was a matter of social necessity. Jefferson, for instance, in his *Notes on Virginia* (1785), had argued that emancipated slaves and whites could not live together without risk of race war growing out of the recollection of past injustices. What is more, it seemed clear that blacks could not be expected to work if freed. They were too shiftless and improvident, the argument went. White workers, on the other hand, feared their competition.

In 1856 William J. Grayson of Charleston published a long poem, *The Hireling and the Slave*, which defended slavery as being better for the worker than the "wage slavery" of northern industry. George Fitzhugh of Virginia developed the same argument, among others, in two books: *Sociology for the South; or, The Failure of a Free Society* (1854) and *Cannibals All! or, Slaves Without Masters* (1857). Few if any socialists ever waxed more eloquent over the evils of industrial capitalism than these proslavery theorists. The factory system had brought abuses and neglect far worse than those of slavery, they contended.

Slavery, Fitzhugh argued, was the truest form of socialism, for it provided security for the workers in sickness and old age, whereas workers in the North were exploited for profit and then cast aside. Men were not born equal, he insisted: "It would be far nearer the truth to say that some were born with saddles on their backs, and others booted and spurred to ride them—and the riding does them good." Fitzhugh argued for an organic, hierarchical society, much like the family, in which each had a place with both rights and obligations. John C. Calhoun endorsed slavery with the more popular argument that it freed masters from drudgery to pursue higher things, and thus made possible a Greek democracy—or what one historian has more aptly tagged a "Herrenvolk [master race] democracy."

Within one generation such ideas had triumphed in the white South over the postrevolutionary apology for slavery as an evil bequeathed by the forefathers. Opponents of the orthodox faith in slavery as a positive good were either silenced or exiled. Freedom of thought in the Old South had become a victim of the nation's growing obsession with slavery.

MAKING CONNECTIONS

- The abolition movement never represented the majority of northerners. As Chapter 15 shows, however, by the end of the 1850s most voters in the North could support the idea of limiting the expansion of slavery westward, if not the abolition of it in the southern states.

- The Civil War brought great changes to southerners, both black and white. Chapter 16 describes the effect of the war on southern society.

- There are revealing comparisons between the Old South of this chapter and the New South of Chapter 18.

FURTHER READING

Those interested in the problem of discerning myth and reality in the southern experience should consult *Myth and Southern History* (1974), edited by Patrick Gerster and Nicholas Cords, for various essays on the topic. Two works help explain the mind of the Old South and its defense of slavery: Eugene D. Genovese's *The Slaveholders'*

Dilemma: Freedom and Progress in Southern Conservative Thought, 1820–1860 (1992) and Eric H. Walther's *The Fire-Eaters* (1992).

Other works on southern culture and society include Bertram Wyatt-Brown's *Southern Honor* (1982), Elizabeth Fox-Genovese's *Within the Plantation Household: Black and White Women of the Old South* (1988), Catherine Clinton's *The Plantation Mistress: Woman's World in the Old South* (1982),* Joan Cashin's *A Family Venture: Men and Women on the Southern Frontier* (1991),* and Theodore Rosengarten's *Tombee: Portrait of a Cotton Planter* (1987).* For a look at the role of religion in southern political life, see Mitchell Snay's *Gospel of Disunion: Religion and Separatism in the Antebellum South* (1993).

Eugene D. Genovese's *Roll, Jordon, Roll: The World the Slaves Made* (1974),* and Herbert G. Gutman's *The Black Family in Slavery and Freedom, 1750–1925* (1976)* stress the theme of a persisting and identifiable slave culture.

Useful surveys of abolitionism include Ronald G. Walters's *The Antislavery Appeal* (1976)* and James B. Stewart's *Holy Warriors: The Abolitionists and Amerian Slavery* (1976).*

On the role of free blacks in the antislavery movement, see R. J. M. Blackett's *Building an Antislavery Wall: Black Americans in the Abolitionist Movement, 1830–1860* (1983), and Shirley J. Yee's *Black Women Abolitionists: A Study in Activism* (1992). See also Michael P. Johnson and James L. Roark's *Black Masters: A Free Family of Color in the Old South* (1984).*

*These books are available in paperback editions.

15 ∾ THE CRISIS OF UNION

CHAPTER ORGANIZER

This chapter focuses on:

- the politicization of slavery

- how the Compromise of 1850 and the Kansas-Nebraska Act reflected sectional tensions

- the rise of a third generation party system: Republicans and Democrats

- the specific events that led to the secession of the southern states

SLAVERY IN THE TERRITORIES

John C. Calhoun and Ralph Waldo Emerson had little else in common, but both men sensed in the Mexican War the omens of a greater disaster. Mexico was "the forbidden fruit; the penalty of eating it would be to subject our institutions to political death," Calhoun warned. "The United States will conquer Mexico," Emerson conceded, "but it will be as the man swallows the arsenic . . . Mexico will poison us." Wars, as both men knew, have a way of corrupting ideals and breeding new wars, often in unforeseen ways. Indeed, America's winning of the Southwest gave rise in turn to quarrels over newly acquired lands. These quarrels set in motion a series of disputes that would culminate in a crisis of union.

THE WILMOT PROVISO The Mexican War was less than three months old when the seeds of a new conflict began to sprout. On August 8, 1846, a freshman Democrat from Pennsylvania, David Wilmot, stood up in the House of Representatives to discuss Polk's request for $2 million to expedite negotiations with Mexico. He favored expansion, Wilmot explained, even the annexation of Texas as a slave state. But slavery had come to an end in Mexico, and if free soil should be acquired, "God forbid that we should be the means of planting this institution upon it." Drawing upon the words of the Northwest Ordinance, he offered a fateful amendment to Polk's appropriations bill: in lands acquired from Mexico, "neither slavery nor involuntary servitude shall ever exist in any part of said territory."

Within ten minutes an otherwise obscure congressman had immortalized his name. The Wilmot Proviso, although never a law, politicized slavery once and for all. For a generation, since the Missouri Controversy of 1819–1821, the issue had been lurking in the wings, kept there most of the time by politicians who feared its disruptive force. But for the two decades following Wilmot's proposal the question would never be far from center stage.

The first flurry of excitement, however, passed quickly. The House adopted the Wilmot Proviso, but the Senate refused to concur, and Congress adjourned without giving Polk his $2 million. When Congress reconvened in December 1846, Polk prevailed on Wilmot to withhold his amendment, but by then others were ready to take up the cause. When a New York congressman revived the proviso, he signaled a revolt by the Van Burenites in concert with the antislavery forces of the North. Once again the House approved the amendment; again the Senate refused. In March the House finally gave in, but in one form or another Wilmot's idea kept cropping up. Abraham Lincoln later recalled that during one term as congressman, 1847–1849, he voted for it "as good as forty times."

John C. Calhoun meanwhile devised a thesis to counter the proviso, and he set it before the Senate in four resolutions on February 19,

1847. The Calhoun Resolutions, which never came to a vote, argued that since the territories were the common possession of the states, Congress had no right to prevent any citizen from taking slaves into them. To do so would violate the Fifth Amendment, which forbade Congress to deprive any person of life, liberty, or property without due process of law, and slaves were property. By this clever stroke of logic Calhoun took the basic guarantee of liberty, the Bill of Rights, and turned it into a basic guarantee of slavery. The irony was not lost on his critics, but the point became established southern dogma—echoed by his colleagues and formally endorsed by the Virginia legislature.

Senator Thomas Hart Benton of Missouri, himself a slaveholder but also a Jacksonian nationalist, found in Calhoun's resolutions a set of abstractions "leading to no result." Wilmot and Calhoun between them, he said, had fashioned a pair of shears. Neither blade alone would cut very well, but joined together they could sever the ties of union. Within another year Benton was complaining that the slavery issue had become like the plague of frogs in Pharaoh's Egypt, with "this black question, forever on the table, on the nuptial couch, everywhere."

POPULAR SOVEREIGNTY Many others, like Benton, refused to be polarized, seeking to bypass the brewing conflict. President Polk was among the first to suggest extending the Missouri Compromise dividing free and slave territory at latitude 36°30′ all the way to the Pacific. Senator Lewis Cass of Michigan, an ardent Whig expansionist, suggested that the citizens of a territory "regulate their own internal concerns" like the citizens of a state. Such an approach would combine the merits of expediency and democracy. It would take the issue out of the national arena and put it in the hands of those directly affected.

Popular sovereignty, or squatter sovereignty, as the idea was also called, had much to commend it. Without directly challenging the slaveholders' access to the new lands, it promised to open them quickly to non-slaveholding farmers who would almost surely dominate the territories. With this tacit understanding the idea prospered in Cass's Old Northwest, where Stephen A. Douglas of Illinois and other prominent Democrats soon endorsed it.

When the Mexican War ended in 1848, the question of bondage in the new territories was no longer hypothetical—unless one reasoned, as many did, that their arid climate excluded plantation crops and therefore excluded slavery. For Calhoun that was beside the point, since the right to carry slaves into the territories was the South's outer defense line, not to be yielded without opening the way to further assaults. In fact, there is little reason in retrospect to credit the argument that slavery had reached its natural limits of expansion. Slavery had been adapted to occupations other than plantation agriculture. Besides, on irrigated lands, cotton later became a staple crop of the Southwest.

Nobody doubted that Oregon would become free soil, but it too was drawn into the growing controversy. Territorial status, pending since 1846, was delayed because its provisional government had excluded slavery. To concede that provision would imply an authority drawn from the powers of Congress, since a territory was created by Congress. After much wrangling, an exhausted Congress let Oregon organize without slavery, but postponed decision on the Southwest territories. Polk signed the bill on the principle that Oregon was north of 36°30'.

Polk had promised to serve only one term, and having reached his major goals, he refused to run again in 1848. At the Democratic convention Lewis Cass, the author of squatter sovereignty, won nomination, but the platform simply denied the power of Congress to interfere with slavery in the states and criticized all efforts to bring the question before Congress. The Whigs devised an even more artful shift. Once again, as in 1840, they passed over Clay, their party leader, for a general, Zachary Taylor, whose popularity had grown since the Battle of Buena Vista. A legal resident of Louisiana and owner of more than a hundred slaves, he was an apolitical figure who had never voted in a national election. Once again, as in 1840, the party adopted no platform at all.

THE FREE-SOIL COALITION   But the antislavery impulse was not easily squelched. Wilmot had raised a standard to which a broad coalition could rally. People who shied away from the abolitionism of Garrison could readily endorse the exclusion of slavery from all the territories. By doing so, moreover, one could strike a blow for liberty without caring about slavery itself, or about the slaves. One might simply want free soil for white farmers, while keeping the unwelcome blacks far away in the South, where they belonged. Free soil in the new territories, therefore, rather than abolition in the South itself, became the rallying point—and also the name of a new party.

Three major groups entered the free-soil coalition: rebellious Democrats, antislavery Whigs, and members of the antislavery Liberty party.

Disaffection among the Democrats centered in New York, where the Van Burenites seized on the free-soil issue as a moral imperative. Free-soil principles among the Whigs centered in Massachusetts, where a group of "conscience" Whigs battled the "cotton" Whigs. The latter, according to the fiery Massachusetts reformer and future senator Charles Sumner, belonged to a coalition of northern businessmen and southern planters, "the lords of the lash and the lords of the loom." Conscience Whigs rejected the slaveholding nominee of their party, Zachary Taylor.

In 1848 these groups—Van Buren Democrats, Conscience Whigs, and Liberty party followers—organized the Free Soil party in a convention at Buffalo. Its presidential nomination went to Martin Van Buren. The Free Soil party platform pledged the government to abolish slavery whenever such action became constitutional, but the party's main principle was the Wilmot Proviso, and it entered the campaign with the catchy slogan of "free soil, free speech, free labor, and free men."

Its impact on the election was mixed. The Free Soilers split the Democratic vote enough to throw New York to Taylor, and the Whig vote enough to give Ohio to Cass, but Van Buren's total of 291,000 votes was far below the popular totals of 1,361,000 for Taylor and 1,222,000 for Cass. Taylor won with 163 to 127 electoral votes, and both major parties retained a national following.

THE CALIFORNIA GOLD RUSH Meanwhile, a new dimension had been introduced into the question of the territories. On January 24, 1848, gold was discovered in the California territory. The word spread quickly, and Polk's confirmation of the discovery in his last annual message, on December 5, 1848, turned the gold-fever into a worldwide contagion. During 1849 more than 80,000 persons reached California, with 55,000 going overland and the rest by way of Panama or Cape Horn. The influx quickly reduced the Mexicans there to a minority, and sporadic conflicts with the Indians of the Sierra Nevada foothills decimated the native peoples.

Of all the many frontiers in the American experience, the mining frontier was perhaps the most exceptional and unstable. Unlike the land-hungry pioneers who traversed the overland trails, the miners were mostly unmarried young men from a variety of places, representing a wide spectrum of ethnic and cultural backgrounds. Few miners were interested in permanent settlement. They wanted to strike it rich quickly and return home. The mining camps in California valleys, canyons, and along creek beds thus sprang up like mushrooms and disappeared almost as rapidly. Several settlements were named for Ophir, the Biblical site of King Solomon's wealth. Others were called Long Bar, Poverty Bar, or Missouri Bar, after the gravel or sand bars where gold was found. As soon as rumors of a new strike made the rounds, miners converged on the area, followed soon thereafter by a hodgepodge of merchants and camp followers who made their living servicing the Argonauts. Then, when no more gold was found, they picked up and moved on. Said one miner: "There is an excitement connected with the pursuit of gold which renders one restless and uneasy—ever hoping to do something better."

The mining shantytowns were disorderly and often lawless communities where vigilante justice prevailed and leisure time revolved around saloons and gambling halls. One newcomer reported that "in the short space of twenty-four days, we have had murders, fearful accidents, bloody deaths, a mob, whippings, a hanging, an attempt at suicide, and a fatal duel." Women were as rare as liquor was abundant. In 1850 less than 8 percent of California's total population was female, and even fewer women hazarded life in the mining camps. Those who did could demand quite a premium for their work as cooks, laundresses, entertainers, and prostitutes. "A smart woman can do very well in this country," one woman reported to a friend back east. "It is the only country I ever was in where a woman received anything like just compensation for work." Women from back east who rarely had a suitor suddenly found themselves smothered with attention in the mining country. Eliza Wilson noted that she had "men come forty miles over the mountains, just to look at me, and I never was called a handsome woman, in my best days, even by my most ardent admirers."

In the polyglot mining camps, the Americans often looked with disdain upon the Hispanics and Chinese who were most often employed as wage laborers to help in the panning process, separating gold from sand and gravel. But the Americans focused their contempt on the Indians. In the mining culture it was not a crime to kill Indians or work them to death. American miners tried several times to outlaw foreigners in the mining country but had to settle for a tax on foreign miners that was applied to Mexicans in express violation of the treaty ending the Mexican War.

CALIFORNIA STATEHOOD   As civic leaders emerged within the burgeoning California population, they grew increasingly frustrated by the
inability of military authorities to maintain law and order. In this context the new president, Zachary Taylor, thought he saw an ideal opportunity to use California statehood as a lever to end the stalemate in
Congress caused by the slavery issue. Born in Virginia and raised in
Kentucky, Zachary Taylor had been a soldier most of his adult life. Constantly on the move, he had acquired a home in Louisiana and a
plantation in Mississippi. Southern Whigs had rallied to his support,
expecting him to uphold the cause of slavery. Instead they had
turned up a southern man with Union principles, who had no more use
for Calhoun's proslavery abstractions than Jackson had for his nullification doctrine. Honest, forthright, and decisive, "Old Rough and Ready"
had the direct mind of the soldier he was. Slavery should be upheld
where it existed, he felt, but he had little patience with abstract theories about slavery in territories where it probably could not exist. Why
not make the California and New Mexico territories, acquired from
Mexico, into states immediately, Taylor reasoned, and bypass the whole
issue?

But the Californians, in need of organized government, were already
ahead of him. By December 1849, without consulting Congress, California organized a free-state government. New Mexico responded more
slowly, but by 1850 Americans there had adopted another free-state
constitution. In Taylor's annual message on December 4, 1849, he endorsed immediate statehood for California and enjoined Congress to
avoid injecting slavery into the issue.

THE COMPROMISE OF 1850

THE GREAT DEBATE   The spotlight thus fell on the Senate, where
the Compromise of 1850, one of the great dramas of American politics,
was enacted by a stellar cast: the great triumvirate of Clay, Calhoun,
and Webster, with support from William H. Seward, Stephen A. Douglas, Jefferson Davis, and Thomas Hart Benton. Seventy-three-year-old
Henry Clay once again took the role of the "Great Compromiser,"
which he had played in the Missouri and nullification controversies. In
1850 he presented a package of eight resolutions that solved all the dis-

puted issues. He proposed to (1) admit California as a free state, (2) organize the remainder of the Southwest without restriction as to slavery, (3) deny Texas its extreme claim to a Rio Grande boundary up to its source, (4) compensate Texas for this by assuming the Texas debt, (5) uphold slavery in the District of Columbia, but (6) abolish the slave trade across its boundaries, (7) adopt a more effective fugitive slave act, and (8) deny congressional authority to interfere with the interstate slave trade. His proposals, in substance, became the Compromise of 1850, but only after a prolonged debate, the most celebrated, if not the greatest, in the annals of Congress—and the final great debate for Calhoun, Clay, and Webster.

On February 5–6 Clay, haggard in appearance and faltering in speech, summoned all his eloquence in defending the settlement. In the interest of "peace, concord and harmony" he called for an end to "passion, passion—party, party—and intemperance." Otherwise, continued sectional bickering would lead to a "furious, bloody, implacable, exterminating" civil war. To avoid such a catastrophe, he stressed, California should be admitted on the terms that its own people had approved. The debate continued sporadically through February, with Sam Houston rising to support Clay's compromise, Jefferson Davis defending the slavery cause on every point, and none endorsing President Taylor's straightforward plan.

Then on March 4, Calhoun, desperately ill with tuberculosis, from which he would die in a few weeks, dramatically left his sickbed to sit in the Senate chamber, a gaunt, heavy-lidded figure swathed in flannels. A colleague read his defiant remarks. "I have, Senators, believed from the first that the agitation of the subject of slavery would, if not prevented by some timely and effective measure, end in disunion," wrote Calhoun. Neither Clay's compromise nor Taylor's efforts, he declared, would serve the Union. The South needed but an acceptance of its rights: equality in the territories, the return of fugitive slaves, and some guarantee of "an equilibrium between the sections."

Three days later Calhoun returned to hear Daniel Webster. The "godlike Daniel," long since acknowledged the supreme orator in an age of superb oratory, no longer possessed the thunderous voice of his youth, nor did his shrinking frame project its once magisterial aura, but he remained a formidable presence. His weathered face revealed worry and sorrow as he addressed the hushed Senate. He chose as his central theme the preservation of the Union:"I wish to speak today, not as a

Massachusetts man, not as a Northern man, but as an American . . . I speak today for the preservation of the Union." The extent of slavery was already determined, he insisted, by the Northwest Ordinance, by the Missouri Compromise, and in the new lands by the law of nature. Both sections, to be sure, had legitimate grievances: on the one hand the excesses of "infernal fanatics and abolitionists" in the North; and on the other hand southern efforts to expand slavery. But instead of threatening secession, he asked, let people "enjoy the fresh air of liberty and union."

The March 7 speech was a supreme gesture of conciliation, and Webster had knowingly brought down a storm upon his head. New England abolitionists lambasted this new "Benedict Arnold" for not aggressively supporting the free-soil cause and for endorsing the new fugitive slave law. On March 11 William H. Seward, freshman Whig senator from New York, gave the antislavery reply to Webster. Compromise with slavery, he argued, was "radically wrong and essentially vicious." There was "a higher law than the Constitution" that demanded the abolition of slavery.

In mid-April a select Committee of Thirteen bundled Clay's suggestions into one comprehensive bill. The measure was quickly dubbed the "Omnibus bill" because it resembled the vehicle that carried many riders. Taylor continued to oppose Clay's compromise, and their feud threatened to split the Whig party wide open. Another crisis loomed when word came that a convention in New Mexico was applying for statehood, with Taylor's support, and with boundaries that conflicted with the Texas claim to the east bank of the Rio Grande.

TOWARD A COMPROMISE   On July 4, 1850, friends of the Union staged a grand rally at the base of the unfinished Washington Monument. Taylor attended the ceremonies in the hot sun. Back at the White House he quenched his thirst with iced water and milk, ate some cherries or cucumbers, and contracted cholera morbus (gastroenteritis). Five days later he was dead. The outcome of the sectional quarrel, had he lived, probably would have been different, whether for better or worse one cannot know.

Taylor's sudden death, however, strengthened the chances of compromise. The soldier in the White House was followed by a politician, Millard Fillmore. The son of a poor farmer in upper New York, Fillmore had come up through the school of hard knocks. Largely self-educated, he had made his own way as a lawyer and then as a candidate in the rough-and-tumble world of New York politics. Experience had taught him caution, which some thought was indecision, but he had made up his mind to support Clay's compromise and had so informed Taylor. It was a strange switch. Taylor, the Louisiana slaveholder, who had nevertheless stoutly opposed the expansion of slavery, was ready to make war on his native region if it pressed the issue; Fillmore, whom southerners thought was antislavery, was ready to make peace.

At this point young Senator Stephen A. Douglas of Illinois, a rising star of the Democratic party, rescued Clay's faltering compromise. Short and stocky, brash and brilliant, Douglas was known affectionately as the "Little Giant." His strategy was in fact the same one that Clay had used to pass the Missouri Compromise thirty years before. Reasoning that nearly everybody objected to one or another provision of the Omnibus, Douglas worked on the principle of breaking it up into six (later five) separate measures. Few members were prepared to vote for all of them, but from different elements Douglas hoped to mobilize a majority for each.

It worked. Thomas Hart Benton noted that the separate items were like "cats and dogs that had been tied together by their tails for months, scratching and biting, but being loose again, every one of them ran off to his own hole and was quiet." In early September 1850 the main bills passed, and on September 20 Fillmore signed the last of the five measures into law. The Union had muddled through, and the settlement went down in history as the Compromise of 1850. For the time it defused an explosive situation and settled each of the major points at issue.

First, California entered the Union as a free state, ending forever the old balance of free and slave states. Second, the Texas and New Mexico Act made New Mexico a territory and set the Texas boundary at its present location. In return for giving up its claims east of the Rio Grande Texas was paid $10 million. Third, the Utah Act set up another territory. The territorial act in each case omitted reference to slavery except to give the territorial legislature authority over "all rightful subjects of legislation" with provision for appeal to federal courts. For the sake of agreement the deliberate ambiguity of the statement was its merit. Northern congressmen could assume that territorial legislatures might act to exclude slavery on the unstated principle of popular sovereignty. Southern congressmen assumed that they could not do so.

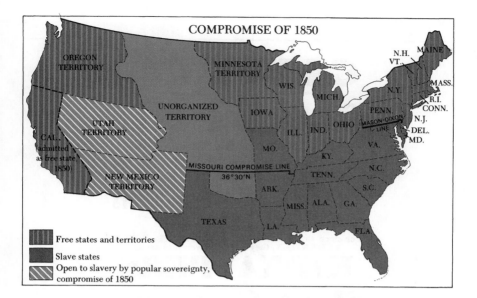

COMPROMISE OF 1850

Free states and territories

Slave states

Open to slavery by popular sovereignty, compromise of 1850

Fourth, a new Fugitive Slave Act put the matter of retrieving runaways wholly under federal jurisdiction and stacked the cards in favor of slave-catchers. Fifth, as a gesture to antislavery forces, the slave trade, but not slavery itself, was abolished in the District of Columbia.

Millard Fillmore's message to Congress in December 1850 pronounced the measures "a final settlement." Still, doubts lingered that either North or South could be reconciled to the measures permanently. In the South the disputes of 1846–1850 had transformed the abstract doctrine of secession into a movement animated by such "fire-eaters" as Robert Barnwell Rhett of South Carolina, William L. Yancey of Alabama, and Edmund Ruffin of Virginia. In their view slavery must expand into the territories or it would wither and die—and southern culture would die along with it. They refused to view the matter as settled, and they would do all in their power to see it returned to the center stage of political debate.

THE FUGITIVE SLAVE LAW   Northern abolitionists were equally determined to keep the issue of slavery's evils in the forefront of public concerns. Southern intransigence in demanding the Fugitive Slave Law had presented abolitionists a new focus for agitation and one that was far more charged with emotion. The law offered a strong temptation to kidnap free blacks by denying alleged fugitives a jury trial and by providing a fee of $10 for each fugitive delivered to federal authorities. "This filthy enactment was made in the nineteenth century, by people who

A notice to the free blacks of Boston to avoid the "watchmen and police officers" who "are empowered to act as kidnappers and slave catchers," 1851.

could read and write," Ralph Waldo Emerson marveled in his journal. He advised neighbors to break it "on the earliest occasion." The occasion soon arose in many places. Within a month of the law's enactment claims were filed in New York, Philadelphia, Harrisburg, Detroit, and other cities. Trouble followed. In Detroit only military force stopped the rescue of an alleged fugitive by an outraged mob in October 1850.

There were relatively few such incidents, however. In the first six years of the fugitive act only three runaways were forcibly rescued from the slave-catchers. On the other hand probably fewer than 200 were returned to bondage during the same years. More than that were rescued by stealth, often through the Underground Railroad. Still, the Fugitive Slave Act had tremendous effect in widening and deepening the antislavery impulse in the North.

UNCLE TOM'S CABIN AND THE 1852 ELECTION   Antislavery forces found their most persuasive appeal not in opposition to the Fugitive Slave Act but in the fictional drama of Harriet Beecher Stowe's *Uncle*

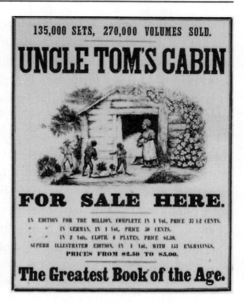

135,000 SETS, 270,000 VOLUMES SOLD.

UNCLE TOM'S CABIN

FOR SALE HERE.

IN EDITION FOR THE MILLION, COMPLETE IN 1 Vol. PRICE 37 1-2 CENTS.
" " IN GERMAN, IN 1 Vol. PRICE 50 CENTS.
" " IN 2 Vols. CLOTH, 6 PLATES, PRICE $1.50.
SUPERB ILLUSTRATED EDITION, IN 1 Vol. WITH 153 ENGRAVINGS,
PRICES FROM $2.50 TO $5.00.

The Greatest Book of the Age.

"The Greatest Book of the Age." Uncle Tom's Cabin, *as this advertisement indicates, was a tremendous commercial success.*

Tom's Cabin (1851), a combination of unlikely saints and sinners, stereotypes and melodramatic escapades—and a smashing commercial success. Slavery, seen through Mrs. Stowe's eyes, subjected its victims either to callous brutality or, at the hands of indulgent masters, to the indignity of extravagant ineptitude and bankruptcy. It took time for the novel to work its effect on public opinion, however. The country was enjoying a surge of prosperity, and the course of the presidential campaign in 1852 reflected a common desire to lay sectional quarrels to rest.

The Democrats, despite a fight over the nomination, had some success in papering over the divisions within their party. As their nominee for president they turned finally to Franklin Pierce of New Hampshire, a personable veteran of the Mexican War with little political experience. Soon they had a catchy slogan to aim at the Whigs: "We Polked you in 1844, we shall Pierce you in 1852." The platform pledged the Democrats to "abide by and adhere to a faithful execution of the acts known as the Compromise measures . . ." Pierce rallied both the Southern Rights men and the Van Burenite Democrats. The Free Soilers, as a consequence, mustered only half as many votes as they had totaled in 1848.

The Whigs were less fortunate. They repudiated the lackluster Fillmore, who had faithfully supported the Compromise, and tried to exploit martial glory by finally choosing Winfield Scott, the hero of Mexico City, a native of Virginia backed mainly by northern Whigs. The convention dutifully endorsed the Compromise of 1850, but with some opposition from the North. Scott, an able field commander but politically inept, had gained a reputation for antislavery and nativism, alienating German and Irish ethnic voters. In the end Scott carried only four states. The popular vote was closer: 1.6 million to 1.4 million.

Pierce, an undistinguished but sincere, boyishly handsome figure, a former congressman, senator, and brigadier in Mexico, was, like Polk, touted as another "Young Hickory." But he turned out to be made of more pliable stuff, unable to dominate the warring factions of his party, trying to be all things to all people, but looking more and more like a "Northern man with Southern principles."

FOREIGN ADVENTURES

CUBA   Foreign diversions now distracted attention from domestic quarrels. Cuba, one of Spain's earliest possessions in the New World, had long been an object of American desire, especially to southerners determined to expand slavery into new areas. In 1854 the Pierce administration instructed Pierre Soulé, the American minister in Madrid, to offer $130 million for Cuba, which Spain peremptorily spurned. Soulé then joined the American ministers to France and Britain in drafting the Ostend Manifesto. It declared that if Spain, "actuated by stubborn pride and a false sense of honor refused to sell," then the United States "shall be justified in wresting it from Spain." Publication of the supposedly confidential dispatch left the administration no choice but to disavow what northern opinion widely regarded as a "slaveholders' plot."

DIPLOMATIC GAINS IN THE PACIFIC   In the Pacific, however, American diplomacy scored some important achievements. In 1844 China signed an agreement with the United States that opened four ports, including Shanghai, to American trade. A later treaty opened eleven more ports and granted Americans the right to travel and trade throughout China. China quickly became a special concern of American Protestant missionaries as well. About fifty were already there by

1855, and for nearly a century, China remained far and away the most active mission field for Americans.

Japan meanwhile had remained for two centuries closed to American trade. Moreover, American whalers wrecked on the shores of Japan had been forbidden to leave the country. Mainly in their interest President Fillmore entrusted a special Japanese expedition to Commodore Matthew Perry, who arrived in Tokyo in July 1853. Perry sought to impress—and intimidate—the Japanese with American military and technological superiority. He demonstrated the cannon on his steamships and presented the Japanese with gifts of rifles, pistols, telegraph instruments, and a working miniature locomotive. For their part the Japanese presented Perry with silk and ornate furnishings. While the Americans paraded their warships, the Japanese offered a performance of sumo wrestlers. Negotiations followed, and Japan eventually agreed to an American consulate, promised good treatment to castaways, and permitted visits in certain ports for supplies and repairs. Broad commercial relations began after the first envoy, Townsend Harris, negotiated the Harris Convention of 1858, which opened five Japanese ports to American trade. Japan continued to ban emigration but found the law increasingly difficult to enforce, and by the 1880s the government abandoned efforts to prevent Japanese from seeking work abroad.

THE KANSAS-NEBRASKA CRISIS

American commercial interests in Asia were in part responsible for the growing interest in constructing a transcontinental railroad line linking the eastern seaboard with the Pacific coast. Other powerful motives were at work as well. Railroad developers and land speculators also promoted this transportation link, as did slaveholders who were eager to expand the area open to slavery. During the 1850s the idea of building a transcontinental railroad, though a great national goal, spawned sectional rivalries in still another quarter and reopened the slavery issue.

DOUGLAS'S PROPOSAL In 1852 and 1853 Congress debated and dropped several likely proposals for the route of the rail line. For various reasons, including terrain, climate, and sectional interest, Secretary of

Sen. Stephen A. Douglas (D-Ill.).

War Jefferson Davis favored a southern route and encouraged what became known as the Gadsden Purchase, a barren stretch of land in present New Mexico and Arizona. In 1853, at a cost of $10 million, the United States acquired the area from Mexico as a likely route for a Pacific railroad.

But midwestern spokesmen had other ideas concerning the path of the railroad. Since 1845, Illinois Senator Stephen A. Douglas and others had offered bills for a new territory in the lands west of Missouri and Iowa, bearing the Indian name Nebraska. In 1854, as chairman of the committee on territories, Douglas put forward yet another Nebraska bill. Unlike the others, this one included the entire unorganized portion of the Louisiana Purchase to the Canadian border. At this point fateful connections began to transform his proposal from a railroad bill to a proslavery bill. To carry his point Douglas needed the support of southerners, and to win that support he needed to make some concession on slavery in the new territories. This he did by writing popular sovereignty into the bill, allowing territories to decide the issue themselves.

It was a clever dodge, since the Missouri Compromise would still exclude slaves until the territorial government had made a decision, preventing slaveholders from getting established before a decision was reached. Southerners quickly spotted the barrier, and Douglas as quickly made two more concessions. He supported an amendment for repeal of the Missouri Compromise insofar as it excluded slavery north of 36°30', and then agreed to organize two territories: Kansas, west of Missouri; and Nebraska, west of Iowa and Minnesota.

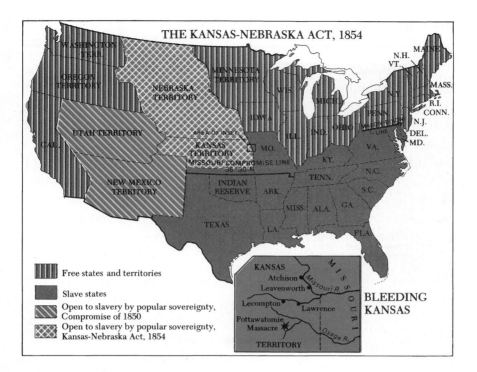

THE KANSAS-NEBRASKA ACT, 1854

WASHINGTON TERR.

OREGON TERRITORY

NEBRASKA TERRITORY

MINNESOTA TERRITORY

WIS.

MICH.

MAINE

N.H.
VT.

N.Y.

MASS.
R.I.
CONN.

UTAH TERRITORY

IOWA

AREA OF INSET

KANSAS TERRITORY

MISSOURI COMPROMISE LINE 36°30'N

CAL.

NEW MEXICO TERRITORY

INDIAN RESERVE

TEXAS

MO.

ILL. IND. OHIO

KY.

TENN.

ARK.

MISS. ALA. GA.

LA.

PENN.

VA.

N.C.

S.C.

FLA.

MASON DIXON LINE

N.J.
DEL.
MD.

Free states and territories

Slave states

Open to slavery by popular sovereignty, Compromise of 1850

Open to slavery by popular sovereignty, Kansas-Nebraska Act, 1854

BLEEDING KANSAS

KANSAS

Atchison
Leavenworth

Lecompton

Pottawatomie Massacre

Lawrence

MISSOURI

Missouri R.

Osage R.

TERRITORY

Douglas's motives remain unclear. Railroads were surely foremost in his mind, but he was influenced also by the desire to win support for his bill in the South, by the hope that popular sovereignty would quiet the slavery issue and open the Great Plains, or by a chance to split the Whigs. But he had blundered, thus damaging his presidential chances and setting his country on the road to civil war. He had failed to appreciate the depth of antislavery feelings. Douglas himself preferred that the territories become free. Their climate and geography excluded plantation agriculture, he reasoned, and he could not comprehend how people could get so wrought up over abstract rights. Yet he had in fact opened the possibility that slavery might gain a foothold in Kansas.

Douglas's move to repeal the Missouri Compromise was less than a week old before six antislavery congressmen published a protest, the "Appeal of the Independent Democrats." Their moral indignation quickly spread among those who opposed Douglas. Across the North editorials, sermons, speeches, and petitions denounced Douglas's bill as a conspiracy to extend slavery. What had been radical opinion was fast becoming the common view of people in the North. But Douglas had the votes and, once committed, forced the issue with tireless energy. President Pierce impulsively added his support, and the bill passed in May 1854 by 37 to 14 in the Senate and 113 to 100 in the House.

Very well, many in the North reasoned, if the Missouri Compromise was not a sacred pledge, then neither was the Fugitive Slave Act. On June 2, 1854, Boston witnessed the most dramatic demonstration against the act. After several attempts had failed to rescue a fugitive named Anthony Burns from being returned south, a force of soldiers and marines marched him to a waiting ship through streets lined with people shouting "Kidnappers!" past buildings draped in black, while church bells tolled across the city. Burns was the last fugitive slave to be returned from Boston, and was himself soon freed through purchase by Boston's black community.

THE EMERGENCE OF THE REPUBLICAN PARTY What John C. Calhoun had called the cords holding the Union together had already begun to splay. The national church organizations of Baptists and Methodists, for instance, had split over slavery by 1845. The national parties, which had created mutual interests transcending sectional issues, were beginning to unravel under the strain. The Democrats managed to postpone disruption for yet a while, but their congressional delegation lost heavily in the North, enhancing the influence of the southern wing.

The strain of the Kansas-Nebraska Act, however, soon destroyed the Whig party. Southern Whigs now tended to abstain from voting, while Northern Whigs moved toward two new parties. One was the new American (Know-Nothing) party, which had raised the banner of native Americanism and the hope of serving the patriotic cause of Union. More Northern Whigs joined with independent Democrats and Free Soilers in spontaneous antislavery coalitions with a confusing array of names, including "anti-Nebraska," "Fusion," and "People's party." These coalitions finally converged in 1854 on the name "Republican," evoking the memory of Jefferson.

"BLEEDING" KANSAS After passage of the Kansas-Nebraska Act, attention swung to the plains of Kansas, where opposing elements gathered to stage a rehearsal for civil war. All agreed that Nebraska would be free, but Kansas soon exposed the potential for mischief in Douglas's concept of popular sovereignty. The ambiguity of the law, useful to Douglas in getting it passed, only added to the chaos. The people of Kansas were "perfectly free to form and regulate their domestic institutions in their own way, subject only to the Constitution." That in itself invited conflicting interpretations, but the law failed to specify the time of decision, adding to each side's sense of urgency about getting control of the territory.

The settlement of Kansas therefore differed from the usual pioneering efforts. Groups sprang up north and south to hurry right-minded settlers westward. The first and best known was the New England Emigrant Aid Society. Southern efforts of the same kind centered in Missouri, a slave state, which was separated from Kansas only by a surveyor's line. When Kansas's first governor arrived in 1854, he found several thousand settlers already in place. He ordered a census and scheduled an election for a territorial legislature in 1855. On election day, several thousand "Border Ruffians" crossed over from Missouri, illegally cast proslavery votes, and pledged to kill every "God-damned abolitionist in the Territory." The governor denounced the vote as a fraud, but did nothing to alter the results. The new legislature expelled the few antislavery members, adopted a drastic slave code, and made it a capital offense to aid a fugitive slave.

Free-state advocates rejected this "bogus" government and quickly formed their own. In 1855 a constitutional convention, the product of an election of dubious legality, met in Topeka, drafted a state constitution excluding both slavery and free blacks from Kansas, and applied for admission to the Union. By 1856 a free-state "governor" and "legislature" were functioning in Topeka. Thus the territory had two illegal governments vying for recognition and control. But the prospect of getting any government to command general authority in Kansas seemed dim, and both sides began to arm. Once armed, they began to fight. In May 1856, 700 proslavery thugs entered the free-state town of Lawrence and smashed newspaper presses, set fire to the free-state governor's home, stole property, and destroyed the Free State Hotel.

The "sack of Lawrence" left just one casualty, but the incident aroused a fanatical Kansas free-soiler named John Brown, who had a history of mental instability. A companion described him as a man "impressed with the idea that God had raised him up on purpose to break the jaws of the wicked." Two days after the sack of Lawrence, Brown, the father of twenty children, set out with four sons and three other men toward Pottawatomie Creek, site of a proslavery settlement, where they dragged five men from their houses and hacked them to death in front of their screaming wives and children, ostensibly as revenge for the deaths of free-state men.

The Pottawatomie Massacre (May 24–25, 1856) set off a running guerrilla war in the territory that lasted through the fall. On August 30, Missouri ruffians raided the free-state settlement at Ossawatomie. They looted the houses, burned them to the ground, and shot John Brown's son Frederick through the heart. The elder Brown, who barely escaped, swore to his surviving sons and followers: "I have only a short time to live—only one death to die, and I will die fighting for this cause." Altogether, by the end of 1856 Kansas lost about 200 killed and $2 million in property destroyed during the territorial civil war.

VIOLENCE IN THE SENATE   Violence in Kansas spilled over into Congress itself. On May 22, 1856, the day after the sack of Lawrence and two days before Brown's Pottawatomie Massacre, a sudden flash of savagery on the Senate floor electrified the whole country. Just two days earlier Senator Charles Sumner of Massachusetts had finished an inflammatory speech in which he described the treatment of Kansas as "the rape of a virgin territory" and blamed it on the South's "depraved longing for a new slave State." Sumner made Senator Andrew P. Butler of South Carolina a special target of his censure. He called Butler a liar and implied that he kept a slave mistress. Sumner also teased him about a speech impediment caused by a stroke.

Sumner's rudeness might well have backfired had it not been for Butler's nephew Preston S. Brooks, a fiery-tempered South Carolina congressman. For two days Brooks brooded over the insults to his uncle, Senator Butler. Knowing that Sumner would refuse a challenge to a duel, he finally confronted Sumner at his Senate desk on May 22. He accused him of libel against South Carolina and Butler, and began beating him about the head with a cane while stunned senators, including Douglas, looked on. Sumner, struggling to rise, wrenched the desk from the floor and collapsed. "Towards the last he bellowed like a calf," a gloating Brooks reported. "I wore my cane out completely but saved the head which is gold."

Brooks had satisfied his rage, but in the process had created a martyr for the antislavery cause. Like so many other men in those years, he betrayed the zealot's gift for snatching defeat from the jaws of victory. For two and a half years Sumner's empty seat was a solemn reminder of the violence done to him. Some thought the senator was feigning injury, others that he really was physically disabled. In fact, although his injuries were bad enough, including two gashes to the skull, he seems to have suffered psychosomatic shock that left him incapable of functioning adequately. When the House censured Brooks, he resigned, but was triumphantly reelected. His admirers presented him with new canes.

SECTIONAL POLITICS Within the span of five days in May 1856 "Bleeding Kansas," "Bleeding Sumner," and "Bully Brooks" had set the tone for another presidential year. The major parties could no longer evade the slavery issue. Already it had split the hopeful American party wide open. Southern delegates, with help from New York, killed a resolution to restore the Missouri Compromise, and nominated Millard Fillmore for president. Later, what was left of the Whig party endorsed him as well.

At its first national convention the new Republican party followed the Whig tradition by seeking out a military hero, John C. Frémont, the "Pathfinder" and leader in the conquest of California. The Republican platform owed much to the Whigs too. It favored a transcontinental railroad and, in general, more internal improvements. It condemned the repeal of the Missouri Compromise and the Democratic policy of expansion. The campaign slogan echoed that of the Free Soilers: "Free soil, free speech, and Frémont." It was the first time a major party platform had taken a stand against slavery.

The Democrats, meeting two weeks earlier, had rejected Pierce, the hapless victim of so much turmoil. They also spurned Douglas because of the damage done by his Kansas-Nebraska Act. The party therefore turned to James Buchanan of Pennsylvania, who had long sought the nomination. The platform endorsed the Kansas-Nebraska Act and urged Congress not to interfere with slavery in either states or territories. The party reached out to its newly acquired Irish and German Catholic voters by condemning nativism and endorsing religious liberty.

The campaign of 1856 resolved itself into two sectional campaigns. The "Black Republicans" had few southern supporters and only a handful in the border states, where fears of disunion held many Whigs in line. Buchanan thus went into the campaign as the candidate of the only remaining national party. Frémont swept the northernmost states with 114 electoral votes, but Buchanan added five free states to his southern majority for a total of 174.

Few presidents before Buchanan had a broader experience in politics and diplomacy. He had been for more than twenty years in Congress, minister to Russia and Britain, and Polk's secretary of state in between. His long quest for the presidency had been built on a southern alliance, and his political debts reinforced his belief that saving the Union depended on concessions to the South. Republicans charged that he lacked the backbone to stand up to the southerners who dominated the Democratic majorities in Congress. To them his choice of four slave-state and only three free-state men for his cabinet seemed another bad omen.

THE DEEPENING SECTIONAL CRISIS

THE DRED SCOTT CASE   During Buchanan's first six months in office he encountered three crises in succession: the Dred Scott decision, new troubles in Kansas, and a business panic. On March 6, 1857, two days after the inauguration, the Supreme Court rendered a decision in the long-pending case of *Dred Scott v. Sandford*. Dred Scott, born a slave in Virginia about 1800, had been taken to St. Louis in 1830 and sold to an army surgeon, who took him as body servant to Illinois, then to the Wisconsin Territory (later Minnesota), and finally returned him to St. Louis in 1838. After his master's death in 1843 Scott apparently tried to buy his freedom. In 1846, with help from white abolitionist friends, he brought suit in Missouri courts claiming that residence in Illinois and Wisconsin Territory had made him free. A jury decided in his favor, reaffirming the widespread notion that "once free, forever free." But the state supreme court ruled against him, arguing that a slave state did not have to honor freedom granted to slaves by free states. When the case rose on appeal to the Supreme Court, the country anxiously awaited its opinion on the issue of whether freedom once granted could be lost by returning to a slave state.

Each of the eight justices filed a separate opinion, except one who concurred with Chief Justice Roger B. Taney. By different lines of reasoning seven justices ruled that Scott reverted to slave status upon his return to Missouri. The aging Taney ruled that Scott lacked standing in court because he lacked citizenship. At the time the Constitution was adopted, Taney added, blacks "had for more than a century been regarded as . . . so far inferior, that they had no rights which the white man was bound to respect."

To clarify the definition of Scott's status, Taney moved to a second major question. He argued that the Missouri Compromise, by ruling that certain new territories were to exclude slaves, had deprived citizens of property in slaves, an action "not warranted by the constitution." The Supreme Court had declared an act of Congress unconstitutional for the first time since *Marbury v. Madison* (1803). Congress had repealed the Missouri Compromise in the Kansas-Nebraska Act three years earlier, but the decision now challenged the concept of popular sovereignty. If Congress itself could not exclude slavery from a territory, then presumably neither could a territorial government created by act of Congress.

Proslavery elements, of course, greeted the court's opinion with glee. Many northerners denounced Taney's ruling. Little wonder that Republicans protested: the Court had declared their free-soil program unconstitutional. It had also reinforced the suspicion that the slavocracy was hatching a conspiracy. Were not all but one of the justices who joined Taney southerners? And had not Buchanan chatted with the chief justice at the inauguration and then urged the people to accept the early decision as a final settlement, "Whatever this may be"?

And what of Dred Scott? Ironically, his owner, now a widow, married a prominent Massachusetts abolitionist, who saw to it that the slave and his family were freed in 1857. A year later Scott died of tuberculosis.

THE LECOMPTON CONSTITUTION   Out in Kansas, meanwhile, the struggle continued through 1857. The contested politics in the territory now resulted in an antislavery legislature and a proslavery constitutional convention. The convention, meeting at Lecompton, drew up a constitution under which Kansas would become a slave state. A referendum on the document was set for December 21, 1857, with rules and officials chosen by the convention.

Although Kansas had only about 200 slaves at the time, free-state men boycotted the election, claiming that it too was rigged. At this point President Buchanan took a fateful step. Influenced by southern advisers and politically dependent upon southern congressmen, he decided to support the action of the proslavery Lecompton Convention. The election went according to form: 6,226 votes for the constitution with slavery, 569 for the constitution without slavery. Meanwhile, the acting governor had convened the antislavery legislature, which called for another election to vote the Lecompton Constitution up or down. The result on January 4, 1858, was overwhelming: 10,226 against the constitution, 138 for the constitution with slavery, 24 for the constitution without slavery.

The combined results suggested a clear majority against slavery, but Buchanan stuck to his support of the Lecompton Constitution, driving another wedge into the Democratic party. Senator Douglas, up for re-election, could not afford to run as a champion of Lecompton. He broke dramatically with the president in a tense confrontation, but Buchanan persisted in trying to drive Lecompton "naked" through the Congress. In the Senate, administration forces held firm, and in March 1858 Lecompton was passed. In the House, enough anti-Lecompton Democrats combined to put through an amendment for a new and carefully supervised popular vote in Kansas. Enough senators went along to pass the House bill. Southerners were confident the vote would favor slavery, because to reject slavery the voters would have to reject the constitution, which would postpone statehood until the population reached 90,000. On August 2, 1858, Kansas voters nevertheless rejected Lecompton by 11,300 to 1,788. With that vote Kansas, now firmly in the hands of its antislavery legislature, largely ended its role in the sectional controversy.

THE PANIC OF 1857 The third crisis of Buchanan's first half year in office, a financial panic, broke in August 1857. It was brought on by a reduction in Europe's demand for American grain, a surge in manufacturing that outran the growth of markets, and the continued weakness and confusion of the state banknote system. Failure of the Ohio Life Insurance and Trust Company precipitated the panic, which brought on a depression from which the country did not emerge until 1859.

Everything in those years seemed to get drawn into the vortex of sectional conflict, and business troubles were no exception. Northern businessmen tended to blame the depression on the Democratic Tariff of 1857, which had put rates at their lowest level since 1816. The agricultural South weathered the crisis better than the North. Cotton prices fell, but slowly, and world markets for cotton quickly recovered. The result was an exalted notion of King Cotton's importance to the world, and apparent confirmation of the growing argument that the southern system was superior to the free-labor system of the North.

DOUGLAS VS. LINCOLN   Amid the recriminations over Dred Scott, Kansas, and the depression, the center could not hold. The Lecompton battle put severe strains on the most substantial cord of Union that was left, the Democratic party. To many, Douglas seemed the best hope, one of the few remaining Democratic leaders with support in both sections. But now Douglas was being whipsawed between the extremes. Kansas-Nebraska had cast him in the role of "doughface," a southern sympathizer. His opposition to Lecompton, the fraudulent fruit of popular sovereignty, however, had alienated him from Buchanan's southern junta. But for all his flexibility and opportunism, Douglas had convinced himself that popular sovereignty was a point of principle, a bulwark of democracy and local self-government. In 1858 he faced reelection to the Senate against the opposition of both Buchanan Democrats and Republicans. The year 1860 would give him a chance for the presidency, but first he had to secure his home base in Illinois.

To oppose him, Illinois Republicans named Abraham Lincoln of Springfield, the lanky, rawboned former Whig state legislator and one-term congressman, a moderately prosperous small-town lawyer. Born in a Kentucky log cabin in 1809, raised on frontier farms in Indiana and Illinois, the young Lincoln had the wit and will to rise above his coarse beginnings. With less than twelve months of sporadic schooling he learned to read, studied such books as came to hand, and eventually developed a prose style as lean and muscular as the man himself. He worked at various farm tasks, operated a ferry, and made two trips down to New Orleans as a flatboatman. Striking out on his own, he managed a general store in New Salem, Illinois, learned surveying, served in the Black Hawk War (1832), won election to the legislature in 1834 at the age of twenty-five, read law, and was admitted to the bar in 1836.

As a Whig regular, Lincoln adhered to the economic philosophy of Henry Clay. He stayed in the legislature until 1842, and in 1846 won a term in Congress. After a single term he retired from active politics to cultivate his law practice.

In 1854 the Kansas-Nebraska debate drew Lincoln back into the political arena. At first he held back from the rapidly growing Republican party, but in 1856 he joined them, getting over 100 votes for their vice-presidential nomination. By 1858 he was the obvious Republican choice to oppose Douglas himself for the Senate, and Douglas knew he was up against a formidable foe. Lincoln resorted to the classic ploy of the underdog: he challenged the favorite to a debate. Douglas had little relish for drawing attention to his opponent, but agreed to meet him in seven sites around the state. The legendary Lincoln-Douglas debates took place that summer and fall.

The two men could not have presented a more striking contrast in appearance. Lincoln was well over six feet tall, sinewy, and craggy-featured, with a singularly long neck, and deep-set, brooding, even melancholy eyes. A fellow lawyer described him as "the ungodliest figure I ever saw." Unassuming in manner, dressed in homely, well-worn clothes and walking with a shambling gait, he lightened his essentially serious demeanor with a refreshing sense of humor. To sympathetic observers Lincoln conveyed an air of simplicity, sincerity, and common sense. Douglas, on the other hand, was short, rotund, bulb-nosed, stern, and cocky, attired in the finest custom-tailored suits and possessed of supreme self-confidence. A man of considerable abilities and even greater ambition, he strutted to the platform with the pugnacious air of a predestined champion.

At the time and since, much attention focused on the second debate, at Freeport, where Lincoln asked Douglas how he could reconcile popular sovereignty with the Dred Scott ruling that citizens had the right to carry slaves into any territory. Douglas's answer, thenceforth known as the Freeport Doctrine, was to state the obvious. Whatever the Supreme Court might say about slavery, it could not exist anywhere unless supported by local police regulations. Thus, if settlers did not want slavery, they simply should refuse to adopt a local code protecting it.

Douglas then tried to set some traps of his own. He sought to pin on Lincoln the stigma of advocating racial equality. Lincoln handled the volatile question with caution. There was, he asserted, a "physical difference between the white and black races," and it would "forever forbid the two races living together on terms of social and political equality." He simply favored the containment of slavery where it existed so that "the public mind shall rest in the belief that it is in the course of ultimate extinction." But the basic difference between the two men,

Lincoln insisted, lay in Douglas's professed indifference to the moral question of slavery.

If Lincoln had the better of the argument, at least in the long view, Douglas had the better of the election, which he won on a vote by the Illinois legislature. Across the nation the elections recorded one loss after another for Buchanan Democrats. The administration had lost control of the House.

JOHN BROWN'S RAID   The gradual return of prosperity in 1859 offered hope that the political storms of the 1850s might yet pass. But the sectional issue still haunted the public mind, and like lightning on the horizon, it warned that a storm was still brewing. In 1859 John Brown once again surfaced, this time in the East. Since the Pottawatomie Massacre in 1856 he had led a furtive existence, engaging in fund-raising, recruiting, and occasional bushwhacking. His commitment to abolish the "wicked curse of slavery," meanwhile, had intensified to a fever pitch.

Finally, on October 16, 1859, Brown launched his supreme gesture. From a Maryland farm he crossed the Potomac with nineteen men, including five blacks, and occupied the federal arsenal in Harper's Ferry, Virginia (now West Virginia). He apparently intended to arm the Maryland slaves he assumed would flock to his cause, set up a black stronghold in the mountains of western Virginia, and provide a nucleus of support for slave insurrections across the South.

John Brown.

What Brown actually did was to take the arsenal by surprise, seize a few hostages, and hole up in the fire-engine house. There he and his band were quickly surrounded by militiamen and town residents. The next morning Brown sent his son Watson and another supporter out under a white flag, but the enraged crowd shot them both. Intermittent shooting then broke out, and another Brown son was wounded. He begged his father to kill him and end his suffering, but the righteous Brown, befuddled and distraught by the unexpected collapse of his glorious insurrection, lashed out: "If you must die, die like a man." A few minutes later the son was dead.

That night Lieutenant-Colonel Robert E. Lee, U.S. Cavalry, arrived with his aide, Lieutenant J. E. B. Stuart, and a force of marines. The following morning, on October 18, Stuart and his troops broke down the barricaded doors and rushed into the fire-engine room. A young lieutenant found Brown kneeling with his rifle cocked. Before the pious patriarch could fire, the marine used the hilt of his sword to beat Brown unconscious. By then the siege was over. Altogether Brown's men killed four people (including one marine) and wounded nine. Of their own force, ten died (including two of Brown's sons), five escaped, and seven were captured.

Brown was quickly tried for treason, convicted on October 31, and sentenced to be hanged on December 2, 1859. "Let them hang me," Brown exulted. "I am worth inconceivably more to hang than for any other purpose." He was never more right. If Brown had failed in his purpose—whatever it was—he had become a martyr for the antislavery cause, and he had set off panic throughout the slave-holding South. At his sentencing he delivered one of the classic American speeches: "Now, if it is deemed necessary that I should forfeit my life for the furtherance of the ends of justice, and mingle my blood further with the blood of my children and with the blood of millions in this slave country whose rights are disregarded by wicked, cruel, and unjust enactments, I say, let it be done."

When Brown, still unflinching, met his end, northern sympathizers held solemn observances. Prominent Republicans, including Lincoln and Seward, repudiated Brown's attempted coup, but the discovery of Brown's correspondence revealed that he had enjoyed support among prominent antislavery leaders who defended his deeds. "That new saint," Ralph Waldo Emerson predicted, ". . . will make the gallows glorious as the Cross." William Lloyd Garrison, the lifelong pacifist, now wished "success to every slave insurrection at the South and in every slave country."

By far the gravest aftereffect of Brown's raid was to leave southerners in no mood to distinguish between John Brown and the Republican party. Southern defenders of the status quo now merged those who would contain slavery with those who would drown it in blood. All through the fall and winter of 1859–1860 rumors of conspiracy and insurrection swept the region. Every northern visitor, commercial traveler, or schoolteacher came under suspicion, and many were driven out. "We regard every man in our midst an enemy to the institutions of the South," said an Atlanta editor, "who does not boldly declare that he believes African slavery to be a social, moral, and political blessing."

THE CENTER COMES APART

THE DEMOCRATS DIVIDE   Amid emotional hysteria the nation approached a presidential election destined to be the most fateful in its history. The Democrats had settled on Charleston, South Carolina, as the site for their 1860 convention. Charleston in April, with the azaleas and dogwoods ablaze, was perhaps the most enticing city in the United States, but the worst conceivable place for such a meeting, except perhaps Boston. It was a hotbed of extremist sentiment and lacked adequate accommodations. South Carolina itself had chosen a remarkably moderate delegation, but the extreme southern-rights men held the upper hand in the delegations from the Gulf states.

Douglas supporters reaffirmed the platform of 1856, which simply promised congressional noninterference with slavery. Southern firebrands, however, now demanded a federal code protecting slavery in the territories. Buchanan supporters, hoping to stop Douglas, encouraged the strategy. The platform debate reached a heady climax when the Alabama fire-eater William L. Yancey informed the northern Democrats that they had erred by failing to defend slavery as a positive good. An Ohio senator offered a blunt reply: "Gentlemen of the South," he declared, "you mistake us—you mistake us. We will not do it."

When the southern planks lost, Alabama's delegation walked out of the convention, followed by delegates from the other Gulf states, Georgia, South Carolina, and parts of the delegations from Arkansas and Delaware. The convention then decided to leave the overwrought atmosphere of Charleston and reassemble in Baltimore on June 18. The Baltimore convention finally nominated Douglas on the 1856 platform. The Charleston seceders met first in Richmond, then in Baltimore, where they adopted the slave-code platform defeated in Charleston, and named Vice-President John C. Breckinridge of Kentucky for president. Another cord of union had snapped: the last remaining national party.

LINCOLN'S ELECTION The Republicans meanwhile gathered in Chicago. There everything suddenly came together for "Honest Abe" Lincoln, "the Railsplitter," the uncommon common man. Lincoln had suddenly emerged in the national view during his senatorial campaign two years before and had since taken a stance designed to make him available for the nomination. He was strong enough on the containment of slavery to satisfy the abolitionists, yet moderate enough to seem less threatening than they were.

Lincoln won the Republican nomination on the third ballot. The party platform foreshadowed future policy better than most. It denounced John Brown's raid as "among the gravest of crimes," and affirmed that each state should "order and control its own domestic institutions." The party repeated its resistance to the extension of slavery, and in an effort to gain broader support, endorsed a higher protective tariff for manufacturers, free homesteads for farmers, a more liberal naturalization law, and internal improvements, including a Pacific railroad. With this platform Republicans made a strong appeal to eastern businessmen, western farmers, and the large immigrant population.

Both major conventions revealed that opinion tended to become more radical in the upper North and deep South. Attitude seemed to follow latitude. In the border states a sense of moderation aroused the diehard Whigs there to make one more try at reconciliation. Meeting in Baltimore a week before the Republicans met in Chicago, they reorganized into the Constitutional Union party and named John Bell of Tennessee for president. Their platform simply called for the preservation of the Constitution and the Union.

Of the four candidates not one was able to command a national following, and the campaign resolved into a choice between Lincoln and

Abraham Lincoln, Republican candidate for president, June, 1860.

Douglas in the North, Breckinridge and Bell in the South. One consequence of these separate campaigns was that each section gained a false impression of the other. The South never learned to distinguish Lincoln from the radicals; the North failed to gauge the force of southern intransigence—and in this Lincoln was among the worst. He stubbornly refused to offer the South assurances or to explain his position on slavery, which he insisted was a matter of public record.

The one man who tried to break through the veil that was falling between the sections was Douglas, who tried to mount a national campaign. Only forty-seven, but already weakened by excessive drink, ill health, and disappointments, he wore himself out in one final glorious campaign. Down through the hostile areas of Tennessee, Georgia, and Alabama he carried appeals on behalf of the Union. "I do not believe that every Breckinridge man is a disunionist," he said, "but I do believe that every disunionist is a Breckinridge man."

By midnight of November 6, however, Lincoln's victory was clear. In the final count he had about 39 percent of the total popular vote, but a clear majority with 180 votes in the electoral college. He carried all eighteen free states by a wide margin. Among all the candidates, only Douglas had electoral votes from both slave and free states, but his total of 12 was but a pitiful remnant of Democratic Unionism. He ran last.

Bell took Virginia, Kentucky, and Tennessee, and Breckinridge swept the other slave states to come in second with 72 electoral votes.

SECESSION OF THE DEEP SOUTH   Soon after the election the South Carolina legislature, which had assembled to choose the state's electors, set a special election for December 6 to choose delegates to a convention. In Charleston on December 20, 1860, the convention unanimously voted an Ordinance of Secession, declaring the state's ratification of the Constitution repealed and the union with other states dissolved. By February 1, 1861, six more states had declared themselves out of the Union. On February 4, a convention of those seven states met in Montgomery, Alabama, and on February 7 it adopted a provisional constitution for the Confederate States of America. Two days later the delegates elected Jefferson Davis its president. He was inaugurated February 18, with Alexander Stephens of Georgia as vice-president.

In all seven states of the southernmost tier a solid majority had voted for secessionist convention delegates, but their combined vote would not have been a majority of the presidential vote in November. What happened, it seemed, was what often happens in revolutionary situations: a determined and decisive minority acted quickly in an emotionally charged climate and carried its program against a confused and indecisive opposition. Trying to decide if a majority of southern whites actually favored secession probably is beside the point—a majority was vulnerable to the decisive action of the secessionists.

Southern Unionists lamented this situation, noting that the "fire-eaters" rather than true statesmen were in control. "Webster and Clay are gone," mourned one Louisianan, "and God has given us over to fools and mad men." Others predicted that secession, instead of conserving traditional southern society, would in fact accelerate its demise. Alexander Stephens had warned in 1860: "Revolutions are much easier started than controlled, and the men who begin them, even for the best purposes and objects, seldom end them."

BUCHANAN'S WAITING GAME   History is full of might-have-beens. A bold stroke, even a bold statement, by the lame-duck president at this point might have defused the crisis, but there was no Jacksonian will in

Buchanan. As Ulysses S. Grant recognized, Buchanan was a "granny of an Executive." Besides, a bold stroke might simply have hastened the conflict. No bold stroke came from Lincoln either, nor would he consult with the administration during the long months before his inauguration on March 4, 1861. He inclined all too strongly to the belief that secession was just another bluff, and kept his public silence.

Buchanan followed his natural bent, the policy on which he had built a career: make concessions, seek a compromise to mollify the South. In his annual message on December 3, 1860, Buchanan made a forthright argument that secession was illegal, but that he lacked authority to coerce a state. "Seldom have we known so strong an argument come to so lame and impotent a conclusion," the *Cincinnati Enquirer* editorialized. There was, however, a hidden weapon in the president's reaffirmation of a duty to "take care that the laws be faithfully executed" insofar as he was able. If the president could enforce the law upon all citizens, he would have no need to "coerce" a state. Indeed Buchanan's position became the policy of the Lincoln administration, which fought a war on the theory that individuals but not states as such were in rebellion.

Buchanan held firmly to his resolve, with some slight stiffening by the end of 1860, when secession became a fact, but he refused to assert federal power provocatively. On the day after Christmas the small garrison at Charleston's Fort Moultrie had been moved into the nearly completed Fort Sumter by Major Robert Anderson, a Kentucky Unionist. Anderson's move, designed to achieve both disengagement and greater security, struck South Carolina authorities as provocative, a violation of an earlier "gentleman's agreement" that the administration would make no changes in its arrangements. Commissioners of the newly "independent" state peremptorily demanded withdrawal of all federal forces, but they had overplayed their hand. Buchanan's cabinet, with only one southerner left, insisted it would be a gross violation of duty, perhaps grounds for impeachment, for the president to yield. His backbone thus stiffened, he sharply rejected the South Carolina ultimatum to withdraw: "This I cannot do: This I will not do." His nearest approach to coercion was to dispatch a steamer, *Star of the West,* to Fort Sumter with reinforcements and provisions. As the ship approached Charleston Harbor, Carolina batteries at Fort Moultrie and Morris Island opened fire and drove it away on January 9. It was in fact an act of war, but

Buchanan chose to ignore the challenge. He decided instead to hunker down and ride out the remaining weeks of his term, hoping against hope that one of several compromise efforts would yet prove fruitful.

LAST EFFORTS AT COMPROMISE   Forlorn efforts at compromise continued in Congress until dawn of Lincoln's inauguration day. On December 18 Senator John J. Crittenden of Kentucky had proposed a series of resolutions that recognized slavery in the territories south of 36°30′ and guaranteed to maintain slavery where it already existed. The fight for a compromise was carried to the floor of each house, and subjected to intensive but inconclusive debate during January and February.

Meanwhile, a peace conference met in a Washington hotel in February 1861. Twenty-one states sent delegates and former president John Tyler presided, but the convention's proposal, substantially the same as the Crittenden Compromise, failed to win the support of either house of Congress. The only compromise proposal that met with any success was a constitutional amendment to guarantee slavery where it existed. Many Republicans, including Lincoln, were prepared to go that far to save the Union, but they were unwilling to repudiate their stand against slavery in the territories. As it happened, after passing the House the amendment passed the Senate without a vote to spare, by 24 to 12, on the dawn of inauguration day. It would have become the Thirteenth Amendment, with the first use of the word "slavery" in the Constitution, but the states never ratified it. When a Thirteenth Amendment was ratified in 1865, it did not guarantee slavery—it abolished slavery.

MAKING CONNECTIONS

- Through the 1850s, most of the debate over slavery concerned its expansion of slavery into the territories; with Lincoln's Emancipation Proclamation, discussed in the next chapter, the issue shifted to slavery itself.

- Many of the Radical Republicans who designed Reconstruction (Chapter 17) had been antislavery Republicans before the war.

- The proposed transcontinental railroad that brought about the Kansas-Nebraska crisis would finally be completed in 1869 (Chapter 19).

FURTHER READING

Surveys of the coming of the Civil War include James M. McPherson's *Battle Cry of Freedom: The Civil War Era* (1988),* and Bruce Levine's *Half Slave and Half Free: The Roots of the Civil War* (1992).* Interpretive essays can be studied in Eric Foner's *Politics and Ideology in the Age of the Civil War* (1980).*

Numerous works cover the crises of the 1850s. Michael F. Holt's *The Political Crisis of the 1850s* (1978)* traces the demise of the Whigs. Eric Foner provides an interpretive introduction to how events and ideas combined in the formation of a new political party in *Free Soil, Free Labor, Free Men: The Ideology of the Republican Party before the Civil War* (1970).* Also good on the Republicans is William E. Gienapp's *The Origins of the Republican Party, 1852–1856* (1987).*

*These books are available in paperback editions.

16 ⤳ THE WAR OF THE UNION

CHAPTER ORGANIZER

This chapter focuses on:

- the main course and major strategies of the Civil War

- how the war affected the home front, North and South

- the reasons for, and results of, Lincoln's Emancipation Proclamation

AN EPIC STRUGGLE

Shrouded in an ever-thickening mist of gallant images and larger-than-life mythology, the Union triumph in the Civil War has acquired the mantle of inevitability. Was not the North destined to win? The Confederacy's fight for independence, on the other hand, has taken on the aura of a romantic lost cause, doomed from the start by the region's sparse industrial development, smaller pool of able-bodied men, paucity of capital resources and warships, and spotty transportation network. But in 1861 the military situation was by no means so clear-cut. For all of the South's obvious disadvantages, it initially enjoyed a captive labor force, superior officers, the prospects of foreign assistance, and the benefits of fighting a defensive campaign on familiar territory. Jefferson Davis and other Confederate leaders were genuinely confident that their cause would prevail on the battlefields. It is important to remember that this epochal event was endowed from the start not with inevitability but with uncertainty, and its outcome was decided as much by human decisions and human willpower as by physical resources.

END OF THE WAITING GAME   In his inaugural address on March 4, 1861, Lincoln reassured southerners that he had no intention of interfering with "slavery in the States where it exists." But secession was another matter. He insisted that the "Union of these States is perpetual," and he promised to hold areas belonging to the government. Still, he pledged that the federal government would use force only if attacked.

But the momentum of secession took control of events. The day after the inauguration word arrived from Charleston that time was running out for the federal garrison at Fort Sumter. The commander, Major Robert Anderson, a Kentuckian with a Georgian wife, had enough supplies for only a month, and the fort was being surrounded by a Confederate "ring of fire." On April 4, 1861, Lincoln decided to resupply Anderson's garrison. A week later the dashing Confederate general Pierre G. T. Beauregard, who had taught artillery to Anderson at West Point, demanded that his former student surrender Sumter. Anderson refused, and just before dawn on April 12, Confederate batteries began shelling the fort. After more than thirty hours, Anderson, his ammunition exhausted, surrendered.

The guns of Charleston thus signaled the end of the tense waiting game. On April 15 Lincoln called upon the loyal states to supply 75,000 militiamen. Volunteers in both the North and the South soon crowded recruiting stations, and huge new armies began to take shape. On April 19 Lincoln proclaimed a blockade of southern ports which, as the Supreme Court later ruled, confirmed the existence of a state of war.

TAKING SIDES   Lincoln's proclamation led four upper South states to join the Confederacy—Virginia, Arkansas, Tennessee, and North Carolina. Each had areas (mainly in the mountains) where both slaves and secessionists were scarce and where Union sentiment ran strong. In fact, Unionists in western Virginia, bolstered by a Union army from Ohio under General George B. McClellan, formed a new state. In 1863

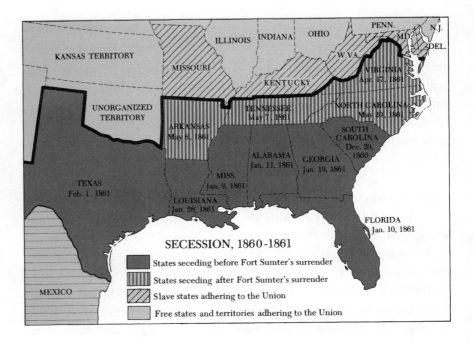

SECESSION, 1860-1861

- States seceding before Fort Sumter's surrender
- States seceding after Fort Sumter's surrender
- Slave states adhering to the Union
- Free states and territories adhering to the Union

Congress admitted West Virginia with a state constitution that provided for emancipation of the few slaves there.

Of the other slave states, Delaware remained firmly in the Union, but Maryland, Kentucky, and Missouri went through bitter struggles for control. The secession of Maryland would have encircled Washington with Confederate states. To hold the state Lincoln took drastic measures: he suspended the writ of habeas corpus (under which judges could require arresting officers to produce their prisoners and justify their arrest) and jailed pro-Confederate leaders. The fall elections ended the threat of Maryland's secession by returning a solidly Unionist majority in the state.

Kentucky, native state of both Lincoln and Jefferson Davis, harbored divided loyalties. The state legislature proclaimed its "neutrality" in the conflict, but that only lasted until September 3, 1861, when a Confederate force captured several towns. General Ulysses S. Grant then moved troops into Paducah. Thereafter, Kentucky for the most part remained with the Union. It joined the Confederacy, some have said, only after the war.

In Missouri, Unionists had a numerical advantage, but secessionist sympathies were strong, and a Confederate militia began to gather near St. Louis. On May 10, 1861, Unionist forces surprised and disarmed the militia at its camp. They finally broke the back of Confederate resistance in Missouri at the battle of Pea Ridge (March 6–8, 1862), just over the state line in Arkansas. Nevertheless, border warfare continued in Missouri, pitting rival bands of gunslingers who kept up their feuding and banditry for years after the war ended.

Robert E. Lee epitomized the agonizing choice facing many border-state residents. Son of "Lighthorse Harry" Lee, a Revolutionary War hero, and married to a descendant of Martha Washington, Lee had graduated second in his class from West Point and had served in the United States army for thirty years. Now a colonel and master of Arlington, an elegant estate facing Washington across the Potomac, he was summoned by Lincoln's seventy-five-year-old general-in-chief, Winfield Scott, another Virginian, and offered command of the new Federal forces. After a sleepless night pacing the floor, he told Scott he could not go against his "country," meaning Virginia. Although Lee failed to "see the good of secession," he could not "raise my hand against my birthplace, my home, my children." Lee resigned his commission, retired to his estate, and soon answered a call to the Virginia—later the Confederate—service.

SOUTHERN UNIONISTS   Many southerners made great sacrifices to remain loyal to the Union. Some left their native region once the fighting began. Others who remained in the South found ways to support the Union. In every Confederate state except South Carolina, whole regiments were organized to fight for the Union, and at least 100,000 men from the southern states fought against the Confederacy. Of course, some of these southern "Tories" changed sides out of expediency rather than loyalty. Confederate soldiers who had been captured occasionally chose to switch sides and serve on the Indian frontier rather than remain in prison.

Others, however, never embraced the Confederate cause. Many of the Southern loyalists were Irish or German immigrants who had no love for slavery or the planter elite. In the Fredericksburg–San Antonio region of Texas, German Americans opposed secession and the war once fighting erupted. The Confederate state government declared six counties in open rebellion in 1862 and sent in troops to suppress Union sentiment. Any German who criticized the Rebel cause was hanged, shot, or whipped. Confederate cavalry units caught one group of Germans trying to escape to Mexico and killed thirty-four of them. In south

Texas almost a thousand Texas-Mexicans fought against Confederate troops. Whatever their motives, these and other southern loyalists played a significant role in helping the Union cause.

BULL RUN   The outbreak of war injected a sudden urgency of meaning into the commonplace routine of everyday life. Caught up in the frothy excitement of military preparation, neither side recognized how deadly earnest the other was; both predicted an easy and quick victory.

Nowhere was this naive optimism more clearly displayed than at the first battle at Bull Run. An impatient public pressured both Lincoln and Davis to strike quickly and decisively. Davis allowed the battle-hungry General Beauregard to hurry his main forces in Virginia to Manassas Junction, about twenty-five miles west of Washington. Lincoln decided that General Irvin McDowell's hastily assembled army of some 30,000 might overrun the outnumbered Confederates and quickly march on to Richmond, the Confederate capital. With buoyant assumptions of victory, Johnny Reb and Billy Yank breezily stumbled into an entangling web of horror. The mood was so breezy, in fact, that hundreds of civilians rode out from Washington to picnic and watch the entertaining spectacle of a one-battle war.

It was a dry summer day on July 21, 1861, when McDowell's forces encountered Beauregard's army dug in behind a meandering, log-strewn little stream called Bull Run. The two generals, who had been classmates at West Point, adopted markedly similar plans—each would try to turn the other's left flank. The Federals almost achieved their purpose early in the afternoon, but Confederate reinforcements led by General Joseph E. Johnston poured in to check the Union offensive. Amid the fury, a South Carolina general rallied his men by pointing to Thomas Jackson's brigade of Virginians: "Look at Jackson standing there like a damned stone wall." It was true, and Jackson was called "Stonewall" thereafter.

Their attack blunted, the exhausted northern troops eventually broke, and their confused and frantic retreat turned into a panic as fleeing soldiers and terrified civilians clogged the Washington road. Lincoln read a gloomy dispatch from the front: "The day is lost. Save Washington and the remnants of this army. The routed troops will not re-form." Fortunately for the Federals, the Confederates were almost as disorganized and demoralized by victory as the Yankees were by defeat, and they failed to give chase. It would have been futile anyway, for the next day a summer downpour turned roads into quagmires.

A MODERN WAR

Bull Run was a sobering experience for both sides. Much of the romance—the splendid uniforms, bright flags, fervent songs—gave way to the agonizing realization that this would be a long, mean, and costly struggle. *Harper's Weekly* bluntly warned: "From the fearful day at Bull Run dates war. Not polite war . . . but war that breaks hearts and blights homes." The sobering defeat "will teach us in the first place . . . that this war must be prosecuted on scientific principles."

Indeed, the Civil War was thereafter conducted on "scientific" principles. It was in many respects the first modern war. First of all, its scope was tremendous. One out of every twelve adult American males served in the war, and few families were unaffected by the event. Over 630,000 men were killed or died of disease, more than in all other American wars combined. Almost any stomach or head wound proved fatal, and gangrene was rampant. Of the survivors, 50,000 returned home with one or more limbs amputated. The Civil War was not tidy and self-contained; it was a total war, fought not solely by professional armies but by and against whole societies. As Nathaniel Hawthorne recognized in 1862, "There is no remoteness of life and thought, no hermetically sealed seclusion, except, possibly, that of the grave, into which the disturbing influences of this war do not penetrate."

THE REALITY OF MODERN WAR   The Civil War was also a modern war in the sense that much of the killing was distant, impersonal, and mechanical. Hand-to-hand combat was the exception rather than the rule. The increasing use of rifled cannons and muskets meant that the carnage occurred mostly at long distance rather than face to face. By etching spiral grooves (rifles) in the barrels, gun manufacturers increased the effective range of firearms. Either attacking infantrymen were decimated by minié balls or grapeshot, or the defenders simply broke and ran. One general observed that the glittering bayonets were "rarely reddened with blood. The day of the bayonet is passed." Combatants armed with rifles frequently never got close enough to see each

Civil War firearms. *The Spencer repeating carbine (top), with its continuous firing capability, brought a new technology to war.*

other. As a participant in the ferocious Union assault on Port Hudson in 1864 remembered, "Many men in the regiment never laid eyes on a Rebel during the whole action."

The Civil War was thus greatly affected by industrial and scientific developments. This first of modern wars brought into use devices and techniques never before used on such a scale: railroad transport, rifled artillery, repeating rifles, ironclad ships, the telegraph, observation balloons, the Gatling gun (a rudimentary machine gun), trenches, and wire entanglements.

WOMEN AND THE WAR   The Civil War was also modern in that its impact penetrated well behind the front lines. While men fought and suffered, women worked, sorrowed, and sacrificed. A Mississippi woman saw her husband and all five sons join the Confederate army at the same time. A North Carolina mother lost seven sons in the fighting; another lost four, all at Gettysburg. The colossal carnage created a generation of widows, spinsters, and wives of disabled husbands.

Women who suffered such grieving losses or who witnessed death on a horrifying scale while serving as nurses were permanently altered by the experience. When war broke out, Mary Newcomb of Illinois was "so full of patriotism that if I had a dozen boys I have no doubt I should have said, 'Go! the country needs you.'" She thereafter became a nurse for the 11th Illinois Regiment. Nursing was as arduous and draining an enterprise as soldiering. A nurse working at a Maryland hospital recorded that she and her peers "endured the cold without sufficient bedding for our hard beds, and with no provision made for our fires. On bitter mornings we rose shivering, broke the ice in our pails, and washed our numb hands and faces, then went out into the raw air, up to our mess room, also without fire, thence to the wards."

The circumstances of war thrust women into new public roles during the conflict. Women became farmers or plantation managers, clerks, munitions-plant workers, and schoolteachers. Said one Georgia woman whose husband was killed in 1863, leaving her to direct three plantations and over a hundred slaves alone, "this cruel war imposes strange duties on us all." She added, however, that "I am willing to stand my lot."

Julia Ward Howe, the women's suffrage activist who composed the "Battle Hymn of the Republic," later observed that many women who were transformed by the war experience in one way or another refused to revert to their "chimney corner life of the fifties." Clara Barton, the tireless nurse, likewise saw in the Civil War an opportunity to end her

Clara Barton (1821–1912), oversaw the distribution of vital medicines to Union troops, and later founded the American Red Cross.

desperate search for "something to do that *was* something." She claimed that the Civil War accelerated by fifty years the involvement of women in traditionally male vocations. This was too optimistic, for after the conflict ended most women reverted to their traditional domestic roles, but many did not or could not, and as such the war did mark a significant change in women's status.

THE DRAFT   As the war gained momentum, each side eventually found it necessary to institute a draft in order to replenish the devastated ranks. The Confederates adopted conscription first. By an act of April 16, 1862, all male white citizens aged eighteen to thirty-five were declared members of the Confederate army for three years. Five months later the upper age was raised to forty-five, and in 1864 the limits were further extended to cover all from seventeen to fifty. One could escape the draft by providing a substitute not of draft age or by paying $500. Those with key civilian jobs were also given exemptions. The exemption of planters with twenty or more slaves led to bitter complaints in the South about "a rich man's war and a poor man's fight."

The North did not mandate a draft until March 1863, when men aged twenty to forty-five were conscripted. As in the South, those unwilling to serve could find substitutes or pay a fee of $300. Eventually the draft in the North produced 46,000 conscripts and 116,000 substitutes, or about 6 percent of the Union armies.

Widespread opposition limited enforcement of the draft acts in both North and South. In New York City draft riots erupted in July 1863, and angry mobs focused their resentment on blacks, lynching several and burning a black orphanage. Seventy-four persons were killed and $2 million in property destroyed before soldiers recalled from Gettysburg could restore order.

Unlike those of today, nineteenth-century armies often organized their units along community and ethnic lines. The Union army, for example, included a Scandinavian regiment (the 15th Wisconsin Infantry), a Scottish Highlander unit (the 79th New York Infantry), a French regiment (the 55th New York Infantry), and a mixed unit of Poles, Hungarians, Germans, Spanish, and Italians (the 39th New York Infantry). There were also numerous German and Irish units. In the Confederate armies, large numbers of Germans served in Texas units. Some 2,500 Texas-Mexicans ("Tejanos") fought for the Rebel cause.

The War's Early Course

The battle of Bull Run demonstrated that the war would not be decided with one sudden stroke. General Winfield Scott, the crusty veteran, had predicted as much, and now Lincoln fell back upon the three-pronged strategy that Scott had long before proposed. It called first for the Army of the Potomac to defend Washington and exert constant pressure on the Confederate capital at Richmond. At the same time, the navy would blockade the southern coast and thereby dry up the Confederacy's access to foreign goods and weapons. The final component of the plan would divide the Confederacy by invading along the main water routes: the Mississippi, Tennessee, and Cumberland Rivers. This so-called Anaconda strategy was intended to entwine and crush the southern resistance.

The Confederate strategy was simpler. If the Union forces could be stalemated, Davis and others hoped, then the British or French might be convinced to join their cause, or perhaps public sentiment in the North would force Lincoln to seek a negotiated settlement. So at the same time that armies were forming in the South, Confederate diplomats were seeking assistance in London and Paris, and Confederate sympathizers in the North were urging an end to the North's war effort.

NAVAL ACTIONS   After the Battle of Bull Run and for the rest of 1861 and early 1862, the most important military actions involved naval war and blockade. The one great threat to the Union navy proved to be short-lived. The Confederates in Norfolk had fashioned an ironclad ship from an abandoned Union steam frigate, the *Merrimack.* Rechristened the *Virginia,* it ventured out on March 8, 1862, and wrought havoc among the Union ships at the entrance to Chesapeake Bay. But as luck would have it, a new Union ironclad, the *Monitor,* arrived from New York in time to engage the *Virginia* on the next day. They fought to a draw and the *Virginia* returned to port, where the Confederates destroyed it when they had to give up Norfolk soon afterward.

Gradually, the northern "Anaconda" tightened its grip on the South. At Fortress Monroe, Virginia, Union forces held the tip of the peninsula between the James and the York Rivers. The navy extended its bases down the Carolina coast in the late summer and fall of 1862. In the

Gulf of Mexico, Flag Officer David Farragut's ships forced open the lower Mississippi and surprised New Orleans in the spring of 1862. The city surrendered on May 1, and Farragut's forces then moved on to take Baton Rouge in the same way.

THE WEST AND THE CIVIL WAR   During the Civil War, western settlement continued. New discoveries of gold and silver along the eastern slopes of the Sierra Nevada and in Montana and Colorado lured thousands of prospectors and their suppliers. As the population grew and dispersed, new transportation and communication networks emerged. Telegraph lines sprouted above the plains, and stagecoach lines fanned out to serve the new communities. Dakota, Colorado, and Nevada gained territorial status in 1861, Idaho and Arizona in 1863, and Montana in 1864. Silver-rich Nevada gained its statehood in 1864.

With the firing on Fort Sumter, many of the regular army units assigned to frontier outposts in the West began to head east to meet the Confederate threat. In Texas, the Indian Territory (Oklahoma), and southern New Mexico, Union soldiers left altogether. Elsewhere they left behind skeleton units to man the forts. Texas was the only western state to join the Confederacy. For the most part, the federal government maintained its control of the other western territories during the war.

But it was not easy. Fighting in Kansas and the Indian Territory was widespread and furious. By 1862 Lincoln was forced to dispatch new volunteer units to the West. He had two primary concerns: to protect shipments of gold and silver and to win over western political support for the war and his presidency. The most intense fighting in the West during the Civil War occurred along the Kansas-Missouri border. There the disputes between proslavery and antislavery settlers of the 1850s turned into brutal guerrilla warfare. The most prominent pro-Confederate leader in the area was William C. Quantrill. He and his proslavery followers, mostly teenagers, fought under a black flag, meaning that they gave no quarter. In destroying Lawrence, Kansas, in 1863, Quantrill ordered his forces to "kill every male and burn every house." They did. By the end of the day, 182 boys and men had been systematically killed. Their opponents—the Jayhawkers—responded in kind. They tortured and hanged prisoners, burned houses, and destroyed livestock.

Many Indian tribes found themselves caught up in the Civil War. Indian regiments fought on both sides, and in the Indian Country they fought against each other. Many Indians among the Five Civilized Tribes living in Indian Territory owned African-American slaves and felt a natural bond with southern whites. Oklahoma's proximity to Texas also influenced the Choctaws and Chickasaws to support the Confederacy. The Cherokees, Creeks, and Seminoles were more divided in their loyalties.

For these tribes, the Civil War served as a wedge that fractured their own unity. The Cherokees, for example, split in two, some supporting the Union and others supporting the South. John Ross, the Principal Chief of the Cherokee Nation, poignantly expressed his dilemma when he responded to a Confederate delegation soliciting an alliance: "I am—the Cherokees are—your friends, but we do not wish to be brought into the feuds between yourselves and your Northern Brethren. Our wish is for peace. Peace at home and peace among you."

Yet eventually Ross acceded to the demands of his followers that they align themselves with the Confederacy. A regiment of Cherokee warriors fought with the Confederates during their victory at Wilson's

Creek, Missouri, in August 1861. By the end of the year, Confederate and Union Cherokee factions were also at war with one another. During 1862, three Choctaw-Chickasaw regiments, a Creek regiment, a Creek-Seminole regiment, and two Cherokee regiments fought alongside white Confederates in Arkansas. One Cherokee leader attained the rank of brigadier general, and in 1865 he would be the last Confederate officer to surrender his troops, two months after Lee surrendered to Grant at Appomattox.

ACTIONS IN THE WESTERN THEATER   Except for the amphibious thrusts in the Chesapeake and along the southern coast, little happened in the Eastern Theater (east of the Appalachians) before May 1862. The Western Theater (from the mountains to the Mississippi), on the other hand, flared up with several clashes and an important penetration of the Confederate states. In western Kentucky, Confederate General Albert Sidney Johnston, a strapping Texan whom Davis considered the South's best general, had perhaps 40,000 men stretched over some 150 miles.

Early in 1862 the relentlessly aggressive Ulysses S. Grant made the first thrust against the weak center of Johnston's overextended lines. Moving out of Cairo and Paducah with a gunboat flotilla, he swung southward up the Tennessee River toward Fort Henry. After a pounding from the Union gunboats, the fort fell on February 6. Grant then moved overland to attack Fort Donelson, and on February 16 captured its 12,000 men. Grant's blunt demand of "immediate and unconditional surrender" and his quick success sent a thrill through the dispirited North.

Ulysses S. "Unconditional Surrender" Grant had not only opened a water route to Nashville but also forced the Confederates thereafter to give up their foothold in Kentucky. The short, slouching, disheveled Grant was now a national hero. But not for long.

SHILOH   As Grant moved his forces southward along the Tennessee River during the early spring of 1862, he made a costly mistake. While planning his attack on Corinth, Mississippi, he clumsily placed his troops on a rolling plateau between two creeks flowing into the Tennessee and failed to set up defensive trenches. General A. S. Johnston shrewdly recognized Grant's oversight, and on the morning of April 6, the tall and confident Johnston ordered an attack on the vulnerable Federals, urging his men to be "worthy of your race and lineage; worthy of the women of the South." The Confederates struck suddenly at Shiloh, a log church in the center of the Union camp. There amid flowering dogwoods, peach trees, and honeysuckle, they found most of Grant's troops still sleeping or eating breakfast. Some died in their bedrolls. Reported one Union officer: "The Rebels are out there thicker than fleas on a dog's back." After a day of bloody carnage and confusion, Grant's men were pinned against the river. But under the cover of gunboats and artillery at nearby Pittsburg Landing, Grant and the brilliant, falcon-eyed general from Ohio, William Tecumseh Sherman, superbly rallied their troops. Reinforcements arrived that night during a torrential rainstorm, and the next day Grant took the offensive. The Confederates withdrew to Corinth, leaving the Union army too battered to pursue.

Shiloh was the costliest battle in American history up to that point, although worse was yet to come. "The scenes on this field," Sherman sadly noted, "would have cured anybody of war." Combined casualties of nearly 25,000 exceeded the total dead and wounded of the Revolution, the War of 1812, and the Mexican War combined. Among the dead was the senior Confederate general, A. S. Johnston, who bled to death when a minié ball severed an artery in his leg. The Union, too, lost for a while the leadership of its finest general. Grant had blundered badly. Some critics charged that he had been drinking and called upon Lincoln to replace him. But the president declined: "I can't spare this man; he fights." Grant's superior, hulking, balding, puffy-eyed General Henry Halleck, however, was not as forgiving. He relieved Grant of his command for several months, and as a result the Union thrust southward ground to a halt.

MCCLELLAN'S PENINSULAR CAMPAIGN   The Eastern Theater remained fairly quiet for nine months after Bull Run. After the Union defeat, Lincoln had replaced McDowell with the brilliant, if theatrical and hesitant, General George B. McClellan. Stonewall Jackson's classmate at West Point, McClellan had served in the army as a captain before resigning and becoming president of a railroad. After the firing on Fort Sumter, he was named a major-general overseeing forces in Ohio, Indiana, and Illinois. Now, as head of the Army of the Potomac, he set about establishing a rigid training regimen, determined to build a pow-

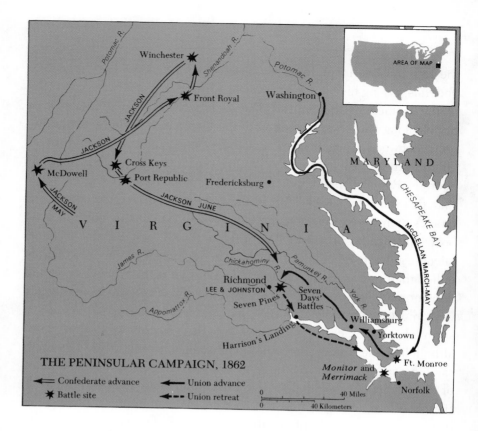

THE PENINSULAR CAMPAIGN, 1862

⬅ Confederate advance   ⬅ Union advance
★ Battle site   ⬅--- Union retreat

erful, well-trained army that would be ready for its next battle. On the surface, the wide-shouldered and broad-chested McClellan exuded confidence and poise, as well as a certain flair for parade-ground showmanship. His troops adored him. Yet for all of McClellan's organizational ability and dramatic flair, his innate caution would prove crippling.

Time passed and McClellan kept building his forces to meet the superior numbers he always claimed were facing him. Lincoln initially gave McClellan his complete support, but the "Young Napoleon" grew more and more enamored of himself and openly contemptuous of the backwoods president. Lincoln, however, refused to respond in kind. "Never mind," he once said after enduring another affront by his general. "I will hold McClellan's horse if he will only bring us success."

But as the weeks passed McClellan brought only more requests for troops and equipment. After nine months of such agonizing preparation, Lincoln and much of the public had grown understandably impatient. The exasperated president, convinced that his general "has got the slows," finally ordered McClellan to begin forward movement by Washington's Birthday, February 22, 1862. McClellan brashly predicted: "I will be in Richmond in ten days." He planned to attack the Confederate capital by the side door, so to speak, up the neck of land between the York and James Rivers, at the tip of which Union forces already held Fortress Monroe.

In mid-March 1862 McClellan's army finally embarked, and before the end of May his advance units sighted the church steeples in Richmond. Thousands of Richmond residents fled the city in panic. President Davis sent his own family to a safe haven west of the city. But McClellan failed to capitalize on his situation. On May 31 Confederate general Joseph E. Johnston struck at Union forces isolated by floodwaters on the south bank of the Chickahominy River. In the battle of Seven Pines (Fair Oaks), only the arrival of reinforcements prevented a disastrous Union defeat. Both sides took heavy casualties, and Johnston was severely wounded.

At this point the fifty-five-year-old Robert E. Lee assumed command of the Army of Northern Virginia, changing the course of the war. Tall, erect, and wide-shouldered, Lee was a reticent Christian gentleman in private, but a slashing, daring leader in uniform. He believed duty to be the "sublimest word in our language." Unlike Johnston, he enjoyed Davis's trust and was adept at assembling a galaxy of superb field commanders: Stonewall Jackson, the fearless, pious mathematics professor from the Virginia Military Institute; James Longstreet, Lee's deliberate but tireless "war horse"; sharp-tongued, tenacious D. H. Hill, the former engineering professor at Davidson College; Ambrose P. Hill, the consummate fighter who challenged one commander to a duel, feuded with Jackson, and kept secret his own mortal disease; and, J. E. B. Stuart, the incurably romantic and recklessly courageous young cavalryman who once said: "All I ask of fate is that I may be killed leading a cavalry charge."

Once in command, Lee quickly decided to hit the Union forces hard north of the Chickahominy River on June 26, 1862, leaving only a token force in Richmond. But heavy losses prevented the Confederates from sustaining their momentum. Lee launched a final desperate attack at Malvern Hill (July 1), where the Confederates were riddled by artillery and gunboats in the James River. As D. H. Hill observed, "It was not war, it was murder." This week of intense fighting, lumped together as the Seven Days' Battles, had failed to dislodge the Union forces. McClellan was still near Richmond.

On July 9 Lincoln visited the front, where McClellan lectured him on the correct strategy to follow. Such insubordination was ample reason to remove the cocky general. Instead Lincoln returned to Washington and on July 11 called Henry Halleck from the west to take charge as general-in-chief, a post that McClellan had temporarily vacated. Thus began what would become a frustrating search on Lincoln's part for a capable and consistent military leader.

SECOND BATTLE OF MANASSAS   The new high command ordered McClellan to return to Washington and join the defending forces there, now under bombastic John Pope, for a new assault against Richmond. As McClellan's Army of the Potomac pulled out, Lee moved northward to strike Pope before the Union forces could be joined. Once again he adopted an audacious strategy. Dividing his forces, he sent Jackson's famous "foot cavalry" on a sweep around Pope's right flank to attack his supply lines.

At Second Bull Run (or Second Manassas), fought on almost the same site as the earlier battle, the Confederates thoroughly confused Pope. J. E. B. Stuart's horsemen raided his headquarters, taking Pope's dress uniform and his strategy book, which outlined the position of his units. Pope then exhausted his own men frantically trying to find the elusive Jackson. By the time they made contact with what they thought were only Jackson's forces, Lee's main army had joined in.

The trap was baited, and the Union army was lured in. On August 30, 1862, as Pope's troops engaged Jackson's line, there came a crushing surprise attack on the Federal flank. James Longstreet's corps of 30,000 Confederates, screaming the Rebel yell "like demons emerging from the earth," drove the Union forces from the field. One New York regiment lost 124 of its 490 men, the highest percentage of deaths in any battle of the war. In the next few days the whipped Union forces pulled back into fortifications around Washington, where McClellan once again took command and reorganized. He displayed his unflagging egotism in a letter to his wife: "Again I have been called upon to save the country." The disgraced Pope was dispatched to Minnesota to fight in the Indian wars.

ANTIETAM   Lee gave his new adversary little time to prepare. Still on the offensive, determined to move the battlefield out of the South and perhaps thereby gain foreign recognition of the Confederacy, he led his troops into western Maryland in September 1862 and headed for Pennsylvania. As luck would have it, however, Lee's bold strategy was uncovered when a Union soldier picked up a bundle of cigars and discovered a secret order from Lee wrapped around them. The paper revealed that Lee had again divided his army, sending Jackson off to take Harper's Ferry. McClellan boasted upon seeing the captured document: "Here is a paper with which, if I cannot whip Bobby Lee, I will be willing to go home." But instead of leaping at his unexpected opportunity, he again delayed for sixteen crucial hours, still worried—as always—about enemy strength, and Lee was thereby able to reassemble most of his tired army behind Antietam Creek. Still, McClellan was optimistic, and Lincoln, too, relished the chance for a truly decisive blow: "God bless you and all with you," he wired McClellan. "Destroy the rebel army if possible."

On September 17, 1862, McClellan's forces attacked, and the furious Battle of Antietam (Sharpsburg) began. Just as the Confederate lines seemed ready to break, A. P. Hill's division arrived from Harper's Ferry, having marched sixteen hot, dusty miles to the battlefield. Bone-weary and foot-sore, they nevertheless plunged immediately into the fray, battering the Union's left flank. It was a ghastly scene. "No tongue can tell, no mind conceive, no pen portray the horrible sights I witnessed this morning," a Pennsylvania soldier reported. Still outnumbered more than two to one, the Confederates were able to force a standoff in the bloodiest single day of the Civil War, a day participants thought would never end.

But in the late afternoon McClellan backed off, letting Lee slip away across the Potomac. Lincoln was disgusted by McClellan's failure to follow up and gain a truly decisive victory, and he fired off the following tart message to the general: "I have just read your dispatch about sore-tongued and fatigued horses. Will you pardon me for asking what the horses of your army have done . . . that fatigues anything?" Later the president sent his commander a one-sentence letter: "If you don't want to use the army, I should like to borrow it for a while." Failing to receive a satisfactory answer, Lincoln removed McClellan and assigned him to recruiting duty in New Jersey. Never again would he command troops.

CAMPAIGNS IN VIRGINIA
& MARYLAND, 1862

◄══ Confederate advance   ◄─── Union advance
◄═ ═ Confederate retreat   ◄─--- Union retreat
✻ Battle site

FREDERICKSBURG   Lee's invasion had failed, and with it failed the Confederacy's hopes of foreign recognition. But the war was far from over. In his search for a fighting general Lincoln now made the worst choice of all. He turned to Ambrose E. Burnside, a handsome, personable, modest figure whose main achievement to that time had been to grow his famous side-whiskers. Burnside had twice before turned down the job on the grounds that he felt unfit for so large a command.

But if the White House wanted him to fight, Burnside would fight, even in the face of the oncoming winter. On a cold December 13, 1862, he sent his men across the icy Rappahannock River to face Lee's forces, well entrenched behind a stone wall and on high ground just west of Fredericksburg on Marye's Heights in Virginia. Watching the massive Union army approaching, an aide asked Stonewall Jackson his intentions. "We will give them the bayonet," he replied. But few Federals ever got close enough for such hand-to-hand fighting. Blessed with a clear field of fire, Confederate artillery and muskets chewed up the valorous blue ranks as they crossed a mile of open bottomland outside the town.

Six times the courageous but suicidal assaults melted under the murderous fire coming from protected Confederate positions above and below them. It was, as a Federal general said, "a great slaughter pen." The scene was both awful and awe-inspiring, prompting Lee to remark: "It is well that war is so terrible—we should grow too fond of it." After seeing his men suffer more than 12,000 casualties, twice as many as the Confederates, Burnside wept as he gave the order to withdraw, and his battered forces sullenly limped back across the river. A northern reporter aptly summarized the battle: "It can hardly be in human nature for men to show more valor, or generals to manifest less judgment."

The year 1862 ended with forces in the East deadlocked and the Federal advance in the West stalled since midyear. Union morale reached a low ebb. Northern Democrats were calling for a negotiated peace, while the so-called Radical Republicans were pushing Lincoln to prosecute the war even more forcefully. Several even questioned the president's competence.

But in the midst of such second-guessing and carping, the deeper currents of the war were in fact turning in favor of the Union: in a lengthening war its superior resources began to tell on the morale of the Confederacy. In both the Eastern and Western Theaters the Confederate counterattack had been repulsed. And while the armies clashed, Lincoln by a stroke of a pen changed the conflict from a war for the Union into a revolutionary struggle for abolition. On January 1, 1863, he signed the Emancipation Proclamation.

EMANCIPATION

The Emancipation Proclamation was the product of long and painful deliberation. Lincoln had always insisted that the purpose of the conflict was to restore the Union, not to free the slaves. The prolonged war forced the issue. Fugitive slaves began to turn up in Union army camps, and generals did not know whether to declare them free or not. Some put these "contrabands" to work building fortifications; others liberated those who belonged to Confederate owners, thus risking

Former slaves, or "contrabands," on a farm in Cumberland Landing, Virginia, 1862.

upsetting border-state slaveholders. Lincoln himself edged toward emancipation. As the war ground on, he eventually decided that complete emancipation was required for several reasons: slave labor bolstered the Confederate cause, sagging morale in the North needed the lift of a transcendent moral ideal, and public opinion was swinging that way as the war continued. Proclaiming a war on slavery, moreover, would end forever any chance that France or Britain would support the Confederacy.

The time to act finally came after Antietam. It was a dubious victory, but it did force Lee's withdrawal from the North. On September 22, 1862, Lincoln issued a preliminary Emancipation Proclamation which warned that on January 1, 1863, all slaves in Confederate states or areas still under active rebellion would be "thenceforward and forever free."

REACTIONS TO EMANCIPATION   The proclamation, with few exceptions, freed only those slaves still under Confederate control, as cynics noted then and later. But critics missed a point that slaves readily grasped. "In a document proclaiming liberty," wrote a black historian, "the unfree never bother to read the fine print." Word of Lincoln's proclamation spread quickly into slave quarters. One South Carolina ex-slave remembered the scene on his plantation: "Some were sorry, some hurt, but a few were silent and glad." Some actively claimed their freedom. One spectacular instance was that of the black river pilot Robert Smalls, who one night in May 1862 took over a small Confederate gunboat and sailed his family through Charleston harbor out to the blockading Union fleet. Later he served in the Union navy and eventually became a congressman.

BLACKS IN THE MILITARY   Lincoln's Emancipation Proclamation reaffirmed the policy that blacks could enroll in the armed services and sparked efforts to organize new all-black units. By mid-1863 black soldiers were involved in significant combat both in the Eastern and in the Western Theaters. Lincoln reported that several of his commanders believed that "the use of colored troops constitutes the heaviest blow yet dealt to the rebels."

Altogether, between 180,000 and 200,000 black men served in the Union army, providing around 10 percent of its total. Some 38,000 gave their lives. Blacks accounted for about a fourth of all enlistments in the navy, and of these, almost 3,000 died. Black women also served in the war. Harriet Tubman and Susie King, for instance, were nurses along with their white counterpart Clara Barton.

As the war entered its final months, freedom emerged more fully as a legal reality. The Thirteenth Amendment, which abolished slavery, was

Sergeant J.L. Baldwin, 56th U.S. Colored Infantry, one of the few black non-commissioned officers in the Civil War. Born in Mississippi, Baldwin escaped slavery and went north to St. Louis, Missouri, where he enlisted in 1863. He was wounded in action in Arkansas, but returned to active duty.

ratified by three-fourths of the states and became part of the Constitution on December 18, 1865, thus removing any lingering doubts about the legality of emancipation. By then, in fact, slavery remained only in the border states of Kentucky and Delaware.

GOVERNMENT DURING THE WAR

Striking the shackles from 3.5 million slaves was a monumental social and economic revolution. But an even broader revolution developed as political power shifted from South to North after secession. Before the war, southern congressmen had been able to frustrate the designs of both Free Soil and Whiggery. But once the secessionists abandoned Congress to the Republicans, a dramatic change occurred. A new protective tariff, a transcontinental railroad to run through Omaha to Sacramento, a homestead act, which granted free homesteads of 160 acres to settlers who occupied the land for five years—all acts that had been stalled by sectional controversy—were adopted before the end of 1862. That year also saw the passage of the Morrill Land Grant Act, which provided federal aid to state colleges of "agricultural and mechanic arts." The National Banking Act, which created a uniform system of banking and banknote currency, followed in 1863. This last act helped the Union address a critical problem: how to finance the war.

UNION FINANCES   Congress had three options for solving this problem: higher taxes, printing paper money, and borrowing. The higher taxes came chiefly in the form of the Morrill Tariff and excise taxes, which fell on manufacturers and nearly every profession. An income tax rounded out the revenue measures.

But tax revenues trickled in so slowly that Congress in 1862 ordered the printing of paper money. Eventually $450 million in "greenbacks" were printed, enough to pay the bills but not unleash the kind of runaway inflation that burdened the Confederacy after Jefferson Davis allowed the unlimited issue of paper money.

Still, paper money and taxes provided only about two-thirds of the money to finance the war. The rest came chiefly from the sale of bonds. A Philadelphia banker named Jay Cooke mobilized a nationwide network of agents and propaganda for the sale of government war bonds. It worked well, and over $2 billion was raised in the process.

All wars provide new opportunities for quick profits, and the Civil War was no different. Many American entrepreneurs reaped quick riches from war contracts. Several cut corners in the process, providing shoddy goods, paying bribes and kickbacks, or in some cases, not delivering supplies at all. Not all wartime fortunes, however, were made dishonestly. Their long-run importance was in promoting the capital accumulation that fueled the phenomenal postwar expansion of the national economy.

CONFEDERATE FINANCES   Confederate finances were a disaster from the start. Tariffs were tried, but imports were low and therefore raised little revenue. In 1863 the Confederate Congress passed a measure which, like the Union's excises, taxed nearly everything. A 10 percent tax on all agricultural products, however, did more to outrage farmers and planters than to supply the army. Enforcement was so lax and evasion so easy that the taxes produced only negligible income.

The last resort, the printing press, was in fact resorted to early. Beginning in 1861 the new Confederate government began an extended inflationary binge for which the only cure was more of the same. Altogether the Confederacy turned out more than $1 billion in paper money, forcing prices up geometrically. By 1864 a wild turkey sold in a Richmond market for $100, flour went for $425 a barrel, and bacon for $10 a pound. Those living on fixed incomes were caught in a merciless squeeze.

CONFEDERATE DIPLOMACY   Civil wars often mushroom into international conflicts. Confederate diplomacy focused on gaining help from foreign governments in the form of supplies, formal recognition, or perhaps even armed intervention. The Confederates indulged the pathetic hope that diplomatic recognition would prove decisive, when in fact it more likely would have followed decisive victory in the field, which never came.

The first Confederate emissaries to England and France took hope when the British foreign minister received them informally after their arrival in London in 1861. In Paris, Napoleon III even promised them that he would recognize the Confederacy if England would lead the way. But when the agents returned to London, the government refused to see them, partly because of Union pressures and partly out of British self-interest.

Confederate negotiators were far more successful at getting supplies than gaining recognition. The most spectacular feat was the procurement of raiding ships. Although British law prohibited the sale of warships to belligerents, a southern agent contrived to have the ships built and then, on trial runs, to escape and be outfitted with guns. In all, eighteen such ships were activated and saw action in the Atlantic, Pacific, and Indian Oceans, where they sank hundreds of Yankee ships and sparked terror in the rest.

UNION POLITICS AND CIVIL LIBERTIES   On the home fronts during the Civil War there was no moratorium on partisan politics, North or South. Within his own party Lincoln faced a Radical wing composed mainly of prewar abolitionists. Led by House members such as Thaddeus Stevens and George Julian, and senators such as Charles Sumner, Benjamin Wade, and Zachariah Chandler, they formed a Joint Committee on the Conduct of the War, which increasingly pressured Lincoln to emancipate the slaves, confiscate southern plantations, and prosecute the war more vigorously. The majority of Republicans, however, supported the president, and the party was virtually united on economic matters.

The Democratic party suffered the loss of its southern wing as well as the death of its leader, Stephen A. Douglas, in June 1861. By and large, northern Democrats supported a war for the "Union as it was" before 1860, giving reluctant support to war policies but opposing wartime constraints on civil liberties and the new economic legislation. "War Democrats" such as Senator Andrew Johnson from Tennessee and Secretary of War Edwin Stanton fully supported Lincoln's policies, however, while a Peace Wing of the party preferred a negotiated end to the fighting, even at the risk of the Union. An extreme fringe among the Peace Democrats even flirted with outright disloyalty. The "Copperheads," as they were called, organized secret societies, mostly in Ohio, Indiana, and Illinois, states with many transplanted southerners, some of whom were pro-Confederate.

Such open sympathy for the enemy provoked Lincoln to crack down hard. Early in the war he assumed certain emergency powers such as the suspension of the writ of habeas corpus, entitling people who had been jailed to demand that a court hear their case. Lincoln also asserted his right to invoke martial law. When critics charged that this violated the Constitution, Lincoln's congressional supporters pushed through the Habeas Corpus Act of 1863, which authorized the suspension of the writ. Some 14,000 arrests of Confederate sympathizers resulted.

In the midterm elections of 1862, the Democrats exploited growing war weariness and resentment of Lincoln's war measures to gain a startling recovery, though not actual control of Congress. When asked his reaction to the election results, Lincoln replied that he felt somewhat "like the boy in Kentucky who stubbed his toe while running to see his sweetheart. The boy said he was too big to cry, and far too badly hurt to laugh." But the political situation made Lincoln even more perplexed as time passed. At their 1864 national convention the Democrats called for an immediate armistice and named General McClellan as their candidate, but he distanced himself from the peace platform by declaring that the two sides must agree on reunion before the fighting should stop.

Radical Republicans, who still regarded Lincoln as being too soft on the traitorous southerners, tried to thwart his renomination, but Lincoln outmaneuvered them at every turn. In a shrewd move he named as his vice-presidential running mate Andrew Johnson, a War Democrat from Tennessee, and called their ticket the "National Union" so as to minimize partisanship. As the war ground on through 1864, with Grant taking heavy losses in Virginia, Lincoln fully expected to lose the election. But key military victories in August and September turned the tide. McClellan carried only New Jersey, Delaware, and Kentucky.

CONFEDERATE POLITICS   Unlike Lincoln, Jefferson Davis never had to contest a presidential election. Both he and his vice-president, Alexander Stephens, were elected for a six-year term. But discontent flourished in the South as events went from bad to worse. A bread riot in Richmond in 1863, for example, ended only when Davis himself persuaded the mob (mostly women) to disperse. After the congressional elections of 1863, about a third of the Confederacy's legislators were openly hostile toward the administration. Although parties as such did not figure in the elections, it was noteworthy that many ex-Whigs and other opponents of secession were chosen.

Jefferson Davis, president of the Confederacy.

Davis, like Lincoln, had to contend with dissenters. Especially troublesome were those committed to states' rights who had supported secession but steadfastly opposed the centralizing tendencies of the government in Richmond. Georgia and North Carolina were strongholds of such sentiment. They challenged, among other things, the legality of conscription, taxes on farm produce, and above all the suspension of habeas corpus. Vice-President Stephens himself carried on a running battle with Davis, accusing the president of trying to establish a "military despotism."

Such internal bickering did not alone cause the Confederacy's defeat, but certainly contributed to it. Where Lincoln was the consummate pragmatist, Davis was a brittle dogmatist with a waspish temper. His fundamental insecurity made him indecisive. But once he made a decision, nothing could change his mind. Davis could never find it in himself to admit that he had made a mistake. Such a personality was ill suited to the chief executive of an infant nation.

THE FALTERING CONFEDERACY

In 1863 the hinge of fate began to close the door on the brief career of the Confederacy. After the Union disaster at Fredericksburg, Lincoln's frustrating search for a capable general turned to one of Burnside's disgruntled lieutenants, Joseph E. Hooker, a handsome, ruddy-faced, hard-drinking character whose pugnacity had earned him the nickname "Fighting Joe." As he planned a new spring campaign, Hooker brashly announced: "May God have mercy on General Lee, for I will have none." But he was no more able to deliver the goods than Burnside. Hooker failed his test at Chancellorsville in May 1863.

CHANCELLORSVILLE   With a force of perhaps 130,000, the largest Union army yet gathered, and a brilliant plan, Hooker suffered a loss of control, a failure of nerve, at the critical juncture. Lee, with perhaps half that number, staged what became a textbook classic of daring and maneuver. Hooker's plan was to leave his base, opposite Fredericksburg, on a sweeping movement upstream across the Rappahannock and Rapidan, and flank Lee's position. A large diversionary force was to cross the Rappahannock below the town. Initially all went well, but Lee sniffed out the ruse. He moved his main force to meet Hooker and dispatched Stuart's cavalry to disrupt the Union lines of communications. Hooker suddenly lost sight of his opponents and was caught by surprise when rebel skirmishers fired on his advance columns. He then ordered his troops to pull back to the Chancellorsville crossroads. "I just lost faith in Joe Hooker," he later admitted, and Lee quickly took advantage of his opponent's failure of nerve. He divided his army again, sending Jackson with more than half the men on a long march to hit the enemy's exposed right flank.

On May 2, Jackson surprised Hooker's right flank at the edge of a densely wooded area called the Wilderness. The Confederates slammed into the Union lines with such furor that the defenders panicked and ran. The thick undergrowth made troop movements more chaotic than usual, and the fighting died out in confusion as darkness fell. The next day was Lee's, however, as his troops forced Hooker's army to recross the Rappahannock. It was the peak of Lee's career, but Chancellorsville was his last significant victory, and his costliest: the South suffered more than 1,600 killed, among them Stonewall Jackson, mistakenly shot by his own men in the confused fighting. "I have lost my right arm," lamented Lee.

VICKSBURG   While Lee held the Federals at bay in the East, Grant, his command now restored, had been groping his way down the Missis-

GRANT
FROM MEMPHIS

AREA OF MAP

Yazoo R.

×CHICKASAW
× BLUFFS

GRANT   Clinton

Vicksburg
PEMBERTON   Vicksburg   Jackson
siege

LOUISIANA

MISSISSIPPI

Mississippi R.

GRANT

Big Black R.

Pearl R.

VICKSBURG, 1863

Grand Gulf   ← Union forces   ✳ Battle site

0   20 Miles
0   20 Kilometers

Bruinsburg

sippi River toward Vicksburg. Located on a bluff 200 feet above the
river, Vicksburg had withstood naval attacks. For months Grant tried to
discover a way to penetrate the city's heavily fortified defenses. The terrain complicated his task: Vicksburg was surrounded by bayous and
marshes that made travel and resupply almost impossible. In May he finally decided to pin down the 30,000 Confederates in Vicksburg and
wear them down or starve them out.

GETTYSBURG   The plight of besieged Vicksburg put the Confederate
high command in a quandary. Lee proposed a diversion. If he could win
a great victory on northern soil, he reasoned, he might do more than
just relieve the pressure on Vicksburg; he might bring an end to the war.
In June 1863 he moved his forces into the Shenandoah Valley and
headed north across Maryland.

Hooker followed, keeping his forces between Lee and Washington,
D.C. But, demoralized by defeat at Chancellorsville, Hooker resigned
his post and was replaced by Major-General George G. Meade, an aristocratic Philadelphian distinctive for his bravery. Neither side chose
Gettysburg, Pennsylvania, as the site for the climactic battle, but a
Confederate foraging party entered the town in search of shoes and encountered units of Union cavalry. The main forces then quickly converged there.

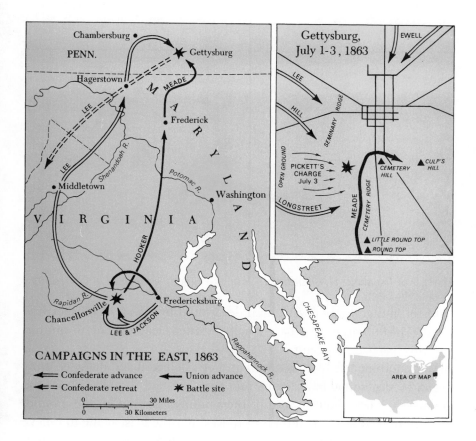

Chamberburg •

PENN.

Gettysburg

MARYLAND

Hagerstown

LEE

MEADE

Frederick

Shenandoah R.

Potomac R.

Middletown

V I R G I N I A

LEE

HOOKER

Washington

Rapidan R.

Chancellorsville

Fredericksburg

LEE & JACKSON

Rappahannock R.

CHESAPEAKE BAY

CAMPAIGNS IN THE EAST, 1863

◄══ Confederate advance   ◄── Union advance
◄═ Confederate retreat   ✳ Battle site

0   30 Miles
0   30 Kilometers

Gettysburg,
July 1-3, 1863

EWELL

LEE

HILL

SEMINARY RIDGE

OPEN GROUND

PICKETT'S
CHARGE
July 3

LONGSTREET

MEADE

CEMETERY RIDGE

▲ CULP'S
   HILL

CEMETERY
HILL

▲ LITTLE ROUND TOP
▲ ROUND TOP

AREA OF MAP ■

On July 1, a hot, steamy day, the Confederates pushed the Federals out of the town, but into stronger positions on high ground to the south. Meade hastened reinforcements to the new lines along the heights. On July 2 Lee, hampered by a lack of information because of the inexcusable absence of Stuart's cavalry, ordered assaults at both the extreme left and the extreme right flanks of Meade's army. The Confederates fought fiercely. Longstreet declared that his corps's assault was "the best three hours' fighting ever done by any troops on any battle-field." But the Federals, who outnumbered their attackers almost two to one, fought just as bravely—and the assaults were repulsed.

The next day Lee staked everything on one final attack on the Union center at Cemetery Ridge. About 2 P.M. Confederate general George E. Pickett's 15,000 troops emerged from the woods west of Cemetery Ridge and began their advance across rising open ground commanded by Union artillery. It was as hopeless and as terribly majestic as Burnside's assault at Fredericksburg. At a distance of 700 yards the Federal artillery homed in on the advancing Virginians. Those who avoided the

Harvest of Death. *T. H. O'Sullivan's grim photograph of the dead at Gettysburg.*

canister and grapeshot were then devastated by a wall of musket fire. Of the 14,000 attackers, barely half returned, leading Lee to mutter: "All this has been my fault."

With nothing left to do but retreat, Lee's dejected and mangled army began to slog south in a driving rain that "washed the blood from the grass." They left about a third of their number behind on the ground. They also had failed in all their purposes, not the least being to relieve the pressure on Vicksburg. On that same day, July 4, the entire Confederate garrison at Vicksburg surrendered. The Confederacy was now irrevocably split. Had Meade aggressively pursued Lee he might have delivered the final blow before the Rebels could get back across the flooded Potomac.

CHATTANOOGA   The third great Union victory of 1863 occurred in fighting around Chattanooga, the railhead of eastern Tennessee and gateway to northern Georgia. On September 9 a Union army led by General William Rosecrans took Chattanooga and then rashly pursued General Braxton Bragg's forces into Georgia, where the two sides clashed at Chickamauga (an old Cherokee word ironically meaning "river of death"). The battle (September 19–20) had the makings of a Union disaster, because it was one of the few times when the Confederates had a numerical advantage (about 70,000 to 56,000). On the second day Bragg smashed the Federal right, and only the stubborn stand on the left under Virginia Unionist George H. Thomas (thenceforth known as the "Rock of Chickamauga") prevented a general rout. The

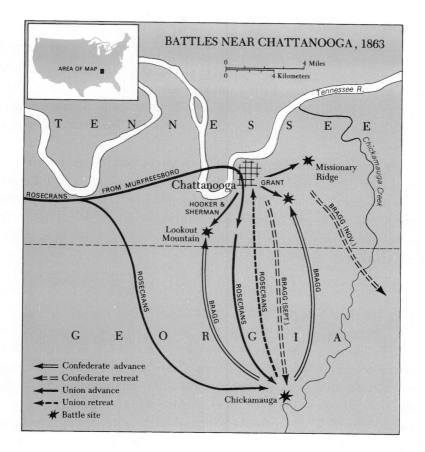

BATTLES NEAR CHATTANOOGA, 1863

AREA OF MAP ■

0 —— 4 Miles
0 —— 4 Kilometers

Tennessee R.

T E N N E S S E E

Chickamauga Creek

Missionary
Ridge

FROM MURFREESBORO

Chattanooga GRANT

ROSECRANS

HOOKER &
SHERMAN

Lookout
Mountain

BRAGG (NOV)

ROSECRANS BRAGG ROSECRANS ROSECRANS BRAGG (SEPT) BRAGG

G E O R G I A

◄══ Confederate advance
◄═ ═ Confederate retreat
◄— Union advance
◄- - - Union retreat
✹ Battle site

Chickamauga

battered Union forces fell back to Chattanooga, while Bragg cut the railroad and held the city virtually under siege.

Rosecrans seemed stunned and immobilized, but Lincoln urged him to hang on: "If we can hold Chattanooga, and East Tennessee, I think rebellion must dwindle and die." The president then dispatched Joe Hooker with reinforcements from Virginia, and Grant and Sherman arrived with more fresh troops from the west. Grant, given overall command of the West on October 16, pushed through the rings of Confederate troops around the city and opened up a supply route in the process. He then replaced Rosecrans with George Thomas. On November 24 the Federals broke out of the city. Hooker's forces took Lookout Mountain in what was mainly a feat of mountaineering. The next day Grant ordered Thomas's troops forward to positions at the foot of Missionary Ridge. But the men did not stop there. Still fuming because the Confederates had jeered them at Chickamauga, they charged toward the crest without orders. One of his aides explained to Grant: "When those fellows get started all hell can't stop them." The attackers could have been decimated, but the Confederates were unable to lower their big guns enough to hit the scrambling Yankees, and, despite Bragg's "cursing like a sailor," his men fled as Thomas's troops reached the summit.

After the Federal victory, as the Union forces consolidated their control of East Tennessee, already full of Unionist sympathizers, Jefferson Davis reluctantly replaced Bragg with Joseph Johnston. Lincoln, on the other hand, had finally found the general he had been searching for in vain for almost three years. In March 1864 Grant was brought to Washington and made general-in-chief.

THE CONFEDERACY'S DEFEAT

The Union's main targets now were Lee's army in Virginia and General Joseph Johnston's in Georgia. Grant personally would accompany Meade, who retained direct command over the Army of the Potomac; operations in the West were entrusted to Grant's longtime lieutenant, William T. Sherman. As Sherman later wrote, Grant "was to go for Lee, and I was to go for Joe Johnston." Grant brought with him a new strategy against Lee. Where his predecessors had all hoped for the climactic single battle, he adopted a war of attrition. He would attack, attack, attack, keeping the pressure on the Confederates, grinding down their numbers and taking away their initiative and will to fight. Victory, he had decided, would come to the side "which never counted its dead." Grant ordered his commanders to wage total war, confiscating or destroying any and all civilian property of military use. It was a brutal, costly, but ultimately effective plan.

GRANT'S PURSUIT OF LEE   In May 1864 the Army of the Potomac, numbering about 115,000 to Lee's 65,000, moved south across the Rappahannock into the Wilderness, where Hooker had earlier come to grief in the Battle of Chancellorsville. In the Battle of the Wilderness (May 5–6), the armies fought blindly through the tangled brush and vines, the horror and agony of the wounded heightened by crackling brush fires. Grant's men suffered heavier casualties than Lee's, but the Confederates were running out of replacements.

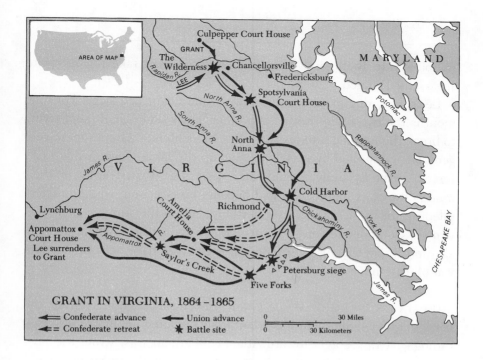

GRANT IN VIRGINIA, 1864–1865

⬅ Confederate advance   ⬅ Union advance
⬅= Confederate retreat   ★ Battle site

Many of the Union officers in the Army of the Potomac whom Grant inherited were in awe of Lee. They feared another decisive counterattack on their flanks. When one of Grant's officers expressed concern about what Lee might do, Grant exploded: "Oh, I am heartily tired of hearing about what Lee is going to do. Some of you always seem to think he is suddenly going to turn a double somersault, and land in our rear and on both flanks at the same time. Go back to your command, and try to think what we are going to do ourselves, instead of what Lee is going to do." Always before, Lee's adversaries had retreated to lick their wounds, but Grant slid off to the left and continued his relentless advance southward, now toward Spotsylvania Court House.

There the armies settled down for five days of carnage, May 8–12. Before it was over, Grant sent word to Lincoln: "I propose to fight it out along this line if it takes all summer." But he soon changed his mind, slid off to his left, and kept moving. Along the Chickahominy, the two sides clashed again at Cold Harbor (June 1–3). In twenty minutes, 7,000 attacking Federals were killed or wounded. Many of them predicted as much. After the failed assault, Confederates retrieved a diary from a dead Massachusetts soldier. The final entry read: "June 3, 1864, Cold Harbor, Virginia. I was killed." Battered and again repulsed, Grant soon had his men moving again, headed for Petersburg, the junction of railroads into Richmond from the south. "I shall take no backward steps," he declared.

Lee's army dug in around the town while Grant laid siege. For nine months the two forces faced each other down while Grant kept trying to break the railroad arteries that were Lee's lifeline. Grant's men were generously supplied by vessels moving up the James River, while Lee's forces, beset by hunger, cold, and desertion, wasted away in their muddy trenches. Petersburg had become Lee's prison, while disasters piled up for the Confederacy elsewhere. "From the summer of 1862," wrote a Confederate veteran, "the war became a war of wholesale devastation. From the spring of 1864, it seemed to have become nearly a war of extermination."

SHERMAN'S MARCH   While Grant was chasing Lee in Virginia, the battle-hardened Sherman was relentlessly pursuing Joe Johnston's army through north Georgia toward Atlanta. Sherman was, wrote the poet Walt Whitman, "a bit of stern open air made up in the image of a man." Tightly strung, profane, and plagued by fits of depression, Sherman was one of the few generals to appreciate the concept of total war. Where Sherman loved a toe-to-toe fight, Johnston preferred retreat and evasion, determined not to risk a single life until the perfect conditions for fighting were obtained.

An impatient President Davis finally exploded at Johnston's retreat and replaced him with the towering, blond-bearded Texan John B. Hood, who did not know the meaning of retreat or evasion. As Lee once noted, he was "all lion, none of the fox." Having had an arm crippled by a ball at Gettysburg and most of one leg shot off at Chickamauga, Hood had to be strapped to his horse. But he remained one of the most tenacious—and impetuous—fighters in the war, and during late July 1864, "the gallant Hood's" army struck three times from his base at Atlanta, each time fighting desperately but meeting a bloody rebuff. Sherman then circled the city and cut off the rail lines, forcing Hood to evacuate on September 1. Sherman's letter to the Atlanta mayor demanding the surrender of the city reflected his military philosophy: "War is cruelty, and you cannot refine it, and those who brought war into our country deserve all the curses and maledictions a people can pour out."

Sherman now resolved to make all of "Georgia howl," as his army embarked on its devastating march southeast through central Georgia.

Hood went in the other direction, cutting through northern Alabama and into Tennessee in the hope of luring Sherman away from the undefended deep South. But Sherman refused to take the bait, although he did dispatch George Thomas with 30,000 men to keep watch on Hood.

They did more than observe, however. In the Battle of Franklin (November 30) Hood sent his army across two miles of open Tennessee ground. Six waves of gray crashed against the Union lines but never broke through. "It is impossible to exaggerate the fierce energy with which the Confederate soldiers . . . threw themselves against the works," recalled a Union colonel. They fought "with what seemed the very madness of despair." A Confederate soldier described the ghastly scene: "We looked over the battlefield, O, my God! What did we see! It was the grand holocaust of death. . . . The dead were piled the one on the other all over the ground. I never was so horrified and appalled in my life." One dead general had been hit by forty-nine bullets. A month later, on December 27, Hood suffered another devastating defeat at Nashville that effectively ended Confederate activity in Tennessee.

During all this, Sherman and the main Union force were marching triumphantly through Georgia, pioneering the modern practice of total war against the enemy's resources and will to resist. "War is war," Sherman bluntly declared, "not a popularity contest." On November 15, 1864, his men burned much of Atlanta and then spread out over a front twenty to sixty miles wide and headed south, living off the land and destroying any crops, livestock, or supplies that might serve Confederate forces. Bands of stragglers and deserters from both armies joined in looting along the flanks.

When, after a month, Sherman's army approached Savannah, they had cut a swath of desolation 250 miles long. Sherman's purpose was clear. He would keep the pressure on "until they are not only ruined, exhausted, but humbled in pride and spirit." Too often, however, his foraging men displayed a wanton brutality that shocked even those they were ostensibly liberating. A Georgia slave reported that he saw Union soldiers "cut the hams off a live pig or ox and go off leavin' the animal groanin'."

On December 21 Sherman rode into Savannah, and three days later he offered the city as a Christmas gift to Lincoln. But Sherman paused only long enough to resupply his forces, who then moved on across the river into that "hell-hole of secession," South Carolina. There his men wrought even greater destruction. More than a dozen towns were torched, including the state capital of Columbia, captured on February 17, 1865. That same day the Confederates defending Charleston abandoned the city and pulled north to join an army Joe Johnston was desperately trying to form.

APPOMATTOX   During this final season of the Confederacy, Grant kept pushing, probing, and battering the Petersburg defenses. News of Sherman's devastating sweep through Dixie only added to the Confederacy's gloom and the impulse to desert. Under siege for almost ten months, their lines around Petersburg were becoming woefully thin, and Lee decided to sneak away and try to join Johnston's forces in North Carolina. In Richmond President Davis, exhausted but still defiant, gathered what papers and treasure he could carry and escaped by train, only to be captured in Georgia on May 10 by Union cavalry.

By then the Confederacy was already dead. Lee pulled his shrunken army out of the trenches around Petersburg with Grant's men in hot pursuit, but he soon found his escape route cut by General Philip Sheridan's cavalry. Although his men shouted their willingness to keep fighting, Lee decided it was senseless to waste any more lives. On April 9 (Palm Sunday), 1865, he donned a crisp dress uniform and met the mud-spattered Grant in the parlor of the McLean home at Appomattox to tender his surrender. Grant, at Lee's request, let the Confederate officers keep their sidearms and permitted soldiers to keep their own horses and mules. Three days later the Confederate troops formed ranks for the last time as they prepared for the formal surrender. Deeply moved by the sight of such solemn splendor, Joshua Chamberlain, the Union general in charge, ordered his men to salute their foes as they paraded past. His Confederate counterpart signaled his troops to do likewise. General Chamberlain remembered that there was not a sound—no trumpets or drums, no cheers or jeers, simply "an awed stillness . . . as if it were the passing of the dead." On April 18 Johnston surrendered his forces to Sherman near Durham, North Carolina.

The debate over why the North won and the South lost the Civil War will probably never end, but Lee's own explanation of the Confederate defeat retains an enduring legitimacy: "After four years of arduous service marked by unsurpassed courage and fortitude, the Army of North-

Robert E. Lee. *Mathew Brady took this photograph in Richmond eleven days after Lee's surrender at Appomattox.*

ern Virginia has been compelled to yield to overwhelming numbers and resources."

BITTERSWEET VICTORY   In Charleston the first occupation troops to arrive in February 1865 were black units, several of whose members had been slaves in the city in 1860. On April 14, 1865, the War Department staged a massive victory celebration at Fort Sumter on the fourth anniversary of its fall. At noon Major Anderson ran up the flag he had lowered previously, while gaily decorated ships and all the forts in the harbor sounded a salute.

The same day President Lincoln spent the afternoon discussing postwar policy with his cabinet. That night he and his wife went to Ford's Theater.

530 · The War of the Union

MAKING CONNECTIONS

- Certain economic and fiscal measures enacted during the Civil War (when southerners were not in Congress to block them) helped fuel the postwar economic growth described in Chapter 19.

- The Confederacy's defeat had a tremendous impact on all dimensions of life in the South, as Chapter 18 (on the New South) demonstrates.

FURTHER READING

The best one-volume overview of the Civil War period is James M. McPherson's *Battle Cry of Freedom: The Civil War Era* (1988).* For emphasis on the South, turn first to Emory M. Thomas's *The Confederate Nation, 1861–1865* (1979). For a sparkling account of the birth of the Rebel nation, see William C. Davis's *"A Government of Our Own": The Making of the Confederacy* (1994).

Recent scholarship on the military conflict includes Steven E. Wordsworth's *Jefferson Davis and His Generals: The Failure of Confederate Command in the West* (1991) and Paul D. Casdorph's *Lee and Jackson: Confederate Chieftains* (1992).

The history of the North is surveyed in Philip S. Paludan's *"A People's Contest": The Union at War, 1861–1865* (1988). The central political figure, Abraham Lincoln, is the subject of Stephen B. Oates's *With Malice toward None* (1977).*

Concerning specific military campaigns, see Stephen W. Sears's *Landscape Turned Red: The Battle of Antietam* (1983) and *To the Gates of Richmond* (1993), James Lee McDonough and James Pickett Jones's *War So Terrible: Sherman and Atlanta* (1992), Robert Garth Scott's *Into*

---

*These books are available in paperback editions.

The Wilderness with the Army of The Potomac (1985), and Albert Castel's *Decision in The West: The Atlanta Campaign of 1864* (1992).

The career of the black soldier is found in Joseph T. Glatthaar's *Forged in Battle: The Civil War Alliance of Black Soldiers and White Officers* (1989).*

For the black woman's experience, see Jacqueline Jones's *Labor of Love, Labor of Sorrow: Black Women, Work and the Family from Slavery to Present* (1985).*

Recent gender and ethnic studies include *Divided Houses: Gender and The Civil War,* edited by Catherine Clinton and Nina Silber (1992), George C. Rable's *Civil Wars: Women and the Crises of Southern Nationalism* (1989), and William L. Burton's *Melting Pot Soldiers: The Union's Ethnic Regiments* (1988).

*These books are available in paperback editions.

17 ✑ RECONSTRUCTION: NORTH AND SOUTH

CHAPTER ORGANIZER

This chapter focuses on:

- the different approaches to Reconstruction

- congressional efforts to reshape southern society

- the role of African Americans in the early postwar years

- national politics in the 1870s

THE BATTLE OVER RECONSTRUCTION

In the spring of 1865 the wearying war was over. At the frightful cost of 620,000 lives and the destruction of the southern economy and much of its landscape, American nationalism emerged triumphant, and some 4 million slaves emerged free. But peace had come only on the battlefields. "Cannon conquer," recognized a northern editor, "but they do not necessarily convert." Now the North faced the imposing task of "reconstructing" a ravaged and resentful South. A few northerners thought the task relatively simple. The poet and professor James Russell Lowell wrote a friend in April 1865: "I worry a little about reconstruction, but am inclined to think that matters will very much settle themselves."

He was wrong. A tangle of difficult issues confronted northern politicians. Should the Confederate leaders be tried for treason? How were new governments to be formed? How and at whose expense was the South's economy to be rebuilt? What was to be done with the freed slaves? Were they to be given land? social equality? education? voting rights? Such complex questions required careful planning, but policy makers did not have the luxury of time or the benefits of consensus.

FORCED DOMESTICITY   The defeat of the Confederacy transformed much of southern society. The freeing of slaves, the destruction of property, and the free-fall in land values left many among the former planter elite destitute and homeless. Amanda Worthington, a plantation mistress from Mississippi, saw her whole world destroyed. In the fall of 1865, she assessed the damage: "None of us can realize that we are no longer wealthy—yet thanks to the yankees, the cause of all unhappiness, such is the case. As long as I thought we would conquer in our just cause, I cared nothing for the loss of property for I felt as if we would be rich if we had *Our Rights & Our Country* left us—but now they are lost too, & *we have* suffered *in vain. In vain!* There is where the bitterness lies!"

Genteel southerners now found themselves forced to rebuild lives and families without the help of slaves. Women accustomed to relying on slaves for their every need were unprepared for the tasks at hand. Those who still had some money after the war often recruited former slaves to work as domestic servants. Now, however, they had to pay for the services. "It seems humiliating to be compelled to bargain and haggle with our servants about wages," wrote one exasperated woman.

BITTER IN DEFEAT   After the Civil War many former Confederates were so embittered by defeat and so resistant to the idea of living under northern rule that they abandoned their native region rather than submit to "Yankee rule." Some migrated to Canada, Europe, Mexico, South America, and Asia. Others preferred the western territories and states. Still others moved north, settling in northern and midwestern cities on the assumption that their educational and economic opportunities would be better among the victors.

Most of those who chose to remain in the South returned to find their farms and homes and communities transformed. One Confederate army captain reported that on his father's plantation "Our negroes are living in great comfort. They were delighted to see me with overflowing affection. They waited on me as before, gave me breakfast, splendid dinners, etc. But they firmly and respectfully informed me: 'We own this land now. Put it out of your head that it will ever be yours again.'"

As Union troops fanned out across the defeated South, it was readily apparent that many former Confederates resented and resisted their presence. People cursed and spat upon the troops as they marched into town. Acts of sabotage kept the federal forces on the alert. Fervent southern nationalists, both men and women, planted in their children a similar hatred of Yankees and a defiance of northern rule. One mother said that she trained her children to "fear God, love the South, and live to avenge her."

LINCOLN'S PLAN AND CONGRESS'S RESPONSE   The problem of reconstruction arose early in the Civil War, as Union forces advanced into the South and were forced to create new local governments. Lincoln in 1862 named military governors for Tennessee, Arkansas, and Louisiana, and by the end of the following year he had formulated a plan for regular civilian governments in those states and any others that might be liberated from the Confederacy.

Acting under his pardon power, President Lincoln issued in 1863 a Proclamation of Amnesty and Reconstruction, under which any Rebel state could form a Union government whenever a number equal to 10 percent of those who had voted in 1860 took an oath of allegiance to the Constitution and Union and received a presidential pardon. Participants also had to swear support for laws and proclamations dealing with emancipation. Excluded from the pardon, however, were certain groups: civil, diplomatic, and high military officers of the Confederacy; judges, congressmen, and military officers of the United States who had left their posts to aid the rebellion; and those accused of failure to treat captured black soldiers and their officers as prisoners of war.

Under this plan loyal governments appeared in Tennessee, Arkansas, and Louisiana, but Congress refused to recognize them. In the absence of any specific provisions for reconstruction in the Constitution, politicians disagreed as to where authority properly rested. Lincoln claimed the right to direct reconstruction under the presidential pardon power, and also under the Constitutional obligation to guarantee each state a republican form of government.

A few conservative and most moderate Republicans supported Lincoln's program of immediate restoration. A small but influential group known as Radical Republicans, however, desired to see a sweeping transformation of southern society that would include making the freedmen full-fledged citizens. The Radicals hoped to reconstruct southern society so as to mirror the North's emphasis on small-scale competitive capitalism. This meant thwarting the efforts of the old planter class to reestablish a caste system and keep the freed blacks in a state of peonage.

The Radicals were talented, earnest men who maintained that Congress, not the president, should supervise the reconstruction program. To this end they helped pass in 1864 the Wade-Davis Bill, sponsored by Senator Benjamin Wade of Ohio and Representative Winter Davis of Maryland. In contrast to Lincoln's 10 percent plan, the Wade-Davis Bill required that a majority of white male citizens declare their allegiance and that only those who swore an "ironclad" oath that they had always remained loyal to the Union could vote or serve in the state constitutional conventions. The conventions, moreover, would have to abolish slavery, deny political rights to high-ranking civil and military officers of the Confederacy, and repudiate Confederate war debts. Passed during the closing days of the 1864 session, the bill went unsigned by Lincoln, and this "pocket veto" provoked the bill's sponsors to issue the Wade-Davis Manifesto, a blistering statement that accused the president of usurping power and attempting to use readmitted states to ensure his reelection.

By early 1865 Lincoln and the Radical Republicans were embroiled in an increasingly heated debate about the direction of reconstruction policy. A few Radicals argued that what the freed blacks needed most was land. But the several proposals for land confiscation and distribution never materialized. Even most dedicated abolitionists shrank from the measures of land reform that might have given the freed slaves more self-support and independence. Citizenship and legal rights were one thing, wholesale confiscation quite another. Instead of land or material help the freedmen more often received age-old advice: work hard and lead sober, honest, and frugal lives. Frederick Douglass, the black abolitionist, suggested that after the war the former slave was left "free from the individual master but a slave of society. He had neither money, property, nor friends. He was free from the old plantation, but he had nothing but the dusty road under his feet. . . . He was turned loose, naked, hungry, and destitute to the open sky." According to a former Confederate general, recently freed blacks had "nothing but freedom."

In March 1865 Congress did establish within the War Department the Bureau of Refugees, Freedmen, and Abandoned Lands, to provide "such issues of provisions, clothing, and fuel" as might be needed to relieve "destitute and suffering refugees and freedmen and their wives and children." The Freedmen's Bureau would also take over abandoned and confiscated land for rental in forty-acre tracts to "loyal refugees and freedmen," who might buy the land at a fair price within three years. But such lands were limited, and by the end of 1865 all confiscated lands were returned to the original owners. Bureau agents were also entrusted with negotiating labor contracts (something new for both freed slaves and planters), providing medical care, and setting up schools. White intransigence and the failure of the bureau to grasp the intensity of white racial prejudice increasingly thwarted the efforts of the Freedmen's Bureau to protect and assist the former slaves.

And Congress was not willing to strengthen the powers of the bureau to deal with such problems. Beyond such temporary measures of relief, no program of reconstruction ever incorporated much more than basic constitutional and legal rights for freedmen. These were important in themselves, of course, but their scope was uncertain, to be settled more by the course of events than by any clear-cut commitment to equality.

Lincoln issued his final statement on reconstruction in his last public address, on April 11, 1865. Speaking from the White House balcony, he dismissed the theoretical question of whether the Confederate states had technically remained in the Union as "good for nothing at all—a mere pernicious abstraction." These states were simply "out of their proper practical relation with the Union," and the object was to get them "into their proper practical relation" as quickly as possible. At a cabinet meeting Lincoln proposed to get state governments in operation before Congress met in December. He worried that Congress might push through a harsher reconstruction program. Lincoln wanted "no persecution, no bloody work," no dramatic restructuring of southern social and economic life.

That evening Lincoln went to Ford's Theater and his rendezvous with death. Shot in the head by John Wilkes Booth, a crazed actor and Confederate zealot, the president died the next morning. Pursued into Virginia, Booth was trapped and shot in a burning barn. His last words were: "Tell mother I die for my country. I thought I did for the best." Three collaborators were tried and hanged, along with Mrs. Mary Surratt, at whose boardinghouse they had plotted. Three others received life sentences, including a Maryland doctor who set the leg Booth had broken when he jumped from Lincoln's box onto the stage. The doctor achieved lasting fame by making common a once obscure expression. His name was Mudd.

JOHNSON'S PLAN   Lincoln's death suddenly elevated to the White House Andrew Johnson of Tennessee, a man whose state remained in legal limbo and whose party affiliation was unclear. He was a War Democrat who had been put on the Union ticket in 1864 as a gesture of unity. Of humble origins like Lincoln, Johnson had moved as a youth from his birthplace in Raleigh, North Carolina, to Greenville, Tennessee, where he became proprietor of a tailor shop. Self-educated with the help of his wife, he had made himself into an effective, salty orator, and he won election as mayor, congressman, governor, and senator, then as military governor of Tennessee before he became vice-president. In the process Johnson had become an advocate of the small farmers against the large planters. He also shared the racial attitudes of most white yeomen. "Damn the negroes," he exclaimed to a friend during the war, "I am fighting those traitorous aristocrats, their masters."

Some of the Radicals at first thought Johnson, unlike Lincoln, to be one of them. Johnson had, for example, asserted that treason "must be made infamous and traitors must be impoverished." Ben Wade loved such harsh talk. "Johnson, we have faith in you," he pledged. "By the gods, there will be no trouble now in running this government." But Wade would soon find him as untrustworthy as Lincoln, if for different reasons. Johnson's very loyalty to the Union sprang from a strict adherence to the Constitution. Given to dogmatic abstractions that were alien to Lincoln's temperament, he nevertheless arrived by a different route at similar objectives. The states should be brought back into their proper relation to the Union, not by ignoring as a pernicious abstraction the theoretical question of their status, but because the states and the

Union were indestructible. By May 1865 he was arguing that "there is no such thing as reconstruction. Those states have not gone out of the Union. Therefore reconstruction is unnecessary."

Johnson's plan to restore the Union thus closely resembled Lincoln's. A new Proclamation of Amnesty (May 29, 1865) added to the list of those Lincoln had excluded from pardon everybody with taxable property worth more than $20,000. These wealthy planters and merchants were the people Johnson believed had led the South into secession. But those in the excluded groups might make special applications for presidential pardon, and before the year was out Johnson had issued some 13,000 such pardons.

In each of the Rebel states not already organized by Lincoln, Johnson named a native Unionist provisional governor with authority to call a convention elected by loyal voters. Lincoln's 10 percent requirement was omitted. Johnson called upon the conventions to invalidate the secession ordinances, abolish slavery, and repudiate all debts incurred to aid the Confederacy. Each state, moreover, was to ratify the Thirteenth Amendment, which ended slavery. Like Lincoln, Johnson endorsed a limited black suffrage. He reminded the provisional governor of Mississippi, for example, that the state conventions might "with perfect safety" extend suffrage to those blacks with education or with military service so as to "disarm the adversary"—the adversary being "radicals who are wild upon Negro franchise."

The state conventions for the most part met Johnson's requirements. But a northern visitor found in the South "an utter absence of national feeling . . . and a desire to preserve slavery . . . as much and as long as possible." Southern whites accepted the situation because they thought so little had changed after all. Emboldened by Johnson's indulgence, they ignored his advice to move cautiously in restoring their political and social traditions. Suggestions of black suffrage were scarcely raised in the conventions, and promptly squelched when they were.

SOUTHERN INTRANSIGENCE   When Congress met in December 1865, for the first time since the end of the war, it had only to recognize the new state governments functioning in the South. But there was the rub: the "new" governments were remarkably like the old. Among the new members presenting themselves to Congress were Georgia's Alexander H. Stephens, late vice-president of the Confederacy, four

Confederate generals, eight colonels, six cabinet members, and a host of lesser Rebels. The Congress forthwith denied seats to all members from the eleven former Confederate states. It was too much to expect, after four bloody years, that Unionists would welcome ex-Confederates back like prodigal sons.

Furthermore, the new southern legislatures, in passing repressive Black Codes regulating the freedom of blacks, baldly revealed that they intended to preserve the trappings of slavery as nearly as possible. As one southerner stressed, the "ex-slave was not a free man; he was a free Negro," and the Black Codes were intended to highlight the distinction. They extended to blacks certain new rights, but also insisted that the freed slaves be set aside as a separate caste subject to special restraints.

The details of the Black Codes varied from state to state, but some provisions were common. Existing black marriages, including common-law marriages, were recognized, and testimony of blacks was accepted in legal cases involving them—in six states in all cases. Blacks could hold property. They could sue and be sued in the courts. On the other hand, blacks in Mississippi could not own farm lands, and in South Carolina they could not own city lots. Blacks were required to enter into annual labor contracts, with provision for punishment in case of

According to a former Confederate general, recently freed blacks had "nothing but freedom."

violation. Dependent children were subject to compulsory apprentice-ship and corporal punishment by masters. Vagrant blacks were pun-ished with severe fines and could be sold into private service if unable to pay. To many people it indeed seemed that slavery was on the way back in another guise.

THE RADICALS   Faced with such evidence of southern intransigence, moderate Republicans drifted more and more toward the Radical camp. Having excluded southern members, the new Congress set up a Joint Committee on Reconstruction, with nine members from the House and six from the Senate, to gather evidence and submit proposals. As a parade of witnesses testified to the Rebels' impenitence, initiative on the com-mittee fell to determined Radicals: Benjamin Wade of Ohio, George W. Julian of Indiana, Henry Wilson of Massachusetts—and most conspic-uously of all, Thaddeus Stevens of Pennsylvania and Charles Sumner of Massachusetts. Stevens, a crusty old bachelor with a chiseled face, thin, stern lips, and brooding eyes, was the domineering floor leader in the House. Driven by a genuine, if at times fanatical, idealism, he angrily insisted that the "whole fabric of southern society *must* be changed."

Sumner, Stevens's counterpart in the Senate, agreed. Now recovered from "Bully" Brooks's 1856 assault, Sumner strove to see the South *reconstructed* rather than simply restored. This put him at odds with Johnson. After visiting the White House, Sumner found the president "harsh, petulant, and unreasonable." He was especially disheartened by Johnson's "prejudice, ignorance, and perversity" regarding the treatment of blacks. Sumner and other Radicals now grew determined to take matters into their own hands. He argued that "Massachusetts could govern Georgia better than Georgia could govern herself." The southern plantations, seedbeds of aristocratic pretension and secession, he later added, "must be broken up, and the freedmen must have the pieces."

Most of these Radical Republicans had long been connected with the antislavery cause, and they approached the question of black rights with a sincere humanitarian impulse. Few, however, could escape the bitterness bred by the long and bloody war or remain unaware of the partisan advantage that would come to the Republican party from "Ne-gro suffrage." But they reasoned that their party, after all, could best guarantee the fruits of victory and that granting suffrage could best guarantee black rights. Stevens reflected the mixed motives of the Radicals when he proclaimed: "I am for negro suffrage in every rebel state. If it be just, it should not be denied; if it be necessary, it should be adopted; if it be a punishment to traitors, they deserve it."

The growing conflict of opinion over reconstruction policy brought about an inversion in constitutional reasoning. Secessionists—and Johnson—were now arguing that their states had in fact remained in the Union, and some Radicals were contriving arguments that they had left the Union after all. Stevens argued that the Confederate states had indeed seceded and were now conquered provinces, subject to the absolute will of the victors. Sumner maintained that the southern states, by their acts of secession, had in effect committed suicide and reverted to the status of unorganized territories subject to the will of Congress. But most congressmen embraced the "forfeited rights theory," which held that the states continued to exist, but by the acts of secession and war had forfeited "all civil and political rights under the Constitution." And Congress was the proper authority to determine conditions under which such rights might be restored.

JOHNSON'S BATTLE WITH CONGRESS   A long year of political battling remained, however, before this idea triumphed. By the end of 1865, Radical views had gained only a slight majority in Congress, insufficient to override presidential vetoes. But the critical year 1866 saw the gradual waning of Johnson's power and influence, much of this self-induced. Johnson first challenged Congress in February, when he vetoed a bill to extend the life of the Freedmen's Bureau. For the moment Johnson's prestige remained sufficiently intact that the Senate upheld his veto.

Three days after the veto, however, Johnson undermined his already weakening prestige by launching an intemperate assault on Radical leaders during an impromptu speech on Washington's Birthday. From that point forward, moderate Republicans backed away from the president, and Radical Republicans went on the offensive. Johnson was now "an alien enemy of a foreign state," Stevens declared.

In mid-March 1866, Congress passed the Civil Rights Act. A direct response to the Black Codes, this bill declared that "all persons born in the United States . . . excluding Indians not taxed," were citizens entitled to "full and equal benefit of all laws." The grant of citizenship to native-born blacks, Johnson claimed, went beyond anything formerly held to be within the scope of federal power. It would, moreover, "foment discord among the races." He vetoed the measure, but this time, in April 1866, Congress overrode the presidential veto. Then in July it enacted a revised Freedmen's Bureau Bill, again overturning a veto. From that point on Johnson's support steadily eroded.

THE FOURTEENTH AMENDMENT   To remove all doubt about the validity of the new Civil Rights Act, the Joint Committee recommended a new constitutional amendment, which passed Congress in 1866 and was ratified in 1868. The Fourteenth Amendment, however, went far beyond the Civil Rights Act, and it would have significant and unforeseen effects long thereafter. The first section asserted four principles: it reaffirmed state and federal citizenship for all persons—regardless of race—born or naturalized in the United States, and it forbade any state (the word "state" was important in later litigation) to abridge the "privileges and immunities" of citizens; to deprive any person (again an important term) of life, liberty, or property without "due process of law"; or to deny any person "the equal protection of the laws." The amendment also voided all Confederate debts.

The last three of these clauses have been the subject of long and involved lawsuits resulting in applications not foreseen at the time. The "due-process clause" has come to mean that state as well as federal power is subject to the Bill of Rights, and it has been used to protect corporations, as legal "persons," from "unreasonable" regulation by the states. Other provisions of the amendment had less far-reaching effects. One section specified that the debt of the United States "shall not be questioned," but declared "illegal and void" all debts contracted in aid of the rebellion. Another section specified the power of Congress to pass laws enforcing the amendment.

Johnson's home state was among the first to ratify the Fourteenth Amendment. In Tennessee, which had harbored probably more Unionists than any other Confederate state, the government had fallen under Radical control. But the rest of the South steadfastly resisted the Radical challenge to Johnson's program. In 1866 bloody race riots in Memphis and New Orleans added fuel to the flames. Both incidents sparked indiscriminate massacres of blacks by local police and white mobs. The rioting, Radicals argued, was the natural fruit of Johnson's policy.

RECONSTRUCTING THE SOUTH

THE TRIUMPH OF CONGRESSIONAL RECONSTRUCTION As 1866 drew to an end, the upcoming congressional elections promised to be a referendum on the growing split between Johnson and the Radicals. Johnson embarked on a speaking tour of the Midwest, a "swing around the circle," which provoked undignified shouting contests between the president and his audiences. Subjected to attacks on his integrity, Johnson responded in kind. In Cleveland he described the Radicals as "factious, domineering, tyrannical" men. Once, while Johnson was speaking from an observation car, the engineer mistakenly pulled the train out of the station, making the president appear quite the fool. Such incidents tended to confirm his image as a "ludicrous boor," which Radical papers eagerly projected. When the election returns came in, the Republicans had well over a two-thirds majority in each house, a comfortable margin with which to override any presidential vetoes.

The Congress actually enacted a new program even before new members took office. On March 2, 1867, two days before the old Congress expired, it passed three basic laws of congressional reconstruction over Johnson's vetoes: the Military Reconstruction Act, the Command of the Army Act, and the Tenure of Office Act.

This cartoon appeared at the time of the 1866 congressional elections. It shows "King Andy I" approving the execution of Radical leaders in Congress.

The first of the three acts prescribed conditions under which new southern state governments should be formed. The other two sought to block obstruction by the president. The Army Act required that all orders from the president, as commander-in-chief, go through the headquarters of the general of the army, then Ulysses S. Grant. The Radicals trusted Grant, who was already leaning their way. The Tenure of Office Act required the consent of the Senate for the president to remove any officeholder whose appointment the Senate had to confirm in the first place. In large measure it was intended to retain Secretary of War Edwin M. Stanton, the one Radical sympathizer in Johnson's cabinet. The Military Reconstruction Act, often hailed or denounced as the triumphant victory of "Radical" Reconstruction, actually fell short of a thoroughgoing transformation. Diluted by moderate Republicans, the Military Reconstruction Act boiled down to little more than a requirement that southern states accept black suffrage and ratify the Fourteenth Amendment.

Tennessee, which had already ratified the Fourteenth Amendment, was exempted from the application of the act. The other ten southern states were divided into five military districts, and the commanding officer of each was authorized to keep order and protect the "rights of persons and property." The Johnson governments remained intact for the time being, but new constitutions were to be framed "in conformity with the Constitution of the United States," in conventions elected by male citizens twenty-one and older "of whatever race, color, or previous condition." Each state constitution had to provide the same universal male suffrage. Then, once the constitution was ratified by a majority of voters and accepted by Congress, and once the state legislature had ratified the Fourteenth Amendment, and once the amendment became part of the Constitution, any given state would be entitled to representation in Congress. Persons excluded from officeholding by the proposed amendment were also excluded from participation in the process. Before the end of 1867 new elections had been held in all the states but Texas.

Having clipped the president's wings, the Republican Congress moved a year later to safeguard its program from possible interference by the Supreme Court. On March 27, 1868, Congress simply removed the power of the Supreme Court to review cases arising under the Military Reconstruction Act, which Congress clearly had the constitutional right to do under its power to define the Court's appellate jurisdiction. The Court accepted this curtailment of its authority on the same day it affirmed the notion of an "indestructible Union" in *Texas v. White* (1868). In that case it also acknowledged the right of Congress to reframe state governments, thus endorsing the Radical point of view.

THE IMPEACHMENT AND TRIAL OF JOHNSON (1868)   Congress's move to restrain the Supreme Court preceded by just two days the trial of the president in the Senate on an impeachment brought in by the House. Johnson, though hostile to the congressional program, had gone through the motions required of him. He continued, however, to pardon former Confederates in wholesale lots and transferred several of the district military commanders who had displayed Radical sympathies. Nevertheless a lengthy investigation by the House Judiciary Committee, extending through most of the year 1867, failed to convince the House that grounds for impeachment existed.

Johnson himself provided the occasion for impeachment when he deliberately violated the Tenure of Office Act in order to test its constitutionality. Secretary of War Stanton had become a thorn in the president's side, refusing to resign despite his disagreements with Johnson's reconstruction policy. On August 12, 1867, during a congressional recess, Johnson suspended Stanton and named General Grant in his place. When the Senate refused to confirm Johnson's action, however, Grant returned the office to Stanton. On February 24, 1868, the House voted impeachment.

Of the eleven articles of impeachment, eight focused on the charge that Johnson had unlawfully removed Stanton and had failed to give the Senate the name of a successor. Article 9 accused the president of issuing orders in violation of the Army Act. The last two articles in effect charged him with criticizing Congress by "inflammatory and scandalous harangues." Article 11 also accused Johnson of "unlawfully devising and contriving" to violate the Reconstruction Acts, contrary to his obligation to execute the laws. At the very least, it stated, Johnson had tried to obstruct Congress's will while observing the letter of the law.

The Senate trial opened on March 5, 1868, and continued until May 26, with Chief Justice Salmon P. Chase presiding. On May 16 enough Republican senators joined their pro-Johnson colleagues to prevent conviction by the narrowest of margins—one vote. These Republicans had broken ranks with their party largely because they feared the consequences of removing a president essentially for political rather than criminal reasons, and they opposed the economic and social agenda of the Radicals. Impeachment of Johnson was in the end a great political mistake, for the failure to remove the president damaged Radical morale and support. Nevertheless, the Radical cause did gain something. To blunt the opposition, Johnson agreed not to obstruct the process of Reconstruction, and thereafter Radical Reconstruction began in earnest.

REPUBLICAN RULE IN THE SOUTH   In June 1868 Congress agreed that seven states had met the conditions for readmission, all but Virginia, Mississippi, and Texas. Congress rescinded Georgia's admission, however, when the state legislature expelled twenty-eight black members and seated some former Confederate leaders. The military commander of Georgia then forced the legislature to reseat the black members and remove the Confederates, and the state was compelled to ratify the Fifteenth Amendment before being admitted in July 1870. Mississippi, Texas, and Virginia had returned earlier in 1870, under the added requirement that they too ratify the Fifteenth Amendment. This amendment, ratified in 1870, forbade the states to deny any citizen the vote on grounds of race, color, or previous condition of servitude.

Long before the new governments were established, partisan Republican groups began to spring up in the South, promoted by the Union League, an organization founded in 1862 to rally support for the Union. League representatives enrolled blacks and loyal whites as members, initiated them into the secrets and rituals of the order, and instructed them "in their rights and duties." These Union Leagues became a powerful source of Republican political strength in the South and as a result drew the ire of unreconstructed whites.

BLACKS IN THE RECONSTRUCTED SOUTH

To focus solely on what white Republicans did to reconstruct the defeated South creates the false impression that the freed slaves were simply pawns in the hands of others. Such a stereotype appeared early. "The Negroes are to be pitied," wrote South Carolinian Julius J. Fleming, a white teacher, minister, and public official. "They do not understand the liberty which has been conferred upon them."

In fact, however, southern blacks were active agents in affecting the course of Reconstruction. Although many of them found themselves liberated but destitute after the fighting ended, the mere promise of freedom raised their hopes about achieving a biracial democracy, equal justice, and economic opportunity. "Most anyone ought to know that a man is better off free than as a slave, even if he did not have anything," said the Reverend E. P. Holmes, a black Georgia preacher and former domestic servant. "I would rather be free and have my liberty."

Participation in the Union army or navy gave many freedmen a training ground in leadership. Black military veterans would form the core of the first generation of African-American political leaders in the postwar South. Military service provided many former slaves the first opportunities to learn to read and write. "A large portion of the regiment have been going to school during the winter months," wrote a black sergeant from Virginia in 1865. Army life also alerted them to alternative social choices and to new opportunities for advancement and respectability. "No negro who has ever been a soldier," reported a northern official after visiting a black unit, "can again be imposed upon; they have learnt what it is to be free and they will infuse their feelings into others." Fighting for the Union cause also instilled a fervent sense of nationalism. "We are Americans," announced a gathering of Virginia blacks, "we know no other country, we love the land of our birth." Another Virginia freedman explained that the United States was "now *our* country—made emphatically so by the blood of our brethren."

The pent-up desire among former slaves for freedom from white control led them to establish independent black churches after the war, churches that would serve as the foundation of African-American community life. In war-ravaged Charleston, South Carolina, the first new building to appear after the war was a black church on Calhoun Street; by 1866 ten more had been built. Blacks preferred Baptist churches over other denominations, in part because of their decentralized structure that allowed each congregation to worship in its own way. By 1890 there were over 1.3 million black Baptists in the South, nearly three times as many as any other black denomination. For many former slaves, churches were the first institutions they owned and controlled. In addition to forming viable new congregations, freed blacks organized thousands of fraternal, benevolent, and mutual-aid societies, clubs, lodges, and associations. Memphis, for example, had over two hundred such organizations; Richmond boasted twice that number.

The freed slaves, both women and men, also hastened to reestablish and reaffirm families. Marriages that had been prohibited were now legitimized through the assistance of the Freedmen's Bureau. By 1870 a preponderant majority of former slaves lived in two-parent households. One white editor in Georgia, lamenting the difficulty of finding black women to serve as house servants, reported that "every negro woman wants to set up house keeping" for herself and her family. To do so they often chose to be sharecropping farmers. With little money or technical training, freed slaves faced the prospect of becoming wage laborers. Yet in order to retain as much autonomy over their productive energies and those of their children on both a daily and seasonal basis, many husbands and wives chose sharecropping. This enabled mothers and wives to devote more of their time to domestic needs while still contributing to family income.

Black communities in the postwar South also quickly sought to establish schools. The antebellum planter elite had denied education to blacks because they feared that literate slaves would organize uprisings. After the war the white elite feared education programs would encourage both poor whites and blacks to leave the South in search of better social and economic opportunities. Economic leaders wanted to protect the competitive advantage afforded by the region's low-wage labor market.

The general resistance among the former slaveholding class to new education initiatives forced the freed slaves to rely on northern assistance or to take their own initiative. A Mississippi Freedmen's Bureau agent noted in 1865 that when he told a gathering of some 3,000 former slaves that they "were to have the advantages of schools and education, their joy knew no bounds. They fairly jumped and shouted in gladness." Black churches and individuals helped raise the money and often built the schools and paid the teachers. Soldiers who had acquired some reading and writing skills often served as the first teachers, and the students included adults. A Florida teacher reported that a sixty-year-old former slave woman in her class was so excited by literacy that she "spells her lesson all the evening, then she dreams about it, and wakes up thinking about it."

BLACKS IN SOUTHERN POLITICS   The new role of blacks in politics caused the most controversy, then and afterward. If largely illiterate and inexperienced in the rudiments of politics, they were little different from millions of whites enfranchised in the age of Jackson or immigrants herded to the polls by political bosses in New York and other cities after the war. Some freedmen frankly confessed their disadvantages. Beverly Nash, a black delegate in the South Carolina convention of 1868, told his colleagues: "I believe, my friends and fellow-citizens, we are not prepared for this suffrage. But we can learn. Give a man tools and let him commence to use them, and in time he will learn a trade. So it is with voting."

Several hundred black delegates participated in the statewide political conventions. Most had been selected by local political meetings or by churches, fraternal societies, Union Leagues, and black army units, although a few simply appointed themselves. "Some bring credentials," explained a North Carolina black leader, "others had as much as they could to bring themselves, having to escape from their homes stealthily at night" to avoid white assaults. The black delegates "ranged all colors and apparently all conditions," but free mulattoes from the cities played the most prominent roles. At Louisiana's Republican state convention, for instance, nineteen of the twenty black delegates had been born free.

By 1867, however, former slaves began to gain political influence, and this led to debates that revealed emerging tensions within the black community. Some southern blacks resented the presence of northern brethren, while others complained that few ex-slaves were represented in leadership positions. Northern blacks and the southern free black elite, most of whom were urban dwellers, tended to oppose efforts to confiscate and redistribute land to the rural freedmen, and many insisted that political equality did not mean social equality. As an Alabama black leader stressed, "We do not ask that the ignorant and degraded shall be put on a social equality with the refined and intelligent." In general, however, unity rather than dissension prevailed, and blacks focused on common concerns such as full equality under the law.

Brought suddenly into politics in times that tried the most skilled of statesmen, many blacks nevertheless served with distinction. Yet the derisive label "black Reconstruction" used by later critics exaggerates black political influence, which was limited mainly to voting, and overlooks the large numbers of white Republicans, especially in the moun-

A lithograph depicting five of the major black political figures of the Reconstruction period: Hiram Revels (top left) and Blanche K. Bruce (center) served in the U.S. Senate, Joseph H. Rainey (bottom left), John R. Lynch (bottom right), and James T. Rapier (top right) in the House of Representatives.

tain areas of the upper South. Only one of the new conventions, South Carolina's, had a black majority, 76 to 41. Louisiana's was evenly divided racially, and in only two other conventions were more than 20 percent of the members black: Florida's, with 40 percent, and Virginia's, with 24 percent. The Texas convention was only 10 percent black, and North Carolina's 11 percent—but that did not stop a white newspaper from calling it a body consisting of "baboons, monkeys, mules . . . and other jackasses."

In the new state governments, any black participation was a novelty. Although some 600 blacks—most of them former slaves—served as state legislators, no black man was ever elected governor and few served as judges, although in Louisiana, Pinckney B. S. Pinchback, a northern black and former Union soldier, won the office of lieutenant-governor and served as acting governor when the white governor was indicted for corruption. Several blacks were elected lieutenant-governors, state treasurers, or secretaries of state. There were two black senators in Congress, Hiram Revels and Blanche K. Bruce, both from Mississippi, and fourteen black members of the House during Reconstruction. Among these were some of the ablest congressmen of the time.

REPUBLICANS IN THE SOUTH   The top positions in southern state governments went for the most part to white Republicans, whom the opposition soon labeled "carpetbaggers" and "scalawags," depending on their place of birth. Northern opportunists who allegedly came south with all their belongings in carpetbags to reap political spoils were more often than not Union veterans who had arrived as early as 1865 or 1866, drawn south by the hope of economic opportunity. Others were lawyers, businessmen, editors, teachers, social workers, or preachers who came on missionary endeavors.

The "scalawags," or southern white Republicans, were even more reviled and misrepresented. A Nashville editor called them the "merest trash that could be collected in a civilized community, of no personal credit or social responsibility." Most "scalawags" had opposed secession, forming a Unionist majority in many mountain counties as far south as Georgia and Alabama, and especially in the hills of eastern Tennessee. Though many were indeed crass opportunists who indulged in corruption at the public's expense, several were quite distinguished figures. They included former Confederate general James A. Longstreet, who decided after Appomattox that the Old South must change its ways. To that end, he became a successful cotton broker in New Orleans, joined the Republican party, and supported the Radical reconstruction program. Others were former Whigs who found the Republican party's expansive industrial and commercial program in keeping with Henry Clay's earlier American System.

THE REPUBLICAN RECORD   The new state constitutions were objectionable to adherents of the old order more because of their origin than because of their content, excepting their provisions for black suffrage and civil rights. Otherwise the documents were in keeping with other state constitutions of the day, their provisions often drawn from the basic laws of northern states. Most remained in effect for some years after the end of Radical control, and later constitutions incorporated many of their features. Conspicuous among Radical innovations were such steps toward greater democracy as requiring universal manhood suffrage, reapportioning legislatures more nearly according to population, and making more state offices elective.

Given the hostile circumstances in which the Radical governments arose and operated, they made a surprisingly good record. In most of the South they established the first state school systems, however inadequate and ill supported at first. Some 600,000 black pupils were in schools by 1877. State governments under the Radicals also gave more attention than ever before to poor relief and to public institutions for the disadvantaged and handicapped, such as orphanages, asylums, institutions for the deaf, dumb, and blind of both races. Public roads, bridges, and buildings were repaired or rebuilt. Blacks achieved new rights and opportunities that would never again be taken away, at least in principle: equality before the law, and the right to own property, carry on business, enter professions, attend schools, and learn to read and write.

Yet several of these Republican regimes also practiced systematic corruption. In Louisiana, the carpetbag governor acknowledged the situation: "Why," he said, "down here everybody is demoralized. Corruption is the fashion." Public money and public credit were often voted to privately owned corporations, notably railroads, under conditions that invited influence peddling. Contracts were let at absurd prices, and public officials took their cut. Taxes and public debt rose in every state. Still, the figures of taxation and debt hardly constitute an unqualified indictment of Radical governments, since they then faced unusual and inflated costs for the physical reconstruction of public works in the South. Corruption was not invented by the Radical regimes, nor did it die with them. In Mississippi, the Republican governments of Reconstruction were quite honest compared to their Democratic successors.

WHITE TERROR   The case of Mississippi suggests that whites were hostile to Republican regimes less because of their corruption than their inclusion of blacks. Most white southerners remained unreconstructed, so conditioned by slavery that they were unable to conceive of blacks as citizens or even free agents. White women in the postwar South were as violently opposed as men to northern rule. "I have always been down on Reconstruction," declared Ella Cooper, "and never should one Southern man accept it with my consent. I opposed it to the last. They can force it on us, but I say 'never accept it.'" In some places hostility to the new regimes took the form of white terror. Efforts to oust Republican rule focused largely on violence. Said one unreconstructed Mississippian, "Carry the election peaceably if we can, forcibly if we must."

This Thomas Nast cartoon chides the Ku Klux
Klan and the White League for promoting conditions "worse than slavery" for southern blacks after the Civil War.

The prototype of terrorist groups was the Ku Klux Klan, first organized in 1866 by some young men of Pulaski, Tennessee, as a social
club with the costumes, secret ritual, and mumbo-jumbo common to
fraternal groups. At first a group of pranksters, they soon began to intimidate blacks and white Republicans, and the KKK spread rapidly
across the South in answer to the Union League. Klansmen rode about
the countryside hiding under masks and robes, spreading horrendous
rumors, harassing assertive blacks, and occasionally running amok,
wreaking violence and destruction.

In Mississippi Klansmen mutilated a black Republican leader in
front of his family. Three white "scalawag" Republicans were murdered
in Georgia in 1870. That same year, an armed mob of whites assaulted a
Republican political rally in Alabama, killing four blacks and wounding
fifty-four. In South Carolina the Klan was especially active. Virtually
the entire white male population of York County joined the Klan, and
they were responsible for eleven murders and hundreds of whippings.
In 1871 some 500 masked men laid siege to the Union County jail and
eventually lynched eight black prisoners. Although most Klansmen
were poor farmers and tradesmen, middle-class whites—planters, mer-

chants, bankers, lawyers, doctors, even ministers—also joined the group and participated in its brutalities.

Congress struck back with three Enforcement Acts (1870–1871) to protect black voters. The first of these measures levied penalties on persons who interfered with any citizen's right to vote. A second placed the election of congressmen under surveillance by federal election supervisors and marshals. The third (the Ku Klux Klan Act) outlawed the characteristic activities of the Klan—forming conspiracies, wearing disguises, resisting officers, and intimidating officials. President Grant, in 1871, singled out nine counties in upcountry South Carolina as an example, and pursued mass prosecutions that brought an abrupt halt to Klan terrorism. The program of federal enforcement broke the back of the Klan, whose activities declined steadily as recalcitrant southerners resorted to more subtle methods of racial intimidation.

CONSERVATIVE RESURGENCE   The Klan in fact could not take credit for the overthrow of Republican control in any state. Perhaps its most important effect was to weaken the morale of blacks and Republicans in the South and strengthen in the North a growing weariness with the whole "southern question." Americans had other fish to fry anyway. Western expansion, Indian wars, industrial development, and political controversy over the tariff and the currency distracted attention from southern outrages. Republican control in the South gradually loosened as "Conservative" parties—Democrats used that name to mollify former Whigs—mobilized the white vote. Scalawags, and many carpetbaggers, drifted away from the Radical ranks under pressure from their white neighbors. Few of them had joined the Republicans out of concern for black rights in the first place. And where persuasion failed to work, Democrats were willing to use chicanery. As one enthusiastic Democrat boasted, "the white and black Republicans may outvote us, but we can outcount them."

Such factors led to the collapse of Republican control in Virginia and Tennessee as early as 1869, in Georgia and North Carolina in 1870. Reconstruction lasted longest in the Deep South states with the heaviest black population, where whites abandoned Klan hoods for barefaced intimidation in paramilitary groups like the Mississippi Rifle Club and the South Carolina Red Shirts. In overwhelmingly black Yazoo County, Mississippi, vengeful whites used violence to reverse the political bal-

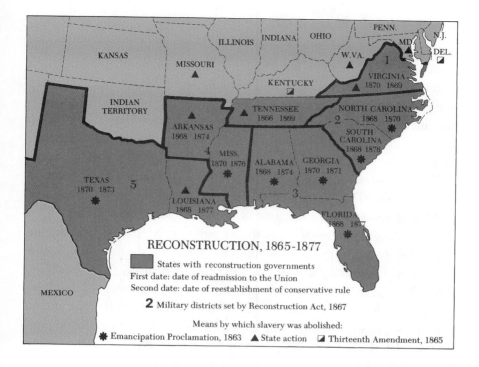

RECONSTRUCTION, 1865–1877

States with reconstruction governments
First date: date of readmission to the Union
Second date: date of reestablishment of conservative rule

2 Military districts set by Reconstruction Act, 1867

Means by which slavery was abolished:
✳ Emancipation Proclamation, 1863   ▲ State action   ☑ Thirteenth Amendment, 1865

ance of power. In the 1873 elections the Republicans cast 2,449 votes and the Democrats 638; two years later the Democrats polled 4,049 votes, the Republicans 7. By 1876 Radical regimes survived only in Louisiana, South Carolina, and Florida, and these all collapsed after the elections of that year.

THE GRANT YEARS

GRANT'S ELECTION   Ulysses S. Grant, who presided over the collapse of Republican rule in the South, brought to the presidency less political experience than any man who had ever occupied the office, except perhaps Zachary Taylor, and arguably less political judgment than any other. But in 1868 the rank-and-file voter could be expected to support "the Lion of Vicksburg" because of his brilliant record as a war leader. Both parties wooed him, but his falling-out with President Johnson pushed him toward the Republicans and built trust in him among the Radicals. They were, as Thad Stevens said, ready to "let him into the church."

When the Republicans gathered in Chicago, they named Grant their unanimous choice. The platform endorsed Radical Reconstruction, cautiously defending black suffrage as a necessity in the South but a matter each northern state should settle for itself. It also urged payment of the nation's war debt in gold rather than in the new "greenback" paper currency printed during the war. More important than the platform were the great expectations of a soldier-president and his slogan: "Let us have peace."

The Democrats took an opposite position on both Reconstruction and the debt. The Republican Congress, the platform charged, had "subjected ten states, in the time of profound peace, to military despotism and Negro supremacy." As to the public debt, the party endorsed Representative George H. Pendleton's "Ohio idea" that, since most bonds had been bought with depreciated greenbacks, they should be paid off in greenbacks unless they specified payment in gold. With no conspicuously available candidate in sight, the convention turned to Horatio Seymour, war governor of New York and chairman of the convention. The Democrats made a closer race than expected, attesting to the strength of traditional party loyalties. While Grant swept the electoral college by 214 to 80, his popular majority was only 307,000 out of a total of over 5.7 million votes. More than 500,000 black voters accounted for Grant's margin of victory.

Grant had proven himself a great leader in the war, but in the White House he seemed blind to the political forces and influence peddlers around him. Shy and withdrawn, he was uncomfortable around intellectuals and impatient with idealists. Grant preferred watching horse races to reading about complex issues. Although personally honest, he was dazzled by men of wealth and unaccountably loyal to greedy subordinates who betrayed his trust. In the formulation of policy he passively followed the lead of Congress. This approach endeared him at first to party leaders, but it left him at last ineffective and caused others to grow disillusioned with his leadership. At the outset Grant consulted nobody on his cabinet appointments. Some of his choices indulged personal whims; others simply reflected bad judgment. Secretary of State Hamilton Fish of New York turned out to be a fortunate exception; he masterfully guided foreign policy throughout the Grant presidency.

THE GOVERNMENT DEBT Financial issues dominated the political agenda during Grant's presidency. After the war the Treasury had assumed that the $400 million worth of greenbacks issued during the conflict would be retired from circulation. Congress in 1866 granted the Treasury discretion to do so gradually. Many agrarian and debtor groups resisted this contraction, believing that a larger money supply would mean rising farm prices and easier-to-pay debts. They were joined by a large number of Radicals who thought a combination of high tariffs and inflation would generate more rapid economic growth. In 1868 "soft money" supporters in Congress halted the retirement of greenbacks, leaving $356 million outstanding. There matters stood when Grant took office.

The "sound" or "hard" money advocates, mostly bankers, merchants, and other creditors, claimed that Grant's election was a mandate to save the country from the Democrats' "Ohio idea." Quite influential in Republican circles, they also had the benefit of a deeply ingrained popular assumption that hard money was morally preferable to paper currency. Grant agreed, and in his inaugural address he endorsed payment of the national debt in gold as a point of national honor.

SCANDAL AND REFORM   Within less than a year of his election Grant fell into a cesspool of scandal. In the summer of 1869 two brilliant, if crass, young railroad entrepreneurs, the crafty Jay Gould and the flamboyant Jim Fisk, connived with the president's brother-in-law to corner the gold market. Gould concocted an argument that the government should refrain from selling gold on the market because the resulting rise in gold prices would raise temporarily depressed farm prices. Grant apparently smelled a rat from the start, but was seen in public with the speculators. As the rumor spread on Wall Street, gold rose from $132 to $163 an ounce. Finally, on "Black Friday," September 24, 1869, Grant ordered the Treasury to sell a large quantity of gold, and the bubble burst. Fisk got out by repudiating his agreements and hiring thugs to intimidate his creditors. "Nothing is lost save honor," he said.

The plot to corner the gold market was only the first of several scandals that rocked the Grant administration. In 1872 the public first learned about the financial buccaneering of the Crédit Mobilier, a construction company that had milked the Union Pacific Railroad for exorbitant fees to line the pockets of insiders who controlled both firms. Rank-and-file Union Pacific shareholders were left holding the bag. This chicanery had transpired before Grant's election in 1868, but it

The People's Handwriting on the Wall. *An 1872 engraving comments on the corruption engulfing Grant.*

now touched a number of prominent Republicans who had been given shares of Crédit Mobilier stock in exchange for favorable votes. Of thirteen Congressmen involved, only two were censured.

Even more odious disclosures soon followed, and some involved the president's cabinet. Grant's secretary of war, it turned out, had accepted bribes from merchants at army posts in the West who traded with Indians. He was impeached, but resigned in time to elude trial. Post-office contracts, it was revealed, went to carriers who offered the highest kickbacks. In St. Louis a "Whiskey Ring" bribed tax collectors to bilk the government of millions in revenue. Grant's private secretary was enmeshed in that scheme, taking large sums of money and other valuables in return for inside information. There is no evidence that Grant himself participated in any of the fraud, but his poor choice of associates earned him widespread censure.

Long before Grant's first term ended, a reaction against the Radical Reconstruction measures, and against incompetence and corruption in the administration, had incited mutiny within the Republican ranks. Open revolt broke out first in Missouri, where Carl Schurz, a German immigrant and war hero, led a group that elected a governor with Democratic help in 1870 and sent Schurz to the Senate.

In 1872 the Liberal Republicans (as they called themselves) held a clamorous national convention in Cincinnati, which produced a compromise platform condemning the party's "vindictive" southern policy and favoring civil service reform, but which remained silent on the protective tariff. The delegates stampeded toward an anomalous presidential candidate: Horace Greeley, editor of the *New York Tribune,* a strong protectionist and enthusiastic reformer. During his long journalistic career he had promoted vegetarianism, brown bread, free-thinking, socialism, and spiritualism. His image as a visionary eccentric was complemented by his open hostility to Democrats, whose support the Liberals needed. One reporter suggested that there had been "too much brains and not enough whiskey" at the convention. The Democrats nevertheless swallowed the pill and gave their nomination to Greeley as the only hope of beating Grant.

The 1872 election result surprised no one. Republican regulars duly endorsed Radical Reconstruction and the protective tariff. Grant still had seven carpetbag states in his pocket, generous support from business and banking interests, and the stalwart support of the Radicals. Above all he still evoked the glory of Vicksburg and Appomattox. Greeley, despite an exhausting tour of the country—still unusual for a presidential candidate—carried only six southern and border states and none in the North. Devastated by his crushing defeat and the simultaneous death of his wife, Greeley entered a mental sanitarium and died three weeks later.

PANIC AND REDEMPTION   A paralyzing economic panic followed close upon the public scandals besetting the Grant administration. Contraction of the money supply brought about by the Treasury's postwar withdrawal of greenbacks and the reckless overexpansion of the railroads into sparsely settled areas helped precipitate a financial crisis. During 1873 some twenty-five strapped railroads defaulted on their interest payments. Caught short, the prominent investment firm of Jay Cooke and Company went bankrupt on September 18, 1873. The ensuing stampede of selling forced the stock market to close for ten days. The Panic of 1873 set off a depression that lasted for six years, the longest and most severe that Americans had yet suffered, marked by widespread bankruptcies, chronic unemployment, and a drastic slow-down in railroad building.

Hard times and corruption hurt Republicans in the midterm elections of 1874, allowing the Democrats to win control of the House of Representatives and gain in the Senate. The new Democratic House immediately launched inquiries into the Grant scandals and unearthed further evidence of corruption in high places. The panic meanwhile focused attention once more on greenback currency. Since greenbacks were valued less than gold, they had become the chief circulating medium. Most people spent greenbacks first and held their gold or used it to settle foreign accounts, which drained much gold out of the country. To relieve this deflationary spiral and stimulate business, therefore, the Treasury reissued $26 million in greenbacks previously withdrawn.

For a time the advocates of paper money were riding high. But Grant vetoed an attempt to issue more greenbacks in 1874, and in his annual message he called for their gradual withdrawal. Congress obliged the president by passing the Resumption Act of 1875. The resumption of paying gold to customers who turned in their greenbacks began on January 1, 1879, after the Treasury had built a gold reserve for the purpose and reduced the value of greenbacks in circulation. This act infuriated those promoting an inflationary monetary policy and provoked the formation of the National Greenback party. The much debated "money question" would remain one of the most divisive issues in American politics until the end of the century.

THE COMPROMISE OF 1877 Grant yearned to run again in 1876, but the recent scandals precluded any challenge to the two-term tradition. James G. Blaine of Maine, former Speaker of the House, emerged as the Republican front-runner, but he too bore the taint of scandal. Letters in the possession of James Mulligan of Boston linked Blaine to some dubious railroad dealings. Newspapers soon published these "Mulligan Letters," and Blaine's candidacy was dealt a body blow.

The Republican convention in Cincinnati therefore eliminated Blaine and several other hopefuls in favor of Ohio's favorite son, Rutherford B. Hayes. Three times governor of Ohio and an advocate of hard money, Hayes had a sterling character and had been a civil service reformer. But his chief virtue, as Henry Adams put it, was "that he is obnoxious to no one."

The Democratic convention in St. Louis was abnormally harmonious from the start. The nomination went on the second ballot to Samuel J. Tilden, millionaire corporation lawyer and reform governor of New York, who had directed a campaign to overthrow first the corrupt Tweed Ring in New York City and then another ring in Albany that had bilked the state of millions.

The campaign generated no burning issues. Both candidates favored the trend toward restoring conservative rule in the South. During one of the most corrupt elections ever, both candidates favored civil service reform. In the absence of strong differences, Democrats waved the Republicans' dirty linen. In response, Republicans waved the bloody shirt, which is to say that they engaged in verbal assaults on former Confederates and the spirit of rebellion, linking the Democratic party with Secession and with the outrages committed against both black and white Republicans in the South. As one Republican speaker insisted, "Every man that tried to destroy this nation was a Democrat. . . . The man that assassinated Abraham Lincoln was a Democrat. . . . Soldiers, every scar you have on your heroic bodies was given you by a Democrat!"

Early election returns pointed to a Tilden victory. Tilden had 184 electoral votes, just one short of a majority, but Republicans claimed nineteen doubtful votes from Florida, Louisiana, and South Carolina, while Democrats laid a counterclaim to one of Oregon's three votes. The Republicans had clearly carried Oregon, but the outcome in the South was less certain, and given the fraud and intimidation perpetrated on both sides, nobody will ever know the truth of the matter. In all three of the disputed southern states, rival canvassing boards sent in different returns. The Constitution offered no guidance in this unprecedented situation. Even if Congress were empowered to sort things out, the Democratic House and the Republican Senate proved unable to reach an agreement.

The impasse dragged on for months, and there was even talk of public violence. Finally, on January 29, 1877, the two houses decided to set up a special Electoral Commission. It had fifteen members, five each from the House, the Senate, and the Supreme Court. The decision on each contested state went by a vote of 8 to 7, along party lines, in favor of Hayes. After much debate and threat of filibuster by Democrats, the

House voted on March 2 to accept the report and declare the Republican Hayes the victor by an electoral vote of 185 to 184.

Critical to this outcome was the defection of southern Democrats who had made several informal agreements with the Republicans. On February 26, 1877, a bargain was struck between prominent Ohio Republicans and powerful southern Democrats. The Republicans promised that, if elected, Hayes would withdraw federal troops from Louisiana and South Carolina, letting the Republican governments there collapse. In return the Democrats pledged to withdraw their opposition to Hayes, to accept in good faith the Reconstruction amendments, and to refrain from partisan reprisals against Republicans in the South.

With this agreement in hand, southern Democrats could justify deserting Tilden. This so-called Compromise of 1877 brought a final "redemption" from the "Radicals" and a return to "home rule," which actually meant rule by native white Democrats. Other, more informal promises bolstered the secret agreement. Hayes's friends pledged more support for Mississippi levees and other internal improvements, including federal subsidy for a transcontinental railroad along a southern route. Southerners extracted a further promise that Hayes would name a white southerner as postmaster-general, the cabinet position with the most patronage jobs at hand. In return, southerners would let Republicans make James A. Garfield Speaker of the new House.

THE END OF RECONSTRUCTION   After Hayes took office, most of these promises were either renounced or forgotten. In 1877, Hayes withdrew federal troops from the state houses in Louisiana and South Carolina, and the Republican governments there soon collapsed— along with much of Hayes's claim to legitimacy. Hayes chose a Tennessean as postmaster-general. But after southern Democrats failed to permit the choice of Garfield as Speaker, Hayes expressed doubt about any further subsidy for railroad building, and none was voted.

As to southern promises regarding the civil rights of blacks, only a few Democratic leaders remembered them for long. Over the next three decades those rights crumbled under the pressure of white rule in the South and the force of Supreme Court decisions narrowing the application of the Fourteenth and Fifteenth Amendments. Radical Reconstruction never offered more than an uncertain commitment to racial equality before the law. Yet it left an enduring legacy, the Thirteenth,

Fourteenth, and Fifteenth Amendments—not dead but dormant, waiting to be warmed back into life. If Reconstruction did not provide social equality or substantial economic opportunities for blacks, it did create the opportunity for future transformation. It was a revolution, sighed North Carolina Governor Jonathan Worth, and "nobody can anticipate the action of revolutions."

MAKING CONNECTIONS

- The political, economic, and racial policies of the Bourbons, the conservatives who overthrew the Republican governments in the southern states, are described in Chapter 18.

- Several of the political scandals mentioned in this chapter were related to the railroads, a topic discussed in greater detail in Chapter 19.

- This chapter ends with the election of Rutherford B. Hayes; for a discussion of Hayes's administration, see Chapter 21.

FURTHER READING

Reconstruction has long been "a dark and bloody ground" of conflicting interpretations. The best synthesis is Eric Foner's *Reconstruction: America's Unfinished Revolution, 1863–1877* (1988).*

More specialized works give closer scrutiny to the aims of the principal political figures. For a study of Andrew Johnson, see Hans L. Trefousse's *Andrew Johnson: A Biography* (1989). Why Johnson was impeached is detailed in Hans L. Trefousse's *Impeachment of a President* (1975).

Scholars have been fairly sympathetic to the aims and motives of the Radical Republicans. See, for instance, Richard Nelson Current's

*These books are available in paperback editions.

Those Terrible Carpetbaggers: A Reinterpretation (1988).* The ideology of the Radicals is explored in Michael Les Benedict's *A Compromise of Principle: Congressional Republicans and Reconstruction* (1974).

The intransigence of southern white attitudes is examined in Michael Perman's *Reunion without Compromise* (1973).* Allen W. Trelease's *White Terror* (1971)* covers the various organizations that practiced vigilante tactics, chiefly the Ku Klux Klan. The difficulties former planters had in adjusting to the new labor system are documented in James L. Roark's *Masters without Slaves* (1977).*

Numerous works have appeared on the freed blacks' experience in the South. Start with Leon F. Litwack's *Been in the Storm So Long* (1979).* The situation of freed slave women, which was often quite different from that of freed slave men, is discussed in Jacqueline Jones's *Labor of Love, Labor of Sorrow: Black Women, Work and the Family from Slavery to Present* (1985) and Dorothy Sterling's *We Are Your Sisters* (1984).*

The politics of corruption outside the South is depicted in William S. McFeely's *Grant: A Biography* (1981).* The political maneuvers of the election of 1876 and the resultant crisis and compromise are explained in C. Vann Woodward's *Reunion and Reaction* (1951)* and William Gillette's *Retreat from Reconstruction, 1869–1879* (1979).*

*These books are available in paperback editions.

APPENDICES

THE DECLARATION
OF INDEPENDENCE

WHEN IN THE COURSE OF HUMAN EVENTS, it becomes necessary for one people to dissolve the political bands which have connected them with another, and to assume the Powers of the earth, the separate and equal station to which the Laws of Nature and of Nature's God entitle them, a decent respect to the opinions of mankind requires that they should declare the causes which impel them to the separation.

We hold these truths to be self-evident, that all men are created equal, that they are endowed by their Creator with certain unalienable rights, that among these are Life, Liberty, and the pursuit of Happiness. That to secure these rights, Governments are instituted among Men, deriving their just powers from the consent of the governed. That whenever any Form of Government becomes destructive of these ends, it is the Right of the People to alter or to abolish it, and to institute new Government, laying its foundation on such principles and organizing its powers in such form, as to them shall seem most likely to effect their Safety and Happiness. Prudence, indeed, will dictate that Governments long established should not be changed for light and transient causes; and accordingly all experience hath shown, that mankind are more disposed to suffer, while evils are sufferable, than to right themselves by abolishing the forms to which they are accustomed. But when a long train of abuses and usurpations, pursuing invariably the same Object evinces a design to reduce them under absolute Despotism, it is their right, it is their duty, to throw off such Government, and to provide new Guards for their future security.— Such has been the patient sufferance of these Colonies; and such is now the necessity which constrains them to alter their former Systems of Government. The history of the present King of Great Britain is a history of repeated injuries and usurpations, all having in direct object the establishment of an absolute Tyranny over these States. To prove this, let Facts be submitted to a candid world.

He has refused his Assent to Laws, the most wholesome and necessary for the public good.

He has forbidden his Governors to pass Laws of immediate and pressing importance, unless suspended in their operation till his Assent should be obtained; and when so suspended, he has utterly neglected to attend to them.

He has refused to pass other Laws for the accommodation of large districts of people, unless those people would relinquish the right of Representation in the Legislature, a right inestimable to them and formidable to tyrants only.

He has called together legislative bodies at places unusual, uncomfortable, and distant from the depository of their public Records, for the sole purpose of fatiguing them into compliance with his measures.

He has dissolved Representative Houses repeatedly, for opposing with manly firmness his invasions on the rights of the people.

He has refused for a long time, after such dissolutions, to cause others to be elected; whereby the Legislative powers, incapable of Annihilation, have returned to the People at large for their exercise; the State remaining in the mean time exposed to all dangers of invasion from without, and convulsions within.

He has endeavoured to prevent the population of these States; for that purpose obstructing the Laws of Naturalization of Foreigners; refusing to pass others to encourage their migrations hither, and raising the conditions of new Appropriations of Lands.

He has obstructed the Administration of Justice, by refusing his Assent to Laws for establishing Judiciary powers.

He has made Judges dependent on his Will alone, for the tenure of their offices, and the amount and payment of their salaries.

He has erected a multitude of New Offices, and sent hither swarms of Officers to harass our People, and eat out their substance.

He has kept among us, in times of peace, Standing Armies without the Consent of our legislature.

He has affected to render the Military independent of and superior to the Civil Power.

He has combined with others to subject us to a jurisdiction foreign to our constitution, and unacknowledged by our laws; giving his Assent to their Acts of pretended Legislation:

For quartering large bodies of armed troops among us:

For protecting them, by a mock Trial, from Punishment for any Murders which they should commit on the Inhabitants of these States:

For cutting off our Trade with all parts of the world:

For imposing taxes on us without our Consent:

For depriving us of many cases, of the benefits of Trial by jury:

For transporting us beyond Seas to be tried for pretended offences:

For abolishing the free System of English Laws in a neighbouring Province, establishing therein an Arbitrary government, and enlarging its Boundaries so as to render it at once an example and fit instrument for introducing the same absolute rule into these Colonies:

For taking away our Charters, abolishing our most valuable Laws, and altering fundamentally the Forms of our Governments:

For suspending our own Legislatures, and declaring themselves in vested with Power to legislate for us in all cases whatsoever.

He has abdicated Government here, by declaring us out of his Protection and waging War against us.

He has plundered our seas, ravaged our Coasts, burnt our towns, and destroyed the lives of our people.

He is at this time transporting large armies of foreign mercenaries to compleat the works of death, desolation, and tyranny, already begun with circumstances of Cruelty & perfidy scarcely parallel in the most barbarous ages, and totally unworthy the Head of a civilized nation.

He has constrained our fellow Citizens taken Captive on the high Seas to bear Arms against their Country, to become the executioners of their friends and Brethren, or to fall themselves by their Hands.

He has excited domestic insurrections amongst us, and has endeavoured to bring on the inhabitants of our frontiers, the merciless Indian Savages, whose known rule of warfare, is an undistinguished destruction of all ages, sexes, and conditions.

In every stage of these Oppressions We have Petitioned for Redress in the most humble terms: Our repeated Petitions have been answered only by repeated injury. A Prince, whose character is thus marked by every act which may define a Tyrant, is unfit to be the ruler of a free people.

Nor have We been wanting in attention to our British brethren. We have warned them from time to time of attempts by their legislature to extend an unwarrantable jurisdiction over us. We have reminded them of the circumstances of our emigration and settlement here. We have appealed to their native justice and magnanimity, and we have conjured them by the ties of our common kindred to disavow these usurpations, which, would inevitably interrupt our connections and correspondence. They too must have been deaf to the voice of justice and of consanguinity. We must, therefore, acquiesce in the necessity, which denounces our Separation, and hold them, as we hold the rest of mankind, Enemies in War, in Peace Friends.

WE, THEREFORE, the Representatives of the UNITED STATES OF AMERICA, in General Congress, Assembled, appealing to the Supreme Judge of the world for the rectitude of our intentions, do, in the Name, and by Authority of the good People of these Colonies, solemnly publish and declare, That these United Colonies are, and of Right ought to be FREE AND INDEPENDENT STATES; that they are Absolved from all Allegiance to the British

Crown, and that all political connection between them and the State of Great Britain, is and ought to be totally dissolved; and that as Free and Independent States, they have full Power to levy War, conclude Peace, contract Alliances, establish Commerce, and to do all other Acts and Things which Independent States may of right do. And for the support of this Declaration, with a firm reliance on the Protection of Divine Providence, we mutually pledge to each other our Lives, our Fortunes, and our sacred Honor.

The foregoing Declaration was, by order of Congress, engrossed, and signed by the following members:

John Hancock

NEW HAMPSHIRE
Josiah Bartlett
William Whipple
Matthew Thornton

MASSACHUSETTS BAY
Samuel Adams
John Adams
Robert Treat Paine
Elbridge Gerry

RHODE ISLAND
Stephen Hopkins
William Ellery

CONNECTICUT
Roger Sherman
Samuel Huntington
William Williams
Oliver Wolcott

NEW YORK
William Floyd
Philip Livingston
Francis Lewis
Lewis Morris

NEW JERSEY
Richard Stockton
John Witherspoon
Francis Hopkinson
John Hart
Abraham Clark

PENNSYLVANIA
Robert Morris
Benjamin Rush
Benjamin Franklin
John Morton
George Clymer
James Smith
George Taylor
James Wilson
George Ross

DELAWARE
Caesar Rodney
George Read
Thomas M'Kean

MARYLAND
Samuel Chase
William Paca
Thomas Stone
Charles Carroll, of Carrollton

VIRGINIA
George Wythe
Richard Henry Lee
Thomas Jefferson
Benjamin Harrison
Thomas Nelson, Jr.
Francis Lightfoot Lee
Carter Braxton

NORTH CAROLINA
William Hooper
Joseph Hewes
John Penn

SOUTH CAROLINA
Edward Rutledge
Thomas Heyward, Jr.
Thomas Lynch, Jr.
Arthur Middleton

GEORGIA
Button Gwinnett
Lyman Hall
George Walton

Resolved, That copies of the Declaration be sent to the several assemblies, conventions, and committees, or councils of safety, and to the several commanding officers of the continental troops; that it be proclaimed in each of the United States, at the head of the army.

ARTICLES OF
CONFEDERATION

To ALL TO WHOM these Presents shall come, we the undersigned Delegates of the States affixed to our Names send greeting.

Whereas the Delegates of the United States of America in Congress assembled did on the fifteenth day of November in the Year of our Lord One Thousand Seven Hundred and Seventy-seven, and in the Second Year of the Independence of America agree to certain articles of Confederation and perpetual Union between the States of Newhampshire, Massachusetts-bay, Rhodeisland and Providence Plantations, Connecticut, New York, New Jersey, Pennsylvania, Delaware, Maryland, Virginia, North-Carolina, South-Carolina and Georgia in the Words following, viz.

Articles of Confederation and perpetual Union between the States of Newhampshire, Massachusetts-bay, Rhodeisland and Providence Plantations, Connecticut, New-York, New-Jersey, Pennsylvania, Delaware, Maryland, Virginia, North-Carolina, South-Carolina and Georgia.

ARTICLE I. The stile of this confederacy shall be "The United States of America."

ARTICLE II. Each State retains its sovereignty, freedom and independence, and every power, jurisdiction and right, which is not by this confederation expressly delegated to the United States, in Congress assembled.

ARTICLE III. The said States hereby severally enter into a firm league of friendship with each other, for their common defence, the security of their liberties, and their mutual and general welfare, binding themselves to assist each other, against all force offered to, or attacks made upon them, or any of them, on account of religion, sovereignty, trade or any other pretence whatever.

ARTICLE IV. The better to secure and perpetuate mutual friendship and intercourse among the people of the different States in this Union, the free inhabitants of each of these States, paupers, vagabonds and fugitives from justice excepted, shall be entitled to all privileges and immunities of free citizens in the several States; and the people of each State shall have free ingress and regress to and from any other State, and shall enjoy therein all the privileges of trade and commerce, subject to the same duties, impositions and restrictions as the inhabitants thereof respectively, provided that such restrictions shall not extend so far as to prevent the removal of property imported into any State, to any other State of which the owner is an inhabitant; provided also that no imposition, duties or restriction shall be laid by any State, on the property of the United States, or either of them.

If any person guilty of, or charged with treason, felony, or other high misdemeanor in any State, shall flee from justice, and be found in any of the United States, he shall upon demand of the Governor or Executive power, of the State from which he fled, be delivered up and removed to the State having jurisdiction of his offence.

Full faith and credit shall be given in each of these States to the records, acts and judicial proceedings of the courts and magistrates of every other State.

ARTICLE V. For the more convenient management of the general interests of the United States, delegates shall be annually appointed in such manner as the legislature of each State shall direct, to meet in Congress on the first Monday in November, in every year, with a power reserved to each State, to recall its delegates, or any of them, at any time within the year, and to send others in their stead, for the remainder of the year.

No State shall be represented in Congress by less than two, nor by more than seven members; and no person shall be capable of being a delegate for more than three years in any term of six years; nor shall any person, being a delegate, be capable of holding any office under the United States, for which he, or another for his benefit receives any salary, fees or emolument of any kind.

Each State shall maintain its own delegates in a meeting of the States, and while they act as members of the committee of the States.

In determining questions in the United States, in Congress assembled, each State shall have one vote.

Freedom of speech and debate in Congress shall not be impeached or questioned in any court, or place out of Congress, and the members of Congress shall be protected in their persons from arrests and imprisonments, during the time of their going to and from, and attendance on Congress, except for treason, felony, or breach of the peace.

ARTICLE VI. No State without the consent of the United States in Congress assembled, shall send any embassy to, or receive any embassy from, or enter into any conference, agreement, alliance or treaty with any king, prince or state; nor shall any person holding any office of profit or trust under the United States, or any of them, accept of any present, emolument, office or title of any kind whatever from any king, prince or foreign state; nor shall the United States in Congress assembled, or any of them, grant any title of nobility.

No two or more States shall enter into any treaty, confederation or alliance whatever between them, without the consent of the United States in Congress assembled, specifying accurately the purposes for which the same is to be entered into, and how long it shall continue.

No State shall lay any imposts or duties, which may interfere with any stipulations in treaties, entered into by the United States in Congress assembled, with any king, prince or state, in pursuance of any treaties already proposed by Congress, to the courts of France and Spain.

No vessels of war shall be kept up in time of peace by any State, except such number only, as shall be deemed necessary by the United States in Congress assembled, for the defence of such State, or its trade; nor shall any body of forces be kept up by any State, in time of peace, except such number only, as in the judgment of the United States, in Congress assembled, shall be deemed requisite to garrison the forts necessary for the defence of such State; but every State shall always keep up a well regulated and disciplined militia, sufficiently armed and accoutred, and shall provide and constantly have ready for use, in public stores, a due number of field pieces and tents, and a proper quantity of arms, ammunition and camp equipage.

No State shall engage in any war without the consent of the United States in Congress assembled, unless such State be actually invaded by enemies, or shall have received certain advice of a resolution being formed by some nation of Indians to invade such State, and the danger is so imminent as not to admit of a delay, till the United States in Congress assembled can be consulted: nor shall any State grant commissions to any ships or vessels of war, nor letters of marque or reprisal, except it be after a declaration of war by the United States in Congress assembled, and then only against the kingdom or state and the subjects thereof, against which war has been so declared, and under such regulations as shall be established by the United States in Congress assembled, unless such State be infested by pirates, in which case vessels of war may be fitted out for that occasion, and kept so long as the danger shall continue, or until the United States in Congress assembled shall determine otherwise.

ARTICLE VII. When land-forces are raised by any State of the common defence, all officers of or under the rank of colonel, shall be appointed by the

Legislature of each State respectively by whom such forces shall be raised, or in such manner as such State shall direct, and all vacancies shall be filled up by the State which first made the appointment.

ARTICLE VIII. All charges of war, and all other expenses that shall be incurred for the common defence or general welfare, and allowed by the United States in Congress assembled, shall be defrayed out of a common treasury, which shall be supplied by the several States, in proportion to the value of all land within each State, granted to or surveyed for any person, as such land and the buildings and improvements thereon shall be estimated according to such mode as the United States in Congress assembled, shall from time to time direct and appoint.

The taxes for paying that proportion shall be laid and levied by the authority and direction of the Legislatures of the several States within the time agreed upon by the United States in Congress assembled.

ARTICLE IX. The United States in Congress assembled, shall have the sole and exclusive right and power of determining on peace and war, except in the cases mentioned in the sixth article—of sending and receiving ambassadors—entering into treaties and alliances, provided that no treaty of commerce shall be made whereby the legislative power of the respective States shall be restrained from imposing such imposts and duties on foreigners, as their own people are subjected to, or from prohibiting the exportation or importation of and species of goods or commodities whatsoever—of establishing rules for deciding in all cases, what captures on land or water shall be legal, and in what manner prizes taken by land or naval forces in the service of the United States shall be divided or appropriated—of granting letters of marque and reprisal in times of peace—appointing courts for the trial of piracies and felonies committed on the high seas and establishing courts for receiving and determining finally appeals in all cases of captures, provided that no member of Congress shall be appointed a judge of any of the said courts.

The United States in Congress assembled shall also be the last resort on appeal in all disputes and differences now subsisting or that hereafter may arise between two or more States concerning boundary, jurisdiction or any other cause whatever; which authority shall always be exercised in the manner following. Whenever the legislative or executive authority or lawful agent of any State in controversy with another shall present a petition to Congress, stating the matter in question and praying for a hearing, notice thereof shall be given by order of Congress to the legislative or executive authority of the other State in controversy, and a day assigned for the appearance of the parties by their lawful agents, who shall then be directed to appoint by joint consent, commissioners or judges to constitute a court for hearing and determining the matter in question: but if they cannot agree, Congress shall name three persons out of each of the United States, and from the list of such persons each party shall alternately strike out one, the petitioners beginning, until the number shall be reduced to thirteen; and from that number not less than seven, nor more than nine names as Congress shall direct, shall in the presence of Congress be drawn out by lot, and the persons whose names shall be so drawn or any five of them, shall be commissioners or judges, to hear and finally determine the controversy, so always as a major part of the judges who shall hear the cause shall agree in the determination: and if either party shall neglect to attend at the day appointed, without reasons, which Congress shall judge sufficient, or being present shall refuse to strike, the Congress shall proceed to nominate three persons out of each State, and the Secretary of Congress shall strike in behalf of such party absent or refusing; and the judgment and sentence of the court to be appointed, in the manner before prescribed, shall be final and conclusive; and if any of the parties shall refuse to submit to the authority of such court, or to appear or defend their claim or cause, the court shall nevertheless proceed to pronounce sentence, or judgment, which shall in like manner be final and decisive, the judgment or sentence and other proceedings being in either case transmitted to Congress, and lodged among the acts of Congress for the security of the parties concerned: provided that every commissioner, before he sits in judgment, shall take an oath to be administered by one of the judges of the supreme or superior court of the State where the case shall be tried, "well and truly to hear and determine the matter in question, according to the best of his judgment, without favour, affection or hope of reward:" provided also that no State shall be deprived of territory for the benefit of the United States.

All controversies concerning the private right of soil claimed under different grants of two or more States, whose jurisdiction as they may respect such lands, and the states which passed such grants are adjusted, the said grants or either of them being at the same time claimed to have originated antecedent to such settlement of jurisdiction, shall on the petition of either party to the Congress of the United States, be finally determined as near as may be in the same manner as is before prescribed for deciding disputes respecting territorial jurisdiction between different States.

The United States in Congress assembled shall also have the sole and exclusive right and power of regulating the alloy and value of coin struck by their own authority, or by that of the respective States—fixing the standard of weights and measures throughout the United States—regulating the trade and managing all affairs with the Indians, not members of any of the States, provided that the legislative right of any State within its own limits be not infringed or violated—establishing and regulating post-offices from one State to another, throughout all of the United States, and exacting such postage on the papers passing thro' the same as may be requisite to defray the expenses of the said office—appointing all officers of the land forces, in the service of the United States, excepting regimental officers—appointing all the officers of the naval forces, and commissioning all officers whatever in the service of the United States—making rules for the government and regulation of the said land and naval forces, and directing their operations.

The United States in Congress assembled shall have authority to appoint a committee, to sit in the recess of Congress, to be denominated "a Committee of the States," and to consist of one delegate from each State; and to appoint such other committees and civil officers as may be necessary for managing the general affairs of the United States under their direction—to appoint one of their number to preside, provided that no person be allowed to serve in the office of president more than one year in any term of three years; to ascertain the necessary sums of money to be raised for the service of the United States, and to appropriate and apply the same for defraying the public expenses—to borrow money, or emit bills on the credit of the United States, transmitting every half year to the respective States an account of the sums of money so borrowed or emitted,—to build and equip a navy—to agree upon the number of land forces, and to make requisitions from each State for its quota, in proportion to the number of white inhabitants in such State; which requisition shall be binding, and thereupon the Legislature of each State shall appoint the regimental officers, raise the men and cloath, arm and equip them in a soldier like manner, at the expense of the United States; and the officers and men so cloathed, armed and equipped shall march to the place appointed, and within the time agreed on by the United States in Congress assembled: but if the United States in Congress assembled shall, on consideration of circumstances judge proper that any State should not raise men, or should raise a smaller number of men than the quota thereof, such extra number shall be raised, officered, cloathed, armed and equipped in the same manner as the quota of such State, unless the legislature of such State shall judge that such extra number cannot be safely spared out of the same, in which case they shall raise officer, cloath, arm and equip as many of such extra number as they judge can be safely spared. And the officers and men so cloathed, armed and equipped, shall march to the place appointed, and within the time agreed on by the United States in Congress assembled.

The United States in Congress assembled shall never engage in a war, nor grant letters of marque and reprisal in time of peace, nor enter into any treaties or alliances, nor coin money, nor regulate the value thereof, nor ascertain the sums and expenses necessary for the defence and welfare of the United States, or any of them, nor emit bills, nor borrow money on the credit of the United

States, nor appropriate money, nor agree upon the number of vessels to be built or purchased, or the number of land or sea forces to be raised, nor appoint a commander in chief of the army or navy, unless nine States assent to the same: nor shall a question on any other point, except for adjourning from day to day be determined, unless by the votes of a majority of the United States in Congress assembled.

The Congress of the United States shall have power to adjourn to any time within the year, and to any place within the United States, so that no period of adjournment be for a longer duration than the space of six months, and shall publish the journal of their proceedings monthly, except such parts thereof relating to treaties, alliances or military operations, as in their judgment require secresy; and the yeas and nays of the delegates of each State on any question shall be entered on the Journal, when it is desired by any delegate; and the delegates of a State, or any of them, at his or their request shall be furnished with a transcript of the said journal, except such parts as are above excepted, to lay before the Legislatures of the several States.

ARTICLE X. The committee of the States, or any nine of them, shall be authorized to execute, in the recess of Congress, such of the powers of Congress as the United States in Congress assembled, by the consent of nine States, shall from time to time think expedient to vest them with; provided that no power be delegated to the said committee, for the exercise of which, by the articles of confederation, the voice of nine States in the Congress of the United States assembled is requisite.

ARTICLE XI. Canada acceding to this confederation, and joining in the measures of the United States, shall be admitted into, and entitled to all the advantages of this Union: but no other colony shall be admitted into the same, unless such admission be agreed to by nine States.

ARTICLE XII. All bills of credit emitted, monies borrowed and debts contracted by, or under the authority of Congress, before the assembling of the United States, in pursuance of the present confederation, shall be deemed and considered as a charge against the United States, for payment and satisfaction whereof the said United States, and the public faith are hereby solemnly pledged.

ARTICLE XIII. Every State shall abide by the determinations of the United States in Congress assembled, on all questions which by this confederation are submitted to them. And the articles of this confederation shall be inviolably observed by every State, and the Union shall be perpetual; nor shall any alteration at any time hereafter be made in any of them; unless such alteration be agreed to in a Congress of the United States, and be afterwards confirmed by the Legislatures of every State.

And whereas it has pleased the Great Governor of the world to incline the hearts of the Legislatures we respectively represent in Congress, to approve of, and to authorize us to ratify the said articles of confederation and perpetual union. Know ye that we the undersigned delegates, by virtue of the power and authority to us given for that purpose, do by these presents, in the name and in behalf of our respective constituents, fully and entirely ratify and confirm each and every of the said articles of confederation and perpetual union, and all and singular the matters and things therein contained: and we do further solemnly plight and engage the faith of our respective constituents, that they shall abide by the determinations of the United States in Congress assembled, on all questions, which by the said confederation are submitted to them. And that the articles thereof shall be inviolably observed by the States we respectively represent, and that the Union shall be perpetual.

In witness thereof we have hereunto set our hands in Congress. Done at Philadelphia in the State of Pennsylvania the ninth day of July in the year of our Lord one thousand seven hundred and seventy-eight, and in the third year of the independence of America.

THE CONSTITUTION OF
THE UNITED STATES

WE THE PEOPLE OF THE UNITED STATES, in order to form a more perfect Union, establish Justice, insure domestic Tranquility, provide for the common defence, promote the general Welfare, and secure the Blessings of Liberty to ourselves and our Posterity, do ordain and establish this Constitution for the United States of America.

ARTICLE. I.

Section. 1. All legislative Powers herein granted shall be vested in a Congress of the United States, which shall consist of a Senate and House of Representatives.

Section. 2. The House of Representatives shall be composed of Members chosen every second Year by the People of the several States, and the Electors in each State shall have the Qualifications requisite for Electors of the most numerous Branch of the State Legislature.

No Person shall be a Representative who shall not have attained to the Age of twenty five Years, and been seven Years a Citizen of the United States, and who shall not, when elected, be an Inhabitant of that State in which he shall be chosen.

Representatives and direct Taxes shall be apportioned among the several States which may be included within this Union, according to their respective Numbers, which shall be determined by adding to the whole Number of free Persons, including those bound to Service for a Term of Years, and excluding Indians not taxed, three fifths of all other Persons. The actual Enumeration shall be made within three Years after the first Meeting of the Congress of the United States, and within every subsequent Term of ten Years, in such Manner as they shall by Law direct. The Number of Representatives shall not exceed one for every thirty Thousand, but each State shall have at Least one Representative; and until such enumeration shall be made, the State of New Hampshire shall be entitled to chuse three, Massachusetts eight, Rhode-Island and

Providence Plantations one, Connecticut five, New-York six, New Jersey four, Pennsylvania eight, Delaware one, Maryland six, Virginia ten, North Carolina five, South Carolina five, and Georgia three.

When vacancies happen in the Representation from any state, the Executive Authority thereof shall issue Writs of Election to fill such Vacancies.

The House of Representatives shall chuse their Speaker and other Officers; and shall have the sole Power of Impeachment.

Section. 3. The Senate of the United States shall be composed of two Senators from each State, chosen by the legislature thereof, for six Years; and each Senator shall have one Vote.

Immediately after they shall be assembled in Consequence of the first Election, they shall be divided as equally as may be into three Classes. The Seats of the Senators of the first Class shall be vacated at the Expiration of the second Year, of the second Class at the Expiration of the fourth Year, and of the third Class at the Expiration of the sixth Year, so that one third maybe chosen every second Year; and if Vacancies happen by Resignation, or otherwise, during the Recess of the Legislature of any State, the Executive thereof may make temporary Appointments until the next Meeting of the Legislature, which shall then fill such Vacancies.

No Person shall be a Senator who shall not have attained to the Age of thirty Years, and been nine Years a Citizen of the United States, and who shall not, when elected, be an Inhabitant of that State for which he shall be chosen.

The Vice President of the United States shall be President of the Senate, but shall have no Vote, unless they be equally divided.

The Senate shall chuse their other Officers, and also a President pro tempore, in the Absence of the Vice President, or when he shall exercise the Office of President of the United States.

The Senate shall have the sole Power to try all Impeachments. When sitting for that Purpose, they shall be on Oath or Affirmation. When the President of the United States is tried, the Chief Justice shall preside: And no Person shall be convicted without the Concurrence of two thirds of the Members present.

Judgment in Cases of Impeachment shall not extend further than to removal from Office, and disqualification to hold and enjoy any Office of honor, Trust or Profit under the United States: but the Party convicted shall nevertheless be liable and subject to Indictment, Trial, Judgment and Punishment, according to Law.

Section. 4. The Times, Places and Manner of holding Elections for Senators and Representatives, shall be prescribed in each State by the Legislature thereof; but the Congress may at any time by Law make or alter such Regulations, except as to the Places of chusing Senators.

The Congress shall assemble at least once in every Year, and such Meeting shall be on the first Monday in December, unless they shall by Law appoint a different Day.

Section. 5. Each House shall be the Judge of the Elections, Returns and Qualifications of its own Members, and a Majority of each shall constitute a Quorum to do Business; but a smaller Number may adjourn from day to day, and may be authorized to compel the Attendance of absent Members, in such Manner, and under such Penalties as each House may provide.

Each House may determine the Rules of its Proceedings, punish its Members for disorderly Behaviour, and, with the Concurrence of two thirds, expel a Member.

Each House shall keep a Journal of its Proceedings, and from time to time publish the same, excepting such Parts as may in their Judgment require Secrecy; and the Yeas and Nays of the Members of either House on any question shall, at the Desire of one fifth of those Present, be entered on the Journal.

Neither House, during the Session of Congress, shall, without the Consent of the other, adjourn for more than three days, not to any other Place than that in which the two Houses shall be sitting.

Section. 6. The Senators and Representatives shall receive a Compensation for their Services, to be ascertained by Law, and paid out of the Treasury of the United States. They shall in all Cases, except Treason, Felony and Breach of the Peace, be privileged from Arrest during their Attendance at the Session of their respective Houses, and in going to and returning from the same; and for any Speech or Debate in either House, they shall not be questioned in any other Place.

No Senator or Representative shall, during the Time for which he was elected, be appointed to any civil Office under the Authority of the United States, which shall have been created, or the Emoluments whereof shall have been encreased during such time; and no Person holding any Office under the United States, shall be a Member of either House during his Continuance in Office.

Section. 7. All Bills for raising Revenue shall originate in the House of Representatives; but the Senate may propose or concur with Amendments as on other Bills.

Every Bill which shall have passed the House of Representatives and the Senate shall, before it become a Law, be presented to the President of the United States; If he approve he shall sign it, but if not he shall return it, with his Objections to that House in which it shall have originated, who shall enter the Objections at large on their Journal, and proceed to reconsider it. If after such Reconsideration two thirds of that House shall agree to pass the Bill, it shall be sent, together with the Objections, to the other House, by which it shall likewise be reconsidered, and if approved by two thirds of that House, it shall become a Law. But in all such Cases the Votes of both Houses shall be determined by yeas and Nays, and the Names of the Persons voting for and against the Bill shall be entered on the Journal of each House respectively. If any Bill shall not be returned by the President within ten Days (Sundays excepted) after it shall have been presented to him, the Same shall be a Law, in like Manner as if he had signed it, unless the Congress by their Adjournment prevent its Return, in which Case it shall not be a Law.

Every Order, Resolution, or Vote to which the Concurrence of the Senate and House of Representatives may be necessary (except on a question of Adjournment) shall be presented to the President of the United States; and before the Same shall take Effect, shall be approved by him, or being disapproved by him, shall be repassed by two thirds of the Senate and House of Representatives, according to the Rules and Limitations prescribed in the Case of a Bill.

Section. 8. The Congress shall have Power To lay and collect Taxes, Duties, Imposts and Excises, to pay the Debts and provide for the common Defence and general Welfare of the United States; but all Duties, Imposts and Excises shall be uniform throughout the United States;

To borrow Money on the credit of the United States;

To regulate Commerce with foreign Nations, and among the several States, and with the Indian Tribes;

To establish an uniform Rule of Naturalization, and uniform Laws on the subject of Bankruptcies throughout the United States;

To coin Money, regulate the Value thereof, and of foreign Coin, and fix the Standard of Weights and Measures;

To provide for the Punishment of counterfeiting the Securities and current Coin of the United States;

To establish Post Offices and Post Roads;

To promote the Progress of Science and useful Arts, by securing for limited Times to Authors and Inventors the exclusive Right to their respective Writings and Discoveries;

To constitute Tribunals inferior to the supreme Court;

To define and punish Piracies and Felonies committed on the high Seas, and Offences against the Law of Nations;

To declare War, grant Letters of Marque and Reprisal, and make Rules concerning Captures on land and Water;

To raise and support Armies, but no Appropriation of Money to that Use shall be for a longer Term than two Years;

To provide and maintain a Navy;

To make Rules for the Government and Regulation of the land and naval Forces;

To provide for calling forth the Militia to execute the Laws of the Union, suppress Insurrections and repel Invasions;

To provide for organizing, arming, and disciplining, the Militia, and for governing such Part of them as may be employed in the Service of the United States, reserving to the States respectively, the Appointment of the Officers, and the Authority of training the Militia according to the discipline prescribed by Congress.

To exercise exclusive Legislation in all Cases whatsoever, over such District (not exceeding ten Miles square) as may, by Cession of Particular States, and the Acceptance of Congress, become the Seat of the Government of the United States, and to exercise like Authority over all Places purchased by the Consent of the Legislature of the State in which the Same shall be, for the Erection of Forts, Magazines, Arsenals, dock-Yards, and other needful Buildings;—And

To make all Laws which shall be necessary and proper for carrying into Execution the foregoing Powers, and all other Powers vested by this Constitution in the Government of the United States, or in any Department or Officer thereof.

Section. 9. The Migration or Importation of such Persons as any of the States now existing shall think proper to admit, shall not be prohibited by the Congress prior to the Year one thousand eight hundred and eight, but a Tax or duty may be imposed on such Importation, not exceeding ten dollars for each Person.

The Privilege of the Writ of Habeas Corpus shall not be suspended, unless when in Cases of Rebellion or Invasion the public Safety may require it.

No Bill of Attainder or ex post facto Law shall be passed.

No Capitation, or other direct, Tax shall be laid, unless in Proportion to the Census or Enumeration herein before directed to be taken.

No Tax or Duty shall be laid on Articles exported from any State.

No Preference shall be given by any Regulation of Commerce or Revenue to the Ports of one State over those of another: nor shall Vessels bound to, or from, one State, be obliged to enter, clear, or pay Duties in another.

No Money shall be drawn from the Treasury, but in Consequence of Appropriations made by Law; and a regular Statement and Account of the Receipts and Expenditures of all public Money shall be published from time to time.

No Title of Nobility shall be granted by the United States: And no Person holding any Office of Profit or trust under them, shall, without the Consent of the Congress, accept of any present, Emolument, Office, or Title, of any kind whatever, from any King, prince, or foreign State.

Section 10. No State shall enter into any Treaty, Alliance, or Confederation; grant Letters of Marque and Reprisal; coin Money; emit Bills of Credit; make any Thing but gold and silver Coin a Tender in Payment of Debts; pass any Bill of Attainder, ex post facto Law, or Law impairing the Obligation of Contracts, or grant any Title of Nobility.

No State shall, without the Consent of the Congress, lay any Imposts or Duties on Imports or Exports, except what may be absolutely necessary for executing its inspection Laws: and the net Produce of all Duties and Imposts, laid by any State on Imports or Exports, shall be for the Use of the Treasury of the United States; and all such Laws shall be subject to the Revision and Controul of the Congress.

No State shall, without the Consent of Congress, lay any Duty of Tonnage, keep Troops, or Ships of War in time of Peace, enter into any Agreement or Compact with another State, or with a foreign Power, or engage in War, unless actually invaded, or in such imminent Danger as will not admit of delay.

ARTICLE. II.

Section. 1. The executive Power shall be vested in a President of the United States of America. He shall hold his Office during the term of four Years, and, together with the Vice President, chosen for the same Term, be elected, as follows:

Each State shall appoint, in such Manner as the Legislature thereof may direct, a Number of Electors, equal to the whole Number of Senators and Representatives to which the State may be entitled in the Congress: but no Senator or Representative, or Person holding an Office of Trust or Profit under the United States, shall be appointed an Elector.

The Electors shall meet in their respective States, and vote by Ballot for two Persons, of whom one at least shall not be an Inhabitant of the same State with themselves. And they shall make a List of all the Persons voted for, and of the Number of Votes for each; which List they shall sign and certify, and transmit sealed to the Seat of the Government of the United States, directed to the President of the Senate. The President of the Senate shall, in the Presence of the Senate and House of Representatives, open all the Certificates, and the Votes shall then be counted. The Person having the greatest Number of Votes shall be the President, if such Number be a Majority of the whole Number of Electors appointed; and if there be more than one who have such Majority, and have an equal Number of Votes, then the House of Representatives shall immediately chuse by Ballot one of them for President; and if no Person have a Majority, then from the five highest on the List the said House shall in like Manner chuse the President. But in chusing the President, the Votes shall be taken by States, the Representation from each State having one Vote; A quorum for this Purpose shall consist of a Member or Members from two thirds of the States, and a Majority of all the States shall be necessary to a Choice. In every Case, after the Choice of the President, the Person having the greatest Number of Votes of the Electors shall be the Vice President. But if there should remain two or more who have equal Votes, the Senate shall chuse from them by Ballot the Vice President.

The Congress may determine the Time of chusing the Electors, and the Day on which they shall give their Votes; which Day shall be the same throughout the United States.

No Person except a natural born Citizen, or a Citizen of the United States, at the time of the Adoption of this Constitution, shall be eligible to the Office of President; neither shall any Person be eligible to that Office who shall not have attained to the Age of thirty five Years, and been fourteen Years a Resident within the United States.

In Case of the Removal of the President from Office, or of his Death, Resignation, or Inability to discharge the Powers and Duties of the said Office, the Same shall devolve on the Vice President, and the Congress may by Law provide for the Case of Removal, Death, Resignation or Inability, both of the President and Vice President, declaring what Officer shall then act as President, and such Officer shall act accordingly, until the Disability be removed, or a President shall be elected.

The President shall, at stated Times, receive for his Services, a Compensation, which shall neither be encreased or diminished during the Period for which he shall have been elected, and he shall not receive within that Period any other Emolument from the United States, or any of them.

Before he enters on the Execution of his Office, he shall take the following Oath or Affirmation:—"I do solemnly swear (or affirm) that I will faithfully execute the Office of President of the United States, and will to the best of my Ability, preserve, protect and defend the Constitution of the United States."

Section. 2. The President shall be Commander in Chief of the Army and Navy of the United States, and of the Militia of the several States, when called into the actual Service of the United States; he may require the Opinion, in writing, of the principal Officer in each of the executive Departments, upon any Subject relating to the Duties of their respective Offices, and he shall have Power to grant Reprieves and Pardons for Offences against the United States, except in Cases of Impeachment.

He shall have Power, by and with the Advice and Consent of the Senate, to make Treaties, provided two thirds of the Senators present concur; and he shall nominate, and by and with the Advice and Consent of the Senate, shall appoint Ambassadors, other public Ministers and Consuls, Judges of the supreme Court, and all other Officers of the United States, whose Appointments are not herein otherwise provided for, and which shall be established by Law;

but the Congress may by Law vest the Appointment of such inferior Officers, as they think proper, in the President alone, in the Courts of Law, or in the Heads of Departments.

The President shall have Power to fill up all Vacancies that may happen during the Recess of the Senate, by granting Commissions which shall expire at the End of their next Session.

Section. 3. He shall from time to time give to the Congress Information of the State of the Union, and recommend to their Consideration such Measures as he shall judge necessary and expedient; he may, on extraordinary Occasions, convene both Houses, or either of them, and in Case of Disagreement between them, with Respect to the Time of Adjournment, he may adjourn them to such Time as he shall think proper; he shall receive Ambassadors and other public Ministers; he shall take Care that the Laws be faithfully executed, and shall Commission all the Officers of the United States.

Section. 4. The President, Vice President and all civil Officers of the United States, shall be removed from Office on Impeachment for, and Conviction of, Treason, Bribery, or other high Crimes and Misdemeanors.

ARTICLE. III.

Section. 1. The judicial Power of the United States, shall be vested in one supreme Court, and in such inferior Courts as the Congress may from time to time ordain and establish. The Judges, both of the supreme and inferior Courts, shall hold their Offices during good Behavior, and shall, at stated Times, receive for their Services, a Compensation, which shall not be diminished during their Continuance in Office.

Section. 2. The judicial Power shall extend to all Cases, in Law and Equity, arising under this Constitution, the Laws of the United States, and Treaties made, or which shall be made, under their Authority;—to all Cases affecting Ambassadors, other public Ministers and Consuls;—to all Cases of admiralty and maritime Jurisdiction;—the Controversies to which the United States shall be a Party;—to Controversies between two or more States;—between a State and Citizens of another State;—between Citizens of different States;—between Citizens of the same State claiming Lands under Grants of different States, and between a State, or the Citizens thereof, and foreign States, Citizens or Subjects.

In all cases affecting Ambassadors, other public Ministers and Consuls, and those in which a State shall be Party, the supreme Court shall have original Jurisdiction. In all the other Cases before mentioned, the supreme Court shall have appellate Jurisdiction, both as to Law and Fact, with such Exceptions, and under such Regulations as the Congress shall make.

The Trial of all Crimes, except in Cases of Impeachment, shall be by Jury; and such Trial shall be held in the State where the said Crimes shall have been committed; but when not committed within any State, the Trial shall be at such Place or Places as the Congress may by Law have directed.

Section. 3. Treason against the United States, shall consist only in levying War against them, or in adhering to their Enemies, giving them Aid and Comfort. No Person shall be convicted of Treason unless on the Testimony of two Witnesses to the same overt Act, or on Confession in open Court.

The Congress shall have Power to declare the Punishment of Treason, but no Attainder of Treason shall work Corruption of Blood, or Forfeiture except during the Life of the Person attainted.

ARTICLE. IV.

Section. 1. Full Faith and Credit shall be given in each State to the public Acts, Records, and judicial Proceedings of every other State. And the Congress may by general Laws prescribe the Manner in which such Acts, Records and Proceedings shall be proved, and the Effect thereof.

Section. 2. The Citizens of each State shall be entitled to all Privileges and Immunities of Citizens in the several States.

A Person charged in any State with Treason, Felony, or other Crime, who shall flee from Justice, and be found in another State, shall on Demand of the executive Authority of the State from which he fled, be delivered up, to be removed to the State having Jurisdiction of the Crime.

No Person held to Service or Labour in one State, under the Laws thereof, escaping into another, shall, in Consequence of any Law or Regulation therein, be discharged from such Service or Labour, but shall be delivered up on Claim of the Party to whom such Service or Labour may be due.

Section. 3. New States may be admitted by the Congress into this Union; but no new State shall be formed or erected within the Jurisdiction of any other State; nor any State be formed by the Junction of two or more States, or Parts of States, without the consent of the Legislatures of the States concerned as well as of the Congress.

The Congress shall have Power to dispose of and make all needful Rules and Regulations respecting the Territory or other Property belonging to the United States; and nothing in this Constitution shall be so construed as to Prejudice any Claims of the United States, or of any particular States.

Section. 4. The United States shall guarantee to every State in this Union a Republican Form of Government, and shall protect each of them against Invasion; and on Application of the Legislature, or of the Executive (when the Legislature cannot be convened) against domestic Violence.

ARTICLE. V.

The Congress, whenever two thirds of both Houses shall deem it necessary, shall propose Amendments to this Constitution, or, on the Application of the Legislatures of two thirds of the several States, shall call a Convention for proposing Amendments, which, in either Case, shall be valid to all Intents and Purposes, as Part of this Constitution, when ratified by the Legislatures of three fourths of the several States, or by Conventions in three fourths thereof, as the one or the other Mode of Ratification may be proposed by the Congress; Provided that no Amendment which may be made prior to the Year One thousand eight hundred and eight shall in any Manner affect the first and fourth Clauses in the Ninth Section of the first Article; and that no State, without its Consent, shall be deprived of its equal Suffrage in the Senate.

ARTICLE. VI.

All Debts contracted and Engagements entered into, before the Adoption of this Constitution, shall be as valid against the United States under this Constitution, as under the Confederation.

This Constitution, and the Laws of the United States which shall be made in Pursuance thereof; and all Treaties made, or which shall be made, under the Authority of the United States, shall be the supreme Law of the Land; and the Judges in every State shall be bound thereby, any Thing in the Constitution or Laws of any State to the Contrary notwithstanding.

The Senators and Representatives before mentioned, and the Members of the several State Legislatures, and all executive and judicial Officers, both of the United States and of the several States, shall be bound by Oath or Affirmation, to support this Constitution; but no religious Test shall ever be required as a Qualification to any Office or public Trust under the United States.

ARTICLE. VII.

The Ratification of the Conventions of nine States, shall be sufficient for the Establishment of this Constitution between the States so ratifying the Same.

Done in Convention by the Unanimous Consent of the States present the Seventeenth Day of September in the Year of our Lord one thousand seven hundred and Eighty seven and of the Independence of the United States of America the Twelfth. In witness thereof We have hereunto subscribed our Names,

G°. WASHINGTON—Presd^t.
and deputy from Virginia.

| New Hampshire | John Langdon |
| | Nicholas Gilman |

| Massachusetts | Nathaniel Gorham |
| | Rufus King |

| Connecticut | Wm Saml Johnson |
| | Roger Sherman |

| New York: . . . | Alexander Hamilton |

New Jersey	Wil: Livingston
	David A. Brearley.
	Wm Paterson.
	Jona: Dayton

Pennsylvania	B Franklin
	Thomas Mifflin
	Robt Morris
	Geo. Clymer
	Thos FitzSimons
	Jared Ingersoll
	James Wilson
	Gouv Morris

Delaware	Geo: Read
	Gunning Bedford jun
	John Dickinson
	Richard Bassett
	Jaco: Broom

Maryland	James McHenry
	Dan of St Thos Jenifer
	Danl Carroll

| Virginia | John Blair— |
| | James Madison Jr. |

North Carolina	Wm Blount
	Richd Dobbs Spaight.
	Hu Williamson

South Carolina	J. Rutledge
	Charles Cotesworth Pinckney
	Charles Pinckney
	Pierce Butler.

| Georgia | William Few |
| | Abr Baldwin |

AMENDMENTS TO THE CONSTITUTION

ARTICLES IN ADDITION TO, and Amendment of the Constitution of the United States of America, proposed by Congress, and ratified by the Legislatures of the several States, pursuant to the fifth Article of the original Constitution.

AMENDMENT I.

Congress shall make no law respecting an establishment of religion, or prohibiting the free exercise thereof; or abridging the freedom of speech, or of the press; or the right of the people peaceably to assemble, and to petition the Government for a redress of grievances.

AMENDMENT II.

A well regulated Militia, being necessary to the security of a free State, the right of the people to keep and bear Arms, shall not be infringed.

AMENDMENT III.

No Soldier shall, in time of peace be quartered in any house, without the consent of the Owner, nor in time of war, but in a manner to be prescribed by law.

AMENDMENT IV.

The right of the people to be secure in their persons, houses, papers, and effects, against unreasonable searches and seizures, shall not be violated, and no Warrants shall issue, but upon probable cause, supported by Oath or affirmation, and particularly describing the place to be searched, and the persons or things to be seized.

AMENDMENT V.

No person shall be held to answer for a capital, or otherwise infamous crime, unless on a presentment or indictment of a Grand Jury, except in cases arising in the land or naval forces, or in the Militia, when in actual service in time of War or public danger; nor shall any person be subject for the same offence to be twice put in jeopardy of life or limb; nor shall be compelled in any criminal case to be a witness against himself, nor be deprived of life, liberty, or property, without due process of law; nor shall private property be taken for public use, without just compensation.

AMENDMENT VI.

In all criminal prosecutions, the accused shall enjoy the right to a speedy and public trial, by an impartial jury of the State and district wherein the crime shall have been committed, which district shall have been previously ascertained by law, and to be informed of the nature and cause of the accusation; to be confronted with the witnesses against him; to have compulsory process for obtaining witnesses in his favor, and to have the Assistance of Counsel for his defence.

AMENDMENT VII.

In Suits at common law, where the value in controversy shall exceed twenty dollars, the right of trial by jury shall be preserved, and no fact tried by a jury, shall be otherwise re-examined in any Court of the United States, than according to the rules of the common law.

AMENDMENT VIII.

Excessive bail shall not be required, nor excessive fines imposed, nor cruel and unusual punishments inflicted.

AMENDMENT IX.

The enumeration in the Constitution, of certain rights, shall not be construed to deny or disparage others retained by the people.

AMENDMENT X.

The powers not delegated to the United States by the Constitution, nor prohibited by it to the States, are reserved to the States respectively, or to the people. [The first ten amendments went into effect December 15, 1791.]

AMENDMENT XI.

The Judicial power of the United States shall not be construed to extend to any suit in law or equity, commenced or prosecuted against one of the United States by Citizens of another State, or by Citizens or Subjects of any Foreign State. [January 8, 1798.]

AMENDMENT XII.

The Electors shall meet in their respective states, and vote by ballot for President and Vice-President, one of whom, at least, shall not be an inhabitant of the same state with themselves; they shall name in their ballots the person voted for as President, and in distinct ballots the person voted for as Vice-President, and they shall make distinct lists of all persons voted for as President, and of all persons voted for as Vice President, and of the number of votes for each, which lists they shall sign and certify, and transmit sealed to the seat of the government of the United States, directed to the President of the Senate;—The President of the Senate shall, in the presence of the Senate and House of Representatives, open all the certificates and the votes shall then be counted;—The person having the greatest number of votes for President, shall be the President, if such number be a majority of the whole number of Electors appointed; and if no person have such majority, then from the persons having the highest numbers not exceeding three on the list of those voted for as President, the House of Representatives shall choose immediately, by ballot, the President. But in choosing the President, the votes shall be taken by states, the representation from each state having one vote; a quorum for this purpose shall consist of a member or members from two-thirds of the states, and a majority of all the states shall be necessary to a choice. And if the House of Representatives shall not choose a President whenever the right of choice shall devolve upon them, before the fourth day of March next following, then the Vice-President shall act as President, as in the case of the death or other constitutional disability of the President.—The person having the greatest number of votes as Vice-President, shall be the Vice-President, if such number be a majority of the whole number of Electors appointed, and if no person have a majority, then from the two highest numbers on the list, the Senate shall choose the Vice-President; a quorum for the purpose shall consist of two-thirds of the whole number of Senators, and a majority of the whole number shall be necessary to a choice. But no person constitutionally ineligible to the office of President shall be eligible to that of Vice-President of the United States. [September 25, 1804.]

AMENDMENT XIII.

Section 1. Neither slavery nor involuntary servitude, except as a punishment for crime whereof the party shall have been duly convicted, shall exist within the United States, or any place subject to their jurisdiction.

Section 2. Congress shall have power to enforce this article by appropriate legislation. [December 18, 1865.]

AMENDMENT XIV.

Section 1. All persons born or naturalized in the United States, and subject to the jurisdiction thereof, are citizens of the United States and of the State wherein they reside. No State shall make or enforce any law which shall abridge the privileges or immunities of citizens of the United States; nor shall any State deprive any person of life, liberty, or property, without due process of law; nor deny to any person within its jurisdiction the equal protection of the laws.

Section 2. Representatives shall be apportioned among the several States according to their respective numbers, counting the whole number of persons in each State, excluding Indians not taxed. But when the right to vote at any election for the choice of electors for President and Vice President of the United States, Representatives in Congress, the Executive and Judicial officers of a State, or the members of the Legislature thereof, is denied to any of the male inhabitants of such State, being twenty-one years of age, and citizens of the United States, or in any way abridged, except for participation in rebellion, or other crime, the basis of representation therein shall be reduced in the proportion which the number of such male citizens shall bear to the whole number of male citizens twenty-one years of age in such State.

Section 3. No person shall be a Senator or Representative in Congress, or elector of President and Vice President, or hold any office, civil or military, under the United States, or under any State, who, having previously taken an oath, as a member of Congress, or as an officer of the United States, or as a member of any State legislature, or as an executive or judicial officer of any State, to support the Constitution of the United States, shall have engaged in insurrection or rebellion against the same, or given aid or comfort to the enemies thereof. But Congress may by a vote of two-thirds of each House, remove such disability.

Section 4. The validity of the public debt of the United States, authorized by law, including debts incurred for payment of pensions and bounties for services in suppressing insurrection or rebellion, shall not be questioned. But neither the United States nor any State shall assume or pay any debt or obligation incurred in aid of insurrection or rebellion against the United States, or any claim for the loss or emancipation of any slave; but all such debts, obligations and claims shall be held illegal and void.

Section 5. The Congress shall have power to enforce, by appropriate legislation, the provisions of this article. [July 28, 1868.]

AMENDMENT XV.

Section 1. The right of citizens of the United States to vote shall not be denied or abridged by the United States or by any State on account of race, color, or previous condition of servitude—

•

Section 2. The Congress shall have power to enforce this article by appropriate legislation.—[March 30, 1870.]

AMENDMENT XVI.

The Congress shall have power to lay and collect taxes on incomes, from whatever source derived, without apportionment among the several States, and without regard to any census or enumeration. [February 25, 1913.]

AMENDMENT XVII.

The Senate of the United States shall be composed of two senators from each State, elected by the people thereof, for six years; and each Senator shall have one vote. The electors in each State shall have the qualifications requisite for electors of the most numerous branch of the State legislature.

When vacancies happen in the representation of any State in the Senate, the executive authority of such State shall issue writs of election to fill such vacancies: *Provided,* That the legislature of any State may empower the executive thereof to make temporary appointments until the people fill the vacancies by election as the legislature may direct.

This amendment shall not be so construed as to affect the election or term of any senator chosen before it becomes valid as part of the Constitution. [May 31, 1913.]

AMENDMENT XVIII.

After one year from the ratification of this article, the manufacture, sale, or transportation of intoxicating liquors within, the importation thereof into, or the exportation thereof from the United States and all territory subject to the jurisdiction thereof for beverage purposes is hereby prohibited.

The Congress and the several States shall have concurrent power to enforce this article by appropriate legislation.

This article shall be inoperative unless it shall have been ratified as an amendment to the Constitution by the legislatures of the several States, as provided in the Constitution, within seven years from the date of the submission thereof to the States by Congress. [January 29, 1919.]

AMENDMENT XIX.

The right of citizens of the United States to vote shall not be denied or abridged by the United States or by any State on account of sex.

The Congress shall have power by appropriate legislation to enforce the provisions of this article. [August 26, 1920.]

AMENDMENT XX.

Section 1. The terms of the President and Vice-President shall end at noon on the twentieth day of January, and the terms of Senators and Representatives at noon on the third day of January, of the years in which such terms would have ended if this article had not been ratified; and the terms of their successors shall then begin.

Section 2. The Congress shall assemble at least once in every year, and such meeting shall begin at noon on the third day of January, unless they shall by law appoint a different day.

Section 3. If, at the time fixed for the beginning of the term of the President, the President-elect shall have died, the Vice-President-elect shall become President. If a President shall not have been chosen before the time fixed for the beginning of his term, or if the President-elect shall have failed to qualify, then the Vice-President-elect shall act as President until a President shall have qualified; and the Congress may by law provide for the case wherein neither a President-elect nor a Vice-President-elect shall have qualified, declaring who shall then act as President, or the manner in which one who is to act shall be selected, and such person shall act accordingly until a President or Vice-President shall have qualified.

Section 4. The Congress may by law provide for the case of the death of any of the persons from whom the House of Representatives may choose a President whenever the right of choice shall have devolved upon them, and for the case of the death of any of the persons from whom the Senate may choose a Vice-President whenever the right of choice shall have devolved upon them.

Section 5. Sections 1 and 2 shall take effect on the 15th day of October following the ratification of this article.

Section 6. This article shall be inoperative unless it shall have been ratified as an amendment to the Constitution by the legislatures of three-fourths of the several States within seven years from the date of its submission. [February 6, 1933.]

AMENDMENT XXI.

Section 1. The eighteenth article of amendment to the Constitution of the United States is hereby repealed.

Section 2. The transportation or importation into any State, Territory or possession of the United States for delivery or use therein of intoxicating liquors, in violation of the laws thereof, is hereby prohibited.

Section 3. This article shall be inoperative unless it shall have been ratified as an amendment to the Constitution by convention in the several States, as provided in the Constitution, within seven years from the date of the submission thereof to the States by the Congress. [December 5, 1933.]

AMENDMENT XXII.

Section 1. No person shall be elected to the office of the President more than twice, and no person who has held the office of President, or acted as President, for more than two years of a term to which some other person was elected President shall be elected to the office of the President more than once. But this Article shall not apply to any person holding the office of President when this Article was proposed by the Congress, and shall not prevent any person who may be holding the office of President, or acting as President, during the term within which this Article becomes operative from holding the office of President or acting as President during the remainder of such term.

Section 2. This article shall be inoperative unless it shall have been ratified as an amendment to the Constitution by the legislatures of three-fourths of the several states within seven years from the date of its submission to the States by the Congress. [February 27, 1951.]

AMENDMENT XXIII.

Section 1. The District constituting the seat of government of the United States shall appoint in such manner as the Congress may direct:

A number of electors of President and Vice-President equal to the whole number of Senators and Representatives in Congress to which the District would be entitled if it were a State, but in no event more than the least populous State; they shall be in addition to those appointed by the States, but they shall be considered, for the purposes of the election of President and Vice-President, to be electors appointed by a State; and they shall meet in the District and perform such duties as provided by the twelfth article of amendment.

Section 2. The Congress shall have the power to enforce this article by appropriate legislation. [March 29, 1961.]

AMENDMENT XXIV.

Section 1. The right of citizens of the United States to vote in any primary or other election for President or Vice President, for electors for President or Vice President, or for Senator or Representative in Congress, shall not be denied or abridged by the United States or any State by reason of failure to pay any poll tax or other tax.

Section 2. The Congress shall have power to enforce this article by appropriate legislation. [January 23, 1964.]

AMENDMENT XXV.

Section 1. In case of the removal of the President from office or of his death or resignation, the Vice President shall become President.

Section 2. Whenever there is a vacancy in the office of Vice President, the President shall nominate a Vice President who shall take office upon confirmation by a majority vote of both Houses of Congress.

Section 3. Whenever the President transmits to the President pro tempore of the Senate and the Speaker of the House of Representatives his written declaration that he is unable to discharge the powers and duties of his office, and until he transmits to them a written declaration to the contrary, such powers and duties shall be discharged by the Vice President as Acting President.

Section 4. Whenever the Vice President and a majority of either the principal officers of the executive departments or of such other body as Congress may by law provide, transmit to the President pro tempore of the Senate and the Speaker of the House of Representatives their written declaration that the President is unable to discharge the powers and duties of his office, the Vice President shall immediately assume the powers and duties of the office as Acting President.

Thereafter, when the President transmits to the President pro tempore of the Senate and the Speaker of the House of Representatives his written declaration that no inability exists, he shall resume the powers and duties of his office unless the Vice President and a majority of either the principal officers of the executive departments or of such other body as Congress may by law provide, transmit within four days to the President pro tempore of the Senate and the Speaker of the House of Representatives their written declaration that the President is unable to discharge the powers and duties of his office. Thereupon Congress shall decide the issue, assembling within forty-eight hours for that purpose if not in session. If the Congress, within twenty-one days after receipt of the latter written declaration, or, if Congress is not in session, within twenty-one days after Congress is required to assemble, determines by two-thirds vote of both Houses that the President is unable to discharge the powers and duties of his office, the Vice President shall continue to discharge the same as Acting President; otherwise, the President shall resume the powers and duties of his office. [February 10, 1967.]

Amendment XXVI.

Section 1. The right of citizens of the United States, who are eighteen years of age or older, to vote shall not be denied or abridged by the United States or by any State on account of age.

Section 2. The Congress shall have power to enforce this article by appropriate legislation [June 30, 1971.]

Amendment XXVII.

No law, varying the compensation for the services of the Senators and Representatives shall take effect, until an election of Representatives shall have intervened. [May 8, 1992.]

PRESIDENTIAL ELECTIONS

Year	Number of States	Candidates	Parties	Popular Vote	% of Popular Vote	Electoral Vote	% Voter Participation
1789	11	**GEORGE WASHINGTON**	No party designations			69	
		John Adams				34	
		Other candidates				35	
1792	15	**GEORGE WASHINGTON**	No party designations			132	
		John Adams				77	
		George Clinton				50	
		Other candidates				5	
1796	16	**JOHN ADAMS**	Federalist			71	
		Thomas Jefferson	Democratic-Republican			68	
		Thomas Pinckney	Federalist			59	
		Aaron Burr	Democratic-Republican			30	
		Other candidates				48	
1800	16	**THOMAS JEFFERSON**	Democratic-Republican			73	
		Aaron Burr	Democratic-Republican			73	
		John Adams	Federalist			65	
		Charles C. Pinckney	Federalist			64	
		John Jay	Federalist			1	
1804	17	**THOMAS JEFFERSON**	Democratic-Republican			162	
		Charles C. Pinckney	Federalist			14	

Year	Number of States	Candidates	Parties	Popular Vote	% of Popular Vote	Electoral Vote	% Voter Participation
1808	17	**JAMES MADISON**	Democratic-Republican			122	
		Charles C. Pinckney	Federalist			47	
		George Clinton	Democratic-Republican			6	
1812	18	**JAMES MADISON**	Democratic-Republican			128	
		DeWitt Clinton	Federalist			89	
1816	19	**JAMES MONROE**	Democratic-Republican			183	
		Rufus King	Federalist			34	
1820	24	**JAMES MONROE**	Democratic-Republican			231	
		John Quincy Adams	Independent			1	
1824	24	**JOHN QUINCY ADAMS**	Democratic-Republican	108,740	30.5	84	26.9
		Andrew Jackson	Democratic-Republican	153,544	43.1	99	
		Henry Clay	Democratic-Republican	47,136	13.2	37	
		William H. Crawford	Democratic-Republican	46,618	13.1	41	
1828	24	**ANDREW JACKSON**	Democratic	647,286	56.0	178	57.6
		John Quincy Adams	National-Republican	508,064	44.0	83	

Year	Number of States	Candidates	Parties	Popular Vote	% of Popular Vote	Electoral Vote	% Voter Participation
1832	24	**ANDREW JACKSON**	Democratic	688,242	54.5	219	55.4
		Henry Clay	National-Republican	473,462	37.5	49	
		William Wirt	Anti-Masonic ⎱	101,051	8.0	7	
		John Floyd	Democratic ⎰			11	
1836	26	**MARTIN VAN BUREN**	Democratic	765,483	50.9	170	57.8
		William H. Harrison	Whig ⎱	739,795	49.1	73	
		Hugh L. White	Whig			26	
		Daniel Webster	Whig			14	
		W. P. Mangum	Whig ⎰			11	
1840	26	**WILLIAM H. HARRISON**	Whig	1,274,624	53.1	234	80.2
		Martin Van Buren	Democratic	1,127,781	46.9	60	
1844	26	**JAMES K. POLK**	Democratic	1,338,464	49.6	170	78.9
		Henry Clay	Whig	1,300,097	48.1	105	
		James G. Birney	Liberty	62,300	2.3		
1848	30	**ZACHARY TAYLOR**	Whig	1,360,967	47.4	163	72.7
		Lewis Cass	Democratic	1,222,342	42.5	127	
		Martin Van Buren	Free Soil	291,263	10.1		
1852	31	**FRANKLIN PIERCE**	Democratic	1,601,117	50.9	254	69.6
		Winfield Scott	Whig	1,385,453	44.1	42	
		John P. Hale	Free Soil	155,825	5.0		
1856	31	**JAMES BUCHANAN**	Democratic	1,833,955	45.3	174	78.9
		John C. Frémont	Republican	1,339,932	33.1	114	
		Millard Fillmore	American	871,731	21.6	8	

Year	No.	Candidates	Party	Popular Vote	% Popular	Electoral Vote	% Participation
1860	33	**ABRAHAM LINCOLN**	Republican	1,865,593	39.8	180	81.2
		Stephen A. Douglas	Democratic	1,382,713	29.5	12	
		John C. Breckinridge	Democratic	848,356	18.1	72	
		John Bell	Constitutional Union	592,906	12.6	39	
1864	36	**ABRAHAM LINCOLN**	Republican	2,206,938	55.0	212	73.8
		George B. McClellan	Democratic	1,803,787	45.0	21	
1868	37	**ULYSSES S. GRANT**	Republican	3,013,421	52.7	214	78.1
		Horatio Seymour	Democratic	2,706,829	47.3	80	

Candidates receiving less than 1 percent of the popular vote have been omitted. Thus the percentage of popular vote given for any election year may not total 100 percent.

Before the passage of the Twelfth Amendment in 1804, the Electoral College voted for two presidential candidates; the runner-up became vice-president.

ADMISSION OF STATES

Order of Admission	State	Date of Admission	Order of Admission	State	Date of Admission
1	Delaware	December 7, 1787	26	Michigan	January 26, 1837
2	Pennsylvania	December 12, 1787	27	Florida	March 3, 1845
3	New Jersey	December 18, 1787	28	Texas	December 29, 1845
4	Georgia	January 2, 1788	29	Iowa	December 28, 1846
5	Connecticut	January 9, 1788	30	Wisconsin	May 29, 1848
6	Massachusetts	February 7, 1788	31	California	September 9, 1850
7	Maryland	April 28, 1788	32	Minnesota	May 11, 1858
8	South Carolina	May 23, 1788	33	Oregon	February 14, 1859
9	New Hampshire	June 21, 1788	34	Kansas	January 29, 1861
10	Virginia	June 25, 1788	35	West Virginia	June 30, 1863
11	New York	July 26, 1788	36	Nevada	October 31, 1864
12	North Carolina	November 21, 1789	37	Nebraska	March 1, 1867
13	Rhode Island	May 29, 1790	38	Colorado	August 1, 1876
14	Vermont	March 4, 1791	39	North Dakota	November 2, 1889
15	Kentucky	June 1, 1792	40	South Dakota	November 2, 1889
16	Tennessee	June 1, 1796	41	Montana	November 8, 1889
17	Ohio	March 1, 1803	42	Washington	November 11, 1889
18	Louisiana	April 30, 1812	43	Idaho	July 3, 1890
19	Indiana	December 11, 1816	44	Wyoming	July 10, 1890
20	Mississippi	December 10, 1817	45	Utah	January 4, 1896
21	Illinois	December 3, 1818	46	Oklahoma	November 16, 1907
22	Alabama	December 14, 1819	47	New Mexico	January 6, 1912
23	Maine	March 15, 1820	48	Arizona	February 14, 1912
24	Missouri	August 10, 1821	49	Alaska	January 3, 1959
25	Arkansas	June 15, 1836	50	Hawaii	August 21, 1959

POPULATION OF THE UNITED STATES

Year	Number of States	Population	% Increase	Population per Square Mile
1790	13	3,929,214		4.5
1800	16	5,308,483	35.1	6.1
1810	17	7,239,881	36.4	4.3
1820	23	9,638,453	33.1	5.5
1830	24	12,866,020	33.5	7.4
1840	26	17,069,453	32.7	9.8
1850	31	23,191,876	35.9	7.9
1860	33	31,443,321	35.6	10.6
1870	37	39,818,449	26.6	13.4
1880	38	50,155,783	26.0	16.9
1890	44	62,947,714	25.5	21.1
1900	45	75,994,575	20.7	25.6
1910	46	91,972,266	21.0	31.0
1920	48	105,710,620	14.9	35.6
1930	48	122,775,046	16.1	41.2
1940	48	131,669,275	7.2	44.2
1950	48	150,697,361	14.5	50.7
1960	50	179,323,175	19.0	50.6
1970	50	203,235,298	13.3	57.5
1980	50	226,504,825	11.4	64.0
1985	50	237,839,000	5.0	67.2
1990	50	250,122,000	5.2	70.6
1995	50	263,411,707	5.3	74.4

IMMIGRATION TO THE UNITED STATES, FISCAL YEARS 1820–1990

Year	Number	Year	Number	Year	Number	Year	Number
1820–1989	**55,457,531**	**1871–80**	**2,812,191**	**1921–30**	**4,107,209**	**1971–80**	**4,493,314**
1820	8,385	1871	321,350	1921	805,228	1971	370,478
1821–30	**143,439**	1872	404,806	1922	309,556	1972	384,685
1821	9,127	1873	459,803	1923	522,919	1973	400,063
1822	6,911	1874	313,339	1924	706,896	1974	394,861
1823	6,354	1875	227,498	1925	294,314	1975	386,914
1824	7,912	1876	169,986	1926	304,488	1976	398,613
1825	10,199	1877	141,857	1927	335,175	1976	103,676
1826	10,837	1878	138,469	1928	307,255	1977	462,315
1827	18,875	1879	177,826	1929	279,678	1978	601,442
1828	27,382	1880	457,257	1930	241,700	1979	460,348
1829	22,520	**1881–90**	**5,246,613**	**1931–40**	**528,431**	1980	530,639
1830	23,322	1881	669,431	1931	97,139	**1981–90**	**7,338,062**
1831–40	**599,125**	1882	788,992	1932	35,576	1981	596,600
1831	22,633	1883	603,322	1933	23,068	1982	594,131
1832	60,482	1884	518,592	1934	29,470	1983	559,763
1833	58,640	1885	395,346	1935	34,956	1984	543,903
1834	65,365	1886	334,203	1936	36,329	1985	570,009
1835	45,374	1887	490,109	1937	50,244	1986	601,708
1836	76,242	1888	546,889	1938	67,895	1987	601,516
1837	79,340	1889	444,427	1939	82,998	1988	643,025
1838	38,914	1890	455,302	1940	70,756	1989	1,090,924
1839	68,069	**1891–1900**	**3,687,564**	**1941–50**	**1,035,039**	1990	1,536,483
1840	84,066	1891	560,319	1941	51,776		
1841–50	**1,713,251**	1892	579,663	1942	28,781		
1841	80,289	1893	439,730	1943	23,725		
1842	104,565	1894	285,631	1944	28,551		
		1895	258,536	1945	38,119		
		1896	343,267	1946	108,721		

Year	Number	Year	Number	Year	Number
1843	52,496	1897	230,832	1947	147,292
1844	78,615	1898	229,299	1948	170,570
1845	114,371	1899	311,715	1949	188,317
1846	154,416	1900	448,572	1950	249,187
1847	234,968	**1901–10**	**8,795,386**	**1951–60**	**2,515,479**
1848	226,527	1901	487,918	1951	205,717
1849	297,024	1902	648,743	1952	265,520
1850	369,980	1903	857,046	1953	170,434
1851–60	**2,598,214**	1904	812,870	1954	208,177
1851	379,466	1905	1,026,499	1955	237,790
1852	371,603	1906	1,100,735	1956	321,625
1853	368,645	1907	1,285,349	1957	326,867
1854	427,833	1908	782,870	1958	253,265
1855	200,877	1909	751,786	1959	260,686
1856	200,436	1910	1,041,570	1960	265,398
1857	251,306	**1911–20**	**5,735,811**	**1961–70**	**3,321,677**
1858	123,126	1911	878,587	1961	271,344
1859	121,282	1912	838,172	1962	283,763
1860	153,640	1913	1,197,892	1963	306,260
1861–70	**2,314,824**	1914	1,218,480	1964	292,248
1861	91,918	1915	326,700	1965	296,697
1862	91,985	1916	298,826	1966	323,040
1863	176,282	1917	295,403	1967	361,972
1864	193,418	1918	110,618	1968	454,448
1865	248,120	1919	141,132	1969	358,579
1866	318,568	1920	430,001	1970	373,326
1867	315,722				
1868	138,840				
1869	352,768				
1870	387,203				

Source: U.S. Immigration and Naturalization Service, 1991.

IMMIGRATION BY REGION AND SELECTED COUNTRY OF LAST RESIDENCE, FISCAL YEARS 1820–1989

Region and Country of Last Residence[1]	1820	1821–30	1831–40	1841–50	1851–60	1861–70	1871–80	1881–90
All countries	8,385	143,439	599,125	1,713,251	2,598,214	2,314,824	2,812,191	5,246,613
Europe	7,690	98,797	495,681	1,597,442	2,452,577	2,065,141	2,271,925	4,735,484
Austria-Hungary	—[2]	—[2]	—[2]	—[2]	—[2]	7,800	72,969	353,719
Austria	—[2]	—[2]	—[2]	—[2]	—[2]	37,124	63,009	226,038
Hungary	—[2]	—[2]	—[2]	—[2]	—[2]	[3]484	9,960	127,681
Belgium	1	27	22	5,074	4,738	6,734	7,221	20,177
Czechoslovakia	—[4]	—[4]	—[4]	—[4]	—[4]	—[4]	—[4]	—[4]
Denmark	20	169	1,063	539	3,749	17,094	31,771	88,132
France	371	8,497	45,575	77,262	76,358	35,986	72,206	50,464
Germany	968	6,761	152,454	434,626	951,667	787,468	718,182	1,452,970
Greece	—	20	49	16	31	72	210	2,308
Ireland[5]	3,614	50,724	207,381	780,719	914,119	435,778	436,871	655,482
Italy	30	409	2,253	1,870	9,231	11,725	55,759	307,309
Netherlands	49	1,078	1,412	8,251	10,789	9,102	16,541	53,701
Norway-Sweden	3	91	1,201	13,903	20,931	109,298	211,245	568,362
Norway	—[6]	—[6]	—[6]	—[6]	—[6]	—[6]	95,323	176,586
Sweden	—[6]	—[6]	—[6]	—[6]	—[6]	—[6]	115,922	391,776
Poland	5	16	369	105	1,164	2,027	12,970	51,806
Portugal	35	145	829	550	1,055	2,658	14,082	16,978
Romania	—[7]	—[7]	—[7]	—[7]	—[7]	—[7]	11	6,348
Soviet Union	14	75	277	551	457	2,512	39,284	213,282
Spain	139	2,477	2,125	2,209	9,298	6,697	5,266	4,419
Switzerland	31	3,226	4,821	4,644	25,011	23,286	28,293	81,988
United Kingdom[5,8]	2,410	25,079	75,810	267,044	423,974	606,896	548,043	807,357
Yugoslavia	—[9]	—[9]	—[9]	—[9]	—[9]	—[9]	—[9]	—[9]
Other Europe	—	3	40	79	5	8	1,001	682

Asia	6	30	55	141	41,538	64,759	124,160	69,942
China[10]	1	2	8	35	41,397	64,301	123,201	61,711
Hong Kong	—[11]	—[11]	—[11]	—[11]	—[11]	—[11]	—[11]	—[11]
India	1	8	39	36	43	69	163	269
Iran	—[12]	—[12]	—[12]	—[12]	—[12]	—[12]	—[12]	—[12]
Israel	—[13]	—[13]	—[13]	—[13]	—[13]	—[13]	—[13]	—[13]
Japan	—[14]	—[14]	—[14]	—[14]	—[14]	186	149	2,270
Korea	—[15]	—[15]	—[15]	—[15]	—[15]	—[15]	—[15]	—[15]
Philippines	—[16]	—[16]	—[16]	—[16]	—[16]	—[16]	—[16]	—[16]
Turkey	1	20	7	59	83	131	404	3,782
Vietnam	—[11]	—[11]	—[11]	—[11]	—[11]	—[11]	—[11]	—[11]
Other Asia	3	—	1	11	15	72	243	1,910
America	387	11,564	33,424	62,469	74,720	166,607	404,044	426,967
Canada & Newfoundland[17,18]	209	2,277	13,624	41,723	59,309	153,878	383,640	393,304
Mexico[18]	1	4,817	6,599	3,271	3,078	2,191	5,162	1,913[19]
Caribbean	164	3,834	12,301	13,528	10,660	9,046	13,957	29,042
Cuba	—[12]	—[12]	—[12]	—[12]	—[12]	—[12]	—[12]	—[12]
Dominican Republic	—[20]	—[20]	—[20]	—[20]	—[20]	—[20]	—[20]	—[20]
Haiti	—[20]	—[20]	—[20]	—[20]	—[20]	—[20]	—[20]	—[20]
Jamaica	—[21]	—[21]	—[21]	—[21]	—[21]	—[21]	—[21]	—[21]
Other Caribbean	164	3,834	12,301	13,528	10,660	9,046	13,957	29,042
Central America	2	105	44	368	449	95	157	404
El Salvador	—[20]	—[20]	—[20]	—[20]	—[20]	—[20]	—[20]	—[20]
Other Central America	2	105	44	368	449	95	157	404
South America	11	531	856	3,579	1,224	1,397	1,128	2,304
Argentina	—[20]	—[20]	—[20]	—[20]	—[20]	—[20]	—[20]	—[20]
Colombia	—[20]	—[20]	—[20]	—[20]	—[20]	—[20]	—[20]	—[20]
Ecuador	—[20]	—[20]	—[20]	—[20]	—[20]	—[20]	—[20]	—[20]
Other South America	11	531	856	3,579	1,224	1,397	1,128	2,304
Other America	—[22]	—[22]	—[22]	—[22]	—[22]	—[22]	—[22]	—[22]
Africa	1	16	54	55	210	312	358	857
Oceania	1	2	9	29	158	214	10,914	12,574
Not specified[22]	300	33,030	69,902	53,115	29,011	17,791	790	789

Region and Country of Last Residence[1]	1891–1900	1901–10	1911–20	1921–30	1931–40	1941–50	1951–60	1961–70
All countries	3,687,564	8,795,386	5,735,811	4,107,209	528,431	1,035,039	2,515,479	3,321,677
Europe	3,555,352	8,056,040	4,321,887	2,463,194	347,566	621,147	1,325,727	1,123,492
Austria-Hungary	592,707[23]	2,145,266[23]	896,342[23]	63,548	11,424	28,329	103,743	26,022
Austria	234,081[3]	668,209[3]	453,649	32,868	3,563[24]	24,860[24]	67,106	20,621
Hungary	181,288[3]	808,511[3]	442,693	30,680	7,861	3,469	36,637	5,401
Belgium	18,167	41,635	33,746	15,846	4,817	12,189	18,575	9,192
Czechoslovakia	—[4]	—[4]	3,426[4]	102,194	14,393	8,347	918	3,273
Denmark	50,231	65,285	41,983	32,430	2,559	5,393	10,984	9,201
France	30,770	73,379	61,897	49,610	12,623	38,809	51,121	45,237
Germany	505,152[23]	341,498[23]	143,945[23]	412,202	114,058[24]	226,578[24]	477,765	190,796
Greece	15,979	167,519	184,201	51,084	9,119	8,973	47,608	85,969
Ireland[5]	388,416	339,065	146,181	211,234	10,973	19,789	48,362	32,966
Italy	651,893	2,045,877	1,109,524	455,315	68,028	57,661	185,491	214,111
Netherlands	26,758	48,262	43,718	26,948	7,150	14,860	52,277	30,606
Norway-Sweden	321,281	440,039	161,469	165,780	8,700	20,765	44,632	32,600
Norway	95,015	190,505	66,395	68,531	4,740	10,100	22,935	15,484
Sweden	226,266	249,534	95,074	97,249	3,960	10,665	21,697	17,116
Poland	96,720[23]	—[23]	4,813[23]	227,734	17,026	7,571	9,985	53,539
Portugal	27,508	69,149	89,732	29,994	3,329	7,423	19,588	76,065
Romania	12,750	53,008	13,311	67,646	3,871	1,076	1,039	2,531
Soviet Union	505,290[23]	1,597,306[23]	921,201[23]	61,742	1,370	571	671	2,465
Spain	8,731	27,935	68,611	28,958	3,258	2,898	7,894	44,659
Switzerland	31,179	34,922	23,091	29,676	5,512	10,547	17,675	18,453
United Kingdom[5,8]	271,538	525,950	341,408	339,570	31,572	139,306	202,824	213,822
Yugoslavia	—[9]	—[9]	1,888[9]	49,064	5,835	1,576	8,225	20,381
Other Europe	282	39,945	31,400	42,619	11,949	8,486	16,350	11,604

Asia	74,862	323,543	247,236	112,059	16,595	37,028	153,249	427,642
China[10]	14,799	20,605	21,278	29,907	4,928	16,709	9,657	34,764
Hong Kong	—[11]	—[11]	—[11]	—[11]	—[11]	—[11]	15,541[11]	75,007
India	68	4,713	2,082	1,886	496	1,761	1,973	27,189
Iran	—[12]	—[12]	—[12]	241[12]	195	1,380	3,388	10,339
Israel	—[13]	—[13]	—[13]	—[13]	—[13]	476[13]	25,476	29,602
Japan	25,942	129,797	83,837	33,462	1,948	1,555	46,250	39,988
Korea	—[15]	—[15]	—[15]	—[15]	—[15]	107[15]	6,231	34,526
Philippines	—[16]	—[16]	—[16]	—[16]	528[16]	4,691	19,307	98,376
Turkey	30,425	157,369	134,066	33,824	1,065	798	3,519	10,142
Vietnam	—[11]	—[11]	—[11]	—[11]	—[11]	—[11]	335[11]	4,340
Other Asia	3,628	11,059	5,973	12,739	7,435	9,551	21,572	63,369
America	38,972	361,888	1,143,671	1,516,716	160,037	354,804	996,944	1,716,374
Canada & Newfoundland[17,18]	3,311	179,226	742,185	924,515	108,527	171,718	377,952	413,310
Mexico[18]	971[19]	49,642	219,004	459,287	22,319	60,589	299,811	453,937
Caribbean	33,066	107,548	123,424	74,899	15,502	49,725	123,091	470,213
Cuba	—[12]	—[12]	—[12]	15,901[12]	9,571	26,313	78,948	208,536
Dominican Republic	—[20]	—[20]	—[20]	—[20]	1,150[20]	5,627	9,897	93,292
Haiti	—[20]	—[20]	—[20]	—[20]	191[20]	911	4,442	34,499
Jamaica	—[21]	—[21]	—[21]	—[21]	—[21]	—[21]	8,869[21]	74,906
Other Caribbean	33,066	107,548	123,424	58,998	4,590	16,874	20,935[21]	58,980
Central America	549	8,192	17,159	15,769	5,861	21,665	44,751	101,330
El Salvador	—[20]	—[20]	—[20]	—[20]	673[20]	5,132	5,895	14,992
Other Central America	549	8,192	17,159	15,769	5,188	16,533	38,856	86,338
South America	1,075	17,280	41,899	42,215	7,803	21,831	91,628	257,954
Argentina	—[20]	—[20]	—[20]	—[20]	1,349[20]	3,338	19,486	49,721
Colombia	—[20]	—[20]	—[20]	—[20]	1,223[20]	3,858	18,048	72,028
Ecuador	—[20]	—[20]	—[20]	—[20]	337[20]	2,417	9,841	36,780
Other South America	1,075	17,280	41,899	42,215	4,894	12,218	44,253	99,425
Other America	—[22]	—[22]	—[22]	31[22]	25	29,276	59,711	19,630
Africa	350	7,368	8,443	6,286	1,750	7,367	14,092	28,954
Oceania	3,965	13,024	13,427	8,726	2,483	14,551	12,976	25,122
Not specified[22]	14,063	33,523[25]	1,147	228	—	142	12,491	93

Region and Country of Last Residence[1]	1971–80	1981–89	1984	1985	1986	1987	1988	1989	Total 170 Years 1820–1989
All countries	4,493,314	5,801,579	543,903	570,009	601,708	601,516	643,025	1,090,924	55,457,531
Europe	800,368	637,524	69,879	69,526	69,224	67,967	71,854	94,338	36,977,034
Austria-Hungary	16,028	20,152	2,846	2,521	2,604	2,401	3,200	3,586	4,338,049
Austria	9,478	14,566	2,351	1,930	2,039	1,769	2,493	2,845	1,825,172[3]
Hungary	6,550	5,586	495	591	565	632	707	741	1,666,801[3]
Belgium	5,329	6,239	787	775	843	859	706	705	209,729
Czechoslovakia	6,023	6,649	693	684	588	715	744	526	145,223
Denmark	4,439	4,696	512	465	544	515	561	617	369,738
France	25,069	28,088	3,335	3,530	3,876	3,809	3,637	4,101	783,322
Germany	74,414	79,809	9,375	10,028	9,853	9,923	9,748	10,419	7,071,313
Greece	92,369	34,490	3,311	3,487	3,497	4,087	4,690	4,588	700,017
Ireland[5]	11,490	22,229	1,096	1,288	1,757	3,032	5,121	6,983	4,715,393
Italy	129,368	51,008	6,328	6,351	5,711	4,666	5,332	11,089	5,356,862
Netherlands	10,492	10,723	1,313	1,235	1,263	1,303	1,152	1,253	372,717
Norway-Sweden	10,472	13,252	1,455	1,557	1,564	1,540	1,669	1,809	2,144,024
Norway	3,941	3,612	403	386	367	372	446	556	800,672[6]
Sweden	6,531	9,640	1,052	1,171	1,197	1,168	1,223	1,253	1,283,097[6]
Poland	37,234	64,888	7,229	7,409	6,540	5,818	7,298	13,279	587,972
Portugal	101,710	36,365	3,800	3,811	3,804	4,009	3,290	3,861	497,195
Romania	12,393	27,361	2,956	3,764	3,809	2,741	2,915	3,535	201,345
Soviet Union	38,961	42,898	3,349	1,532	1,001	1,139	1,408	4,570	3,428,927
Spain	39,141	17,689	2,168	2,278	2,232	2,056	1,972	2,179	282,404
Switzerland	8,235	7,561	795	980	923	964	920	1,072	358,151
United Kingdom[5,8]	137,374	140,119	16,516	15,591	16,129	15,889	14,667	16,961	5,100,096
Yugoslavia	30,540	15,984	1,404	1,521	1,915	1,793	2,039	2,464	133,493
Other Europe	9,287	7,324	611	719	771	708	785	741	181,064

Asia	1,588,178	2,416,278	247,775	255,164	258,546	248,293	254,745	296,420	5,697,301
China[10]	124,326	306,108	29,109	33,095	32,389	32,669	34,300	39,284	873,737
Hong Kong	113,467	83,848	12,290	10,795	9,930	8,785	11,817	15,257	287,863[11]
India	164,134	221,977	23,617	24,536	24,808	26,394	25,312	28,599	426,907
Iran	45,136	101,267	11,131	12,327	12,031	10,323	9,846	13,027	161,946[12]
Israel	37,713	38,367	4,136	4,279	5,124	4,753	4,444	5,494	131,634[13]
Japan	49,775	40,654	4,517	4,552	4,444	4,711	5,085	5,454	455,813[14]
Korea	267,638	302,782	32,537	34,791	35,164	35,397	34,151	33,016	611,284[15]
Philippines	354,987	477,485	46,985	53,137	61,492	58,315	61,017	66,119	955,374[16]
Turkey	13,399	20,028	1,652	1,690	1,975	2,080	2,200	2,538	409,122
Vietnam	172,820	266,027	25,803	20,367	15,010	13,073	12,856	13,174	443,522[11]
Other Asia	244,783	557,735	55,998	55,595	56,179	51,793	53,717	74,458	940,099
America	1,982,735	2,564,698	208,111	225,519	254,078	265,026	294,906	672,639	12,017,021
Canada & Newfoundland[17,18]	169,939	132,296	15,659	16,354	16,060	16,741	15,821	18,294	4,270,943
Mexico[18]	640,294	975,657	57,820	61,290	66,753	72,511	95,170	405,660	3,208,543
Caribbean	741,126	759,416	68,368	79,374	98,527	100,615	110,949	87,597	2,590,542
Cuba	264,863	135,142	5,699	17,115	30,787	27,363	16,610	9,523	739,274[12]
Dominican Republic	148,135	209,899	23,207	23,861	26,216	24,947	27,195	26,744	468,000[20]
Haiti	56,335	118,510	9,554	9,872	12,356	14,643	34,858	13,341	214,888[20]
Jamaica	137,577	184,481	18,997	18,277	18,916	22,430	20,474	23,572	405,833[21]
Other Caribbean	134,216	111,384	10,911	10,249	10,252	11,232	11,812	14,417	762,547
Central America	134,640	321,845	27,626	28,447	30,086	30,366	31,311	101,273	673,385
El Salvador	34,436	133,938	8,753	10,093	10,881	10,627	12,043	57,628	195,066[20]
Other Central America	100,204	187,907	18,873	18,354	19,205	19,739	19,268	43,645	478,319
South America	295,741	375,026	38,636	40,650	42,650	44,782	41,646	59,812	1,163,482
Argentina	29,897	21,374	2,287	1,925	2,318	2,192	2,556	3,766	125,165[20]
Colombia	77,347	99,066	10,897	11,802	11,213	11,482	10,153	14,918	271,570[20]
Ecuador	50,077	43,841	4,244	4,601	4,518	4,656	4,736	7,587	143,293[20]
Other South America	138,420	210,745	21,208	21,724	24,601	26,452	24,201	33,541	623,454
Other America	995	458	2	2	2	11	9	3	110,126
Africa	80,779	144,096	13,594	15,236	15,500	15,730	17,124	22,485	301,348
Oceania	41,242	38,401	4,249	4,552	4,352	4,437	4,324	4,956	197,818
Not specified[22]	12	582	295	12	8	63	72	86	267,009

Source: U.S. Immigration and Naturalization Service, 1991.

[1]Data for years prior to 1906 relate to country whence alien came; data from 1906–79 and 1984–89 are for country of last permanent residence; and data for 1980–83 refer to country of birth. Because of changes in boundaries, changes in lists of countries, and lack of data for specified countries for various periods, data for certain countries, especially for the total period 1820–1989, are not comparable throughout. Data for specified countries are included with countries to which they belonged prior to World War I.

[2]Data for Austria and Hungary not reported until 1861.

[3]Data for Austria and Hungary not reported separately for all years during the period.

[4]No data available for Czechoslovakia until 1920.

[5]Prior to 1926, data for Northern Ireland included in Ireland.

[6]Data for Norway and Sweden not reported separately until 1871.

[7]No data available for Romania until 1880.

[8]Since 1925, data for United Kingdom refer to England, Scotland, Wales, and Northern Ireland.

[9]In 1920, a separate enumeration was made for the Kingdom of Serbs, Croats, and Slovenes. Since 1922, the Serb, Croat, and Slovene Kingdom recorded as Yugoslavia.

[10]Beginning in 1957, China includes Taiwan.

[11]Data not reported separately until 1952.

[12]Data not reported separately until 1925.

[13]Data not reported separately until 1949.

[14]No data available for Japan until 1861.

[15]Data not reported separately until 1948.

[16]Prior to 1934, Philippines recorded as insular travel.

[17]Prior to 1920, Canada and Newfoundland recorded as British North America. From 1820 to 1898, figures include all British North America possessions.

[18]Land arrivals not completely enumerated until 1908.

[19]No data available for Mexico from 1886 to 1893.

[20]Data not reported separately until 1932.

[21]Data for Jamaica not collected until 1953. In prior years, consolidated under British West Indies, which is included in "Other Caribbean."

[22]Included in countries "Not specified" until 1925.

[23]From 1899 to 1919, data for Poland included in Austria-Hungary, Germany, and the Soviet Union.

[24]From 1938 to 1945, data for Austria included in Germany.

[25]Includes 32,897 persons returning in 1906 to their homes in the United States.

—represents zero.

NOTE: From 1820 to 1867, figures represent alien passengers arrived at seaports; from 1868 to 1891 and 1895 to 1897, immigrant aliens arrived; from 1892 to 1894 and 1898 to 1989, immigrant aliens admitted for permanent residence. From 1892 to 1903, aliens entering by cabin class were not counted as immigrants. Land arrivals were not completely enumerated until 1908. For this table, fiscal year 1843 covers 9 months ending September 1843; fiscal years 1832 and 1850 cover 15 months ending December 31 of the respective years; and fiscal year 1868 covers 6 months ending June 30, 1868.

PRESIDENTS, VICE-PRESIDENTS, AND SECRETARIES OF STATE

	President	Vice-President	Secretary of State
1.	George Washington, Federalist 1789	John Adams, Federalist 1789	T. Jefferson 1789 E. Randolph 1794 T. Pickering 1795
2.	John Adams, Federalist 1798	Thomas Jefferson, Dem.-Rep. 1797	T. Pickering 1797 John Marshall 1800
3.	Thomas Jefferson, Dem.-Rep. 1801	Aaron Burr, Dem.-Rep. 1801 George Clinton, Dem.-Rep. 1805	James Madison 1801
4.	James Madison, Dem.-Rep. 1809	George Clinton, Dem.-Rep. 1809 Elbridge Gerry, Dem.-Rep. 1813	Robert Smith 1809 James Monroe 1811
5.	James Monroe, Dem.-Rep. 1817	D. D. Tompkins, Dem.-Rep. 1817	J. Q. Adams 1817
6.	John Quincy Adams, Dem.-Rep. 1825	John C. Calhoun, Dem.-Rep. 1825	Henry Clay 1825
7.	Andrew Jackson, Democratic 1829	John C. Calhoun, Democratic 1829 Martin Van Buren, Democratic 1833	M. Van Buren 1829 E. Livingston 1831 Louis McLane 1833 John Forsyth 1834
8.	Martin Van Buren, Democratic 1837	Richard M. Johnson, Democratic 1837	John Forsyth 1837
9.	William H. Harrison, Whig 1841	John Tyler, Whig 1841	Daniel Webster 1841

President	Vice-President	Secretary of State
10. John Tyler, Whig and Democratic 1841		Daniel Webster 1841 Hugh S. Legare 1843 Abel P. Upshur 1843 John C. Calhoun 1844
11. James K. Polk, Democratic 1845	George M. Dallas, Democratic 1845	James Buchanan 1845
12. Zachary Taylor, Whig 1849	Millard Fillmore, Whig 1848	John M. Clayton 1849
13. Millard Fillmore, Whig 1850		Daniel Webster 1850 Edward Everett 1852
14. Franklin Pierce, Democratic 1853	William R. D. King, Democratic 1853	W. L. Marcy 1853
15. James Buchanan, Democratic 1857	John C. Breckinridge, Democratic 1857	Lewis Cass 1857 J. S. Black 1860
16. Abraham Lincoln, Republican 1861	Hannibal Hamlin, Republican 1861 Andrew Johnson, Unionist 1865	W. H. Seward 1861
17. Andrew Johnson, Unionist 1865		W. H. Seward 1865
18. Ulysses S. Grant, Republican 1869	Schuyler Colfax, Republican 1869 Henry Wilson, Republican 1873	E. B. Washburne 1869 H. Fish 1869

CHRONOLOGY OF
SIGNIFICANT EVENTS

16,000–14,000 B.C.	Likely period for first crossing of land bridge from Old World to New World
5000 B.C.	Hunting and gathering established as a way of life in New World
2000–1500 B.C.	Permanent towns appear in Mexico
800 B.C.–A.D. 600	Adena-Hopewell culture (northeast United States)
400 B.C.–present	Pueblo-Hohokam culture (southwest United States)
A.D. 300–900	Mayan culture
600–1500	Mississippian culture (southeast United States)
1000	Leif Ericsson sights Newfoundland
1215	Magna Carta adopted in England
1300–1519	Aztec culture
1300–1598	Inca culture
1440	Gutenberg invents movable type
1477	Marco Polo's *Travels* published
1492–1504	Columbus's four voyages to New World
1493	Pope declares demarcation line
1517	Martin Luther launches Protestant Reformation
1519	Cortés conquers Aztec empire
1536	John Calvin publishes *The Institutes*
1558–1603	Reign of Queen Elizabeth I
1565	Town of St. Augustine founded by the Spanish
1587	Sir Walter Raleigh's "lost colony" at Roanoke
1588	Defeat of the Spanish Armada by the English
1603–1625	Reign of James I, first of England's Stuart kings
1606	Virginia Company chartered
1607	Jamestown founded
1614	Dutch trading post set up on Manhattan Island

1616	Tobacco becomes an export staple for Virginia
1619	Virginia's General Assembly first convenes
1619	First Africans brought to English America
1620	*Mayflower* lands at Plymouth
1625	Population of English colonies in America at 2,000
1625–1649	Reign of Charles I in England
1630	Gov. John Winthrop leads the Puritan migration to Massachusetts Bay
1634	First settlement in Maryland
1636	Harvard College founded
1638	Anne Hutchinson banished from Massachusetts in Antinomian controversy
1642–1649	English Civil War
1649–1660	The Commonwealth and Protectorate in England
1651	William Bradford completes *Of Plymouth Plantation*
1660	English monarchy restored under Charles II
1662	Half-Way Covenant adopted by New England Congregational churches
1664	Dutch New Netherland colony becomes English New York
1675	King Philip's War
1676	Bacon's Rebellion
1681	Pennsylvania founded
1685–1688	Reign of James II
1687	Newton's *Principia* published
1688	England's Glorious Revolution
1689	John Locke's *Two Treatises on Civil Government* published
1689–1697	King William's War (War of the League of Augsburg)
1692	Salem witch trials
1700	Population of English colonies in America at 250,000
1702–1713	Queen Anne's War (War of the Spanish Succession)
1704	First enduring newspaper published in America
1732	Georgia founded

1732–1757 Benjamin Franklin publishes *Poor Richard's Almanack*
1734 Great Awakening begins in colonies
1735 Trial of John Peter Zenger
1740–1748 King George's War (War of the Austrian Succession)
1754–1763 French and Indian War (Seven Years' War)
1763 Proclamation of 1763
1764 The Sugar Act
1764 The Currency Act
1765 The Stamp Act
1766 Declaratory Act
1767 Townshend Act
1768 John Dickinson publishes *Letters of a Pennsylvania Farmer*
1768 Samuel Adams's Massachusetts Circular Letter
1769 Virginia Resolves
1770 Boston Massacre
1773 Boston Tea Party
1774 Coercive Acts
1774 First Continental Congress
1775 Battles of Lexington and Concord
1775 Second Continental Congress
1775 Battle of Bunker Hill
1776 Thomas Paine's *Common Sense*
1776 Declaration of Independence
1777 American victory at Saratoga
1777 Congress adopts the Articles of Confederation
1778 Franco-American alliance set
1781 Battle of Yorktown
1782 Crèvecoeur's *Letters from an American Farmer*
1783 Peace of Paris
1784 *Empress of China* sails for Canton
1787 Shays's Rebellion
1787 The Constitutional Convention meets and submits the Constitution to states for ratification
1787 Northwest Ordinance
1788 Hamilton, Madison, and Jay publish *The Federalist*
1788 The Constitution ratified by the states
1789 George Washington elected president

1789	Bill of Rights submitted to the states
1790–1791	Hamilton's *Reports*
1790	Samuel Slater's cotton mill set up in Rhode Island
1793	Eli Whitney invents the cotton gin
1794	Whiskey Rebellion
1794	Jay Treaty
1795	Pinckney Treaty
1795	North Carolina opens first state university
1796	John Adams elected president
1797	XYZ Affair
1797–1810	Revivalism on the frontier
1798–1800	Undeclared war with France
1798	Alien and Sedition Acts
1798	Kentucky and Virginia Resolutions
1800	Thomas Jefferson elected president
1803	*Marbury v. Madison*
1803	Louisiana Purchase
1803–1806	Lewis and Clark expedition
1807	Embargo Act
1809	Non-Intercourse Act
1811	Battle of Tippecanoe
1811	National Road started
1812	Congress declares war on Great Britain
1814	Hartford Convention
1815	Battle of New Orleans
1815	Peace of Ghent
1817–1825	Construction of the Erie Canal
1819	*McCulloch v. Maryland*
1819	Adams-Onis Treaty
1820	Washington Irving's *The Sketch Book*
1820	Missouri Compromise
1820	Significant Irish immigration begins
1821	Boston opens first public secondary school
1821–1822	Santa Fe Trail opened
1822	Cotton mills opened in Lowell, Massachusetts
1823	Monroe Doctrine
1826	James Fenimore Cooper's *The Last of the Mohicans*
1828	Andrew Jackson elected president
1828	Calhoun's *South Carolina Exposition and Protest*

1829–1837	Battle over recharter of the Bank of the United States
1830	Webster-Hayne debate
1830	Indian Removal Act
1830–1847	The Mormon trek west
1830–1860	Hudson River school of painting
1831	*Cherokee Nation v. Georgia*
1831	William Lloyd Garrison begins publication of *The Liberator*
1831	Nat Turner's rebellion
1832	South Carolina Ordinance of Nullification
1833	Chicago founded
1836	Siege of the Alamo
1836	Texas declares its independence
1836–1850	Transcendentalism spreads in New England
1836	Ralph Waldo Emerson's *Nature*
1837	Panic of 1837
1837	*Charles River Bridge v. Warren Bridge*
1840	Edgar Allan Poe's *Tales of the Grotesque and Arabesque*
1842	Webster-Ashburton Treaty
1844	Samuel F. B. Morse invents the telegraph
1844–1846	Dispute with Great Britain over Oregon Territory
1845	United States annexes Texas
1846	Americans declare California an independent republic
1846	United States declares war on Mexico
1846	Wilmot Proviso
1846	Potato famine in Ireland
1848	Gold discovered in California
1848	Treaty of Guadalupe Hidalgo
1848	Seneca Falls convention on women's rights
1850	Compromise of 1850
1850	Nathaniel Hawthorne's *The Scarlet Letter*
1850	Clayton-Bulwer Treaty
1851	Herman Melville's *Moby-Dick*
1852	Harriet Beecher Stowe's *Uncle Tom's Cabin*
1853	Gadsden Purchase
1854	Perry's reopening of Japan
1854	Henry David Thoreau's *Walden*
1854	Ostend Manifesto

1854	Kansas-Nebraska Act
1855	Walt Whitman's *Leaves of Grass*
1856	"Bleeding Kansas"
1857	Dred Scott decision
1858	Lincoln-Douglas debates
1859	John Brown's Raid
1859	Charles Darwin's *Origin of Species*
1860	Abraham Lincoln elected president
1860–1861	Southern states secede from the Union
1861	The Civil War breaks out
1861	First Battle of Bull Run
1861–1890	Indian wars in the West
1862	Battle of Antietam
1862	Battle of Shiloh
1862	The Homestead Act
1863	Battle of Gettysburg
1863	New York City Draft Riots
1863	Lincoln issues the Emancipation Proclamation
1864	Sherman's March to the Sea
1865	Lee surrenders to Grant at Appomattox Courthouse
1865	Freedmen's Bureau established
1865	Assassination of President Lincoln
1866–1868	Fourteenth Amendment passed and ratified
1867	First Reconstruction Act
1867–1877	Congressional Reconstruction of the South
1867	United States purchases Alaska
1868	Impeachment of President Andrew Johnson
1869	Completion of first transcontinental railroad
1869	National Woman Suffrage Association founded
1870	Standard Oil Company of Ohio established by John D. Rockefeller
1873	Crédit-Mobilier Scandal

ILLUSTRATION CREDITS

CHAPTER 1: **p. 8,** Milwaukee Public Museum; **p. 12,** Courtesy of the British Museum; **p. 14,** Neg. No. 286821, courtesy Department of Library Services, American Museum of Natural History; **p. 26,** Library of Congress; **p. 28,** Huntington Library; **p. 33,** American Antiquarian Society; **p. 43,** The New York Public Library: Astor, Lenox, and Tilden Foundations.

CHAPTER 2: **p. 58,** (left) Worcester Art Museum, (right) Worcester Art Museum; **p. 63,** American Antiquarian Society; **p. 64,** Statue of Liberty National Monument; **p. 65,** The Abby Aldridge Rockefeller Folk Art Center, Williamsburg, Virginia; **p. 76,** From Ralph Gardiner, *England's Grievance Discovered,* 1655; **p. 83,** Harvard University.

CHAPTER 3: **p. 101,** The Library Company of Philadelphia; **p. 106,** Public Archives of Canada.

CHAPTER 4: **p. 118,** Courtauld Institute of Art; **p. 123,** The Historical Society of Pennsylvania; **p. 128,** (top) Library of Congress, (bottom) Boston Public Library; **p. 132,** Library of Congress; **p. 134,** The New York Public Library: Astor, Lenox, and Tilden Foundations; **p. 142,** American Antiquarian Society; **p. 144,** Library of Congress.

CHAPTER 5: **p. 155,** Brown Brothers; **p. 156,** The Historical Society of Pennsylvania; **p. 163,** Library of Congress; **p. 166,** The New-York Historical Society; **p. 171,** The British Library; **p. 180,** The Massachusetts Historical Society; **p. 181,** National Gallery of Art; **p. 183,** Museum of Art, Rhode Island School of Design.

CHAPTER 6: **p. 200,** Library of Congress; **p. 207,** Independence National Historical Park Collection.

CHAPTER 7: **p. 216,** Museum of the City of New York; **p. 225,** Independence National Historical Park Collection; **p. 232,** The New York Public Library: Astor, Lenox, and Tilden Foundations; **p. 235,** The American Antiquarian Society; **p. 237,** Huntington Library.

CHAPTER 8: **p. 245,** The New York Public Library: Astor, Lenox, and Tilden Foundations; **p. 248,** The Cincinnati Historical Society; **p. 252,** Library of Congress; **p. 259,** The New York Public Library: Astor, Lenox, and Tilden Foundations; **p. 262,** American Museum of Natural History; **p. 267,** Library of Congress; **p. 270,** The Warder Collection, N.Y.

CHAPTER 9: **p. 275,** Maryland Historical Society; **p. 286,** The Metropolitan Museum of Art Rogers Fund, 1942, (42.95.7) (c) by The Metropolitan Museum of Art; **p. 293,** The New-York Historical Society.

CHAPTER 10: **p. 303,** Historical Society of Pennsylvania; **p. 304,** National Museum of American History; **p. 306,** National Portrait Gallery, Smithsonian Institution/Art Resource, N.Y.; **p. 314,** American Antiquarian Society; **p. 317,** Boatmen's National Bank of St. Louis; **p. 319,** The New-York Historical Society; **p. 324,** Library of Congress; **p. 327,** Library of Congress.

CHAPTER 11: **p. 332,** Amon Carter Museum; **p. 337,** Statue of Liberty National Monument; **p. 340,** The New-York Historical Society; **p. 343,** Library of Congress; **p. 348,** The New York Public Library: Astor, Lenox, and Tilden Foundations.

CHAPTER 12: **p. 363,** Library of Congress; **p. 369,** *New England* Magazine; **p. 370,** Concord Free Public Library; **p. 374,** Amon Carter Museum; **p. 381,** Library of Congress; **p. 383,** National Portrait Gallery, Smithsonian Institution/Art Resource, N.Y.; **p. 385,** The Warder Collection, N.Y.

CHAPTER 13: **p. 399,** Museum of New Mexico; **p. 410,** Library of Congress.

CHAPTER 14: **p. 428,** The New-York Historical Society; **p. 430,** Library of Congress; **p. 437,** Library of Congress; **p. 439,** Chicago Historical Society; **p. 440,** Peabody Museum, Harvard University; **p. 442,** South Carolina Historical Society; **p. 452,** (left) National Portrait Gallery, Smithsonian Institution/Art Resource, N.Y., (right) The New-York Historical Society.

CHAPTER 15: **p. 468,** Library of Congress; **p. 469,** The New-York Historical Society; **p. 472,** Library of Congress; **p. 483,** Boston Athenaeum; **p. 487,** Chicago Historical Society.

CHAPTER 16: **p. 498,** Chicago Historical Society; **p. 499,** Library of Congress; **p. 512,** Library of Congress; **p. 513,** Chicago Historical Society; **p. 518,** The National Archives; **p. 522,** Library of Congress; **p. 529,** Library of Congress.

CHAPTER 17: **p. 539,** Library of Congress; **p. 543,** National Portrait Gallery, Smithsonian Institution/Art Resource, N.Y.; **p. 550,** The National Archives; **p. 553,** Library of Congress; **p. 558,** Library of Congress.

INDEX

abolitionism, *see* antislavery movements
Acadia, 105
Acoma Indians, 397
Act for the Impartial Administration of Justice
    (1774), 133
Adams, Abigail, 143, 181, 197, 217, 234, 379
Adams, Henry, 561
Adams, John, 126, 143, 148, 159, 172,
    173–74, 181, 185–86, 189, 199–200
    as ambassador to Great Britain, 195
    background of, 235
    Boston Massacre and, 129
    domestic discontent and, 238–40
    foreign policy under, 236–38
    judicial appointments of, 241–42, 246
    political philosophy of, 235
    in presidential elections, 234–35, 240
    as vice-president, 215, 217
Adams, John Quincy, 188, 252, 279, 350, 394,
    415
    abolitionism and, 453
    party affiliation of, 321
    presidency of, 291–92
    in presidential elections, 289–90, 295
    as secretary of state, 278, 281, 287, 288
Adams, Samuel, 126–27, 129, 131, 133, 137,
    143, 185, 209
African-Americans:
    in American Revolution, 178–79
    in antebellum southern society, 435–43
    in Civil War, 500, 513–14
    constitutional rights of, 218
    racial riots and, 542
    Reconstruction and, 538–41, 542, 546–55,
        562–63
    segregation of schools and, 453
    as soldiers in Civil War, 547
    stereotypes and caricatures of, 427–28, 454
    suffrage for, 538, 541, 544, 549, 556
    violence against, 500, 542, 552–54
    as voters, protection of, 554
    see also slavery; slaves; slave trade
agriculture:
    in colonial period, 56–57, 61–62, 106
    crop rotation in, 61

exchanges between New and Old Worlds
    and, 11–13
growth of (early 1800s), 330–33, 341
of Indians, 397–98
in pre-Columbian civilizations, 11–13, 56
sharecropping in, 548
in South, 61–62, 214, 429–30
in West Africa, 64
see also cotton production; farmers; tobacco
    production
Alabama, 302, 310, 553
Alamance, battle of (1771), 130–31
Alamo, battle of (1836), 408–10
Alaska, Russian claim to, 287, 402–3
alcohol consumption, prohibition and early
    temperance movements, 380–81
Alcott, Bronson, 368
Algeria, 248, 270–71
Algerian pirates, 237
Algonquian Indians, 100–104
Alien and Sedition Acts (1798), 238–40
Allen, Ethan, 130, 139
America, naming of, 11
American and Foreign Anti-Slavery Society,
    451
American Anti-Slavery Society, 449, 450–51
American Colonization Society, 447–48
American Crisis, The (Paine), 153
American party, 353, 474, 477
American Revolution, 137–73
    arts and, 184
    Boston Tea Party and, 132–33
    causes of, assessed, 144–45
    civilians during, 158–59
    as civil war, 154
    fighting in, 137–41, 144–45
    financing of, 157–58
    French aid in, 148, 162, 163–64, 170–71,
        172–73
    ideologists of, 173–74
    independence issue in, 142–45
    Indians in, 161, 164–66, 192
    loyalists and, 137, 154–56, 161, 164–66,
        168–69, 173, 175, 178, 179, 194–95
    mercenaries (Hessians) in, 141, 152, 154

THE WORLD